IMAGES
OF THE PAST

Jim Selley

IMAGES
OF THE PAST

T. DOUGLAS PRICE
GARY M. FEINMAN
UNIVERSITY OF WISCONSIN

MAYFIELD PUBLISHING COMPANY
MOUNTAIN VIEW, CALIFORNIA
LONDON • TORONTO

FOR ANNE BIRGITTE GEBAUER AND LINDA NICHOLAS

Price, T. Douglas (Theron Douglas)
    Images of the past / T. Douglas Price, Gary M. Feinman.
        p.   cm.
    Includes bibliographical references and index.
    ISBN 0-87484-814-8
    1. Man, Prehistoric.   2. Agriculture, Prehistoric.   3. Culture—
Origin.   4. Indians—Origin.   5. State, The—Origin.   I. Feinman,
Gary M.   II. Title.
GN740.P75   1992
930.1—dc20
                                                    92-15785
                                                       CIP

Manufactured in the United States of America
10 9 8 7 6 5 4

Mayfield Publishing Company
1240 Villa Street
Mountain View, California 94041

Sponsoring editor, Janet M. Beatty; *production editor,* Sharon Montooth; *copyeditor,* Betsy Dilernia; *text and cover designer,* Jeanne M. Schreiber; *illustrators,* Joan Carol, Judith Ogus; *photo researcher,* Lynn Rabin Bauer; *cover photographer,* Nathan Benn; *manufacturing manager,* Martha Branch. The text was set in 10/12 Berkeley Oldstyle Book by Thompson Type and printed on 50# Mead Pub Matte by Arcata Graphics in Kingsport, Tennessee.

Text and Photo Credits appear on a continuation of the copyright page, p. 526.

PREFACE

Images of the Past is an introduction to prehistoric archaeology that aims to capture the excitement and visual splendor of archaeology while at the same time providing insight into current research methods, interpretations, and theories in the field.

A number of introductory books on the subject of archaeology already exist. Such volumes generally take one of two directions; they offer either a comprehensive survey of world prehistory or a primer on method and theory. Surveys of world archaeology summarize what archaeologists have learned, but they often tend to be rather dry encyclopedias of information on the many places and times that people have lived in the past. That vast body of data is formidable to the beginning student. Primers on method and theory, on the other hand, are compilations of the history, techniques, concepts, and principles of archaeology: how to search for archaeological remains, how excavations are done, how to determine the age of prehistoric materials, who Louis Leakey was, and the like.

We assume that most beginning students of archaeology want to know what archaeologists have learned about the past. It is our goal, then, to discuss *what* archaeologists have learned more than *how* they have learned it. But you can't have one without the other. We believe that a combination of what has been discovered and how it was found will prove to be of most value for those beginning to learn about archaeology.

For this reason we are taking a new tack in this book. Our focus is on more than eighty archaeological sites from a variety of times and places around the world. Rather than try to cover all of prehistoric archaeology, we have chosen to emphasize certain discoveries that have resulted in important insights into prehistory. These sites, then, are signposts through the past.

We begin this journey with the evidence for the first humans, some four million years ago, and we conclude with the stirrings of written history in the Old World and the European conquest of the New World. The sites are grouped in ten chapters organized along chronological and/or geographic lines. The first four chapters are in chronological order, from the earliest human remains several million years ago to the beginnings of farming around 10,000 years ago. These chapters follow the expansion of the human species from its original home in Africa into Asia, Europe, and eventually Australia and the Americas. Chapter Five covers the beginnings of agriculture in the Old and New Worlds.

Chapters Six through Ten treat the rise of large, complex societies and early states. This second half has a geographic focus, with chapters on North America, Mesoamerica, South America, Old World states, and Europe. Within each of these chapters we have generally followed the sequence of development through time, from earlier to later. Although the earliest state societies arose in the Old World, we have arranged the chapters from the New World to the Old in order to emphasize and compare the rise of states in both areas. This arrangement of the chapters is intended to enhance comprehension of major processes such as the origins and spread of agriculture and the rise of more complex societies.

Each chapter contains a prolog and an epilog. The prologs provide an overview of the time period and developments that are discussed in the chapter. The prologs also offer continuity between the sections and contain essential maps and chronological charts for the chapter. The epilogs vary in content — some provide a summary, others introduce new information and concepts, others are theoretical, and yet others are more comparative. Examples of discussions included in the epilogs are the behavioral correlates of cold climate adaptations, the origins of language, and the nature of cultural complexity. The prologs and epilogs should be read with some care, for they provide the glue that binds the site descriptions together.

Interspersed among the site descriptions are highlighted sections that cover some of the who, how, and why of archaeology: biographies of interesting individuals, essential methods, debates about archaeological interpretation, or simply certain spectacular finds. In these sections, we illustrate some of the more interesting questions archaeologists ask about the past and show various new methods employed to decipher the archaeological record.

Because prehistory is a very visual subject, we have included more than 500 illustrations. It is essential to see and study the maps, plans, artifacts, and places that comprise the archaeological record. The basic framework of archaeology is the location of prehistoric materials in time and space. For this reason there is a series of coordinated maps and time lines to show readers where these sites and materials fit in terms of geography and chronology. In addition, we've included a number of full color photographs in a separate section of the text to provide some impression of the captivating beauty of the past.

Throughout the text we provide a number of learning aids to help students better understand the material that is presented. Following difficult site names, we have included a pronunciation guide in parentheses. Technical terms and important concepts in archaeology are indicated in bold type; these words can be found in a glossary at the end of the book. Where appropriate, we have tried to provide some sense of the size of areas and structures from archaeological sites with reference to modern features such as city blocks, football fields, and the like. A list of general suggested readings appears at the end of each chapter, while more detailed lists of references are found in the bibliography. Specific citations were not used in the text for the sake of continuity, but references for the information can be found under the name of the individual associated with the work in the bibliography at the back of the book. Finally, an appendix offers some English-metric measure conversions and equivalents to help make sizes more concrete.

A note on dates: The age of archaeological materials in the text is given in two ways. Dates from the Pliocene and Pleistocene are given in years before the present, or b.p. Dates from the last 10,000 years or so are given in calendar years before Christ, B.C., or Anno Domini, A.D. Because corrected radiocarbon (calibrated) dates can only be extended back a few thousand years from the present, we have not used such corrections for the dates in this text. This subject is discussed in more detail in Chapter 1. The more recent dates are given in uncalibrated radiocarbon years unless otherwise noted.

Finally a note on the creation of this book. We began this project because we were generally dissatisfied with the texts available for introductory archaeology. We divided up the book according to our own areas of knowledge and activity. Doug Price is interested in prehistoric foragers and the transition to agriculture; Gary Feinman is concerned with the rise of complex societies and the organization of states. Price works primarily in the Old World with stone tools and hunter-gatherers; Feinman does fieldwork largely in Mexico and the American Southwest. We hope that our interest and enthusiasm for archaeology carry over to you in this book and that you enjoy these *Images of the Past*.

ACKNOWLEDGMENTS

Any project like this one is the culmination of the efforts and contributions of a multitude of individuals and institutions. We want to thank the many individuals who have helped with this book in a variety of different ways from reviewing the text, providing new data, supplying photographs, helping us locate a variety of materials, and general support. We have done our very best to contact the copyright holders of the original work included herein and to secure their permission to reprint their material; if we have overlooked anyone, we offer our sincere apologies.

This project has been long and complex and would not have been feasible without the help of these friends and colleagues: Kim Aaris-Sørensen, Melvin Aitkens, Niels Andersen, Larry Bartram, Gert Jan Bartstra, John Bennet, C. K. Brain, Robert Brightman, Brian Byrd, Christopher Chippendale, Tim Champion, Grahame Clark, Desmond Clark, Carmen Collazo, George Dales, Jack Davis, Hilary and Janette Deacon, John de Vos, Preben Dehlholm, Tom Dillehay, Scott Fedick, Lisa Ferin, Kent Flannery, Melvin Fowler, George Frison, Anne Birgitte Gebauer, Jon Gibson, Peter Christian Vemming Hansen, Frank Hole, Vance Holliday, F. Clark Howell, Tom Jacobsen, Dick Jeffries, Greg Johnson, Ken Karstens, Larry Keeley, Mark Kenoyer, Susan Kepecs, J. E. Kidder, Jr., Richard Klein, Henry de Lumley, Tom Lynch, Joyce Marcus, Alexander Marshack, Ray Matheny, Alan May, A. T. M. Moore, Chris O'Brien, John Parkington, Peter Vang Petersen, Theron D. Price, Jeffrey Quilter, John Reader, Charles Redman, Merle Green Robertson, Gary Rollefson, Denise Schmandt-Besserat, Jeff Shokler, Ralph Solecki, Charles Spencer, Dragoslav Srejovic, Jim Stoltman, J. F. Thackeray, David Hurst Thomas, Donald Thompson, B. L. Turner II, Patty Jo Watson, Huang Weiwen, J. Peter White, Edwin Wilmsen, and Peter Woodman.

Several individuals deserve special mention. Linda Nicholas helped greatly with many parts of the project, but especially with finalizing large parts of the text and illustrations. Jennifer Blitz spent much of a year obtaining illustrations and permissions with extraordinary energy and care. The book likely would not have been completed without Jennifer's help. Our editor at Mayfield, Jan Beatty, inspired and cajoled at the appropriate times to get the job done. Jan has become a valued friend in the process. The production team—Sharon Montooth, Jeanne Schreiber, and Lynn Rabin Bauer—labored long, hard, and well to put all of this together.

We'd like to thank our reviewers, who provided help, ideas, inspiration, and motivation to revise and refine the text: J. M. Beaton, University of California, Davis; Richard Blanton, Purdue University; G. A. Clark, Arizona State University; Steven Falconer, Arizona State University; Kenneth L. Feder, Central Connecticut State University; William A. Haviland, University of Vermont; John W. Hoopes, University of Kansas; Gary W. Pahl, San Francisco State University; Donald A. Proulx, University of Massachusetts, Amherst; John W. Rick, Stanford University; Ralph M. Rowlett, University of Missouri-Columbia; Katharina J. Schreiber, University of California, Santa Barbara; William Turnbaugh, University of Rhode Island; Randall White, New York University; David J. Wilson, Southern Methodist University; and Richard W. Yerkes, Ohio State University.

To all of these individuals goes our sincere appreciation. We hope that you find the result worth your efforts.

Contents

IMAGES
OF THE PAST

INTRODUCTION

Images of the Past is a survey of world archaeology, covering more than 4 million years and all the continents except Antarctica. It is not possible to describe the entirety of human **prehistory** in a single volume such as this; that would be a little like trying to see Washington, D.C. in fifteen minutes. We have to be selective and visit only some of the more interesting and important places, so we have chosen some of the archaeological sites that have increased our understanding of the past. It is our hope that the pathway that begins in the next pages will provide you with a sense of what archaeologists know about the past and how they have come to know it.

The threads that run through this volume and tie the past to the present are the major trends in our development as a technological species: growth and diversification. Growth in the number of people on the planet and diversification in the kinds of environments that the human species inhabits, specialization in the tools and techniques used to obtain food and manufacture objects, growth in the complexity of human organizations, and diversity in the roles and positions that exist in society. The story of our human past is the story of these changes through time as we evolved from small, local groups of people living close to nature to large nation states involved in global trade.

Archaeology is the study of the human past, combining the themes of time and change. The major themes of time and change — change in our biology and change in our behavior through time — are also the focus of this book. Archaeology is the closest thing we have to a time machine. This machine moves backward through the mists of time. These mists become denser the further back we go and the windows of our time machine become more obscured. In the next chapter we are going as far back as we as humans can go, some 4 to 5 million years, when we took our first steps in Africa. But first we need to examine change through time in more detail in terms of biological and cultural evolution.

BIOLOGICAL EVOLUTION

Change, modification, variation — these themes describe the process through which humans have evolved from the earliest replicating molecules. The theory of natural selection, formulated by Charles Darwin and Alfred Russell Wallace in the middle of the last century, accounts for this process of change. Darwin and Wallace were strongly influenced by the ideas of Thomas Malthus, an English clergyman and philosopher. In his 1798 *Essay on the Principle of Population*, Malthus observed that the growth of human populations potentially exceeded the quantity of food available. He argued that because famine, war, disease, and the like naturally controlled the size of human populations, the number of people would not exceed the resources available to feed them; thus not everyone who was born would survive to reproduce.

Darwin coined the term *natural selection* to account for the increase in offspring of those individuals who did survive. The concept was put forth in his 1859 publication *On the Origin of Species by Means of Natural Selection*. On his global voyage aboard the

exploration ship *Beagle,* Darwin had observed that most species of plants and animals showed a great deal of variation — that individuals were distinct and exhibited different characteristics. Following Malthus, Darwin pointed out that all organisms produce more offspring than can survive. High rates of mortality are often observed among the young, and Darwin argued that the individuals that survive do so because of certain beneficial characteristics they possess.

In other words, the surviving organisms are those that are best adapted to the world that confronts them. For example, offspring with sharp hearing or eyesight can more readily avoid a predator than those without. Nature's choice of better adapted individuals — *"selection of the fittest,"* according to Darwin — leads to continual change in the species, as the more advantageous characteristics are passed genetically from one generation to the next. This basic process gave rise to the myriad creatures that occupy our world today. Evolutionary change is often described as differential reproductive success, and natural selection is the principal, though not the exclusive, mechanism responsible for it. Of course, as environmental conditions change, physical characteristics that enhance survival and successful parenting may also vary.

Views on the process of biological evolution evolve as well. Today there is some debate about the pace of change — whether major evolutionary developments occurred gradually, as Darwin emphasized, or rather abruptly and suddenly. Steven Jay Gould, of Harvard University, has termed such rapid jumps in the rate of evolution *punctuated equilibria.* It now seems that some biological shifts do occur gradually, while others may occur in rather rapid spurts following long periods of *stasis,* or little change.

CULTURAL EVOLUTION

For humans, there is also an important non-genetic, or cultural, component of variation and long-term change. What was selected for during the biological evolution of human

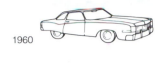

1960

1950

1930

1920

1900

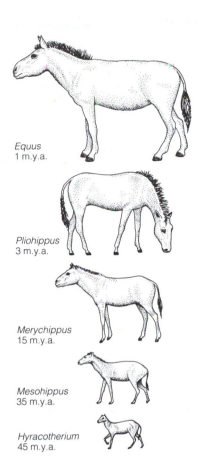

Equus
1 m.y.a.

Pliohippus
3 m.y.a.

Merychippus
15 m.y.a.

Mesohippus
35 m.y.a.

Hyracotherium
45 m.y.a.

Biological organisms and cultural artifacts evolve over time. The evolution of the horse from Hyracotherium, 45 m.y.a., to Equus, 1 m.y.a. The evolution of the automobile from A.D. 1900 to 1960.

beings was an unusual capability for adaptation based on learning, experience, and the use of tools, collectively known as **culture**. Within limits, culture enables us to modify and enhance our physiology and activities without a corresponding change in our genetic composition. As a consequence, natural selection by itself is neither adequate nor appropriate for explaining the culturally acquired traits of the human species.

The record of our species and its immediate ancestors is characterized by important episodes of both biological and cultural evolution. Biological, rather than cultural, changes dominated the first several million years of our existence. The evolution of our earliest ancestors is highlighted by key physical modifications in moving, teeth, and in the size and organization of the brain. The last 100,000 years or so of our presence on the planet, however, are marked primarily by cultural changes. The transmission of cultural traits occurs much more rapidly through learning than through the process of Darwinian evolution. The rates of recent changes are unmatched in the entire history of life. In tens of thousands of years, the human species has spiraled from a few tens of thousands of individuals using stone implements to billions of people with cars, airplanes, cities, satellites, frozen foods, computers and the hydrogen bomb — all without significant genetic changes in the species.

For centuries, scholars have tried to understand and explain cultural evolution and change, yet no single approach has been widely accepted (at least in the way that Darwin's concept of natural selection has been adopted in contemporary biology). Like biological evolution, cultural change is neither unilinearly directed nor inevitable. There is an opportunistic aspect to both processes. Yet over the course of human history, we see general (albeit not uniform) increases in the scale and complexity of human societies. These changes are illustrated in the chapters of this book, in which we see that humans aggregated in larger and more hierarchically arranged organizations through time. These communities were often part of more expansive and populous societies that included a number of different groups and institutions. To examine these processes of development, we must begin at the beginning — with the very first humans.

Man is only one of the earth's "manifold creatures" and he cannot understand his own nature or seek wisely to guide his destiny without taking account of the whole pattern of life.

George Gaylord Simpson,
The Meaning of Evolution (1967)

THE FIRST HUMANS

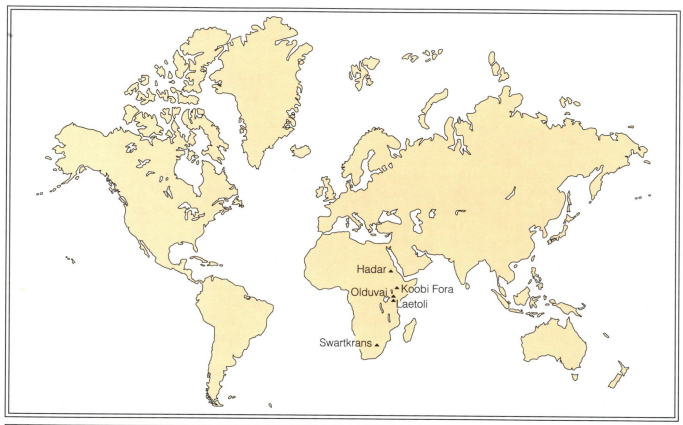

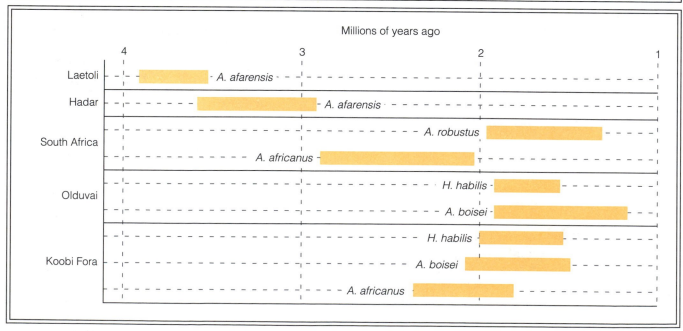

PROLOG
THE DAWN OF HUMANITY

*Our place on the planet in terms of geological
time, our relationship to other animals, and
our distinctively human characteristics*

Try to imagine the unimaginable. Around 15 billion years ago, an explosion of cosmic proportions ripped time and space apart and created our universe. Hydrogen and helium hurtled through emptiness, cast out of that original Big Bang. Clouds of these gases began to coagulate and attract other passing clouds. As these concentrations were compacted further by gravity, temperatures rose, and the energy created in the nuclear furnaces of the first stars lit up the universe.

More complex reactions in these evolving stars gave rise to heavier atoms of carbon, oxygen, magnesium, silicon, sulfur, and the other elements of the periodic table. Massive eruptions and disintegrations tore these early elements out of the stars and spewed them across space, creating newer and heavier stars. As they condensed, smaller conglomerations, lacking the mass or temperature to ignite, gathered around the edges of the brightly burning stars. Some of these cold and infinitesimal outliers became hard, metallic globes; others were frigid balls of gas. The planets were born. Some gases remained on the harder planets and condensed into oceans or enveloped the surface as a primordial atmosphere. Violent electrical storms, driven by energy from the stars and massive volcanic activity rifting the surface of the forming planet, tore apart and reconstituted these elements in the early seas and atmospheres.

On the planet we call Earth, this alchemy of primeval forces churned out new molecules in an atmosphere of methane, ammonia, hydrogen sulfide, water, and hydrogen. Among the multitude of new chemistries created in the soup of the early Earth's oceans was a remarkable combination of atoms. This new molecule was able to reproduce itself — to make a copy of its original. Life had emerged. Like the broom of the sorcerer's apprentice, once begun, the copying process filled the seas with duplicates. Reproducing molecules grew and achieved more complex forms. Molecules became bacteria that spread and diversified roughly a billion years after the formation of our planet. Reproducing molecules became the building blocks of more elaborate organisms that developed metabolic and sexual reproductive functions. Systems for eating and internal metabolism enabled organisms to obtain energy from other life forms. Sexual reproduction allowed for a tremendous diversity in offspring, and thus a greater capacity for adapting to changing environments and conditions.

Plants appeared in the oceans and spread to the land. The atmosphere fed carbon dioxide to the plants, which in turn replenished the air with oxygen through the process of photosynthesis. Swimming cooperatives of molecules in the oceans moved onto the land and began to breathe the oxygen. Fish, amphibians, reptiles, insects, mammals, and birds spread across the face of the Earth. And then, only a moment ago in geological time, a human creature evolved from this great chain of beings.

GEOLOGICAL TIME

The universe is approximately 15 billion years old. Planet Earth is roughly 4.5 billion years old. The idea of either 15 billion years or 4.5 billion years is incomprehensible,

CONTENTS

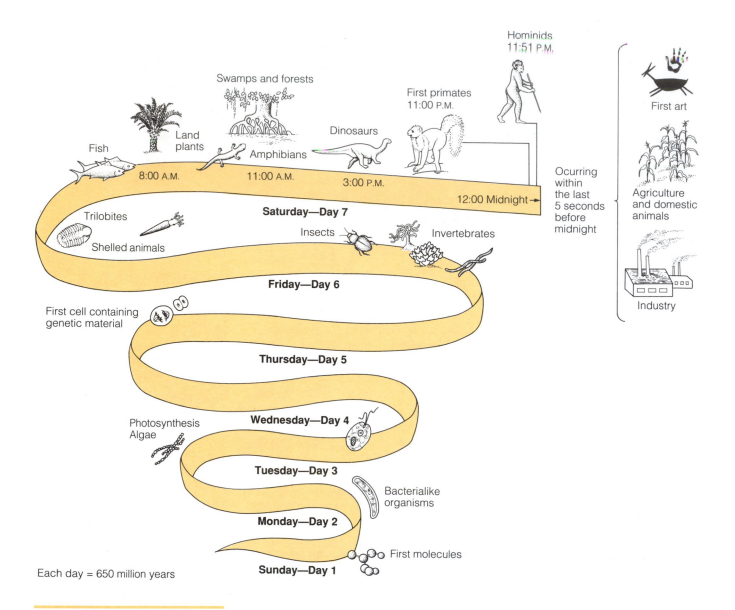

Hominids
11:51 P.M.

First primates
11:00 P.M.

Swamps and forests

First art

Dinosaurs

Land plants

Amphibians

Fish

8:00 A.M.   11:00 A.M.   3:00 P.M.

Ocurring within the last 5 seconds before midnight

Agriculture and domestic animals

12:00 Midnight

Saturday—Day 7

Trilobites

Insects

Invertebrates

Shelled animals

Friday—Day 6

Industry

First cell containing genetic material

Thursday—Day 5

Wednesday—Day 4

Photosynthesis Algae

Tuesday—Day 3

Bacterialike organisms

Monday—Day 2

First molecules

Each day = 650 million years

Sunday—Day 1

The evolution of life on Earth as a single week in time. The Earth forms at 12:01 A.M. Sunday morning, life appears on Monday morning, fish evolve on Saturday morning, and the first bipedal hominids show up at 11:51 P.M. Saturday night.

but some appreciation of this vast span of time is essential to an understanding of our past and of our place in the cosmos. If we can theoretically compress the eons that have passed into meaningful units of time, the events of our evolutionary history may make more sense.

Consider a single week, from Sunday morning to Saturday night, as a metaphor for our countdown to today. If one day in this 4.5-billion-year week represents over 650 million years, one hour would be 25 million years, one minute would be 400,000 years, and the passage of a single second would take more than 6000 years. Roughly 4.5 billion years ago, the seven days of our metaphorical week, the Earth formed in our solar system. The time was early Sunday morning at 12:01 A.M. By Sunday evening, a primitive atmosphere and ocean had appeared, and the first molecules began to coalesce. By Monday morning the first traces of life emerged in the shape of bacteria that evolved and multiplied. More complex bacteria, utilizing photosynthesis, began the task of converting the poisonous, primordial atmosphere to an oxygen base on Tuesday. Not until Thursday were the first cells carrying genetic material created. Late Friday morning the first invertebrate animals — resembling jellyfish, sponges, and worms — evolved. Before dawn on Saturday morning, the seas were teeming with shell-bearing animals, such as the trilobites. Around breakfast time on Saturday, fish and small land plants appeared. By

Era	Period	Epoch	Millions of years ago (m.y.a.)	Important Events
CENOZOIC	Quaternary	Recent	.01	Modern genera of animals.
		Pleistocene	2	Early humans and giant mammals now extinct.
	Tertiary	Pliocene	5.1	Anthropoid radiation and culmination of mammalian speciation.
		Miocene	25	
		Oligocene	38	Expansion and modernization of mammals.
		Eocene	54	
		Paleocene	65	
MESOZOIC	Cretaceous		135	Dinosaurs dominant; marcupial and placental mammals appear; first flowering plants spread rapidly.
	Jurassic		180	Dominance of dinosaurs; first mammals and birds; insects abundant, including social forms.
	Triassic		225	First dinosaurs and mammal-like reptiles, with culmination of large amphibians.
PALEOZOIC	Permian		270	Primitive reptiles replace amphibians as dominant class; glaciation.
	Carboniferous		350	Amphibians dominant in luxuriant coal forests; first reptiles and trees.
	Devonian		400	Dominance of fishes; first amphibians.
	Silurian		440	Primitive fishes; invasion of land by plants and arthropods.
	Ordovician		500	First vertebrates, the jawless fish; invertebrates dominate the seas.
	Cambrian		600	All invertebrate phyla appear and algae diversify.
PRE-CAMBRIAN			4500	A few multicellular invertebrates; earliest fossils at 3.6 m.y.a.

11:00 A.M., amphibians began to move onto the land, and insects appeared in a warm landscape of swamps and forests. Late that same afternoon, the first dinosaurs crawled about. Smaller, warm-blooded dinosaurs began to produce live young and nurse them. Sixty-seven minutes before midnight, the common ancestor of apes and humans found its home in dense forests. The first recognizable human, walking on two legs, made an appearance at 11:51 P.M. The earliest art was created less than five seconds before midnight. Agriculture and animal domestication were discovered only two seconds before the end of the week, and the industrial revolution began just as the last bell for midnight tolled.

In order to help make this vastness of time comprehensible, geologists have divided the Earth's history into a series of **eras** representing major episodes, usually distinguished by significant changes in the plant and animal kingdoms. The Precambrian is the first major era of geologic time and extends from the origin of the Earth to about 600 million years ago. The succeeding Paleozoic Era witnessed the appearance of the first vertebrate species: fish and early amphibians. Plants spread onto the land and reptiles began to appear. Around 225 million years ago the Mesozoic Era, the age of the dinosaurs, began. The **Cenozoic**, our current era, began about 65 million years ago with the rise of mammals, birds, and flowering plants.

The Cenozoic is further divided by geologists into a series of seven **epochs**, only the last three of which are relevant to the evolution of the human species. The **Pliocene**, beginning around 5 or 6 million years ago, is the geological epoch in which the first **hominid**, or humanlike creature, appeared. The **Pleistocene** Epoch, beginning about 2 million years ago, was marked by a series of major climatic fluctuations. Completely modern forms of the human species appeared toward the end of this epoch. The **Recent** (also called the Holocene, Postglacial, or Present Interglacial) Epoch, beginning only 10,000 years ago, witnessed the origins of agriculture and the industrial age, and includes our present time.

THE EVOLUTION OF THE ANIMAL KINGDOM

Zoologists classify the members of the animal kingdom according to their similarities and differences. We are animals because we move and eat with a mouth; we are vertebrates because of backbones, and mammals because of warm blood and breast feeding. We are **primates** because of grasping hands, flexible limbs, and a highly developed sense of vision, which we share with the other members of the primate order: lemurs, tarsiers, monkeys, and apes. We are called **Hominoidea** — the taxonomic group that includes the apes and humans — because of the shape of our teeth, our lack of a tail, and our swinging arms. Human molars display a distinctive Y5 pattern on the surface with five cusps; the molars of apes have a + 4 pattern with only four cusps. Hominoidea include all present and past apes and humans, while the term hominids refers specifically to present and past humans. Humans share a common ancestor with the chimps and gorillas that appeared at some point in the last five to ten million years.

Present evidence suggests the following scenario for primate evolution during the Cenozoic. The first primates on Earth were recognized about 65 m.y.a. (million years ago) at the beginning of the era, when the air temperature was warming and extensive tropical forests covered much of the land surface. These early primates began as tree-dwelling insect eaters. They had such adaptive characteristics as stereoscopic color vision, which provided depth perception and enhanced their ability to move in three dimensions from branch to branch and to spot insects; and a grasping ability, so they could hold on to the branches and grab the bugs. This heritage has provided us with extraordinary vision and large centers in the brain to process the mass of information absorbed by the eyes. Along with the ability to hold and manipulate objects with dexterity came other changes. Arms and shoulders became more flexible for swinging in the trees, and internal organs and bones were engineered toward a more vertical arrangement.

The earliest fossil apes appeared approximately 25 million years ago. Apes are generally distinguished from monkeys and other primates by larger size, distinctive teeth, greater sociability, the absence of tails, and a reduced sense of smell. From one of these early apes, a new group of animals — known as the **dryopithecines** — emerged in the Miocene Epoch some 20 million years ago. These creatures had a number of features, known primarily from the fossil teeth that have survived, suggesting that they were the probable ancestors of both the living apes and humans. Dryopithecines were apparently very successful in their adaptation, ranging over much of Africa, Asia, and Europe. During this time the Earth changed dramatically. Increased activity in the Earth's crust created new mountain ranges. Volcanoes and earthquakes were recurrent. Rainfall increased, and air temperature dropped. Widespread tropical forests began to shrink, taken over by expanding grasslands and savannas.

Around 14 million years ago, a new series of fossil primates evolved from the dryopithecines. These creatures are generally regarded as the likely ancestors of both humans and apes, such as the chimpanzee and gorilla. Although the remains are rare and fragmentary, the size and shape of the teeth and jaw and the thickness of the tooth enamel indicate a mouth designed for heavy chewing and a diet of seeds, nuts, grasses, and insects — foods found in the forest and at the juncture of forest and open grassland.

At some point in the later Miocene, an African contemporary of these primates took the path toward humanness, as seen in the evidence for more upright posture and

In each great region of the world the living mammals are closely related to the extinct species of the same region. It is, therefore, probable that Africa was formerly inhabited by extinct apes closely allied to the gorilla and chimpanzee; and as these two species are now man's nearest allies, it is somewhat more probable that our early progenitors lived on the African continent than elsewhere.

Charles Darwin, *The Descent of Man* (1871)

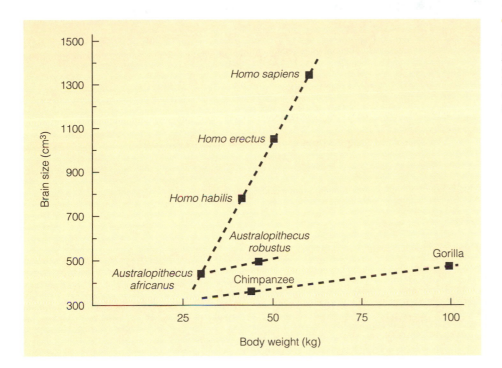

Brain size and body weight in the higher primates and hominids. Body weight is estimated for the fossil hominid forms. Note the increase in both body weight and brain size in the line of human evolution.

smaller canine teeth. Richard Klein, of the University of Chicago, perhaps best described the situation: "Proto-people probably diverged from proto-chimpanzees" between 5 and 10 million years ago (Klein, 1989, p. 180). The fossil record from this time period is very scanty. A recent fossil find in the Sumburu Hills of Kenya may represent this creature. A fragment of an upper jaw, dating to 8 or 9 million years ago, shows characteristics of a generalized chimpanzee-gorilla-hominid ancestor. By the beginning of the Pliocene, approximately 5.5 million years ago, recognizably hominid members of our lineage had appeared in Africa. The sites described in the following pages of this chapter tell that story.

ON BEING HUMAN

But what is human? What makes us distinct among other species of animals? We are human because we have a skeleton designed for upright walking. We have grasping thumbs, capable of both strength and precision movement. But we are also human because we have lost the grasping, opposable toe of the other apes. We are human because we have small, flat teeth and lack the large, slashing canines of other primates. We have distinct noses compared to apes, and a face that sits beneath our brain case rather than in front of it. We are human because we lack fur and have more sweat glands than hair follicles. We have conspicuous penises and breasts, and we care for our young over a lengthy period of infancy and childhood. We have large brains relative to our body size and enhanced intelligence embedded in a complex repertoire of behaviors known as culture. We are human because we often act on reason rather than instinct, and because we make and use tools to alter our environment and make our lives more secure and comfortable. We are human because we speak a language full of meaning and metaphor.

Upright posture, large brain size, and tool use are generally considered the three primary indicators of humanness among those in the list above. The major questions in human evolution, then, concern when, where, and why these distinctive characteristics appeared. What of us is preserved in the layers of geological time? **Paleoanthropology**, the study of human evolution, is an attempt to answer these and other questions, using the fossil evidence of bones and stones from the Pliocene and Pleistocene Epochs. For this study we turn to Africa; our oldest ancestors are known only from that continent. Some of the best evidence comes from sites at Laetoli, Hadar, Swartkrans, Olduvai, and Koobi Fora.

LAETOLI

*The best evidence for the first steps
toward humanness*

Before 1970 there was relatively little evidence for the earliest human ancestors other than a few skulls and pieces of bone. The characteristics of upright posture, large brain size, and tool use were thought to have evolved simultaneously as large primates moved out from the forest into the savanna. In the last twenty years or so, however, discoveries in East Africa have reshaped and redefined our family tree. All the evidence for the early hominids before 1 million years ago comes from Africa. New fossils from Ethiopia, Kenya, and Tanzania have pushed back the age of the earliest known hominids and considerably modified our understanding of their behavior and appearance.

There is a long gap in the fossil record of human evolution between 10 and 5 million years ago. The evolutionary sequence toward humanness is unclear because of the lack of fossils from this crucial interval. The known remains include only a few isolated teeth and fragments of jaws, the hardest bones in the skeleton. Perhaps conditions for the burial and preservation of fossil bones were not good during this time, or perhaps we have not yet looked in the right places.

Shortly after 5 million years ago, however, during the Pliocene Epoch, the first recognizably human remains began to appear in East Africa. Many of the early hominid fossils date to the later Pliocene and the beginning of the Pleistocene, a time often described as the **Plio/Pleistocene**. The brain size of these earliest hominids from the Pliocene was not larger than that of the modern apes, nor had their teeth changed a great deal from their earlier ape ancestors. What was different,

however, was a new form of movement. The earliest human fossils in the Pliocene showed definite indications of **bipedalism**—walking on two feet rather than four.

The most dramatic evidence for this new posture comes not from the fossil bones, however, but from actual footprints preserved at the site of Laetoli (lay-toe'-lee) in Tanzania, discovered by Mary Leakey in 1976. Laetoli is located about 70 km (40 mi) southeast of Olduvai Gorge. Sometime around 3.6 million years ago, an active volcano near Laetoli covered the area with a layer of volcanic ash. Following a light rain shower, various animals moved across the damp layer of ash. A chemical reaction between rainwater and the ash quickly hardened their tracks; even the impressions of the raindrops are preserved in some areas at the site. Spring hares, birds, extinct elephants, pigs, buffalos, rhinoceros, a saber-toothed tiger, and lots of baboons left their footprints. The numerous sets of tracks do not often overlap one another, suggesting that this layer of footprints was quickly buried by more ash, ensuring its preservation. Radiopotassium dating was used to measure the age of the ash layers to between 3.5 and 3.8 m.y.a. for these footprints. (See "Dating Methods," p. 12.)

Early hominids walked across the fresh ash as well. The seventy or so human footprints continued over a distance of more than 6 m (20 ft) and were made by three individuals. The longest track contains about thirty prints of an individual walking on two feet with a stride and balance that is clearly human. A second, smaller individual followed in the foot-

They are the most remarkable find I have made in my entire career. . . . When we first came across the hominid prints I must admit that I was skeptical, but then it became clear that it could be nothing else. They are the earliest prints of man's ancestors, and they show us that hominids three-and-three-quarters million years ago walked upright with a free-striding gait, just as we do today.

Mary Leakey, in R. Leakey (1981)

prints of the first, and a third set of prints lies alongside the first. The footprints look human, with a well-defined arch and an absence of the diverging toe that is characteristic of the great apes. Studies of the size and depth of the prints suggest that two of the individuals were approximately 1.4 m (4′8″) tall, and the third was 1.2 m (4′) tall. Mary Leakey, the excavator of these fossil footprints, noted the child-size steps and speculated on the scene:

> At one point [the child] stops, pauses and turns to the left to glance at some possible threat or irregularity, and then continues to the north. This motion, so intensely human, transcends time. 3,600,000 years ago, a remote ancestor — just as you or I — experienced a moment of doubt.
>
> (R. Levin, 1988, p. 57)

Thus the evidence indicates that three early hominids strolled across this area of damp, volcanic ash. Walking on two feet appears to have been the normal mode of locomotion, very similar to our modern stride. No stone tools have been found in deposits of this age at Laetoli; such equipment was apparently not yet a part of the human condition. Hominid fossil remains, particularly fragments of skulls from Laetoli and elsewhere in East Africa, also demonstrate that the human brain had not yet begun its major expansion. In fact, these earliest humans might best be portrayed with the head and face of an apelike creature atop a small, upright human body, stepping into the future. As Mary Leakey went on to say: "The outstanding evolutionary question now is: What was the selection pressure that produced bipedalism?" (R. Levin, 1988, p. 57).

A view of the ash surface at Laetoli, with at least two pairs of hominid footprints and the track of an extinct form of horse running from lower left to upper right.

DATING METHODS

Measuring the age of archaeological remains

In the first half of this century, there was almost no way to determine the age of the remains of early humans and their artifacts. A few **relative dating** techniques were used to estimate the age of bones and stones in a long sequence, but it was generally impossible to establish the absolute age of a layer or artifact in calendar years. Relative dating methods often use stratigraphic relationships to order older and younger materials; lower layers of sediments in the ground, in caves, and elsewhere are, not surprisingly, older than the layers on top.

Relative dating methods also rely on the **association** of various items. The bones of extinct animals, such as elephants in France found with stone tools, were clear evidence that the artifacts were as old as the animals, even if the exact age was uncertain. In a contemporary situation, glass bottles have changed over the last 200 years. Bottles have become seamless, with shorter necks and narrower bodies. The known dates for certain types of bottles can be used to determine the age of other materials found with them. The thickness of the stem and bore of clay smoking pipes from the eighteenth and nineteenth centuries followed a steady decline, as the technology for manufacturing these items improved. Thus the age of an historic trading post in Canada can be estimated by measuring the broken pieces of pipe stem found there. Photographs can be approximately dated by the known age of the automobile or other objects that are pictured.

Relative dating methods, however, are limited. It is often necessary to know the ages of archaeological materials more precisely in calendar years — **absolute dating** — in order to answer most questions about the past. Although many methods for determining absolute dates are now available, the most common techniques rely on the properties of radioactive decay in certain elements. Many elements have both stable and radioactive atomic forms, known as **isotopes**. The techniques used for determining absolute dates with these elements are referred to as **isotopic techniques**. Perhaps best known among these is radiocarbon dating, but certain other elements — potassium, uranium, or calcium, for example — can also be used. Radiopotassium, or potassium-argon, dating, for determining the age of early human ancestors and their remains, and radiocarbon dating, for dating archaeological events in the last 40,000 years, are described below.

RADIOPOTASSIUM DATING

Radiopotassium dating, also known as **potassium-argon dating**, is a technique of crucial importance for determining the age of the earliest human remains. This technique can date most of the Earth's history and has been used to measure the age of the oldest rocks on our planet, as well as samples of moon rocks. The first potassium-argon dates from the lava at the base of Olduvai Gorge — 1.75 m.y.a. — startled the scientific community in the 1960s. These fossil remains were almost 1 million years older than previously believed. Other early hominid remains in East Africa from Laetoli, Koobi Fora, Hadar, and elsewhere have also been dated using the radiopotassium technique. Bones and artifacts are not themselves directly dated; rather, the newly formed volcanic rocks or ash deposits that lie directly under or over the prehistoric materials are analyzed. These dates thus bracket the archaeological materials in time.

The technique is based on the following principles. Potassium (chemical symbol K) is found in abundance in granites, clays, and basalts in the minerals of the Earth's crust. Potassium occurs in several stable forms and has one radioactive isotope, ^{40}K, with a half-life of approximately 1.3 billion years. **Half-life** is a measure of the rate of decay in radioactive materials. Essentially, half the radioactive materials will disappear within the period of one half-life. Because this isotope has such a very long half-life, it is not possible to date materials that are younger than 500,000 years or so, because too little decay has taken place to measure.

The radioactive isotope ^{40}K decays into argon (^{40}Ar), an inert gas, and calcium (^{40}Ca). About 11% of ^{40}K becomes ^{40}Ar as it decays. The materials generally dated by the $^{40}K/^{40}Ar$ technique are limited to rocks, volcanic ashes, and other substances that contain radioactive potassium and trap the argon gas that is produced. The molten state of the rock permits the release of trapped gas in the parent rock and resets the argon reservoirs in the new rock to zero. ^{40}Ar begins to accumulate as soon as a rock is formed. By measuring the amount of ^{40}Ar to ^{40}K remaining, it is possible to determine how much ^{40}K has decayed and thus the amount of time that has elapsed since the rock was created. Measurements are done with sophisticated counters that record the amount of radioactivity remaining.

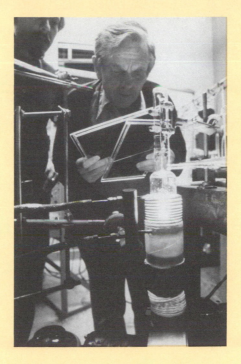

Garniss Curtis, developer of the radio-potassium dating method, examining the laboratory apparatus as a sample is heated to extract gases for the measurement of isotopes in a potassium-argon dating laboratory.

RADIOCARBON DATING

The Manhattan Project was the most secret and expensive weapons development effort of the U.S. government during World War II. Laboratories in Chicago, New York, Tennessee, New Mexico, and elsewhere employed thousands of scientists and technicians to develop the first atomic bomb. Many of the unknowns of radioactivity were revealed for the first time during this work. One of the spinoffs was the discovery that some radioactive elements could be used to measure the age of various materials. Willard Libby, a physicist at the University of Chicago, announced the first age determinations from radioactive carbon in 1949 and received the Nobel Prize for his discovery.

The key to the procedure known as **radiocarbon dating** lies in the half-life of radioactive elements. Radioactivity is a process of instability and decay. In the decay process, a radioactive isotope changes from one elemental form into another and emits an electron. Some radioactive isotopes, such as potassium, have an extremely long half-life. Others have very brief half-lives; ^{90}Sr (strontium-90), for example, has a half-life of twenty-eight

years. In order to determine the age of prehistoric materials, the half-life of an element must be of an appropriate period to measure the age of the material. For example, a material with a brief half-life would be gone in just a few years; in very old material, none would remain to be measured.

Carbon is the most useful element for isotopic dating; it is present in all living things. Carbon has several stable isotopes, including ^{12}C and ^{13}C, and the critical radioactive isotope, ^{14}C, also known as carbon-14 or radiocarbon, with a half-life of approximately 5730 years. However, because of this rather short half-life, materials older than about 40,000 years do not contain sufficient remaining radiocarbon to be dated.

Carbon-14 is produced in the atmosphere by cosmic radiation, which is assumed to have been at a constant level in the past, as it is today. The radioactive carbon combines with oxygen into carbon dioxide and is incorporated into plants and animals in the same ratio as it is found in the atmosphere. When a plant or animal dies, the intake of carbon ceases,

Table 1.1   Some of the Major Dating Techniques in Archaeology

Technique	Materials	Range	Principle	Limitations
Radiocarbon	Wood, charcoal, bone, carbonate	100 to 40,000 years	Radioactive decay	Contamination, calibration
Radiopotassium	Volcanic rock or minerals	Unlimited but approximate	Radioactive decay	Appropriate samples are rare
Uranium Series	Coral, molluscs, travertine	30,000 to 300,000 years	Radioactive decay	Few labs, technical problems, contamination
Geomagnetism	Undisturbed sediment or volcanic rocks	Unlimited but approximate	Alignment of particles with pole reversals	Few labs
Archaeomagnetism	Intact hearths, kilns, burned areas	2000 years	Alignment with changes in location of the Earth's magnetic pole	Few labs, calibration
Thermoluminescence (TL)	Pottery, heated stones, calcite	1,000,000 years	Accumulation of TL in crystals	Environmental irradiation rate, few labs
Electron Spin Resonance	Heated crystalline stones, calcites, bones, shell	1,000,000 years	Accumulation of unpaired electrons in crystals	Few labs, experimental technique
Obsidian Hydration	Obsidian artifacts	35,000 years	Accumulation of weathering rind on artifact	Requires local calibration
Dendrochronology	Tree rings in preserved logs and lumber	8000 years	Counting of annual growth rings	Region-specific
Fission Track	Volcanic rock, crystalline materials	100,000 to 1,000,000 years	Radioactive decay leaves microscopic track in crystals at known rate	Materials rare in archaeological context

and the decay process begins. Thus the amount of radiocarbon in prehistoric material is a direct function of the length of time the organism has been dead.

A variety of organic materials can be assayed by radiocarbon dating, including wood, bone, shell, charcoal, antler, and other items. Carbon-14 often survives best at prehistoric sites in the form of charcoal, and this material has been most commonly dated by the radiocarbon dating method. However, wood charcoal can come from very old trees or wood and may not date the actual archaeological material accurately. If charcoal from the older rings of the tree is used for dating, the age may be off by several hundred years. For more reliable dates, plants other than trees are used. Materials with a short life — such as nutshells, corncobs, small twigs — are preferable to wood charcoal.

The actual measurement of radiocarbon is straightforward. A sample of known weight is cleaned carefully and burned, to create a pure gas of carbon dioxide. The radioactive carbon isotopes in that gas are then counted. In simple terms, a Geiger counter is used to record radioactive emissions from the gas. Several grams of organic material are normally required to produce enough gas for counting.

New technology, however, has resulted in a reduction in the amount of material that is measured. Atomic **accelerator mass spectrometers (AMS)** are now being used to measure the ratio of carbon isotopes in very small samples. Rather than measuring radioactivity through a Geiger counter, an AMS involves the separation and counting of individual carbon atoms by their weight, a much more accurate process. Moreover, less than 0.01 g of sample is needed, and individual pieces of charcoal or a single nutshell or a cereal grain can be dated directly. AMS dating is now being used to provide new dates from many sites and materials that could not previously be measured. The technique, implemented in 1980, has already produced very important results.

One example of AMS dating concerns the first domestication of wheat. In 1978, Fred Wendorf, of Southern Methodist University, and Roman Schild, of the Polish Institute for the History of Material Culture, reported that they had found the earliest domesticated wheat in the world at the Wadi Kubbaniya in Egypt. The radiocarbon age of the site was measured as 19,060 years ago, a date obtained from charcoal in a hearth near where several grains of the cereal were found. A major discovery, this wheat was almost twice the age of the earliest known domestic cereal, and it came from a location outside the Fertile Crescent, the expected homeland. Needless to say, there was controversy and doubt. For this reason, Wendorf and Schild subsequently used the new AMS dating technique to measure the age of one of the individual cereal grains. The new date of 2800 B.C. clearly indicated that the wheat was much younger than originally thought. The grains of wheat had likely moved down through the ground near a very old and deeply buried hearth.

There are certain problems with radiocarbon dating, some involving contamination of the sample. However, as the number of actual measurements increased, it became clear to investigators that there were often regular errors in the dates, and a detailed study was undertaken to assess this error factor. Tree rings of known age from the bristlecone pine tree were compared against radiocarbon measurements of the same material. The bristlecone pine is one of the oldest living organisms on Earth, reaching ages of up to 4000 years. Individual growth rings from the tree could be counted from the outer bark to the inner core, and the exact age of a ring could be measured in calendar years. That same ring could also be dated by radiocarbon to determine the relationship between calendar years and radiocarbon years.

This study resulted in the recognition of changes in the amount of radioactive carbon in the atmosphere over time and the need for a correction, or calibration, factor for radiocarbon dates to convert them to true calender years. It appears that the assumption that radiocarbon has always been produced at a constant rate in the atmosphere is incorrect and that differences between radiocarbon years and calendar years are related to changes in the rate of cosmic ray bombardment. Radiocarbon dates that have been converted to calendar years are called **calibrated dates**.

The dates in this book are given in two ways. Dates from the Pliocene and Pleistocene are given in years before the present (B.P.). Dates from the last 10,000 years or so are given in calendar years before Christ, B.C., or Anno Domini, A.D. Because of the fact that calibrated radiocarbon dates can only be extended back 5000 or 6000 years from the present, we have not used calibrated dates. Thus the more recent dates are given in uncalibrated radiocarbon years unless otherwise indicated. Another term for periods of time used in the latter part of the book is **millennium** (plural **millennia**). A decade is 10 years; a century is 100 years; a millennium is 1000 years. The millennia before Christ run in reverse — the first millennium B.C. goes from 0 B.C. to 1000 B.C.

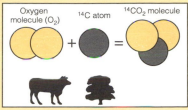

(1) ^{14}C and oxygen enters living organisms.

(2) ^{14}C begins to deplete.

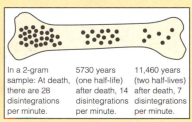

In a 2-gram sample: At death, there are 28 disintegrations per minute.

5730 years (one half-life) after death, 14 disintegrations per minute.

11,460 years (two half-lives) after death, 7 disintegrations per minute.

(3) ^{14}C continues to disintegrate at an orderly, predictable rate.

The principles of radiocarbon dating.

Hadar

More fragments of early humans from northeastern Ethiopia

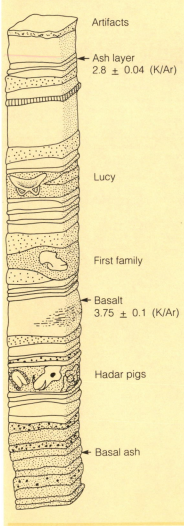

The severely eroded badlands of Pliocene and Pleistocene deposits in the Hadar region of Ethiopia.

- Artifacts
- Ash layer 2.8 ± 0.04 (K/Ar)
- Lucy
- First family
- Basalt 3.75 ± 0.1 (K/Ar)
- Hadar pigs
- Basal ash

Pliocene stratigraphy at Hadar showing the approximate age of the layers where Lucy and the "first family" were found. These layers are exposed by erosion, and the fossil finds appear on the eroded surface of the layer.

New **fossil** discoveries continue to come out of East Africa, causing paleoanthropologists to continue to redraw our family tree. One of the most productive areas of research is in a region known as the Hadar (huh-dar'), northeast of Addis Ababa in Ethiopia. In this geologically active zone, the combination of faulting, rapid deposition, and continued erosion has exposed numerous layers from the Pliocene and Pleistocene that contain some of the earliest human fossils yet discovered. Donald Johanson, a paleoanthropologist at the Institute for Human Origins in Berkeley, California, and Maurice Taieb, a French geologist, began a search for early hominid fossils in this area in 1972. One of the most complete early human skeletons ever discovered was found by this team in 1974.

Johanson spotted a small arm bone on the ground while on a survey walk. He picked it up and immediately noticed other bits of skull and bone. As he continued, more pieces were collected—fragments of vertebrae, limbs, and jaws. The next day he returned with a large crew and carefully sifted the earth at the site in order to recover all the fragments they could find. The finds of Pliocene hominids are commonly of a single tooth or at most a few bones. Instead of the usual few tiny pieces of jaw, skull, or teeth, almost 100 fragments were found after two weeks of sifting and searching—almost 40% of a complete skeleton.

For the first time, a reasonably intact early hominid was available, enough to reconstruct virtually the entire skeleton. Lucy, as this individual was dubbed by her discoverers, provided much new detail on the anatomy of torso and limbs. Lucy was probably female, small in stature—1.2 m, only 4' tall—small brained, and about 20 years old when she died. Absolute age for the skeleton is estimated as somewhat more than 2.9 m.y.a.

Earlier still from Hadar, dating perhaps to 3.2 m.y.a., are the skeletal parts of what has been described as "the first fam-

ily"—over 200 bones from at least seven individuals, five adults and two children, found together. This is an absolutely remarkable discovery. Johanson's own description of the discoveries conveys the sense of excitement and importance:

> Anthropology student John Kolar spotted an arm-bone fragment. From some distance away Mike Bush, a medical student, shouted that he had found something just breaking the ground surface. It was the very first day on survey for Mike.
>
> "Hominid teeth?" he asked, when we ran to him. There was no doubt. . . .
>
> Michèle Cavillon of our motion-picture crew called to me to look at some bones higher up the hill.
>
> Two bone fragments lay side by side, one a partial femur and the other a fragmentary heel bone. Both were hominid. Carefully we scoured the hillside. Two more leg bones—fibulae—showed up, but each from the same side. The same side? That could only indicate two individuals. . . .
>
> Time was of the essence. Rainstorms during the months of our absence could wash away fragments that would be lost forever down the ravines. Each day produced more remains. . . .
>
> So we had evidence of young adults, old adults, and children—an entire assemblage of early hominids. All of them at one place. Nothing like this had ever been found!
>
> (Johanson, 1976, p. 805)

These individuals apparently died as a group, possibly in a local flash flood, and their bodies were then washed into a location where their bones were preserved until their discovery. The sediments in which the fossils were discovered were lakeshore and riverine deposits, and there are very few remains from other species in these layers. There is no sign that the hominid bones were gnawed or eaten by other animals.

The discovery of these bones from a *group* suggests new answers to a number of questions. The presence of so many individuals together indicates that our earliest ancestors did indeed live in groups. These individuals were relatively small (1.2 to 1.5 m, or 3′ to 4′ tall) but strong and sturdy. The heads were small, with human molars and small canine teeth. There was still present, however, an ape-like gap between the incisor teeth and canines. The skeleton below the neck was almost completely human, but the arms were long and the bones of the hand were heavy with large muscle attachments. The anatomy of the leg and pelvis indicates that they walked erect. Other information on early hominid patterns of growth, differences between children and adults and between males and females, the dexterity of the hands, and more, will emerge as the study of these extraordinary remains continues.

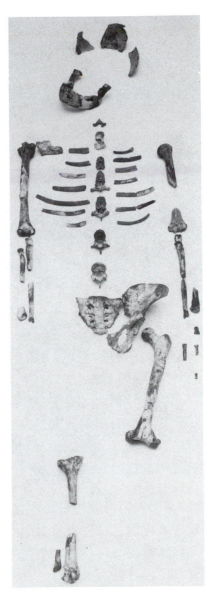

The skeleton known as Lucy from Hadar, one of the most complete of an early hominid. Almost 40% of the bones are present. A member of Australopithecus afarensis, Lucy was approximately 1.2 m tall and 3 million years old.

AN UNCERTAIN FAMILY TREE

The changing evidence and interpretation of our earliest biology

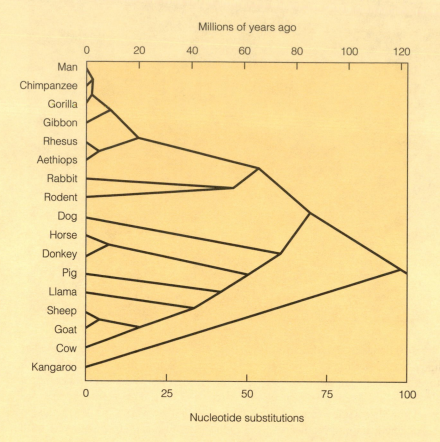

Millions of years ago

Nucleotide substitutions

Relative distances among various species in terms of nucleotide substitutions. The number of substitutions is shown at the bottom of the graph and the estimated age of evolutionary divergence between the species and a common ancestor is shown at the top.

Human evolution—the changes in the skeleton and biology of our species over the last several million years—is a fascinating subject, yet one for which there is only sparse evidence. In almost every instance the fossil remains for our earliest hominid ancestors are very fragmentary, poorly preserved, and disturbed by natural forces. This is due largely to the age of the remains; time and nature have taken their toll. The absence of evidence is particularly obvious between about 10 and 2 million years ago, the period when early hominids first appeared.

Fortunately, not all the information on this subject comes from fossil bones. Evidence from molecules helps provide some insight about the point in time at which certain hominoids became hominids—when humans became a species distinct from an apelike ancestor. Scientists have developed a "molecular clock" that provides an estimate of the time at which certain modern species separated from a common ancestor in the past. The

mechanism for this clock is the change over time in the amino acids, which make up animal protein. Known as nucleotide substitutions, these changes represent mismatches in the genetic material of two species. The number of differences in the amino acids in the chromosomes of two species correlates closely with the evolutionary distance between them. Chemically and genetically, in terms of the composition of chromosomes, our closest relative is the chimpanzee. Comparison of amino acids in humans and chimps indicates that the two species diverged 4 to 5 million years ago—a date very close to that for the earliest fossil hominids.

Determination of the genus and species of the fossil bones of early humans, however, is very difficult. There are no more than a few hundred separate individuals represented among all the finds of *Australopithecus* and early *Homo*. Because it is so difficult to determine the age of many of these fossils, questions exist about whether these species were contem-

Table 1.2   Major Characteristics of the Plio/Pleistocene Hominids

	A. afarensis	A. africanus	A. robustus	A. boisei	H. habilis
Dates	4 to 3 m.y.a.	3 to 2.5 m.y.a.	2.2 to 1.5 m.y.a.	2.2 to 1 m.y.a.	2.2 to 1.6 m.y.a.
Sites	Hadar Omo Laetoli	Taung Sterkfontein Makapansgat Lake Turkana (?) Omo (?)	Kromdraai Swartkrans	Olduvai Lake Turkana Omo	Olduvai Lake Turkana Omo Sterkfontein (?) Swartkrans (?)
Cranial capacity	380 to 500 cc $\bar{x}$ = 440 cc	435 to 530 cc $\bar{x}$ = 450 cc	520 cc (based on one specimen)	500 to 530 cc $\bar{x}$ = 515 cc	500 to 800 cc $\bar{x}$ = 680 cc
Size	3′6″ 50 lb (♀) (♂ to 100 lb?)	Similar to *afarensis*	5′ + to 150 lb	5′ + to 150 lb	Limited evidence; may have been size of *afarensis*
Skull	Very prognathous; receding chin; large teeth; pointed canine with gap; arcade between ape and human; hint of crest	Less prognathous than *afarensis*; jaw more rounded; large back teeth; canines smaller than *robustus*, larger than *afarensis*; no crest	Heavy jaws; small canines and front teeth; large back teeth; definite crest	Very large jaws; very large back teeth; large crest	Flatter face; less sloping forehead; teeth similar to *africanus*; no crest
Postcranial skeleton	Long arms; short thumb; curved fingers and toes; bipedal	—	Hands and feet more like modern humans; retention of long arms	—	Limited evidence; retention of long arms; maybe retention of primitive features of hand and foot

$\bar{x}$ = mean value.

Source: Adapted from Feder, K. L., and M. A. Park. 1989. *Human antiquity*. Mountain View, CA: Mayfield.

poraneous or sequential in time. Not surprisingly, there are a number of controversies over just what to call these first hominid forms and how to identify them. As Richard Klein has noted, paleoanthropology is more like a court of law than a physics laboratory. It sometimes seems that whenever a new fragment is discovered, our entire family tree is reassessed and often redrawn. New fossils are found almost every year that modify current ideas.

Since the initial work of the Swedish natural historian Carolus Linnaeus during the mid-1700s, scientists have classified newly discovered members of the plant and animal kingdoms according to a system that organizes these living things into species, genus, family, order, class, phylum, and kingdom, from most specific to more general — a family tree of life.

Modern humans are members of the family *Hominidae* in the genus *Homo* and the species *sapiens*. The early members of the family *Hominidae,* from 2 to 3 million years ago, include two genera, *Australopithecus* and *Homo*. The *Australopithecus* forms take several names — *africanus, robustus, boisei* — with one evolving into the other; the *Homo* is named *habilis*. The line of **australopithecines** (the generic term for the various forms of *Australopithecus*) eventually became extinct around 1 million years ago. The major difficulties in the classification of the early hominids lie in the features of the skull and lower jaw. The most important traits that help distinguish the early hominids include various bony ridges on the top, front, and back of the skull; the shape and size of the skull, jaws, and teeth; the size of the brain case and face; and the presence of a chin. There

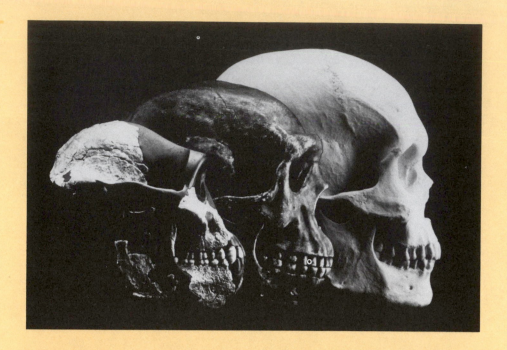

The skulls of Australopithecus afarensis *(left),* Homo erectus *(center), and* Homo sapiens sapiens.

is little consensus on which of these features distinguish which fossils forms, however, so disagreements are common and changes in hominid lineages are frequent.

The generally accepted view of Donald Johanson and Tim White, of the University of California, Berkeley, is that an *Australopithecus* called *afarensis* existed between 3 and 4 million years ago and was the ancestor of all later hominid forms. The specimens from Laetoli and Hadar are examples of this early species. Certainly the palate of this australopithecine suggests a close relationship with an ape ancestor. The palate and upper teeth of modern humans have a parabolic shape — a smooth curve — while this area has a distinctive U-shape in the apes. *Australopithecus afarensis* in East Africa at 3.5 million years ago had a U-shaped jaw. *Afarensis* evolved into later forms such as *africanus, robustus,* and *boisei.*

Richard Leakey, of the National Museum of Kenya; Alan Walker, of Johns Hopkins University; and others suggest a different scenario. Leakey's father Louis always argued that the genus *Homo* had its roots deep in the Pliocene, and eventually he discovered several early *Homo*

specimens at Olduvai and elsewhere. This view is maintained by his son Richard and others, who would push the evolutionary split from a common ancestor of the *Australopithecus* and *Homo* lines much further back in time, perhaps to near the beginning of the Pliocene, around 6 million years ago. They imagine that two or more different australopithecine groups (*robustus* and *africanus*) and one line of *Homo* (*habilis*) evolved at this point in time. The first stone tools are almost certainly associated with a form of *Homo* that survived and continued to make artifacts. There is very little fossil evidence between 4 and 7 million years ago, because geological deposits dating to this period in Africa are extremely rare. Thus the common ancestor that Leakey and others envision far back in the Pliocene remains hypothetical.

The 1986 discovery by Johanson and White of over 300 pieces of a skeleton of *Homo habilis* in beds at Olduvai Gorge dating to 1.8 million years ago redrew part of this picture. For the first time, there are enough fragments of the arms and legs of a *habilis* creature to provide an indication of height and the proportions of the limbs. Surprisingly, this female *habilis* was less

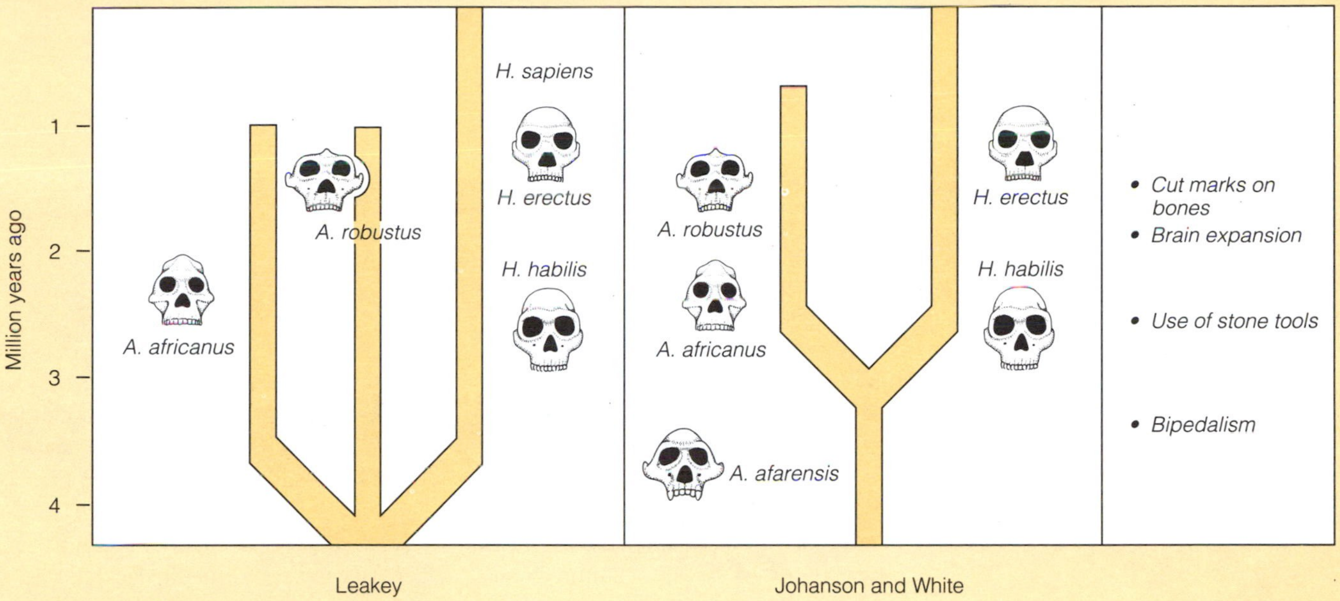
H. sapiens
1
2
3
4
Million years ago
A. africanus
A. robustus
H. erectus
H. habilis
A. robustus
A. africanus
A. afarensis
H. erectus
H. habilis
• Cut marks on bones
• Brain expansion
• Use of stone tools
• Bipedalism
Leakey
Johanson and White

Two current models of human evolution, as seen by Richard Leakey and by Donald Johanson and Tim White. The first evidence for important events in human evolution is indicated on the right of the chart.

than 1 m (3′3″) tall and had very long arms, similar to Lucy and other australopithecines. Such evidence suggests (1) that *habilis* may still have been spending part of its life in the trees, (2) that sexual dimorphism was still very pronounced, and (3) that major changes in behavior and habitat of the early hominids may have taken place in the period between 1.5 and 2 m.y.a. Thus it appears that *Homo habilis* "represents a mosaic of primitive and derived features, indicating an early hominid which walked bipedally . . . but also retained the generalized hominoid capacity to climb trees" (Sussman and Stern, 1982, p. 931).

There are, of course, other schools of thought; indeed, there are almost as many views on the classification of early hominids as there are scientists considering the question. It is clear, however, that early human evolution was characterized by two adaptive pathways in the tropics of Africa: one that led to big teeth and a heavy jaw for chewing vegetable foods, and the other toward expansion of the brain case and the use of tools.

The middle portion of our family tree is relatively straightforward and uncontested. A form known as *Homo erectus* gradually evolved from *Homo habilis* about 1.8 million years ago, again in Africa. *Erectus* was the first early human form found not just in Africa but also in Asia and probably in Europe. *Homo erectus* evolved into what has been termed archaic *Homo sapiens*. The earliest examples of these archaic *sapiens* forms are known from sub-Saharan Africa and must have appeared before 200,000 years ago. There are two forms of archaic *Homo sapiens,* called (1) *Homo sapiens* in Africa and most of Asia, and (2) *Homo sapiens neanderthalensis* in Europe and Southwest Asia. Neanderthal populations were likely absorbed by expanding groups of *Homo sapiens sapiens* between 40,000 and 30,000 years ago. This issue of the evolution of modern humans will arise again in Chapter Three.

SWARTKRANS

South African caves with many early humans

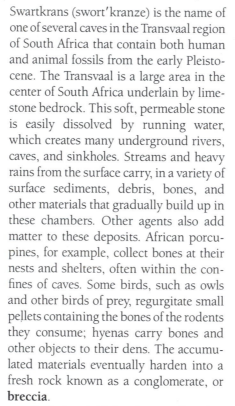

Swartkrans (swort′kranze) is the name of one of several caves in the Transvaal region of South Africa that contain both human and animal fossils from the early Pleistocene. The Transvaal is a large area in the center of South Africa underlain by limestone bedrock. This soft, permeable stone is easily dissolved by running water, which creates many underground rivers, caves, and sinkholes. Streams and heavy rains from the surface carry, in a variety of surface sediments, debris, bones, and other materials that gradually build up in these chambers. Other agents also add matter to these deposits. African porcupines, for example, collect bones at their nests and shelters, often within the confines of caves. Some birds, such as owls and other birds of prey, regurgitate small pellets containing the bones of the rodents they consume; hyenas carry bones and other objects to their dens. The accumulated materials eventually harden into a fresh rock known as a conglomerate, or **breccia**.

Early hominid fossils were first discovered when the breccias in these caves were commercially quarried for lime, used to make plaster and cement. Dense bone concentrations were discarded in order to get to the purer deposits of limestone. Eventually the importance of these bones was recognized, and expeditions from museums and universities in South Africa and elsewhere conducted excavations to uncover more fossil materials. All together these excavations have uncovered the remains of more than 150 individual hominids of several species.

There are four major problems associated with the study of these materials: (1) extracting the fossils from the rock in which they are encased, (2) estimating the age of the fossils and the deposits, (3) determining the cause of death of the animals and how they got in the caves, and (4) designating the genus and species for the hominid remains.

The fossil bones are found in breccia and, in fact, have become rock themselves. Removal of the fossils from these deposits is very difficult. Jackhammers, and even dynamite, have been used to break apart the breccia to get at the mineralized bones. In recent years, large blocks of the breccia have been removed to a laboratory where acid treatments gradually dissolve the rock and permit the removal of the fossils. Because these materials are buried in the earth, geological forces have often acted to modify and distort the stone and the fossils. The weight of deposits sometimes flattens or warps bone or crushes these materials together.

The limestone deposits in these caves do not provide anything that can be directly dated. There are no fresh volcanic ash or rocks for potassium-argon dating; the bones are too old for radiocarbon measurement. The majority of dates from the caves are based on the known ages of extinct animals that were once found throughout much of Africa. For example, changes in the size of the teeth of fossil pigs over time can be used to estimate the ages of the various deposits. Such dating is done by the association of hominid remains with pig teeth of known age found in the same breccia. On this basis, the early Pleistocene breccia at Swartkrans is thought to date between 1.7 and 1 million years ago.

C. K. Brain, a paleontologist in South Africa, has been excavating at the site of Swartkrans for some fifteen years and is beginning to understand the deposits in the cave. Brain notes two major episodes of breccia accumulation, apparently of

Skull of an **Australopithecus robustus** *from Swartkrans cave.*

short duration on the order of 10,000 years each. Dating of the deposits is complicated by the manner in which the breccias form. There is no simple stratigraphy in which materials are piled up in regular horizontal layers. Continuing water flow erodes and partially dissolves older deposits, then new episodes of accumulation fill the solution cavities in the old deposits. Each cave thus contains a honeycomb of deposits from various periods.

These deposits are the source for fossils of both *Australopithecus robustus* and *Homo erectus*. Partial remains of at least eighty *Australopithecus robustus* individuals have been recovered from the deposits at Swartkrans, along with fragments of bone and teeth from six individuals of *Homo erectus*. These two hominid forms appear to be contemporary at Swartkrans, as at Olduvai. This astounding number of individuals from a single deposit raises the question of how so many came to be in one place—a question that has yet to be answered.

The shape and structure of the hand bones from several *robustus* individuals indicates that this creature made and used the stone tools that also occur commonly in the cave deposits. A developed Oldowan assemblage accompanied the remains of the australopithecines and *Homo* individuals. In addition to the stone tools, there are bone artifacts with polishes that resulted from being used as digging implements, probably to obtain the roots and bulbs of plants growing in the area. New data from Swartkrans, from approximately 1 million years ago, suggests that the individuals in the cave used fire, perhaps to keep preying leopards at bay. If this evidence is reliable, it records the earliest instance of the intentional use of fire.

Investigations at this important South African cave have served to document the contemporaniety of *Australopithecus robustus* and *Homo erectus,* to demonstrate that *robustus* almost certainly made and used tools, that bone tools were an important part of the equipment for these early hominids, that plants were likely important in the diet, and that fire may have been used, at least for defensive purposes.

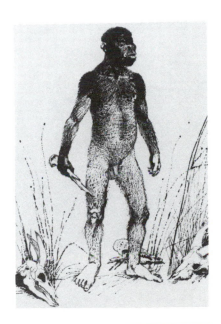

An artist's interpretation of an australopithecine.

RAYMOND DART AND THE TAUNG CHILD

Early hominids in South Africa and the question of hunting

Raymond Dart in 1978 with the Taung fossil. The 1927 announcement of this find of the first early hominid in Africa was either ridiculed or largely ignored. It was more than thirty years before the importance of this find was generally accepted.

In 1925, Raymond Dart, an anatomist in South Africa, published a five-page paper describing the discovery of a fossil he called *Australopithecus africanus,* or "southern ape of Africa," at a limestone quarry near a place called Taung (tong). The find included most of the small skull of a juvenile and a cast of the inside of the brain case. Dart noted that the animal had an exceptionally large brain for its size and that the canine teeth were small. In addition, the structure of the skull suggested that the creature had walked on two feet.

At the time Dart made the public announcement of the discovery, the origins of humans were thought to lie in eastern Asia approximately 500,000 years ago. Dart's announcement of this specimen "intermediate between living anthropoids [apes] and man" was greeted with disbelief and derision (Dart, 1925, p. 195). Several leading authorities, including Dart's former professor, argued that the skull belonged to a gorilla; one individual even suggested that it was the "distorted skull of a chimpanzee." Sir Arthur Keith, the leading physical anthropologist of the day, called Dart's claims preposterous. In scientific circles these are very strong words.

Dart's work was then ignored for more than a decade until another adult australopithecine was found in 1937. This

discovery provided more evidence for the presence in Africa of a true early hominid. This individual was small in size, about 1.2 m (4′) tall and weighing perhaps 35 kg (75 lb). Then in 1938, a new type of fossil hominid — *Australopithecus robustus* — was reported. This was a larger individual, perhaps 68 kg (150 lb) and 1.5 m (5′) tall, heavy-boned, but likely a vegetarian with huge molar teeth for grinding plants. Additional discoveries since have vindicated Dart's original claims, establishing an age of more than 2 million years for the specimen from Taung.

The rejection that Dart experienced and the controversy that his discovery engendered are not unusual in the field of paleoanthropology. The origin of our species is a subject of great interest; yet the available evidence is fragmentary, scarce, and very costly to recover. Apart from isolated finds of teeth, there are no more than a few thousand pieces of bone from a few hundred individuals represented among the early human fossils found to date. Thus each new find brings discussion, debate, and often controversy.

Dart continued to work in South Africa for almost fifty years, until his death in 1988. He proposed a number of theories regarding the life and times of *Aus-*

tralopithecus that have provoked significant debate and more investigations. Dart, the original discoverer of the australopithecines, believed that the early hominids had been extraordinary predators, hunting many animals and bringing their carcasses back to the limestone caves. Dart argued that animal bones found in the caves were the remains of meals and evidence of the prowess of *Australopithecus* as a hunter of even the largest animals.

Dart's graphic depiction conveys his image of our earliest ancestors: "Man's predecessors . . . seized living quarries by violence, battered them to death, tore apart their broken bones, dismembered them limb from limb, slaking their ravenous thirst with the hot blood of victims and greedily devouring living writhing flesh" (Dart, 1953, p. 209).

To do this before the invention of stone tools, he suggested they used an **osteodontokeratic** tool kit, picking up pieces of animal bone, tooth, and horn lying on the ground and wielding these as clubs, knives, and saws: "found" tools rather than "made" tools. Dart pointed as examples to the depressed fractures on the fossil skulls of baboons from the South African caves as evidence that they had been killed by club-wielding australopithecines. These clubs, he thought, might have been the heavy leg bones of antelope and other creatures.

Dart further suggested that the high number of hominid skulls in the caves, often with the bases broken away, were evidence that early man also hunted his neighbors, that the *robustus* groups may have been prey to the smaller, smarter *africanus*:

> These protomen . . . were mighty hunters. They were also callous and brutal. The most shocking specimen was the fractured lower jaw of a 12-year-old son of a manlike ape. The lad had been killed by a vicious blow delivered with calculated accuracy on the point of the chin, either by a smashing fist or a club.
>
> (Dart, 1956, pp. 325–326)

However intriguing Dart's ideas may be, they have stirred significant contro-

versy. The question is one of hunter or hunted, according to Brain. Brain's detailed studies provide a number of insights regarding the processes of deposition in the limestone caves, and they contradict some of the arguments of Dart. Many of the cracks and breaks in the fossil remains that Dart interpreted as evidence of violent death more likely resulted from geological distortion after burial, according to Brain. Brain argues that the vast majority of larger fossils came into the cave as the remains of carnivore meals, especially leopards. Brain points out that leopards often drag their kills into trees to protect them from other predators. The damp entrance shafts to caves such as Swartkrans would have likely been overgrown with trees, and these trees may have been lairs for satiated leopards. Over 40% of the human fossils are immature individuals who may have been vulnerable to leopard attacks. Brain also points to a hominid skull with two crushing indentations in the forehead, punctures that fit precisely with the huge canine teeth of the leopard.

No diamond cutter ever worked more lovingly or with such care on a priceless jewel — nor, I am sure, with such inadequate tools. But on the seventy-third day, December 23, the rock parted. I could view the face from the front, although the right side was still embedded. The creature which had contained this massive brain was no giant anthropoid ape such as a gorilla. What emerged was a baby's face, an infant with a full set of milk teeth and its permanent molars just in the process of erupting. I doubt if there was any parent prouder of his offspring than I was of my Taung baby on that Christmas."

Raymond Dart, in Pfeiffer (1985)

OLDUVAI

*A trail of biological and behavioral evolution
from the early Pleistocene to the recent past*

Olduvai Gorge, cutting 100 m into the Serengeti Plain and 2 million years into human evolution.

Flying low across north Tanzania, one crosses an enormous wilderness of grassland and solitary trees, an arena filled with herds of wildebeest, giraffe, elephant, and many other animals. This is the fabled Serengeti (ser-in-get'ee) Plain — the place of safari. The level surface of the plain results from the long and gradual accumulation of geological sediments, especially volcanic materials such as ash and lava. Two million years ago this area was a large bowl-shaped basin, ringed by a series of volcanic mountains and uplands. Active volcanoes filled the air with ash and covered the ground with molten lava, which hardened into new rock. The basin trapped rainfall, forming lakes and wetlands during the beginning

of the Pleistocene. Silts and sands, carried by running water, were deposited in these lakes, which grew over time or disappeared as rainfall amounts varied with changes in the Earth's climate. Along the shores of these lakes, the creatures of the early Pleistocene of East Africa found food, reproduced, and died; occasionally their bones were buried and preserved in the accumulating layers of sediment.

The richness of the lakeshore environment is demonstrated by the abundance of fossil animal bones that are found here. Antelope, giant buffalo, and wild sheep occur in large numbers, along with aquatic species, such as the giant crocodile, hippopotamus, fish, and fowl. The layers of lava, ash, and lake deposits

Waterbuck

Okapi

Oryx

Porcupine

Sivatherium

Deinotherium

Some of the more common early Pleisto-cene animal species at Olduvai Gorge.

continued to build up until the basin became relatively level — the surface of the Serengeti today.

About 200,000 years ago, a particularly violent series of quakes and volcanic activity opened a crack in this surface. Through this new rift ran seasonal streams, cutting and eroding a large gulley into the layers of sediment. Gradually a miniature grand canyon, some 40 km (25 mi) long and almost 100 m (325 ft) deep, wound its way from the top of the Serengeti Plain through the layer cake of deposits. This canyon is Olduvai (ol-dew-vie') Gorge, one of the most famous prehistoric sites on Earth. Today, each step down into the gorge takes us back 6000 years in time to the layer of basalt at the very bottom, dating to 1.75 million years ago.

Along the steep sides of this gorge, two archaeologists named Louis and Mary Leakey began an extended vigil, in quest of the remains of the earliest humans. Starting in 1931, the Leakeys made the arduous journey from Nairobi each summer to spend several weeks at the rugged exposures of Olduvai. Accompanied by their dogs, and later their children, they sought fossil hominids. Louis Leakey had found numerous crude stone tools in the lower layers at the gorge and was convinced that the bones of their makers would also appear in this remarkable series of deposits. Not until 1959, however, twenty-eight years after the first visit, was their persistence rewarded by Mary's discovery of a very early hominid fossil, initially named *Zinjanthropus*. At the time the fossil was thought to be approximately 1 million years old — twice the age of the then earliest known hominid remains from Java.

The Leakeys' discovery brought the search for the first humans to Africa and eventually back into the Pliocene Epoch. The Leakeys' find of *Zinj* also brought world recognition for their efforts in the form of acclaim and funding, providing for further investigations at Olduvai. With this funding, the Leakeys were able to examine a larger area of the gorge in two years than had previously been possible in twenty years. This intensive work paid off in the discovery of more fossils and a whole series of archaeological sites.

The first standardized objects of human manufacture (stone artifacts) appeared in the lower layers at Olduvai. Olduvai provided the first clear documentation that crude stone tools and the bones of very early hominids were to be found at the same point in geological time. Over seventy prehistoric localities with stones or bones or both have been recorded in the geological layers of the gorge to date; perhaps ten of these represent actual living areas where tools were made and used. Some of the stones are unmodified and may have been used as anvils and for other purposes. By means of bashing stone on stone, intentionally shaped and manufactured pieces—stone artifacts—could be created from rocks. These tools had strong, sharp edges, providing cutting equipment for a species lacking sharp teeth or claws.

The materials for these artifacts were often brought from the rocky hills some 10 km (6 mi) away. Raw materials were selected on the basis of specific properties. Fine-grained stone was used to make small cutting tools, while basalt and quartz were used for heavy chopping equipment. Tools described as choppers, spheroids, and discoids were created by knocking off flakes of stone from a rounded cobble or large pebble. These sharp-edged cobbles are about the size of a tennis ball and are known as Oldowan pebble tools, named after the gorge itself.

The flakes that had been struck off these pebble tools also had sharp edges and were likely used as tools.

One of the Olduvai sites contains a large quantity of broken and fragmented bone, along with stone tools. Many of the bone fragments are clustered in an area of about 5 by 10 m (16 by 33 ft) (a large room), with an empty zone several feet wide surrounding this concentration. Perhaps a thorn hedge or barricade was placed in this area to protect the inhabitants in the center.

At another site in Olduvai Gorge there is a group of stones, several hundred rocks, in a roughly circular arrangement, surrounded by the bones of giraffe, hippopotamus, antelope, and elephant. The reasons for such concentrations are unknown; it is not even clear if early hominids were responsible for killing the animals represented by the bones. However, the hominids almost certainly collected the bones. Two other sites at Olduvai are known to have been places of animal butchering. At one of the sites, known as FLK North, the bones of an elephant lie scattered on the ground along with stone artifacts. The elephant would have been much too heavy to move and must have been butchered at the spot where it died. Most of the bones from the elephant are present, disarranged by the butchering, and surrounded by stone tools and flakes. Striations and cutting marks on the bones document the use of stone flakes to remove meat from the skeleton.

Comparison of animals represented at sites in Olduvai with prey of modern hunters in the Kalahari Desert of southern Africa provides further information. The range of prey types and the sizes of prey are very similar, strongly suggesting that the Olduvai hominids were hunters, like those of the Kalahari, rather than scavengers. Other evidence suggests that most of the living floors at Olduvai were occupied during the wet season. Tortoise hibernate during the dry season, making them difficult to capture, yet their remains are common at most of the sites at Olduvai. Such information suggests that our early ancestors may have been absent from the Olduvai lakeshore during the dry season, pursuing other activities and perhaps other game elsewhere in the region.

A schematic cross section through the 100 m of deposits at Olduvai Gorge, showing the various fossil forms, types of stone tools, and approximate dates.

	m.y.a.
	100 m
	400,000
Hand-axes *Homo erectus* Bed IV	
	72 m / 700,000
Bed III	
	60 m / 1,200,000
Handaxes pebble tools *Homo erectus Homo habilis*	
Bed II	
	32 m / 1,650,000
Pebble Tools	
Homo habilis Australopithecus boisei	
	1,800,000
Bed I	0 m
Basal basalt layer	1,900,000

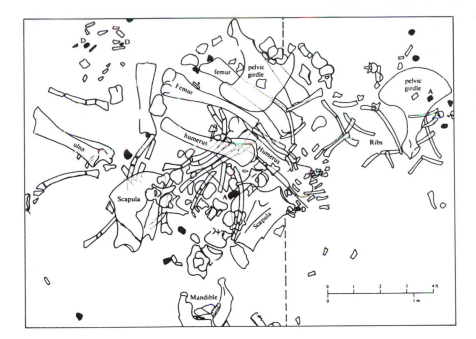

The plan of part of an excavated deposit at Olduvai, containing a concentration of elephant and other bones, with stone tools shown in solid black. This site likely represents the place where parts of these animals were butchered.

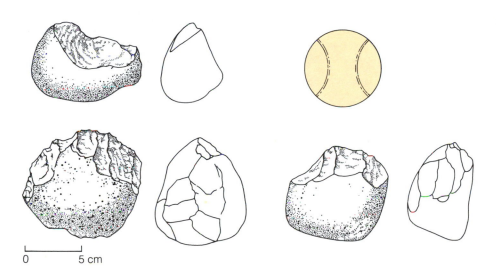

Typical Oldowan pebble tools, shown with a tennis ball for scale.

Olduvai will remain one of the most important archaeological sites in the world because it contains the information that may help to answer many questions—the human fossils, the early Pleistocene deposits, the presence of both animal bone and stone artifacts, and the fact that these materials are sometimes found where they were dropped by our ancestors.

THE LEAKEY FAMILY

A dynasty of paleoanthropologists

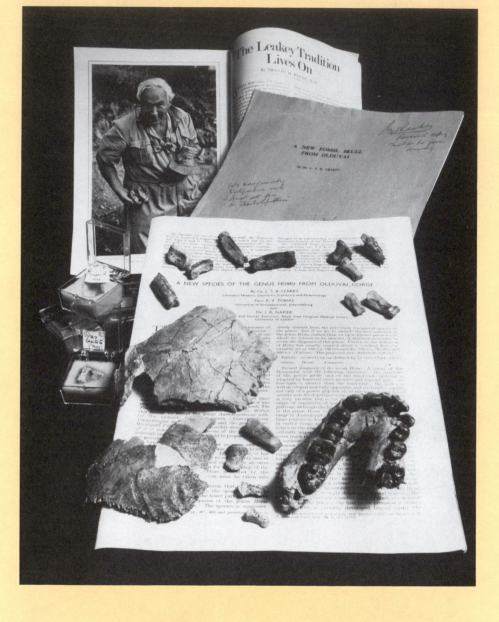

Louis Leakey and the remains of Homo habilis *from Olduvai Gorge. This find demonstrated that Africa was the cradle of early human evolution and brought fame to the Leakeys.*

Born to British missionary parents in Kenya in 1903, Louis Leakey became interested in prehistoric artifacts as a child. At age 16, Leakey left for England to attend Cambridge University. A rugby injury forced a break in his studies, and he returned to East Africa on a year-long fossil-hunting expedition, engendering his interests in bones and paleontology. Leakey then returned to Cambridge, taking high honors in archaeology and modern languages.

Leakey then received a six-year research fellowship from Cambridge to conduct archaeological investigations in East Africa. The first expedition involved excavations at a Neolithic site, the results of which were published in *Nature,* an important British science journal. A second expedition centered on Gamble's Cave and provided one of the first sequences of the development of stone artifacts in East Africa. In 1931, Leakey led his third expedition to Olduvai Gorge. Here, early handaxes were found soon after his arrival; the fragment of a human jaw was discovered nearby. Leakey argued for great antiquity for this bone, but a

The Leakey family at work in Olduvai Gorge.

British geologist, Percy Boswell, accused Leakey of incompetence in a letter to a scientific magazine. This incident left Leakey determined to be more exact in his statements.

Much of Leakey's research was guided by his belief that Africa was the cradle of the human race, in contrast to generally accepted scientific belief. One of the members of Leakey's fourth expedition included Mary Nicol, an archaeologist and illustrator, who would become his wife in 1936. Mary and Louis Leakey then began their lifelong research on early human history in East Africa. The Leakeys continued their investigations at Olduvai Gorge because of the abundance of stone tools that were found there. Leakey was convinced that human fossils would also be found, which would demonstrate the fact that early hominids had made the stone tools. Leakey was appointed Director of the National Museum of Kenya in Nairobi in 1945, and each summer the Leakeys would return to the search for evidence of early humans in the layers of the gorge.

Finally, in 1959, after more than two decades of dogged and difficult prospecting, Mary Leakey spotted the fragments of a heavy jaw that belonged to an early hominid from the beginning of the Pleistocene. The Leakeys had finally proven that East Africa indeed witnessed the emergence of the human species. Worldwide recognition of that discovery provided the financial backing that permitted the Leakeys to expand their programs of excavation and prospecting, resulting in the discovery of numerous new sites and fossil remains.

The discovery in 1972 of a very early, large-brained human skull (*Homo habilis*) by the Leakeys' son Richard at Lake Turkana reaffirmed Louis' conviction that large-brained hominid forms had a very long history in East Africa. Two days later, on the first of October, Louis Leakey died in London. Since his death, Mary Leakey and her sons have continued the search for human origins in Africa. Richard Leakey continues his father's work today as director of the museum in Kenya.

KOOBI FORA

Important evidence for on-the-spot stone tool use and meat eating by early hominids

The majority of archaeological finds from the Plio/Pleistocene are stone tools and isolated fragments of bone. The chances of materials of this age being preserved to the present and exposed for discovery range between slim and none. There are only a very few examples of **living floors,** actual locations where early hominids stayed for a while and left evidence of their presence. One of the best examples comes from deposits near Lake Turkana in northern Kenya.

Flying north from Olduvai, one reaches a series of rugged hills and gullies cut through geological sediments on the east side of Lake Turkana. This region is known as Koobi Fora (coo-bee-for'ah). The area today is a harsh landscape of thornbush savanna, with only scattered vegetation amid the scars of heavy erosion. Some 4 million years ago, however, these sediments were being deposited by major rivers flowing into the lake basin. The rivers carried gravel, sand, silt, and clay that were laid down as they reached the quiet, deeper waters of the lake. Large deltas were created, offering a propitious habitat for plants, animals, and early hominids. In the rapidly accumulating deposits of this delta environment, bones and artifacts were quickly buried and occasionally preserved.

More recently, as the basin has filled and lake levels have dropped, these deposits are now above water and extend to the east of the present lake for more than 30 km (20 mi). In today's arid environment, seasonal streams cut gullies through the geological layers and occasionally expose the former surfaces of the delta, along with various archaeological

materials. Since the early 1970s, over twenty localities have been found where stones and/or bones from human activities have been exposed. One of these sites, designated as FxJj50, or site 50, was found eroding at the edge of a gulley some 20 km (13 mi) east of the lakeshore. The almost fresh condition of the bone here indicated the importance of this site and resulted in a more detailed study of the location.

A major program of excavation under the direction of Glynn Isaac, of the University of California, Berkeley, and later of Harvard University, was conducted from 1977 to 1979. Nine months of digging over that three-year period by a crew of six to ten people resulted in the exposure of almost 200 sq m (2000 sq ft) of deposits containing a variety of stones and bones. Radiopotassium dates on volcanic ash in the deposits indicated an age of 1.5 million years. The groups of stones and bones found on an actual living surface suggest that a small hominid group used this spot for a few hours or days, eating, sleeping, and making tools. Scientific research into the questions raised by the excavations at Koobi Fora continue today, pursued by the students Isaac trained. These questions include the following:

1. What were the climate and environment, the landscape and vegetation, at the time of the occupation of the site?

2. How did the stones and bones get here? Are they the result of human activities? What kinds of activities?

3. How were these objects buried, and have they been disturbed in the 1.5 million years since they were covered?

4. How were the stone tools made and used?

5. What can we learn from the animal bones?

6. What can be said about diet and how meat was obtained?

A variety of approaches, from such fields as geology, geography, zoology, ethnoarchaeology, and ethology, have been employed to understand the area around Koobi Fora, the site itself, and the materials found buried there.

Some 1.5 million years ago this area was quite different. Site 50 was in the center of a large river flood plain, level for miles around. The river itself likely flowed directly by the site, because the deposits indicate that it was a spit or sand bar along the bank at a large bend. The region was rich in animal life; the bones of many species similar to those in East Africa today were found at the site. The bones at site 50 were generally in very good condition, lacking the fractures and cracks that appear as bone begins to dry out and decompose. Of the more than 2000 bones recovered in the excavations, approximately 1000 could be identified as to the species of animal. A variety of animals were represented, including those from riverine environments, such as hippopotamus, catfish, and waterbuck; and a number of larger terrestrial species, such as giraffe, wild pig, porcupine, and gazelle.

The well-preserved condition of the bones argues that the site was buried rapidly after its abandonment. Nevertheless, the presence of fossil carnivore excrement, gnaw marks on the bones, and the absence of the soft ends of many of the bones indicate that such animals as hyenas and other scavengers consumed some of the bones left behind by the hominid group, prior to the burial of the site. Studies of patterns of breakage indicate that many of the bones were intentionally fragmented by the early hominids.

Excavations at Koobi Fora exposing the bone and stone evidence of early hominid activities.

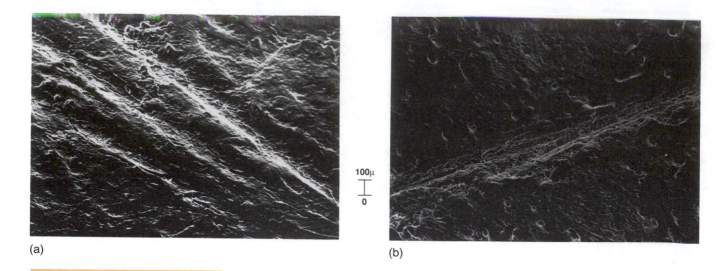

(a)

(b)

Cutmarks on bone at very high magnification. (a) The grooves in this photomicrograph are round-bottomed, indicating a tooth mark. (b) This micrograph shows modern bone experimentally cut by a stone tool. The grooves are sharp and have a V-shaped bottom.

Stone tools at Koobi Fora come in the form of numerous small flakes, tools and cores, and **manuports**, unmodified pieces of rock and stone that were transported into the site from elsewhere. Materials for the tools and manuports include basalt, chert, and other stones, some of which were brought from locations 8 to 10 km (5 or 6 mi) away. The vast majority of the artifacts are, in fact, the small, sharp flakes. Originally these flakes were thought to be waste products from the making of pebble tools, but today it is recognized that they were important cutting tools. Lacking slashing canines or sharp claws, humans needed artificial cutting equipment in order to penetrate the thick skins of the larger animals of Africa to obtain meat.

Studies by Nicholas Toth, of Indiana University, and Lawrence Keeley, of the University of Illinois, Chicago, have provided important clues about the use of these flakes. Keeley used a high-powered microscope to examine the edges of stone artifacts from Koobi Fora. Experimental work demonstrated that different materials leave different kinds of traces in the form of polish on the edges of these tools. At a magnification of $400\times$, Keeley observed microscopic polish and wear distinctive of meat cutting, slicing soft plant material, and scraping and sawing wood on about 10% of the flakes. Two of the flakes with evidence of meat butchering were found within 1 m (3 ft) of a large herbivore bone exhibiting **cutmarks**. Such evidence strongly supports the use of these stone artifacts as butchering tools.

The evidence for woodworking is also of great interest and suggests that wooden tools were being made as well, perhaps crude digging sticks to obtain roots and tubers. This indirect information, however, is the only evidence for the use or consumption of plant materials.

One aspect of the study of such early sites involves putting back together as many of the pieces of stone and bone as possible. **Refitting** the broken pieces into their original form requires skill and great patience. It is like trying to solve a three-dimensional jigsaw puzzle with no picture and lots of missing pieces. Nevertheless, the reassembled pieces provide significant information about the site and the activities that took place there:

1. Different pieces of individual objects were generally found close to one another, indicating that the disturbance of the site by natural processes following abandonment was minimal. Such a pattern suggests that this was indeed a living surface, and the objects were left close to where they were dropped.

2. The distribution of pieces of matched sets indicates that the entire area of site 50 was used by its inhabitants. This pattern strengthens the argument that the remains at this site represent a single episode of human activity.

3. Missing pieces from objects that have been reassembled suggest

that certain tools and flakes made at the site may have been transported elsewhere for later use.

4. The refitted sets of items also indicate how stones and bones were fractured originally and provide details of the motor coordination and skills of these early hominids. (See "The First Archaeology," p. 36.)

In the following passage, Isaac discusses his impressions from the studies of Koobi Fora site 50:

The site has provided particularly clear evidence of some things that early hominids *were* doing: they repeatedly carried stones to certain favored places and made simple sharp-edged implements from them. To those same places they seem to have carted parts of animal carcasses. Once there they presumably ate the meat and they certainly broke the bones to get at the marrow. When people ask why the hominids did not eat their meat where they obtained it, I can point out a number of potential reasons. It is possible that they simply came to eat in the shade, but it seems even more likely that they carried food to special places like site 50 for social reasons — very particularly in order to feed youngsters, or even to feed their mates and relatives. Such food-sharing behaviours certainly became a universal part of the human pattern at some stage in evolution and many archaeologists are inclined to think it might have begun by the time that site 50 formed.

(Isaac, 1984, p. 75)

The question of prehistoric human diet is difficult, because generally the remains of meals are not well preserved. The wild plants of East Africa must have supplied a ready source of food, but the importance of fruits, nuts, and other vegetables in the diet is simply unknown.

Another difficult matter, and one of the major controversies in paleoanthropology, is the question of hunting versus scavenging: How did early hominids obtain meat? Some scholars believe that early hominids were primarily scavengers, raiding the kills of lions and other predators, taking the morsels that remained, competing with hyenas and vultures. Others argue that early hominids were hunters — stalking, killing, butchering, and eating the creatures of Plio/Pleistocene East Africa. The evidence is scanty and open to debate. There are only a few known facts: (1) Chimpanzees and baboons occasionally hunt, kill, and consume small animals; (2) by the end of the Pleistocene, humans were major predators and large game hunters, responsible in part for the extinction of certain species, such as the wooly mammoth; and (3) early hominids ate some meat.

However, exactly how early hominids obtained meat during the Pliocene and early Pleistocene is unknown. The evidence from site 50 certainly suggests that humans brought various animal parts back to a common location and removed the meat and marrow with stone tools. In one instance, the large leg bone of an antelope-size creature had been broken into ten pieces, in a fashion that modern hunters in the area today use to obtain the nutritious and tasty marrow. On this same bone, tiny scratches made by stone tools are visible. These cutmarks are usually found at places where large pieces of meat are attached to the bone. This evidence strongly suggests that early hominids were indeed hunters with access to the best cuts of meat from their prey.

Nevertheless, some would still argue that the remains at site 50 are not evidence for meat eating or predation. A few would even say that the association of bones and stones at site 50 was fortuitous, that the bones were brought there later by the river. Some would argue that the cutmarks and breakage patterns were caused by natural forces, and that the bones bear no evidence of human modification. Studies and debates continue. Through such controversies, new information and new ideas come to light, and our knowledge grows.

THE FIRST ARCHAEOLOGY

Simple, intentionally broken pebbles: the earliest preserved evidence for tool making

Hello to all intelligent life forms everywhere, and to everyone else out there, the secret is to bang the rocks together guys.

Douglass Adams, *The Hitchhiker's Guide to the Galaxy* (1980)

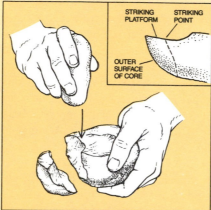

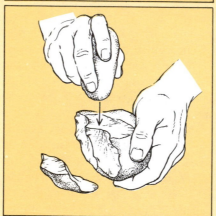

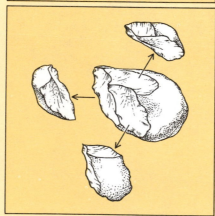

Percussion flaking, used by early hominids to create cutting edges on stone tools. One stone (the hammerstone) was bashed against another (the core) to remove one or more flakes.

Stone tools appeared first in Africa between 2 and 3 million years ago, probably associated with the increasing importance of meat in the human diet. Such tools provided access to the carcasses of animals, allowing early humans to cut through thick, tough animal skins to remove the meaty tissue — actions simply not possible without some kind of sharp implement. Stone tools provided useful cutting edges for a species that lacked either teeth or claws for slicing meat, shredding plants, or digging. As Nicholas Toth says, "sharp-edged stones became the equivalent of canines and carnassials [meat-cutting teeth] and heavier rocks served as bone-crunching jaws" (Toth, 1987, p. 121).

The Leakeys returned to Olduvai again and again in search of human fossils because of the abundance of simple stone tools they found there. They were convinced that early hominids made these artifacts. The earliest stone tools are remarkably simple, almost unrecognizable unless found together in groups or alongside other objects. Small round cobbles, the size of a large egg or tennis ball 5 to 8 cm (2 to 3 in.) in diameter, weighing about 1 kg (a pound or two), were collected from streambeds, lakeshores, and beaches; and they appeared to have been struck with another stone.

This process, called **percussion flaking**, results in a piece (a **flake**) being removed from the parent cobble (a **core**) by the blow from another stone (a **hammerstone**) or hard object. Both the flake and the core have fresh surfaces with sharp edges and can be used for cutting. Initially the fractured cobbles themselves were thought to be the intended **artifacts** and were called pebble tools. The flakes were thought to be by-products of the manufacturing process, a kind of waste material (the French word *débitage* is often used for this category). Today it is clear that flakes were equally important as cutting tools and as tools for making other tools, such as shaping wood, bone, or antler to new forms for new purposes. The simple action of striking one stone against another to remove a flake and create a sharp edge was a very successful invention, one that was used and refined for 2 million years, until the introduction of metals just 6000 years ago.

The best raw materials for stone tools in the early Pleistocene had to be brittle enough to break, and hard and smooth enough to provide a cutting edge. The stone also had to be fine-grained so that it would break in a predictable fashion, resulting in large flakes, rather than hundreds of shattered fragments. Various rocks were used during the early Pleistocene, including basalt (a hard volcanic lava), quartz, and **flint**. Flint is one of the best and most common materials used for making stone tools.

The kinds of pebble tools found at Olduvai, Koobi Fora, and elsewhere in Africa have been defined as Oldowan — a tradition of tool making. The term **Oldowan** is applied to the entire group, or **assemblage**, of different stone objects found together at sites from the first part of the Pleistocene. These stone, or **lithic**, artifacts include pebbles flaked on one side only (**unifacial**) or on both sides (**bifacial**). The flakes are also occasionally further modified by additional flaking (**retouching**) along their edges, to shape them. Such modified flakes include scrapers, burins, and awls from Olduvai and elsewhere.

Other kinds of information are also available from the stone artifacts, the most durable of the remains of our ancestors. Studies by Toth have suggested that many of these flakes were made by holding the core stone in the hand and striking it with another hammerstone. Indeed, Toth argues, on the basis of the shape of the flakes, that the majority of the flakes from Koobi Fora were produced by right-handed individuals. This handedness is not seen in the very earliest stone tools from 2.4 m.y.a., but emerged in the period between 1.9 and 1.4 m.y.a., likely correlated with the changes in the organization of the cerebral cortex. The brain of modern humans is divided into two hemispheres that control different areas of thought and behavior, and handedness is a result of this lateralization. In right-handed people, the left hemisphere controls such sequential events as talking and more quantitative activities, while the right hemisphere regulates spatial conceptualization and more abstract behavior. These functions are reversed in left-handed people. Thus, the predominance of right-handedness in stone tool manufacture after 2 million years ago suggests that this organizational change had already taken place in the brain.

Tools provide an interface between humans and the environment, enabling us to manipulate and change our surroundings. One of the more remarkable things about stone tools is the investment they represent: a vision of the future, an anticipation of action. An object was made at one time and place often to be used later elsewhere.

EPILOG
BIOLOGY AND BEHAVIOR

*Bones, Stones, Sex, and Love in
the Plio/Pleistocene*

As we have noted, the evidence for early hominids consists of pieces of bones and teeth, along with some small broken stones, from a few locations in East Africa and South Africa. There is really very little information for the reconstruction of our early pedigree and manners. The fact that there are any reasonable explanations of the earliest human evolution is testimony to the diligence and ingenuity of the paleoanthropologists. In spite of the sparseness of evidence for the biology and behavior of early hominids, there are still a number of ideas and theories about how and why we became human. Part of this understanding comes from comparisons with our nearest relatives, the chimpanzees and gorillas, and part from inferences made from the evidence of the stones and bones themselves. Much of the following discussion involves such speculative reconstruction of human behavior — based on little evidence, and subject to considerable revision and modification.

The modern human brain is roughly 1000 cc (60 cu in.) larger than that of other primates (similar to comparing a large grapefruit to a lemon). We have a much greater brain-to-body-size ratio than almost any other species, suggesting the importance of our brains for our survival. Yet human infants are born with remarkably small, underdeveloped brains, only about 25% of the adult size. Whereas the chimpanzee brain at birth is about 65% of fully adult size, the human brain does most of its growing after birth, because of the narrow birth canal. Because of the underdeveloped infant brain, a human requires a long period of maternal care and attention, while a newborn foal, in contrast, can run and feed itself after just a few days. In humans, the long period of infant dependence fosters a strong bond between mother and child and also enables children to know their brothers and sisters. Language and learning may also be enhanced as a result of such an extended and intimate relationship.

Lengthy periods of maternal care, however, are expensive. Small children limit the mobility and activity of the mother, including acquiring food. Extended care during brain growth also requires longer nursing and delayed weaning. In turn, such behaviors require more food for the mother; nursing may increase her metabolic demands by 50% or more. At the same time, the average life expectancy among the australopithecines appears to have been low, around 20 years of age. Such an early age of death may well have meant that children were often orphaned and had to be nurtured by the group rather than by single sets of parents; communal child care and feeding may well have been concomitant with the advancement of our species.

Differences between humans and the apes are also evident in the secondary sex characteristics. Human female breasts are significantly larger than male breasts, a difference more pronounced than in any other species. Breast size is not related to effective feeding of young. The human male penis is far larger than that of other primates, including gorillas. Human females have softer skin and higher voices and lack much of the body hair that often characterizes other primate females. The vagina in the human female points sufficiently toward the front of the body, to permit face to face sexual intercourse.

Another biological difference lies in the absence of an **estrus** cycle in human females. The female members of most animal species are sexually active only for limited intervals, a period known as estrus, a few days each month or each year. Female apes display sexual receptivity by means of flaring or brightly colored sexual organs, but ovulation is concealed in human females. Clearly there have been strong selective forces favoring these characteristics.

Beyond biological similarities and differences with other animals and our closest relatives among the apes, are humans indeed closer to the angels? We possess other attributes that distinguish us from the animals. Our large brains and intelligence enable us to make decisions and act rationally beyond what our basic instincts might direct. Humans have moved from purely instinctual behavior to reason and thought: We may flee a fire, but we may also turn back into that fire to save others.

Large brains and intelligence support our ability to communicate in a spoken language. Language offers an enormous repository of learning. With words and abstract concepts, we can communicate an entire range of experience and reactions to those experiences. Learning without experience becomes possible, and hence an ability to anticipate the future. We can learn a range of potential responses to impending situations or risks.

Humans have technology: making and using a wide range of tools and other devices that increase our chances for survival. Tool use has often been considered the single most distinctive characteristic of our species, even though we know that other animals may use or even make simple tools. For example, the sea otter wields a rock to break open the shell of an abalone. Jane Goodall has observed chimpanzees using a variety of tools: thrashing about with branches for display, using clubs and missiles for defense, selecting a twig and stripping its bark to probe the nests of termites and attract them to the stick, to then be eaten by the wise chimp. Tool use may not be unique to humans, but using tools to make other tools does distinguish the human animal.

The question of priority concerns the sequence in which the most obvious human traits — tool use, large brains, and bipedalism — appeared. Some years ago, the evidence from Olduvai suggested that all three traits appeared simultaneously in a serendipitous development. As our earliest ancestors moved on to the expanding savannas of Africa, standing upright provided a view across the grasslands while at the same time liberated

Table 1.3 Average Cranial Capacity of Some Primates and Fossil Hominids

	Cubic Centimeters
Modern human	1400
Neanderthal	1450
Homo erectus	1000
Homo habilis	630
Australopithecine	450
Gorilla	600
Chimpanzee	400
Orangutan	400
Gibbon	100

A chimpanzee using a simple tool for immediate reward. Here an adult chimp in a tree uses a twig to extract insects from a hole. Humans make tools in order to make other tools for later use, a unique distinction.

the hands to wield tools. Larger brains developed because vision centers expanded and because tool use required intelligence, and vice versa.

Today new evidence from Africa provides a sharper picture of the sequence of events at the dawn of humanity. It now seems clear from such sites as Laetoli that hominids were upright for perhaps 2 million years prior to either the use of stone tools or significant increases in brain size. Apparently standing upright was very important to early survival. Explanations must now be sought as to why that was the case.

Discussion focuses on whether it was the feet or the hands that were changing. Mary Leakey and her colleagues have suggested that we became upright in order to pursue migratory animal herds on the savanna. Bipedalism and powerful strides would be advantageous for the long-distance movements for following herds to acquire food. And upright posture would free the hands for carrying young offspring. This hypothesis ignores the fact that the teeth in the australopithecines were adapted to an increasingly vegetarian diet, becoming bigger and flatter over time. Walking around, however, could also be useful for collecting scattered plant foods.

Microscopic analysis of wear patterns on fossil teeth by Alan Walker, of Johns Hopkins University, indicates that the tooth enamel among early hominids more closely resembles that of fruit eaters, not carnivores. Study of the anatomy of the wrist, shoulder, pelvis, and thigh of the early australopithecines indicates a pattern of movement (**loco-motion**) different from both the modern apes and humans. Henry McHenry, of the University of California, Davis, also notes the curvature in the hand and foot bones, concluding that these creatures must have spent some time in the trees.

Other ideas regarding the evolution of bipedal locomotion relate to food getting, carrying, or sharing. Clifford Jolly, of New York University, has proposed that bipedalism was adaptive because it provided a means for gathering and eating young leaves, seeds, and pods of the African thornbush growing on the plain. Owen Lovejoy, of Case Western Reserve University, has proposed that our ancestors became two-footed in order to carry food back to a central location to be shared with kin:

> Both an advanced material culture and the Pleistocene acceleration in brain development are sequelae to an already established hominid character system, which included intensified parenting and social relationships, monogamous pair bonding, specialized sexual-reproductive behavior, and bipedality. . . . The nuclear family and human sexual behavior may have their ultimate origin long before the dawn of the Pleistocene.
>
> The proposed model accounts for the early origin of bipedality as a locomotor behavior directly enhancing reproductive fitness, not as a behavior resulting from occasional upright feeding posture. It accounts for the origin of the home base in the same fashion as it has been acquired by numerous other mammals. It accounts for the human nuclear family, for the distinctive human sexual epigamic features, and the species' unique sexual behavior.
>
> (Lovejoy, 1981, p. 350)

We do not yet know why, in fact, humans became bipedal.

In the final analysis, it is culture that distinguishes the human creature. Culture is what the anthropologist Leslie White called our "extrasomatic means of survival" — the nonbiological, nongenetic behavior and sociability that have carried us through the millennia and spread us into diverse environments across the planet. Clifford Geertz of Princeton University has said that humans are toolmaking, talking, symbolizing animals. Only they laugh; only they know when they will die; only they disdain to mate with family members; only they contrive those visions of other worlds called art. They have not just mentality but consciousness, not just needs but values, not just fears but conscience, not just a past but a history. Only they have culture.

Culture is a constellation of ideas and actions that are learned and transmitted from generation to generation. Human culture embodies the totality of behaviors and experiences that are summarized in our language and taught us by our parents and peers — a kind of group personality that provides a repertoire of actions in situations of choice. It is as impossible to have human identity without social contact as it is to have

With the stimulus of constantly available sex, protohominids had begun the most fundamental exchanges the human race would ever make. Males and females were learning to divide their labor, to exchange meat and vegetables, to share their daily catch. Constant sex had begun to tie them to one another and economic dependence was tightening the knot.

Helen Fisher, *The Sex Contract* (1983)

Kingdom: Animalia

Phylum: Chordata

Class: Mammalia

Order: Primates

Suborder: Anthropoidea

Superfamily: Hominoidea

Family: Hominidae

Genus: *Homo*

Species: *sapiens*

Subspecies: sapiens

Subspecies: neanderthalensis

Species: *erectus*

Species: *habilis*

Genus: *Australopithecus*

Species: *robustus*

Species: *afarensis*

Species: *africanus*

Species: *boesei*

Classification of the hominids in the animal kingdom.

biological existence without progenitors. Tarzan was an ape until he met Jane. Culture permits us to eulogize our place in the universe, to create gods, to anticipate death, to travel to the stars — and to study archaeology.

SUGGESTED READINGS

Brain, C. K. 1981. *The hunters or the hunted? An introduction to African cave taphonomy*. Chicago: University of Chicago Press. The classic detective story of the early human fossil remains in the caves of South Africa.

Day, Michael. 1977. *Guide to fossil man*. Chicago: University of Chicago Press. An illustrated compendium of fossil human remains known prior to 1977.

Fisher, Helen E. 1983. *The sex contract*. New York: Quill. Another view of the origin of the species.

Klein, Richard G. 1989. *The human career: Human biological and cultural origins*. Chicago: University of Chicago Press. A recent summary of the evidence and arguments concerning human evolution; detailed, accurate, and readable.

Lewin, Roger. 1987. *Bones of contention*. New York: Simon and Schuster. A popular account of the finds of fossils and feuds among paleoanthropologists over the last twenty-five years or so.

Michels, J. W. 1973. *Dating methods in archaeology*. New York: Seminar Press. A discussion of the variety of dating methods used in archaeology, including radiocarbon and potassium-argon.

2

Out of Africa: *Homo Erectus*

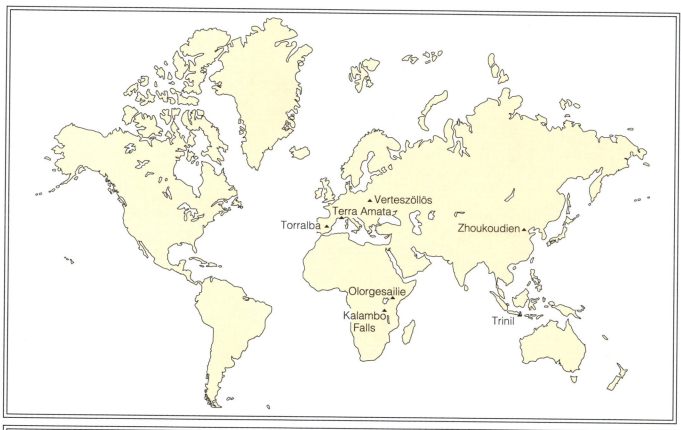

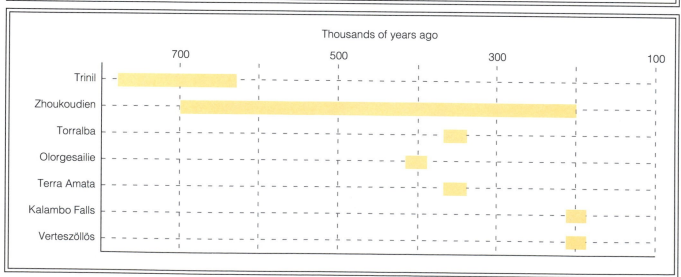

FROM HOMINID TO HUMAN

*The movement of human populations from
Africa to other continents 750,000 years ago*

After several million years in Africa, our ancestors began to move into the cooler continents of Asia and Europe and to encounter new environments. Hands and simple tools had been sufficient to obtain the foods available in the benign warmth of much of Africa. Expansion out of the tropics, however, required new skills and inventions for survival where cold weather or lack of food or shelter could bring hasty death. It became necessary for our ancestors to modify the environment to fit their needs.

By this time, a new species of human had evolved in Africa, known as *Homo erectus.* The earliest *erectus* fossil comes from Koobi Fora in East Africa, dating to 1.5 million years ago. *Erectus* individuals were robust, with large bones and teeth; they also had larger bodies and significantly larger brains — around 1000 cc — than their *Homo habilis* ancestors. *Erectus* skulls are characterized by a low sloping forehead, prominent brow ridges, and protruding face. Cranial capacity changed relatively little between 1.5 million and 500,000 years ago. These humans were almost fully modern in terms of movement and locomotion; they differed very little, if at all, from modern anatomy below the neck.

During the time of *Homo erectus,* we see the first evidence for the controlled use of fire, for systematic and cooperative hunting, for traces of constructed dwellings, and for the use of wooden spears. This was a time of significant changes in stone tools, as well. Handaxes were invented as a general, all-purpose tool and were used at many sites.

The precise chronology for this important period in human evolution is not known; accurate dates are rare. It is a time too recent for radiopotassium dating and too old for radiocarbon methods. Moreover, many archaeological sites from this period have barely survived time and the elements. Deposits have often been badly disturbed; sites have suffered erosion and redeposition, as the landscape has changed. Most of what we know about the period between 700,000 and 120,000 years ago, known as the Middle Pleistocene, comes from Europe and the Near East. Caves and rock shelters in these areas have preserved remains from this period, attracting archaeologists interested in the Paleolithic.

CONTENTS

Table 2.1   Major Characteristics of *Homo erectus* Compared to *Homo sapiens sapiens*

Trait	Homo erectus	Homo sapiens sapiens
Forehead	Absent	Vertical and rounded
Face	In front of cranium	Under cranium
Cranial capacity	1000 cc	1400 cc
Lower jaw	Larger and heavier; no chin	Smaller and lighter; distinct chin
Teeth	Larger	Smaller
Brow ridge	Heavy, extends across the eyes	Absent
Limb bones	Larger and heavier	Smaller and lighter

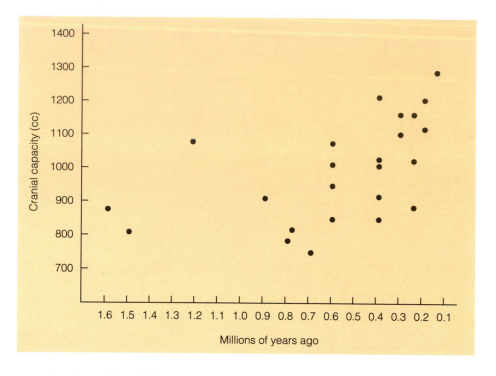

Cranial capacity versus time for Homo erectus *skulls. Two patterns emerge: (1) There is relatively little change between 1.5 and 0.5 m.y.a., and (2) there is a dramatic increase in cranial capacity after 0.5 m.y.a., perhaps associated with the evolution of modern* Homo sapiens.

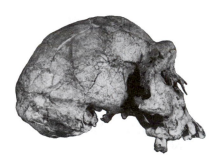

The nearly complete skull of a Homo erectus *from Koobi Fora, dating to approximately 1.5 m.y.a.*

Our knowledge of this period is greatly constrained by our limited understanding of the human mind and behavior at this time. *Homo erectus* populations were neither apes nor modern humans in terms of cranial capacity and cerebral organization. We cannot know how they approached their world nor exactly what kinds of activities they pursued beyond those related to eating and sleeping. We thus have only a very small, obscure window on the prehistory of *Homo erectus*.

What is essential to understand, nevertheless, is that during this period our ancestors began to exert their influence on nature. The move out of the tropics demanded solutions to new problems in northern regions, especially cold weather and a lack of plant foods. Populations that survived easily in warm climates where roots, seeds, and nuts were often available had to find new and improved ways to stay warm and obtain food. An efficient cooling system for the tropics, abundant sweat glands were of little help to furless humans in the temperate reaches of the Old World. Almost certainly, fire, constructed shelter, and clothing — if only in the form of animal skins wrapped around the body — were used by *Homo erectus* in the course of movement into the more northern continents.

Fire may have been the major factor in the increasing success of human adaptation and the expansion into new, colder habitats. Fire was used for light, warmth, protection, and cooking. Cooking with fire provides a number of advantages in addition to making food more tender and palatable. Cooking improves the digestibility of many foods and destroys harmful toxins and microorganisms. Boiling removes juices and fats from plants and animals that are otherwise inedible. For *Homo erectus,* cooking likely made it possible to add new foods to the diet that could not have been eaten previously.

Longer, colder winters also put a premium on successful predation. Meat had to be eaten in the winter when roots, nuts, leaves, and other vegetables were not available for sustenance. Hunting became essential to the human way of life in more temperate, cooler areas. It is unlikely that females with infants and young children could successfully hunt regularly to provide their own food. By this point in time a viable relationship between males and females, incorporating food sharing as part of pair bonding, necessarily emerged to ensure the continuance of the human species. Modern relationships between males and females and basic family structure must be related to these necessary, adaptive changes. These connections — person to person, male to female, parents to offspring, kin to kin, group to group — are links in the chain of human society and survival.

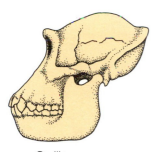
Gorilla

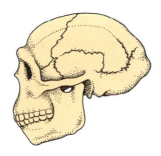
Homo erectus

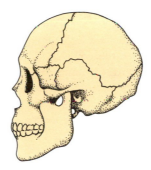
Homo sapiens sapiens

The skulls of a gorilla, Homo erectus, *and modern* Homo sapiens sapiens, *shown at the same scale. The face moves under the brain case as cranial capacity expands; the teeth and jaws become smaller.*

The **sexual division of labor** emphasizes the cooperative relationship between males and females. Roles for males, faster and larger, as food hunters and females as food gatherers emerged to create an efficient and synergistic system that maximized biological capabilities. Then, as now, sex and love bonded males and females together for food sharing and reproduction; maternal instincts and extended childhoods bonded mothers to children and siblings to one another. We have no idea of the precise nature of prehistoric male–female relationships — whether monogamous, several females to one male, or several males to one female. But the present universality of the human family suggests a substantial time depth for this unit of society.

Almost certainly some form of proto-family emerged among *Homo erectus* populations. Pair bonding may have helped to ensure the survival of offspring, as males began to recognize individual children as their own. Incest taboos, another human universal, may well have arisen at the same point in time, to promote and solidify relationships beyond the group. Marriage or mating outside the family ensures alliances with other families and groups, reducing the potential for conflict within the immediate family.

The move out of Africa was one of the most important developments in human prehistory. Following the initial appearance in southern and eastern Africa, the human species gradually increased in number and inhabited most of the more hospitable zones of the continent. Population continued to expand, as did the geographic range of the species. The earliest dates for the existence of humans outside of Africa are generally younger than 750,000 years ago. Evidence of these early humans and their activities has been found at the sites described in this chapter. Trinil and Zhoukoudien document the presence of *Homo erectus* in Eastern Asia. Terra Amata, Torralba, and Ambrona are among the earliest sites in Europe. Kalambo Falls and Olorgesailie demonstrate the continued development of the human species in Africa. These sites take us from around 500,000 years ago to about 150,000 years ago, along our journey through time.

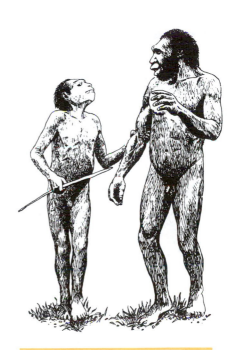

An artist's interpretation of an adolescent and adult Homo erectus.

THE PALEOLITHIC PERIOD

Archaeological divisions of time

Artifacts from the Lower Paleolithic include handaxes (top row), from the Middle Paleolithic a flake core, flake tool, and Levallois point (middle row), and from the Upper Paleolithic a blade core, blade, and Solutrean point. There were many bone and antler tools in use in the Upper Paleolithic as well.

Just as geologists divide up the history of the Earth into periods and epochs, archaeologists break up the prehistory of human society into more manageable and understandable units. The scheme used by archaeologists to compartmentalize prehistory focuses on changes in artifacts and material culture. Differences in the types of material used to make tools, and changes in the shapes of tools, are often the main criteria for distinguishing time periods.

In 1836, Christian Thomsen proposed a Three Age system for organizing the exhibits in the National Museum of Denmark, with separate rooms for stone, bronze, and iron objects. This system was quickly adopted elsewhere in Europe to designate the ages of prehistory: the Stone Age, Bronze Age, and Iron Age. These basic divisions are still used in Europe and in many other areas of the world.

The Stone Age was subsequently further divided in 1865 by English naturalist John Lubbock, who coined the terms Paleolithic and Neolithic to distinguish the Old Stone Age and the New Stone Age. The Paleolithic is characterized by tools of flaked flint, while the Neolithic is represented by polished stone tools and pottery. Further divisions of the Paleolithic were made as the age and complexity of the period became known. In 1872, the French prehistorian Gabriel de Mortillet proposed three major subdivisions of the Paleolithic: Lower, Middle, and Upper.

Since then, an even earlier subdivision of the Paleolithic has been designated with the discovery of the earliest stone artifacts in Africa. The Basal Paleolithic includes the pebble and flake tools of the Oldowan industry from around 2.5 million years ago until the appearance and spread of handaxes. The Lower Paleolithic includes the Acheulean and Clactonian industries generally associated with *Homo erectus* and early *Homo sapiens*. (See "The Acheulean Handaxe," p. 62.) Handaxes and flake tools characterize these periods. The Lower Paleolithic thus extends from approximately 1.5 million years ago to the beginning of the Middle Paleolithic, about 120,000 years ago. The Middle Paleolithic is associated with Neanderthals and other forms of archaic *Homo sapiens*, and is characterized by a predominance of flake tools in artifact assemblages. In Europe and the Near East, Middle Paleolithic assemblages are known as Mousterian. (See "The Problem of the Mousterian," p. 96.) The Upper Paleolithic begins around 35,000 years ago with an emphasis on tools made on very long thin flakes of stone, known as blades, and on tools made from a number of other materials, including bone and antler. The finale of the Upper Paleolithic generally coincides with the end of the Pleistocene, around 10,000 years ago. (See "The Upper Paleolithic," p. 112.)

Major developments during the Paleolithic include the appearance of the first stone tools around 2.5 million years ago, the controlled use of fire around 0.75 million years ago, definitive evidence for the hunting of large game and the first definite structures and shelters perhaps 350,000 years ago, the intentional burial of the dead beginning around 100,000 years ago, the first art and decoration 30,000 years ago, and the dispersal of human populations throughout most of the world by the end of the Pleistocene. Our human ancestors lived as hunter-gatherers for more than 99% of prehistory, successfully harvesting the wild foods of the landscape. Domestication — the planting of crops and the herding of animals — doesn't begin until the very end of the Paleolithic, after 8000 B.C.

Some important technological trends occurred during the Paleolithic, one of which was the specialization of tools. The earliest stone artifacts were general-purpose tools extremely simple in form. Over time there is a definite increase in the kinds of tools present and in the total number of tools at the largest sites. There is also an increase in the efficiency of the use of stone and in the amount of cutting edge produced by flaking stone. For example, 0.5 kg (1 lb) of flint would produce about 8 cm (3 in.) of edge on an Oldowan pebble tool, about 30 cm (12 in.) around the circumference on a handaxe from the Lower Paleolithic, about 90 cm (30 in.) of

Epoch	Years before present	Climate (Warmer ← → Colder)	Period	Stone Industry	Archaeological Sites	Hominid Species	Major Events
Post-Galacial							Farming
	10,000		Neolithic				
Upper Pleistocene			Upper Paleolithic	Blade tools	Lascaux Pincevent Dolni Vestonice Tabun	Homo sapiens sapiens	Art
	100,000		Middle Paleolithic	Mousterian flake tools	Shanidar Klasies River Verteszöllös Kalambo Falls	Homo sapiens neanderthalensis Archaic Homo sapiens	Burial of dead Oldest dwellings
Middle Pleistocene	200,000				Torralba Terra Amata Olorgesailie		
	500,000		Lower Paleolithic		Zhoukoudien Trinil		Use of fire Spread out of Africa
Lower Pleistocene				Clactonian chopping tools			
	1,000,000			Acheulean handaxes	Koobi Fora	Homo erectus	Handaxes
				Oldowan pebble tools	Olduvai		
	2,000,000				Swartkrans	Homo habilis	Large brains First stone tools
Pliocene			Basal Paleolithic		Hadar	Australopithecines	Oldest hominid fossils
	3,000,000				Laetoli		

edge on the flake tools of the Middle Paleolithic, and in the Upper Paleolithic, the long, thin flakes would result in almost 9 m (30 ft) of cutting edge. An increase in the types of materials used to make tools is also evident during the Paleolithic. Bone, antler, ivory, and wood are commonly used by the end of the Paleolithic, although this may be a result of better preservation at more recent sites.

The Paleolithic witnessed the achievement of humanness, a heritage that has been passed on to the inhabitants of the most recent 10,000 years of our species' past. The major developments in this recent past would not have been possible without the gradual population expansion, innovative technology, and developing language, social relations, and ritual that marked the journey of our ancestors through the Paleolithic.

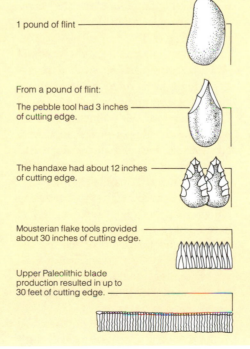

1 pound of flint

From a pound of flint:

The pebble tool had 3 inches of cutting edge.

The handaxe had about 12 inches of cutting edge.

Mousterian flake tools provided about 30 inches of cutting edge.

Upper Paleolithic blade production resulted in up to 30 feet of cutting edge.

Major divisions of the Pleistocene and the Paleolithic.

A major trend through the Paleolithic: increasing efficiency in the production of cutting edge. Pebble tools, handaxes, flakes, and blades were likely produced from the same original piece of flint. Blade production provides an enormous increase in the amount of cutting edge available from the same amount of material.

TRINIL

The discovery of Homo erectus *in Java*

The first discovery of the fossil remains of *Homo erectus* is an unusual tale of individual intuition and conviction. The hero of this episode is Eugene Dubois, born in the Netherlands in 1858, just before the appearance of Charles Darwin's first book on natural selection. English biologist Alfred Russell Wallace was promoting a similar theory on the evolution of species at this same time. Both Wallace and Darwin argued that the progenitors of the human species had come from a "warm, forest-clad land." Wallace had lived for almost a decade on the islands of Sumatra and Borneo in Malaysia. In 1869, he published a book entitled *Malay Archipelago,* in which he wrote about the orangutans in this area and the potential there for human evolution: "With what interest must every naturalist look forward to the time when the caves of the tropics be thoroughly examined, and the past history and earliest appearance of the great manlike apes be at length made known" (Wallace, 1869, p. 72).

Heavily influenced by the words of Wallace, Dubois carefully studied the evidence for human evolution. He wisely realized that early human remains would be found in areas with limestone caves, where the chances for preservation were greatest. He reasoned that Europe had been too cold for these early humans. He also knew that large parts of northern Europe had been scoured by erosion during the glacial periods and were unlikely to have retained the earliest evidence. (See "Climate and Environment During the Pleistocene," p. 82.) Thus, he was convinced that he should go to the Dutch colonies in the East Indies and find human fossils — and he did.

Dubois' views were highly heretical in the context of European paleoanthropology in the latter half of the nineteenth century. Early hominid remains, such as Cro-Magnon and Neanderthal, had just been discovered in Europe, and their qualifications for "humanness" were being debated. At this time the concept of a missing link — the fossil connection between the apes and man — dominated perspectives on human evolution. Many scientists did not believe that apes had sired the human species because evidence for the connection was lacking.

Dubois had grown up in an enquiring family atmosphere. His father, a pharmacist, had taught him the scientific classification of all the plants and trees in their neighborhood. As a high school student he attended an influential lecture on evolution, and an interest in natural history and evolution dominated his subsequent intellectual life. Dubois trained as a surgeon and anatomist at the University of Amsterdam.

To pursue his interests in early hominids, he gave up his university position, joined the army as a surgeon in the Dutch East Colonial forces, and left for Sumatra with his wife and their infant in 1887. A Dutch colony and an obvious destination for the adventurer in Dubois, Sumatra was a tropical land with limestone caves and living great apes. His duties at the small hospital allowed him time to explore the countryside. He spent two years looking for fossil materials without success. In 1890, stricken with malaria, he was transferred to the island of Java, where the drier climate might improve his condition. There, the colonial administration provided a crew for his investigations and two officers to supervise the workers. The area was rich in fossils, and Dubois immediately began to ship specimens of extinct mammals back to the Netherlands.

Eugene Dubois and the fossil finds from Java. The skullcap of the Homo erectus found by Dubois in Java is shown, along with a photo of Dubois as a young man.

One of the most productive fossil sites Dubois found was located along the eroding bank of the Solo River in north-central Java, near the village of Trinil (trin′el). Here the 15-m-high (50-ft) bank exposed layers of volcanic ash, river sediments, and sandstone. Hundreds of bones from deer, rhinoceros, elephant, pig, tiger, hyena, crocodile, and other species were recovered in the layers. Finally in 1891, a tooth and then a skull were recovered that documented the presence of fossil hominids in Java. Dubois described both specimens as great man-like apes. In the next year, a human thigh bone was uncovered some 15 m (50 ft) from the skull. The femur was essentially identical to the modern form, although slightly heavier. This evidence led Dubois to designate the species as *Pithecanthropus erectus*. The term *erectus*, the species name, indicates upright posture, and *Pithecanthropus*, the genus name, is from the Greek *pithecos* (ape) and *anthropos* (man). A second skull was found in the area in 1937. Today, after more than seventy-five specimens have been discovered throughout Africa, Asia, and Europe, the individuals from Java are included in the category *Homo erectus*, to indicate their similarity to ourselves.

Dubois' discovery was of paramount importance, because it indicated that Asia,

The location of Trinil. At the time that early hominids were on Java, sea level was lower and the island was part of the mainland of Southeast Asia. Darker shaded areas indicate land masses during that time. Lighter shaded areas indicate current land masses.

The bank of the river where the skull of Java man was found by Dubois.

not Europe, might be the ancestral home of the human species. He returned to Europe in 1895 with the materials he had found and was met with substantial criticism and doubt. Even today, a controversy seems to arise in paleoanthropology whenever new and distinctive fossil forms are uncovered. Various authorities of Dubois' day argued that the thigh bone was too modern and could not belong with the skull. Others were unsure whether it was closer to an ape or to a human. Soon there were more than fifteen different written opinions on the matter, espousing various ape, man, or ape–man interpretations. By the turn of the century, the controversy had driven Dubois to his home in the Netherlands, where he buried the fossils under the floor and withdrew from scientific circles until his death. Toward the end of his life he became more and more convinced that the remains of Java man were in fact those of an ancestor to the apes, and not human after all. The end of the Dubois story is all the more poignant in light of the fact that it was subsequently determined that he had indeed been the first to discover the remains of our direct ancestor, *Homo erectus*.

At the time of its initial colonization, Java would not have been an island as it is today, but rather an extension of the peninsula of Southeast Asia, connected to the continent by land bridges during a period of lower sea level. The precise date for this colonization, or for the hominid fossils themselves, is difficult to specify. Methods such as radiopotassium dating have not proven very successful. Estimates place the age of the hominid materials at around 0.75 m.y.a., but this date remains speculative.

The evidence for the initial presence of hominids outside Africa comes from early *Homo erectus* sites such as Trinil. The spillover of humans out of an African homeland sometime after 1 million years ago must have been a gradual process related to growing population and a fairly mobile lifestyle. Even at a rate of expansion of just 15 km (10 mi) per generation of twenty years, it would take only some 20,000 years to cover the distance between East Africa and Southeast Asia — around 15,000 km (10,000 mi). That brief period of time is indistinguishable with current dating techniques.

Another puzzling aspect of the Java discoveries is the absence of tools or other materials associated with the human fossils. No stone artifacts have been found that can definitely be connected with the *Homo erectus* population. Although excavations in the last century might well have ignored odd-shaped pieces of stone, even more recent work has been unable to determine whether flakes or core tools were being made and used in the same period as the *Homo erectus* fossils. In other parts of the world during the Middle Pleistocene, stone artifacts in the form of handaxes, choppers, and flakes were used widely. A number of *Homo erectus* habitation sites document both the tools and the food debris of these groups.

A microscopic study of the scratches and wear on the teeth of the Java hominids suggests the consumption of thin, chewy vegetable foods. Perhaps such a diet, largely dependent upon plants, would not require even the simplest tools. Perhaps bamboo was employed for making tools, split into pieces, and the sharp edges used. But the mystery of the missing artifacts on Java has not been solved; more exploration and excavation must be undertaken there to determine how these *Homo erectus* groups survived.

ZHOUKOUDIEN

Bones of the dragon

For centuries, many Chinese have believed that fossil bones have medicinal and curative powers. Called dragon's teeth, such fossils are ground into powder and sold at apothecaries throughout the country. For nearly a century, paleontologists and other natural scientists have often visited such shops to look for the bones of new species and to learn about potential new fossil sites. In 1899, a European doctor in Beijing found an unusual fossil tooth at an apothecary and identified it as the upper third molar of either human or ape origin. The tooth came from a place called Dragon Bone Hill, a large limestone ridge near the town of Zhoukoudien (Joe-ko-tee-en'), 50 km (30 mi) southwest of Beijing. Before the doctor returned to Europe, he passed the tooth and the information to a Swedish geologist, John Gun-

nar Andersson. Andersson and his friend Davidson Black, a Canadian anatomist, were convinced they could find an early human fossil where the tooth was found. When Andersson returned to Sweden, Black continued the project and persuaded the Rockefeller Foundation to sponsor excavations at the site. On the basis of two hominid teeth that were found, Black announced the discovery of *Sinanthropus pekinensis* (Chinese man of Peking) in 1927. Later in the same year the first skull was found, confirming Black's bold proclamation.

For ten years, a large workforce essentially mined the deposits in the complex of caves at Zhoukoudien, removing over half a million tons of material in the quest for fossils. Almost 2000 days, more than six months each year, were spent

blasting out the limestone and removing rock and sedimentary deposits over a vertical distance of 55 m (180 ft), as high as a seventeen-story building. The large limestone chamber that is the center of the Zhoukoudien caves is enormous, 140 m (450 ft) north to south, by 40 m (130 ft) east to west, by approximately 40 m (125 ft) high, the size of a supertanker. The deposits in this chamber were almost completely excavated in the course of the project. The crude excavation methods and untrained labor meant that stone tools and other materials were often missed, and that important information on context of the deposits was not recorded.

In his report, Black described dense layers of ash, baked sediments, and charred bone resulting from fires in the cave. These materials were thought to be the evidence for humans in the caves, where people lived, made tools, built fires, ate, and died and left their bones. Over 20,000 stone tools, including flakes, scrapers, and choppers (but no handaxes), were found, made from quartz, sandstone, rock crystal, and flint. These materials do not occur naturally in limestone areas and must have been brought into the caves. The artifacts are generally very crude and irregular but do improve in quality toward the top of the deposits.

The abundant bones in the deposits came from both large and small species. Most of the large animal bones came from an extinct form of deer with enormous horns, and from wild horses and giant boars, elephants, water buffalo, hyenas, such carnivores as bears and saber-toothed tigers, and others — a total of ninety-six mammalian species. These animals suggest that the climate was somewhat warmer than today. Moreover, the habitat requirements for these animal species suggest that the area around Zhoukoudien was a mosaic of forested hills, open plains, lakes, and rivers. The forest was likely dominated by pine, cedar, elm, hackberry, and the Chinese redbud tree. Charred seeds of hackberry fruits found in the deposits at Zhoukoudien led to the suggestion that such plant foods may have formed part of the diet of the human inhabitants.

By far the most important finds at Zhoukoudien were the remains of the early hominids, today designated as *Homo erectus*. A total of six skullcaps (the face and lower portion of the crania are missing), twelve skull fragments, fifteen mandibles, 157 teeth, seven thigh bones, one fragment of shinbone, three bones from the upper arm, one collarbone, and one wrist bone have been recovered to date. As in the South African caves, hominid

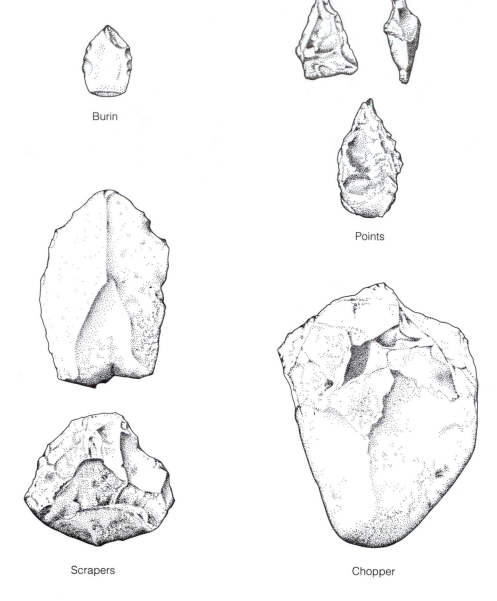

Stone artifacts found at Zhoukoudien.

Burin

Points

Scrapers

Chopper

skulls are more common than the other bones of the skeleton, in part because they are more resistant to destruction and in part because they are more readily recognized. These fragments came both from adult males and females and from children. An increase in brain size over time may be seen in the materials from Zhoukoudien. Skulls at the lower end of the deposits have a cranial capacity of about 900 cc, while those from the upper levels are closer to 1100 cc on average, within the range of variation of modern *Homo sapiens sapiens*.

The investigations conducted by Black, and since 1949 by the Chinese, have revealed at least thirteen stratified layers in the deep deposits at Zhoukoudien. The deposits themselves date to at least 700,000 years ago at the bottom to roughly 200,000 years ago at the top of the sequence by various dating methods. The time span covered by the finds of *Homo erectus* is about 250,000 and 550,000 years ago.

Unfortunately these important fossils have been lost. The excavations at Zhoukoudien had to be closed in 1937 with the outbreak of war between the Japanese and Chinese. A decision was made to move the fossils to the United States for safekeeping. They were packed carefully in

Geological Period	Stratigraphy Depth (m)	Layer
Upper / Middle Pleistocene	5	Breccia travertina
	10	Breccia with ashes
	15	Ashes
		Hard travertine
Middle	20	Hard breccia
	25	Fine sand
	30	Breccia with ashes
		Upper red clay
Lower	35	Lower ash
		Breccia
		Coarse sand
	40	Reddish clay sand
Lower Pleistocene		Basal gravel

● Homo erectus fossil

The stratigraphy of 40 m (130 ft) of deposits at Zhoukoudien, showing the location of the Homo erectus skeletal remains.

The stratigraphy of 40 m (130 ft) of deposits at Zhoukoudien, showing the location of the Homo erectus *skeletal remains.*

crates and placed in the hands of a detachment of U.S. Marines. Somewhere between the consulate in Beijing and the port of departure from China, the fossils disappeared. Today they may be destroyed, still in China, in Japan, in the United States, or at the bottom of the Pacific—no one knows. A reward of $150,000 was posted for their return. Fortunately, plaster casts were made before the fossils were lost, so that there is at least some information on their size, shape, and important features. In addition, the more recent Chinese excavations since 1949 have uncovered a few more examples. Nevertheless, these priceless relics of some of our earliest ancestors would be a marvelous rediscovery.

THE FIRST EUROPEANS

An uncertain date of arrival

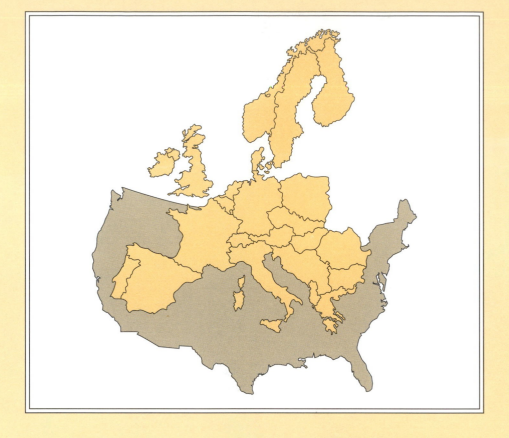

The latitudinal relationship between
Europe and the United States.

New York City lies at the same latitude as Madrid and Rome. In fact, most of the European continent is further north than the U.S.–Canadian border. Very cold climates would have prevailed in Europe during parts of the last 1 million years, making the northernmost portions of the continent generally inhospitable to human occupation. Large glaciers extended across the Pyrenees, the Alps, Scandinavia, and Britain, and a permafrost tundra dominated the northern half of Europe during these colder periods.

The earliest archaeological sites in Europe are younger than 750,000 years B.P. and contain simple pebble-tool assemblages. The best-dated early site is from Italy, at a place known as Isernia. Simple stone tools and animal bones were found together there in deeply buried lake deposits underlying a volcanic ash dating to 730,000 years ago by radiopotassium methods. The stone tools, largely limestone pebble tools and small flint flakes,

were found in the thousands. The archaeological materials were quickly covered by the fall of volcanic ash, so that the date should be reasonably accurate for the occupation. Large animals associated with the deposit are bison, rhinoceros, elephant, bear, hippopotamus, pig, goat, and deer.

A few sites in Europe may be even older than Isernia, but there are no absolute dates for them, and their ages remain controversial. By 400,000 years B.P., however, most of Europe had been occupied. Lower Paleolithic sites are found throughout the central and southern parts of the continent at places such as Bilzingsleben in Germany, Terra Amata in France, and Torralba and Ambrona in Spain. Bilzingsleben lies in an area of natural mineral springs; human and animal bones and small stone tools were found preserved in the hardened deposits of travertine around the springs. Isotopic dates for the site indicate an age of approximately

The locations and ages (thousands of years ago) of some of the earliest hominid sites in Europe.

Map labels:
- Clacton (245)
- Swanscombe (325)
- Bilzingsleben (350)
- Steinheim (250)
- Verteszöllös (350)
- Arago (250)
- Terra Amata (350)
- Torralba and Ambrona (350)
- Isernia (730)

200,000 years B.P., during an interglacial period. Human skull fragments were found in the deposits, along with numerous animal bones. A site very similar to Bilzingsleben was found in Hungary at Verteszöllös, roughly 50 km (30 mi) west of Budapest. Here again, the stone artifacts are curious because of their small size, likely due to an absence of larger pieces of raw material in the area. Short cutting edges were produced on thousands of tiny pebbles, often only 2.5 cm (1 in.) in diameter. Charcoal and burned animal bone document the use of fire at this site. As at Bilzingsleben, fragments of skull from early European hominids were found in the layers at Verteszöllös. The species designation of these forms, either *Homo erectus* or archaic *Homo sapiens,* is a matter of some dispute.

TERRA AMATA

Europe's oldest beach hut

Located along the Mediterranean shore in the city of Nice, France, the site of Terra Amata (tare'aha-mot'ah) was initially uncovered in 1965 during the construction of a high-rise apartment building, located at the intersection of Boulevard Carnot and a side street called Terra Amata, meaning beloved land. The latter name was given to the archaeological site. The director of a national archaeological research center in nearby Marseilles, Henry de Lumley, was called in to look at the materials, and he immediately recognized their importance. The site is exceptional because of the antiquity of the remains; the remarkable preservation of bone, charcoal, shell, and other artifacts; and the possible presence of dwelling structures.

De Lumley convinced the builders to stop work for six months in order to rescue the remains, which overlapped the edges of the foundation trenches. A crew of around 300 volunteers was quickly organized. Over 270 cu m (350 cu yd) of earth were moved to expose 125 sq m (1350 sq ft) of the occupation area; 35,000 prehistoric objects were uncovered, and the location of each was plotted on charts. As many as twenty-one hut constructions were defined during the excavation.

Today the apartment building stands on top of what is perhaps the oldest dwelling structure in Europe. Fortunately, a portion of the underground parking area was set aside as a museum to protect and display one of the huts and its contents. Recordings available on headsets describe the significance of the various features on the living floor in several languages, while spotlights capture each place for the eyes of the visitor. Modern France displays

The site of Terra Amata, discovered during the digging of the foundation for a new apartment building in Nice, France.

Prevailing wind from northwest

Pebble windscreen

Artist's reconstruction of a possible hut on the beach at Terra Amata with location of the hearth and flint working areas.

some of its oldest evidence of human habitation.

Terra Amata sits at the foot of Mont Boron, one of the dominant landmarks along the coastline of Nice. This 240-m-high (800-ft) limestone ridge carries the scars of beaches formed during various high stands of the Mediterranean, during periods of higher sea level between glacial periods. In places the sea had created small coves at the base of the mountain, piling sand and pebbles into beaches at the shore.

The section exposed by the excavations at Terra Amata has at least eight layers over a vertical height of 25 m (80 ft). Red clays over 3 m (10 ft) thick dominate the surface sediments. Beneath this horizon of soils and slope wash are a series of layers of sand and silts, marking warmer periods of the Pleistocene when sea level was higher and beaches were cut into Mont Boron. The youngest of these layers contains at least three fossil beaches and sand bars. This layer dates to approximately 350,000 years ago. At the time of occupation, the site was located on the delta of the Paillon River, near the mouth, at the coast of the Mediterranean. The environment at that time was slightly cooler than today, and the water level in the Mediterranean was about 25 m (80 ft) higher.

Traces in the sands of this fossil beach mark a series of dwelling structures and the remains of meals, tools, and building materials, dating to the Lower Paleolithic.

Saplings or branches were apparently used for the construction of this structure. Large cobbles from the beach and blocks of limestone from the nearby hillside were used to buttress the sides of the huts. In one case a complete oval of stones remained intact, filled with organic matter and ash. Several larger logs were used in the center of these oval huts to support the roof of branches pulled together from the sides. The branches and posts are gone, but their impressions in the sand and the cobbles remain to mark the location. In addition, the tools and bones are found within the confines of the structure. What is surprising is the size of these oval structures, roughly 6 by 13 m (20 ft by 40 ft), the size of an average classroom. Twenty people, or more, might have shared such a shelter.

Shallow fireplaces were built in each hut with a small windscreen of pebbles and sand to protect the fire from drafts. Scorched earth and scatters of broken and burned bones mark these hearths in the sand. Artifacts and food refuse concentrate around the fireplaces, decreasing in density toward the margins of the huts. These peripheral areas were likely used for sleeping. Food remains in the form of discarded bones document a diet that included red deer (like the North American elk), an extinct form of elephant, rhinoceros, ibex (mountain goat), wild boar, and wild cattle. Many of the animals represented in this group appear to have been

A small fireplace inside one of the structures at Terra Amata. The sand is black and red from the ash and heat of the fire. Pebbles were piled up on one side of the fire, perhaps to shield the flames from the wind.

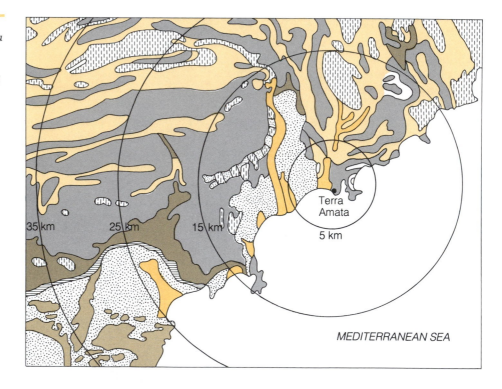

Geological map of the area around Terra Amata. The stone for the artifacts found at the site came from several different sources up to 25 km away. (The shading represents different rock types.) Clearly these Acheulean hunter-gatherers were carrying raw materials some distance.

35 km   25 km   15 km

Terra
Amata

5 km

MEDITERRANEAN SEA

hunted and killed as juveniles. In addition, the inhabitants collected foods from the sea; burned shells from oysters, mussels, and limpets have been found in the refuse at Terra Amata, as well as fish bones. There is little evidence for plants preserved at the site, although such foods must have also been important.

The artifacts are often simple pebble tools, but a few crude handaxes and cleavers were being used as well. Most of the artifacts were made from materials locally available on the beach, but some of the stone came from a distance of 25 km (40 mi) or more inland. In some places inside the structure, the waste material from tool making can be seen clustered around a small open area, as though an individual sat making tools as the debris accumulated around him. The stone tools belong to the early part of the Acheulean period. (See "The Acheulean Handaxe," p. 62.)

De Lumley also reported impressions of wooden bowls in the sandy floor of one of the huts, and in another area suggested that the remains of a hide or skin could be detected on the floor. A fragment of human skull and the impression of a footprint in the sand were found in one of the huts. One of the most remarkable finds from the site was a series of what were thought to be **coprolites** — fossilized human excrement — in and around the huts. Pollen in these paleofeces came from plants that flower and produce pollen in the late spring and early summer, leading the investigators to suggest that this was the time of year that the huts were occupied. Reanalysis of the coprolites has shown that the coprolites were in fact tree roots that had grown down through the layers at the site. Thus the original suggestion that the site was occupied in the late spring and early summer likely has no basis. Indeed, the antler found at the site had been naturally shed by the deer, an event that normally takes place during the colder months of the year. We do not know for sure when the inhabitants were at the site.

De Lumley also argued that the structures were occupied for only a brief time each year, abandoned, and gradually covered by around 10 cm (several inches) of sand and sediment from winter storms. What is surprising is that the human group apparently returned to the same spot year after year to rebuild the same hut. Superimposed layers in the hearths suggest this pattern of repeated construction, and de Lumley suggests that one of the huts has evidence for eleven episodes of rebuilding.

Reevaluation of evidence is always important in archaeology. More recent studies of Terra Amata have provided some corrections, cautions, and revisions of the earlier interpretations. Analysis of the location and distribution of the individual pieces of stone and bone that fit together by Paola Villa, of the University of Colorado, is very informative. The location of these refitted pieces indicates that they were recovered from different layers over vertical distances of 30 cm (1 ft) or more. Thus many of the levels originally distinguished at Terra Amata may not actually have been originally distinct but perhaps formed as later features at the site. The superimposed living floors that indicated possible reoccupation of the huts annually cannot be confirmed.

In spite of these cautions and some problems with the original data, Terra Amata remains one of the most important Paleolithic sites in the world. Most archaeological interpretation is subject to reevaluation and revision, as new information comes to light. It is clear that early Europeans stayed at this place and ate a variety of food. They likely built several large huts, and exploited the rich resources of the Mediterranean shoreline.

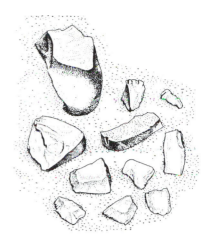

Refitted stone artifacts. Flakes from the same original nodule at Terra Amata have been refitted by archaeologists to study manufacturing techniques and the object of the tool-making activity.

THE ACHEULEAN HANDAXE

The Swiss Army knife of the Lower Paleolithic

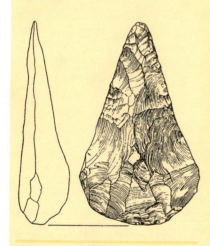

An Acheulean handaxe.

While pebble tools do have a cutting edge, they are extremely simple and unwieldly. These basic tools changed, evolved, and improved through time as early hominids began to remove more and more flakes from the core of raw material, completely reshaping it and creating longer, straighter cutting edges. When such a core assumes a distinctive teardrop shape, with two opposing convex faces—pointed at one end, rounded at the other, retouched all over to a desired size, shape, and heft—it is known as a **handaxe**, the hallmark of *Homo erectus* and early *Homo sapiens* technology. The name derives from the French phrase *coup de poing*, an axe wielded in the hand. But the handaxe is truly an all-purpose piece of equipment that was used for cutting meat, sawing, digging, bashing, and boring large holes, among other things.

The handaxe is, in fact, a more complex tool than it may first appear. The form is a shape inside a piece of stone, in the mind of the maker; a cobble must be completely modified in order for the handaxe to emerge. Moreover, the handaxe is symmetrical in outline, reflecting purpose, skill, and foresight in manufacture. Handaxes are often made on small cobbles 10 to 15 cm (4 to 6 in.) long. A number of much larger examples, however, are also known, up to 30 cm (1 ft) or more in length.

The 700,000-year-old site of Kilombe in Kenya provides interesting data on the manufacture of handaxes. Here, hundreds of handaxes were discovered eroding out of the same geological layer. What is remarkable is that most of the handaxes are very similar in size and shape. Stone artifacts are made by a process called a **reduction technique**—the removal of flakes from a core—and errors or mistakes cannot be erased. Nevertheless, the symmetry and relationship between length and width in the handaxes from Kilombe is remarkable. Small and large implements have the same length-to-width ratio, indicating the importance of the mental image the makers had of what a handaxe should look like.

Handaxes and associated tools are referred to as **Acheulean** (ash-oo-lee'an) artifacts, after the original site at St. Acheul on the Somme River in northern France. Abundant meltwater at the end of each glacial period downcut the rivers of northern Europe, creating a series of terraces in the river valleys. On these terraces near the towns of Abbeville and St. Acheul, prehistorians during the nineteenth century collected these hallmark tools of the Lower Paleolithic. Objects on the higher, older terraces were crude handaxes, with irregular edges and heavy flake scars on their surfaces. Acheulean handaxes from the lower, younger terraces were more symmetrical, with straighter edges. A **hard hammer technique** (stone-on-stone) was used to make the more irregular tools of the early part of the Acheulean period. A **soft hammer technique** was used to make the younger, more regular artifacts. Mallets of bone, antler, or even wood can be used to remove flakes from stone. Lighter, soft hammers are easier to control, and the flakes that are removed are both thinner and wider.

Acheulean assemblages include not only handaxes but a variety of other tools, both heavy-duty pieces and smaller ones. **Cleavers**—a kind of handaxe with a broad, rather than pointed, leading edge—are also quite distinctive of the period. Other artifacts include a variety of flake tools, such as scrapers, **burins**, and borers.

Some years ago, Harvard archaeologist Hallam Movius described the distribution of handaxes as limited to Africa, the southern two-thirds of Europe, and western Asia. More recent research, however, has expanded the known distribution of these tools. While they do not appear everywhere, handaxes are now known from most of Africa, Asia, and Europe. They tend to be more common in temperate and tropical areas and perhaps less useful in cooler climates.

In Britain, and in some areas of the European continent, the term **Clactonian** has been used to refer to the nonhand-

axe assemblages of the Lower Paleolithic. These assemblages represent an evolved Oldowan series of artifacts, including simple pebble tools and flakes. The term is taken from the site of Clacton-on-Sea in England, where a distinctive set of tools, with heavy choppers and notched and saw-toothed pieces, but lacking handaxes, was described during the nineteenth century. Flake tools in these assemblages are generally blocky and irregular in shape, unlike the regularly shaped core and flake artifacts of the Acheulean.

The distinction between handaxe and nonhandaxe assemblages is of considerable interest in prehistory, and its significance is still not clear. Mary Leakey has found both kinds of assemblages, with and without handaxes, in the same levels of Bed II at Olduvai Gorge, suggesting that the differences in the assemblages are likely due to the activities performed, rather than change through time. However, the actual reasons for the presence or absence of handaxes on sites of the Lower Paleolithic are yet to be determined.

Torralba and Ambrona

Twin sites in the center of Spain providing dramatic evidence for large game hunting

Central Spain is dominated by the Castillian Plateau, a relatively level and arid plain with an elevation of slightly more than 1000 m (3250 ft). Surface water is limited in this porous limestone landscape, most of the rain simply soaking deep into the ground. Some 150 km (100 mi) northeast of Madrid a steep-sided valley cuts through this plateau, creating one of the few routes between north and south in the region. During the Pleistocene, this valley almost certainly would have been an important route of migration for large animals moving between the north in summer and the south in winter. Moreover, the less-permeable rocks on the valley floor held springs and wetlands, providing an important source of water in this dry region.

In 1888, workmen digging a ditch for water pipes encountered the buried bones of elephants in this valley. Initially these were thought to be the animals that Hannibal lost on his march to Rome. It was quickly realized, however, that these pachyderms with straight tusks almost 3m (10 ft) long (*Elephas antiquaus*) had lived in Spain in the very distant past. In 1907, a Spanish nobleman, the Marqués de Cerralbo, became interested in the elephant bones and began excavations. Working on at the project for four years, he uncovered the remains of at least twenty-five elephants and other animals, along with a number of stone and bone objects of human manufacture. The Marqués published his discoveries and ideas about these materials, and for the first half

The location of the Ambrona site in the Castillian Plateau. The location of the excavations is marked by the piles of earth and the van.

The linear arrangement of bones and tusks during the excavations at Ambrona.

Excavators removing the earth from around the bones and stone artifacts at the Ambrona site. The ditch for the waterpipe in the foreground was responsible for the original discovery of the site at the turn of the century.

of this century his finds were recognized as the oldest known human artifacts in Europe.

In 1960, Clark Howell, of the University of California, Berkeley, came across the Marqués' reports and further investigated the sites where the elephants had been uncovered. Excavations were reopened, and new information about the area became available. Two separate sites were recognized on the facing hillsides of Torralba (tore-all'ba) and Ambrona (am-brone'ah) in the valley. Both sites are located on a natural terrace about 40 m (130 ft) above the present valley floor.

The bones and stones that accumulated here did so during a colder episode of the Pleistocene, probably during a glacial period, perhaps 350,000 years ago. There is geological evidence of extreme cold in fossil frost cracks in the ground and the presence of frost-weathered gravels, suggesting temperatures at least 5–6°C (8–12°F) colder than today. Pollen evidence from the sites suggests an open, steppelike landscape with small pines and a few deciduous trees in low, sheltered areas with sedge swamps along the valley floor.

Certain species of animals were more common than others at the kill sites of the Lower Paleolithic. At Torralba and Ambrona, for example, there were fifty-five elephants, twenty-six horses, twenty-five

An excavated surface at Ambrona showing the distribution of elephant and other bones. Many of the elephant bones are in approximate anatomically correct position.

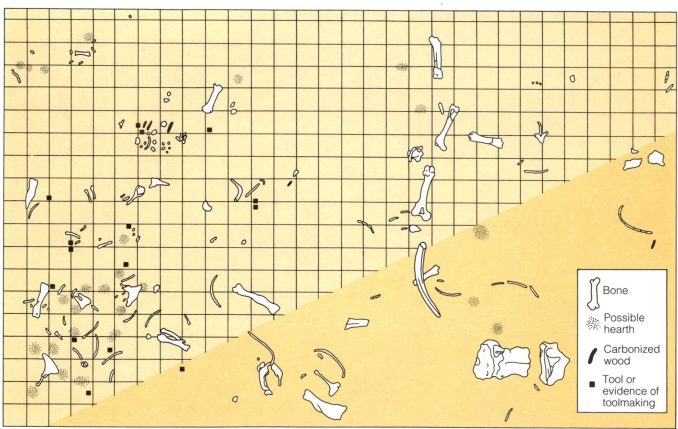

A blueprint of a portion of the site at Ambrona showing the location of artifacts and bones.

Legend:
- Bone
- Possible hearth
- Carbonized wood
- Tool or evidence of toolmaking

deer, ten aurochs (wild cattle), six rhinoceros, and four carnivores. The massive bones of larger animals obviously have a greater chance both of surviving and of being discovered. Some smaller animals were also found, however, including the weasel, wolf, and hare, and various birds and reptiles. The majority of these species would have lived in a grassland habitat.

Many of the artifacts and animal bones at Torralba and Ambrona were in **secondary position**, that is, moved from their *in situ* (original or primary) location of deposition by natural forces. In this case, it appears that a small stream carried many of the bones and stones downstream from their primary deposit, to be buried in sand and other water-lain sedi-

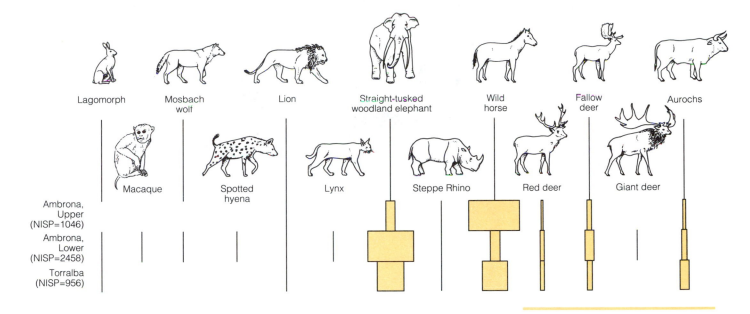

The species of animals represented in the bones at Torralba and Ambrona. The width of the bar for each site and level indicates the abundance of the species. Elephants and horses are by far most common at these sites. NISP stands for the number of identifiable bones per species.

ments. In one or two spots, however, the partially **articulated** (connected) bones of elephants suggest a pattern of dismemberment and butchering. Scattered among the animal bones at these locations were the tools likely used to remove meat from the skeleton. The artifacts at the sites included objects made of stone, bone, ivory tusk, and wood. The stone artifacts belong to the early Acheulean; handaxes were made and used here, along with cleavers and a variety of other flake and core tools. Some of the stone used for making these artifacts came from some distance away.

The evidence suggests that this area was used for thousands of years as a place for stalking, ambushing, and killing game animals. There is no evidence of huts or even fireplaces, but small charcoal pieces are densely scattered in the levels with the bones and artifacts. It has been suggested that fire may have been used to drive these large animals toward the marshly bottoms of the valley, to mire them in the mud so they could be more easily killed. Such conjectures are very difficult to prove, because the remains of natural fires would resemble those of intentionally set ones.

The evidence at Torralba and Ambrona does seem to indicate that these early Spaniards were successful hunters, taking the lives of a variety of different animals. Several interesting questions are raised by the discoveries. How many people does it take to kill and eat an elephant?

The fact that such large animals were being hunted suggests that a fairly large group of hunters was involved, perhaps thirty or more people. Did the hunting groups return to the valley of Torralba and Ambrona each year to intercept the migrating animal herds? The animals seem to have been killed individually over time, suggesting a long series of repeated hunts over the years in the area. Where were these groups during the remainder of the year, and what were their sources of food? Future investigations in central Spain may provide some answers.

THE PLEISTOCENE MAMMALS OF EUROPE

Prehistoric species now extinct

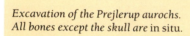

Excavation of the Prejlerup aurochs. All bones except the skull are in situ.

While the Pleistocene witnessed the evolution of a number of our modern mammals (e.g., elephants, horses, and cattle), there were also many animals present then that are now extinct. Woolly mammoth and rhinoceros; cave bear, cave lion, and cave hyena; giant deer and beaver; bison and aurochs (wild cattle) — all roamed over much of Europe during the colder periods of the Pleistocene. These species were generally much larger than their modern equivalents, and all of them are now extinct.

The cave lion, *Felis leo,* and cave bear, *Ursus spelaeus,* are generally well known because of the large number of bones that have been found in caves. The cave bear was enormous, at least the size of a modern Alaskan grizzly, with a very large head and huge canine teeth. This creature ranged over much of Europe, and many of its bones have been found in caves at high elevations in the Alps. Thousands of skeletons of cave bears that died during hibernation have been preserved. The Drachenhöhle in Austria, for example, is estimated to have contained the remains of over 30,000 bears. Tight crevices in the cave were polished by the passage of bears over tens of thousands of years.

The woolly mammoth, *Mammuthus primigenius,* is also well known, both from the skeletal material that has been found and from a few examples of almost complete animals — soft parts, skin, and hair — found frozen in the permafrost of Siberia and Alaska. In Alaska, frozen mammoth hairs in the ground sometimes clog the equipment of gold miners. This animal had a huge domed head, enormous curved ivory tusks, and humped shoulders. Standing approximately 3 to 4 m (10 to 12 ft) at the shoulder, its body was covered with a short woolly undercoat and long, hairy overcoat. The mammoth required an arctic steppe environment and consumed a diet of tundra grasses. This species ranged from western Europe across northern Asia and into North America during the Upper Pleistocene and was apparently quite common at that time.

The giant Irish deer, from the bogs of Ireland and northern Europe, is known for the enormous antlers that it carried, as much as 4 m (12 ft) across. This animal was about the size of the North American moose but more closely resembled the elk. Wild cattle, known as aurochs (*Bos primigenius*) were common game animals

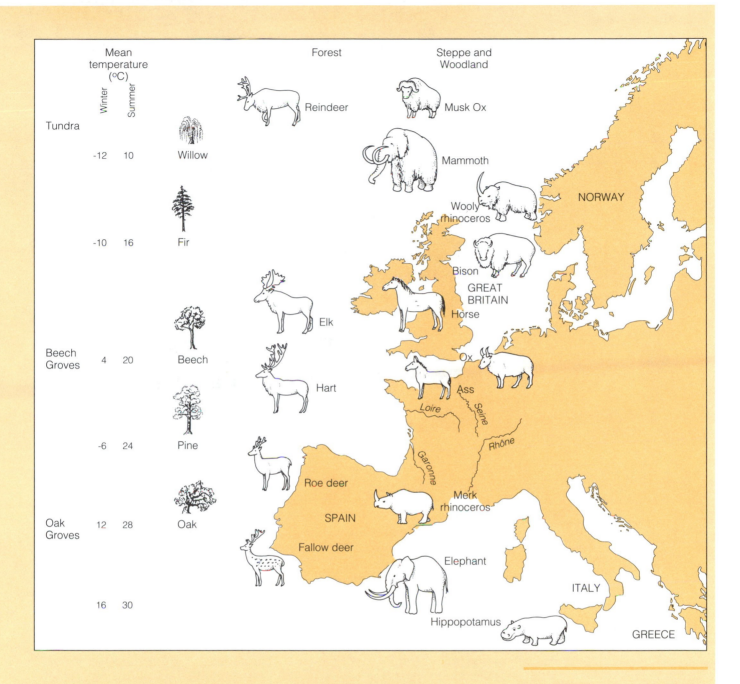

Mean temperature (°C)					
	Winter	Summer		Forest	Steppe and Woodland
Tundra				Reindeer	Musk Ox
	-12	10	Willow		Mammoth
					Wooly rhinoceros
	-10	16	Fir		Bison
				Elk	Horse
Beech Groves	4	20	Beech	Hart	Ox
					Ass
	-6	24	Pine	Roe deer	Merk rhinoceros
Oak Groves	12	28	Oak	Fallow deer	Elephant
	16	30			Hippopotamus

during the warmer periods of the Pleistocene. These animals were likely adapted to grasslands and open woodlands and were particularly common in the early Postglacial.

Many of these species disappeared around the end of the Pleistocene; mammoths, cave bears, and others were extinct by 10,000 B.C. (The causes of these extinctions are discussed in Chapter Three.) The last of the aurochs, a female, died in a game forest in Poland in A.D. 1627. The giant Irish deer may have survived in the Black Sea area until 2000 or 3000 years ago, long after it had disappeared from the European continent. The large-headed Prezwalski horse, depicted in Paleolithic cave paintings, still exists in several European zoos. Other important Pleistocene species — such as reindeer, red deer, elk, musk ox, and brown bear — have survived to the present and continue to survive at the margins of civilization.

KALAMBO FALLS

East Africa 200,000 years ago

Nutshells excavated at Kalambo Falls.

The Kalambo River flows peacefully through the plateau country of East Africa, until its waters suddenly leap over the edge of the East African Rift Valley at the border between Tanzania and Zambia. There the river falls over 250 m (800 ft) into a spectacular gorge close to the present shore of Lake Turkana. Deposits in the valley above the falls have provided one of the longest archaeological sequences anywhere in East Africa, or even in the world. Over 200,000 years of successive human occupations are preserved in the waterlain deposits from the floods and backwaters of the river.

The site of Kalambo (ka-lam′bo) Falls was first discovered in 1953 by Desmond Clark, of the University of California, Berkeley, while he was examining a steeply eroded bank of the river. Preserved tree trunks and branches were present in the layers at the bottom of the bank, along with handaxes and cleavers of the Acheulean tradition in almost fresh condition. This lowest level, designated at Bed I, is over 3 m (10 ft) thick, composed of alternating layers of white sand and

dark clay. The excavations were designed to expose the living surfaces in the lower beds by first removing the overlying sterile sands and clays, allowing all the objects on a single level to be seen and mapped.

Kalambo Falls is a very unusual site for two reasons. First, evidence for the early use and consumption of plants is preserved, and second, evidence for meat eating in the form of animal bones is not represented. The acidic sediments at the Kalambo sites removed all traces of bone, but the waterlogged condition of the lower layers permitted the preservation of a variety of plant materials. Bed I contains several living floors from the late Acheulean, along with a remarkable set of plant materials, including leaves, nuts, seeds, fruits, and some of the oldest wooden objects in the world. A club, a smoothed and pointed piece, and other wooden objects that were modified by humans were recovered from the lowest Acheulean layers. Evidence for fire is also preserved in charred logs found on the living floors at this site.

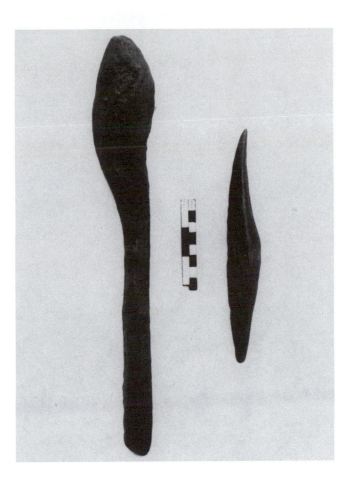

Wooden artifacts including a wooden club (left) and a sharpened wooden object (right) from Kalambo Falls.

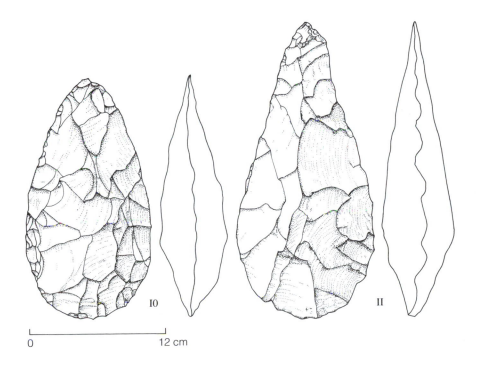

Upper Acheulean handaxes from Kalambo Falls shown in plan view and cross-section.

0   12 cm

Olorgesailie

A Middle Pleistocene lake basin in Kenya

The site of Olorgesailie. The roof at the back of the site covers a part of the excavated area. The stone for many of the artifacts came from the mountain in the background.

Visitors use a raised boardwalk to tour the layers of hundreds of Acheulean artifacts at the site. The man on the ground is Glynn Isaac.

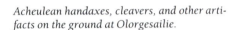

Acheulean handaxes, cleavers, and other artifacts on the ground at Olorgesailie.

Modern baboons spend much of their time in trees, as did their ancestors at Olorgesailie.

Mount Olorgesailie (o-lor-ga-sigh'lee), a dormant volcano in the geologically active area of East Africa, lies about 60 km (40 mi) southwest of Nairobi, Kenya. Although today this region is arid, a large lake basin once filled the rift valley beneath the mountain during the Middle Pleistocene, some 400,000 years ago. During the 1940s, Mary and Louis Leakey found many handaxes and animal bones eroding from sediments along the former lakeshore, marking the location of an important series of early sites.

Major excavations at the site of Olorgesailie were undertaken by Glynn Isaac, then Deputy Director at the Centre for Prehistory and Paleontology in Nairobi. The most important site at Olorgesailie was designated DE/89, located along a sandy streambed at the edge of the former lake. The archaeological materials recovered there included over 400 handaxes and numerous animal bones. Much of the stone raw material for the handaxes came from nearby Mount Olorgesailie. The quantity of lithic material transported to the site — over 1 ton — is testimony to the importance of stone tools for these Acheulean groups.

Bone preservation is exceptionally good at Olorgesailie, better than at many of the sites in this part of the world. Most of the animal bones come from at least sixty-five individuals of an extinct species of very large baboon, known as *Theropithecus*. All the skeletal elements of the baboons are represented, both large and small bones. Some of the bones are heavily weathered and appear to have been exposed on the surface for some time, while others appear fresher and may have been buried rapidly. Although a small portion of the bone and lithic remains at DE/89 may have been moved by intermittent water in the stream channel and deposited together, most of the materials appear to lie at the spot where they were discarded — strong evidence for one or more episodes of humans hunting baboons along the tree-lined stream banks.

Isaac has suggested that these baboons may have been hunted when they were together in a group, perhaps resting in a tree at night. The large number of individuals is likely evidence both for the importance of meat in the diet and for the hunting skills of these human groups, involving coordination and cooperation. Gorilla-size baboons would be a formidable prey for lightly armed human groups. The baboon bones show cutmarks from stone tools, and many were broken in a very specific manner, presumably to extract marrow.

ASSEMBLAGE VARIATION

Stone tools reflect past human activity

A number of Lower Paleolithic assemblages have been mapped and excavated at Olorgesailie and elsewhere in East Africa. The differences in the contents of these sites are most interesting. It is, in fact, striking how different the sets of stone artifacts from Middle Pleistocene African sites can be. Major differences in the assemblages are seen in terms of cores versus flakes, tools versus nontools, large versus small tools, and used versus unused pieces. Some of the sites contain hundreds of large tools, particularly handaxes; others are composed predominantly of small tools such as scrapers; still others contain a mixture of the two.

The causes of such differences are unknown. The effects of erosion, of different raw materials, and changes through time all play a role. The sites under discussion span a period of several hundred thousand years, during which time a number of changes could be expected. Nevertheless, a major source of such differences must also lie in the functions of the artifacts and the activities for which they were used. The presence of the many handaxes with the baboon bones at Olorgesailie suggests that perhaps the larger tools were used for butchering meat. Studies of microscopic traces on handaxes from England by Lawrence Keeley, of the University of Illinois, Chicago, showed meat polish from butchering. At Kalambo Falls, however, where bones are not preserved but plant remains are abundant, large bifaces are also common, even more so than at Olorgesailie. In areas of higher rainfall, heavier vegetation, and poor-quality raw material, large tools are very irregular and poorly made.

Sites that are clearly locations where animals were butchered, such as the partially dismembered hippopotamus at Olorgesailie, have a very high proportion of large cutting tools and very little waste material from their manufacture. However, other sites with a predominance of heavy-duty tools have very little bone. Sites with a wide range of small, large, used, and unused artifacts are likely to be localities where a group of individuals carried out a number of different activities, perhaps campsites.

	Spheroids	Choppers	Light-duty tools	Heavy-duty tools	Large cutting tools	Misc.	Utilized/ modified	Total artifacts
Kalambo								6696
Olorgasailie 7								5059
Olorgasailie 1								850
Olduvai Bed IV								494
Olduvai Upper Bed II								6801
Olduvai Upper A Bed II								5180
Olduvai Middle Bed II								4399
Olduvai Middle Bed II								52

Different kinds of tools and other artifacts from Lower Paleolithic sites in East Africa. The width of each bar represents the abundance of the type at the site. The total number of artifacts from each site is given in the far-right column.

EPILOG
The Origins of
Language

The evolution, not emergence, of speech

The origin of human speech and language is one of the more intriguing aspects of human adaptation and evolution, yet perhaps the most difficult to resolve. Modern languages contain approximately 150,000 words and add several new words each week. Shakespeare's vocabulary is estimated to have been about 24,000 words; a newspaper reporter uses about 6000 words; the average person on the street has a speaking vocabulary of 3000 words or less. We have a natural interest in when and where our ability to communicate with the spoken word originated.

It is not possible to dig up the words or thoughts of preliterate peoples from the past. Large brain size alone does not demonstrate intelligence or speech. Brain size certainly increased as our early ancestors evolved, but so did body size. Brain size also varies greatly today, without a clear relationship to intelligence. Just how much the brain grew in response to bigger bodies, or how much due to added brainpower, is unclear.

The problem may lie in the question we have asked — When and where did language appear? — rather than in the subject of the *evolution* of language. In fact, the Linguistic Society of Paris banned discussion of the origin of language in 1866 because of the heated debate and the small amount of data that were generated. The origin of language is best understood as a process of development, rather than as an event of discovery — a process that began with the vocalizations of our primate ancestors and that continues today as our languages grow and change.

Language did not appear suddenly a few million years ago without antecedents, but evolved gradually from the utterances and cries of early primates to its modern form. On the one hand, language today is a mammoth complex of vocabulary, grammar, and structure, to which many new words are added each year. On the other hand, most animals make sounds that reflect involuntary reactions. Monkeys vocalize to express emotion, but they do not have voluntary control over their sounds. Chimpanzees, however, have a repertoire of twenty or more vocalizations and gestures for expressing emotions and needs. Although these chimps can control their expressions, they are unable to connect more than two or three concepts in a single phrase.

To understand the evolution of language from gestures and cries to its complexity today, we must appreciate the path of its development. Recent studies of the physical remains of early humans offer substantial information about language use by early hominids. Endocasts provide the only direct evidence of brain organization. An **endocast** is a copy or cast of the inside of a fossil skull, reflecting the general shape and arrangement of the brain and its various parts. The cerebrum, the upper portion of the brain, is primarily concerned with the complexities of behavior. This area is large and developed in higher primates. The size of the cerebrum and its convoluted surface — the degree of wrinkling — increases through the evolution of the human species from our primate ancestors.

The organization of the cerebrum is critically important. In modern humans, the front of the brain is much larger than the rear, and the sides of the brain are well developed, in contrast to chimpanzees and other apes. The two sides of the modern

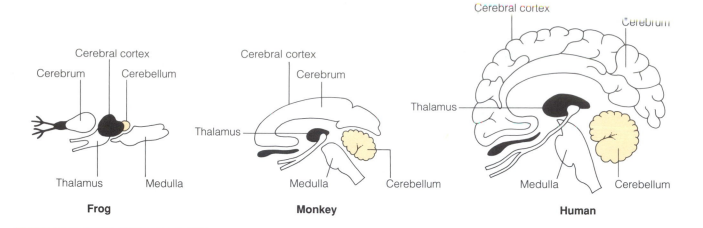

Frog

Monkey

Human

The evolution of the brain, showing amphibian, monkey, and human examples. Conscious mental activity takes place at the surface of the cerebrum. The massive wrinkles in the human cerebrum illustrate the importance of this area of the brain.

Endocasts from South African australopithecines. Note the details of the blood vessels and other structures that have been preserved in the fossil casts.

brain operate in cooperation to direct and control different aspects of behavior and activity. This division in the organization and operation of the brain is called lateralization. One side controls language, while the other is largely responsible for motor skills and perception. Lateralization of the brain is essential for language use, because the processing of strings of words must be done in close physical proximity in the neurons of the brain. Some individuals with speech problems are probably sequencing words and controlling speech from both sides of the brain.

Studies by Ralph Holloway, of Columbia University, have shown that the pattern of lateralization in fossil endocasts goes back well into the Pleistocene and likely to australopithecines as well. Dean Falk, of the State University of New York, Buffalo, has also been involved in the study of endocasts, pointing out that Broca's area, involved in the control of language, is larger in *Homo habilis* than in the brain of their contemporaries, the australopithecines from East Africa.

Certainly many of the activities of our Pleistocene ancestors would have required some form of communication. Repeated visits to the beach at Terra Amata would have to be planned and discussed. The elephant hunts at Torralba would have required cooperation and communication in order to be successful. Food sharing, social organization, and other distinctly human characteristics imply a sophisticated system of verbal expression. These abilities must have evolved and expanded through time, as both brain power permitted and need required.

One of the major issues remaining in the development of language is the reason for the shift from a primitive language like that of small children to a syntactic one with grammatical rules and structure. This development may be related in part to the evolution of the human brain and organizational changes therein. Some radical linguists suggest that all the languages on Earth spring from a common "mother tongue," and a few would even suggest a date of 100,000 years ago for this common language. Needless to say, this view is highly speculative; but it does suggest that future research in this area may provide more information.

SUGGESTED READINGS

Gamble, Clive. 1986. *The Palaeolithic settlement of Europe*. Cambridge: Cambridge University Press. A recent summary of the European Paleolithic, including the first inhabitants.

Howells, W. W. 1980. *Homo erectus* — who, when, and where: A survey. *Yearbook of Physical Anthropology* 23:1–23. A discussion of the characteristics of *Homo erectus*.

Lieberman, Philip. 1991. *Uniquely human: The evolution of speech, thought, and selfless behavior*. Cambridge, MA: Harvard University Press. A recent work on the evolution of language and other very human behaviors.

Pfeiffer, J. 1985. *The emergence of humankind*. New York: Harper & Row. A popular and very readable account of human and cultural evolution in the Paleolithic.

Sutliffe, A. J. 1985. *On the track of Ice Age mammals*. Cambridge, MA: Harvard University Press. A detailed study of the mammals of Pleistocene.

WINTER HUNTERS

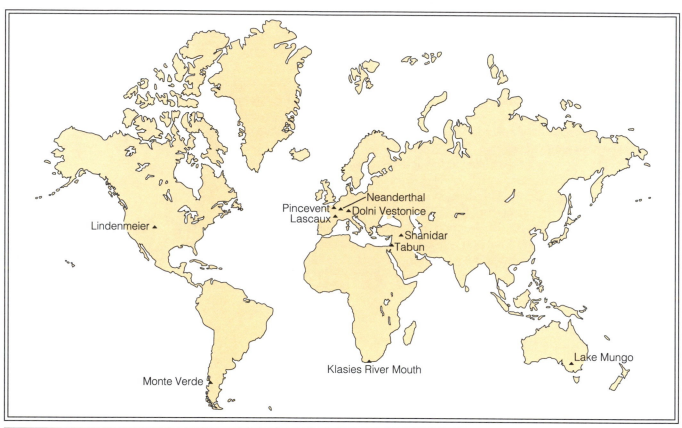

Lindenmeier ▲

Pincevent ▲ ▲ Neanderthal
Lascaux ▲ ▲ Dolni Vestonice

▲ Shanidar
▲ Tabun

Monte Verde ▲

Klasies River Mouth

▲ Lake Mungo

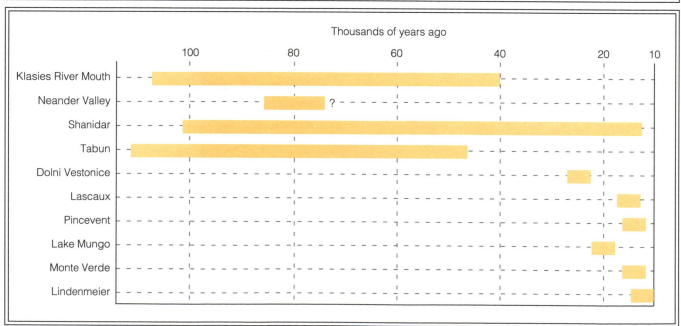

Thousands of years ago

	100	80	60	40	20	10

Klasies River Mouth

Neander Valley   ?

Shanidar

Tabun

Dolni Vestonice

Lascaux

Pincevent

Lake Mungo

Monte Verde

Lindenmeier

PROLOG

THE APPEARANCE OF
HOMO SAPIENS

Modern human forms in the Upper Pleistocene

Major changes in human biology and culture took place during the Upper Pleistocene, from approximately 130,000 to 10,000 years ago, a period that includes both the Middle and the Upper Paleolithic. Environmental variation in the temperate parts of the Old World required significant adjustment by human populations that had previously been accustomed to warmer, less-hostile environments. For the first time, early humans began to exhibit behaviors that were more than just instinctual, beyond the basic necessities for survival. In the Middle Paleolithic these behaviors included burial of the dead, ritual hunting, cannibalism, and the nurturing of the weak and elderly. The Upper Paleolithic witnessed the first art, the invention of many new tools, and tailored clothing. And early human populations expanded to almost all parts of the globe.

As we have discussed, *Homo erectus* was the first early human form found outside of Africa. *Homo erectus* evolved into what is termed archaic *Homo sapiens*. At the beginning of the Middle Pleistocene, around 700,000 years ago, only *erectus* fossils are known; by the end of this period, 130,000 years ago, only *sapiens* were present. The earliest examples of these archaic *sapiens* are known from sub-Saharan Africa before 200,000 years ago. In all likelihood, *Homo erectus* became archaic *Homo sapiens* shortly after 500,000 years ago. There are two forms of early *Homo sapiens*: archaic *Homo sapiens* and *Homo sapiens neanderthalensis*.

In Europe, fragments of human bone have been found at a number of sites dating to between 400,000 and 100,000 years ago. The earlier of these European fossils (from Bilzingsleben and Verteszöllös) are more similar to *Homo erectus* than to *Homo sapiens*. Later fossil fragments from such sites as Swanscombe in England, Steinheim in Germany, and Arago in France suggest that a larger brained, more modern form had emerged. These later forms have features that are closer to the Neanderthals than to *Homo erectus*, suggesting that an archaic form of *Homo sapiens* was present in Europe by at least 200,000 years ago. Skulls from 125,000 to 100,000 years ago begin to exhibit the distinctive bulge on the back of the skull and the projecting face and teeth that characterize the Neanderthals. Fully modern humans did not appear in Europe until after 35,000 years ago. It is essential to remember the distinction between archaic *Homo sapiens* and fully modern *Homo sapiens sapiens*. Archaic *Homo sapiens* evolved from *Homo erectus* between 700,000 and 200,000 years ago. Fully modern *Homo sapiens* emerged in the last 200,000 years from the archaic form. Modern evolved from archaic; when and how are less clear.

There is controversial genetic evidence to suggest that the modern form *Homo sapiens sapiens* appeared approximately 200,000 years ago. This evidence comes from studies of **mitochondrial DNA**, genetic material that mutates at a relatively constant rate. Because mitochondrial DNA is inherited only from the mother, it can provide a line back into the past. The number of different mutations separating two individuals should be a function of how far back in time they share a common maternal ancestor. Analysis of the DNA of a number of women from around the world showed few differences and

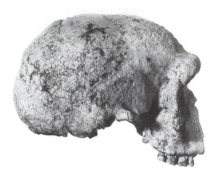

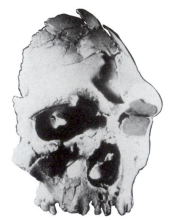

Early hominid skulls in Europe: Steinheim (top) and Arago (bottom). Dating to between 300,000 and 200,000 years ago, these specimens likely represent an intermediate form between Homo erectus *and fully modern* Homo sapiens. *Thus they are now considered to represent archaic* Homo sapiens *and the ancestors of* Homo sapiens neanderthalensis.

suggested that they shared a relatively recent ancestry. Based on the number of accumulated mutations in the DNA, the researchers concluded that modern *Homo sapiens sapiens* evolved in southern Africa between 140,000 and 200,000 years ago. This is known as the African Eve hypothesis.

The fossil evidence is less definitive. A few fragments from the Klasies River Mouth Caves and another site called Border Cave in South Africa indicate that anatomically modern humans were present in southern Africa by 100,000 years ago. These are the earliest known fully modern *Homo sapiens sapiens;* the fossil evidence suggests that the African Eve hypothesis may not be wrong. It seems clear that fully modern humans appeared, probably in Africa initially, before 100,000 years ago.

Today the Neanderthals are generally considered to be a specialized form of archaic *Homo sapiens* that developed in the colder, more isolated areas of Europe and western Asia during the last glaciation. The Neanderthals occupied Europe and western Asia from about 125,000 to around 35,000 years ago, when over a period of 5000 years, they were rather suddenly replaced by fully modern *Homo sapiens sapiens*. In Africa and most of Asia during this time, fully modern humans appear to have been present. Europe and the Near East were exceptions. Current evidence from newly dated sites in the Near East suggests that fully modern humans appeared in this area about 90,000 years ago. At Qafzeh Cave in Israel, and elsewhere in the Near East, the bones of modern *sapiens sapiens* have been found in layers dating to 90,000 years ago with tools also found at Neanderthal sites. At other sites, such as Kebara and Tabun, Neanderthal skeletons have been found dating to between 60,000 and 45,000 years ago. Thus it appears that fully modern humans were present in the Near East shortly after 100,000 years ago and that they coexisted with Neanderthals for some length of time. Evidence from several sites in the Near East (e.g., Boker Tachtit and K'sar Akil) indicates a local evolution in stone tool technology from Middle to Upper Paleolithic, suggesting that there is no direct correlation between Neanderthal and the Middle Paleolithic and between modern humans and the Upper Paleolithic.

In Europe the transition is less clear, and the evidence for the first fully modern humans indicates a much later date. The earliest modern humans did not appear in Europe until 40,000 years ago. A Neanderthal burial was discovered in 1981 in a layer of Upper Paleolithic artifacts from St. Césaire in France dating to 32,000 years ago. The skulls from St. Césair appear to document the arrival of Upper Paleolithic technology in Europe prior to the spread of *Homo sapiens sapiens* into this area. The rapid disappearance of Neanderthals and their replacement by fully modern humans appears to have taken place between 40,000 and 30,000 years ago from east to west in Europe. One scenario would thus have fully modern humans coming out of Africa and into the Near East and the rest of Asia shortly after 100,000 years ago. Modern and Neanderthal forms apparently coexisted in the Near East for 50,000 years. In Europe, however, modern forms appeared quite late, quickly replacing the Neanderthals.

Several theories exist on the nature of this transition. Some believe that the Neanderthals simply evolved everywhere into modern humans under homogeneous selective pressures. It is unlikely that the replacement process involved a massive invasion or conquest of Neanderthals by moderns, as has been suggested in the popular media. Erik Trinkhaus, of the University of New Mexico, and others argue that the evolution of fully modern humans likely occurred in a limited area under specific selective pressures. The new traits would then have spread from the point of origin. Trinkhaus points out that the genetic characteristics that define Neanderthal evolved over a period of more than 50,000 years, yet disappeared in 5000 years in Europe. Such a rapid change makes uniform selective force unlikely as an explanation for the Neanderthals' disappearance. Thus Trinkhaus would argue for the expansion of anatomically modern populations first into the Near East and later into Europe, replacing and absorbing the existing Neanderthals.

This chapter tells the story of the appearance, expansion, and spread of *Homo sapiens* (archaic, Neanderthal, and fully modern forms) to virtually all parts of the globe, as evidenced by such sites as Klasies River Mouth Caves in South Africa, the Valley of the

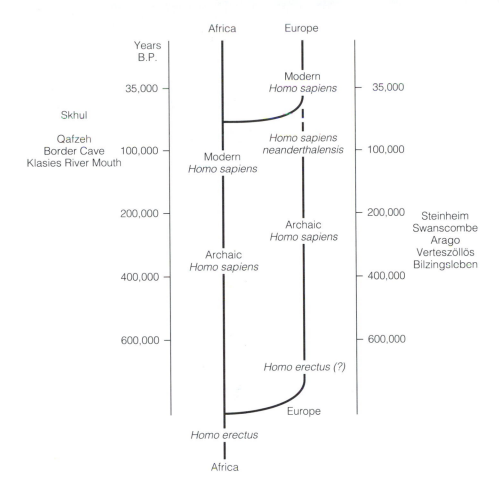

Years B.P.

Africa   Europe

35,000 —   Modern
                 Homo sapiens   — 35,000

Skhul

Qafzeh
Border Cave   100,000 —   *Homo sapiens*   — 100,000
Klasies River Mouth   Modern   *neanderthalensis*
                 Homo sapiens

200,000 —   Archaic   — 200,000   Steinheim
                 Homo sapiens   Swanscombe
                                        Arago
            Archaic   Verteszöllös
            Homo sapiens   Bilzingsleben
400,000 —   — 400,000

600,000 —   — 600,000

                 Homo erectus (?)

                 Europe

Homo erectus

Africa

Human evolution in the Middle Pleistocene, 700,000 to 35,000 years ago. Current evidence suggests a model in which Homo erectus *entered Europe and Asia after 700,000 years ago, archaic forms of* Homo sapiens *appearing soon thereafter. Archaic* Homo sapiens *evolved into modern* Homo sapiens sapiens *in Africa and apparently moved into the Near East after 100,000 years ago and into Europe, replacing the Neanderthals, after 40,000 years ago.*

Neander in Germany, Shanidar Cave in northern Iraq, and the cave of Tabun in Israel dating between 50,000 and 100,000 years ago. The human burials from Lake Mungo in Australia document the spread of *Homo sapiens* to Australia during this period. The settlements at Dolni Vestonice in Czechoslovakia, and Lascaux and Pincevent in France, come from the Upper Paleolithic and date between 35,000 and 10,000 years ago. The land bridge of Beringia, along with two important archaeological sites in the western hemisphere, Monte Verde in Chile and Lindenmeier in Colorado, provide evidence for the peopling of the New World sometime before the end of the Pleistocene. The Pleistocene and the Paleolithic came to an end some 10,000 years ago. As the Paleolithic closed, the human species on six continents began to adapt to the warmer conditions of the Present Interglacial.

CLIMATE AND ENVIRONMENT IN THE PLEISTOCENE

Challenging conditions for human survival from cycles of changing temperature

In parts of northern Canada, summer temperatures are cool, with lows at night around 5°C (40°F). The last snowfall of the winter is often in June, and the first flakes of the autumn come in September. A drop in average summer temperature in this area of 5–6°C (10°F) would mean that not all the winter's snow would melt each year. Even if these snowbanks increased by only a few centimeters each summer, they would grow substantially over the course of time. For example, just 10 cm (4 in.) of snow every year for 10,000 years would build an enormous snowdrift over 1 km (.6 mi) high.

Ice would form under the piles of accumulating snow. A mound of ice is very heavy, and the weight causes the mass to spread at the edges. In such manner huge sheets of ice expanded horizontally during the Pleistocene, as more and more snow and ice accumulated. It has been estimated that these ice sheets may have expanded across the landscape at a rate of as much as 100 to 150 m (350 to 500 ft) per year. In 1000 years, such a growing ice mass would cover a distance of 100 km (62 mi). In 20,000 years of accumulation, the ice would spread 2000 km (1250 mi) from its original center.

Today about 10% of the land surface of the Earth is covered by glaciers. These glaciers are in Antarctica, Greenland, northern Canada, Europe, and Asia, as well as in the high mountain regions. During the colder episodes of the Pleistocene, continental ice sheets expanded from these same areas to cover 30% of the land surface. During the last 1 million years, sheets of continental ice more than 1.5 km (1 mi) thick grew in the Northern Hemisphere.

In North America, these ice masses covered most of Canada and extended into the United States as far south as St. Louis, Missouri. In northern Europe, a similar sheet moved from the Baltic Sea basin to cover Scandinavia, northern Great Britain, and parts of the Netherlands, northern Germany, Poland, and the northwestern part of the former Soviet Union. These sheets of ice acted as enormous bulldozers, grinding down the landscape as they advanced and depositing huge blankets of homogenized earth and rock as they retreated. The weight of the ice also pushed down the land surface, often to great depths. In Greenland today, for example, where the ice sheet is 2 km (1.2 mi) thick, the land surface resembles a very deep bowl, higher at the edges where the ice is thinner. The land surface in the interior of Greenland is far below present sea level; it is one of the lowest spots on Earth.

As the continental ice sheets melted at the end of the Pleistocene, the land surface has rebounded to its former state in a gradual process. The coast of Finland today is expanding at an astounding rate of several meters (10 ft) per century, as this area comes back from the weight of the glacial ice. The mass of ice also reduced the Earth's water reservoir, particularly the oceans. During the time of maximum cold when water was frozen in huge continental sheets, global sea level was reduced as much as 100 to 150 m (300 to 500 ft), completely changing the outlines of the continents and often creating connections between former islands and separate land masses.

The Pleistocene began approximately 2 million years ago at a time characterized by active volcanoes, cooling temperatures, and the appearance of a number of modern species of animals. Although the term Ice Age in the singular has been popular, there were, in fact, a number of glacial periods, or ice ages, during the Pleistocene. There have been at least nine, and probably more, alternations between colder and warmer conditions, known as **glacials** and **interglacials**, during the past million years. Warmer, interglacial periods appear to last between 10,000 and 30,000 years, much shorter than the intervals of cold weather, the glacial periods. A graph of atmospheric temperatures for the last 60 million years indicates that while there has been a general cooler trend, dramatic swings from warmer to colder are most pronounced in the last 1 to 2 million years.

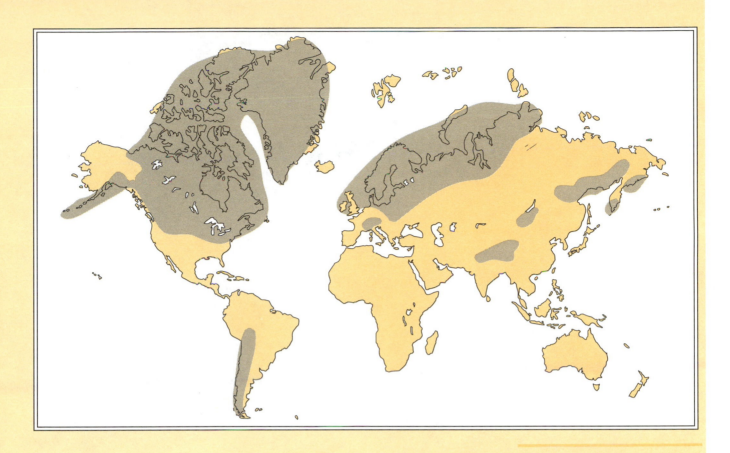

The causes of Pleistocene climatic change and continental glaciation have been debated for many years. Volcanic plumes filling the air with ash and smoke and shading the Earth, or changes in the level of solar radiation, were once thought to be responsible for the onset of the Pleistocene. Recent attention has been given to the role of mountain uplift in cooling the Earth's climate. Walter Ruddiman and John Kutzbach suggest that the uplift of the North American Rocky Mountains and the Himalayas of South Asia resulted in global disruption of weather patterns and the onset of cooler, drier climate. By approximately 3 million years ago, the cooling had reached the level where continental glaciers began to form.

Fluctuations in air and water temperatures were common during the Pleistocene and were cyclical in nature. In the 1920s, Yugoslavian mathematician Milutin Milankovitch argued that the variations in the Earth's orbit changed climate in a cyclical fashion. Slight variation in the precession of the Earth's axis and shifts in the eccentricity of the orbit change the distribution and intensity of sunlight reaching the Earth, just as changes in our seasons are caused by movement along the orbit. Milankovitch predicted cycles of 100,000, 40,000, and 20,000 years for these climatic changes, based on his calculations of the Earth's orbital variation. Such a cyclical pattern seems to fit the information on climatic change found in the ocean cores. Thus it appears that minor changes in such factors as the distance between the Earth and the sun and the tilt of the Earth's axis play a major role in the amount of sunlight reaching the Earth, the atmospheric temperature, and ultimately the expansion and retreat of continental glaciation. This phenomenon, now known as **Milankovitch forcing**, is considered to be the prime reason for the fluctuations of glaciation and climatic change during the Pleistocene.

The maximum distribution of continental glaciation during the colder periods of the Pleistocene. Ice sheets are more common in the Northern Hemisphere in part because there is much more land at the higher northern latitudes.

A modern glacier

The impact of glaciation has been felt most strongly in the Northern Hemisphere, where most of the Earth's land surface is located. In Europe, glaciations from the last several hundred thousand years are reasonably well detailed. In the last century, two Swiss geologists, A. Penck and E. Brückner, recognized four repeated glaciations in Europe from a series of Alpine moraines and river terraces.

They named these glacial stages after local rivers — the Günz, Mindel, Riss, and Würm — from oldest to most recent, with the intervening, interglacial periods designated as Günz/Mindel, Mindel/Riss, and Riss/Würm. These four glacial periods, and the interglacials, cover the last 700,000 years in Europe, including the period when that continent was first inhabited by humans. Major changes in the

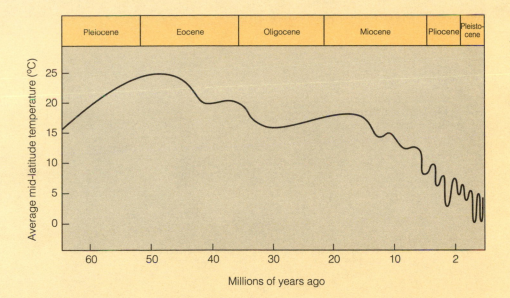

Pleiocene	Eocene	Oligocene	Miocene	Pliocene	Pleisto-cene

Average global air temperature through the Cenozoic. Note the gradual decline in the earth's atmospheric temperature since the Eocene and the more dramatic oscillations in the late Pliocene and Pleistocene.

landscape, and in the plants and animals inhabiting it, occurred with the climatic cycles of cold and warm.

Substantial evidence for human occupation in Europe does not appear until after 350,000 years ago, during the Mindel/Riss interglacial. Sea level was some 25 m (80 ft) higher than today, and warmth-loving animals and plants were present throughout the continent. The subsequent Riss period extended from roughly 300,000 to 130,000 years ago as a very long interval of cold climate and continental glaciation. The last interglacial period—Riss/Würm—dates to approximately 130,000 to 120,000 years ago and was characterized by a climate similar to that of today or even slightly warmer. Sea level was 5 to 8 m (16 to 25 ft) higher than at present, and deciduous trees, such as oak and elm, were growing in northern Europe. Hippopotamus bones have been found in England from this time. Other mammals, including elephant, rhinoceros, hyena, and lion, roamed the plains and forests of the continent.

The last glacial began as a long period of cool, wet weather around 115,000 years ago in Europe. Temperatures during the coldest parts of the Würm were 8–12°C (14–20°F) lower than today. The presence of the continental ice sheets and the cooler weather caused major changes in the wind patterns and storm tracks across Europe, Asia, and Africa. Just as the ice sheets expanded to the south, so did the major environmental zones shrink from the advancing front. Temperate forests migrated to warmer regions, as the tundra in front of the ice expanded. Tundra covered a broad band of western and central Europe. In southwestern France, however, the environment was not a pure arctic tundra but rather a slightly warmer, drier region where maximum daytime summer temperatures may have averaged 16°C (60°F), although temperatures cooled very rapidly at night. Herds of reindeer, woolly mammoth, and horses roamed the treeless elevations and wooded low, sheltered areas.

The end of the Pleistocene has been designated as 10,000 years ago (8000 B.C.), when the last ice sheets retreated. The last 10,000 years, including today, geologists call the Holocene, or simply the Postglacial. Another term that is sometimes used is Present Interglacial. It is not at all clear that the glacial cycles of the Pleistocene have ended; we may presently be witnessing one of the warmer intervals between periods of glaciation.

Notable among the animals found in the later Pleistocene were a beaver the size of a small bear, woolly mammoths, mastodons, a bird with a 12-foot wingspan that is a cousin to the modern condor, extinct species of horses and wolves, and musk ox (still found in the Arctic areas).

THE KLASIES RIVER MOUTH CAVES

Possibly the longest continuous sequence of human habitation in the world

A series of caves cluster at the mouth of the Klasies (class′ease) River, where it empties into the Indian Ocean in South Africa. The caves were originally cut by wave action against the high sandstone and shale cliffs in this area at a time when sea level was higher than it is today. The caves and the sandy area in front of them were a suitable place for human residence from about 120,000 to 60,000 years ago. At one location, the accumulated debris from these occupations had completely buried the opening of another, lower cave. The attractions of the site for repeated residence over this period included the shelter of the caves; the moderate climate; immediately available marine foods, such as shellfish, seals, even beached whales; the

abundant fresh water; access to large and small mammals living along the river; and good quality stone for tools.

The 60,000 years of deposits are 20 m (65 ft) deep (the height of a six-story building) and span the entire Middle Stone Age (MSA) of southern Africa. In Africa, the terms Early, Middle, and Late Stone Age distinguish the archaeological divisions of the Paleolithic. Although these deposits are enormously deep, they accumulated at a rate of only 5 to 10 cm (2 to 4 in.) every 100 years. Dating these deposits is difficult. In the lower layers there is insufficient radiocarbon remaining in the organic materials to be measured and other dating techniques have been employed, including oxygen iso-

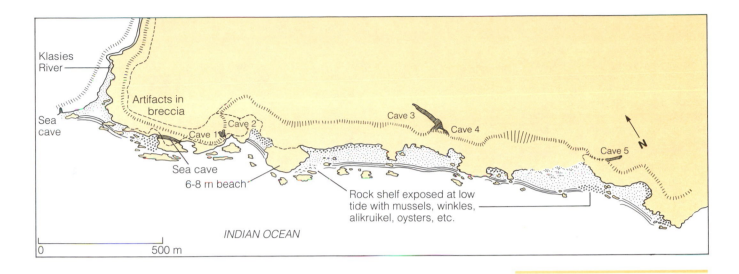

The Klasies River Mouth coastline with the location of caves, artifacts, and resources.

The Klasies River Mouth Caves and the archaeological deposits.

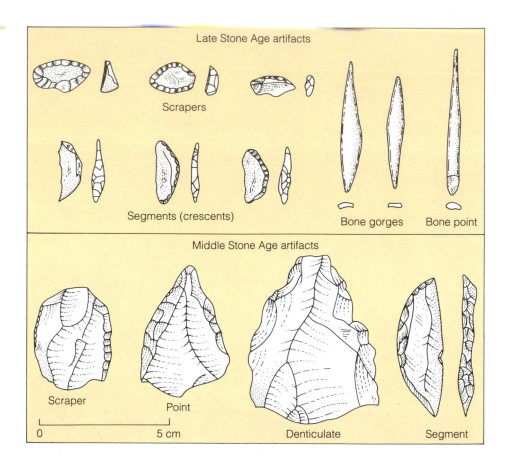

Late Stone Age artifacts

Scrapers

Segments (crescents)

Bone gorges

Bone point

Middle Stone Age artifacts

Scraper

Point

0   5 cm

Denticulate

Segment

Artifacts from the excavations at the Klasies River Mouth Caves. The Middle Stone Age assemblage is dominated by flake tools and was replaced by Late Stone Age materials in the upper levels at KRM. The Late Stone Age artifacts appear in association with fully modern humans after approximately 100,000 years B.P.

topes. Oxygen isotope ratios ($^{18}O/^{16}O$) in a seashell can be used to record the temperature of the water at the time that shell formed. Geological cores removed from deep ocean sediments contain microscopic shells that have been measured for water temperature. It is thus possible to construct graphs of changing water temperature extending hundreds of thousands of years into the past.

It is also possible to measure the oxygen isotope ratio in shells found in archaeological sites. The shells in stratigraphic layers from the Klasies River Mouth (KRM) Caves were measured and the results compared to the ocean sediment curve for which the age was already known. This correlation and other dating methods—including electron spin resonance, uranium disequilibrium, and amino acid dating—suggest that the age of the Middle Stone Age deposits extend from 120,000 to 60,000 years ago.

Excavations over a number of years by Ronald Singer and John Wymer, of the University of Chicago, and Hilary Deacon, of the University of Stellenbosch in South Africa, have exposed the buried oc-

cupation layers and revealed a number of pieces of evidence of major importance for understanding Old World prehistory. A handful of fossil fragments from Klasies and another site, Border Cave, indicate that anatomically modern humans were present in southern Africa by 100,000 years ago. Anatomically modern humans (*Homo sapiens sapiens*) appear here earlier than anywhere else in the world and may well be the ancestors of the San peoples of Africa. The human remains from Klasies are fragmentary and show breakage, cutmarks, and burning that suggest cannibalism.

The evidence from the animal bones, studied by Richard Klein, documents a successful economy throughout the Middle Stone Age. A wide range of animal species is represented, with large and small mammals abundant. Porcupine, grysbok (small antelope), eland (large antelope), giant buffalo, rock hyrax (a small mammal), and the Cape fur seal are the most common. The site also records early human use of marine foods, evidenced by limpet and mollusk shells, and the bones of penguins and seals. The shells could

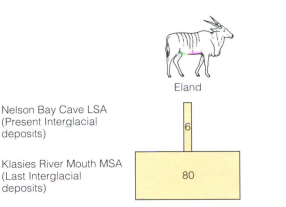

Eland   Cape buffalo   Bushpig

Nelson Bay Cave LSA
(Present Interglacial
deposits)

Klasies River Mouth MSA
(Last Interglacial
deposits)

6

39

38

80

29

3

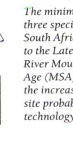

The minimum number of animals of three species from two coastal caves in South Africa. Nelson Bay Cave belongs to the Late Stone Age (LSA); Klasies River Mouth dates to the Middle Stone Age (MSA). The decrease in eland and the increase in bushpig at the younger site probably reflects improved hunting technology in the Late Stone Age.

have been collected along the coast by wading at low tide. There are abundant carbonized organic remains in the deposits, and Deacon believes that these may represent roots and tubers that were collected and eaten by the inhabitants.

The faunal evidence from KRM can also be used to examine the hunting abilities of these Stone Age people in South Africa. Consider two patterns of death for a population of animals: (1) attritional, in which death is by natural causes, such as predation, disease, accident, or old age; and (2) catastrophic, in which a natural disaster, such as flood or epidemic disease, simultaneously kills most of the members of the population. The catastrophic pattern would provide an almost complete picture of the age and sex of the living population, while an attritional profile would be dominated by young and old animals, those more susceptible to predation and disease. Prime-age adults would be largely missing in the attritional profile.

Comparison of the remains of two species of animals from KRM indicates that the eland, a large antelope, is represented by a catastrophic death pattern, while the pattern for Cape buffalo is attritional. The eland is a relatively docile animal that can be driven into traps or falls by hunters, which probably explains the catastrophic profile. Cape buffalo are much more recalcitrant and dangerous. The high proportion of young in the pattern for the Cape buffalo was likely the result of selective hunting. Thus animals that could be driven are represented by catastrophic death patterns, while more aggressive species were likely hunted

individually with weapons. The higher number of elands at KRM — even though this species is much less common than the Cape buffalo in the environment — suggests that the MSA people were not particularly good hunters, and that drives by groups of people may have been more effective than stalking.

If we compare the remains of these two species from a younger site at Nelson Bay Cave, dating to about 10,000 years ago, the pattern for the buffalo is the same, and eland remains are very rare. This pattern suggests that the later groups of people were better hunters than their counterparts at the KRM Caves. The evidence is supported by the presence of the bow and arrow at the later sites. On the other hand, Deacon believes that people of the Middle and Late Stone Age were behaviorally similar, hunting smaller animals and both hunting and scavenging larger ones. His perspective suggests that the general way of life in this area may not have changed from 100,000 years ago until the end of the Pleistocene.

THE VALLEY OF
THE NEANDER

Close relatives with strange habits

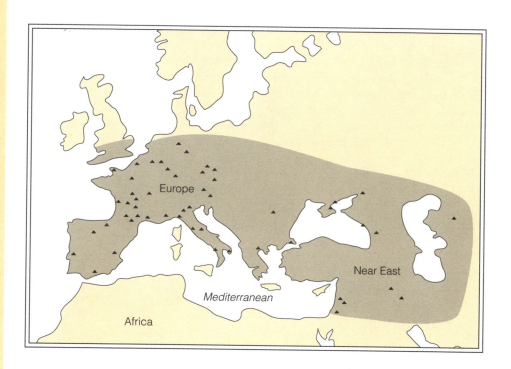

The distribution of the sites of Homo sapiens neanderthalensis *in Europe and the Near East.* Homo sapiens sapiens *existed in the rest of Asia and Africa during this time.*

In 1856, three years before Charles Darwin published his extraordinary treatise *On the Origin of Species,* proposing natural selection as a mechanism for evolution, pieces of an unusual skeleton were unearthed in a limestone cave in the Neanderthal (the Valley of the Neander River) near Düsseldorf, Germany. Prior to this discovery there had been no recognition of human forms older than a few thousand years and only a limited awareness of a concept like human evolution. Leading authorities described the bones from the Neander Valley variously, as those of a deceased Prussian soldier, a victim of Noah's flood, or a congenital idiot, but definitely not an early ancestor. Gradually, however, more examples of these in-

dividuals came to light. In 1886, at the cave of Spy in Belgium, two similar skeletons were discovered in association with early stone tools and the bones of extinct animals, proving the antiquity of the humans in Europe.

In 1913, the French physical anthropologist Marcellin Boule published a study of an arthritic Neanderthal skeleton from the site of La Chapelle-aux-Saints. In this report, he described the finds from Europe as a new species, designated *Homo neanderthalensis.* Unfortunately Boule did not acknowledge the discoveries of *Homo erectus* in Java and saw the Neanderthals as somewhere between ape and human. Boule described the creature's muscular and clumsy body and heavy-jawed skull

Side view of a classic Neanderthal skull from the site of La Ferrassie, France. Typical features include pronounced brow ridges above the eye orbits, a sloping forehead, and a generally robust appearance.

and declared that Neanderthals had little intellectual prowess. His work resulted in a view of Neanderthals as slow in wit, gait, and habit—an idea that continues in some quarters even today.

Gradually, however, as more *Homo erectus* and australopithecine specimens were reported and accepted into the family tree, Neanderthals have come to be recognized as closer to modern humans. Today they are classified as a member of our own genus and species but are distinguished at the subspecies level, as *Homo sapiens neanderthalensis.*

Neanderthals were short and stocky, averaging about 1.5 m (5 ft) in height, with bowed limbs and large joints supporting a powerful physique. Fossil skeletons of Neanderthals are recognized today by several distinctive features in the skull and teeth. The cranium is relatively low and the face is long. Prominent **brow ridges** (bony ridges above the eye orbits) and heavy bone structure give the skull a distinctive look. The average brain size of Neanderthals is slightly larger than that of modern humans, a likely consequence of their generally larger muscle mass and heavier bone structure. The distinctive

shelf or protrusion at the back of the Neanderthal skull is known as an occipital bun. The face is large, the forehead slopes sharply backward, and the nose and teeth sit further forward than in any other hominid, giving the entire face a swept-back appearance. This face is probably the result of a combination of factors, including adaptation to the cold and heavy chewing.

The front teeth are often heavily worn, suggesting that they were used for grasping or heavy mastication. Frequently there are intriguing small scratches on the front teeth, generally running in a diagonal direction. These marks are thought to be the result of "stuff and cut" table manners, in which a piece of meat is grasped in the teeth and a stone knife is used to cut off a bite-size piece at the lips. Occasionally these knives must have slipped and scratched the enamel of the front teeth. The majority of the scratches run from upper right to lower left, although about 10% are in the opposite direction. Such evidence confirms that handedness among humans was common by that time.

The skeleton of Neanderthals differs somewhat from fully modern forms, al-

Table 3.1   Major Characteristics of Neanderthals Compared to Modern Humans

Trait	Homo sapiens neanderthalensis	Homo sapiens sapiens
Forehead	Sloping	Vertical
Brow ridges	Moderate	Absent
Face	Slightly forward	Below forehead; under cranium
Cranial capacity	1400 cc	1400 cc
Protrusion on back of skull	Present	Absent
Chin	Absent	Present
Appearance of skeleton	Robust	Gracile

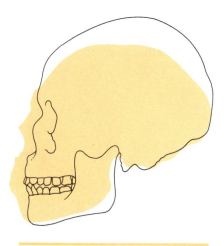

Differences between the skulls of Neanderthals and modern Homo sapiens. *The bulging forehead, the presence of a chin, reduced brow ridges, and the absence of a large protrusion on the back of the skull (known as an occipital bun) characterize modern humans.*

though they had the same posture, dexterity, and mobility. The bones of the Neanderthal are generally described as robust, having heavier limb bones than our own, suggesting much greater muscular strength and a more powerful grip. This strength also appears in the shoulder blade, neck, and on the back of the skull where heavy muscle attachments are noticeable. Muscles on the shoulder blade would have provided the Neanderthals with strong, controlled downward movements for making stone tools or for thrusting spears. The more robust appearance of the Neanderthals may be related to the strength and endurance required for long-distance travel over irregular terrain. Neanderthal skeletal remains also exhibit more traumatic damage from accident or violence than many modern populations. The Neanderthals lived to their late thirties and mid-forties or more, a rather long life expectancy. An eleven-month gestation period has been suggested on the basis of the sizes of the pelvic opening and birth canal in Neanderthal females.

Cultural innovations during the Middle Paleolithic included the first intentional burial of the dead in graves, sometimes accompanied by flowers, tools, or food. The presence of remains of these materials in graves implies the concepts of death as sleep or of life after death. Other, more exotic, practices emerged as well, difficult to understand or to explain from our modern perspective. One of the most extraordinary of these was the intentional killing of cave bears, the enormous denizens of the rocky areas of Europe during the Pleistocene but now extinct. Trophy skulls and bones from these huge bears were placed in special niches and stone-lined crypts, in a fashion more elaborate than any human burial.

Finally, there are a number of examples of broken and burned human bones among the remains of other animals in deposits belonging to the Middle Paleolithic. At the cave of Krapina in Yugoslavia, the bones of at least thirteen human individuals were found along with those of various herbivores and other animals. The human bones had been burned, split to extract marrow, and treated like the bones of the animals that had provided meals for the occupants of this site. At the Grotte de l'Hortus in southwestern France, similar evidence of cannibalism has been found. Heavily fragmented Neanderthal bones from at least twenty people are scattered among the numerous bones of small wild goats. Most of the human bones are skull and jaw fragments, and many of the human individuals were over 50 years old. Whether such practices represent rituals of consecration of the dead or simply the killing of individuals from enemy groups that were added to the larder is unclear. It seems most likely that what we witness in this evidence is a rare behavior likely associated with ritual consumption of dead relatives. Human flesh as a component of the daily diet is extremely detrimental to the success of the species.

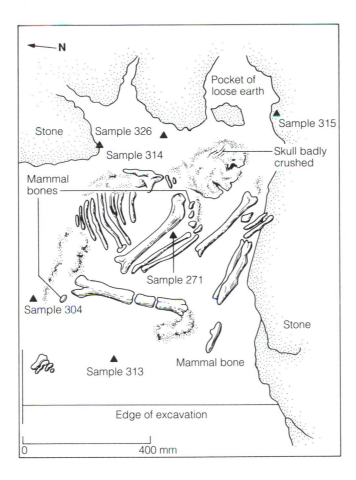

Burial IV from Shanidar, associated with large amounts of flower pollen. The drawing shows the position of the burial in the cave and the location of the pollen samples that were taken.

An artist's reconstruction of the Neanderthal burial ground at La Ferrassie, France. The graves of infants and adults were uncovered here during the last century.

The Problem of the Mousterian

Puzzling differences among Neanderthal sites

Typical flake tools from the European Mousterian. Used with permission from François Bordes, 1968, The Old Stone Age. *Courtesy of McGraw-Hill Book Company. Figure 34, page 100.*

Neanderthal populations are generally associated with the manufacture of a variety of flake tools in groups of artifacts termed **Mousterian** (moose-teer′e-an) assemblages. Although handaxes continued to be made, large retouched flakes and **Levallois** pieces, from a technique for making thin flakes with lots of cutting edge, are the major hallmarks of the Middle Paleolithic. Flakes were shaped into a variety of tools for more special purposes.

The French prehistorian Gabriel de Mortillet first defined the Mousterian in 1866 from materials excavated at the classic site of Le Moustier and elsewhere in southwestern France. De Mortillet noted that there were different kinds of layers of Mousterian tools, which he characterized as being dominated by scrapers, points, or handaxes. He further suggested a chronological sequence for these assemblages based on the fact that handaxes were thought to be older.

Around the turn of the century another French prehistorian, Denis Peyrony, excavated a number of Middle Paleolithic caves and shelters. Peyrony pointed out that there was no order to these assemblages, that layers with handaxes could be found on top of layers with points. The differences in these groups of tools were not due to change over time, as had been suggested by de Mortillet.

Understanding these tools and the differences in assemblages of Mousterian artifacts is a significant problem in archaeology. A major contributor to this debate was François Bordes, Professor of Geology and Prehistory at the University of Bordeaux. A brilliant archaeologist, Bordes was also a talented flintknapper, making copies of the stone tools he excavated to better understand how they had been produced. Several generations of archaeology students from Europe and North America attended his excavations in France. Long lunches, bouts with "baboons," as Bordes called the huge stones that had to be removed from the excavations, and a hundred other stories have added to the legend of Bordes, who died in 1981. (See "François Bordes," p. 108.)

Bordes' investigation of the Mousterian was remarkable. He moved away from an emphasis on individual artifacts, such as handaxes or scrapers, as indicators of differences. This approach had been borrowed from paleontology, where the single bone of an extinct species could provide the age for an entire group of fossils. In the 1950s, Bordes developed a list of some sixty-two different types of stone artifacts from the Middle Paleolithic. This list provided a way of describing entire assemblages or layers; all the materials that were excavated could be counted on the list, rather than just a few obvious forms, such as handaxes or points.

Then Bordes compared different layers in terms of the total assemblage of artifacts on his type list. He did this through the use of "cumulative curves." The percentages of each of the sixty-two types of artifacts can be graphed as single lines by adding each percentage to the next until all are accounted for and total 100%. Each line then represents a single assemblage. Lines of the same shape indicate similar assemblages of artifacts. Using this method, Bordes was able to distinguish four major groups of Mousterian artifacts, which he called Denticulate, MTA (Mousterian of Acheulian Tradition), Typical, and Charentian. Charentian assemblages were subdivided into Quina and Ferrassie, based on the types of scrapers present.

Bordes sought to explain the cause of the differences between the groups of assemblages. He had a definite flair. When asked, for example, if the type of stone raw material could affect the kind of tool that was made, he would reach in his pocket and take out a piece of glass, a piece of concrete block, and a piece of flint, each made into the same type of small handaxe. He dismissed evolution over time as a factor in the differences in the assemblages. He argued that assemblages succeeded one another without relation to geological strata, in the deep cave deposits he had excavated. This was a time period for which there are few reliable dating methods. Bordes also argued that these assem-

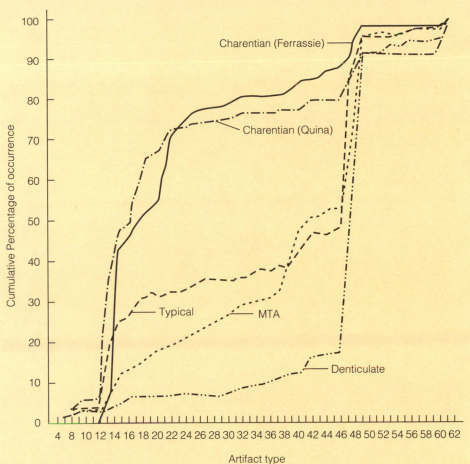

blages were not a result of different seasons of the year or different activities in those seasons. Deep, black layers a meter or more thick in some of the caves suggested to Bordes that people had lived there year-round. Moreover, study of reindeer teeth in these deposits indicated that the animals had been killed and their carcasses brought to the cave throughout the year.

Finally, Bordes settled on an "ethnic" or "tribal" explanation of the differences in the Mousterian assemblages. He viewed the area of southwestern France during the Middle Paleolithic as one with a relatively low population, in which "a man from one tribe might not encounter another individual more than a few times in his lifetime" (Bordes, 1970, p. 65). Bordes felt that the variability in Mousterian assemblages reflected different ways of doing things—just as the British take tea and scones, use a spanner instead of a wrench, and drive on the left side of the road. But this explanation fails to account for why the same kind of assemblage— one with lots of scrapers, for example— can be found in both France and Syria, thousands of kilometers apart.

The debate over the Mousterian highlights alternative explanations of differences in material culture. How do we explain two different sets of artifacts, made from the same materials, from the same general area, and at the same time? Differences in either the use of the items (function) or in the tradition (style) of the people who made them appear to be the best possibilities.

One of the major antagonists in this debate was Lewis Binford, an American archaeologist, now at Southern Method-

Table 3.2   A Summary of the Binfords' Study of Assemblage Variability During the Mousterian

Factor	Artifact Types from Bordes List	Suggested Activity	Type of Activity	Analogy to Bordes Variants
I	Borers, scrapers, burins	Manufacture of tools from nonflint materials	Base camp, maintenance tasks	Typical Mousterian
II	Points and scrapers	Hunting and butchery	Work camp, extractive tasks	Ferrassie
III	Flakes and knives	Cutting and incising, food processing	Base camp, maintenance tasks	MTA
IV	Utilized flakes, denticulates	Shredding and cutting of plant materials	Work camp, extractive tasks	Denticulate
V	Point, blade, scrapers	Killing and butchering	Work camp, extractive tasks	Ferrassie

Source: L. Binford and S. Binford. 1966.

ist University. Binford used a statistical technique known as factor analysis to examine the various kinds of tools that dominated the different assemblages. Binford argues that the different layers of the Mousterian represent different activities, perhaps not seasonal, but task-specific. Certain layers may have accumulated from the use of caves for hunting trips; other groups of tools are more representative of general-purpose domestic activities at a residential site; still others may reflect activities involving woodworking and the processing of plant materials. Although Binford's argument has never been demonstrated, it does provide a feasible counter to Bordes.

Recent work by Nicholas Rolland, of the University of Victoria, and Harold Dibble, of the University of Pennsylvania, has pointed out that many of the differences in Bordes' cumulative curves, hence in the Mousterian assemblages, are caused by the percentage of scrapers found in the various layers. Rolland and Dibble carefully examined the scrapers and argue that many of their differences are due to the intensity of use. Scrapers used for a long time for heavy-duty purposes are deeply retouched and distinctly convex—the kind of scrapers that typify the Charentian. Other scrapers, lacking such intense use, characterize the Typical Mousterian. Thus factors such as the availability of flint raw material or the length of occupation at a site may determine how intensively scrapers were used. Roland and Dibble also point out that scrapers and denticulated (notched) pieces are inversely correlated; that is, scrapers are rare in assemblages with denticulates, and vice versa.

It appears that the differences among Mousterian assemblages may not be as great as originally perceived, and that factors such as intensity of use and function of the scrapers and denticulates may be quite important. A number of variables—including time, style, and function—have likely contributed to the differences that are seen among the Mousterian layers.

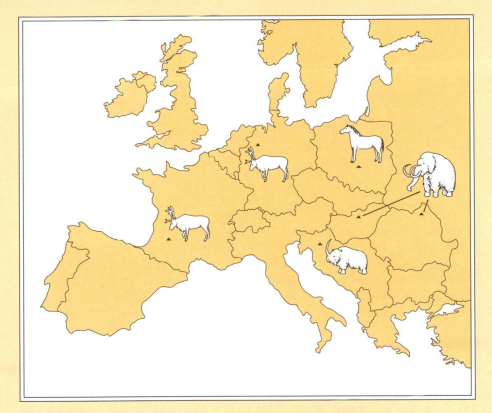

Map of some Neanderthal sites showing primary prey species. There was a predominance of mammoth hunting on the steppes of Eastern Europe. Some sites show an emphasis on one or a few species while others contain a variety of different animals in the faunal assemblages.

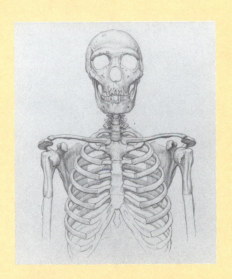

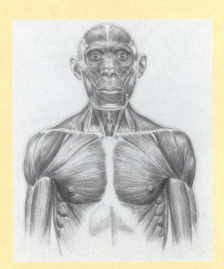

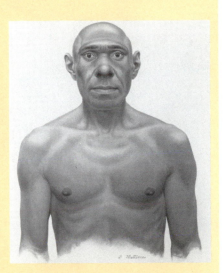

Reconstruction of the facial tissue of a neanderthal skull. A few forensic scientists have studied the attachment of soft tissue to the bones of the face and skull and are able to reconstruct a likeness of the individual. Such skills have been applied to a neanderthal with the result you see here. Body hair was not added to the reconstruction.

SHANIDAR CAVE

*Evidence of the life and death of Neanderthals
in northeastern Iraq*

A common misconception represents our Pleistocene ancestors as creatures of the caves, a view that has prevailed because much of the evidence from the later part of the Pleistocene comes from caves. Archaeological materials are well preserved in these places, but not necessarily because our ancestors were their constant occupants. While the mouths and entrances of caves may have provided shelter and residence for some groups, the inner recesses were almost certainly used only for special and short-term, limited purposes.

Most of the early hominids' time was spent at open-air camps and settlements, along streams, rivers, lakes, and seas. Such places were subject, however, to destructive forces — erosion, deep burial, submergence under the sea — and rarely survived to the present. It is, in fact, remarkable that there are so many traces of the past remaining.

Caves are excellent repositories for human debris. Deeply stratified deposits accumulate over millennia, incorporating all kinds of trash and food remains discarded by people living at their entrances and overhangs. The natural accumulation of sand and other sediments in caves is very slow, perhaps 1 to 5 cm (0.5 to 2 in.) of deposits per 100 years. This means that the materials left behind after numerous brief visits over a long period of time lie close together in the deposits. Often deposits that have accumulated over thousands of years can be found in the same archaeological layer.

One of the most important prehistoric caves in the Near East was discovered and excavated by Ralph Solecki, of Texas A&M University. In 1951, Solecki joined an expedition to northern Iraq to help record ancient inscriptions on historic monuments dating from 800 B.C. Solecki, however, was really interested in even older things, particularly from the Paleolithic, that might be found in this region. At the end of the expedition, Solecki stayed on to investigate a few caves in the area in search of an early site. One of these was the cave of Shanidar (shan'-a-dar). Solecki visited the site during the summer, returning in the fall. He described his experience as follows:

> My first reconnaissance of the cave left me with a very favorable impression. I spent no more than ten minutes there on the initial visit, making some rough measurements. . . . The next step was to make a test pit, or "sondage," in the earthen deposits of the cave. . . . I made some rough calculations of costs and estimated that it would take about three hundred dollars and a truck to do about a month of excavation at Shanidar Cave. I wondered about labor, since I did not see many men around the small village. But I was cheerful in the thought that at last we have found what looked like the ideal cave site.
>
> (Solecki, 1971, pp. 68–69)

The Zagros Mountains are a heavily folded series of sedimentary rocks that run from southwestern Iran to northeastern Iraq, dividing the high plateau of Iran from the arid stretches of Mesopotamia between the Tigris and Euphrates rivers. The northern end of the Zagros range in Iraq is rolling, rugged countryside, covered with *maqui* vegetation — scattered shrubs and dwarf oak — and tall poplars growing along the valley floors and flowing streams. In the spring the valley is colored by abundant wildflowers — red anemones and poppies, irises, grape hyacinth, and blue hollyhocks. A number of caves and rock shelters lie at the boundary between harder and softer limestone formations found in this valley.

The cave of Shanidar, carved by nature into the softer limestone, is located 750 m (2500 ft) above sea level, a 40-minute climb from the nearest road. The entrance to the large chamber is 8 m (25 ft) high and some 25 m (80 ft) wide. The floor of the chamber inside is large, about the size of four tennis courts, extending back about 110 m (350 ft). The distance from the flat earthen floor to the ceiling is roughly 14 m (35 ft), the equivalent of a three-story building. The ceiling is blackened by deep layers of soot from countless fires, interrupted in places where earthquakes have shaken off large blocks. The mouth faces south, and the morning sun reaches deep into the chamber. It is also well protected from cold, northern winter winds and has probably been occupied off and on for the last 100,000 years or so. In recent times, Kurdish goat herders have spent winters in a series of brush huts at the rear of Shanidar Cave.

Over a series of field seasons from 1951 to 1960, Ralph and Rose Solecki explored the dry layers of Shanidar Cave. Their original test trench in the center of the cave was expanded to roughly 6 by 20 m (20 by 70 ft) and deepened until bedrock was encountered at almost 15 m (50

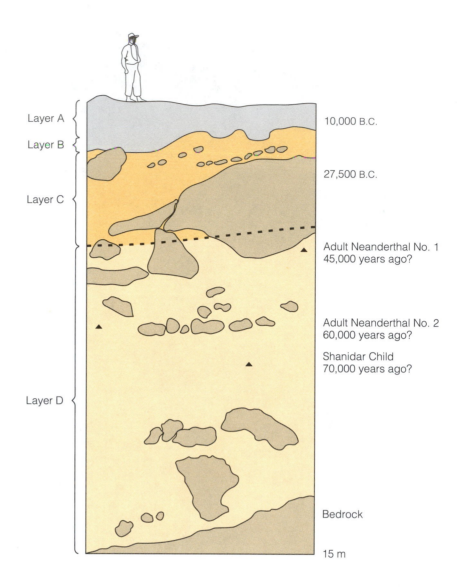

A view in cross-section through the deposits at Shanidar Cave. The dark upper layers are recent, Neolithic, and Mesolithic deposits. The Upper Paleolithic levels make up the rest of the upper third of the layers, while the Mousterian makes up the bottom two-thirds of the deposits. The triangles mark the locations of Neanderthal skeletal remains. The large chunks of rock are pieces of the roof that fell to the floor of the cave.

Layer A

Layer B

Layer C

10,000 B.C.

27,500 B.C.

Adult Neanderthal No. 1
45,000 years ago?

Adult Neanderthal No. 2
60,000 years ago?

Shanidar Child
70,000 years ago?

Layer D

Bedrock

15 m

ft) below the surface. It was like digging a five-level basement.

The excavations exposed four major layers of deposits in the cave, designated A through D. These materials accumulated in the cave at a rate of only about 2 cm (1 in.) per 100 years. Layer A was the top 1.5 m (5 ft) of deposit, a black, greasy soil containing pottery, bones of domestic animals, and grinding stones, going back from the present to the earliest farmers in the area, perhaps 7000 years ago. Layer B was made up of brown-stained sediments containing materials from the preceding period, between 7000 and 12,000 years ago. In this layer, snail shells and a few wild animals represented the kinds of foods that were eaten. There is very little

evidence for occupation in the cave during the next 17,000 years. A yellow soil with a group of massive boulders near the top, Layer C dates from 29,000 to 34,000 years ago. Solecki had to use dynamite to blast through these boulders and go deeper into the cave deposits. The boulders fell from the roof about 29,000 years ago and may be the reason that the cave was not occupied for such a long period. Layer C contains stone and bone materials from the early part of the Upper Paleolithic.

Layer D was the primary deposit in the cave, some 9 m (30 ft) of sediments dating from 35,000 to perhaps 100,000 years ago, spanning the time of Neanderthal and the Middle Paleolithic. Deep ash deposits in these levels testify to the large hearths that burned in the cave. The stone artifacts belong to the Mousterian and are similar in fashion to those from other sites in the Near East. The bones of wild goat, wild pig, and tortoise occur commonly in Layer D. The most important and best reported finds from this layer, however, are the skeletons of seven adults and two infants that were encountered during the excavations.

Several of the individuals in Shanidar died as a result of rock fall from the ceiling of the cave. One of the skeletons, a 40-year-old male, had a withered humerus (upper arm bone), which would have made his arm largely useless from birth. He also suffered from arthritis and was blind in one eye, likely the result of a blow to the left side of the head. This individual could not have been a successful hunter. Nevertheless he survived with the help of the rest of the group. A second male was found somewhat lower in the layer, also crushed by falling rock in the cave. Sometime after the rockfall, the companions of this individual returned, covered the spot with more stones, and built a large fire above his final resting place. A third male was also crushed by the collapse of the roof at another time. The ribs of this individual were scarred by a wooden spear of some kind, wounds received shortly before he died.

Four individuals were found in a single grave, two females and an infant lying beneath a male. Detailed study of two of the skulls from Shanidar by Erik Trinkhaus indicated that the backs of the heads were misshapen, perhaps from the use of some kind of cradling board during infancy.

Other burials at Shanidar were intentional. Pollen samples from one of the graves, identified by Arlette Leroi-Gourhan, suggest that garlands of eight different spring flowers, including grape hyacinth, bachelor buttons, and hollyhocks, had been placed around the head. These plants would not have grown in the cave and must have been brought there as a part of the grave offerings for the deceased male. Evidence for both compassion and aggression are thus documented in the Neanderthal burials from Shanidar.

A skull of Homo sapiens neanderthalensis *from Shanidar Cave. This individual was likely killed by rocks falling from the roof of the cave.*

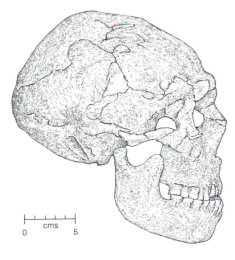

cms
0   5

One of the Neanderthal skulls from Shanidar.

PALYNOLOGY

Clues to prehistoric vegetation

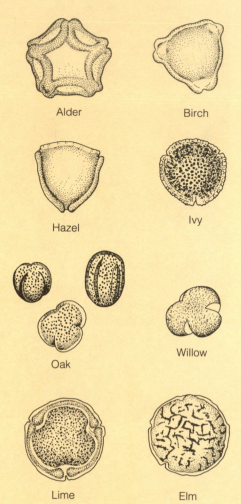

Alder
Birch
Hazel
Ivy
Oak
Willow
Lime
Elm

Examples of magnified pollen grains from several plant species. Identification of pollen from stratigraphic deposits provides information on changes in vegetation over time.

Although the vagaries of preservation normally remove the stems, flowers, and other parts of plants from archaeological sites, the pollen those plants produce is frequently preserved. Pollen is a microscopic sexual germ that many kinds of seed-bearing plants send into the air for fertilization. Wind or insect pollination is common to most trees, shrubs, grasses, and some flowering plants. Tree pollen generally travels farther than that of flowering plants. Pollen "rain" is carried everywhere, as hay-fever sufferers know well. Some types of pollen can be transported hundreds of kilometers and high up into the atmosphere.

In spite of their microscopic size, pollen grains are protected by a shell of material called sporopollenin, one of the most resistant substances in nature, impervious to water and soil acids. As long as sediments protect pollen grains from oxidation, they will be preserved for thousands of years. Deposits in lakes and bogs often provide the best pollen records, but many types of sediments will preserve these grains. Pollen is also preserved in coal and has been found in rocks 500 million years old.

Pollen is produced in enormous quantities by plants and can be found in densities reaching several thousand grains per cubic centimeter of soil. Pollen is very specific in shape and size and can be identified to the genus and even species of plant that produced it. Thus the pollen that accumulates in the sediments surrounding an archaeological site can be used to provide a picture of the area's past vegetation, climate, and environmental conditions; such study is called **palynology,** or pollen analysis.

In the field, samples of sediment for pollen analysis are taken every few centimeters from a stratigraphic column. In the laboratory, pollen grains are removed from sediment samples through a series of acidic and alkaline washes that dissolve minerals, silicates, and organic materials, leaving only the pollen grains as a residue. Microscopic examination enables the palynologist to identify and count the grains. Several hundred grains from each layer produce a spectrum of the pollen species. Each species is recorded in a **pollen diagram,** which summarizes both the species and the proportions of the various groups of plants found in each sample.

Pollen analysis can be applied to the reconstruction of local vegetation, to regional maps of plant distributions, or to the study of climatic change. For example, the ratio of tree (arboreal pollen, or AP) grains to nontree (nonarboreal pollen, or NAP) grains might provide an indication of the density of forest, and even precipitation, in a given area (i.e., the more trees, the greater the precipitation). Certain marker species or changes in the pollen record may aid in the recognition of prehistoric settlements or cultivation prac-

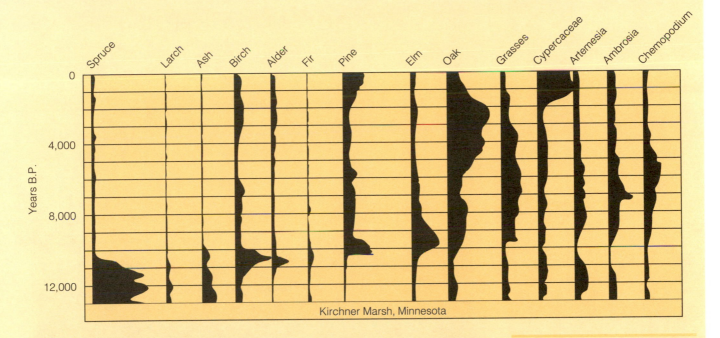

Spruce · Larch · Ash · Birch · Alder · Fir · Pine · Elm · Oak · Grasses · Cypercaceae · Artemesia · Ambrosia · Chemopodium

Years B.P.

Kirchner Marsh, Minnesota

Centimetre 1 2 3

A pollen diagram from Kirchner Marsh, Minnesota, showing the succession of vegetation in this area following the retreat of glacial ice. The major changes include the appearance of spruce, larch, and ash, which are gradually replaced by birch and alder, then by pine, then elm, then oak. Grasses and other nontree species are indicated on the right side of the diagram. The most pronounced changes are seen around 10,000 years ago at the end of the Pleistocene.

An assortment of seeds from the flotation of sediments at an archaeological site.

tices. For example, the beginning of agriculture in northern Europe is often recognized by the appearance of cereal pollen, a reduction in arboreal pollen, and tiny pieces of charcoal from wood burning found in the pollen spectra.

In some situations, pollen may provide information about the presence of certain plants at a specific location. At Shanidar, the extraordinary density of pollen in the area of Burial IV indicated that flowering plants had been placed in the grave inside the cave. Small, bright flowers that bloom in and around June (grape hyacinth, groundsel, and hollyhock) were found in abundance, along with branches from a coniferous shrub; perhaps a kind of wreath was laid alongside the deceased before the grave was filled.

TABUN AND SKHUL

Biological and cultural developments in the Near East between 130,000 and 50,000 years ago

Mount Carmel rises from the Plain of Sharon in Israel, to a maximum elevation of almost 500 m (1600 ft). It extends about 30 km (20 mi) along the eastern Mediterranean shore. The western flank of this limestone ridge is dissected by a number of dry streambeds, known in Arabic as *wadis*. The walls of the Wadi el-Mughara (Valley of the Caves) near the southern end of Mount Carmel are dotted with caves weathered out of the soft limestone. Three of these, the Mugharet el-Wad (moog-ah-rot′el-wad′), the Mugharet et-Tabun (ta-boon′), and the Mugharet es-Skhul (es′ska-hool′), together contain a sequence of prehistoric deposits stretching from the Acheulean to the Neolithic and are among the most famous archaeological sites in Southwest Asia.

Early excavations in the 1930s were conducted by Dorothy Garrod, of Cambridge University, a member of the British School of Archaeology in Jerusalem. Garrod was the first female professor at Cambridge and a remarkable individual. She

led a series of expeditions in the Near East, probing into the deposits in the caves and uncovering both human remains and prehistoric artifacts. Four caves were excavated in the course of her fieldwork from 1929 to 1934. A combined stratigraphy from all the excavations would have 2 m (6.5 ft) of Mesolithic deposits at the top, followed by 2.5 m (8 ft) of Upper Paleolithic, and finally 16.5 m (50 ft) of Middle and Lower Paleolithic remains—a total of 21 vertical m (almost 65 ft) of the most extensive archaeological sequence in the Near East. From Tabun and Skhul also came the human remains that provide important evidence for the transition to *Homo sapiens sapiens*.

Tabun contains two major chambers: a large, unroofed outer zone in front of an inner chamber with a chimney opening on the hillside above it. The cave was filled with a deeply stratified series of layers containing deposits dating from the Lower Paleolithic to the Bronze Age. Layer C, described by Garrod as Levalloiso-Mousterian, contained an assemblage of

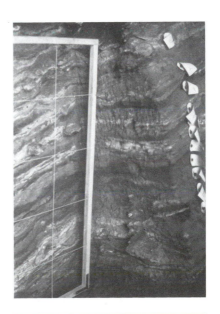

A composite drawing of the current stratigraphic profile at Tabun compared to Garrod's earlier results. The more recent excavations have provided greater detail about the stratigraphy and chronology of the site.

Excavations inside the cave of Tabun. The excavators are working on the vertical face of the cave deposits at the edge of earlier excavations. The square grids are used for drawing the stratigraphy.

Middle Paleolithic artifacts, animal bones, and two important human fossils. Both hominids are similar to the Neanderthals of western Europe and likely date to around 120,000 years ago.

The Mugharet es-Skhul is actually an **abri,** or rock overhang, 150 m (500 ft) east of Tabun. The site contained some 2.5 m (8 ft) of archaeological deposits and the partial skeletons of at least ten individuals. The burials included three children and seven adults, two females and four males (one unknown). One of the buried individuals was holding the jaw of a wild boar. The burials from Skhul are probably 20,000 years younger than the Neanderthal remains at nearby Tabun. The human skeletal materials from Skhul share a robustness with the older Neanderthal populations, but more generally resemble *Homo sapiens sapiens.*

A second series of excavations were undertaken in the cave of Tabun from 1967 to 1972 by Arthur Jelinek, of the University of Arizona, to clarify the chronological relationships among these sites and the layers that composed them. The new studies, combining sophisticated environmental and geological investiga-tions, resulted in many details on the for-mation of the deposits and changes in cli-mate during the occupation of the cave. In addition, careful studies of the artifacts recovered provided new information about stone tools and human behavior.

One of the most striking results of the archaeological investigations came from the analysis of the sizes and shapes of stone flakes found in the layers. Measure-ments indicate that there is a regular de-crease in the ratio of thickness to width, suggesting that over time there was a tendency to make thinner flakes. Jelinek suggests that this trend reflects an in-crease in manual dexterity arising from evolving changes in the organization and structure of the brain. Jelinek further ar-gues that the trend is very strong evidence for continuity in biological evolution as well, indicating that *Homo sapiens sapiens* evolved from *H. sapiens neanderthalensis.* Finally Jelinek remarks on the conserva-tism shown in the lithic evidence from Tabun. The very slow changes in the tech-niques of flake manufacture suggest a lack of innovation and creativity, perhaps one of the reasons that the Neanderthals were replaced by more modern humans.

A portion of the complex cave stratigra-phy at Tabun, showing the sloping deposits.

FRANÇOIS BORDES, 1919—1981

A remembrance, by A. J. Jelinek

"François Bordes, one of the most eminent prehistorians of the last three decades, died of a heart attack in Tucson, Arizona, on April 30, 1981. He was born in a small chateau at Rives in Lot-et-Garonne, France, on December 30, 1919. Bordes' strongest ties throughout his life were with this beautiful region of towering cliffs, green forests, and small villages.

"From an early age Bordes had an intense interest in the natural sciences and in the prehistory of the country around him. As an adventurous boy, with a bicycle for transportation, he became acquainted with Denis Peyrony, Curator of the Museum of Prehistory at [the nearby town of] Les Eyzies. An indication of the seriousness of this early interest was his excavation, with an official permit, at the Roc de Gavaudun [at age 15]. He entered the Université de Bordeaux in 1936, where he majored in geology and botany. The outbreak of World War II interrupted his studies and had a profound influence on his life. Following the German occupation of Vichy France in late 1942, Bordes began one of the most exciting and difficult episodes of his eventful life, as a member of the French Resistance. In early November 1944, he was seriously wounded by a grenade.

"It was during the years immediately following the war that Bordes formulated the idea of a standardized typology for the study of Lower and Middle Paleolithic industries. He saw that this would allow objective comparisons of these industries. . . . This step was of fundamental importance in the development of Paleolithic archaeology, and Bordes's typology is now used as a standard for comparative studies throughout much of the Old World.

"Upon his appointment to the Faculté des Sciences of the Université de Bordeaux in 1956, Bordes began building a research institute that pioneered in the integration of the diverse disciplines of sedimentology, paleontology, palynology, and archaeology. Bordes's best-known excavations, at the sites of Combe Grenal, Pech de l'Azé, and Corbiac are monuments to the patience and persistence that [are] necessary for the careful exposure and documentation of the rich cultural and environmental record that is preserved in sites from this region. Many now mature and younger American and European Paleolithic prehistorians benefitted from experience in his excavations through his continuing generosity and hospitality to all serious students of prehistory. . . .

"Bordes's active imagination was probably most evident in his science fiction stories and novels, mostly written in the 1950s and 1960s. They brought him a modest fame in that literary realm under the pseudonym of Francis Carsac.

"During the 35 years of his scientific career Bordes authored, coauthored, or edited about 170 articles, monographs, and books on Paleolithic archaeology and other aspects of prehistory. . . . There could be no finer monument to the wide range of interests and abilities of this unique scholar than the legacy of professional literature that he has left us.

"Behind the direct approach that was typical of François Bordes in any situation was a complex man of uncompromising integrity and sensitive nature. His lack of patience with what he viewed as unnecessary formality and long-winded or pretentious oration was legendary. His familiar expletives on such occasions were viewed with some amusement by those of like mind. Perhaps the most striking aspect of his personality was his lively and unceasing interest in the universe around him. This continuing inquiry and assimilation of knowledge lent an essential vitality to the man that makes it all the more difficult to believe that he is gone. His work has brought all prehistorians closer to an understanding of the lives of those Paleolithic peoples in whom he was so deeply interested. For those of us who knew him as a person the world will never be quite the same. He is buried in the cemetery at Carsac near his summer home and field headquarters in the heart of the country that he loved so well."

Source: Adapted from A. J. Jelinek. 1982b. François Bordes. *American Antiquity* 47: 785–792.

François Bordes (in the hat) excavating at Pech de l'Azé IV in 1973.

AUSTRALIA

The Spread of Homo sapiens sapiens

Although it may seem strange to find Australia in the middle of a discussion of the Upper Pleistocene, there are several important things to be learned from a consideration of the evidence from the land "down under." Australia was colonized by *Homo sapiens sapiens* at least 40,000 years ago, perhaps even earlier. Rafts or boats of some kind were likely used. These first emigrants somehow crossed a body of water at least 100 km (65 mi) wide, far beyond sight of land, to reach the island continent. There are archaeological sites at least 20,000 years old in all corners of the continent, and the oldest site, on the Upper Swan River, dates to around 38,000 years ago.

At this time, during one of the coldest periods of the Pleistocene, sea level was as much as 150 m (500 ft) lower than it is at present; the continental shelves were exposed, and land bridges connected a number of areas formerly separated by the sea. Australia was connected to New Guinea and Tasmania, comprising a larger continent called Sahul. The Sahul Strait, a body of water that today is several thousand meters deep, lay between Australia and Asia. One of the deepest bodies of water in the world, the Sahul Strait would have always been sea. Thus the earliest inhabitants of Australia were forced to cross a large body of water to reach the continent.

Australia and Southeast Asia during the colder periods of the Pleistocene.

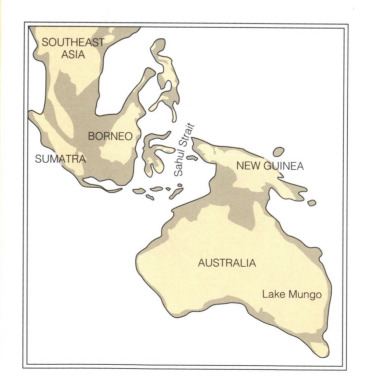

The elaborate art of the Australian Aborigines is found throughout much of the continent and includes a wide variety of human and animal figures.

The fact that there was never a land bridge between Australia and mainland Asia is evidenced by the fact that the animal species in the two areas are very different. Asian placental mammals and Australian marsupial mammals have not been in contact in the last several million years. This difference was originally noted by Alfred Lord Wallace, a British naturalist, and the term "Wallace Line" is used to designate the separation of the two distinct groups.

Some of the oldest sites in Australia are in margins of dried-up lakebeds in the southeastern part of the country, an area known as Lake Mungo. Sites around Lake Mungo contain hearths and shells dating to around 32,000 years ago. This area would have contained a series of lakes and fertile shorelines during the period of initial occupation, when rainfall was higher than today. The sites were discovered in 1968 by a geologist who found human bones in a sand dune that was at least 20,000 years old. The bones appeared to have been buried at a time when the dune was active on the shore of a former lake.

Further examination of the area around the bones on the dune revealed a series of stone artifacts and a number of patches of charcoal, which must have been the locations of hearths. Most of the hearths contained fish and mammal bones. Bird bones, eggshell, and shell from freshwater mollusks were also found in a few fireplaces. Other sites around the fossil lakeshore have revealed concentrations of shellfish and burned areas with charcoal and fired clay lumps, which were probably used for cooking. The material culture of these early inhabitants included both bone and stone tools, with a large number of heavy core and pebble artifacts.

Several burials have been found, one of which is the oldest known example of cremation — the cremated and badly fragmented remains of a woman 20 to 25 years old. Other remains include another female and a male. **Red ochre,** an iron mineral and pigment, was used in some of the graves to cover a portion of the remains. All of these individuals are designated as *Homo sapiens sapiens,* documenting the presence of modern humans in the eastern part of Eurasia, several thousand years prior to their appearance in Europe.

These early inhabitants rapidly occupied all of Australia, as indicated by the spread of radiocarbon dates from across the continent. What is almost equally remarkable, however, is how little change took place here over thousands of years. Foraging was apparently a very successful and stable adaptation in prehistoric Australia. Hunter-gatherers arrived almost 40,000 years ago, and they were still present when Captain Cook "discovered" the continent 200 years ago.

THE UPPER PALEOLITHIC

Homo sapiens sapiens
to the forestage

The Upper Paleolithic is characterized by a variety of innovations that developed over the course of the last 25,000 years of the Pleistocene. These include the appearance of anatomically modern humans in Europe; the extensive use of stone blades; the widespread manufacture of a variety of objects from bone, antler, ivory, and wood; the invention of new equipment, such as the spearthrower and the bow and arrow; the domestication of the dog; and the development of art and decoration. Such extensive changes may reflect a major reorganization of the human brain — one that cannot be detected in the contours and crevices of fossil bones. The Upper Paleolithic also represents an important phase in the expansion of the human species: There were more sites in more places than ever before. Virtually all of the Earth's diverse environments, from tropical rain forest to arctic tundra, were inhabited during this period. Africa, Europe, and Asia were filled with groups of hunter-gatherers; Australia and North and South America were colonized for the first time.

The archaeological materials of this period are best known from Europe, especially from southwestern France, an important hub of archaeological activity in the twentieth century. Here the Upper Paleolithic replaced the Middle Paleolithic, between 35,000 and 30,000 years ago. Excavations over the last 100 years in the deep deposits of caves and rock shelters of this area have exposed layer upon layer of remains from the last part of the Pleistocene. The layers are known as the Aurignacian, Perigordian, Solutrean, and Magdalenian. In central and eastern Europe, the Upper Paleolithic remains are designated as Gravettian, roughly equivalent to the Perigordian in the west.

The skeletal remains of *Homo sapiens sapiens* are found in western Europe after 30,000 years ago, following the appearance of blade tool industries and other distinctively Upper Paleolithic artifacts. These anatomically modern individuals were originally called Cro-Magnon, after the place in France where they were first discovered. In spite of this distinctive name, they were indistinguishable from modern humans. Lacking the heavy brow ridges and protruding jaw of the Neanderthals, the *sapiens sapiens* face sits almost directly under a bulging forehead, with smaller teeth and jaws. A chin developed, to reinforce the smaller, weaker

A chart of the chronology, climatic changes, major cultural periods, and typical artifacts of the Upper Paleolithic. The differences between the European cultures were much greater during the Upper Paleolithic than during the Middle Paleolithic.

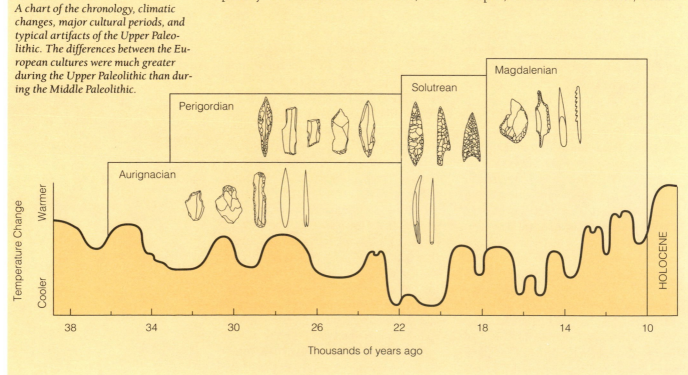

Blades and blade tools during the Upper Paleolithic. Blade manufacture was a kind of mass production of many elongated flakes. A pointed piece of bone or antler was struck with a hammerstone to remove the blade from the core through an indirect percussion technique.

jaw. Cranial capacity is fully modern, and there is no reason to assume any significant intellectual differences from ourselves.

The material remains left by these Upper Paleolithic societies reinforce the idea that by this time the human species had indeed arrived as creative creatures. Blade manufacturing techniques and blade tools characterize the Upper Paleolithic. Stone **blades** are a special form of elongated flake, with a length at least twice the width, and sharp, parallel cutting edges on both sides. Blades could be mass-produced in large quantities from a single nodule of flint, removed from a core in a fashion akin to peeling a carrot. Blades also provided a form, or blank, that could be shaped (retouched) into a number of different tools. Projectile points, burins, knives, drills, and scraping tools can all be made from a basic blade form.

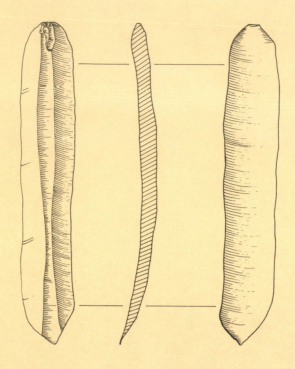

Blades: flakes with a length at least twice their width.

Another distinctive aspect of Upper Paleolithic stone tool manufacture is the appearance of special flaking techniques during the Solutrean, to make very thin, beautiful leaf-shaped points in several different sizes. Some of these points were used for spears and some for arrows, while others may have served as knives. These tools are among the finest examples of the flintknapper's skill from the entire Paleolithic. At the end of the Solutrean, however, these flaking techniques largely disappeared from the craft of stone tool manufacture, not to be used again for thousands of years.

Many new kinds of tools—made of materials such as bone, wood, ivory, and antler—also distinguished the Upper Paleolithic. Spearthrowers, bows and arrows, eyed needles, harpoons, ropes, nets, oil lamps, torches, and many other things have been found. Hafted and composite tools, incorporating several different materials, were also introduced, such as stone tools held in bone or antler handles by resin or other adhesives.

Spearthrowers provide an extension of the arm, enabling hunters to fling their darts with greater force and accuracy.

Prior to this invention, spears may have been used primarily as thrusting weapons, requiring dangerous, close-range attacks. Spearthrowers of bone, wood, or antler have three components: a handle, a weighted balance, and a hook to hold the end of the spear. Spearthrowers are often elaborately decorated, with carved figures of animals used for the weight. By the end of the Upper Paleolithic, the spearthrower was replaced by the bow and arrow as the hunting weapon of choice. The bow provides an even more accurate means of delivering a long-distance, lethal blow to animal prey.

Dogs were domesticated during the Upper Paleolithic, probably for the purpose of hunting. As temperatures warmed at the end of the Pleistocene and the European forests moved back across the continent, woodland species of animals became more common but less visible to the hunter. The strong sense of smell to locate prey that a human hunter lacks is well developed in his faithful companion.

Fine bone needles with small eyes document the manufacture of sewn clothing and other equipment from animal skins. A number of carved artifacts—buttons, gaming pieces, pendants, necklaces, and the like — appeared for the first time, marking a concern with personal appearance and the aesthetic embellishment of everyday objects. This development is closely related to the first appearance of decorative art. Figurines, cave paintings, engravings, and myriad decoration of other objects represent the creative explosion that characterized Upper Paleolithic achievement. There is also compelling evidence for a celebration of the seasons and an awareness of time in the archaeological remains from the Upper Paleolithic. Finally, primitive counting systems and the beginnings of a calendar of sorts, or at least a recording of the phases of the moon, may have appeared at this time.

DOLNI VESTONICE

Mammoth hunters in eastern Europe

Excavations of Dolni Vestonice uncovering the piles of mammoth bones on the south side of the settlement.

The woolly mammoth of Pleistocene Europe was a magnificent creature. As seen in cave paintings and frozen examples from Siberia, this animal had a huge domed head atop a massive body covered with long fur. The mammoth was roughly one-and-a-half times the size of a modern African elephant and must have been a formidable prey for the late Pleistocene hunters of Europe. In addition to mammoth, herds of wild reindeer, horses, woolly rhinoceros, and other species roamed the tundra-covered regions of Europe. The mammoth, however, was the game of choice in the east and provided the bulk of the diet for hunters in this area. At one site in Czechoslovakia, for example, the remains of 800 to 900 mammoths have been uncovered.

The remains of the camps of these mammoth hunters were fortuitously buried under deep deposits of fine silt. This silt had been picked up by the winds at the edges of the ice sheets, carried in the air across central Europe, and gradually deposited as blankets of sediment, known as **loess** (pronounced "luss"). Numerous prehistoric sites were slowly covered by this dust, and bone, ivory, and other materials have been well preserved in it. The major problem with such sites is simply to find them, hidden as they are under 2 or more m (6 to 8 ft) of silt.

Near the town of Dolni Vestonice (dol-nee′ves-toe-neet′za), in south-central Czechoslovakia, the enormous bones of extinct mammoths were first uncovered in the course of removing loess for brickmaking. Although excavations were initially undertaken in 1924, the extent of the prehistoric occupation was not truly recognized until the work that began in 1947 and continues today. Large horizontal excavations have removed the deep loess deposit covering the site, exposing an area containing dwelling structures, mammoth bones, and many intriguing artifacts dating to about 25,000 years ago.

During the late Pleistocene, the area was one of tundra and permafrost, situated north of the treeline in Europe. Little wood was available, except possibly from small stands of willow and other species

in sheltered valleys. Broad expanses of grass, moss, and lichens provided food for the herds of mammoth, horse, and reindeer that were the predominant fauna of the area. The freezing and thawing of the ground resulted in movement of the surface, a phenomenon known as **solifluction**, which disturbed and redeposited many of the remains at Dolni Vestonice. For this reason, interpretation of the evidence from the site is difficult.

The highest layers in the deposits, containing a campsite, are still reasonably well preserved. This camp lay on a projecting tongue of land, along a small stream that becomes a bog just at the southern edge of the site. Part of the site sits on a ridge, providing a good view of the valley of the nearby Dyje River. The complete site covers an area of roughly 60 by 130 m (200 by 500 ft), the size of a soccer field.

The effectiveness of the mammoth hunters is dramatically portrayed in the scatters of bones marking the southern boundary of the settlement along the stream. The bones of at least 100 mammoths were piled up in an area of 12 by 45 m (40 by 140 ft). Stone tools and broken bones suggest that this was a zone where animals, or parts of animals, were butchered and where skins were cleaned and prepared.

Other piles of bones were found throughout the settlement, often sorted according to kind of bone, presumably for use as fuel and raw material for construction. Fires were lit on some of these bone piles, as evidenced by ash, perhaps as a defense against predatory animals. Along with these bone piles are rows of mammoth tusks forming a fence, or defensive wall, along the northern side of the settlement, creating a kind of compound. All of the structures at the site, except one, and most of the artifacts were found inside this compound.

Stone, earth, wooden posts, and mammoth bones were used in construction of the shelters at the site. The first structure to be uncovered was a very large oval, 9 by 15 m (30 by 50 ft) in size, with five regularly spaced fireplaces inside. The

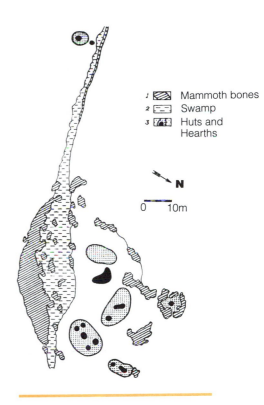

1 Mammoth bones
2 Swamp
3 Huts and Hearths

The plan of the site of Dolni Vestonice, Czechoslovakia, showing the isolated hut to the north of the main camp, and several structures and hearths to the south, along with piles of mammoth bones.

An ivory carving of a mammoth from Vogelherd, Germany (8.8 cm long).

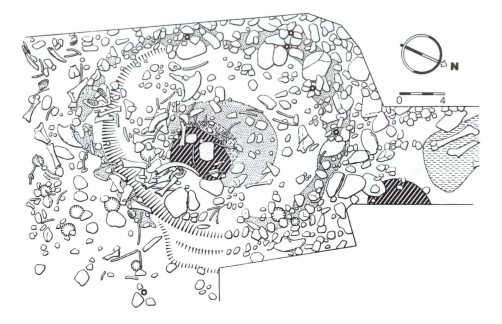

A residential structure from Dolni Vestonice showing the semisubterranean floor, with flat stones, fireplaces, and mammoth bones used for the framework. Postholes are indicated by small dark circles. The bone framework was likely covered with animal hides to complete the structure. The hut is approximately 6 m in diameter.

The rendering of an asymmetrical human face on a small piece of ivory (3 cm high).

The head of a woman with an asymmetrical face, carved in ivory (4.6 cm high).

size of the structure, about half of a tennis court, and its contents suggested to the excavators that this was an open windbreak, without a ceiling, rather than a roofed structure, and that it was occupied primarily in the summertime. The wall posts were supported with limestone blocks and were likely covered with animal hides. At least three roofed huts are thought to have been present inside the area of the settlement as well. These structures are partially dug into the loess; they contain one or two hearths and have numerous large mammoth bones on top of the floor. These bones are probably the remains of the framework for the roof, which would have collapsed after abandonment of the settlement.

In an open area near the center of the compound was found a large hearth, almost 1 m (3 ft) deep and several meters (about 10 ft) across, which may have been a common, central fire for the community at Dolni Vestonice. In the ashes of this fire an ivory carving of a female figure, called the Venus of Vestonice, was found.

Another structure, uncovered in 1951, was found some 80 m (250 ft) along the stream to the west of the main settlement. This structure was smaller, 6 m (20 ft) in diameter, and very unusual. The floor of the hut had been dug into the

loess slope to level it and to provide more protection against the elements. Limestone blocks were placed against the excavated slope to buttress the wall. Posts were also supported by these blocks at the front of the hut, like a lean-to.

Hollow bird bones were found inside; they were cut at the ends and may have functioned as musical instruments. In the center of the hut was a ovenlike fireplace with a domed clay structure raised around it. The oven was made of fire-hardened earth and ground limestone. In the ashes and waste from the oven, standing in a deep pile on the floor were more than 2300 small clay figurines that must have been fired in the oven. This is the earliest example of the use of fired clay in the world, some 15,000 years before the invention of pottery. The figurines consisted of heads, feet, and other fragments of animal effigies and fired lumps of clay. Even the fingerprints of the maker had been preserved in some of the pieces.

The depth and extent of deposits at Dolni Vestonice, along with the presence of both summer and winter huts, suggest that this site may have been occupied year-round. The number and size of the structures and the overall size of the site imply that a substantial group of people made this place their home. Bohuslav

Klima, the excavator of the site, believes that between 100 and 120 people may have lived in this early permanent community. The remarkable artifacts and other materials found at the site confirm the impression that this was indeed an unusual place.

Flint tools at the site belong to the Gravettian, the Upper Paleolithic of eastern Europe. Tools are made on narrow blades in the form of points, knives, burins, and others. There are also numerous tools made from mammoth bone and ivory: awls, needles, knives, spear points, lances, and digging equipment. Ornaments in the form of pendants, necklaces, bracelets, and the like are made of carved bone, ivory, and shell. Some of the species of shell come from the Mediterranean Sea, several hundred kilometers to the south. Other objects carved of antler or ivory, or made of baked clay, have no clear practical purpose and likely served as ritual objects in the ceremonies that took place in the community.

The most remarkable finds may involve the same individual. Excavations in 1936 uncovered a small ivory plaque about 3 cm (1.5 in.) high with a crudely incised human face portrayed on it. The face is asymmetrical, with the left eye and the left half of the lip somewhat lower than the right. A second carved ivory head was found in 1948 in the open summer hut. This three-dimensional head portrays an individual, again, whose left side of the face is somewhat distorted and asymmetrical. Finally, a burial was excavated in 1949, discovered beneath two huge shoulder blades from a mammoth. The skeleton belonged to a female and was covered with red ochre; a flint point was buried near her head. The bones of the white arctic fox were found near her hands. A study of the facial bones of this individual showed that she suffered from partial paralysis of the left side of her face. It seems entirely possible that the two faces carved in ivory are representations of the actual person in the grave. The burial itself was found in a lower layer in the settlement and is likely several hundred years older than the ivory carvings. If the difference in age between the actual burial of the old woman and the carvings is accurate, this individual must have been recounted and described in the oral histories of the group for a very long time indeed.

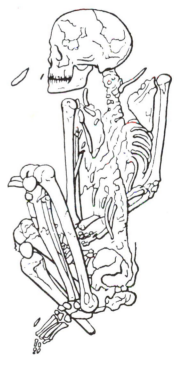

The buried skeleton of an elderly female from Dolni Vestonice. The bones of the left side of the face revealed congenital nerve damage, which would likely have resulted in an asymmetrical face. The woman was buried under two mammoth shoulder blades, and the bones of an artic fox were found next to her in the grave.

THE CAVE OF
LASCAUX

A monument to human creativity

Nestled in the lovely countryside of southwestern France, the Vezere River runs past some of the most important Stone Age sites in the world. This area, known as the Perigord, is a prehistorian's dream. The spectacular landscape contains not only hundreds of important archaeological sites, but also the kitchens and cellars of many superb French chefs. The limestone plateau is dissected by numerous streams and rivers that have carved high cliffs along the courses of the valleys. These cliffs are riddled with caves and rock shelters, which provided residence for generations of Paleolithic groups.

Over time the entrances to many of the caves have collapsed and hidden the caverns completely. The cave of Lascaux (loss'co) was discovered by chance in 1940 when a young boy noticed a hole in the earth where a pine tree had been uprooted by the wind. After dropping some rocks down the hole, he and several friends slid down the opening and into the cave, which we now know contains the most important collection of Upper Paleolithic art in the world. Lascaux had been sealed for around 15,000 years, the outside world completely unaware of the splendor it held.

After World War II, the cave was opened as an underground museum, and for two decades it was one of the major tourist attractions in France, with as many as 1000 visitors a day. Unfortunately the flow of tourists altered the environment of the cave dramatically, raising both the temperature and the humidity, and bringing in dust. These changes caused the growth of a fungus on the walls that began to cover and eventually flake off parts of the paintings. The cave was closed in 1963 and efforts were begun to halt the growth of the fungus, remove it, and preserve the paintings for posterity. The problem was

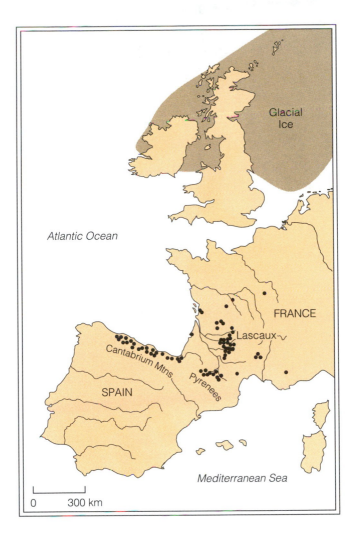

fixed, but the cave has not been reopened to the public. Instead, the French government has built a facsimile of the cave, Lascaux II, where tourists to the Perigord can view copies of the beautiful animal paintings that graced the original walls.

The artwork of the Upper Paleolithic can be divided into two major categories: **mural art** — paintings and engravings on the walls of caves; and **portable art** — carvings, figurines, and other decorated pieces that can be moved from place to place. Mural art is restricted almost exclusively to France and Spain; portable art is found throughout Europe and the rest of the Old World. During the Upper Paleolithic, mural art was placed not only in caves but also at the entrances to caves and along the cliff faces and rock outcrops of the Perigord and elsewhere. Only deep in the caves of this area, however, has the mural art generally survived the erosive forces of nature. These cave interiors were

not living areas but were probably visited only briefly by the artists and others.

The paintings are almost exclusively of animals; humans are rarely represented. Human figures are depicted more commonly in engravings, both on cave walls and in portable objects. Some of the engravings appear to show men wearing the skins and heads of animals. These individuals may have been dancers or participants in some ceremony. Single human hands are found outlined on the cave walls. These hands may be simple signatures or grafitti, but, curiously, they are often missing several knuckles on fingers, or even entire fingers. For example, at the cave of Gargas in the Pyrenees Mountains, all but ten of 217 hand paintings have fingers missing.

The paintings are rendered in outline and colored in monochrome or polychrome. Animals are most often depicted in profile. The paintings are often high on

No matter how many caves one has explored, no matter how magnificent or crude or abstract the figures, it always comes with a catch of breath. It may be a bull or a bison drawn larger than life or an engraved horse no bigger than your little finger. It may appear high in a fissure or down close to the floor, on wide exposed surfaces for all to see or in private crawl-in places, painted bare red or black outline or in rich polychrome, starkly grand or delicate in a low key — a variety of locations and styles, and yet all part of a single tradition that endured for some twenty millenniums.
John Pfeifer, *The Creative Explosion* (1982)

3	11	1	1
9	9	1	1
3	9	1	1
1	59	1	1

Three depictions on the walls of the cave of Les Trois Frères, France, showing humans in animal skins. These individuals may be dancers, sorcerers, or hunters.

the ceiling in the darkest areas of the caves; scaffolding and lighting were essential. Pieces of rope and pine torches have been found along with simple oil lamps made of stone bowls. Over 150 fragments of such lamps have been found at Lascaux.

The quality of the paintings is such that we can assume there were recognized artists in the societies of the Upper Paleolithic. The cave art is generally carefully planned and skillfully executed, capturing both the movement and the power of the animals that are rendered. It is not grafitti, nor is it hastily sketched.

Lascaux is a lengthy, narrow chamber a little longer than a football field. In spite of its rather small size, more than 600 paintings and 1500 engravings grace the walls, making it the most decorated of the magnificent painted caves of Spain and France. The paintings must have had a great impact, viewed in the light of a flickering torch by awed individuals deep in the interior of the Earth.

The opening of the cave leads into a large chamber, some 20 m (65 ft) long, filled with huge animal paintings. Four large bulls, each up to 5 m (16 ft) long, stride across the ceiling. In the adjacent halls and passageways, hundreds of paintings depict bison, deer, horses, wild cattle, and other animals. Very specific characteristics, such as spring molting, are shown in some of the paintings. Animals are often shown as pregnant or with their meaty haunches exaggerated. In several instances, feathered darts are shown flying toward the animals. Certain abstract patterns also appear either in isolation or in association with animals. Rows of dots and multicolor checkerboard patterns are painted at various places in the cave.

Most of the paintings at Lascaux date to around 17,000 years ago, during the Magdalenian. The art is dated from fragments of paints and other artifacts found in archaeological layers of known age in the cave. The paints were a blend of mineral pigments mixed with cave water; the chewed end of a stick, or pieces of hair or fur, were used to apply the paint to the walls. The common colors in the paintings are black (charcoal and manganese oxide), yellow and red (iron oxides and clay), and occasionally white (clay and calcite).

The majority of the paintings show one or a group of animals; there is little attempt at scenery or storytelling. Many of the paintings are often superimposed

Man and bison at Lascaux.

over others, with little apparent regard for the previous work. Large herbivores, which provided much of the meat for these Upper Paleolithic hunter-gatherers, are most frequently shown in large chambers and open areas in the caves; such dangerous animals as carnivores, bears, and rhinoceros are more often seen in the deep recesses of the caves and far-removed crevices. Curiously, however, the most important game animal at this time, the reindeer, is seen only once at Lascaux.

One of the most remarkable groups of paintings is found at the bottom of a narrow 5-m shaft off to the side in the cave. At the bottom of this shaft, a large, woolly rhino with raised tail faces left, a series of dots near its hindquarters. Across a small crevice appears a striking scene of man and beast, the only human figure painted in the cave. A beautiful multicolor bison on the right is mortally wounded, its entrails spilled by a spear. The dying animal is either down on the ground or charging the man to the left. This figure, obviously male, is shown in merest out-

line, depicted with a birdlike face. On the ground nearby lies a long object with several barbs, perhaps a spearthrower, and a bird with a single long leg, perhaps an important symbol. Is this painting a memorial to a hunter killed by the bison, a member of the bird clan or totem? Is the rhino part of the scene? Such questions point out the difficulties involved in trying to read the minds of prehistoric people. We can speculate, but we cannot know what was intended by these paintings.

There are several schools of thought on the meaning of the cave paintings from the Upper Paleolithic. The emphasis on pregnant animals has often been considered to reflect a concern with fertility and reproduction, the bounty of nature, and an awareness of the replenishment of the herds on which these people depended for food. Others point to the exaggerated hips and haunches of the animals and spears in flight and argue for a concern for the hunt for meat. Hunting rites and the ritual killing of animals before a hunt might magi-

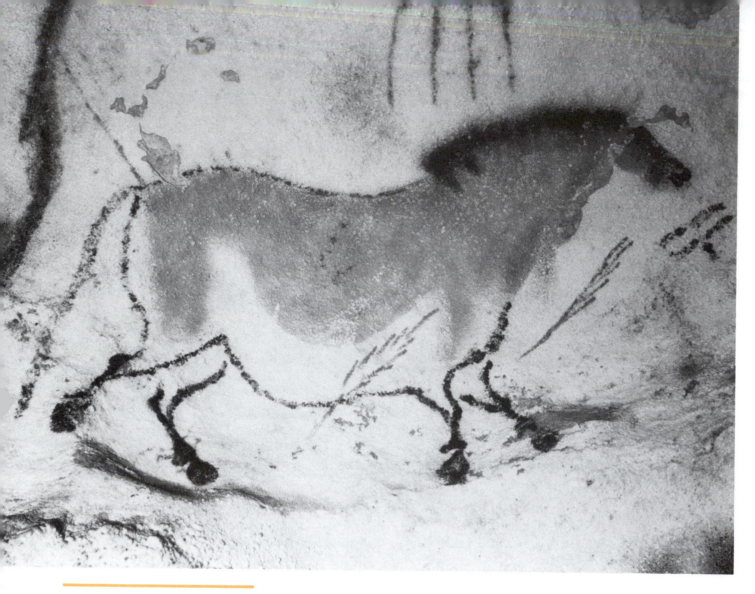

A painting of a running wild horse at Lascaux. Several symbols appear in the painting, including a grid or trap above the horse, an unidentifiable symbol in front of the head, and two spears, arrows, or plants in front of and under the animal.

cally help ensure success in the quest for food.

A few individuals suggest that these cave paintings are simply "art for the sake of art," a means for artists to express themselves and to change the way their fellow humans saw the world. Still others suggest that these caves were primitive temples, sanctuaries for ceremony and ritual, such as the initiation of the young into society. Huge animals flickering in the light of torches and lamps deep in the bowels of the Earth would have provided a staggering experience to the uninitiated. Footprints preserved in the muddy floors of painted caves in France indicate that all sizes of people walked in the cave. Margaret Conkey, of the University of California, Berkeley, argues that these painted caves may have served as a focus of social activity for large groups of people. She suggests that the caves may have been a

permanent symbol on the landscape and a place for the ceremonies and rituals associated with the aggregation of a number of groups of hunter-gatherers.

The magnificent art of the Upper Paleolithic represents an initial awakening of the creative spirit, an explosion of an aesthetic sense. Such a transformation may as well represent major changes either in the minds of Upper Paleolithic people, or in the way they viewed the world and organized their lives and their society, or both.

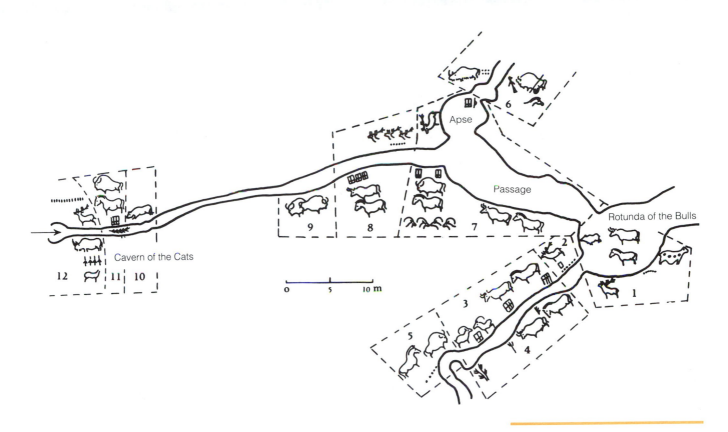

The distribution of animals and designs at Lascaux. The numbers indicate frequency of occurrence. Large prey animals tend to be in the major galleries of the caves, while carnivores and other depictions are in less-accessible areas.

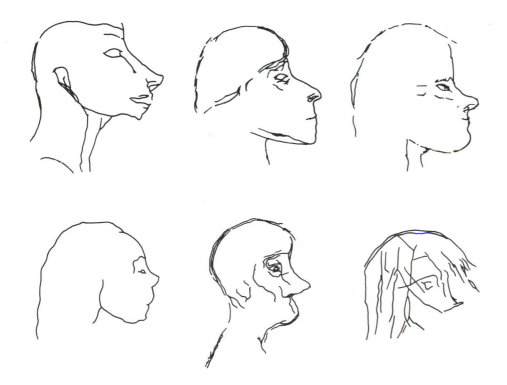

Some of the human heads engraved on the walls of the cave at La Marche, shown at the same size or scale.

PORTABLE ART

A sense of design and beauty

Examples of Upper Paleolithic decoration of bone, antler, ivory, and wood objects. Such decoration was applied to a variety of pieces, some utilitarian and others more symbolic.

The aesthetic sense that appeared during the Upper Paleolithic was expressed in several different media, through a variety of techniques. Carving, sculpting, and molding of clay, antler, wood, ivory, and stone were all practiced throughout this period. While most of the cave paintings appeared toward the end of the Upper Paleolithic, decoration of artifacts and other objects was almost continuous from approximately 35,000 years ago. Prior to the appearance of *Homo sapiens sapiens* in Europe, there is remarkably little evidence for the nonpractical modification of items. Only a handful of decorated objects have been found in Middle Paleolithic contexts.

Beginning in the Aurignacian some 34,000 years ago, however, bone became a common material for human use, modification, and decoration. A variety of bone points date to this early period. Initially simple and plain, such points became heavily barbed and decorated by the end of the Upper Paleolithic. At the same time, carved bone and antler figurines of both humans and animals began to appear in the archaeological record.

Perhaps the most spectacular portable objects from the Upper Paleolithic are the Venus figurines. These small sculptures appeared throughout most of Europe during a brief period around 25,000

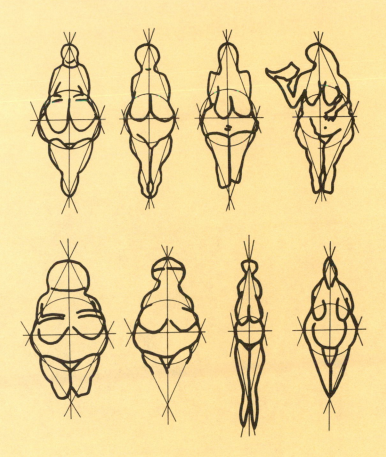

years ago. The figures were either engraved in relief on the walls of caves, carved in the round from ivory, wood, and stone such as steatite, or modeled in clay. The female characteristics of these statuettes are exaggerated; breasts, hips, buttocks, and thighs are very large, while the head, arms, hands, legs, and feet are shown only schematically. The pubic triangle is sometimes outlined; one figurine has a detailed vulva. Some of the figurines appear to be pregnant, while others are holding a horn of plenty, perhaps implying fertility, bounty, and reproduction — Mother Earth figures.

Probably 80% of the prehistoric art known today came from the last stage of the Upper Paleolithic, the Magdalenian. Many cave paintings date to the early part of this period, while most of the portable art may have come later. Engraved bone is common. Objects with a short life were decorated in a cursory fashion, while more important pieces with a longer life expectancy were heavily ornamented.

Portable art was more common in the larger settlements than in the smaller ones. This suggests a connection between art and the ritual activities that occur when large groups of people come together. Hunter-gatherer groups aggregate in large assemblies during a portion of each year to exchange raw materials and learn new information, to find mates, and to celebrate important events, such as marriage or initiation into adulthood. Then, as now, rituals and ceremonies provide a common bond in both physical and psychic realms: dance, trance, and the reaffirmation of common beliefs are very important aspects of such gatherings. Decoration in the form of masks, body painting, and the like are common during such ceremonial occasions, and was likely the case during the Upper Paleolithic as well.

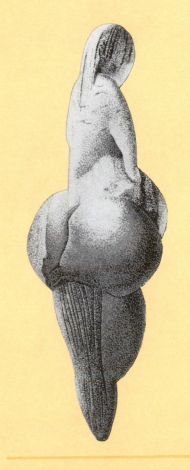

A Venus figurine from Lespugue, France, carved in ivory (14 cm high).

PINCEVENT

*Brief stops by reindeer hunters in
the Upper Paleolithic*

When tundra and permafrost covered northwestern Europe at the end of the Pleistocene, several fords on the River Seine were important crossing points for migrating reindeer herds. The sandbanks and sandbars of the Seine and other rivers were the sites of the camps of Magdalenian reindeer hunters approximately 12,000 years ago. The part of the Seine near Paris lies at the northern end of a major route of reindeer migration, when herds moved north from the south of France each year.

Scatters of stone, bone, antler, hearthstones, and charcoal mark these ephemeral summer encampments of reindeer hunters. A number of such sites, including one called Pincevent (ponce'vaughn), were quickly buried and extremely well preserved. The archaeological remains are found in thin layers of silt, deposited when the river flooded annually. The floods must have been gentle, because minimal disturbance of the materials is evident. Several artifacts were found standing upright, and two crushed birds' eggs remained at the site.

The concentrations of materials average 60 to 70 sq m (650 to 750 sq ft), likely representing single tents or structures as the residence and focus of activity of a few hunters. Each group of structures contains 20,000 to 30,000 stone artifacts and other materials. Stone blades, a major product at these sites, were used for a variety of purposes. At the site of Etiolles, extremely long blades were produced from large nodules of raw material, some more than 80 cm (30 in.) long, weighing 40 kg (90 lb) or more. The blades from these nodules were as long as 50 cm (20 in.). The absence of wear marks on the edges of some of these blades suggests they had not been used and were being stockpiled for some later purpose.

At Pincevent, at least four different levels with archaeological remains have been recognized, extending over an area of 2 hectares (ha), or 5 acres, larger than a soccer field. The excavations were originally directed by A. Leroi-Gourhan and M. Brezillon in 1964 and continue today. The excavators intentionally exposed broad horizontal areas of the site, leaving features, artifacts, and bones in place. In this manner, entire "living floors" could be seen and the pattern of discarded materials studied to determine where people slept, cooked, made tools, and so on. The excavators also made latex rubber casts of many areas, which were then painted to reconstruct and permanently preserve the archaeological remains.

One of the most important areas excavated at Pincevent to date is in Layer IV. This area contains 94,000 kg (200,000 lb) of flint artifacts, the skeletal remains of at least 43 reindeer, fire-cracked rock, ochre, and a number of shallow pits and fireplaces. Red ochre stains are concentrated around three large fireplaces. The excavators suggest that activities were centered around three contemporary huts, each with an associated fireplace. Each hut contains a central zone for actual living space and surrounding zones for domestic activities and refuse disposal. The intensity of activity decreases with distance from the hearths. Small piles of waste material from stone tool manufacture lie on one side of the hearths, while finished tools and red ochre are on the other side.

Near one of the hearths is a large stone that was likely the seat of a flint-worker. Most of the flint is available in the immediate area. A few pieces, however, came from some distance, confirming the mobility of the hunters who stopped here. Reconstruction or refitting of the pieces removed from the flint nodules provides a good indication of how tools were made. Moreover, pieces that are missing and not found at the site provide evidence of which tools were carried elsewhere. Finally, the lines connecting the spots where these joined pieces were found indicates how the tools and waste materials were moved about on the site.

Most of the reindeer at the site were killed and butchered during the summer months. The distribution of bone on the living floor is similar to the flint debris. Larger bones were at the periphery, while smaller pieces and fragments were found near the fireplaces. The bones from a meal were apparently tossed away from the hearth. Fragments of antler were found near the hearths, but larger pieces were discarded at the edge of the activity zone. Most antler working was apparently done at this periphery. The lack of sweeping or clearing of the living area suggests that occupation at Pincevent was very brief.

Lewis Binford, of Southern Methodist University, has questioned the existence of actual tents or structures at Pincevent, arguing that the distribution of materials in arcs of debris around the hearths could just as easily happen in the absence of tents or huts. There is no definitive evidence that the hunters built shelters at the site. Binford also argues that all of the materials at the two largest hearths could have resulted from one or two individuals working and shifting position in response to wind direction. Binford based his suggestions on observation of Eskimo hunters in Alaska and the manner in which they moved away from the smoke of a fire on windy days.

A reconstruction of a possible tent around one of the Pincevent hearths: (a) hearth, (b) concentration of artifacts.

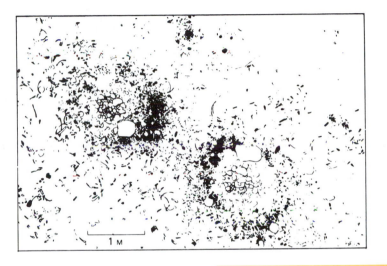

The distribution of stone and bone around two hearths at Pincevent. The large stones were used for sitting during stone tool manufacture, while the scatters of lithic debris were produced as a result.

SYMBOLS AND NOTATION

Evidence of seasonal awareness, numbers, and phases of the moon

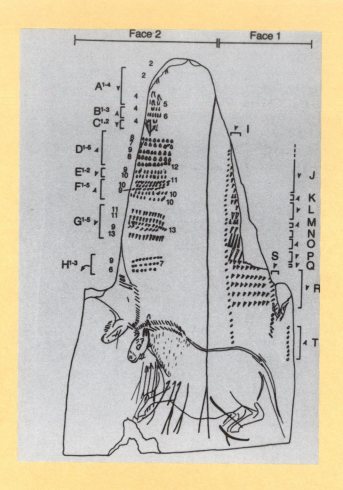

Face 2   Face 1

Marshack's interpretation of an engraved bone piece from the site of La Marche, France. Two horses appear at the bottom of the piece, one with a number of arrows drawn into the animal. The regular sets of marks were made with different tools, suggesting that something was being counted or recorded.

Among the many objects of decorated bone from the Upper Paleolithic are a series of fragments and plaques engraved with unusual images. Many of these engraved bones come from the early Upper Paleolithic Aurignacian. The designs are carved into the polished surface of bone using pointed stone tools. The motifs that often occur together suggest that specific concepts were intended.

One example is a bone knife from the French site of La Vache. The design on one side consists of two animal heads, a doe and an ibex; wavy lines, which may represent water; and three plants. The other side of the knife shows the head of a bison in autumn rut, four plant motifs that may be pine branches, a drooping stem, and three seeds or nuts. Alexander Marshack, of the Peabody Museum at Harvard University, suggests that the designs on the two sides of the knife are intended to convey images of the spring and fall, a recog-

nition of the seasons and their distinctive characteristics.

Other bone artifacts exhibit unusual combinations of notches and patterns of dots that are difficult to comprehend. One example of such an object comes from the cave of La Marche and dates to about 14,000 years ago. The polished fragment of bone, about 15 cm (6 in.) long, is decorated at the base with one entire horse and the head of another. Nine or ten pointed lines are drawn into the complete horse, perhaps symbolically representing the hunt. When the bone with the horses broke, it was reused to flake flint tools, and later elaborate sets of marks were added in a series of rows on both sides of the bone above the horses.

Marshack has undertaken a detailed, microscopic study in order to determine how the notches and dots were placed on the bone. He was able to identify both the type of pointed tool that made the marks

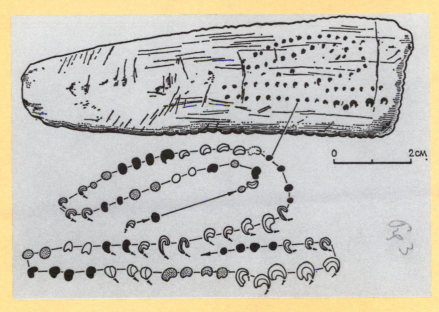

and the order in which at least some of them were made. At least four different tools were used to carve the arrows in the horse on the La Marche bone; the marks all occur in sets or blocks, each of which was made with a different tool in a slightly different shape. The number and pattern of the marks suggest that they were added over a period of time. On other decorated bones from the Upper Paleolithic, Marshack has observed marks in groups of thirty or thirty-one. The number seven also seems to regularly define groups of marks on other objects. Although such marks on bones have been considered decoration, they could signify some kind of tally, a counting of a series of events, or perhaps numbers of hunting kills.

Perhaps the most intriguing decorated bone object yet found is from Abri Blanchard in France. A flat, irregular rectangle, this bone plaque has no animals or figure engravings, but a series of carved and engraved notches and marks. The eighty notches cover about half the perimeter of the object, while the marks form a semicircular pattern of two parallel lines on the flat surface. Microscopic examination indicates that at least twenty-four different tools were used to make the sixty-nine marks on the surface of this bone. Marshack believes that these marks record the phases of the moon. The shape of the marks changes with the moon's phases, and the entire object records a period of about six months. Thus Marshack would argue that our Upper Paleolithic forebears were noting the passage of time, reckoning the year according to the seasons and a lunar calendar. Marshack's discoveries are certainly controversial, but the idea that Upper Paleolithic peoples were capable of counting and notation, as well as symbolic representation, does not seem far-fetched in light of the other evidence of their creativity and accomplishments.

BERINGIA

The arrival of the first inhabitants in the New World

The New World and Beringia, the land bridge between northeast Asia and Alaska, at the end of the Pleistocene, 12,000 years ago. The map shows the location of Beringia, the extent of continental glaciation, the coastline during lower sea level, and the sites mentioned in the text. The dotted arrows show the possible route through a gap in the Canadian ice sheets.

The first colonists of North America walked to their new land sometime before 10,000 years ago. These individuals were not Irish monks in leather canoes, Scandinavian Vikings in long boats, or Italians in tiny ships, but rather small groups of Asians who crossed a land bridge connecting the two continents on their own feet. The ancestors of the American Indians were the first inhabitants of the Western Hemisphere, a fact that was apparent when the Americas were "discovered" by Columbus.

There is no doubt that the first people in the New World came from Asia; the major question is *when* they came. By 8000 B.C. human groups had occupied most of both continents, from Alaska to Tierra del Fuego at the southern tip of South America. The best place to begin considering the question of when this process of colonization started is at the point of entry. There were two possible barriers to the movement of terrestrial animals from northeast Asia into central North America: (1) the Bering Strait, the body of water that separates the two continents today; and (2) an immense sheet of glacial ice that covered much of northern North America in the late Pleistocene.

Siberia and Alaska today are separated by less than 100 km (60 mi) at their closest point across the Bering Strait. The water in the strait is relatively shallow; the sea floor is roughly 40 m (120 ft) beneath the surface. During the colder intervals of the Pleistocene, when global sea levels were as much as 130 m (400 ft) below present levels, the floor of the Bering Strait became dry land. During periods of maximum cold and low sea level, the land area of Beringia as it is called, would have been more than 1000 km (600 mi) wide and indistinguishable from the continents on either side. The warm Japanese Current swept the southern shore and kept most of the area ice-free. The area would have been relatively flat and treeless, a bleak and windswept plain. Scattered groups of mammoth, bison, horse, reindeer, camel, and many other species moved across this region during the cold periods of the Pleistocene. At some point in time, these herds were followed by people from northeast Asia.

When was Beringia exposed as dry land and open for crossing? It is possible to plot the changes in sea level and their effects on the Bering Land Bridge. Beringia was exposed for long periods during the Pleistocene and submerged only briefly during the warmer interglacials. However, in order for people to cross Beringia, they would first have to be present in northeast Asia. The same conditions that produced lower sea levels also meant a very harsh climate and environment in northeastern Asia, which apparently delayed human settlement in the area until perhaps 35,000 years ago. Russian archaeologists have uncovered remains from this time belonging to Upper Paleolithic groups who used bifacially worked stone spear points to hunt large game.

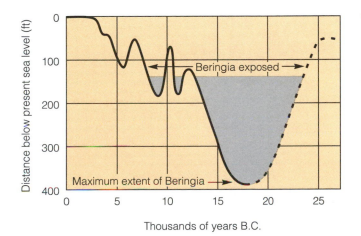

Changes in sea level in the area of the Bering Strait during the last 25,000 years. This area became dry land when sea level dropped below 130 m below present. Thus there were a number of periods when humans could have walked into the New World.

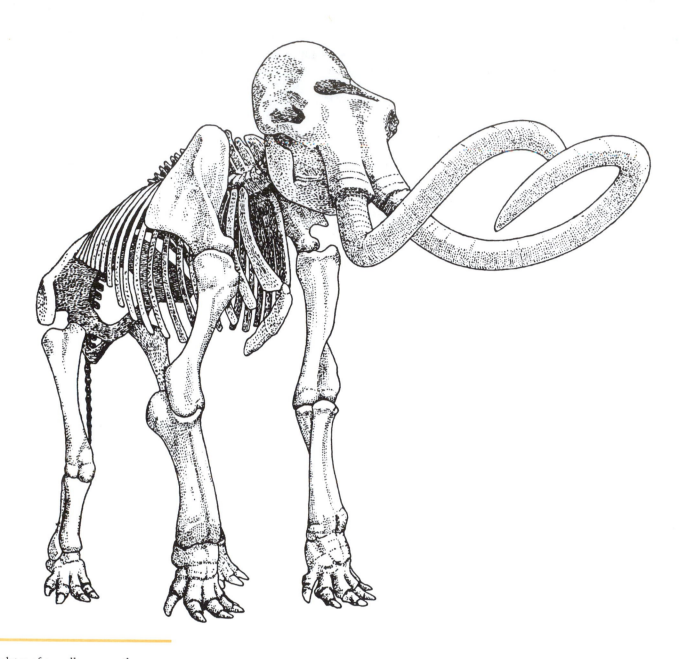

A skeleton of a woolly mammoth. Mammoths roamed the area of Beringia and much of North America at the end of the Pleistocene. This extinct form of elephant is 4 m at the shoulder, about the height of the top of a basketball backboard.

These individuals almost certainly were ancestral to the people who first crossed into North America.

Although the exact timing is debated, Beringia was probably dry land for long periods between 28,000 and 13,000 years ago. After 11,000 B.C. warmer climatic conditions began to melt the continental ice sheets, and the meltwater gradually returned the seas to their present levels. During the period of maximum cold and lower sea level, the continental ice sheets of northern North America stretched from the Aleutian Islands across Canada to Greenland. Alaska was cut off from the rest of North America and was more a part of Asia than of the New World. A gap or corridor between the western and eastern centers of the Canadian ice sheets was probably open only between 28,000 and 25,000 years ago and again shortly after 15,000 B.C. This corridor may have provided the route for these newly arrived hunting groups into the North American continent and points south. Another possible route lay along the western coastline of North America. That rich coastal habitat would have been ice-free and likely accessible to the hunters crossing the Bering Land Bridge.

Paleoindian projectile points were attached to spears. These two Clovis points were found at the Hell Gap site in Wyoming. The smaller of the two was broken and resharpened.

Whatever the route, these emigrants must have been few in number, because they left very little evidence of their presence. Sites from this early period are quite rare and the dates usually debated. Only a few places, such as Monte Verde in Chile, dating to at least 13,000 years ago, provide good evidence for these early inhabitants. Monte Verde contains the remains of extinct elephants and other animals in association with stone tools.

The archaeological remains in North America from the beginning of the Holocene Epoch around 10,000 years ago are generally known as **Paleoindian**. Sites from this period are characterized by the presence of a specific type of stone spear tip, known as a **fluted point**. Paleoindian spear points document the widespread presence of the early Americans in North America between 12,000 and 9,000 years ago.

The best-known points from this period are called **Clovis,** named after the spot where they were originally found in eastern New Mexico. Clovis people were relatively mobile groups of big game hunters, spreading across most of North America east of the Rocky Mountains. New types of projectile points evolved follow-ing the Clovis Period. Distinctive, regional types of Paleoindian points are found throughout the New World. **Folsom** points, for example, are found only in the Great Plains. A number of sites are known where animals were killed and butchered with these points, but only a few actual settlements have ever been found. The Lindenmeier site in northern Colorado is one of the few examples of a Folsom campsite.

It appears that *Homo sapiens sapiens* came to the New World for the first time between 28,000 and 12,000 years ago. Groups of hunters quickly expanded across both continents and were likely involved in the extinction of a number of animal species. It is important to remember that the Bering Strait was probably the point of entry for several migrations into the New World. The colonization of North and South America was not a single event, but rather a series of crossings. Certainly the ancestors of modern Eskimos came across the Strait relatively late, perhaps 4000 years ago in boats. Thus the timing of when the first Americans arrived is a difficult and complex question that will continue to be an important concern in the field of archaeology.

MONTE VERDE

Early inhabitants of South America

Monte Verde, 1983. General view of the site and field laboratory. Excavation trenches can be seen running perpendicular to the creek. The buildings in the center of the photo are part of the excavation headquarters.

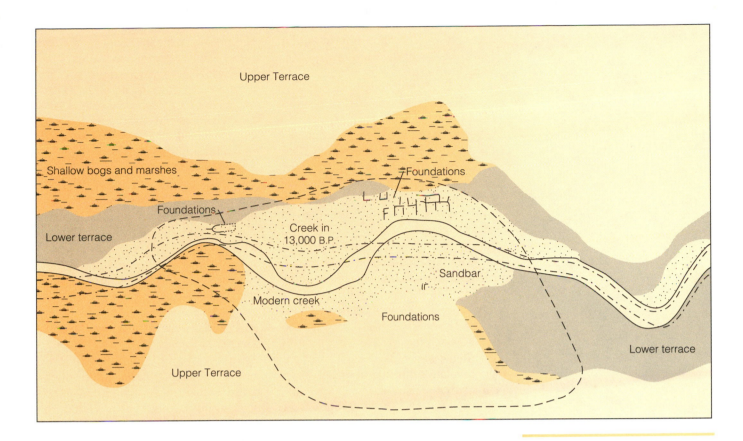

Upper Terrace

Shallow bogs and marshes

Foundations

Foundations

Lower terrace

Creek in
13,000 B.P.

Modern creek

Sandbar

Foundations

Lower terrace

Upper Terrace

Traces of human groups in the Americas prior to 12,000 years ago are almost non-existent. There are only a few examples of archaeological sites in the New World that contain both definite evidence of an early human presence and reliable radiocarbon dates. In many instances, sites that are candidates for very early human occupation have been discounted because of contaminated carbon samples or questionable stone artifacts.

Several of the best examples of human occupation sites before 10,000 B.C. are in South America rather than near the point of entry at the Bering Strait. Monte Verde (mon′tay ver′day) is a 13,000-year-old campsite in Chile, discovered in 1976 by Tom Dillehay, of the University of Kentucky. While surveying in the area, he uncovered bone and stone artifacts in a shallow peat bog along Chinchihuapi Creek, a small, slow stream that drains this part of the rain forests of southern Chile. The site lies along the sandy banks on either side of the creek. Radiocarbon dates on wood and other materials date the site to 13,000 years ago.

Excavations that continued after the original discovery have uncovered a number of remarkable and unexpected finds for such an early site. Conditions of preservation have resulted in the recovery of actual plant remains and a number of wooden objects, along with stone flakes and broken animal bones. Wood is rare at any archaeological site, yet it was preserved in the bog at Monte Verde. Apparently the bog developed shortly after the abandonment of the site and quickly enclosed all the remaining materials in a mantle of peat. Peat provides a waterlogged, oxygen-free environment where such objects can be preserved.

The timber and earthen foundations of perhaps twelve dwelling structures were recovered in the excavations. The rectangular foundations, made of logs and planks held in place with stakes of a different kind of wood, enclose rooms 3 to 4 m (10 to 13 ft) long on each side. Posts placed along the foundation timbers supported a sapling framework, which may have been covered by animal skins. Small pieces of what may be animal hide were preserved next to the timber foundation. Two large hearths and a number of shallow clay basins provided fireplaces for the inhabitants of these huts. Even a child's

The location and plan of the Monte Verde site. The settlement lay on both sides of the creek, covering an area of approximately 7000 sq m, as indicated by the dashed line. Foundations are outlined where they have been located.

footprint was found preserved in the hardened clay of the basin of one of the small fireplaces.

Many of the artifacts at the site were found inside these structures. Wooden artifacts include digging sticks, spears, and a mortar, in addition to the material used for construction. Several kinds of stone tools, both flaked and ground, were found. No stone projectile points were made here, but evidence of other weapons was uncovered. Spherical stones with an encircling groove were probably bola stones, South American throwing weapons with three leather thongs weighted at each end. The bola is thrown in a spinning fashion, and the stone weights wrap the thongs around the prey. Other stone balls without grooves were likely used in a sling as a heavy projectile.

To the west of the living floors was a single, more substantial rounded structure with a pointed end, with a foundation of sand and gravel. The bases of wooden posts at the edges of the foundation mark the walls of the structure, and a kind of yard or patio was marked off with branches near the entrance. Mastodon bones, animal skins, stone and wooden tools, salt, and the remains of several different types of plants were found in this area.

The arrangement of these structures over an area of roughly 70 by 100 m (220 by 400 ft) (approximately the size of a soccer field) suggests that a well-organized community of thirty to fifty individuals lived at the site. Plant remains are from species that ripen throughout the year, suggesting that this was a year-round settlement. The occupants of Monte Verde appear to have relied primarily on plants and large animals for their livelihood. Most of the bones came from mastodons, a close but extinct relative of the mammoth and elephant. The wetlands (marshes, bogs, and streams) of the Monte Verde area are a very rich environment. Many edible plants grow here, and small game are plentiful. Exotic objects — including several of the plants, beach-rolled pebbles, quartz, and bitumen, an adhesive tar — were also brought to the site from the Pacific coast about 25 km (15 mi) to the south.

The plant remains document extensive gathering of local vegetation. A total of forty-two edible species of plants have been identified from the site. Most of the evidence is from tubers and roots that were preserved, including the wild potato. This is the oldest evidence anywhere for the potato, which was later domesticated in the Andes. The products of other plants, including seeds, berries, nuts, and fruits, were also recovered during the excavations. A number of grinding stones further point to the importance of plants in the diet at Monte Verde. Herbaceous plants were also found, which today are used for medicinal, rather than nutritional, purposes.

The evidence from Monte Verde contradicts most traditional views of the peopling of the Americas. The radiocarbon date of 11,000 B.C. for this site in South America documents the fact that early Asians crossed the Bering Strait before 13,000 years ago. Paleoindian sites normally contain small concentrations of stone artifacts, sometimes in association with the bones of large, extinct animals. Paleoindians have been considered to have lived primarily as small, mobile groups of big game hunters.

The information from Monte Verde has forced a reconsideration of our interpretation of the earliest inhabitants of the New World, because it is in direct contrast to what has been observed at most sites where preservation is not nearly as good. The organic materials from Monte Verde indicate the importance of plants, as well as animals, in the diet at that time. The existence of wood and wooden tools, more common at Monte Verde than stone artifacts, provides an intriguing look at the organic component of equipment that is so rarely witnessed in the archaeological record. The suggestive evidence for permanent residence at this site is also in contrast to Paleoindian occupations elsewhere.

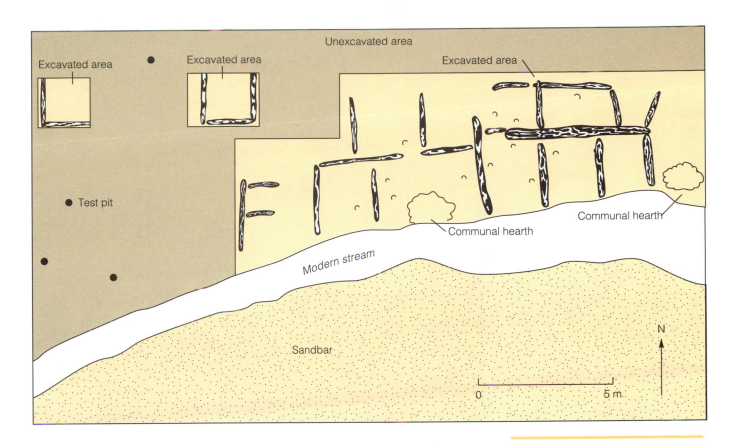

Unexcavated area

Excavated area

Excavated area

Excavated area

● Test pit

Communal hearth

Communal hearth

Modern stream

Sandbar

N

0   5 m.

A detailed plan of structures in the eastern part of the site at Monte Verde. Logs were set in place using wooden pegs to create the foundations of these structures. Shallow, clay-lined hearths were found on the floors inside several of the huts.

Some of the 13,000-year-old wood timber foundations at Monte Verde. Each rectangular enclosure measures about 2.3 by 3.3 m. Note the dark, greasy appearance of the hut floors and the artifacts in place.

LINDENMEIER

Late Pleistocene hunters in Colorado

A drawing of a Paleoindian flintknapper removing the flute from a Clovis point. A chest crutch is used to apply pressure to remove the flake from the end of the point. This flute or channel in the base of the point facilitates the hafting.

Lindenmeier, located in northern Colorado at an elevation of 2000 m (6500 ft) in the foothills of the Rocky Mountains, lies at the intersection of three major environmental zones: the eastern slope of the Rockies, the Colorado piedmont, and the Great Plains. Gullies cutting through sedimentary deposits in this area washed out and exposed the buried bones of large bison and early spear points. The local ranchers who discovered these artifacts in 1924 wrote to the Smithsonian Institution in Washington, D.C., to announce the site's existence.

In 1934, Frank Roberts, of the Smithsonian Institution, was sent to investigate Lindenmeier. Roberts wanted to document the association of hunters and extinct animals in the past. Early sites in North America were almost unknown at the time. His excavations at Lindenmeier continued each year from 1934 through 1940. The field crew spent a total of almost 600 days on the excavations, opening over 1800 sq m in the process, and digging deeply into the buried archaeological deposits. This project eventually uncovered one of the largest Paleoindian

sites in the New World. His careful excavations and recording procedures permitted the final results of Roberts' original investigations to be published by others after his death. The final report on Roberts' work at Lindenmeier was published by Edwin Wilmsen in 1978.

Radiocarbon dates from the site place the occupation of Lindenmeier at 9000 B.C., just before the end of the Pleistocene. The climate at that time was less arid and cooler than it is today. The local environment at the site was more wooded, with stands of juniper and pine. Fragments of charcoal from these species were recovered from fireplaces at Lindenmeier. Ground cover would have been heavier, with thick grasses over much of the area. The area around the site can be envisioned as having been a lush meadow watered by an active spring, which attracted both animals and their predators. The spring, adjacent to the site, must have been the reason this spot was selected as a campsite.

More than 15,000 animal bones were recovered in the excavations. Twelve different species were represented at Lindenmeier, including wolf, coyote, fox, hare,

rabbit, turtle, deer, antelope, and bison; they inhabited all three environments near the site. Antelope, wolf, and fox are native to the Rocky Mountains and the piedmont, while bison, coyote, and jackrabbit are common in the High Plains. The bison was by far the most abundant animal represented at the site and must have provided most of the meat consumed there. This is an extinct form of bison, a huge animal some 2 m (6.5 ft) at the shoulder. In all likelihood the Folsom hunters cooperated to drive these animals into blind canyons and other traps where they could be more easily killed.

More than 50,000 stone artifacts have been counted from the excavated areas at Lindenmeier. Approximately 5000 of these stone pieces and seventy bones are shaped into finished tools. The bone tools include needles and simple pointed pieces. In addition, a number of bone pieces decorated with notches and engraved lines, and several bone beads, were excavated.

More than 600 bifacially worked projectile points were recovered, including almost 250 Folsom points. These Paleoindian spear tips are slender, bifacially worked fluted stone points, shaped carefully on all surfaces by pressure flaking. To finish the fluted point, a single long flake, or flute, is removed from the base of each side as a channel to facilitate attachment to a wooden spear shaft. This fluting flake was probably removed by pressure from a chest crutch and vise. These points are found with the skeletons of such big game animals as giant bison, mastodon,

mammoth, and others. Often broken points were either resharpened or reworked into other tools, such as scrapers and knives. The repair of broken equipment was one of the characteristic activities at the campsites of hunter-gatherers.

Fifteen distinct concentrations of archaeological materials were observed in the excavations at Lindenmeier. Two groups of these concentrations deserve special attention. Area I includes excavation Units A, B, and C, and Area II includes Units F, G, and H. Wilmsen questioned whether these two clusters of artifacts and bones were left by the same group on separate visits, or by two distinct groups perhaps at the same time. Careful measurements of the Folsom points in the two concentrations indicated two different sizes. The points in one area were slightly smaller on average and fashioned in a different manner. These differences led Wilmsen to argue that two different groups of people were responsible for the two concentrations. Further evidence for the differences between the two areas is seen in the original sources for the **obsidian** that was used to make some stone tools. Obsidian is a type of glass produced during volcanic eruptions and highly prized for making stone tools. Obsidian in Area I came from New Mexico, while the material in Area II was from the north, near Yellowstone National Park in Wyoming. Lindenmeier thus seems to provide evidence of two or more different social groups that came together to cooperate in annual bison hunting for a brief time, some 11,000 years ago.

The reconstructed haft and mounting of a Clovis point.

PLEISTOCENE EXTINCTION

Natural versus human causes

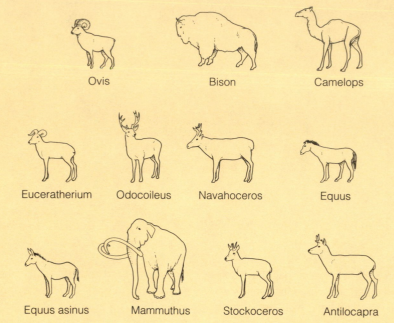

Ovis   Bison   Camelops

Euceratherium   Odocoileus   Navahoceros   Equus

Equus asinus   Mammuthus   Stockoceros   Antilocapra

Some Pleistocene and early Holocene animals of North America.

The neck vertebra of a bison with a Paleoindian point embedded in it.

In various places around North America—the La Brea tar pits, the caves of the Grand Canyon, the bone beds of eastern Missouri—the remains of very large animals that once roamed North America have attracted a great deal of public attention. Many of these animals were large carnivores and herbivores that wandered the continent over the last 2 million years. By the end of the Pleistocene, however, some thirty-five genera of land mammals, nearly half the total number, became extinct in North America.

Such species as the giant sloth and giant beaver, the horse, camel, mammoth and mastodon, lion, cheetah, and short-faced bear, all much larger than their modern counterparts, became extinct before 10,000 years ago. The giant sloth was about the size of a giraffe and weighed up to 3 tons. Caves in the Grand Canyon have preserved many examples of softball-sized giant sloth dung. The giant beaver in the Great Lakes area weighed as much as 140 kg (300 lb). A similar, though not as complete, pattern of extinction in large mammals occurred at the close of the Pleistocene in Europe and Asia, where mammoth, woolly rhino, cave bear, lion, and other species also became extinct.

What caused the demise of so many animals in such a relatively short period of time? Scientists, archaeologists, paleontologists, climatologists, and others have considered this question for decades. Two major scenarios have been proposed: climatic change (a natural cause) and hunting overkill (the human element).

Each position has a set of facts and conjectures that appears to contradict that of the other. For example, those supporting human causes argue that very similar climatic changes during earlier interglacials did not result in the extinction of many species, such as the mammoth, which adapted to a broad range of environments. Also, the widespread appearance of Clovis hunters around 11,000 years ago coincides closely with the demise of a number of the extinct species. Fluted points have been found in association with the bones of extinct mammoth, mastodon, horse, tapir, and camel, suggesting that Paleoindian hunters, with easy access to animals virtually ignorant of human predators, quickly eliminated the large animals they encountered.

Those who doubt the role of human hunters point out that a number of extinct species are never found at kill sites. There

The remains of a mammoth killed and butchered by Paleoindian hunters at the Colby site in Wyoming.

is, in fact, no direct evidence of human predation on such animals as the giant sloth and giant beaver. Other nonmammalian species also suffered extinction at the end of the Pleistocene. For example, almost 45% of the genera of birds in Pleistocene North America disappeared by 11,000 years ago. There is little reason to suspect human intervention in the extinction of these species.

New evidence for increasing aridity at the end of the Pleistocene and its effect on animal populations argues against the role of human hunters as the sole factor in the extinctions. This climatic change caused a shift in the distribution of small species, and perhaps caused the extinction of large animals. Larger animals require more food and more space to live and thus, as a species, are more vulnerable to changes in their environment. Large animals are also found in lower numbers than smaller ones; the loss of a few individuals in an area could have serious consequences during mating season. Larger animals, too, have a longer generation length than smaller ones, so that genetic changes occur more slowly through the population, making them more susceptible to extinction.

Proponents of the climate change theory argue that seasonal differences in climate were not as pronounced in the Pleistocene as they are today. Late Pleistocene winters must have been warmer and summers cooler than they are at present. As seasonal differences increased at the end of the Pleistocene, environmental changes would have been dramatic. Such difficulties, in conjunction with effective human predation, may have been too much for those species of large animals that died out.

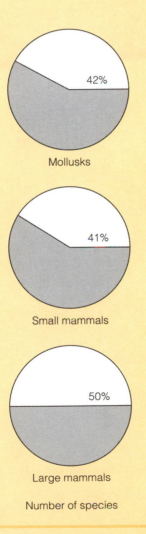

42%

Mollusks

41%

Small mammals

50%

Large mammals

Number of species

Percentages of extinct animals compared to the total number of species in each group.

EPILOG
The End of the Paleolithic

On the threshold of farming

The story of the Paleolithic is a remarkable saga — an evolutionary journey from primate to human. The major changes that occurred in human biology and culture during that period made modern humans essentially what we are today. We began more than 4 million years ago as chimpanzeelike primates living in open grassland environments of subtropical Africa. The climate was mild, plants grew year-round, and large predators killed and ate many animals, leaving behind bits of meat and bone marrow for hungry hominids. Sharp edges of stone helped to remove the meat from the bones, and other stones cracked the heavy bones open to expose the marrow. Biologically — lacking claws, big teeth, and speed — early humans were ill-equipped to defend themselves or their young from the predators of the plains. As social beings, however, with safety in numbers, they may have been able to deter those ferocious carnivores.

The early hominid adaptation successfully spread over most of Africa by about 1 million years ago. Brain size almost doubled during this period, and faces underwent dramatic changes. The handaxe was invented — a marvelous, multipurpose tool sculpted from a slab of stone. As hominid numbers and adaptive success increased, they began to move out of the African cradle to Eurasia. Here cooler, more temperate climates challenged ingenuity. The mysterious force of fire was controlled during this time for heat, light, and cooking, becoming a new ally in the continuing battle with nature. Simple huts were erected for shelter, and some form of covering or clothing almost certainly was in use. Plants were not available during the northern winters, and survival came to depend on hunting ability.

By 100,000 years ago, our ancestors had occupied much of the Old World, including the cold tundras of Pleistocene Europe and Asia. Human brains reached modern size. New tools and ideas prevailed against the harsh environment. Life became something more than eating, sleeping, and reproducing. Burial of the dead and the care of the handicapped and injured illustrated a concern for fellow hominids. A cultlike preoccupation with cave bears and evidence for cannibalism demonstrated an interest in the supernatural; ritual and ceremony achieved an important place among their activities. Hominids probably began to dream.

The Upper Paleolithic was the culmination of many long trends — in biology and culture, in language and communication, in ritual and ideology, in social organization, in art and design, in settlement and technology — that began several million years earlier. Evolution brought humans to the modern form, *Homo sapiens sapiens*. New continents were explored; Australia, North America, and South America were colonized. More kinds of implements were made from a wider variety of materials than ever before. Bows, boats, buttons, fish hooks, lamps, needles, nets, spearthrowers, and many other items were produced for the first time. The dog was domesticated as a faithful hunting companion and occasional source of food. Caves and many artifacts were decorated with painting, carvings, and engravings, as an awareness of art and design erupted in the human consciousness. Sites from the Upper Paleolithic were larger and more common than those from previous periods.

The diversity of the Upper Paleolithic is also seen in the diet. During much of the Paleolithic there was an emphasis on one or a few species of animals, usually large game such as elephant, reindeer, mammoth, or horse. Toward the end of the Paleolithic, however, there was a clear increase in the diversity of plants and animals that were consumed, and in the exploitation of new habitats from which these new foods came; more aquatic and avian species were eaten, for example.

The end of the Paleolithic was likely the apogee of hunter-gatherer adaptations on this planet. Very successful groups of foragers lived and expanded into almost all of the environments on Earth. It is, in fact, this expansion in numbers that is in part responsible for the end of a hunting-gathering way of life. Increasing populations required new and more productive sources of food. The bounty of the land, the wild plants and animals of nature, simply were not enough to feed everyone. Experiments to increase the available amount of food became necessary. The story of the domestication of plants and animals and the beginning of the Neolithic is the subject of Chapter Five. Chapter Four discusses the events after the end of the Pleistocene leading up to the beginnings of agriculture.

SUGGESTED READINGS

Bordes, François. 1968. *The Old Stone Age*. New York: McGraw-Hill. A discussion of the tools and remains of the Old Stone Age by a French prehistorian.

Fagan, B. M. 1987. *The great journey*. London: Thames & Hudson. A very readable and recent account of the arrival of the first Americans.

Pffeifer, John E. 1982. *The creative explosion: An inquiry into the origins of art and religion*. New York: Harper & Row. A popular volume on the investigation and interpretation of Upper Paleolithic art.

Soffer, Olga. 1987. *The Pleistocene Old World*. New York: Plenum Press. A series of technical papers on the state of research, primarily concerned with the Middle and Upper Paleolithic.

White, Randall. 1986. *Dark caves, bright visions: Life in Ice Age Europe*. New York: American Museum of Natural History. A wonderfully illustrated book on the art, both cave paintings and portable objects, of the Upper Paleolithic.

HOLOCENE HUNTER-GATHERERS

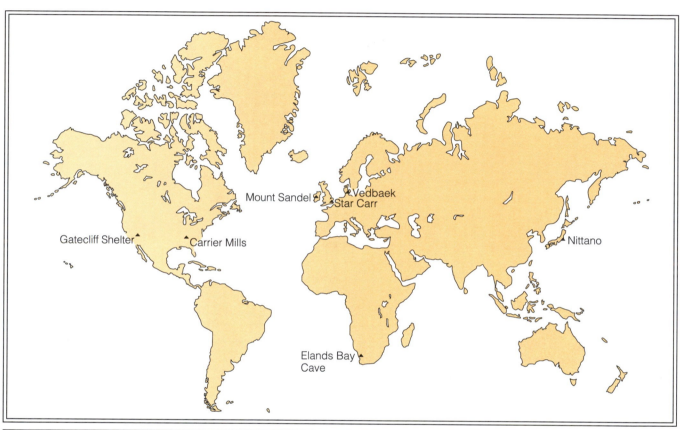

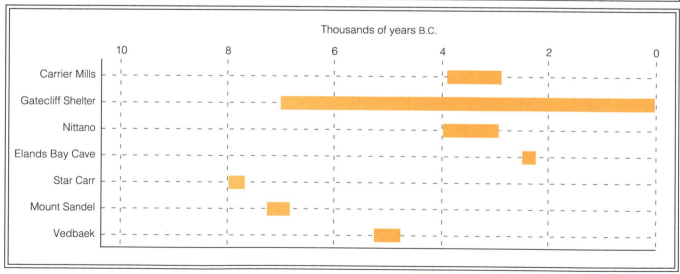

THE WORLD AFTER 8000 B.C.

New solutions to changing environments

The pace of change in human society has increased dramatically over time. For example, there were more innovations in artifacts and advances in human behavior during the Upper Paleolithic than in preceding periods. A number of major changes also took place at the end of the Pleistocene, beginning around 10,000 years ago. Large game hunting, an adaptation that had characterized human prehistory for most of the Middle and Upper Paleolithic, began to decline as certain animal species became extinct, and probably for other reasons as well. The human diet became more diversified and included more species of both plants and animals.

This chapter considers human adaptations at the beginning of the Postglacial. In a few areas—the Near East, the Far East, and parts of the Americas—domestication of plants and animals was beginning to alter the basic hunting-and-gathering pattern of human subsistence. (These origins of agriculture are discussed in Chapter Five.) In most other places, groups of **hunter-gatherers** continued their way of life, adapting to the changing environmental conditions of the Holocene. The term hunter-gatherer describes human groups who use only the wild resources of the Earth, hunting animals and collecting plants, nuts, seeds, shellfish, and other foods for their sustenance.

In North America the Paleoindian period of big game hunting ended approximately 9000 years ago, at the same time many species of big game became extinct. The period between 6000 and 1000 B.C. is known as the **Archaic**. Human groups began to exploit a broad spectrum of food sources. Many new sorts of subsistence pursuits seem to have begun at this time. Ground stone tools such as mortars and grinding stones have been found at some Archaic sites, indicating an increasing reliance on plant foods. Exotic materials in some regions document an increase in long-distance trade for obsidian, copper, and shell. The date for the end of the Archaic varies from area to area in North America. In some regions, such as the arid grasslands of the plains, hunting and gathering persisted until European contact. In other areas, such as major river valleys of the Midwest and Southeast, a more sedentary lifestyle and the use of cultivated plants, or **cultigens**, occurred as early as 500 to 1000 B.C.

The great diversity of Archaic adaptations was also present in eastern North America, although the major emphasis was on fishing, hunting, and plant and nut collecting. Settlements were often located along lakes, rivers, and coastlines to take advantage of aquatic resources. The Archaic sites in the Green River area of Kentucky and at Carrier Mills in southern Illinois document adaptations typical of this region. Piles of freshwater mussel shells along the rivers of the Southeast, the remains of prehistoric meals, are enormous, some examples up to 0.5 km (600 yds) long, 100 m (350 ft) wide, and 6 to 8 m (20 to 25 ft) high. In the Great Lakes region, native copper nuggets from Lake Superior were collected and hammered into knives, spear points, and various pendants and jewelry. Along the eastern seaboard, huge shell middens accumulated, documenting the importance of marine foods in the diet of the hunter-gatherers of New England and the East Coast.

Details of the climate, geology, and archaeological sequence in Europe and North America during the last 12,000 years.

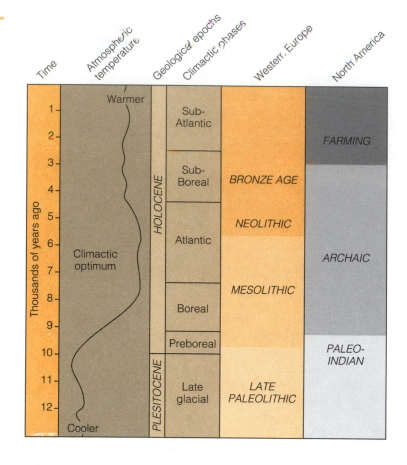

Archaic sites in the Great Plains document a major focus on bison hunting. Sites in the dry, desert West contain artifacts and organic materials that indicate an emphasis on both plant foods and hunting. Groups in the Great Basin collected seeds and nuts and hunted antelope and small game such as rabbit. Gatecliff Shelter in Nevada contains a very deep sequence of deposits and provides a good example of such adaptations.

In Japan, the period between the beginning of the Holocene and the introduction of rice cultivation is known as the Jomon. Thousands of settlements were occupied during this time, and very sophisticated pottery was created by these food-collecting peoples. In fact, the earliest ceramics in the world were made in Japan approximately 12,000 years ago. Nittano, on the edge of Tokyo, provides an example of a Jomon coastal settlement and documents the importance of fishing in this area around 5500 years ago.

In South and East Africa, the term Late Stone Age is used to describe the artifacts and encampments of Holocene hunter-gatherers. Although most studies are concerned with the earlier periods of human prehistory in these areas of Africa, new information from South Africa has offered some indication of the lifestyle of these groups shortly before the introduction of herding and farming. Investigations at Elands Bay Cave on the west coast of South Africa provide such evidence.

The term **Mesolithic** (Middle Stone Age) designates the period between the end of the Pleistocene and the beginning of agriculture in Europe, North Africa, and parts of Asia. These hunter-gatherer societies were similar in adaptation to Archaic groups in North and South America, consuming a wide range of wild plant and animal species and employing a highly specialized technology. An incredible range of fishing gear, including nets, weirs, hooks, and harpoons, was used during this period. Ground stone artifacts appear as axes, plant-processing equipment, and other tools. Projectile weapons were equipped with a variety of different tips made of bone, wood, antler, or stone. In those areas of Europe where bone and other organic materials have been preserved, artifacts are often decorated with fine, geometric designs. Cemeteries that are sometimes present at Mesolithic sites suggest more sedentary occupations.

Examples of Mesolithic settlements discussed in this chapter come from northwestern Europe. Star Carr, an early Holocene site in England, is one of the best-known Mesolithic sites in the world, dating to approximately 7500 B.C. Materials excavated at this waterlogged site document the range of technology in use during the Mesolithic. Mount Sandel is an early Irish Mesolithic site that contains evidence for year-round occupation by 6000 B.C. In Denmark, excavations at Vedbaek have exposed a cemetery and settlement dating to about 5000 B.C.

Many characteristics often associated with early farming groups appear among the hunter-gatherers of the early Postglacial. These include a broad-spectrum diet, permanent settlement in larger communities, and cemeteries. Such developments presage the emergence of the Neolithic and document the changes taking place by this time in human society.

CARRIER MILLS

Middle Archaic in southern Illinois

The location of the Black Earth site, SA-87, at Carrier Mills, Illinois. The dark areas on the ground correspond to the settlement areas at the site.

The Archaeological Resources Protection Act of 1979 (Public Law 96-95; 93 Stat. 712, 16 U.S.C. 470)

This law provided for the protection of archaeological resources located on public lands and Indian lands; defined archaeological resources to be any material remains of past human life or activities that are of archaeological interest and are at least 100 years old; encouraged cooperation between groups and individuals in possession of archaeological resources from public or Indian lands with special permit and disposition rules for the protection of archaeological resources on Indian lands in light of the American Indian Religious Freedom Act; provided that information regarding the nature and location of archaeological resources may remain confidential; and established civil and criminal penalties, including forfeiture of vehicles, fines of up to $100,000, and imprisonment of up to 5 years for second violations for the unauthorized appropriation, alteration, exchange, or other handling of archaeological resources with rewards for furnishing information about such unauthorized acts.

(U.S. Congress, Office of Technology Assessment, 1986)

Environmental protection policy in the United States requires that, prior to the start of federally-supported construction projects, an environmental impact study be done to determine if important archaeological or historical sites are in danger of destruction. This essentially means that both federal agencies and private corporations must provide information on the expected effects of their projects on the history and prehistory of the area. Various kinds of construction—including major reservoirs, highway construction, new sewage systems, powerline rights-of-way, and many others—require such archaeological surveys and environ-

The locations of excavation units in the three areas of the Black Earth site.

mental impact statements. This kind of work, generally termed **cultural resource management**, is an important part of the field of archaeology.

Strip mining results in the complete removal of ground surface in order to excavate deep pits to extract coal. Any buried or surface archaeological sites that are not salvaged prior to strip mining will simply be destroyed. In the early 1980s, the Peabody Coal Company of St. Louis, Missouri, was required to submit an environmental impact study of the Carrier Mills area in southern Illinois prior to an expansion of mining operations there. The area to be surveyed and tested for archaeological and historical sites covered some 57 ha (150 acres). Richard Jeffries, Brian Butler, and David Braun, of the Center for Archaeological Investigations at Southern Illinois University, Carbondale, were the directors of this five-year project.

An archaeological survey involves walking across the landscape looking for stones, **potsherds** (fragments of clay vessels), and bones that are turned up by plowing, animal burrowing, and erosion. In areas where thick grass or dense vegetation make it hard to see the surface of the ground, small test holes may be excavated to determine if buried archaeological remains are present. The survey of the Carrier Mills area discovered three large multiperiod sites, dating to between 4000 B.C. and European contact. These sites were excavated carefully in order to obtain as much information as possible before the mining began.

One of the three major settlements, known as the Black Earth site, dates to the Middle Archaic, from 4000 to 3000 B.C. The site sits along a low ridge, directly adjacent to a series of shallow lakes and swamps to the east and west; the low, rolling Shawnee Hills lie to the south of the site. The occupants utilized the river, lakes, and swamps of the lowlands for aquatic resources and exploited the uplands behind the settlement for deer.

Evidence for human use of these areas and for the activities of the inhabitants comes from the prehistoric **middens** — accumulations of trash and waste material. The site's name comes from the distinct black midden deposits that stand out against the yellow-brown soils of the ridge, the result of charcoal and ash from thousands of campfires. The entire scatter of artifacts at Black Earth covers some 53,000 sq m (13 acres). Three discrete concentrations were recognized within the huge area, designated as A, B, and C. The largest, Area A, is at least 17,000 sq m (4 acres) (the size of two soccer fields), and the cultural horizon extends up to 1.5 m (5 ft) below the present ground surface. Approximately one-third of Area A was excavated during the project.

The middens surround this Middle Archaic community. Deposition appears to be continuous, suggesting that the occupation was relatively uninterrupted.

Extraction tasks that have been identified for the Middle Archaic component include hunting (projectile points, atlatl [spearthrower] components, faunal remains), fishing (fishhooks, fishhook production residue, faunal remains), fowling (faunal remains), procurement of lumber (axes), nut procurement and processing (pitted stones, grinding stones, nutshell), butchering (heavy-duty scrapers, cutmarks on bone), and hide processing (scrapers, bone awls). Maintenance tasks include the manufacture of flaked stone tools (unfinished bifaces, debitage, hammerstones), ground stone tools (unfinished tools), and bone and antler tools (grooved abraders, antlers with scoring marks, production residue), and the recycling of broken tools (scrapers made from broken projectile points). One socially related task can be accounted for in the data, disposal of the dead (burials).
Richard Jeffries and Mark Lynch
(1985)

Excavations at the Black Earth site.

The middens contain much more sand than the surrounding natural soils, suggesting that locally available sandstone may have been brought to the site for various uses. The decomposition of this rock would explain the higher levels of sand in the midden soils. The concentration of ash, excrement, and other organic matter in the sediments changed the chemistry of the soil, resulting in more alkaline conditions favorable for the preservation of bone and other materials.

The preserved plant and animal remains document the diet of the inhabitants. Almost 57,000 pieces of animal bone were excavated, representing some seventy-seven species of mammals, reptiles, birds, and fish. Turtles from the nearby swamp and wetlands are among the most common remains. The bowfin, favoring swampy habitats, is the most common fish among the midden remains. White-tailed deer and turkey are the most important land animals. Raccoon, opossum, elk, rabbit, beaver, and other species also were included in the game larder, but deer must have been the staple. Deer were hunted throughout the year at Black Earth, but more animals were killed in the fall and winter months. Some species were killed for nonfood products such as fur, feathers, or shell.

Hickory nut shells are very common in the middens; acorn shells are also found throughout the occupation area, along with the remains of hazelnuts and walnuts. Available in the fall, these nuts could easily be stored and used through the winter for food. Seeds from hackberry, wild grape, persimmon, bedstraw, and wild bean were also recovered. These plants ripen and are harvested in late summer and fall.

Discarded stone artifacts in the middens include a number of hafted tools — projectile points, drills, and end scrapers. Scraping tools were often made from broken arrowheads, recycled for processing animal hides. Ground stone tools are also common, ranging from grooved axes to grinding slabs, from counterweights for spearthrowers to hammerstones. Bone and antler tools are numerous and include awls, pins, needles, fishhooks, and other

An artist's interpretation of Middle Archaic life at the Black Earth site.

items. Almost one-third of these were made from the antler and bone of white-tailed deer. Turtle shell was used for bowls, cups, and dance rattles. A number of bone pins were found that may have been used as part of clothing or for hair arrangement. These pins are decorated with incised lines in a geometric design. Beads and pendants of shell, antler, and bone were also found.

In addition to the settlement remains, a cemetery was found at the Black Earth site. At least 154 burials from the Middle Archaic have been found in excavated areas. The investigators estimate a total of more than 500 graves for the entire site. Infants accounted for 21% of the burials. Males slightly outnumbered females in the cemetery and had a shorter lifespan. Male life expectancy was only 32 years; for females, 38 years. Adult males averaged 1.7 m (5′6″) in height, while females were 1.6 m (5′2″) tall.

Individuals were buried in shallow pits, and occasionally a cap of clay was used to seal the grave. About half the burials were found in an extended position, and the other half were flexed (curled up). Children and young adults normally were fully laid out in the graves, while older adults were placed in the grave in a flexed position. Four individuals were buried in unusual positions, including one man seated upright and bent over.

Grave goods provide an important sample of the tools and ornamental items of the living population. Everyday objects were generally discarded when they were broken or no longer useful. Materials placed in graves, however, were likely the property of the deceased or placed with the dead as a kind of offering; these objects are generally still intact when discovered at a burial site. (See "Grave Goods," Chapter Six, p. 266.)

Only about 25% of the individuals were buried with objects in their grave. Grave goods were more commonly given to individuals buried in an extended position. Males were buried with a wider array of goods than females or children. Males were generally buried with equipment to obtain food or other resources, while females were buried with tools to

Burial 86 at the Black Earth site, with artifacts at the left shoulder and between the legs.

process or prepare these raw materials. Women were buried with scrapers, bone awls, and needles. Only males were buried with ornamental objects such as bone pins and decorated bones, along with projectile points, worked stone drills and axes, and small animal bones. A "medicine bundle" was placed near the head of a 43-year-old male. This cluster contained forty-five objects including eagle talons, part of a bear paw, a miniature axe, pieces of slate, red ochre, and a dog's tooth. One perforated disk of marine shell, probably from the Atlantic Ocean or the Gulf of Mexico, was found around the neck of a buried infant. Copper from the Great Lakes area was found with an adult male at Carrier Mills. A copper wedge had been placed at the top of the neck of the skeleton. Perhaps this wedge was a substitute for the missing skull of this particular individual.

Table 4.1 Grave Goods Buried with Individuals at the Black Earth Site

Function	Adult Male	Adult Female	Child
Utilitarian	Mussel shell Bone awl Worked antler Unworked deer bone Projectile point Flint core Drill Scraper Utilized flake Axe fragment	Mussel shell Bone awl Worked antler Unworked deer bone Bone needle Hafted scraper Flint biface	Mussel shell Utilized flake Ground stone
Ornamental	Shell pendant Bone pin Shell bead Antler bead Pendant	Shell pendant	Shell pendant Shell bead Mussel shell bead Circular shell disc
Ceremonial	Decorated bone Animal bone (not deer) Elk antler cup Red ochre Fossil Crystal Worked shale Worked stone Hematite Water-worn pebble Banded slate Miniature grooved axe	Worked turtle shell Animal bone (bird) Red ochre	Turtle shell cup Red ochre Water-worn pebble Crystal

Burial 102 at the Black Earth site, with a cache of artifacts near the right shoulder.

THE HUMAN SKELETON

A storehouse of information

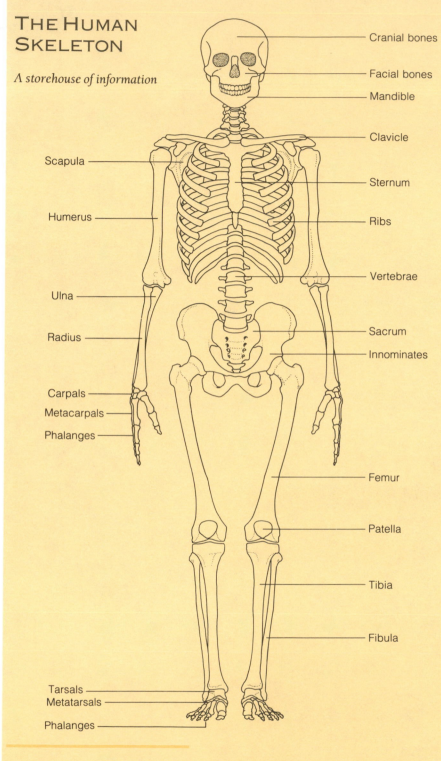

- Cranial bones
- Facial bones
- Mandible
- Clavicle
- Scapula
- Sternum
- Humerus
- Ribs
- Vertebrae
- Ulna
- Radius
- Sacrum
- Innominates
- Carpals
- Metacarpals
- Phalanges
- Femur
- Patella
- Tibia
- Fibula
- Tarsals
- Metatarsals
- Phalanges

The major bones of the human skeleton.

Since the time of the Neanderthals, the human species has buried its dead. As a result, intact human skeletons are sometimes preserved in single graves or cemeteries. Archaeologists and physical anthropologists spend hours carefully uncovering and removing these skeletal remains from the ground. Bones and teeth are taken to the laboratory, where a surprising amount of information can be obtained from the observation and measurement of various features.

The human skeleton is much more than a structural framework for supporting the body. Bone tissue contains a wide variety of information about the individual to whom it belongs. The length and thickness of bone, for example, provide an indication of an individual's size and strength. Evidence of disease or illness is also embedded in bone. It is often possible to determine age at death, cause of death, sex, a history of disease or accident, and nutritional status from the analysis of prehistoric human bone. Diet, too, may be reflected in the chemical composition of bone. (See "Bone Chemistry and Prehistoric Subsistence," p. 182.) Stature can be estimated from measurements of the long bones of the arm or leg. A formula is used to predict a person's living height from the length of these bones. The sex of a skeleton is indicated by several features. Adult males are generally taller than females, but in most cases size alone is insufficient to make this distinction. Several features of the pelvis are most important for determining the sex of skeletal remains. The female pelvis is wider than the male and slightly different in shape.

Consideration of a series of burials from a single cemetery can provide useful information about the entire population, including demography, life expectancy, and genetic inheritance. Several indicators are used to estimate age at death, one of the most important being teeth. The age of children and adolescents is relatively simple to determine from teeth. In many mammals, deciduous teeth of the young are replaced by permanent teeth, and the eruption pattern of permanent teeth is well known. For example, most 6-year-

Table 4.2 Estimating Stature from Femur Length

Femur Length, mm	Stature	
	cm	in.
452	169	66
456	170	66
460	171	67
464	172	67
468	173	68

Adapted from Jurmain, R., H. Nelson, and W. A. Turnbaugh. 1987. *Understanding physical anthropology and archaeology,* 4th ed. St. Paul, MN: West.

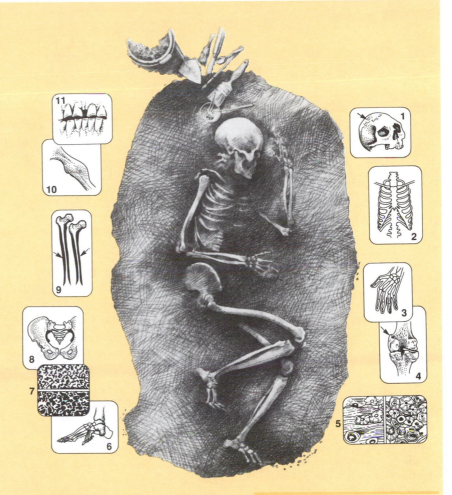

olds are missing their two front teeth; we speak of a 12-year molar.

The size and condition of the bones of the skeleton can also be used to estimate age at death. Body size, as indicated by the length of long bones, is one clue. However, the joint ends of long bones (**epiphyses**) provide even more reliable information. During childhood and early adolescence, as the skeleton grows and hardens, the ends of long bones are separate from the shaft to facilitate growth. At puberty and throughout adolescence the epiphyses harden and unite with the shaft to become a single bone, terminating growth. The age of epiphyses union varies for different bones, and this information can be used to determine the age of death. By the early twenties, the development of teeth and bones is largely complete. Other, less-precise indicators must be used to estimate the age of death from the skeletal material of older individuals. Skeletal features used for adult ages include the pelvis and skull and degenerative changes in bone tissue.

Stress during one's lifetime is also revealed in the skeleton. Malnourishment in childhood causes the disruption of bone growth, which shows up in the skeleton as a series of distinct features, known as Harris lines, in the ends of long bones. Tooth enamel also reflects childhood stress and malnourishment in an irregular series of lines, a condition known as dental enamel hypoplasia. Various diseases and other health problems also are reflected in bone. Arthritis is one of the most common pathological conditions in the bones of adult individuals, resulting in an accumulation of bone tissue around the affected area. Syphilis, tuberculosis, and other infectious diseases may result in bone loss and pitting or deformation of the skull and other bone surfaces.

The skeleton as a storehouse of information. (1) Lesions on the skull suggest scalping at the time of death. (2) Flattened ribs and fused breastbone result from corsets of the eighteenth century. (3) Badly twisted and eroded joints are evidence of arthritis. (4) Bone spurs appear on the knees of riders who were too long in the saddle. (5) Bone cells, or osteons, are denser in middle age (right), than in adolescence (left). (6) Shortened and deformed foot bones document the practice of foot binding in the China of previous centuries. (7) Osteoporosis, a loss of bone density, is more common in the elderly (bottom), than the young (top). (8) The female pelvis is wider than that of the male, for giving birth. (9) More robust femurs are evidence of a diet higher in meat; a thinner cortex suggests a protein-deficient diet. (10) Bumps and irregularities in bone show improperly healed fractures and injuries. (11) Indentations and grooves in the teeth are found among fishermen and wool spinners, who used their teeth for cutting thread.

GATECLIFF SHELTER

*Cave deposits from the Archaic of Nevada
and the Desert*

The Great Basin of North America covers large parts of Nevada, Utah, California, Oregon, and Idaho. This region lies west of the Rocky Mountains and east of the rain shadow of the Pacific Coast ranges, such as the Sierra in California. The Great Basin is, in fact, a whole series of dry, intermontane valleys and basins at relatively high elevation. The area today is essentially semiarid desert with scrub vegetation. Water is available primarily at springs that have been the focus of human settlement for thousands of years. At the end of the Pleistocene and during the early Holocene, however, many of the low areas of the Great Basin were filled with freshwater lakes providing a fairly rich aquatic habitat.

The Monitor Valley in central Nevada is a fairly typical high, intermontane basin. It is here that the site of Gatecliff was found at an elevation of 2300 m (more than 7500 ft). Gatecliff Shelter is one of those archaeological discoveries that offers much more than expected. In 1970, David Hurst Thomas, of the American Museum of Natural History, in New York, was looking for a few good caves that might contain a deep stratigraphic sequence for the area. A local mining engineer told him about a place called Gatecliff where he had seen prehistoric paintings.

Gatecliff Shelter is a large opening at the foot of a steep rocky slope. The ceiling of the shelter is heavily blackened from centuries of smoke, and the walls have been painted with small figures and other designs in various colors. A large **sondage,** or test excavation, into the cave revealed that it indeed contained a very deep, long sequence of human occupation, covering most of the Archaic in this area. Thomas then began a series of annual excavations at the cave that lasted seven seasons and involved over 200 people, 5000 person-days in total. These excavations continued from the top of the ground surface at Gatecliff to a depth of more than 10 m (32 ft), one of the deepest stratigraphies in North America. More than 600 cu m (800 cubic yards, equivalent to several very large rooms) of earth were removed in the excavations.

The deposits at Gatecliff are like a cake with layers or a book with pages. The archaeologists peel back the horizontal layers, or pages, to read the human activities that left the archaeological remains. The layers in the cave are very well defined; sixteen individual cultural horizons can be discerned in the more than fifty layers in the cave. Sterile deposits of silt, up to 0.6 m (2 ft) thick, often buried the abandoned human occupation levels in the cave. The cave was inundated by flash floods. Occasionally alluvial materials, carried by the water, covered the original cave floor and created a new one. This process was repeated a number of times, resulting in the gradual accumulation of deep sediments.

Gatecliff Shelter contains an extensive record of past human activities. More than forty radiocarbon dates indicate that the lowest layers are at least 9000 years old, and the upper part of the deposit contains remains from A.D. 1300. A layer of volcanic ash near the bottom of the deposits is known to have come from the eruption of Mt. Mazama, 6900 years ago.

The earliest evidence for human occupation in the shelter dates to 5500 years

Removal of the sediments from the bottom layers of Gatecliff Shelter by bucket brigade.

An artist's reconstruction of Gatecliff Shelter from the inside, after seven years of excavations. The total depth of the excavations was 12 m, the equivalent of a four-story basement.

Excavations at the very bottom level of Gatecliff Shelter. Part of the stratigraphy shown here is also depicted in the drawing of the section on the next page.

ago, shortly after a piñon pine and juniper woodland began to dominate the Monitor Valley, replacing the previous sagebrush steppe in the area. Most of the archaeological evidence indicates brief, episodic occupations in the shelter, largely associated with male-oriented activities such as hunting and the manufacture and repair of equipment. Careful sifting of the sediments resulted in the recovery of more than 51,000 animal bones. More than 90% of the large mammal bones at the site come from bighorn mountain sheep, suggesting that this animal may have been the major target of such high-altitude hunting. One of the upper layers, Horizon 2, dating to about A.D. 1300, contained the remains of at least twenty-four bighorn sheep that had been killed elsewhere and dragged to the shelter to be butchered.

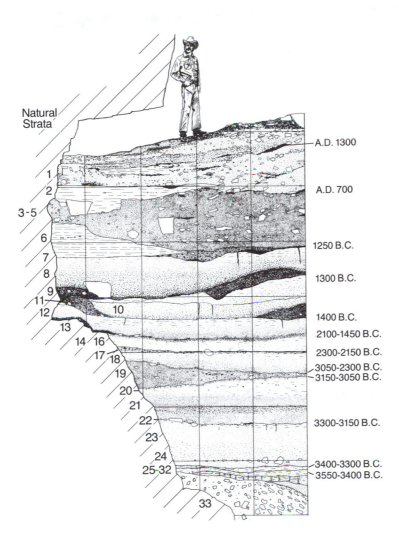

Natural Strata

1
2
3-5
6
7
8
9
11
12
10
13
14 16
17 18
19
20
21
22
23
24
25-32
33

A.D. 1300
A.D. 700
1250 B.C.
1300 B.C.
1400 B.C.
2100-1450 B.C.
2300-2150 B.C.
3050-2300 B.C.
3150-3050 B.C.
3300-3150 B.C.
3400-3300 B.C.
3550-3400 B.C.

A composite drawing of the stratigraphic section at Gatecliff Shelter, with layer designations at left and chronology at right. Each grid unit is 1 sq m. The human figure is shown to scale.

Most of the best cuts of meat — ribs, rump, shoulders, and neck — were taken away, probably to the residential community elsewhere in the valley. The bones of rabbit and hare were numerous.

Because of the normally very dry conditions in the desert, more fragile organic remains are preserved at the site as well, including rope, string, and basketry. Plant remains are rather limited, however, and only a few food species are represented, particularly piñon and *Chenopodium*. Piñon nuts can be harvested in the fall from the piñon pine; *chenopodium* is a kind of grass with small, nutritious seeds that ripen in the late summer.

The area near the back of the cave generally contained smaller objects, discarded and dropped directly after use. Larger pieces of stone, bone, and other material were tossed toward the front of the shelter. This process was simple and basic, probably intended to keep the living floor in the back relatively smooth and level. More than thirty fireplaces were observed in the cultural levels, almost always built about 4 m (14 ft) from the back wall of the shelter. The deposits contained more than 400 projectile points, many made from the locally available dark green stone. Only a few points were made from obsidian, which must have come from somewhere else.

Gatecliff was apparently used only rarely as a residence for entire groups; there is very limited evidence of female activities. Toward the end of the Archaic occupation in the shelter, however, there is a greater emphasis on grinding stones for the preparation of plant foods, along with more than 400 engraved limestone slabs. Thomas suggests that these slabs may have been left when women were in the area collecting seeds.

NITTANO

Coastal hunter-gatherers of Jomon Japan

The Early Postglacial period in Japan represents a long and well-documented sequence of environmental change and cultural development. Dating to between 10,000 and 300 B.C., this period is referred to as the **Jomon**. Over 30,000 Jomon sites have been discovered, concentrated in the eastern part of the country. Subsistence was based primarily on wild resources, although some cultivated plants were included in the diet. The importance of hunting is indicated by the abundance of arrowheads at many Jomon sites. Although the hunting near inland sites focused primarily on deer and boar, hunting of large game such as bear and antelope, as well as monkey, hare, marten, and other small mammals, also was done.

Marine foods and coastal settlements predominated in eastern Japan, particularly after 4000 B.C. Fishing was equally important at sites on the rivers, estuaries, and the ocean. Elaborate fishing gear, and even whole communities specializing in fishing, are evidenced in the archaeological record. Salmon and other freshwater fish were caught in the rivers. Bones from such deepwater species as tuna and shark were also found among the archaeological deposits. Fishing equipment included net floats of bark and pumice, net weights, fishhooks, harpoons, and dugout canoes. Over 30 species of shellfish come from the middens of this period.

The site of Nittano (nit'a-no), near the modern city of Tokyo, is fairly typical of Late Jomon fishing communities along the coast. This extensive shell midden, at the head of a narrow, tidal inlet from the Pacific Ocean, was occupied during the

Stone artifacts from Jomon Japan. Top row: a drill, a stemmed stone knife, and a scraper. The stems are for the attachment of a haft or handle. Bottom row: two projectile points and a small polished stone axe. The example in the upper-right corner is 6 cm long.

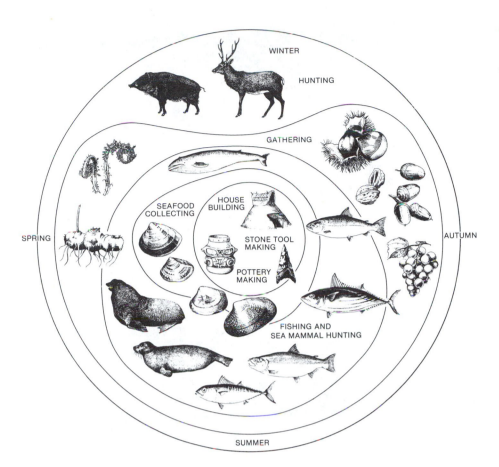

WINTER
HUNTING
GATHERING
SEAFOOD COLLECTING
HOUSE BUILDING
STONE TOOL MAKING
POTTERY MAKING
SPRING
AUTUMN
FISHING AND SEA MAMMAL HUNTING
SUMMER

Early and Middle Jomon, approximately 4000 to 3000 B.C. Excavations exposed ten layers of deposits, with a dense concentration of shells, particularly in the middle layers. Twenty-three species of mollusks and thirteen genera of fish were identified, the majority of which live in the brackish waters of tidal inlets and bays. The most common species of mollusk in the deposits was *Corbicula japonica,* an inhabitant of freshwater streams and estuaries. The mollusks and fish were apparently collected and caught in and near the brackish waters of the estuary directly in front of the site. The species found in highest numbers in the midden come from habitats closest to the site.

Analysis of the mollusk shells from Nittano indicates that the site was occupied year-round. Mollusk shells from creatures such as oysters and limpets grow in a series of increments, added to the shell as *daily* growth rings of calcium carbonate. Under a microscope, these rings can be counted and compared to the month of birth for the species. Thus both the age of the mollusk and the time or year

it died can be determined. Most of the mollusks at Nittano were harvested in the spring and autumn, with a few in summer and almost none in winter. Evidence from several migratory fish species, which spend the summer months in estuaries and the colder months at sea, indicates that most of the fish were caught in the spring, summer, and autumn.

Plant foods were important in the Jomon diet, and more than 180 species have been identified from various settlements. These included such fleshy fruits as grapes, blackberries, and elderberries, and aquatic plants with edible seeds and tubers. Nuts played a major role in subsistence with the remains of walnuts, chestnuts, acorns, and buckeyes found at many sites. The preparation of nuts, seeds, and roots is indicated by the presence of mortars, pestles, milling stones, and other equipment. Plant utilization and even cultivation was much more common in western Japan. In the later Jomon, root crops, such as taro, yams, and arrowroot, may have been under cultivation in this area, along with such cereals as buck-

A large pottery container from the Middle Jomon period. This vessel stands 39 cm high.

wheat and barley. Chipped stone hoes were common at sites from this time. Rice, however, was apparently not cultivated in significant quantities until the end of the Jomon period. Other stone tools included projectile points, scrapers, and drills.

A wide range of other materials, including wood, bone, and antler, were used for various tools and other objects; these items are often heavily decorated with carved designs. Jade was exchanged over long distances to be manufactured into pendants and other jewelry. Pottery containers were invented very early in Japan, probably before the end of the Pleistocene. These fired clay vessels are well represented at Jomon sites, and their form becomes increasingly elaborate through time. Distinct regional varieties can be identified. The word *jomon* means **cord-marking**, referring to the kind of decoration applied to unfired early Jomon pottery. Cord-wrapped sticks were pressed into the west clay to create a design.

Jomon villages were usually small and occupied for a long time, several hundred years or more in some cases. Settlements along the coastline are associated with large accumulations of shells, or **shell middens**. Inland sites are found on higher level ground. The inland settlements generally contained four to eight **pithouses**, although up to fifty structures are known from a single site. These pithouses were substantial, circular structures built from large support posts, containing elaborate, stone-lined hearths. Villages were often arranged in a horseshoe shape and may have been divided into two groups of residential units, one on either side of the horseshoe. Communal structures for various purposes were found around the periphery of the village. Burials occurred individually near houses or in the communal structures. The central open area contained few artifacts, but occasionally standing stones were erected there. In one instance these large standing stones, 1.5 m (5 ft) high, were transported from a quarry some 120 km (80 mi) away.

A ditch, postholes, and hearth from a house construction at a Jomon site. The outer ditch is 6 m in diameter. The roof was likely conical in shape, constructed of timber and thatched with reeds.

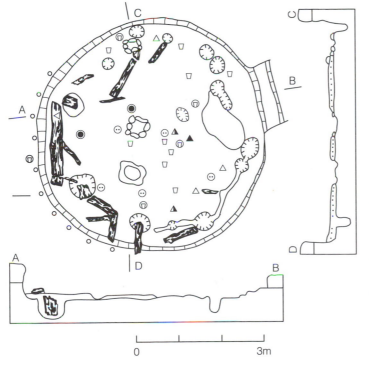

▽ Pot

◉ Buried pot

⊕ Milling stone

⊙ Mortar

▲ Polished stone axe

△ Flaked stone axe

▲ Stone projectile point

0   3m

The plan and sections of a Middle Jomon circular house from central Honshu, Japan.

ELANDS BAY CAVE

Late Stone Age hunter-gatherers in southern Africa

Much of what we know about the prehistory of southern Africa has been discovered only in the last twenty years. In that period, John Parkington, of the Department of Archaeology at the University of Capetown in South Africa, has been studying the artifacts and settlements of Holocene groups in western South Africa. He says:

> We wish to know how the prehistoric populations used the area and its resources, what the relationship was between hunters and herders, what the exploitation strategies were, what precise resources were utilized and how, and what effects the resource pattern had on group size, site location, and seasonal mobility. Archaeology with an ecological viewpoint is the study of the interrelationships of technology, subsistence, and environment.
>
> (Parkington, 1984, p. 92)

An important question facing Parkington (and many archaeologists) is how far these prehistoric hunter-gatherers moved in an annual cycle of resource use. Was their movement between the coast and inland in an east-west direction? Did groups move from north to south within environment zones? Or were these groups relatively sedentary and move only small distances when necessary?

These are difficult questions to answer. One problem is the relationship between the archaeological remains, primarily stone tools and animal bones, and the actual behavior of the prehistoric hunter-gatherers. Connections between static, material objects and dynamic, human activities are needed, and Parkington has used several assumptions to make such connections. He says:

> Environments effectively comprise sets of resources, each with a specific distribution pattern. In order to extract and manipulate chosen resources, prehistoric groups needed to engage in specific activities, some of which involved the use of stone tools. Thus the accumulation of stone tools at a site reflects, albeit in a complex way, the range of activities pursued there. Further, differences between the composition of assemblages reflect the relative importance of tool related activities at those sites.
>
> (1984, p. 96)

A review of Parkington's investigations provides some information on the nature of archaeological research.

This research project focused on an area of some 22,500 sq km (8700 sq mi, about the size of the state of Vermont), between the western coast of the cape of southern Africa and interior mountain plateaus. Four major environmental zones running in north–south bands can be distinguished in the region. To the west, the Atlantic Ocean plays a major role in the climate and environment of the area. Many species of animals are available for food from the sea and the beach, including fish, seals, lobsters, mollusks, and sea birds. Rocky points near the mouths of rivers and estuaries are particularly good locations for obtaining shellfish and other marine species. The Strandveld is a low, sandy band up to 30 km (20 mi) inland, between the beach and the mountains. Vegetation in this zone produces fruit, berries, and roots in season. Animal spe-

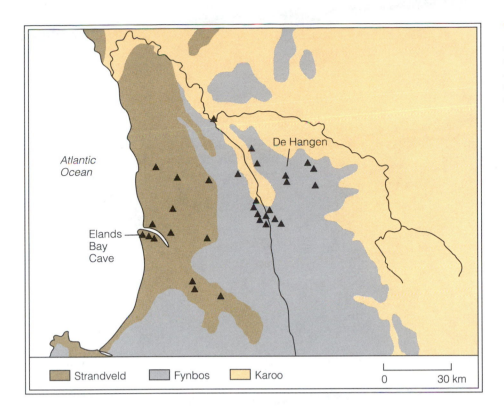

Strandveld Fynbos Karoo

0   30 km

cies in the area include tortoise, hare, small antelope, and ostrich. Other, larger species of game, such as the eland (a kind of antelope), have disappeared since European contact. The Fynbos band covers the sandstone mountains; shrubs predominate, but trees are found along rivers and at higher elevations over 1000 m (3300 ft). Plants and animals are abundant in this zone; fish can be caught in the rivers. The Karoo is a dry lowland between higher elevations, drained by the Doorn River. This area is a rich pasture for winter grazing by many species of herbivores. These same species may have moved west into the Fynbos in the summer when the Karoo veld is burned brown by the sun. The human hunters may have followed the herds in a similar pattern of regular movement or **transhumance**.

Seasonal changes in resources are important for hunter-gatherers who depend on wild plants and animals. Most of the edible species of fruits and berries in the research area ripen in the late spring and summer and are rare in the winter months. Diaries and other records from early European explorers in southern Africa report that the diet of the hunter-gatherers in the inland was dominated by

roots that the women collected daily. Roots and tubers reach maximum size in the later summer and grow smaller during winter.

Animal foods are generally available throughout the year, with some exceptions. Young seals are easily captured in the summer at breeding colonies on the beaches after their birth, or during the winter when they come out of the water. Mollusks are better to eat during the winter months. Certain species of saltwater fish are available only seasonally on the coast. Water is also a concern in southern Africa. Smaller streams and freshwater springs are common in the mountains, but surface water is rare in the Strandveld and the Karoo. Precipitation is much higher in the mountains. Several rivers run through the project area to the sea and do provide freshwater year-round.

Parkington has suggested that the archaeological remains of hunter-gatherers found throughout this area were produced by the same or related groups of people moving seasonally in an annual cycle, from the coast to inland areas and back, to take advantage of resources when they were available. He argues that the Fynbos is best suited to summer resi-

Elands Bay Cave, on the west coast of South Africa.

dence, while both the Karoo and coast provide better sources of food in the winter. Shellfish and marine species substitute for the absence of plant foods during the cooler months of the year.

The archaeological remains for evaluating this hypothesis come from excavations at two sites: Elands Bay Cave on the coast and De Hangen in the inland mountains. Elands Bay Cave is located on the mouth of the Vlie River at the Atlantic Ocean. The archaeological deposits consist largely of a shell midden filled with artifacts, bones, and plant remains. All the evidence suggests that the inhabitants here were on the coast for a brief time in the winter, exploiting a variety of marine and terrestrial animals. The shells of mussels and limpets are the most common food remains in the midden. Near the cave are a series of intertidal, rocky flats where mollusks are still very abundant today. Shells suggest that this site was occupied repeatedly in the winter, because mussels can be toxic if eaten in the summer. A variety of both marine and terrestrial species are also represented in the midden. Marine fish, seals, and birds outnumber the terrestrial animals by ten to one. The presence of commercial lobster fisheries at the river mouth today points to the abundance of this food. Seal bones from Elands Bay Cave were very similar in size and come from yearling seals. These animals tire easily during their first period at sea, and wash up or haul out on the beaches during the late winter. Hare bones are also present at Elands Bay Cave, though not in abundance; most of the individuals are fully grown, and newborns are rare. Although grasses used for bedding, as well as seaweed and twigs, are all preserved in the midden, there is very little evidence for the utilization of plant foods.

De Hangen is located in the Fynbos, some 60 km (40 mi) inland from the coast. Excavations at the site have produced a variety of plant and animal remains. Long grasses were gathered during the late spring and summer for bedding in the caves. Edible plant foods were very common, including seeds, fruits, tubers, and roots. These plant foods are more readily available in the summer months. The animal bones came primarily from tortoise, hare, and small antelope. Most of the hares were juveniles when they were killed during the summer. Bones from freshwater fish and several marine shells were also found. Other connections with the coast are also in evidence. Stone tools

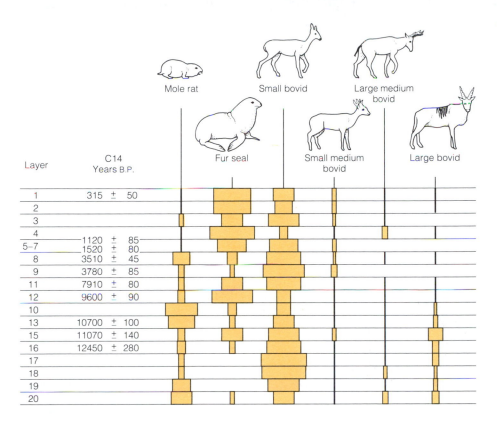

Mole rat Small bovid Large medium bovid

Fur seal Small medium bovid Large bovid

Layer	C14 Years B.P.
1	315 ± 50
2	
3	
4	
5–7	1120 ± 85 / 1520 ± 80
8	3510 ± 45
9	3780 ± 85
11	7910 ± 80
12	9600 ± 90
10	
13	10700 ± 100
15	11070 ± 140
16	12450 ± 280
17	
18	
19	
20	

Changes in the number of animals by species over time at Elands Bay Cave. The layer numbers and radiocarbon dates are shown on the left side. Six species are shown: mole rat, fur seal, and four sizes of bovids (antelopes). Of particular note is the increasing importance of fur seals and the trend toward smaller bovids in the upper layers.

were made from a quartzite material available only from sources in the Strandveld. Rock paintings in the mountains south of De Hangen include sailing ships, which must have been visible from the coast.

Stone tools provide additional information about the pattern of residence. There are major differences in the lithic assemblages between the coastal and inland mountain areas. **Adzes**, associated with woodworking, comprise more than half the tools at sites in the mountains and only about 5% of the assemblages on the coast. Adzes were probably used to make sticks for digging roots and tubers in the Fynbos area. Pieces with one blunted edge are rare in the mountains but more common in the Strandveld. These small stone artifacts were likely used to provide sharp tips and barbs for arrows, and thus are found more often where hunting was the primary source of food.

The archaeological remains suggest a pattern of winter residence on the coast and summer residence in the mountains, supporting Parkington's hypothesis. This evidence also fits the pattern that might be expected given the seasonal availability of certain resources. However, the archaeological evidence does not *prove* this to be the case. Settlement could easily be moved

a few tens of meters as a few tens of kilometers. Winter sites inland, or summer sites along the coast, simply may not yet have been discovered.

Bone chemistry, discussed later in this chapter, provides contradictory information. (See "Bone Chemistry and Prehistoric Subsistence," p. 182.) If the same individuals were moving seasonally from inland to coast, eating seafood for at least part of the year, a marine diet should be represented in the carbon isotope content of their bones. However, analysis of human skeletal material from inland burials has failed to reveal these expected isotope values, suggesting that visits to the coast were not part of a regular pattern.

Thus the questions posed originally in this research remain to be answered. Work to date has better defined the questions and pointed to new topics for study. Further investigation is necessary to define the dominant pattern of residence in this area. Another question regards the time depth of the settlement pattern. How far back in time does the system of residence continue? Is residential mobility between different environment zones characteristic of the entire Holocene? As usual in archaeology, good questions attract others.

STAR CARR

Preserved settlements of Postglacial hunter-gatherers in the bogs of northwestern Europe

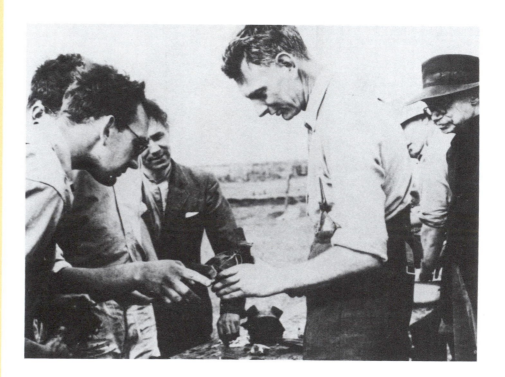

Star Carr, 1951, with the excavator Grahame Clark in the right center of the photo, holding one of the red deer antler headdresses. V. Gordon Childe stands behind Clark in the hat.

The Mesolithic site of Star Carr lies in northeast Yorkshire, England, some 8 km (5 mi) west of the present seaside resort of Scarborough. Excavations were carried out from 1949 to 1951 under the direction of Grahame Clark, of Cambridge University. The project has often been described as a classic example of a **multidisciplinary** study—one in which a number of different scientists participated, including zoologists, palynologists, geologists, and botanists, as well as archaeologists.

Star Carr is dated both by radiocarbon and pollen analysis to the early part of the Mesolithic, around 9500 years ago. The faunal assemblage is clearly of Holocene age, and pollen from the site is typi-

cal of plants in this area around 7500 B.C. The pollen evidence from the peat indicates that birch and pine were the predominant trees, prior to the establishment of a deciduous forest. The excavations exposed an area of almost 350 sq m (or 420 sq yd, the size of a basketball court) and recovered a vast array of archaeological materials. Preservation of organic materials in the peat was remarkable, and the remains include a wooden paddle, rolls of birch bark, stag antler masks, numerous barbed antler points, many animal bones, and a wide range of woodworking and boneworking tools. The remains from Star Carr also include approximately 17,000 flint artifacts, shale and amber beads, and

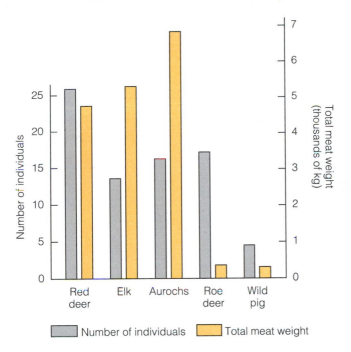

Number of individuals (left axis)

Total meat weight (thousands of kg) (right axis)

| | Number of individuals | Total meat weight |

The animals represented in the bones at Star Carr and the estimated weight of their meat. Note that although the bones of roe deer are the second most common, the meat from this animal provides only a small part of the diet. Aurochs contribute the largest portion of animal protein.

lumps of hematite and iron pyrite. A variety of animal species are represented. Bone remains document the importance of red deer, roe deer, elk, aurochs, and wild pig in the diet. Hazelnuts and water lily seeds at the site were likely used as food. No fishbones were found.

The settlement of Star Carr was located on the south shore of a narrow peninsula that extended into a small lake, marked today by peat deposits. Clark suggested that the site was occupied by three or four families during the winter months of the year:

> The site was evidently occupied by a small hunting band which supported itself during the winter by the culling of red deer stags, supplemented by hunting elk, aurochs, and other game, and which took advantage of a period of settled existence to replenish the equipment needed during the course of the year.
>
> (Clark 1972, p. 16)

Clark's interpretation has been questioned by others. Star Carr has been variously regarded as a specialized area for hide and antler working used over several seasons, as a hunting stand and butchering place used repeatedly for short episodes by a small group, or as only a small dump area for a much larger settlement on the adjacent peninsula. Clearly the same evidence provides for a number of conflicting interpretations, and it may be difficult to determine which correlates most closely to the actual archaeological data.

Two pieces of information are particularly relevant for interpretation of the site: the season of the occupation and the nature of the excavated deposits. The original evidence for seasonality was taken from the presence or absence of antler attached to the skulls of red deer, roe deer, and elk. For example, the antlers of red deer are fully grown and attached to the skull from October through March; they are shed in April and grow again during summer. The stage of development can be determined readily by examination. Roe deer and elk exhibit similar cycles in the growth and loss of their antlers.

The antler evidence from Star Carr, however, represents all seasons of the year. Clark's argument for a winter occupation was based largely on the abundance of red deer antler at the site and the assumption that red deer could have been hunted most readily in the winter. Reexamination of the antler, teeth, and other faunal remains has modified Clark's argument and suggests possible year-round residence at the site but with a clear emphasis on the *summer* months. Thus while members of the group may have been at Star Carr either permanently or intermit-

One of the red deer antler headdresses found at Star Carr.

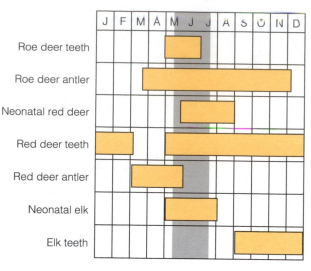

The evidence used to determine the season of occupation at Star Carr. The majority of the information suggests that the site was inhabited during the early summer.

tently during the year, it seems that there was more activity at the site in the warmer months.

The original situation of the excavations at Star Carr is also important. The peninsula on which Star Carr was located would have been a fine spot for a settlement. The artifacts and faunal remains found along the lakeshore attest to a substantial occupation. However, the actual area where people lived was probably on higher ground adjacent to the excavated area. The higher ground has not been explored in detail, part of it having been destroyed by construction, years before an archaeological awareness existed in the region. Most of the remains from Star Carr are large items originally discarded in the muddy waters at the edge of the lake. They were preserved by the waterlogged mud and accumulated peat deposits. Thus much of the excavated area was under water during the time of occupation, and therefore could not have been an actual living floor.

The abundance of materials from Star Carr is, however, evidence for a series of substantial occupations. The large number of animal species at the site supports this suggestion. The stone tools represent all the known types from this period of the Mesolithic, indicating that the site was a base camp where a variety of activities took place. The wide range of bone and antler artifacts is remarkable and include barbed points, bone chisels, and antler mattocks (digging tools).

Intriguing questions about the site remain. Why, for example, are there so many headdresses of stag antler? Twenty-four of these items were found. Possible uses may have been as costumes for ritual activity or for hunting camouflage. Perhaps they were simply stored in the water for future use and never retrieved. They are one of the mysteries of the site.

Star Carr remains a classic study in archaeology. The fact that several different interpretations exist is a testimony to the outstanding quality of the research and the details that have been published. Without such exemplary work in the first place, a new consideration would not be possible.

Although the basic topography of the Earth has not changed significantly since the end of the Pleistocene, the environment itself has undergone dramatic modifications in vegetation, fauna, and sea level. A marked shift in climate at the end of the Pleistocene was largely responsible for such environmental changes. Seasonal differences caused by variation in solar radiation resulted in significant changes in surface temperatures and precipitation. Dramatic deviations from modern conditions are clear. Europe was as much as 6–8°C (20°F) colder during the ice ages some 18,000 years ago, and warmer than at present by 1–2°C (2–5°F) around 7000 years ago during the Early Postglacial.

One of the results of the increasing temperatures at the close of the Pleistocene was the melting of the continental ice sheets and the consequent rise in the oceans. During the maximum cold period of the last glaciation at around 18,000 years ago, the sea was as much as 130 m (500 ft) below its present level. A gradual rise in the level of the oceans began after 16,000 years ago and continued into the Postglacial. The rate of increase was variable, but a rise of as much as one meter per century occurred during the period of maximum warming. The rising Postglacial seas did not reach present beaches until sometime after 5000 years ago.

The higher sea levels of the Postglacial transformed the outline of the continents. Australia separated from New Guinea and Tasmania. The peninsula of Indonesia broke up into islands. The Bering Land Bridge was submerged and filled by the Bering Strait. The East Coast of North America moved west by more than 100 km (60 mi) in some areas. The British Isles separated from the European continent, as the English Channel was flooded by rising seas.

The forest history of Europe records the complexity of vegetational development through the end of the Pleistocene and during the early Holocene. Many of the species that disappeared during glacial conditions in the north survived along the southern coasts of Western Eu-

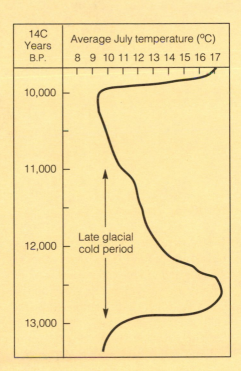

THE POSTGLACIAL ENVIRONMENT OF EUROPE

The conditions of the Present Interglacial

Average July temperatures for the end of the Pleistocene in northern Europe. The dramatic rise in temperature around 13,000 years ago was followed by a cooling spell until the end of the Pleistocene, 10,000 B.P.

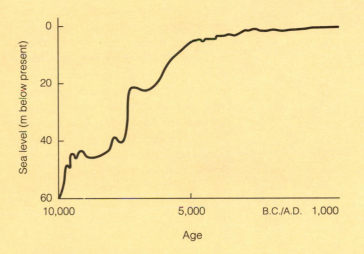

Change in sea level for the last 12,000 years. Holocene sea levels reached modern coastlines only in the last few thousand years.

rope. Late Pleistocene deciduous forests were restricted primarily to southwestern Europe; hazel, oak, and elm survived in western France and northern Spain. A range of species were found in Iberia and Italy during the later Pleistocene. Following the close of the Pleistocene, deciduous forest was found throughout most of western Europe, with the exception of small areas of Mediterranean forest in southern Italy, southern France, northeastern Spain, and the islands of the western Mediterranean.

MOUNT SANDEL

*The first settlement in Ireland,
during the Postglacial*

Ireland, a remote and distinctive outpost of western Europe, is an island of rocky uplands and steeply cut valleys, mantled with dense vegetation that grows almost year-round in a climate tempered by the Gulf Stream. Ireland has long been isolated from Britain. There is no evidence to indicate that a land bridge ever existed either between northern Ireland and Scotland or between southern Ireland and France. This insularity has resulted in an absence of many common European mammals. A distinctly restricted fauna characterizes Irish archaeological sites from the early Postglacial. Although some late Pleistocene fauna—reindeer and giant Irish deer—may have persisted into the Holocene, there is no evidence for human exploitation of these animals. Species of certain economic importance during the Holocene included wild pig, Irish hare, pine marten, beaver, otter, and brown bear. On the coast, fish, birds, shellfish, and sea mammals were incorporated into the diet. Other species common on the continent of Europe at this time—wild cattle, elk, roe deer—did not appear in Ireland.

This insular character also lent a distinctive cast to the Irish Mesolithic that became more pronounced through time. Artifacts at the earliest sites already exhibited features distinct from those in neighboring Scotland, only a few kilometers away across the North Channel. By the end of the Mesolithic, many stone tools were uniquely Irish, indicating an absence of contact with the rest of Britain and the continent. For example, there were no flint arrowheads in the Later Mesolithic of Ireland, objects that were very common in England and on the continent during that period.

Recent investigations have fleshed out a previously vague outline of Irish prehistory. Paleolithic hunters apparently never occupied the island. Radiocarbon evidence for the earliest humans in Ireland dates to 7000 B.C. Two divisions of the Mesolithic can be recognized. The Early Mesolithic, characterized by narrow blades, is known from only a few sites. These materials continued in use for approximately 1000 years, until approximately 6000 B.C. The Later Mesolithic runs from 6000 B.C. to the introduction of agriculture, about 3500 B.C.

The name Mount Sandel was given to an Iron Age fort atop a 30-m (100-ft) bluff on the River Bann, County Antrim, in Northern Ireland. Amateur archaeologists have collected Mesolithic artifacts from the fields around the fort for a century, demonstrating the potential for early remains. The area was excavated in the 1970s, prior to housing construction, by Peter Woodman, of the University of Cork, to determine what, if any, Mesolithic remains could be salvaged. What started as a minor rescue operation quickly grew into a major project, as the excavations required some forty weeks of work over five seasons, opening an area of more than 1000 sq m (1200 sq yd).

These investigations provided the earliest evidence for human settlement in Ireland, dating to 7000 B.C. Excavations at the site on the bluff exposed a series of large, circular structures, roughly 6 m in diameter (or 20 ft, the size of a large

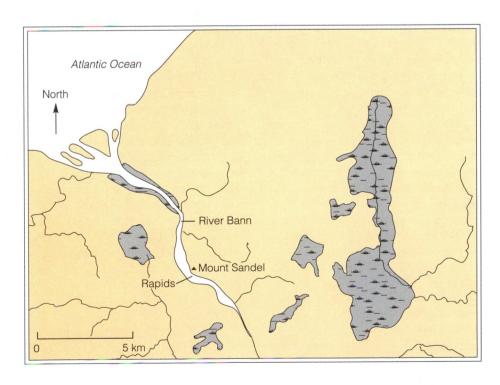

The Bann Valley and the location of Mount Sandel. The River Bann at Mount Sandel was a series of narrow rapids where fish were easily caught by the inhabitants of the site. The shaded areas indicate wetlands and small lakes.

Excavations at Mount Sandel, revealing the post holes, pits, and hearths associated with a large circular structure, 6 m in diameter.

room), with a central fireplace and interior pits. The investigations showed that at least four huts had been rebuilt successively on the same spot. The huts were marked by peripheral rows of post holes, many more than 20 cm (8 in.) deep, set at an angle in the ground. A circle of saplings or branches had been shoved into the ground and then brought together in the center to form this structure. The ground was cleared to the subsoil in the interior of the hut, and sod may have been used to cover the outside of the structure. Estimates by Woodman suggest that eight to twelve people may have inhabited this hut.

Stone artifacts in the huts included a substantial amount of waste material, along with worn or broken and discarded arrow tips and drills. Around the edges of the huts, hollow axes and scraping tools were discarded. A number of flint blades with traces of red ochre were also found here; their use is an enigma. Evidence for tool manufacture was also found outside the huts to the west. A concentration of waste and cores and an absence of finished tools characterized this area.

Fireplaces in the huts were used for cooking and heating. Their contents included stone artifacts, burned animal bones, and large quantities of carbonized hazelnut shells. The seeds of water lily and wild apple were also recovered in excavations. The majority of identifiable bones from the site were those of wild boar; hare was present but rare. Bird and fish bones were common. Duck, pigeon, dove, goshawk, and grouse were taken by the Mesolithic hunters of Mount Sandel. Sea bass, eel, and especially salmon were well represented. Freshwater fish were not found in the bone assemblage.

The River Bann runs into the sea some 5 km (3 mi) north of the site. Today the tidal ebb and flow of the sea create

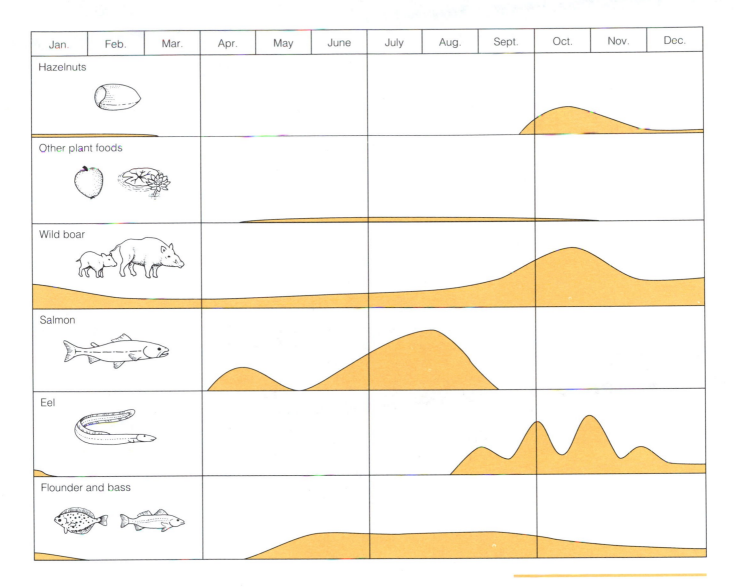

	Jan.	Feb.	Mar.	Apr.	May	June	July	Aug.	Sept.	Oct.	Nov.	Dec.
Hazelnuts												
Other plant foods												
Wild boar												
Salmon												
Eel												
Flounder and bass												

A graph of the seasonality of occupation at Mount Sandel. Evidence indicated that the site was likely inhabited year-round. The inhabitants could have concentrated on wild boar in the winter, salmon and sea fish in the spring and summer, and hazelnuts, eel, and pig in autumn.

an estuary below Mount Sandel, but this would not have been the case during the Mesolithic, when sea level was lower. The Bann would likely have been a series of rapids below Mount Sandel during the period of Mesolithic occupation, and the mouth of the estuary would have been a few more kilometers to the north.

The substantial nature of the residential structure, the numerous pits and rebuilding episodes, along with evidence from the plant remains and animal bones, all suggest that Mount Sandel was occupied year-round. Various foods would have been available throughout much of the year, enabling the occupants to remain at the site for most or all of the seasons. Salmon were present in the streams and rivers during the summer months; eels ran downstream in autumn when hazelnuts were ripe. Water lily seeds were best collected in September. Most of the pig bones came from young animals killed in the winter.

VEDBAEK

*Prehistoric communities
in Mesolithic Denmark*

Denmark, northern Germany, and southern Sweden were occupied only briefly during prehistoric time, essentially since the close of the Pleistocene and the retreat of the ice sheets from northern Europe. At that time, as temperatures rose, the tundra gave way to open woodlands of birch and pine, and eventually to a mixed forest of lime, oak, elm, and other deciduous species. These forests were occupied initially by herbivores such as the aurochs and moose (the European elk), followed soon after by wild pig, elk (the European red deer), roe deer, and many small mammals and birds. Inhabiting the streams and lakes were large numbers and varieties of fish. The inlets and islands of the seas around southern Scandinavia offered a propitious food source for the prehistoric people of this area, and were the locations of human settlement during the Later Mesolithic. Wild animals and plants from the land, sea, and air were the focus of their hunting and gathering activities. The inland forests were probably quite dense and supported little wildlife.

By 7000 years ago, there had been a dramatic shift in human social arrangements in this area from the first small, scattered groups of inland, tundra-dwelling reindeer hunters to concentrations of more sedentary societies along the coastlines. These groups expanded their resource base, eating fish, seals, porpoise, small whales, oysters, mussels, clams, and the like. Settlements became more permanent and the dead began to be buried in cemeteries.

An example of such a situation can be seen from an important archaeological area near the town of Vedbaek (vay-bek′)

near Copenhagen, Denmark. Following the retreat of the ice sheets, the Vedbaek Valley was filled with a freshwater system of lakes and streams. Warming trends continued, and the rising sea filled the mouth of the Vedbaek River sometime around 5500 B.C., creating a brackish inlet. The shallow waters around the shoreline and islands of the inlet were covered with stands of reeds and sea grass. Gradually the inlet filled up with deposits of reeds and leaves and other organic materials, becoming the layer of peat that it is today.

In 1975, a Mesolithic graveyard was discovered here during the construction of a new school. The cemetery is radiocarbon dated to approximately 4000 B.C. and contains the graves of at least twenty-two males and females of various ages. All the burials were fully extended, with one slightly curled up exception. Powdered ochre was used to adorn individuals in many of the graves. Racks of red deer antler were placed with elderly individuals; males were buried with flint knives; females often were interred with jewelry of shell and animal teeth. Incisor teeth from bear, aurochs, and the European elk were obtained by trade with or expedition to northern Sweden and used in such jewelry.

In another grave, a newborn was found buried on the wing of a swan next to his mother, whose head had been placed on a cushion of material such as an animal skin elaborately decorated with ornaments of snail shells and deer teeth. Similar materials were found around her waist, suggesting a skirt or costume of some kind. The cemetery also contained

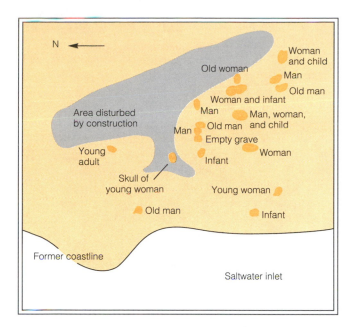

N

Old woman

Woman and child

Man

Old man

Woman and infant

Area disturbed by construction

Man

Man, woman, and child

Old man

Man

Empty grave

Young adult

Woman

Infant

Skull of young woman

Young woman

Old man

Infant

Former coastline

Saltwater inlet

The Mesolithic cemetery at Vedbaek, near the coastline of the former inlet. The disturbed area is the location of the construction activities that resulted in the discovery of the burials.

The grave of a young woman and infant at Vedbaek. Note the knife blade at the infant's waist and the deer teeth behind the woman's head. The deer teeth were part of the decoration on a hide or skin placed under her head (above). An artist's interpretation of the mother and child burial at Vedbaek (below).

dramatic evidence of conflict among the groups occupying northern Europe at this time. The simultaneous burial of three individuals in a single grave — an adult male with a bone point in his throat, an adult female, and a child — suggests both the violent death of all three and the existence of a nuclear family. (See page 149.)

Since the discovery of the cemetery, Vedbaek has been the focus of an intensive investigation. Over fifty archaeological sites have been located around the shore of the inlet. Some sixty species of fish, reptiles, birds, and mammals have been identified in the bone remains from these sites. These species come from every environment — the forest, streams, lakes, wetlands, the inlet, the sound, and the sea. Terrestrial fauna are dominated by red deer, roe deer, and wild pig. Marine foods, however, provided a major portion of the diet; fish and seal bones are very common at the sites.

Mesolithic sites were always located on the shore, emphasizing the importance of the sea. Distinct zones of artifact deposition can be seen at such sites. The actual living floor on dry land is characterized by the presence of hearths, pits, construction stone, and some artifacts. Stone tools and other artifacts are generally small in size, suggesting that larger refuse may have been swept up and tossed or discarded elsewhere. Organic materials such as bone and plant remains generally do not survive on the surface of the ground

in temperate climates. A second zone of refuse, originally discarded in the water, can be recognized in the layers adjacent to the occupation floor. The larger materials in this zone are well preserved, including bone, antler, and sometimes wooden artifacts. Because much of the shoreline of the Vedbaek inlet was occupied during the Mesolithic, this second zone often contains a vertical stratigraphy of tools and other debris. This information has been used to construct a detailed chronology for the area. Changes in artifact types and manufacturing methods can be traced through time.

Repeated residence at the same location, however, tends to obscure information about the horizontal arrangement of the prehistoric settlement, the locations of structures and associated hearths and pits. For this reason, an excavation was organized to uncover a settlement of brief occupation where horizontal patterns of the use of living space might be examined. Several factors pointed to a site called Vaenget Nord (ving-it-nord). Today the location of this site is marked by a grove of birch trees growing on a slight rise in the landscape. The rise had been a small island during the period when an inlet of the sea filled the Vedbaek Valley around 7000 years ago. This island was flooded and eventually submerged by rising sea level shortly after that date. Thus the period of time when it could have been a platform for human occupation was limited. Excavations revealed that the number of artifacts per square meter was lower at this site than at the heavily used shoreline sites. Evidence from the age of the

artifacts and radiocarbon dating reinforced these impressions.

Major excavations were begun in 1980 and concluded in 1983 by teams of Danish and American archaeologists. The excavation strategy was twofold. Narrow trenches were cut into the deep marine deposits off the former shore of the island to expose the refuse zone. Broad horizontal units were opened on the surface of the island to expose the living floor and to map the distribution of artifacts, pits, fireplaces, and other items.

The surface sediments of the island are light sandy clays. The darker traces of past human activities, such as digging, fire building, or the placement of posts, are often retained in this light soil. On top of this natural surface of the island is a layer of cultural materials, made up of ash and charcoal, seaweed, organic refuse, and the like. The thickness of this layer varied across the top of the island, deeper along the sloping shoreline.

There are two areas at the southern and eastern margins of the island where large boulders have been fractured into a number of pieces to create a kind of pavement or landing area. In addition, there are several intact boulders on the site, concentrated in the northwest section. A number of very large posts were also exposed in the course of the excavation. These posts are the trunks of elm or alder trees, roughly 30 cm (12 in.) in diameter, that were sharpened to a point and driven into the surface of the island.

The distribution of flint artifacts on the island is of major importance in understanding the activities that took place

A variety of marine foods were consumed by the inhabitants of Vedbaek. Some of these species and their preferred habitats are indicated here.

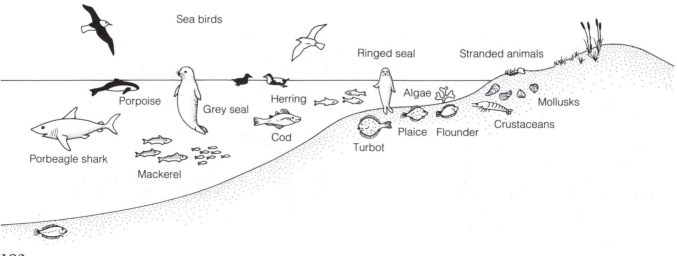

at the site. The artifacts can initially be divided into the waste products of manufacturing and repair and the actual finished tools that were in use. The finished tools are primarily adzes, arrowheads, and burins; only a few scrapers have been recovered. Waste materials include cores for producing flakes and blades, core shaping flakes, and a great quantity of shattered flint as a by-product of the flaking technique.

Most of the pits and hearths found in the excavation lie on the southwestern, landward side of the island. Several large fireplaces were present, often associated with concentrations of burned cooking stones and charcoal. Also in this area was a large, shallow depression that may have been the location of a structure of some sort. A dense cluster of small stake holes was also observed in this area, perhaps related to the construction. Some small pits are scattered around the site. One human-size pit with a blade knife and two axes was probably a grave.

The center of the island has several distinctive features, including the large depression, numerous pits, and stake holes. Artifacts found here were varied, and most of the projectile points came from this zone. This was likely the primary focus of the occupation. The northeast portion of the island contains evidence for hide working; most of the scrapers, truncated pieces, and unretouched blades come from this zone. Adjacent to this area is a zone of intensive stone tool making, rich in both *débitage* and flint tools. The majority of refitted pieces come from this area. To the south, behind these areas, is a zone of garbage dumping, containing abundant charcoal, fire-cracked stones, and only a few dispersed flakes. On the north shore of the island is a zone of erosion, which was the beach during the time of occupation. North of the island, in what was the inlet, is the refuse zone of larger stone and organic materials discarded in the waters adjacent to the island.

Density plots of the waste material reveal areas of tool manufacture. Flint axes were made as core tools by shaping a heavy nodule of flint into an elongated implement with a sharp leading edge. These axes, averaging 1 kg (2 lbs) or more in weight, were attached to long, elm han-

dles and used to fell trees, to hollow logs, and to butcher meat. Arrowheads were made on rhombic-shaped segments of flint blades. Analysis of the microscopic wear on the edges of the stone artifacts indicates the function of certain tools and blades. Some 25% of the blades showed evidence for use on such materials as plants and wood, fresh and dry hide, and meat and bone. Distribution of the blades points to the areas of the site where these activities took place. Hide-working tools were more common in the central and northeast parts of the island.

Vaenget Nord was likely a small and specialized camp for the Mesolithic inhabitants whose more permanent homes were along the shoreline of the inlet. This small island was probably used for certain activities at certain times of the year. Plant and animal remains indicate the utilization of a variety of environments, presumably during the warmer months of the year. Hazelnut shells are also common at the site, documenting fall habitation. The island situation and the presence of bones from garfish, mackerel, and dogfish, indicate the importance of the inlet and the sea to the inhabitants. Vaenget Nord was the focus of activities that involved hunting (the presence of arrowheads), the butchering of animals (butchered bones, meat polish on blades), the manufacture of tools and equipment from animal by-products such as bone (wear marks on burins) and hide (polish on scrapers and blades) and some woodworking (the presence of axes). The variety of hearths, pits, and heaps of cooking stones reinforce the impression of diverse activities.

Excavations at Vaenget Nord. The excavators removed the topsoil, leaving the Mesolithic artifacts in place to map their location and distribution.

BONE CHEMISTRY AND PREHISTORIC SUBSISTENCE

Information about past diet contained in human bones

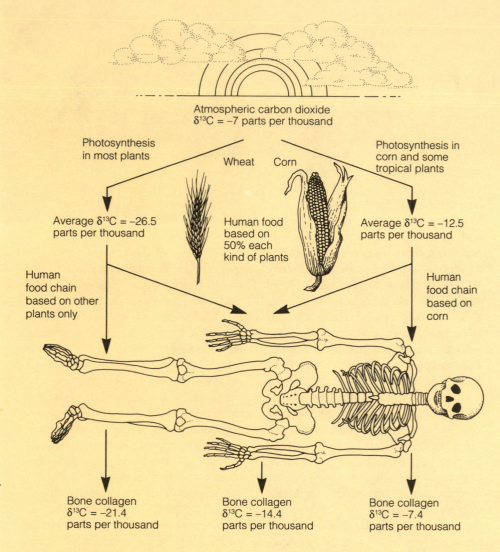

Atmospheric carbon dioxide
$\delta^{13}C = -7$ parts per thousand

Photosynthesis in most plants

Photosynthesis in corn and some tropical plants

Wheat   Corn

Average $\delta^{13}C = -26.5$ parts per thousand

Human food based on 50% each kind of plants

Average $\delta^{13}C = -12.5$ parts per thousand

Human food chain based on other plants only

Human food chain based on corn

Bone collagen $\delta^{13}C = -21.4$ parts per thousand

Bone collagen $\delta^{13}C = -14.4$ parts per thousand

Bone collagen $\delta^{13}C = -7.4$ parts per thousand

The movement of carbon isotopes through the food chain. Differences in the types of plants consumed or the presence of marine foods in the diet will result in changes in the carbon isotope ratio ($\delta^{13}C$) in human bone. This information is used to estimate the diet of prehistoric human groups.

The nature of past human diet is one of the most important subjects of archaeological research. The quest for food directly affects many aspects of human behavior and society, including group size and social organization, residence patterns, technology, and transportation. Evidence for diet has traditionally come from a number of areas of analysis: the study of preserved animal bones, plant remains, fecal matter, tooth wear and disease, and the physical characteristics of the human skeleton. New methods involving the chemical analysis of human bone offer a means for obtaining more information about paleonutrition.

Human bone is composed of organic and mineral compounds and water. Isotopic studies of the composition of bone focus on the organic portion, primarily in the form of the protein collagen. The carbon atoms in collagen occur in two major stable forms, ^{12}C and ^{13}C (carbon-12 and carbon-13). The ratio of ^{13}C to ^{12}C (defined as $\delta^{13}C$) in bone is measured with an instrument known as a mass spectrometer and reported as a value ranging from about 0 to -30. The ratio of these two carbon isotopes in bone reflects the content of the diet.

Carbon-13 is more common in certain kinds of terrestrial plants, such as

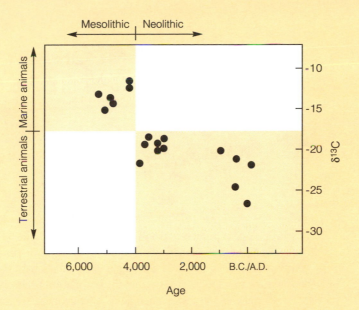

Carbon isotope measurement of human bone from Mesolithic and Neolithic Denmark. A dramatic decline in the use of marine foods came with the on-set of agriculture, around 4000 B.C.

corn, and in marine plants and animals. People who eat corn have higher ratios of carbon isotopes in their bones. Changes in this isotope ratio in prehistoric bone can indicate when corn became an important component of the diet. Such studies have been done both in Mexico, to ascertain when corn was first domesticated, and in North America, to record when this important staple first arrived. Analysis of carbon isotopes from human bone from the Tehuacán Valley in Mexico indicates that a heavy dependence on corn began around 4500 B.C.

Marine plants, and the marine animals that consume them, exhibit carbon isotope ratio values ranging between -10 and -18 $\delta^{13}C$. Values more positive than -20 indicate a predominance of marine foods in the diet, while lower values are more closely related to the consumption of terrestrial plants and animals. Henrik Tauber, of the National Museum of Denmark, measured the carbon isotope ratio in the bones of skeletons from Vedbaek, along with a number of other burials from Scandinavia and Greenland. The ratios from Vedbaek range from -13.4 to -15.3 $\delta^{13}C$ and are close to values for historical Eskimo skeletal material. Greenland Eskimos con-

sumed marine foods extensively, perhaps as much as 70% to 90% of the diet, and a similar proportion of seafoods may have characterized the diet of the Later Mesolithic. Saltwater fish, seals, propoise, whales, and mollusks comprised a major part of the diet at Vedbaek. Analysis of a dog bone from the Vedbaek area gave a reading of -14.7 $\delta^{13}C$, within the human range, suggesting a similar diet for the canine. Neolithic burials in Denmark show a sharp decline in carbon isotope ratios, indicative of a decrease in the importance of seafoods among these early agriculturalists.

EPILOG
CONTEMPORARY
HUNTER-GATHERERS

*A disappearing way of life at the margin
of civilization*

Anthropologists point out that 99.5% of past human life has been spent as hunter-gatherers. Hunter-gatherers are simple, egalitarian people who live in small groups and move around following a seasonal cycle in the quest for wild foods. Such adaptations are thought to represent the foundations of human society, from which more recent social and political arrangements have evolved. Group size and organization are highly flexible among hunter-gatherers in order to permit rapid response to seasonal changes in the food supply. For example, the Copper Eskimo of northern Canada followed a seasonal round of residential moves that focused on seal hunting in the winter, fishing in the warmer months, and caribou hunting in autumn. Such an annual cycle defines the basic pattern of subsistence and settlement for many groups of hunter-gatherers.

Among these groups, leadership is ephemeral and gained through the recognition of one's abilities. Relationships between individuals are determined by kinship; status differences are negligible, and everyone has access to the resources of the group. Private property is limited; labor, goods, and food are shared communally. Essential tasks for food collecting are divided by sex; men are normally hunters of larger animals, while women collect plant foods, fish, and trap small animals.

This picture of hunter-gatherers is too simple, however, and reflects relatively recent changes in human society. Ten-thousand years ago, hunter-gatherers occupied all the continents except Antarctica; everyone was a hunter-gatherer. Theirs was generally a very successful adaptation, one that had provided for the enormous expansion of the human species into a wide range of environments across the face of the Earth. Hunter-gatherer societies exhibited a diverse range of forms from large, sedentary populations with hierarchical leadership to very small, egalitarian groups moving across the land in search of food. In most areas wild food was readily available to support large numbers of people. Such adaptations have been described as the "original affluent society" by anthropologist Marshall Sahlins (1968, p. 89). Leisure time was plentiful, and life must have been reasonably good. Health conditions were significantly better than among early farming populations.

We have an enormous amount to learn from such traditional societies of hunter-gatherers. These people offer encyclopedic knowledge about the landscape and environment in which they live. Oral traditions and living memory can provide archaeologists with marvelous insights into the hunting way of life and the manner in which these groups coped with their environment and their neighbors.

Such studies must be done quickly, however. It seems unlikely that any traditional forager adaptations will remain after the turn of this century. Today, the spread of farming societies and the tentacles of the industrialized world have enormously reduced the number of extant hunter-gatherer societies. These groups now live in the most marginal environments on the planet — only those areas that are of little interest or use to agricultural and industrial society. The San, or Bushmen, of the Kalahari Desert of South Africa; the Efe, or Pygmy, of the Congo rain forest in Africa; the Hadza in the tsetse fly-ridden areas of East Africa; the Inuit, or Eskimo, of northern North America; and the Aborigines

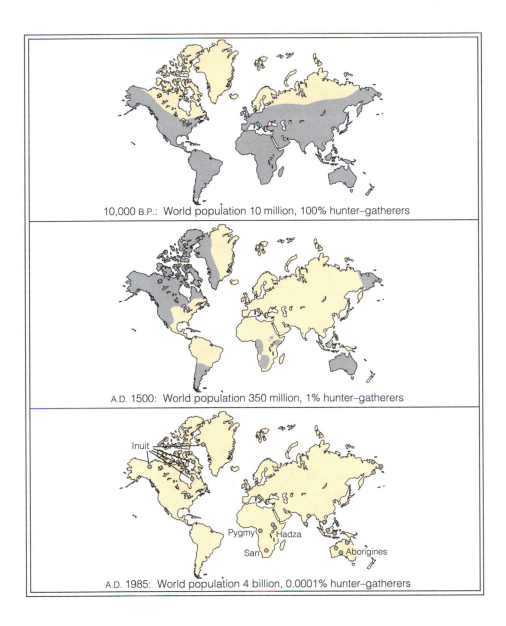

10,000 B.P.: World population 10 million, 100% hunter–gatherers

A.D. 1500: World population 350 million, 1% hunter–gatherers

Inuit

Pygmy Hadza

San Aborigines

A.D. 1985: World population 4 billion, 0.0001% hunter–gatherers

The estimated population and distribution of hunter-gatherers over the last 10,000 years. The figures for 1985 probably overestimate the remaining numbers of hunter-gatherers.

of western Australia are among the few remaining groups of hunter-gatherers. Even these societies are rapidly losing their traditional way of life, as national governments seek to settle them in permanent communities for purposes of education and health care.

SUGGESTED READINGS

Akazawa, T. and C. M. Aikens, eds. 1986. *Prehistoric hunter-gatherers in Japan*. Tokyo: University of Tokyo Press. A series of articles on the archaeology of early Japan.

Brothwell, D. R. 1981. *Digging up bones*. Ithaca, NY: Cornell University Press. One of the best manuals on the excavation and analysis of human skeletal material.

Jeffries, Richard W. 1987. *The archaeology of Carrier Mills*. Carbondale: Southern Illinois University Press. A popular account of the excavations of the Archaic site at Carrier Mills, Illinois, and of the general archaeology of this area.

Price, T. D., and J. A. Brown, eds. 1985. *Prehistoric hunter-gatherers*. Orlando, FL: Academic Press. A set of papers on early Holocene foragers in a variety of places around the globe.

Zvelebil, Marek ed. 1986. *Hunters in transition*. Cambridge: Cambridge University Press. A series of papers on foragers becoming farmers during the early Holocene.

Kua hunter-gatherers of the Kalahari Desert of Botswana, southern Africa. Hunter-gatherers today occupy only the most marginal places on Earth and are rapidly disappearing.

THE ORIGINS OF AGRICULTURE

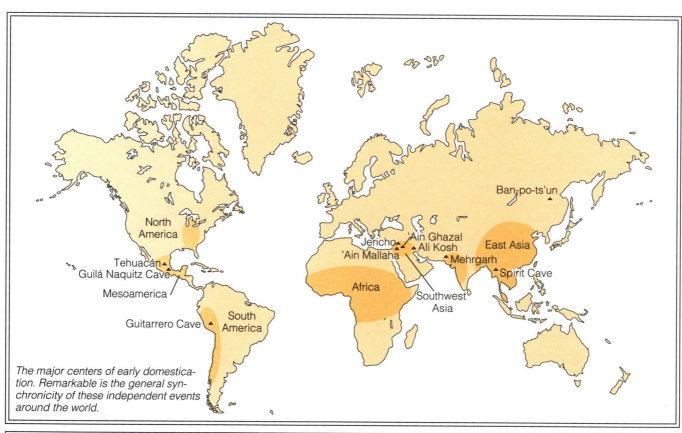

The major centers of early domestication. Remarkable is the general synchronicity of these independent events around the world.

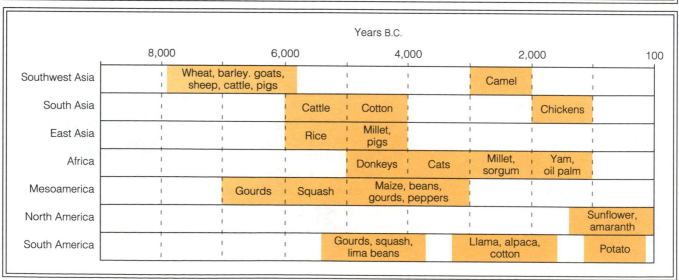

	Years B.C.							
	8,000		6,000		4,000		2,000	100
Southwest Asia		Wheat, barley. goats, sheep, cattle, pigs					Camel	
South Asia				Cattle	Cotton			Chickens
East Asia				Rice	Millet, pigs			
Africa					Donkeys	Cats	Millet, sorgum	Yam, oil palm
Mesoamerica			Gourds	Squash	Maize, beans, gourds, peppers			
North America								Sunflower, amaranth
South America				Gourds, squash, lima beans		Llama, alpaca, cotton		Potato

PROLOG
THE FIRST FARMERS

*The major transition in the course
of human prehistory*

The vast majority of our history as a species was spent as hunter-gatherers. Our ancestry as food collectors, consuming the wild products of the earth, extends back at least 4 million years. Nevertheless, shortly after the end of the Pleistocene, some human groups began to produce food rather than collect it, to domesticate and control wild plants and animals. Perhaps the most remarkable transition in our prehistory is the almost simultaneous appearance of domesticated plants and animals in several different areas of the world between about 10,000 and 7000 years ago.

Agriculture is a way of obtaining food that involves domesticated plants and animals. But the transition to farming is much more than simple herding and cultivation. It also entails major, long-term changes in the structure and organization of the societies that adopt this new way of life, as well as a totally new relationship with the environment. While hunter-gatherers largely live off the land in an *extensive* fashion, generally exploiting a diversity of resources over a broad area, farmers *intensively* utilize a smaller portion of the landscape and create a milieu that suits their needs. Humans began to truly master the Earth.

Just because a species is exploited intensively by humans does not automatically mean it will become domesticated. Although oak trees have supplied acorns to humans for thousands of years, they have not been domesticated. **Domestication** changes the physical characteristics of the plant or animal involved. The domestication process is a combination of both the nature of the plant or animal species (generational length, life cycle, plasticity) and the intensity and nature of the human manipulation.

Agriculture requires several major practices for long-term success: (1) *propagation,* the selection and sowing of seeds or breeding of animals; (2) *husbandry,* the tending of plants or animals during the growth period; (3) the *harvesting* of plants when ripe or the *slaughter* of animals at appropriate times; and (4) the *storage* of seeds and *maintenance* of animals through their nonproductive periods to ensure annual reproduction. Propagation and husbandry of plants involves **cultivation:** clearing fields, preparing soil, weeding, protecting them from animals, and providing water.

The evidence for early domesticated plants is biased toward seed crops. The best known early domesticates are the cereals — the grasses that produce large, hard-shelled seeds; nutritious kernels of carbohydrate that can be stored for lengthy periods. The hard cereal grains, and occasionally the stems of these plants, were often burned during preparation or cooking in the past and thereby preserved to the present.

Root crops are not well documented in the archaeological record because they lack hard parts that are resistant to decay. Such plants include potatoes, yams, manioc, taro, and others that may have been domesticated quite early. Root crops reproduce asexually from shoots or cuttings, and for this reason domesticated varieties are harder to distinguish from their wild ancestors. Asexually reproducing plants may maintain exactly the same genetic structure through many generations, because a piece of the mother plant is used to start the daughter. Such plants can also show great variation within a species, making domestication difficult to document.

187

Animals were apparently domesticated initially for meat, with the exception of the dog. Dogs were tamed from wolves very early, perhaps 14,000 years ago in the Old World, and used for hunting and as pets, or even for food. Subsequently, however, a number of other species of animals were domesticated and herded for food and/or kept as beasts of burden. Goats and sheep appear to be the first animals domesticated, followed shortly by cattle, pigs, and others. The secondary products (milk, horn, leather) of these domesticated species also became important, as did their function as beasts of burden.

Domestication of both plants and animals may be related to the storage of food. Such cereals as wheat and barley have hard outer coverings that protect the nutritious grain for some months, permitting the seed to survive until the growing season and offering very good possibilities for storage. Meat can be stored, too, in the form of living, tame animals that are always available for slaughter. As such, storage provides a means to regulate the availability of food and to accumulate surplus.

THE PRIMARY CENTERS OF DOMESTICATION

Questions concerning the origins of agriculture must focus on *primary* centers, where individual species of plants and/or animals were first domesticated. *Secondary* areas of agricultural development received plants and animals from elsewhere, although in many of these regions some local plants and animals were domesticated and used along with the introduced varieties. Primary centers for domestication were in the Near East, East Asia, Mexico, and South America. The earliest known domesticates — wheat, barley, peas, beans, goats, and sheep — appeared in the Old World, between the eastern Mediterranean Sea and Afghanistan, around 8000 B.C. Many other plants and animals — pigs, cattle, bread wheat, rye, figs, olives, grapes, flax — were later added to this list. The origins of agriculture in the Near East are discussed in detail in this chapter because the archaeology is well known and the process of domestication took place somewhat earlier than elsewhere.

Agriculture was also invented in the Far East, perhaps in two or three different areas, sometime before 5000 B.C. Millet was first cultivated and pigs were domesticated in North China in early villages dating to around 6000 B.C. Rice was initially cultivated in southern China and Southeast Asia about the same time before 5000 B.C. In all probability, root crops were under cultivation in this area, along with rice, sometime between 7000 and 3000 B.C. Recent evidence from New Guinea suggests that agriculture may have been practiced very early in this area. Radiocarbon dates from a digging stick found in what appears to be an ancient agricultural field indicate an age of around 6000 B.C. This evidence suggests that we may expect the dates for all of East Asia to be pushed back somewhat earlier with future research.

In the New World, agriculture developed in Mexico, in northwestern South America, and in eastern North America. In Mexico, gourds, squash, avocados, chili peppers, beans, and corn were cultivated before 5000 B.C. These crops provide all the essential nutrients for a healthy diet, and meat protein may not have been necessary. Domesticated animals never provided an important part of the diet in this area, although turkeys, dogs, and the stingless honeybee were domesticated.

Sites in the highlands of Peru contain evidence for the early domestication of gourds, tomatoes, beans, and potatoes by 5000 B.C. Some of these plants may have reached the mountains from an original habitat in the lowland jungles, but little is known about the prehistory of the Amazon Basin and other tropical areas of South America. Potatoes certainly were an indigenous crop; hundreds of varieties of wild and domesticated potatoes grow in this area today. In addition to plants, several animals were domesticated. The guinea pig was used for food, while the **llama** was probably domesticated for use as a beast of burden to transport goods around the mountains of South America. The **alpaca**, a **camelid** like the llama, may have been domesticated for both meat and wool.

In addition to the four major centers of domestication—the Near East and Far East in the Old World, and South America and Mexico in the New World—there were also beginnings of horticulture or agriculture in other areas, shortly after the end of the Pleistocene. There are early dates for swamp drainage for agricultural fields in New Guinea; these fields probably grew fruit and tuber crops, such as yams. In eastern North America, several local plants—such as marshelder, sunflower, and chenopod—were domesticated by 1000 B.C., long before the introduction of corn from Mexico. In sub-Saharan Africa, species such as sorghum and millet may have been independently domesticated. Clearly there was a trend toward domestication and agriculture on a global scale at the beginning of the Holocene.

EXPLANATIONS FOR THE ORIGINS OF AGRICULTURE

Remarkable is the fact that this process of domesticating plants and animals appears to have taken place separately and independently in several different areas at about the same point in time. Given the long prehistory of our species, why should the transition to agriculture happen within such a brief period, within a 3000-year segment of four or more million years of human existence? Such a dramatic shift in the trajectory of cultural evolution requires explanation.

Both the views about, and the evidence for, the origins of agriculture continue to be revised and updated. Ideas about the origins of agriculture can be best understood from an historical perspective, considering the early theories first. These hypothetical explanations of why domestication occurred can be described according to the major emphasis of each one: the oasis hypothesis, the natural habitat hypothesis, the population pressure hypothesis, the edge or marginal zone hypothesis, and the social hypothesis. A consideration of these ideas also reveals much about the nature of archaeology and archaeologists. Theories on the origin of agriculture have often focused on the earliest evidence from the Near East and, for that reason, may not be appropriate to all places where early domestication occurred.

During the first fifty years of this century, farming was thought to have originated on the dry plains of Mesopotamia, where the early civilizations of the Sumerians and others arose. The best evidence for early farming villages at that time came from riverine areas or oases with springs in the Near East, such as along the Nile River in Egypt or at Jericho in the Jordan Valley. At this time, the end of the Pleistocene was thought to be a period of increasing warmth and dryness in the Earth's climate. Because the ice ages (glacial periods) were cold and wet, the reasoning went, they should have ended with higher temperatures and less precipitation. Given this view of past climate, logic suggested that areas like the Near East—a dry region to begin with—would have witnessed a period of aridity at the end of the Pleistocene when vegetation grew only around limited water sources. The **oasis hypothesis** suggested a circumstance in which plants, animals, and humans would have clustered in confined areas near water. Proponents of this theory, like the late V. Gordon Childe, argued that the only successful solution to the competition for food in such situations would be for humans to domesticate and control both the animals and the plants. In this sense, domestication emerged as a symbiotic relationship for survival.

During the 1940s and 1950s, however, new evidence suggested that there had been no major climatic changes in the Near East at the close of the Pleistocene—no crisis during which life would concentrate at oases. The new information forced a reconsideration of the origins of agriculture. Robert Braidwood, of the University of Chicago, suggested that domestication did not occur first in the lowlands of Mesopotamia, but pointed out—in his **natural habitat hypothesis**—that the earliest domesticates likely appeared where their wild ancestors lived and that this area, the "hilly flanks" of the Fertile Crescent in the Near East, should be the focus of investigations. Braidwood and a large team of researchers excavated at the site of Jarmo in northern Iraq. The evidence from this early farming village supported his hypothesis that domestication did indeed

The conditions of incipient desiccation . . . would provide the stimulus towards the adoption of a food-producing economy. Enforced concentration by the banks of streams and shrinking springs would entail an intensive search for means of nourishment. Animals and men would be herded together in oases that were becoming increasingly isolated by desert tracts. Such enforced juxtaposition might promote that sort of symbiosis between man and beast implied by the word domestication.

(Childe, 1951, p. 23)

begin in the natural habitat. Braidwood did not offer a specific reason as to why domestication occurred, other than to point out that technology and culture were ready by the end of the Pleistocene, that humans were familiar with the species that were to be domesticated. At that time, farming was considered to be a highly desirable and welcome invention that provided security and leisure time. Archaeologists thought that once human societies recognized the possibilities of domestication, they would immediately start farming.

Lewis Binford, of the University of New Mexico, challenged these ideas in the 1960s. Binford argued that farming was back-breaking, time-consuming and labor-intensive. He pointed to studies of living hunter-gatherers indicating that these groups spent only a few hours a day obtaining food; the rest of the time was for visiting, talking, gambling, and the general pleasures of life. Even in very marginal areas, such as the Kalahari Desert of southern Africa, food collecting was a successful adaptation, and people rarely starved. Binford argued, therefore, that human groups would not become farmers unless they had no other choice—that the origin of agriculture was not a fortuitous discovery, but a last resort.

Binford made his point in terms of an equilibrium between people and food, a balance that could be upset either by a decline in available food or an increase in the number of people. Since climatic and environmental changes appeared to be minimal in the Near East, Binford thought that it must have been an increase in the number of people that upset the balance. Population pressure was thus introduced as a causal agent for the origins of agriculture: more people, more mouths to feed, requiring more food. The best solution to that problem lies in domestication, which provides higher yields of food per acre of land. But at the same time, agricultural intensification requires more labor to extract the food.

Binford further suggested that the effects of population pressure would be felt most strongly not in the core of the natural habitat zone, where dense stands of wild wheat and large herds of wild sheep and goats were available, but rather at the margins, where wild foods were less abundant. This theory, incorporating ideas about population pressure and the margins of the Fertile Crescent, has become known as the **edge hypothesis**.

Binford's concern with population has been elaborated by Mark Cohen, of the State University of New York, Plattsburgh. Cohen argued for an inherent tendency for growth in human population, a pattern responsible for the initial spread of the human species out of Africa, the colonization of Asia and Europe, and eventually of the New World as well. After about 15,000 B.C., according to Cohen, all the inhabitable areas of the planet were occupied, and population continued to grow. At that time there was an increase in the use of less preferred resources in many areas. In addition to large game, land snails, shellfish, birds, and many more plant species were incorporated into the diet around the end of the Pleistocene, after 10,000 years ago. Cohen argues that the only way for a very successful, but rapidly increasing, species to cope with declining resources was for them to begin to cultivate the land and domesticate its inhabitants, rather than simply to collect the wild produce. Domestication for Cohen was a solution to problems of overpopulation on a global scale.

Others, who have recently argued that we cannot understand the transition to farming and food storage and surplus simply in terms of environment and population, have developed a **social hypothesis** for explaining the origins of agriculture. Barbara Bender, of the University of London, for example, has suggested that the success of food production may lie in the ability of certain individuals to accumulate food surplus and to transform those foods into more valued items, such as rare stones and metals. From this perspective, agriculture was a solution to a social problem.

There are a number of other theories about why human societies adopted agriculture at the end of the Pleistocene. Geographer Carl Sauer suggested that agriculture began in the hilly tropics of Southeast Asia, where sedentary groups with knowledge of the rich plant life of the forest might have domesticated plants for poisons and fibers. Botanist David Rindos argues that domestication is a process of interaction between humans and plants, evolving together toward a more beneficial symbiotic relationship.

There are problems with all of these hypotheses, some of which can be seen in a brief consideration of the evidence from the Near East. The earliest agriculture villages — places like Jericho, 'Ain Ghazal, and Ali Kosh — were indeed located at the margins of the natural habitat. Attempts to artificially reproduce dense stands of wild wheat in this area may have resulted in domestication. However, population was not particularly high just prior to agriculture. Several sites show signs of abandonment in the levels just beneath those layers that contain the first domesticated plants. The most recent climatic evidence indicates that there was, in fact, a period of slightly cooler and moister temperatures in the Near East at the end of the Pleistocene that may have greatly expanded the geographic range of wild wheat and barley, making them available to more human groups, and fostering the process of domestication.

It is very difficult to excavate information like social relations or population pressure, a fact that makes many of the current theories hard to evaluate. Any adequate explanation of the Neolithic transformation should deal not only with how it all began, but also why it happened rather suddenly around 10,000 years ago. Such factors as population and climatic change certainly play a role in cultural evolution. But we cannot yet say precisely why plants and animals began to be domesticated shortly after the end of the Pleistocene. Some theories may seem reasonable in one of the primary centers of domestication, but not in another.

The sequence of events in two areas is of interest here. In the Near East, permanent settlements are known from 10,000 B.C., prior to the presence of direct evidence for domesticated plants or animals. Cultivated plants appeared about 8500 B.C.; animals were not herded until perhaps 7500 B.C. Pottery did not come into general use until around 6500 B.C. In Mesoamerica, however, the archaeological sequence reveals domesticated plants first, followed by pottery and permanent villages about 3000 years later. Domesticated animals were not important here. The differences in these two areas suggest that neither **sedentism** (permanently settled communities) nor cultivation is totally dependent one upon the other. It is also clear that domesticated animals are not essential in all areas. Livestock may have served in part to store surplus plant foods.

Simply put, there is no single, accepted, general theory for the origins of agriculture. There is no common pattern of development in the various areas where domestication first took place. The how and why of the Neolithic transition remains one of the more intriguing questions in human prehistory. This chapter examines the origins of agriculture in more detail in the several primary centers where it first appeared: the Near East, the Far East, Mexico, and South America. Because of the quantity and quality of archaeological information from the Near East, much of the discussion will concentrate on this area.

The Epilog considers the spread of agriculture from the primary centers, like the ripples from a pebble thrown in a pond, to other areas, such as sub-Saharan Africa and elsewhere around the ancient globe, where domesticates were introduced from other areas. Subsequent chapters will explore the expansion of agriculture into Europe and parts of North America. We will also discuss the consequences of this major change in human subsistence in terms of economy, organization, settlement, and ideology. Human society was never again the same following the beginnings of domestication. Even societies that continued to hunt and gather after the Neolithic were dramatically affected by neighboring farmers.

> *Technology and demography have been given too much importance in the explanation of agricultural origins; social structure too little. . . . Food production is a question of techniques; agriculture is a question of commitment. . . . Commitment is not primarily a question of technology but of changing social relations. This account has chosen to emphasize the social properties of gatherer-hunter systems; to show how alliance structures, and the individuals operating within these structures, make demands on the economic productivity of the system; how demography and technology are products of social structure rather than independent variables.*
>
> (Bender, 1978, p. 204)

Wheat, Barley, Goats, and Sheep

The appearance of the first farmers at the end of the Pleistocene in Southwest Asia

Discussions of the origins of the agriculture often focus on the Near East for several reasons: (1) The earliest evidence for plant domestication from anywhere in the world is found here; (2) there is a reasonable amount of information available from excavations and other studies; and (3) the Near East has often been considered the "cradle of Western civilization."

The Near East, or Southwest Asia, as it is also known, is a fascinating region. Known today for the political problems that beset it, the area is also the home of the earliest domesticated plants and animals, as well as some of the world's earliest civilizations. Southwest Asia is an enormous triangle of land, approximately the size of the contiguous United States. The area is bounded on the west by Turkey and the Mediterranean, on the south by Saudi Arabia and the Indian Ocean, on the north by the Black Sea and Caspian Sea, and on the east by Afghanistan, at the edge of South Asia. The climate and environment are similar to New Mexico, Arizona, Utah, and Colorado.

Southwest Asia is also a series of contrasts. Some of the highest and lowest places on Earth are found there, along with both rain forest and arid desert. Snow-capped mountains are visible from burning hot wastelands. Water is an important resource; arable land with fertile soil is scarce. The environment of this area can be visualized as a series of bands, driest in the south, and moister to the north. Arabia is largely sand and desert; Mesopotamia, the region between the Tigris and Euphrates rivers, is too dry for farming unless some form of irrigation is used. Many plants cannot survive in areas with less than 300 mm (1 ft) of rain each year. The 300-mm isobar stretches along an arc of mountains that surround Mesopotamia. The Zagros Mountains of western Iran, the Taurus Mountains of southern Turkey, and the highlands of the Levant along the eastern Mediterranean shore form a region where more rainfall and a variety of plants can be found. This region is the natural habitat for many of the wild ancestors of the first species of plants and animals that were domesti-cated at the end of the Pleistocene — the wild wheats and barleys, the wild legumes, the wild sheep, goats, pigs, and cattle that hunter-gatherers began to exploit in large numbers at the time of the origin of agriculture.

Some 20,000 years ago, a series of developments began in the Near East that set the stage for village farming — the shift from the collection of wild food, characteristic of hunter-gatherers for the previous several million years, to the production of domesticated plants and animals. Climatic conditions during this period are not completely understood, but some general patterns are known. In 18,000 B.C., global temperatures were 6°C (10°F) cooler than they are today. A warming trend began about 13,000 B.C. and increased to a maximum around 3000 B.C. Climate at the very beginning of the Neolithic was somewhat variable. Precipitation changes were not dramatic, but in an arid area, minor changes in rainfall can have a significant impact on vegetation. Rainfall was lowest during the periods of maximum cooling around 18,000 B.C. As temperature and precipitation increased, the forest zone expanded in the Near East, and the number of species was greater than it is today. After 7000 B.C. or so, however, continuing increases in temperature likely resulted in more evaporation, so that effective precipitation began to decline and the forest cover shrank.

The archaeology of the later Pleistocene and early Holocene in the Near East is best understood in terms of the time before and the time after the beginning of domestication. The general pattern of the shift to cultivation and herding appears to be one in which a broad-spectrum diet, based on the many wild species of the region, very gradually narrowed to a few domesticated plants and animals.

The story starts about 20,000 years ago, during the late Paleolithic, and continues up to 8000 years ago, during the early Neolithic. In the late Paleolithic, groups of hunter-gatherers lived in small, seasonal camps throughout the area. These groups exploited a range of resources but focused primarily on certain species of animals, such as gazelle. Plant foods are not common in the archaeological sites from this period.

The period just before agriculture, from about 10,000 to 8500 B.C., is referred to as the Natufian in the Levant. The period was characterized by an increase in the number of sites and therefore people, coinciding with a period of increased rainfall and abundant vegetation. The natural habitat was rich in wild plants and animals, resources that supported permanent settled communities before any evidence for domestication. 'Ain Mallaha was one such village in the prefarming period.

In the period just prior to the Neolithic, there was more intense utilization of plant foods. Particularly noticeable is the range of equipment for processing plants: sickle blades and grinding stones for preparing plant foods, along with storage pits and roasting areas for processing wild wheat. Sites were often located in areas of cultivable land, but such settlements were dependent on wild cereals, as evidenced by the remains of wild wheat and barley. These same locations were occupied during the Neolithic, too, probably because of the quantity or quality of arable land. It is entirely possible that these plants were tended or cultivated at this time, but simply did not show signs of domestication in this early stage. Hunting continued and more immature animals were taken among the hunted species, such as gazelle or wild goat.

By 8500 B.C., changes in the size, shape, and structure of several cereals indicate that they have been domesticated. The archaeological data from Jericho and Abu Hureyra, for example, mark this transition. The Neolithic, defined by the appearance of domesticated plants, began at this time. The specific reasons why these wild foods were domesticated, however, is not known. The archaeological evidence can tell us when and where but not why or how. The transition to the Neolithic is not marked by abrupt changes but rather by increasing emphasis on patterns that appeared during the Natufian.

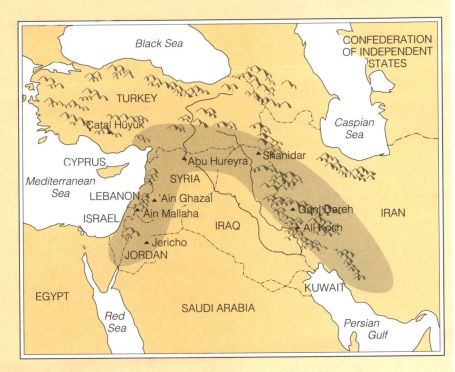

The locations of Near East sites mentioned in the chapter. The shaded area represents the Fertile Crescent.

The number and size of prehistoric communities expanded greatly in the early Neolithic, as populations were apparently concentrated in fewer settlements. The first towns appeared. Major changes in human diet, and probably in the organization of society as well, began to take place. By 7600 B.C., domesticated animals, particularly sheep and goats, made their first appearance in the Levant, and a number of changes in architecture were seen. Good evidence comes from Jericho, 'Ain Ghazal, and Ali Kosh. The early Neolithic is often divided into two periods, referred to as the Pre-Pottery Neolithic A (PPNA) and Pre-Pottery Neolithic B (PPNB). Pottery was probably invented in the Near East in the seventh millennium B.C. as a kind of easily produced, waterproof container. These dishes were useful for holding liquids, for cooking the gruel made from wheat and barley (bread was a somewhat later invention), and for storage of materials. The complete Neolithic package of domesticates, village architecture, and pottery was thus in place shortly before 6000 B.C., as the Neolithic revolution began to spread to Europe and Africa.

'AIN MALLAHA

Pre-Neolithic developments in the Near East

Excavations at 'Ain Mallaha exposing burials in the house floors.

The Natufian site of 'Ain Mallaha (ein'-ma-la'ha) lies beside a natural spring on a hillside overlooking the swamps of Lake Huleh in the upper Jordan Valley of Israel. Excavations from 1955 to 1973 by Jean Perrot, of the French Archaeological Mission in Jerusalem, uncovered three successive layers, with the remains of permanent villages. Each layer contained a number of round houses, ranging from 3 to 8 m (10 to 25 ft) in diameter, even larger in the lowest level. House entrances faced downhill toward the water. Although the structures were built close together, the community had a centrally located open area with round storage pits.

'Ain Mallaha is one of the earliest "villages" anywhere in the world, dating to between 11,000 and 9000 B.C. The entire settlement covers an open area of about 2000 sq m (½ acre, the size of a large hockey rink), with a population estimated at 200 to 300 people. The remarkable architecture consists of large substantial houses with stone foundations, standing to a height of almost 1 m (3 ft). Wooden center posts may have supported conical roofs. Stone-lined square or oval hearths and bins were found in the centers of the rooms or against the walls. **Querns** and mortars — grinding surfaces for preparing grain — were occasionally set into the floor.

The ground stone artifacts are elaborate: plates, bowls, mortars, pestles, and more. This production points to a need for containers at this time. A number of the objects are decorated with elaborate geometric designs. Carved limestone figurines of a human body, a human face, a stylized face, and a tortoise were also found. The flaked stone industry is rich, with more than 50,000 pieces. The bone tools include awls, skewers, needles, and fishhooks.

The animal bones found at the site come from wild pig, three kinds of deer, wild goat, wild cattle, wild horse, and gazelle. Gazelle is the most common and was often the primary game animal at the sites

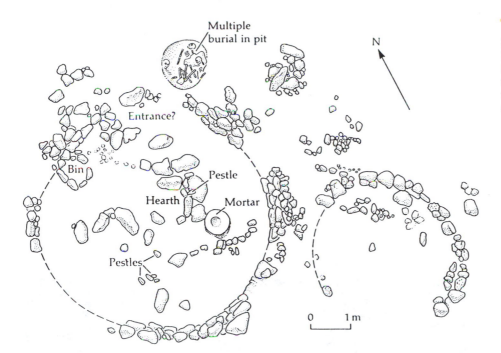

Multiple burial in pit

Entrance?

Bin

Pestle

Hearth

Mortar

Pestles

N

0   1 m

Two circular houses at 'Ain Mallaha. These structures have rock wall foundations and often contain grinding equipment, storage bins, and pits. Burials were often placed in abandoned storage pits.

of this period. Bird, fish, tortoise, and shellfish remains were also found. The lake was clearly an important resource for these people, indicated by the presence of net sinkers at the site. The high incidence of tooth decay in individuals buried at 'Ain Mallaha suggests that carbohydrates from cereals or other plants were consumed in quantity. Wild barley and almonds were found charred in excavations, and it is clear from the abundance of sickle blades and other plant-processing equipment that wild cereals played a very important role in the diet.

Two different kinds of burials were found at 'Ain Mallaha: (1) individual interments, including child and infant burials beneath stone slabs under the house floors; and (2) collective burials in pits, either intact or as secondary reburials after soft tissue had disappeared. Most of the eighty-nine graves were found outside the houses. Abandoned storage pits were often reused for burial purposes. Many of the graves contain red ochre; limestone slabs covered several of the simple graves. Four horns from gazelle were found in one grave, and in another, an old woman was buried with a puppy. Shell from the Mediterranean and rare greenstone beads or pendants from Syria or Jordan were occasionally placed in the burials, but grave goods were generally rare.

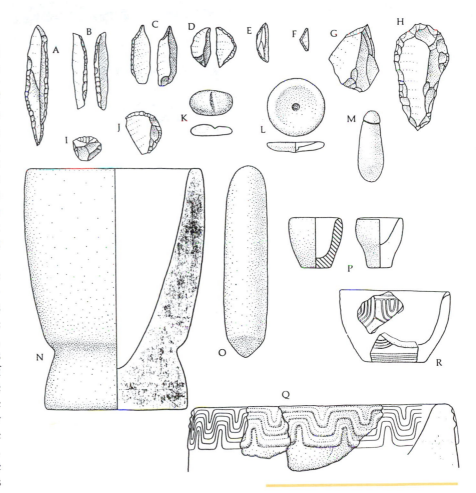

Various artifacts from 'Ain Mallaha: A–J: chipped stone tools. N, P–R: ground stone containers. K–M, O: ground stone tools.

JERICHO

One of the oldest continuously inhabited places on Earth

The ancient tell of Jericho lies near a major spring at the northern end of the Jordan Valley in the Near East. The tell is a mound of the accumulation of 10,000 years of human occupation.

And it came to pass at the seventh time, when the priests blew with the trumpets, Joshua said unto the people, Shout; for the Lord hath given you the city. . . . And the people shouted with a great shout. . . . The wall fell down flat . . . and they utterly destroyed all that was in the city . . . with the edge of the sword . . . and they burnt the city with fire, and all that was therein.

(Josh. 6:16)

The walls of Jericho (jer'ih-coe) fell to Joshua and the Israelites sometime around 1300 B.C. The place had been occupied, however, for thousands of years prior to their arrival. In fact, the walls of Jericho tumbled down almost twenty times in the course of its history, from either earthquake or siege. Jericho is a **tell**, a massive mound of 2.4 ha (6 acres) composed of mud-bricks and trash, accumulated to a height of 22 m (70 ft) during its long history of occupation. The layers of the tell built up at a rate of roughly 26 cm per 100 years, almost a foot every century.

Jericho, or Tel es' Sultan as it is known in Arabic, is one of the oldest continuously inhabited places on Earth. Since at least 10,000 B.C., Elisha's Fountain, the spring at Jericho, has witnessed virtually continuous human settlement. The freshwater spring floods the area beneath it and supports an oasis of luxuriant vegetation in the midst of the hot and arid Jordan Valley, lying at a depth of 275 m (900 ft) below sea level. The mound itself was abandoned sometime before the birth of Christ, as settlement spread to the surrounding low area.

The biblical connection has made Jericho a place of major interest and importance for archaeologists in the Near East. Today the tell resembles the surface of the moon. Craters and trenches mark the excavations of many archaeological projects that have explored these accumulated layers since 1873.

Beneath biblical Jericho, British archaeologist Dame Kathleen Kenyon exposed a number of levels containing remains from the Bronze Age, the Neolithic, and the Mesolithic. In the following discussion, we will concentrate on the remains from the early Neolithic, from 8500 to 7600 B.C. Because the mound is so deep, these lowest levels were reached only by narrow trenches. Kenyon estimated from these small exposures that the early Neolithic community at Jericho covered approximately 2.4 ha (6 acres), the size of several soccer fields, with a population of perhaps 600 people.

The residential structures and artifacts exposed in Kenyon's excavations were similar to those from other Near Eastern sites from this period. Closely packed round houses contained interior hearths and grinding equipment. Headless burials were also uncovered in the houses at Jericho; skulls were found separated from the rest of the skeleton.

Gazelle bones were abundant in early layers at Jericho. This important game animal was probably exploited by large drives that captured a number of animals simultaneously. Aurochs, wild boar, and fox were also eaten. Many animals present in the surrounding hills were not hunted, including wild goat, oryx, hartebeest, and wild camel. The presence of equipment for processing grain (sickles and grinding stones) and storage bins suggests that cereals were important at this time. In the early Neolithic, these cereals were domesticated and likely were cultivated in the fertile soil of the Jericho oasis.

The inhabitants of early Neolithic Jericho were involved in the trade of various items over long distances. Such materials as salt, tar, and sulfur came from the area around the Dead Sea; turquoise was brought from the Sinai peninsula, cowry shells from the Red Sea, obsidian from Turkey, and greenstone from Jordan. The reasons for such exchange probably lie in the importance of contacts with neighboring communities and in the accumulation

A plastered and painted skull from Jericho. The plaster remodeling of the features of human heads is found at several early Neolithic sites in the Near East and may reflect an increasing reverence for ancestors.

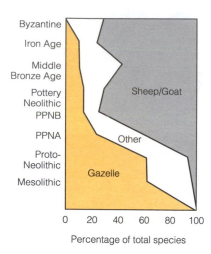

Changes in the consumption of animals over time at Jericho. Note especially the shift from wild gazelle to domesticated sheep and goat. PPNA and PPNB stand for Pre-Pottery Neolithic A and Pre-Pottery Neolithic B.

of status items as wealth for some portion of the community.

Most remarkable among Kenyon's discoveries from this period were a large stone tower, wall, and ditch, which appeared to encircle the site. These structures were built at the beginning of the eighth millennium B.C., or around 8000 B.C. The wall itself is 1.8 m (6 ft) thick at the base, narrowing to 1.1 m (3.5 ft) at the top, and stands 3.6 m (12 ft) high today, buried under the accumulated deposits of Jericho. The rubble-filled stone tower was also completely buried, at a height of 8.2 m (27 ft). Built inside the wall with a diameter at the base of 9 m (30 ft), the tower has an interior staircase with twenty-two steps leading from the bottom to the top. In front of the wall was a deep ditch, which added greatly to the height of the total structure. The ditch was some 2 m (6.5 ft) deep and 8.5 m (28 ft) wide, cut into the bedrock under the site. Such a construction project would have been a major undertaking by a small community in the eighth millennium B.C. The tower and wall were abandoned by 7300 B.C. and rapidly disappeared under the accumulating layers of the tell.

The significance of these structures has been the focus of discussion and debate. Kenyon suggested that the tell was completely encircled by the wall and ditch, with towers placed at regular intervals. However, only the one tower was exposed in the excavations and the wall was not found on the southern, lower side of the mound. Numerous unanswered questions have arisen regarding the nature of the enemy, the materials to be protected, the location of the tower *inside* the wall, the reason for abandonment, and the size of the population. Comparable fortifications are not seen at other early Neolithic sites in the Near East, and the massive defensive structure seems out of place.

Ofer Bar-Yosef, of Harvard University, has examined the evidence for fortifications at Jericho and found it lacking. Bar-Yosef would rather understand the tower, wall, and ditch in terms of a series of defenses against nature, rather than humans. In this arid region, each rainfall moves a great deal of sand and silt from higher ground to lower areas. Such erosion and deposition would have been aggravated through land clearing by the inhabitants of the site. Sediments may have accumulated on the upslope side of the tell of Jericho and at other early Neolithic sites.

To counteract the rapid accumulation of sediments at the edge of their community, the inhabitants of Jericho, Bar-Yosef argues, built the wall and then dug the ditch to hold back these materials. The rock-cut ditch at Jericho filled with water-transported sediments shortly after it was built. The wall was thickest in the middle portion where the deposit was heaviest. The large tower inside the wall is another matter. Bar-Yosef has noted the excellent preservation of the tower to its total height in the tell. He argues that there was likely a mud-brick structure on top of the stone structure, a building for communal storage or religious activities that made the tower a very special structure in the settlement. The tower thus may represent an early shrine or temple for the community, a concept that was later transformed into the monumental ziggurats of the Mesopotamian states.

Around 7500 B.C., there were major changes in the architecture, artifacts, and animals at Jericho. Houses became square, constructed with what have been described as hog-backed bricks — large, cigar-shaped, mud-bricks with a herringbone pattern of thumbprints on the top. Domesticated animals became important at this time; sheep and goat comprised almost one-half of the animal bones, along with a few wild cattle and pigs, gradually replacing gazelle. Pig and cattle were possibly in the process of change at this time, because their bones were slightly smaller than the wild forms but not as small as the domesticated variety.

KATHLEEN KENYON, 1906—1978

Archaeologist of the Holy Land

Dame Kathleen Kenyon and D. Tushingham at the excavations in the lower levels of Jericho.

Kathleen Mary Kenyon, one of the doyens of British archaeology in the Near East, was the daughter of the Director of the British Museum. She read history at Oxford and was the first president of the Oxford University Archaeological Society. Her first fieldwork was done at the age of 23 on Dr. Gertrude Caton-Thompson's expedition to Great Zimbabwe, in what was then southern Rhodesia. From 1930 until around 1950, she spent summers excavating Roman towns, Iron Age hill forts, and many other sites in England. During this period, Dame Kenyon was a founding member of the Institute of Archaeology at the University of London, first as Secretary and then as Acting Director during World War II.

She was introduced to Near Eastern archaeology from 1931 to 1934 through her participation in excavations at the site of Samaria in Israel. Kenyon's interests returned to the Near East in 1951, the beginning of a period of intense fieldwork and writing. Through her efforts in the British Academy, the British School of Archaeology in Jerusalem was reopened with Kenyon as Honorary Director. Her research project at Jericho lasted from 1952 until 1958. In 1962, excavations were begun in Jerusalem, uncovering the sequence of massive walls that defined the city in the first and second millennia B.C. Her work in the Near East and elsewhere is the subject of a number of books and professional monographs, including *Beginning in Archaeology* (1952), *Digging Up Jericho* (1957), *Archaeology in the Holy Land* (1960), and *Digging Up Jerusalem* (1974).

As a personality Miss Kenyon was a forceful character but was greatly loved by all who worked with her. Her energy, her warmth of heart, her cool imagination and her impeccable craftsmanship will long be remembered by a multitude of colleagues and pupils from many parts of the world.

The London Times, August 25, 1978

Obsidian and Long-Distance Trade

The rise of a Turkish city

The distribution of obsidian in the Near East from two major sources. Note the proximity of Çatal Hüyük in Turkey to one of the sources. The overlapping area represents approximate distribution of obsidian from each source.

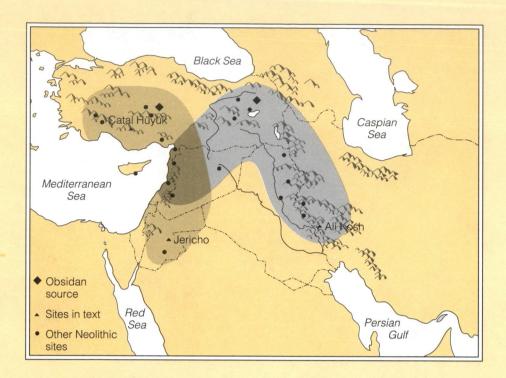

Obsidian is a translucent, hard, black glass, produced by volcanoes. Molten silica sometimes flows out of a volcanic core and hardens into this stone, which was highly sought after by prehistoric makers of stone tools. Obsidian, like glass and flint, fractures easily and regularly, creating very sharp edges. Because of their sharpness, obsidian scalpels have been used in modern surgery. In the past, obsidian was often traded or exchanged over long distances, hundreds of kilometers or more.

Obsidian is also interesting because it is available from only a few places, limited by the proximity to volcanic mountains and the chance formation of a silica flow. Most sources for obsidian are known because they are rare and the material is unusual. It is also possible to fingerprint different flows of obsidian through minor variations in the chemical composition of the material, which is specific to one source, allowing pieces found elsewhere to be traced to the places where they originated. The sources of obsidian — the Near East, the Aegean area, North America, Mexico, and elsewhere — have been studied using these methods.

Most of the Near East obsidian comes from the mountains of Turkey (Anatolia) or northern Iran (Armenia), both outside the Fertile Crescent. Information on the sources of obsidian found at early Neolithic sites provides data on both the direction and the intensity of trade. Sites in the Levant generally contained obsidian from Anatolia, while tool makers at sites in the Zagros used Armenian material. The percentage of obsidian in the total flaked stone assemblages indicates that sites closest to the sources used a great deal of obsidian, while those farthest away had only a small amount available. At Jericho, for example, 700 km (400 mi) from the Anatolian sources, only about 1% of the stone tools are made from obsidian; the situation is similar at Ali Kosh, 800 km (500 mi) from the Armenian sources.

At the site of Çatal Hüyük in south-central Turkey, however, most of the chipped stone tools are obsidian. Occupied between 6500 and 5500 B.C. this site was excavated by James Mellaart, of the University of London, during the 1950s. Several obsidian quarries were located within 150 km (100 mi) of Çatal Hüyük. In addition to finished tools,

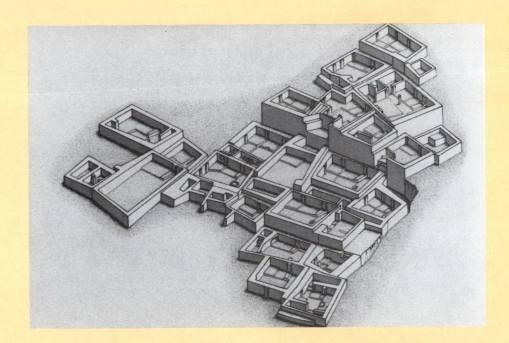

many unfinished obsidian tools were found, along with large amounts of raw material. It appears that obsidian was moved in very large quantities from the Anatolian sources to Çatal Hüyük and other sites in the area. From here the obsidian was traded over a wide area of the Near East. In return, the inhabitants of Çatal Hüyük received copper, shell, and other exotic materials.

Çatal Hüyük (sha-tal'who-yuk') was clearly a prosperous center, probably because of its control of the obsidian trade. The tell of Çatal Hüyük is 500 m (1600 ft) long, 150 m (500 ft) wide, and 15 m (50 ft) high. At least twice as large as early Neolithic Jericho, covering some 13 ha (32 acres), the site was a large town, and the stone foundations of rectangular houses can be seen on the surface of the mound. These houses were built closely together in one, two, or three stories around small courtyards. The roofs were flat, and access to the houses was likely through the roofs. One of the remarkable things at Çatal Hüyük is the fact that a large number of the structures, perhaps 20%, appear to have been shrines. The walls of these shrines are elaborately dec-

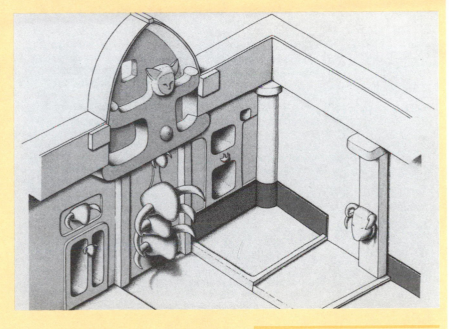

orated and painted with a variety of figures, including vultures, bulls, and humans. Some of the paintings show women giving birth to bulls. Clearly the importance of obsidian as a desired object in trade was an essential factor in the rise of Çatal Hüyük. Trade and exchange of materials accelerated greatly in the Neolithic.

An artist's reconstruction of one of the shrine rooms at Çatal Hüyük. A goddess form gives birth to a ram above three bull's heads.

'AIN GHAZAL

New communities and early farming in the Near East

'Ain Ghazal (ein′ga-zel′) is a large, early Neolithic site at the edge of the modern city of Amman in Jordan. The site was accidentally discovered in 1981 when layers of houses and burials were exposed by construction for a new road. Neolithic structures were found sitting on artificial terraces along the banks of the Wadi Zarqa, over a length of almost 600 m (2000 ft). Investigations were conducted from 1982 to 1989 by Gary Rollefson, of San Diego State University; Alan Simmons, of the University of Nevada; and Zeidan Kafafi, of Yarmouk University in Jordan. Long trenches were used to determine the limits of the settlement. 'Ain Ghazal (meaning "the spring of the gazelle") is very large, covering almost 12 ha (30 acres). This site is twice as large as contemporary levels at similar Pre-Pottery Neolithic B sites dating from 7000 to 6000 B.C.

Excavations exposed numerous pits, house floors, burials, and a range of artifacts and debris. Domestic houses were generally of one form, a long rectangular room with an entrance on one side. The room contained built-in benches or counters along the walls and a central hearth set in a plastered basin. A change in this basic pattern was probably the result of remodeling due to an increase or decrease in the size of the family occupying the house.

Initial house construction involved site preparation and the leveling of the slope, requiring movement of a substantial amount of earth and the construction of a stone retaining wall for the front of the terrace. House walls of stone were then

An artist's reconstruction of houses at 'Ain Ghazal. These houses had rock wall foundations, and walls and roofs of timber and reeds covered with mud.

erected, laid directly on the level surface of the terrace. The area between an inner and outer row of large stones was filled with rubble of earth and small stones. These walls were up to 60 cm (18 in.) thick at the base. Some of the walls uncovered during the excavations were still standing to a height of 1.5 m (5 ft). Wooden posts were also used as structural elements, either along the walls or in the middle of the room, to support roof beams. Roofs were light and flat, likely made of brush and reeds covered with a layer of earth. A smooth mud coating was the final surface for the roof, resulting from the packing of the earth after rain.

For the floor of the house, the builders dug a shallow pit for a fireplace and then covered the entire surface and the lower part of the inside walls and posts with plaster made with lime, sand, and small stones, often burnished with red ochre. To make this plaster, they heated limestone to at least 750°C to convert it to calcium carbonate in a simple lime kiln. Then they mixed the lime ash with water and tempered it with sand. The walls themselves were coated with mud and a thin layer of lime plaster. Walls and floors were occasionally decorated with paintings or colors. The outside of the house was probably coated with mud as well, to make a rain-resistant structure.

Modifications to the original structures were made during the course of occupation. House 4 is an example of such remodeling. Initially a big room, 6 by 7 m (20 by 25 ft), was modified by enlarging the exterior walls, dividing it into two rooms, and adding a storage pit. In the next stage, the entire floor was removed, along with some of the subfloor soil to make the house deeper on the terrace. Four posts were then used to support the roof, and a deeper hearth was built. Later, the west room was removed and a terrace built at that end of the house, along with a new entrance. A new hearth was centered in the east room and new plaster laid down in the smaller and deeper house.

Houses are a dynamic expression of the needs of the inhabitants. This pattern of remodeling houses is repeated several times at 'Ain Ghazal. Renovation was likely a more reasonable solution than moving or building completely new structures.

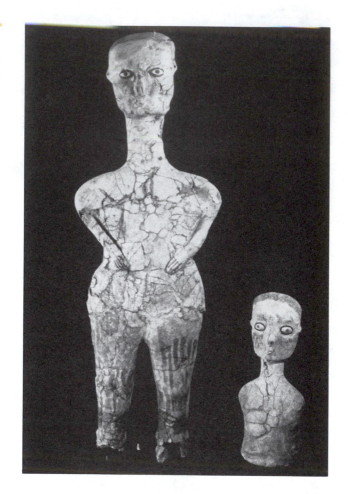

Two of the decorated statues from 'Ain Ghazal after reconstruction. The statues have a skeleton of straw covered by plaster. The bodies are often painted, and the eyes are cowrie shells set in bitumen. The taller statue is 90 cm high.

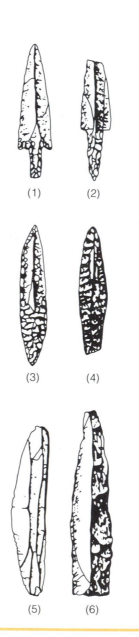

(1)   (2)

(3)   (4)

(5)   (6)

Chipped stone artifacts from 'Ain Ghazal. Included here are points (1-4), a sickle (5), and a knife (6). The sickle blade is 4 cm long.

Family growth required the addition of a new room, while a decrease in family size resulted in the removal of a portion of the original structure.

Relatives were often buried beneath the floor of the houses, adjacent to the hearth. A total of eighty burials have been excavated, including twenty-two infants. At the same time nearly 20% of the population lived beyond age 50. A number of the burials lack skulls, while four skulls were found together in a single pit at the site, all facing southwest. Facial features had been restored with plaster, and tar had been applied to the eye sockets, perhaps to attach shells or other materials to represent the eyes. Another skull from the site had been scraped with a flint knife and coated with red ochre.

Plant and animal remains provide information on the varied diet and subsistence activities of the inhabitants. Goats are the most abundant, but cattle, gazelle, wild pig, and such small carnivores as fox, hare, and turtle are also common. Although the evidence for domestication is meager, several changes in the goat and

cattle skeletons and the patterns of butchering suggest that these animals were herded. Other animals present—such as marten, badger, squirrel, and goshawk—required forest habitats, a more pleasant environment than exists in this rather arid zone today. A number of plants were being cultivated by the residents of 'Ain Ghazal, including barley, wheat, peas, and beans.

Flint **sickles** for harvesting grain comprised almost 10% of all the stone tools; spear and arrow points made up another 6%. A cache of eighty-four flint blades was found hidden under one house floor. Bone artifacts were not common, but those present were used primarily for sewing and making cloth: needles, a thimble, awls, and weaving tools.

Although pottery was not yet used by these early farming villagers, there is a type of whiteware vessel, a crude, plaster container at 'Ain Ghazal. Ceramic figurines, both human and animal in form, were made for religious purposes. The animal effigies are primarily cattle, with a few goats and pigs. The human figures are mostly female, reminiscent of the "fertil-

The statuary cache at 'Ain Ghazal during the excavations. The scale is 15 cm long.

ity" or Venus figurines from the Upper Paleolithic, some of which are decorated with geometric lines and designs. In addition, there are a number of clay tokens, geometric objects in the form of cones, balls, cylinders, and the like that are thought to represent some form of early counting and recording system.

Pendants of polished limestone were made, as were beads of bone, stone, and shell. Stone beads were made from turquoise, **carnelian**, amber, and greenstone; the shell beads of cowrie and mother of pearl came from the Red Sea some 250 km (150 mi) away, while clam and cockleshell beads were from the Mediterranean, 110 km (70 mi) to the west.

Perhaps the most spectacular finds are two groups of plaster statues. One group, found beneath a house floor, includes twelve complete human figures and thirteen heads made of plaster. The second group contains as many as twenty large statues, 0.7 to 0.9 m (2'5" to 3') tall. The busts are 0.3 to 0.5 m (1' to 1'5") tall. Carefully arranged in two layers, the figures were made with a frame of twigs and reeds, bound together with twine, on which plaster was modelled to create a human figure. The bodies are highly schematic and featureless with oversize, flat heads. Each face is different, however, suggesting that specific individuals were being copied, that the figures were intended as portraits. Blue-green paint is applied around very white areas for the eyes, and a small bit of asphalt is attached to the center of the white eye, creating a stunning affect. The features resemble those found on the plaster skulls, in this early form of ancestor worship or veneration. Most of the standing figures are male, while the separate heads represent all ages and both sexes. There is at least one female figure, apparently holding one breast in her right hand. Most remarkable of all, the feet of one of the statues depicts an individual with six toes—a genetic rarity also seen on statues from contemporary levels at Jericho. Clearly, there was a great deal of communication between these towns, as trade, religious beliefs, and interaction increased in the early Neolithic.

Paleoethno-botany

The study of prehistoric plant remains

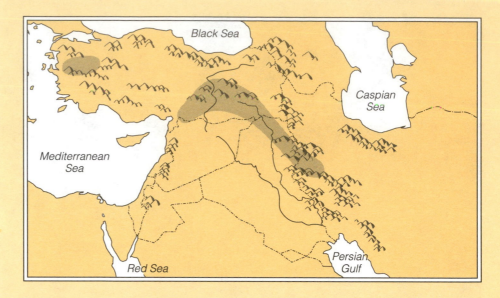

The natural habitat of wild einkorn wheat (Triticum boeoticum) in the Near East.

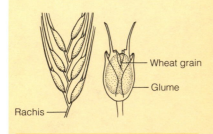

Rachis

Wheat grain

Glume

The main characteristics of cereal grains.

Preservation of plants is rare unless the remains have been carbonized, generally through burning or oxidation. Plant remains are usually obtained from excavations through a process called **flotation**, in which the lighter, carbonized plant pieces float to the top of a container of water into which sediments have been poured. Major issues in **paleoethnobotany** (the study of the prehistoric use of plants), in addition to the kinds of plants used, include the contribution of plants to the diet, medicinal uses, and domestication: the origins of agriculture.

The paleoethnobotany of the Near East is of particular interest because of the early evidence for domestication in this area. Two varieties of wheat (emmer and einkorn), two-row barley, rye, oats, lentils, peas, chickpeas, and other plants were originally cultivated in the Near East. The wild forms of these species are common in the Near East, both today and in the past. Wild emmer wheat has a restricted distribution in the southern Levant. Einkorn was probably domesticated in the south of Turkey, while emmer may have been first cultivated in the Jordan Valley. Wild barley grows throughout the Fertile Crescent. Wild einkorn wheat is relatively widespread in the northern and eastern sections of this region. All of these wild grasses grow well in disturbed ground around human settlements.

Jack Harlan, an agronomist participating in an archaeological project in southern Turkey during the 1960s, experimented to determine how much food was available from wild wheat. Dense stands of einkorn, grow on the slopes of the mountains in this area. This wild einkorn is more nutritious than the hard winter red wheats grown in the United States today. Harvesting the wheat, Harlan collected more than a kilogram of cereal grain per hour with his hands, and even more with the sickle. He estimated that a family of four could harvest enough grain in three weeks to provide food for an entire year. If this wild food is so abundant and nutritious, why was wheat domesticated? The answer likely lies in the fact that wild wheats do not grow everywhere in the Near East, and some communities may have transplanted the wild form into new environments.

Although artifactual evidence for the use of plants (e.g., sickles, milling stones, storage pits, and roasting areas) exists in a number of areas, domesticated varieties cannot be distinguished from wild types without actual plant parts or grain impressions in clay bricks or pottery. Paleoethnobotanist Gordon Hillman, of the University of London, studied wild einkorn and observed that simple harvesting had no major impact on the genetic structure of the wheat. Only when specifically

Patty Jo Watson and Louise Robbins, of Washington University of St. Louis, operating flotation equipment. Site sediments are stirred into water to separate the heavier from the lighter particles, which may include carbonized plant remains.

Table 5.1 Common Food Plants in the Early Neolithic Near East

Einkorn wheat,
  wild and domesticated forms
Emmer wheat,
  wild and domesticated forms
Rye, wild and domesticated forms
Barley, wild and domesticated forms
Chickpeas, domesticated form
Field peas, domesticated form
Lentils, wild and domesticated forms
Common vetch
Bitter vetch
Horse bean
Grape, wild and domesticated forms
Caper
Prosopis
Fig
Hackberry
Turpentine tree
Wild pistachio

selective harvesting and other cultivation techniques were applied could changes in the morphology of the seeds be noted. Such a pattern suggests that certain characteristics of domesticated wheat and barley, which show definite morphological differences from the wild ancestral forms, must have been intentionally selected. Hillman has also conducted experimental studies suggesting that the changes from wild to domesticated wheat might occur in a brief period, perhaps 200 years or less.

According to Hans Helbaek, a leading paleoethnobotanist who worked on the issue of plant domestication, the most important characteristic of a domesticated species is the loss of natural seeding abilities. The plant comes to depend on human intervention to reproduce. This change also permits humans to select the characteristics of those plants to be sown and reproduce, leading to preferred characteristics. Another characteristic of domesticated plants was the presence of plants outside their natural habitat, in new environmental zones. New conditions of growth obviously select for different characteristics among the members of the plant species. Certain varieties do very well when moved to a new setting.

Wheat is an annual grass with large seed grains that concentrate carbohydrates inside a hard shell. Grains are connected together by the **rachis,** or stem. Each seed is covered by a husk, or **glume**. The major changes that distinguish wild and domesticated wheat are found in the rachis and glume. In wild wheat (*Triticum boeoticum*), the stems of the seed cluster are brittle, so that the grains can be naturally dispersed as a seeding mechanism. The glumes covering the seeds are tough, to protect the grain until the next growing season. These two features, however, are counterproductive to effective harvesting and consumption by humans. Because of the brittleness of the rachis, many seeds fall to the ground before and during harvesting, and collection is difficult. The tough glume is hard to remove and must be roasted to make it brittle enough that winnowing can remove it. Domesticated wheats exhibit a reverse of these characteristics: a tough rachis and a brittle glume. These changes enable the seed to stay on the plant so it can be harvested in quantity and the glume to be removed by threshing without roasting. These changes also mean that the wheat is dependent upon humans for seeding and therefore, by definition, domesticated.

ALI KOSH

*A small tell in southwestern Iran, occupied at
the time of the origins of agriculture*

*Excavations at Ali Kosh. The middle
(right) and lower (left) levels reveal
early Neolithic deposits.*

Nestled in the foothills of the Zagros Mountains in the southwestern corner of Iran, the Deh Luran Plain is an arid region at the edge of the 300-mm (12-in.) rainfall isobar. Today dry seasons cause crop failure three years out of five. The area lies at the periphery of the Fertile Crescent, outside the natural habitat of the ancestors of domesticated plants and animals. This inauspicious region, however, was the focus of a major archaeological project in the early 1960s, concerned with prehistory and human ecology between 8000 and 4000 B.C. The project was directed by Frank Hole, of Yale University, in collaboration with Kent Flannery, of the University of Michigan, and James Neely, of the University of Texas. The investigation was primarily concerned with the beginnings

of successful plant and animal domestication, village life, and irrigation agriculture; it was the first archaeological project in the Near East to emphasize the recovery of carbonized plant remains by the method of flotation.

Although it is surprising to find early Neolithic settlements in the center of this marginal region, the area has a very high density of prehistoric sites. Excavations at several sites have provided an almost continuous sequence of evidence for the period of time between the origins of agriculture and the beginnings of the Bronze Age. The site of Ali Kosh (ah-lee-kosh′) was the focus of one of these excavations, which uncovered the earliest Neolithic site in the area, and one of the earliest Neolithic occupations in the Zagros,

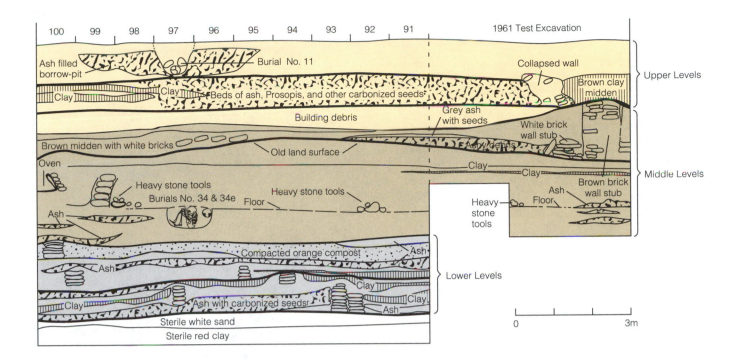

The stratigraphic sections at Ali Kosh, showing the three major levels of the site, dating from about 7500 B.C. at the lowest level to about 5600 B.C. at the upper levels.

perhaps 500 years younger than similar sites in the Levant.

Ali Kosh is a low mound, or tell, some 7 m (22 ft) deep and 135 m (450 ft) in diameter, with three distinct periods represented in its stratigraphy. The lowest level, dating to between 7500 and 6750 B.C., contains a few rectangular houses with walls made of unfired slabs of clay. The houses have several small rooms, each about 2 by 2.5 m (6 by 8 ft) in size, with floors of stamped earth. The size of the houses, and of the tell itself, suggests a community of perhaps fifty to a hundred people. The evidence indicates only that the site was occupied in the cooler months of the year; it is possible that the villagers left Ali Kosh each summer to take their herds to pasture in the cooler, higher steppes east of the site. The presence of pistachio nut shells, which grow only in the hills, among the food remains at Ali Kosh indicates that these nuts were collected by groups away from the village, perhaps at the end of summer. Some trade is indicated by the presence of obsidian imported from Turkey, about 700 km (400 mi) away. Obsidian comprises about 1% of the flaked stone at Ali Kosh. However, most of the food and raw materials that were used come from the adjacent steppe.

Over 45,000 seeds from forty species of plants and 10,000 bones from thirty-five species of animals were found in the excavations at the tell. Very small seeds from wild alfalfa, vetch, canary grass, and oat grass were recovered. Domestic emmer wheat and two-row barley were cultivated. Carbonized seeds from reeds found with the wheat and barley suggest that the fields were located at the edge of a nearby marsh. Wild wheat and barley are winter-ripening plants in the Near East, so harvesting was probably in March or April.

Domestic goats were kept at Ali Kosh; the surrounding plain would have provided excellent winter grazing for these herds. The morphological changes associated with domestication are not yet apparent in these animals. However, most of the bones came from young male goats, a slaughter pattern suggesting the intentional culling of specific animals. Sheep were present in much smaller numbers. Hunting and fishing were important subsistence activities, and the remains of gazelle, aurochs, and wild boar were present in the deposits. Catfish, carp, mussels, turtle, and migratory waterfowl were also included in the food larder.

In the upper levels at Ali Kosh, dating to between 6000 and 5600 B.C., a number

The tell at Ali Kosh. The 1963 excavations exposed the upper level.

of trends are apparent. Construction was more substantial, and larger mud-bricks were used; houses were larger and had stone foundations. Wild legumes and hunted animals were less common among the plant remains. Wheat and, especially, barley increased in importance in the diet. Weedy plant remains suggest that cultivated fields were also used for pasture and left fallow at times. Sheep were becoming more common and beginning to compete with goats for fodder. Sheep are better adapted than goats to warm climates, and their increase may suggest a more permanent occupation of the tell. In the lowest level, domestic plants and animals were about one-third of the total seed and bone remains; in the upper level, domestic plants were roughly 40% of the total, and herded animals, primarily sheep, provided more than 50% of the meat.

Trade networks brought obsidian (2% to 3% of the flaked stone tools), copper, seashells, and turquoise from long distances during the later period, perhaps in exchange for **bitumen,** a local asphalt, which was used for waterproofing and as an adhesive. Clay figurines of humans and animals were now common. Pottery appeared for the first time, replacing stone bowls and asphalt-lined baskets. A number of burials were found in the upper level; males wore a girdle, or G-string, with a fringe of stone beads and a bell-shaped pubic ornament of stone, asphalt, or baked clay. By now there were at least two other communities in the Deh Luran Plain.

Over a period of some 2000 years, we can observe the success of the agricultural enterprise, as domesticated plants and animals became more important in the diet. The process was a gradual one, however, as the new species replaced wild forms as the focus of subsistence. The growth of Ali Kosh and the appearance of new Neolithic settlements suggests significant population increase in the context of the successful agricultural adaptation; the population of the Deh Luran Plain tripled over a 2000-year period. However, the long-term use of the fields likely led to soil exhaustion and reduced productivity, factors that may be responsible for the abandonment of Ali Kosh after 5600 B.C. and resettlement of the population elsewhere in the Deh Luran area.

The companion of paleoethnobotany in the investigation of the preserved organic remains from the past, **archaeozoology** is the study of the animal remains from archaeological sites. Focusing on the hard body parts that survive—bone, teeth, antler, ivory, scales, and shell, archaeozoologists attempt to answer questions about whether animals were hunted or scavenged, how animals were butchered, how much meat contributed to the diet, and the process of domestication.

Archaeozoologists can identify the genus or species of an animal from small fragments of bone, as well as age and sex, how the bone was broken, and how many individual animals are represented in a bone assemblage. Fracture patterns in long bones may reveal intentional breakage to remove marrow. Analysis of cut-marks on bone may provide information on butchering techniques. Herded animals show certain changes in size and body parts that provide direct evidence for domestication. Domesticated species are generally smaller than their wild ancestors; the shape of the horns often changes in the domestic form; the microscopic structure of bone also undergoes modification in domestic animals. Other traits may also be selected by herders to increase yields of milk, wool, or meat. However, because it can take many generations to establish a biological change, the earliest stages of domestication may not have been recorded in the bones and horns that remain.

Brian Hesse, of the University of Alabama, Birmingham, estimated the age and sex of animals that had been killed at a prefarming site in the Zagros Mountains of western Iran. He used this information to study whether hunting or herding was practiced. Herded animals are slaughtered when the herder decides; for most species, this means that the average age of death for domesticated animals is younger than that for wild animals. Hunted animals are taken by chance encounter, and the percentage of adult animals is higher among wild groups.

The ages of animals are most frequently determined by an assessment of

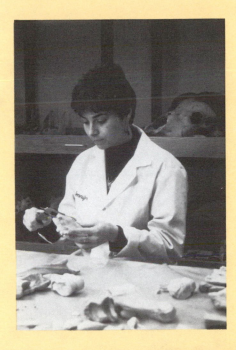

Archaeozoologists measure a variety of characteristics on prehistoric animal bones.

tooth eruption and wear, along with information about changes in bone. Before 10,000 years ago, all the known sites in the Zagros Mountains of Iran show similar slaughter patterns for sheep, goats, and red deer; bone assemblages contain primarily adult animals, indicating that all were hunted in the wild. After 10,000 years ago, however, a number of sites contain assemblages dominated by the bones of younger animals. In each case, sheep or goat is represented by the young animals, proportionately higher than in a normal wild herd.

Ganj Dareh (ganjh′dar-ah′) is a small tell, approximately 1 ha (2.5 acre) in area, high in the Zagros Mountains. The earliest Neolithic layer in the 8 m (25 ft) of deposits was extensively burned, so preservation is exceptional. The site contains the earliest ceramics in the Near East, dated to around 7000 B.C., in the form of both pottery and clay figurines. Ganj Dareh provides dramatic evidence for early animal domestication. The footprints of sheep or goats were found in the hardened mud-brick used in house construction; the animals had stepped on these bricks while they were drying. The abundant animal bones are dominated by young ani-

Table 5.2 Important Animal Species in the Neolithic Near East

Common Name	Genus Name
Gazelle	*Gazella*
Goat, wild and domesticated forms	*Capra*
Sheep, wild and domesticated forms	*Ovis*
Roe deer	*Capreolus*
Fallow deer	*Dama*
Cattle, wild and domesticated forms	*Bos*
Pig, wild and domesticated forms	*Sus*
Onager	*Equus*
Bear	*Ursos*
Jackal	*Canis*
Hare	*Lepus*
Wild cat	*Felis*
Fish	—
Bird	—

The distribution of wild goats (Capra aegagrus) in the Near East and Egypt.

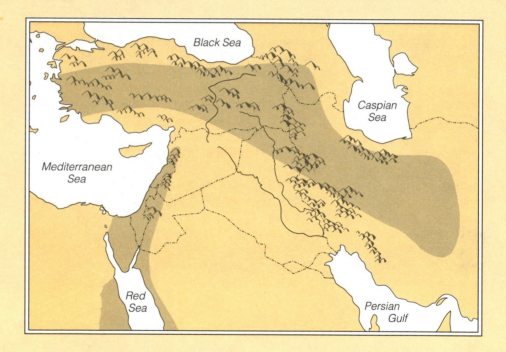

mals, primarily male goats. Goats outnumber sheep six or more to one. It thus seems likely that goats were the first livestock species to be domesticated in the Zagros area sometime after 7500 B.C.

At the site of Abu Hureyra (a'boo-hoo-ray'rah) in Syria, a study of the bones of wild gazelle and domesticated goats and sheep has also provided new information on the process of animal domestication. Around 11,000 years ago, the site was occupied by prefarming hunter-gatherers who hunted gazelle in large numbers, as evidenced by the bones and teeth of many young gazelle. The teeth, in particular, indicated that both newborn and year-old animals were common in the faunal assemblage, along with adults of all ages. This pattern of newborns, yearlings, and adults, and the absence of ani-

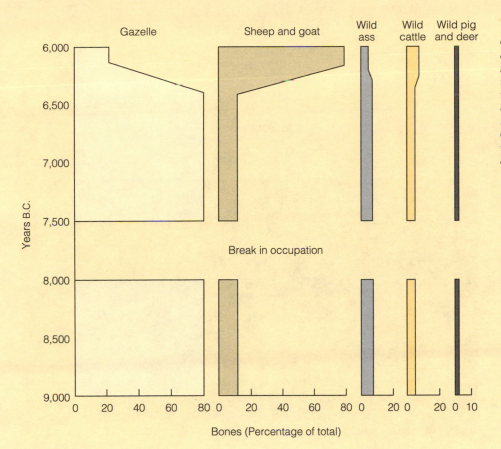

Years B.C.

Gazelle — Sheep and goat — Wild ass — Wild cattle — Wild pig and deer

Break in occupation

Bones (Percentage of total)

Changes in animal species at Abu Hureyra, Syria, between 9000 and 6000 B.C. The width of the bars indicates the relative abundance of the species. The most pronounced change is the decrease in gazelle and the increase in sheep and goats between 6500 and 6000 B.C. There was an absence of human occupation at this site between 8000 and 7500 B.C.

mals of ages in between, indicates that most of them were killed during the same time each year, shortly after the calving period in late April and early May. Hunters were taking entire herds of gazelle, as the animals migrated north during early summer. They probably used a drive technique that would force a herd into an enclosure or series of pitfalls, where all the animals could be killed. These hunters were so effective that the number of gazelle in the area dropped dramatically — to less than 20% of all the animals at the site — by 6500 B.C.

Goat and sheep domestication may have been a solution to the problem of decreasing numbers of gazelle. Sheep and goats were slaughtered throughout the year, in contrast to the seasonal hunting of gazelle at Abu Hureyra. Goat and sheep bones are present as about 10% of the faunal assemblage until 6500 B.C., when very rapidly they became the predomi-

nant component, reaching almost 80% of the fauna. This point in time was about 1500 years after plant domestication had been initiated at the site; wheats and barley were providing a significant portion of the diet. It was also some 3500 years after the initial occupation of the site, documenting the sequential stages of sedentism, plant cultivation, and animal domestication that were typical in the Near East.

MEHRGARH

*New evidence for the early Neolithic
in South Asia*

A view of Mehrgarh.

A grave with five young goats.

The Indus civilization, one of the world's early urban societies, emerged in South Asia, the subcontinent now composed of India, Pakistan, Bangladesh, and Nepal. The largest communities of this ancient civilization — the cities of Harappa, Mohenjo-daro and others — were centered on the Indus River system now in Pakistan. (See Chapter Nine.) Until the 1970s, however, little was known about the antecedents of this ancient society. In the late 1960s, it was suggested that plant and animal domestication did not reach the subcontinent of South Asia until after 4000 B.C. The prevailing opinion was that migrants from the west, who made metals and wheel-thrown pottery, brought an agricultural way of life to South Asia just a few centuries before the rise of the Indus civilization.

Recent archaeological findings, however, have revealed an older, more indigenous picture of agricultural origins in the Indus River drainage. One key for this new perspective has come from a long-term research program, conducted by the French Archaeological Mission and the

Pakistani Department of Archaeology, at the site of Mehrgarh (meh-her-gar'), located in the Kachi Plain about 200 km (120 mi) northwest of the Indus River. The site is also interesting because of its location immediately below the Bolan Pass through the mountains, connecting the Indus River Valley with the Near East.

In 1974, the first fieldwork at Mehrgarh by Jean-François Jarrige and his collaborators focused on a small mound. At that time, however, older pottery was collected over an area of several hundred hectares adjacent to the mound. Large-scale excavations in this area have yielded a sequence of deposits dating to the seventh millennium B.C. The earliest occupation level at Mehrgarh lacked pottery, although clay was used to make bricks for the construction of substantial, multiroom, quadrangular structures and **anthropomorphic** (having human form) figurines. A count of plant impressions in the mud-bricks by Lorenzo Costantini found that barley was the most abundant cultigen in this early level. This barley had several, distinctive local characteristics and may not have been completely domesticated. Other cereals grown at that time included smaller amounts of einkorn, emmer, and a kind of bread wheat.

As in the early Neolithic sites of Southwest Asia, gazelle was the most abundant of the wild animal species, which included sheep, goat, cattle, swamp deer, and a large South Asian antelope. Some goats have been recognized anatomically as domesticated. In each of two burials from an early level of the occupation, five young goats were placed at the foot of an adult male, whose body was covered with red ochre. These early graves also contained a diverse combination of body ornaments made from exotic materials like seashell, turquoise, and **lapis lazuli**.

After 6000 B.C., important subsistence shifts occurred at Mehrgarh, and the first ceramic vessels were found. Richard Meadow, of Harvard University, has noted a reduction in the body sizes of the goat, sheep, and humped cattle (*Bos indicus*) at the site, which he interprets as evidence for domestication. While the relative abundance of wild species decreased, the proportion of cattle bones increased greatly, suggesting that cattle husbandry may have begun about the same time at Mehrgarh as at sites to the west. Between 6000 and 4000 B.C., domesticated barley, well adapted to floodplain irrigation, was the predominant cultigen. Charred seeds of the plumlike jujube (*Zizyphus jujuba*) fruit and date (*Phoenix dactylifera*) pits also have been recovered. Cotton (*Gossypium*) seeds were found with wheat and barley grains at about 5000 B.C., the earliest date for cotton in the world.

At this time, Mehrgarh was a well-planned, permanent community composed of compartmentalized, mud-brick structures that served primarily as storage rooms. Features found in other parts of the settlement include circular fireplaces (containing heavily burned rocks for **stone boiling**) with piles of bone and other debris nearby. These areas may have been used for large-scale food processing or cooking, or some other kind of communal activity.

Both the specialized craft production and the extensive long-distance trade, so evident at the major centers of the later Indus civilization, had clear antecedents

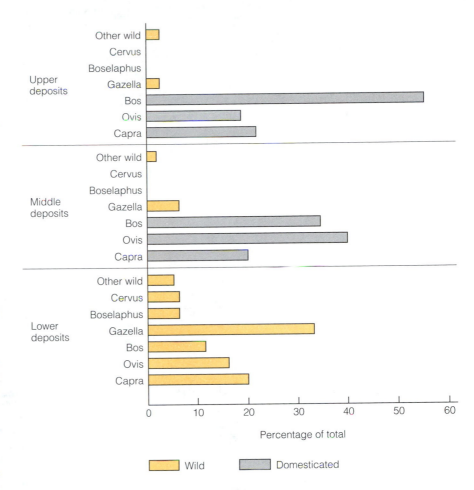

Percentage of total

☐ Wild   ☐ Domesticated

millennia earlier at Mehrgarh. By 4000 B.C., the site spread over tens of hectares and included specialized centers where fine ceramic ware was made. For roughly the next 1500 years, Mehrgarh was an important craft center. Wheel-thrown pottery was mass-produced, and beads of lapis lazuli, turquoise, and carnelian were perforated with green **jasper** bits rotated by a **bow-drill**. (See "Pottery," p. 216.) Fragments of crucibles used to melt copper also were uncovered.

The archaeology at Mehrgarh, along with recent studies at other contemporary sites, has revised South Asian prehistory. No longer can we envision the inhabitants of the Indus River drainage as simple recipients of advances brought from the west. Nor can the rise of the Indus civilization after 3000 B.C. be attributed to the precipitous blossoming of these nonindigenous traits. We now recognize a sequence in South Asia that documents a preceramic Neolithic phase, the manipulation of cereal grains, and the indigenous domestication of cattle, along with the development of highly specialized local craft industries.

The transition from hunting to herding at Mehrgarh. In the lower deposits, all the species present are wild, including gazelle (Gazella), wild goat (Capra), wild sheep (Ovis), wild cattle (Bos), antelope (Boselaphus), and swamp deer (Cervus). After 6000 B.C. (middle deposits), the reduced size of cattle, goat, and sheep bones at Mehrgarh indicates that these animals were domesticated. After the Neolithic (upper deposits), domesticated cattle were dominant.

Pottery

Ancient containers: a key source for archaeological interpretation

A Mexican woman making pottery vessels.

"Pottery is . . . the greatest resource of the archaeologist," wrote the famed Egyptologist W. M. Flinders Petrie (Flinders Petrie, 1904, pp. 15–16). Indeed, ceramics are the most common kind of artifact found at most post-Paleolithic sites. Since pottery has several purposes — cooking, storage, serving, or carrying materials — many different pieces can be used by a single household at the same time. Moreover, pottery vessels are fragile and often have to be replaced. However, fragments of pottery, or **potsherds**, are very durable and normally preserve better than many other ancient materials found in archaeological contexts.

Ceramics also are important because they can be good **temporal markers**, indicators of specific time periods. In his study of ancient Egyptian pottery, Flinders Petrie was one of the first archaeologists to recognize how decorative styles change. In addition to chronological sensitivity, pottery vessels have a whole series of distinctive technical, formal, and decorative attributes that can tell us many different things about the lives of the people who made, traded, and used them.

Fired-clay containers provide clean and sturdy storage for food and drink and can serve to prepare food over a fire. Yet the earliest securely dated pottery vessels,

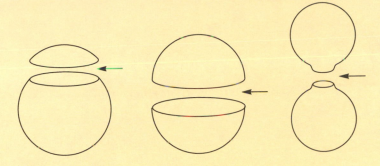

found at Jomon sites in Japan, are less than 10,000 to 12,000 years old. Why did they occur so late in human history? Ceramic vessels do have liabilities; they are relatively heavy and often fragile. Many mobile foragers do not use ceramics, preferring lighter containers like net bags, gourds, and baskets. In the preceramic levels at Mehrgarh, for example, the inhabitants used baskets coated with water-resistant bitumen. Clearly, the development of and reliance on ceramic vessels is associated with more settled communities. Yet some sedentary groups, such as the Indians of northwestern North America, did not use pottery, relying instead on a diverse array of woven baskets for storage. Pottery did not simply appear with agriculture. In both Mexico and Southwest Asia, plant domestication preceded the use of ceramics by more than a thousand years. Conversely, the world's oldest ceramic containers were made by the nonagricultural Jomon fisher-foragers of ancient Japan.

The late advent of pottery is curious because ceramic technology had been used by human societies for some time. Baked clay figurines were made at Paleolithic sites in the former Soviet Union and Eastern Europe as early as 20,000 to 30,000 years ago. Clay figurines and mud-bricks were made in the Levant 10,000 years ago, yet pottery did not appear locally until around 7000 B.C. Settled farming villagers used ground stone bowls long before they made ceramic containers. In the Americas, ceramic vessels were not made until several thousand years later, when they first appeared in lowland South America. The earliest pottery containers in Mexico and North America date between 3000 and 2000 B.C., before the advent of fully sedentary villages.

The earliest pottery from both the Old and the New Worlds was crafted by hand. Generally, early pottery vessels were built up in a series of clay coils or molded using gourds. However, by roughly 4000 B.C., **wheel-thrown pottery** became an important commodity throughout the Near East and South Asia. The potter's wheel permits a single worker to make a greater number of vessels more quickly. Such pottery is also highly uniform in size, shape, and appearance. In the Americas, fired clay vessels continued to be handmade (sometimes at a high level of technological sophistication) until the European introduction of the potter's wheel in the sixteen century A.D. Some scholars have attributed the Old World invention of the potter's wheel to the presence of wheeled vehicles, absent in the New World. Yet the pottery wheel may have preceded the use of the wheel for transport in the Old World. Furthermore, we know that some Native American groups were familiar with the concept of the wheel, because wheeled toys have been found in archaeological contexts. The absence of the potter's wheel may be related to the relative difficulty and inefficiency of transporting ceramic vessels long distances in the aboriginal Americas, where there were few domesticated beasts of burden, no wheeled vehicles, and generally less widespread sea transport than was employed in the Old World.

BAN-PO-TS'UN

A Neolithic village in northern China

Botanists have long recognized that many Chinese food plants were indigenous to the region. Until recently, however, archaeologists believed that the "idea" of agriculture (along with the knowledge for domesticating animals and making pottery) had diffused to the rich soil of the middle Huang Ho River Valley in northern China from elsewhere. Prior to 1960, the few known Neolithic sites with their characteristic black-and-red pottery were assigned to the Yangshao culture and presumed to date to roughly 3000 B.C. The general view that Near East products arrived in China about this time was supported by the presence of small amounts of foreign domesticates, such as wheat and barley, at known Yangshao sites, along with larger quantities of a locally domesticated grain (millet) and domesticated pigs.

In the last thirty years, however, information about the Chinese Neolithic has undergone a major transformation.

A map of China, with sites mentioned in the text.

Thousands of new Neolithic sites have been discovered during surveys conducted across a large area of the country. Dozens of these sites have been excavated, and a number of earlier sites have been recorded. Early Neolithic sites in North China with millet and pigs have now been dated to the sixth millennium B.C., while the age for some Yangshao sites has been pushed back to 5000 B.C. Equally significant has been the discovery of Neolithic sites, such as Hemudu in South China, that predate 5000 B.C. At these more southerly sites, the staple food plant was rice, not millet. The origin of agriculture now appears to have been an indigenous process in both North and South China, since in both areas local cultigens have been found to be both more abundant and earlier than exotic domesticates.

The best known Chinese Neolithic site, Ban-po-ts'un (ban-pot'sun), is not the oldest, but rather the first to have been excavated extensively (with work completed between 1953 and 1955). Located on a loess terrace about 9 m (30 ft) above a tributary of the Huang Ho near the city of Xian, Ban-po-ts'un covers 5 to 7 ha (12.5 to 17.5 acres). Roughly a hundred houses, some circular and others square, were surrounded by a defensive and drainage ditch. Many of these structures were excavated, and the evidence indicates that the occupation at Ban-po was long and continuous. In one instance, five superimposed house floors were uncovered.

Many of the houses were semisubterranean, 3 to 5 m (10 to 16 ft) in diameter, with the house floors sunk roughly a meter below the ground surface. Each house had timber beams that rested on stone bases, supporting a steeply pitched thatched roof. Floors and interior walls were plastered with clay and straw. One or two circular or pear-shaped fire pits, modeled in clay, were sunk at the center of most of the dwellings. Storage pits and

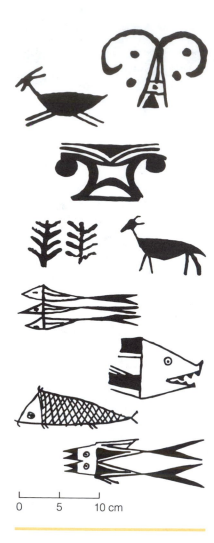

Examples of painted designs on Ban-po-ts'un pottery.

A drawing of a reconstructed section of a pottery kiln at Ban-po-ts'un.

animal pens were interspersed among the houses at the center of the settlement.

At Ban-po, the principal crop was millet (*Setaria italica*), which was cultivated in the rich, soft-textured loess soils that surround the village. Such agricultural tools as bone hoes, polished stone adzes, axes, knives, and digging-stick weights were abundant at the site. Chestnuts, hazelnuts, and pinenuts were collected to supplement the grain diet. **Hemp** was grown by the inhabitants of Ban-po-ts'un, probably to use as a fiber. Silk production also is suggested by a neatly sliced silkworm cocoon that was recovered. Numerous **spindle whorls** (for spinning thread) and bone needles also were found. Impressions of cloth, as well as baskets and mats, provide more evidence of weaving.

Pigs and dogs were the principal domesticated animals, although cattle, sheep, and goat also were present. Bone and quartz arrow points, bone fishhooks, and net-sinkers all were found, and the bones of several varieties of deer were plentiful. Thus hunting and fishing contributed to the diet at Ban-po.

Ban-po-ts'un has yielded more than 500,000 pieces of pottery. Six pottery **kilns** were recovered beyond the ditch at the east side of the settlement, outside the residential zone. Most of the vessels were handmade into a distinctive red ware. While cooking pots tended to be coarse and gritty, water vessels and food-serving bowls were made of a finer paste. Cord marking was the most common surface decoration, although basket, textile, and finger-nail impressions also were employed. The black painted geomorphic and zoomorphic Yangshao designs were applied primarily to bowls and jars.

The inhabitants of Ban-po were buried in one of two ways. Infants and small children were placed in large redware pottery jars and interred near the houses. The cemetery for adults was located outside the enclosing ditch at the north end of the settlement, where corpses were placed in 2-m (6.5 ft) deep pits and arranged in rows. With very few exceptions, each individual was buried separately in an extended position. Ceramic vessels were included with the body in the majority of graves. In a few instances, larger quantities of goods were found. The most elaborate burial was of a child, who was placed in a wooden tomb that included a green jade pendant, a string of sixty-three bone disc beads, four ceramic vessels, and three stone pellets.

Toward the end of the occupation at Ban-po, a large rectangular structure was erected on a manmade platform (20 by 12.5 m, or 65 by 41 ft) at the center of the village. The platform was ringed by a low wall that originally may have been the foundation for a higher wall of posts. Unlike the residential dwellings, this structure was plastered with a white limy substance that had been hardened by baking. The structure also had a hard earthen floor that appears to have been destroyed in a fire. While some archaeologists might consider this special, central structure to be a possible indicator of emergent social inequalities, Chinese archaeologists interpret the building as a communal assembly hall or clan house.

The purposefully planned layout of Ban-po-ts'un, with a large central building surrounded by a nucleated residential area inside a ditch, and exterior pottery-making and cemetery facilities, was very similar to other contemporary Yangshao villages. For example, Chiang-chai, near Ban-po, had concentric circles of oblong and rectangular houses surrounding four large structures that faced the village center. Chiang-chai also was ringed by trenches, and the cemetery area and pottery kilns were located outside these earthworks. At all well-studied Yangshao sites, the dwelling and cemetery areas are spatially distinct.

Today, 11% of the world's arable land is planted with rice. This staple grain provides half the diet for 1.6 billion people; an additional 400 million people depend on the plant for at least 25% of their food. In fact, among the world's major grain crops, rice is the only plant that is harvested almost solely for human consumption.

Yet despite its worldwide significance, archaeologists know relatively little about how or where rice was first domesticated. Although the plant is now cultivated in a variety of environments, it was originally indigenous to the tropics. Rice is an annual grass that shares many characteristics with wheat, barley, oats, and rye. The rice plant belongs to the genus *Oryza*. *Oryza* contains two cultivated species, the Asian *Oryza sativa* and the West African *Oryza glaberrima,* each of which includes a multitude of variants. While archaeologists know less about *Oryza sativa* than they do about early domesticated wheat, barley, or corn, *Oryza glaberrima* is even more of an unsolved mystery.

The Far East seems to have been the focus for early experimentation and cultivation of *Oryza sativa.* Recent archaeological research in South China has suggested that rice was already an important component of the diet at sites along the shores of Lake Dongting by 6000 to 5000 B.C. Also in South China, large quantities of rice stalks, grains, and husks were preserved at the waterlogged prehistoric village of Hemudu, excavated between 1973 and 1978. The settlement contains houses raised on wooden piles above a lakeshore. Excavations revealed rice in stratigraphic levels extending back to the late sixth and early fifth millennia B.C. In one place, the rice remains were 25 to 50 cm (10 to 20 in.) thick, suggesting that a threshing floor may have been preserved. Both wild and domesticated varieties have been identified at Hemudu, making this the earliest domesticated rice in the world. Remains of the bottle gourd, water chestnut, and the sour jujube were recovered, as were acorns and other nuts. The faunal assemblage includes wild deer, elephant, rhinoceros, tiger, and turtle, as well as the domesticated water buffalo, dog, and pig.

Cord-impressed pottery was found at Hemudu, and similar ceramic wares have been recovered, along with rice, at other recently excavated sites in southern China. These sites are later, dating to the mid-fifth millennium B.C. Rice, with both wild and domesticated characteristics, also has been recovered at excavated sites in Thailand, where it may pertain to as early as the late fourth millennium B.C. In Southeast Asia, even earlier evidence of rice domestication may lie under water, as rising sea levels have covered many Neolithic sites. In sum, we still have fewer answers than questions about rice domestication. In the years ahead, earlier dates for rice, both wild and domesticated, will surely be found, as the archaeological records for Southeast Asia and South China are reconstructed and interpreted.

RICE

One of the world's most important grains

A drawing of Oryza sativa, *the cultivated Asian species of the rice plant.*

SPIRIT CAVE

*The intensive exploitation of plants
in early Holocene Thailand*

Excavation at Non Nok Tha.

In 1952, geographer Carl Sauer proposed that the cradle for the world's earliest agriculture should lie in mainland Southeast Asia, rather than in Southwest Asia, as most scholars still believe. Sauer thought that the highly diverse, tropical, and riverine environments of Southeast Asia would have provided a superb locale for the fishing and farming ways of life (or lifeways) that he surmised constituted the earliest stage in the transition to agriculture. Like the Russian botanist Nikolai Ivanovich Vavilov before him, Sauer was aware that the wild ancestors for a wide array of modern cultigens (root, tree, and seed crops) had been traced to Southeast Asia.

For over a decade, few prehistorians gave serious consideration to Sauer's ideas because of the absence of information to evaluate them. Moreover, his proposal did not conform to the traditional views of mainland Southeast Asia as a kind of cultural recipient or backwater area that ob-

tained most technological advances from India or China. For Thailand, traditional archaeological reconstructions suggested that the earliest domesticates came from North China after 3000 B.C.

During the 1950s, the most relevant archaeological materials for tropical Southeast Asia belonged to the Hoabinhian complex, known from a series of limestone caves and shell middens. As this complex was not well dated, the presence of cord-marked pottery with edge-ground stone axes in the upper deposits of several Hoabinhian sites was presumed to signal the introduction of agriculture from North China.

By the 1960s, however, new information revised the traditional Southeast Asian picture of a conservative Hoabinhian way of life, punctuated by a series of infusions from the north. An archaeological research program, under the general direction of Wilhelm G. Solheim II, of the University of Hawaii, produced evidence

A map of Southeast Asia, with sites mentioned in the text.

that intensive plant exploitation, pottery, and metallurgy had a much earlier history in Southeast Asia. Perhaps the most important findings came from Spirit Cave, an upland Hoabinhian site in northwestern Thailand, and Non Nok Tha, a later habitation mound in the lower northeastern part of the country.

Spirit Cave was discovered and excavated by Chester Gorman, a student of Solheim's. While reconnoitering through rugged hilly terrain near the Burmese border in 1966, Gorman learned from the villagers about a nearby cave site. He found both Hoabinhian stone tools and cord-marked pottery on the surface inside the limestone chamber. Excavations revealed a stratigraphic sequence that Gorman divided into two cultural levels. The lower deposits contained standard Hoabinhian chipped stone artifacts, while polished adzes, cord-marked and burnished pottery, and polished slate knives were found in the upper soil layers. The slate knives, similar to tools used to harvest rice in Java today, had not been found previously in the Hoabinhian. The most unexpected findings resulted from a careful study of plant remains and from the absolute dates generated by carbon-14 analyses of charcoal.

The first archaeologist to carefully sieve the excavated soil from a Hoabinhian site, Gorman found a great variety of seeds, shells, husks, and other plant parts. Such food plants as butternut, almond, cucumber, water chestnut, a few beans, and peppers were recovered, as was candlenut, which may have been used for lighting. Remains of the stimulant betel nut and the bottle gourd, a probable container, also were found. Interestingly, neither of these two latter plants is now native to this area. None of the recovered plant species differs significantly from its wild prototype, indicating that none of them was domesticated. Nonetheless, an intensive utilization (and possibly tending) of a wide variety of plants was indicated. The Spirit Cave occupation also was much older than expected. The earliest levels were at least 11,000 years old, while the ceramic occupation began roughly 3000 to 4000 years later.

Significantly, the remains of rice were absent at Spirit Cave. However, rice husks were recovered in the earliest (4000 to 3000 B.C.) occupational levels at the site of Non Nok Tha, where clear impressions and carbonized remnants of rice chaff were found in potsherds. Apparently the ancient potters, like their modern counterparts, mixed the plant materials into their clay as a fiber **temper** (or additive) to improve the workability of the clay and to reduce breakage. Intensive micro-

Excavation at Spirit Cave.

suggested that plant collecting and tending were supplemented by broad-based hunting, with deer, wild pig, and arboreal species like monkeys the principal targets.

During the last three decades, knowledge about the early Holocene in Southeast Asia has expanded significantly. We have learned that the broad-spectrum Hoabinhian complex extended more deeply into the past than had been previously believed, and that plant-tending may have contributed importantly to the diet. By the seventh millennium B.C. (also much earlier than previously expected), new technologies, including pottery, were in evidence at Spirit Cave. However, an even more dramatic transition occurred during the next several millennia. At settled villages, like Non Nok Tha and Ban Chiang, the inhabitants lived in houses built on piles or wooden stilts, buried their dead in low mounds, made socketed spearpoints and adzes as well as adornments of bronze (this was some of the world's earliest known bronzeworking). At these later settlements, cultivated wild or hybrid rice and domesticated animals comprised the bulk of the diet.

While much has been learned, many questions remain. The importance of indigenous tropical domesticates, like yam and taro, presently cannot be evaluated because these root crops preserve so poorly in the archaeological record. The specifics of the domestication process for rice also remain largely unknown. Some answers may emerge from very recent excavations done by Higham at the ancient village of Khok Phanom Di, located in a coastal mangrove swamp in southern Thailand. Between 5000 and 2000 B.C., a 12-m (39 ft) high midden accumulated at the site, where the inhabitants ate fish and shellfish, buried their dead sprinkled with red ochre, and made pottery (at least some of which was tempered with rice chaff). Higham has hypothesized that villagers may have begun to cultivate (and perhaps domesticate) the plant when a drop in sea level left the settled inhabitants at some distance from the coast. According to Higham, the lowering of sea levels may have exposed coastlines and left the settled villages far from the shore and marine resources. Perhaps the environmental shift was one factor that triggered an increasing reliance on rice.

scopic studies of rice impressions in ceramics by Douglas Yen, of the University of Hawaii–Honolulu, and others indicate that the grains were not completely domesticated and may have been hybrids, or intermediate between wild and domesticated varieties.

Rice became an increasingly important plant by the end of the several-thousand-year period between the upper levels at Spirit Cave and the lowest occupations at Non Nok Tha. Charles Higham's (University of Otago, New Zealand) analyses of the animal remains from Non Nok Tha (and contemporary levels at the more northerly site of Ban Chiang) indicate an increasing importance for domesticated animals — cattle, pigs, chickens, and dogs — at these later sites as well, although hunting and fishing did continue. For Spirit Cave, Higham's identifications

Perhaps the most surprising and significant result from archaeological research at the sites of Non Nok Tha and Ban Chiang in northeastern Thailand is the evidence for metalworking shortly after 4000 B.C. **Metallurgy**, unlike the working of clay, bone, wood, or stone, requires a greater understanding and manipulation of raw materials; metals first have to be extracted from crystalline ores before they can be made into useful objects. The extraction or smelting of copper ores cannot be accomplished with the heat (600–800°C, 1100–1500°F) obtained from a typical cooking fire. Both higher temperature and a **reducing atmosphere** (oxygen-deficient) are required for the necessary chemical reaction to take place. In addition to smelting, metalworking also involves other techniques: mining, **annealing** (gradual heating followed by gradual cooling to reduce brittleness and enhance toughness), casting, and **alloying**.

More than 800 metal ornaments and weapons were uncovered at Ban Chiang, and many more were found at Non Nok Tha. **Optical emission spectroscopy** of these objects was used to determine elemental composition. Mixing other metals (particularly tin) with copper produces alloys (such as bronze) that are harder, more enduring, and easier to cast. The characteristics of a specific metal object are affected by the proportions of different metals in the particular piece. The earliest metal object from Ban Chiang, a socketed spearhead dating to 3600 B.C., contained less than 2% tin; the presence of such a small amount of tin suggests that the alloying may not have been deliberate. However, most of the objects from both sites clearly were composed of normal tin bronze (intentionally alloyed to include about 10% tin).

The expertise of the ancient Thai metalsmiths was investigated through other procedures that examined the grain, or microstructure, of the different specimens using **photomicrographs**. The very early fourth millennium (mostly copper) socketed spearpoint, found in a grave at Ban Chiang, was cast in a two-piece mold with a core inserted during casting to create the socket. Subsequently, the point was cold-worked and annealed. The internal structure of a third-millennium bronze axe from Non Nok Tha showed that its manufacture required alloying, casting, cold-hammering, and annealing.

In addition to bronze tools and ornaments, iron bracelets and bangles—some of the oldest iron objects in East Asia—were discovered in later first-millennium B.C. deposits at Ban Chiang. The incorporation of iron into local metallurgy is just one indication that these early metalsmiths continually experimented and expanded their abilities to create a wider assortment of better-made tools and ornaments.

EARLY METALLURGY IN THAILAND

Bronze ornaments and weapons

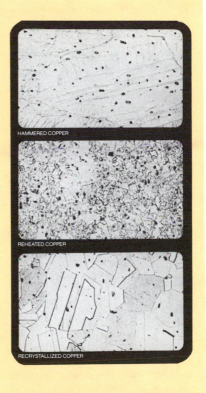

Photomicrographs of specimens of copper, showing how different ancient metalworking techniques affect the structure of the metals.

Specimens of pure copper and four copper alloys, showing marked differences when viewed through a microscope. Without magnification, the specimens display only subtle differences in hue and texture.

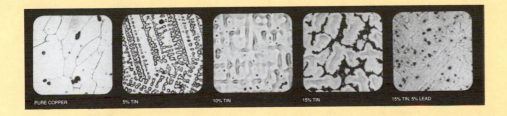

TEHUACÁN

The evolution of early maize

From a personal point of view, and closely connected with satisfying my innate curiosity, has been the thrill of discovery of art and artifact and the fact that these objects have remained unknown to anyone until my little trowel or paintbrush uncovered them — often after long periods of searching for these new and thrilling finds. I have been doing archaeology now for over forty years but the thrill is still there and I feel that this thrill should happen to anyone and everyone.

(MacNeish, 1978, p. xii)

In the early 1960s, when Richard Mac-Neish began his fieldwork in the highland Tehuacán (tay-wa-con') Valley in Puebla, Mexico, little was known about either the preceramic occupation of Mesoamerica or the beginnings of agriculture in the New World. (See "Mesoamerica," p. 229.) MacNeish chose to look for the origins of maize (*Zea mays*) in the relatively small Tehuacán Valley for two reasons. First, due to the region's dryness, preservation was unusually good. Preliminary excavations unearthed fragments of basketry and plant materials in limestone cave deposits. Second, MacNeish already had recovered tiny 5000-year-old corncobs in caves in both the northeastern Mexican state of Tamaulipas and the southern state of Chiapas. He reasoned that the earliest domesticated *Zea* should be still older and would be found in a highland region like Tehuacán, located between Tamaulipas and Chiapas.

MacNeish designed his Tehuacán research to examine two critical questions: (1) What led to the domestication of maize? (2) How did these changes lay the foundation for later Mesoamerican civili-

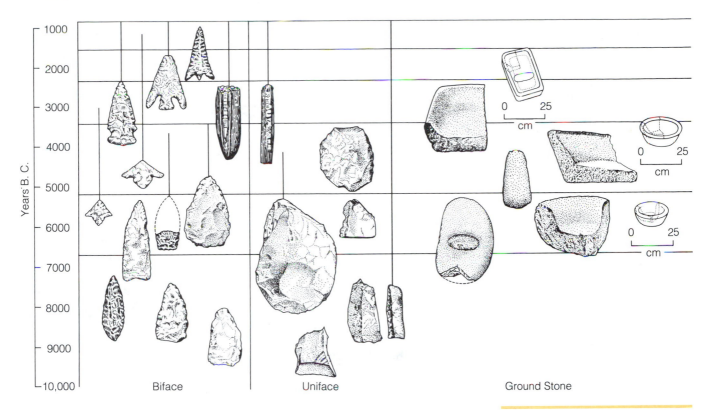

Date

Years B.C.: 1000, 2000, 3000, 4000, 5000, 6000, 7000, 8000, 9000, 10,000

Biface   Uniface   Ground Stone

Changes in the flaked and ground stone industry in Tehuacán, from 10,000 to 1000 B.C.

zation? He undertook a large survey that located more than 450 prehispanic sites (over the 1500 sq km, or 575 sq mi, of the valley) and excavated at a series of twelve cave and open-air deposits. Controlled stratigraphic excavations, combined with a large number of radiocarbon dates, allowed MacNeish to reconstruct an unbroken 12,000-year sequence of occupation, at that time the longest recorded in the New World. For the first time, a picture of early presedentary, preceramic society in Mesoamerica could be sketched, using both artifacts and the plant and animal remains preserved in the dry caves of Tehuacán.

During the preceramic era, according to MacNeish, the few people of the Tehuacán Valley lived in small bands that dispersed periodically. Some camps accommodated only a single nuclear family, while others sheltered much larger groups. The plant and animal remains recovered from preceramic sites in Tehuacán's diverse topographic zones led to the recognition that **seasonality** (of resource availability) and **scheduling** (of resource extraction) were critically important in

determining the annual regime. More specifically, the early inhabitants of Tehuacán scheduled their seasonal movements across the highland region, from the river banks to the foothills to the moutains, to coincide with the periodic availability of local plant and animal species.

For most of the preceramic era, such game as rabbits and deer supplemented plants in the diet. During the May-to-October rainy season, edible plants were more abundant and a diversity of seeds, cactus fruits, and berries were exploited, in addition to the bountiful seedpods of the **mesquite** tree. Rabbits, rodents, lizards, and other small animals were consumed at this time of year, when the size of human groups was generally larger. Although some fruits were still available in the early part of the dry season (November and December), cactus leaves and deer apparently were the staples during the dry spells that lasted from January to April.

Although this way of life was basically persistent for almost 6500 years, from 8000 to 1500 B.C., several important dietary changes did take place. A wild ancestor of the domesticated squash was

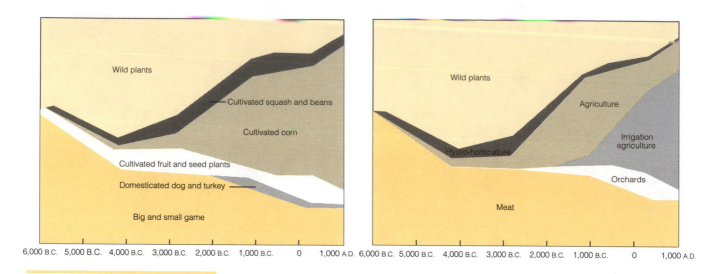

Changes in diet and farming strategies in the Tehuacán Valley, from 6000 B.C. to 1000 A.D.

used by 8000 years ago, probably as a container or for its protein-rich seeds. Shortly thereafter, domesticated varieties of squash and the earliest known maize appeared in Tehuacán. The archaeological evidence suggests that these early domesticated plants did not provide a large portion of the diet, which still was based primarily on wild plants and animals. Thus these initial experiments toward plant domestication occurred among a population that was largely mobile, and remained so for thousands of years.

Somewhat enigmatically, the bone chemistry assay of human bone from the Tehuacán excavations provides a rather different picture for the period after 5000 B.C. (See "Bone Chemistry and Prehistoric Subsistence," Chapter Four, p. 182.) These studies indicate a smaller amount of meat in the diet than is seen in the archaeological deposits, as well as a greater role for either early cultigens or wild *setaria* grass, the seeds of which were present but not recovered in abundance in the archaeological record. Yet the relative importance of meat inferred from archaeological deposits is not surprising, given that bone generally preserves better in ancient deposits than do smaller plant materials.

In addition to the gradual increase in the overall proportion of both wild and domesticated plant foods in the diet, the Tehuacán sequence also reveals an increase in population and a decrease in residential mobility. Based on the size and number of sites known from the prece-

ramic phases, the total population density for the Tehuacán Valley, though low, may have increased severalfold during this period. While the earliest sedentary villages in Tehuacán did not occur until 3000 to 4000 years ago, the length of site occupation increased, and the size of sites grew during the preceding millennia. A single circular pithouse, the earliest known in Mesoamerica, was found in a 5000-year-old level at an open-air site in the region. Later preceramic occupations also tend to have more storage features.

There is little question that the Tehuacán research of Richard MacNeish has revolutionized our knowledge of early Mesoamerica, as well as our understanding of the diversity of situations in which early agriculture developed. In the Tehuacán Valley, the first experiments toward plant domestication occurred among people who remained residentially mobile for thousands of years, a sequence that is very different from what has been long known for early farming in Southwest Asia.

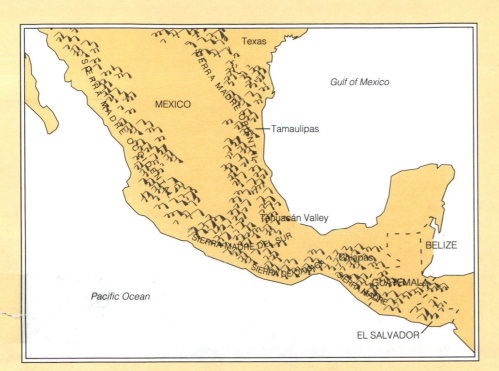

A map of Mesoamerica, with regions and places mentioned in text.

Mesoamerica is the term suggested by geographer Paul Kirchhoff to describe the region — consisting of southern and central Mexico, Guatemala, Belize, El Salvador, and the western parts of Honduras and Nicaragua — that was the focus of complex, **hierarchical** states at the time of Spanish contact. (See Chapter Seven.) Kirchhoff drew up a list of cultural traits that generally defined the prehispanic societies of Mesoamerica (also referred to as Middle America) and distinguished them from other large cultural regions in the New World, such as the Andean area in South America. Ancient Mesoamerican peoples shared a reliance on a series of indigenous cultigens (including maize, beans, squash, and chili peppers) that they had farmed for millennia before the arrival of the Europeans.

Although situated entirely in the tropics, the environment of Mesoamerica is highly diverse, a mosaic of landscapes, vegetation, and fauna. The principal contrast is between the highlands and the lowlands. While the Yucatán, the Isthmus of Tehuantepec, and coastal lowland zones tend to be flat, warm, and heavily vegetated, highland areas are generally drier, cooler, and more rugged. The highlands are composed of large basins surrounded by high areas of elevated mountain crests. For the most part, both topographic zones are affected by significant seasonal variation in rainfall. Most of the annual precipitation falls between May and October, creating a very different climatic regime than in Europe or North America, where the most important seasonal dichotomy is between winter cold and summer heat.

The wild ancestors of the major cultigens — maize, beans, and squash — were all highland plants. Thus it is not surprising that the earliest archaeological evidence for Mesoamerican agriculture has been found in highland valleys like Tehuacán and Oaxaca. The dry caves in these upland valleys are recognized for their superb archaeological preservation. Yet some of Mesoamerica's earliest sedentary villages were established in the lowlands, where the highland cultigens eventually were incorporated into a coastal subsistence economy that also included marine resources and lowland plants.

GUILÁ NAQUITZ CAVE

A preceramic seasonal campsite in Mexico

We have indicated that the research problem we chose for ourselves at Guilá Naquitz was to develop a model that would not only deal with some of the underlying and more universal aspects of early domestication but also tie that process into the specific cultural pattern for the Valley of Oaxaca.

K. V. Flannery (1986)

Kent Flannery spent the day before Christmas, 1964, in the foothills of the eastern Valley of Oaxaca, 150 km (90 mi) south of the Tehuacán Valley, searching for the best sites to continue a study of agricultural origins in Mesoamerica. Having just completed several seasons of fieldwork as the faunal analyst on MacNeish's interdisciplinary team in arid Tehuacán, Flannery wanted to see what form early agriculture might have taken in a more humid valley with greater farming potential. On that December day, Flannery found a preceramic occupation at Cueva Blanca, a site that he says more than any other launched his Valley of Oaxaca Human Ecology project.

On Christmas day, heartened by the previous day's finds, Flannery began to prepare a research proposal. A year later, with support from the Smithsonian Research Foundation, he returned to Oaxaca. On January 26, 1966, less than a week after beginning a reconnaissance of caves in the area, he found a rock shelter with lots of chipped stone debris and half of a projectile point on the ground surface. This small overhang named Guilá Naquitz (gē-la'nah-keets'; "the white cliff," in the native Zapotec language of Oaxaca) was completely excavated.

At Guilá Naquitz, Flannery and his field crew carefully peeled away the layers of preceramic occupations dating between 8750 and 6670 B.C. Based on the careful retrieval and analysis of the floral, faunal, and artifactual remains found in the cave strata, Flannery suggested that the shelter of Guilá Naquitz was occupied seasonally between August and December by small groups, perhaps a series of nuclear families, or what MacNeish had called **microbands**. As in the Tehuacán Valley, the ancient inhabitants of Oaxaca were mobile, living in several different camps during the course of their yearly activities.

The location of Guilá Naquitz Cave and Cueva Blanca in the Valley of Oaxaca.

The archaeological contents of the cave strata indicate that the inhabitants of Guilá Naquitz consumed a diversity of plant foods, such as acorns and the roasted heart of **maguey** (the source of tequila and mescal today), which could have been collected in the thorn forest surrounding the site. Other plant foods, such as the seeds of the mesquite tree and hackberries, were brought back to the cave from the flatter grassland below. A small part of the diet, one that increased slightly through time, came from squash and bean plants, which may have been tended or cultivated in the disturbed terrain around the site. Although neither maize cobs nor *Zea* kernels were recovered in the preceramic levels at Guilá Naquitz, *Zea* pollen was identified in several of the ancient levels. The variety of nuts, seeds, fruits, and cactus eaten during late summer and early autumn was supplemented by a small amount of venison and rabbit meat. Although deer and rabbit bones were not abundant at Guilá Naquitz, this meat still provided much of the protein consumed in the cave.

The subsistence activities of the inhabitants of Guilá Naquitz were rather conservative, changing little over the millennia of intermittent occupations.

Perhaps this continuity should not be surprising. Two nutritionists, J. R. K. Robson and J. N. Elias, concluded that the diet of the cave occupants compared favorably with the contemporary diet in the United States, providing similar levels of nutrients and exceeding caloric requirements with less intake of food.

While seasonally abundant plant foods could have been collected near the cave, stone for making tools was taken from quarries up to 50 km (30 mi) away. This better raw material was used principally for projectile points, while more local, but less suitable, rock sources were used for more disposable tools, such as scrapers and worked flakes.

Besides recording the collection and processing of plant foods and the butchering and consumption of animals, the archaeologists at Guilá Naquitz documented the manufacture of tools, the digging of pits to store acorns, the use of fire pits to prepare food, and even the collection of leaves for bedding in the cave. Years of multidisciplinary study by Flannery and his colleagues illustrate how archaeologists can reconstruct the events of the past into a credible picture of society just prior to the advent of agriculture in the highlands of ancient Mexico.

A fragment of knotted net from Guilá Naquitz Cave. Such nets were used as bags to transport food to the cave.

ZEA MAYS

The mysterious ancestry of corn

Teosinte

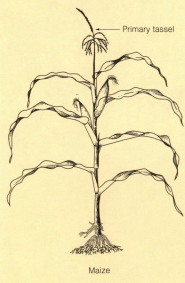

Maize

The teosinte and maize plants.

Maize—or corn, as it is popularly known in the United States—was unknown in Europe prior to the arrival of Columbus in the New World in 1492. By that time, the plant was cultivated by the native inhabitants over much of the tropical and temperate portions of the Western Hemisphere. The great adaptability and plasticity of maize is evidenced by its position as the second or third most important food plant on Earth and its current worldwide distribution. Botanical studies, however, indicate that the ancestor of modern corn (*Zea mays*) was native to southern Mexico.

Botanists and archaeologists have puzzled over the ancestry of maize. Domesticated varieties of such cereals as wheat, barley, and rice are structurally nearly identical to living wild species. The principal difference is that while in the domesticated varieties the edible seeds tend to remain fastened on the plant, the wild varieties have shattering **inflorescences**. Shattering is a mechanism by which the seeds of the plant are dispersed naturally. The most recognizable feature of domesticated maize, the massive husked ear, is not present even in wild grasses most closely related to maize. In fact, the nonshattering ear of domesticated corn, with its surrounding husks, inhibits seed dispersal, so that without farmers to remove and plant the kernels from the ear, modern maize could not reproduce for even one or two years. Because of its structure, the late George Beadle, a renowned plant geneticist, referred to domesticated maize as a "biological monstrosity."

Because of this pronounced difference between domesticated maize and related wild grasses (the **teosintes**), the debates over the origins of maize have been more contentious, and until recently have achieved less consensus, than discussions concerning the origins of most other seed plants. Although a few experts still hold the view that there was a wild species of maize (with an ear) that has since become extinct, most participants in the debate have returned to the previously popular position that the ancestor of maize was a variety of teosinte, a wild grass so closely related to *Zea mays* that some botanists place it with corn in the same species. Teosinte still grows in the foothills and highlands of Mexico and Guatemala, and, in fact, is the only large-seeded wild grass in the neotropical Americas. Some annual teosintes have an ear of six to twelve seeds that are not fused into a cob. Otherwise, certain teosinte varieties are very similar to maize and produce fully fertile offspring when interbred with the domesticated plant. Teosinte and maize have nearly identical tassels, as well as highly similar DNA, amino acid, and nutritional compositions. Even studies with a scanning electron microscope cannot distinguish the pollen of annual types of teosinte from small seeded varieties of corn (such as early domesticated maize).

New evidence for the ancestral role of the plant that the Aztec called *teocentli* ("God's ear of corn") has emerged, yet debates have continued over both the specific morphological changes that were necessary for the evolution from teosinte to maize and the mechanisms that might have triggered the process. Walton Galinat and George Beadle have hypothesized that the maize ear evolved directly from teosinte's female ear, perhaps through human selection of initially rare variants. Alternatively, plant systemacist Hugh Iltis, of the University of Wisconsin–Madison, sees the formation of the cob as the result of more rapid changes during which the terminal branch of the teosinte tassel was transformed into an ear of corn.

To date, archaeological findings have supplemented but not resolved these debates. Archaeological deposits at Guilá Naquitz, dating to the seventh or eighth millennium B.C., contained bean and squash seeds and grains of *Zea* pollen. Yet we do not know whether the pollen came from maize or teosinte, or how the pollen was transported into the cave. Today, teosinte often grows in the same fields with beans, squash, and maize. Teosinte is a weedy pioneer that thrives in disturbed

Increasing corncob size through time.

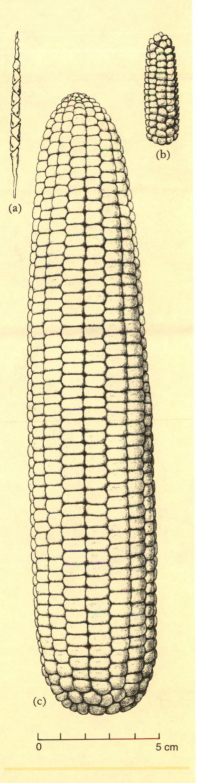

The domestication of corn. In teosinte (a), the kernels are not fused into a cob, as they are in early maize (b) and modern maize (c). Drawn to scale.

areas, such as seasonally wet streambeds and abandoned campsites. Although teosinte seeds can be neither popped nor ground into flour as easily as maize, the wild plant is occasionally eaten as a low choice, or "starvation" food, in times of need. Seasonally, teosinte stems may have been (and are still) eaten, because they store a rich, sugary liquid.

According to MacNeish's Tehuacán research, the earliest domesticated corn remains appear in cave deposits dating to the end of the sixth millennium B.C. Recently these early dates for maize have been contested, based on carbon-14 dating of the early maize cobs themselves. These recent assays place the early maize only at the fourth millennium B.C. However, the possibility exists that in the decades since their recovery, these cobs were contaminated by exposure to more recent carbon. Regardless, these early ears were small (about the size of an index finger) and contained no more than eight rows of kernels. Not surprisingly, this relatively primitive maize was not a preceramic dietary staple. Although we cannot directly determine the role of human selection in the evolution of these early cobs, the Tehuacán evidence has provided a marvelous record of increasing ear size, from the earliest tiny cobs to the much larger and more productive ears (with bigger kernels and more seed rows) grown today. The role of human selection in this latter process is obvious.

GUITARRERO CAVE

*The origins of domestication in
the high Andes*

A century before the arrival of the Spanish in the sixteenth century A.D., the prehispanic New World's largest empire was in place along the western side of South America. This political domain stretched from the Inca capital of Cuzco, in Peru's southern highlands, down into Chile and northwestern Argentina and up through Ecuador. It encompassed high Andean mountain slopes, Pacific coastal deserts, and the western fringes of the Amazonian tropics. The Inca established a network of roads and trails to move people and goods across these diverse topographic zones.

Thousands of years before the beginnings of Inca expansion, the earliest steps toward agriculture were taken in this part of South America, where the high Andes are sandwiched by a coastal desert and a tropical rain forest. Although roads were not yet built, communication between these environments also was critical to Andean domestication. By 8000 to 10,000 years ago, Amazonian plants were introduced into the Andes. After 6000 B.C., morphologically wild plants and animals from the rain forest and mountains were found at sites along the Pacific. Yet the earliest indications for cultivation and domestication appear in the mountains.

As mentioned in the discussion of Monte Verde, human groups first arrived in South America as mobile hunters and gatherers, using stone implements and eating a variety of foods. They spread rapidly across the continent. Although earlier sites have been reported, archaeologists have a much more complete understanding of the last 10,000 to 12,000 years in the Andean highlands. One of the important sites for the early period is Guitarrero (gē-ta-rare′o) Cave, a large natural rock shelter at 2580 m (8500 ft) above sea level in the mountains of northern Peru. First occupied more than 10,000 years ago, Guitarrero Cave served as a campsite for thousands of years, accumulating a valuable record of the beginnings of domestication in the Andes.

Excavations in the cave during the late 1960s were directed by Thomas Lynch, of Cornell University. The dry highland cave environment preserved many organic materials, and polished bone knives, fragments of gourd bowls, cordage, basketry, and textiles were recovered. The late C. Earle Smith noted that the total bulk of the inedible fibrous plants was roughly equivalent to that of the food plant remains at the site, suggesting that the Andean utilization of fibers and textiles had a very early origin. The basic twining or finger-weaving technique, used to create many of the textiles at Guitarrero Cave, is clearly an important step toward the elaborate techniques used for later prehispanic Andean fabrics.

Organic remains also revealed continuity in another important Andean cultural pattern: communication and exchange between different environmental areas. Guitarrero Cave, on the western slope of the Andes, sits in the middle of the three principal ecological zones. The high-altitude shelter faces the exceedingly dry, narrow Pacific coastal zone. To the east, over the Andes, are the wetter, tropical eastern slopes, or **montaña** zone, which grades down to the Amazon jungle. The presence of lima beans, a plant native to the Amazon basin, in archaeological levels dating to roughly 8000 years ago reveals both the antiquity of pan-Andean connections, at least in an indirect, down-the-line fashion (passing from person to person, group to group over long distances), and the origins of cultivation in South America.

As with the lima bean, many of the wild ancestors of the major South American domesticated plants, including manioc, peanuts, guava, and coca, were native to the eastern side of the Andes. Yet because of the poor archaeological preser-

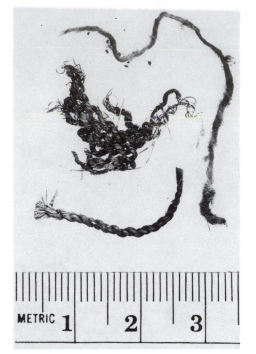

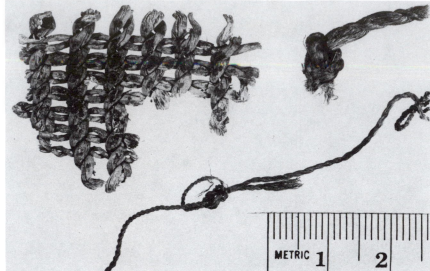

Cordage recovered from Guitarrero Cave.

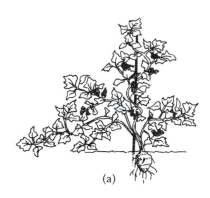

(a)

(b)

Jicama, a common native South American tuber and root plant: (a) plant, and (b) tuberous root.

vation in the *montaña* zone, we know little about the first stages in the cultivation/domestication process. Other root crops like the potato are indigenous to the mountain zone. Unfortunately, efforts to learn about the origins of root crops are hampered by the asexual strategies for reproduction (vegetative propagation) that characterize these plants. Ten thousand years ago, Andean **tubers** and **rhizomes** (rootlike stems) were prime sources of carbohydrates for the occupants of Guitarrero Cave. Yet these plants may have been wild, collected from higher elevations.

As in highland Mesoamerica, the first steps toward cultivation and domestication in the Andean highlands resulted in few immediate changes in society. In both regions, the preceramic era was characterized for thousands of years by continued mobility and rather resilient diets. At Guitarrero Cave, the earliest inhabitants relied for generations on a variety of tubers, rhizomes, and squash for carbohydrates, several kinds of beans for plant protein, and wild fruits, along with a variety of chili peppers, for minerals and vitamins.

The long archaeological record at Guitarrero Cave also documents the incorporation of maize into the preceramic highland diet. This major subsistence shift dates to the fourth millennium B.C., which corresponds well with early maize found at sites in the Ayacucho Basin of

Peru and to the north in Ecuador. As expected, the earliest Guitarrero maize, known solely from cob remains, resembles other early South American maize specimens. However, the small cobs also show a generic resemblance to the Tehuacán cobs. This is not surprising if one accepts teosinte as the ancestor of maize. As more botanists and archaeologists recognize this evolutionary relationship, the ultimate ancestor of maize in South America most likely will be seen as coming from the highlands of Mexico.

Analysis of the faunal remains from Guitarrero by Elizabeth Wing, of the University of Florida, indicates that deer, camelids, rabbits, and a range of different small animal and bird species were hunted. Wing observed a steady decline in the number of deer bones and an increase in camelids through time, a pattern also seen at other Andean sites from this time and particularly at sites in the higher grassland, or *puna*, region. In the Andes, the increase in camelid remains is only part of the evidence for manipulation and eventual domestication (for both meat and wool) of the larger llama and the smaller alpaca. The larger llama also served as a pack animal, carrying goods across the Andes. Another Andean species, the guinea pig, also was domesticated for meat but was not abundant at Guitarrero Cave.

Archaeological evidence indisputably shows that the beginnings of farming and sedentary life were associated with increased rates of population growth. Because the reasons for this rapid growth are difficult to understand through the archaeological record alone, archaeologists and physical anthropologists have looked to demographic and physiological analyses of contemporary peoples to gain insight into factors that may have prompted this post-Pleistocene transition.

Like all significant demographic shifts, the post-Pleistocene changes theoretically could have resulted from changes in migration, mortality, or fertility. Although migration may have become an important factor in certain later agricultural regions, like Neolithic Europe, it alone cannot account for the rapid growth evidenced across much of the globe following food production and sedentism. Although post-Pleistocene mortality rates are difficult to evaluate, several conditions actually may have promoted increased mortality following agriculture and sedentism. In most instances, agricultural diets were less balanced than hunting and gathering regimes. In several regions, tooth decay is found in adult burials only after the transition to agriculture. Animal domestication brought people and animals closer, and may have led to the genesis of contagious human diseases, apparently beginning as animal viruses or infections. Sedentary populations and higher population densities also may have increased the human susceptibility to certain contagious diseases. Thus although longer lifespans may have contributed to demographic shifts in some areas, fertility changes seem to be a more likely impetus.

Demographic studies of contemporary human groups usually, though not always, indicate that settled agriculturalists have higher fertility rates than mobile hunters and gatherers. In human populations numerous factors — including age at marriage, length of a woman's reproductive period, birth spacing, coital frequency, and the importance of contraception — can affect the number of births each female has during her lifetime. In contemporary studies of recently settled hunters and gatherers, different sets of factors seem to contribute to the frequently noted rise in fertility with the introduction of agriculture and sedentism.

Despite these differences, shortened nursing and earlier child weaning often do occur among recently settled foraging populations. Shorter periods of breast feeding prompt hormonal changes that increase chances of conception and pregnancy, so spacing between births often declines when women adopt a shorter nursing period. Alternatively, nursing may stimulate hormones in a manner that suppresses ovulation and menstruation, a phenomenon known as **lactational amenorrhea**. Thus prolonged breast feeding is frequently associated with longer spacing between births.

The Gainj of highland Papua New Guinea, a horticultural village population, have a birth-spacing pattern, without contraception, that is more similar to contemporary hunter-gatherers than to other farmers. James Wood and Patricia Johnson found that Gainj women breast-feed their infants for an extended period, more than three years on average. In part, the Gainj women breast-feed because they lack adequate weaning foods (a characteristic of many hunter-gatherers as well). The Gainj agricultural staples — sweet potatos, yams, and taro — are not easy to digest, nor are they the compact sources of nutrients required for weaning, since infants generally consume only small amounts of food daily.

In contrast, the Neolithic staples of Southwest Asia provided considerably better alternatives and supplements to mother's milk than are available to the agricultural Gainj. Not only were the high carbohydrate, easy-to-digest cereals (like wheat and barley) available, but milk from sheep, goats, and cattle also could be fed to infants. Thus the increased rate of demographic growth in the post-Pleistocene Near East could have been linked to changing patterns of weaning, nursing, and hence the spacing of births.

BREAST FEEDING AND BIRTH SPACING

Ideas about post-Pleistocene demographic growth

EPILOG
THE SPREAD OF AGRICULTURE

*The success and consequences
of food production*

Different concepts and methods are used by researchers who study the Paleolithic and those who investigate agricultural societies. Paleolithic archaeologists tend to excavate in natural stratigraphic levels, often in caves, paying careful attention to the distributions of bone and stone materials. Researchers focused on later agricultural peoples concentrate more on the stratigraphic levels revealed in the architectural remains of past structures, such as temples and houses. The latter must analyze pottery and metalwork, as well as stone and bone. Because pre-Neolithic sites have fewer artifacts and are often deeply buried, systematic regional surveys, which find and map archaeological remains visible on the land surface, are rarely as practical or useful for the specialist in the Pleistocene as they are for many archaeologists who study later periods.

These differences in archaeological perceptions and practices reflect real changes in the nature of the archaeological record that began between 10,000 and 4000 years ago in many (although not all) areas of the world. In most regions, Paleolithic sites tend to be small, thin scatters of lithic materials, reflecting generally lower populations and the tendency for occupations to involve fewer people over shorter periods of time. The low artifactual densities and the general absence of substantial structures at prefarming sites also suggests greater residential mobility.

In many regions, the presence of residential and civic architecture and cemeteries at archaeological sites is unique to prehistoric farming societies. In addition, while the artifacts of the Paleolithic — spear points, knives, and scrapers — tended to be largely for harnessing or capturing energy (food), "facilities" or materials (stone bowls, ceramic containers) and features (pits) to store energy became much more important in later eras. Kent Flannery aptly noted that there are more storage facilities at 'Ain Mallaha alone than are known from all earlier Southwest Asian sites, indicating a sudden transition to residential stability with its implied social and economic adjustments.

The archaeological record indicates that more sedentary ways of life, plant and animal domestication, and pottery were not adopted simultaneously, nor did these changes occur in a single or uniform sequence in all regions. For example, sedentary villages preceded any evidence for plant domestication in Southwest Asia, while the domestication of maize, beans, and squash occurred several millennia prior to the earliest Mesoamerican villages. Furthermore, although the Mesoamerican combination of beans and corn provides a complete protein source as well as adequate calories, some of the other agricultural grains (barley, rice) were staples high in carbohydrate but low in protein. In addition, the domestication of animals clearly was a much more significant part of the Neolithic transition in the Old World than in the Americas.

Nevertheless, given the varied climatic, demographic, and cultural conditions of the early Holocene, the successful adoption and rapid spread of food production is most evident. In regions where indigenous resources were not domesticated, exotic cultigens and animals were often quickly introduced and adopted. Once domesticated, wheat and barley were transmitted rapidly to the Nile Valley, many parts of Europe, and to North China as a supplement to millet. In the river valleys of eastern North America, maize and

Some of the major African food crops:
from left to right, yam, finger millet, and
sorghum.

some species of squash from Mexico were incorporated into local agricultural complexes that included different combinations of oily seed plants, like sunflower, marshelder, and chenopodium.

The Neolithic transition apparently was an even more complex mosaic in sub-Saharan Africa. Imported sheep and goat were introduced from Southwest Asia into diverse economies that locally domesticated more than a dozen different plant species, including finger millet (Ethiopia, northern Uganda), sorghum (Lake Chad to the Nile), African rice (middle delta of the Niger), tiny-seeded teff (Ethiopia), and yams (West Africa). While domesticated sheep and goat clearly were foreign, the origins of the domesticated cattle in sub-Saharan Africa are less certain; they are either exotic or domesticated independently in north Africa, where they were present by the fifth millennium B.C. As in Japan, where ceramics preceded food production, pottery vessels were found at sites occupied by semisedentary fishers and foragers from the fifth and sixth millennia in the Sudan, as well as along the margins of now dry lakebeds south of the Sahara Desert.

From a global perspective, food production emerged at a time of major cultural changes that have shaped the course of recent human history. Just as the Neolithic creates a divide in the archaeological record and among archaeologists, the beginnings of domestication are generally linked in time with more permanent or sedentary communities, changing social and political relations, larger and denser populations, new technologies, and shifting networks of exchange and communication. Although the complexity of these relationships make it difficult to decipher the exact causes for these prehistoric changes, archaeologists have gained some ideas by studying contemporary peoples, particularly those who have recently shifted from a mobile hunting-and-gathering way of life to more sedentary, agricultural pursuits.

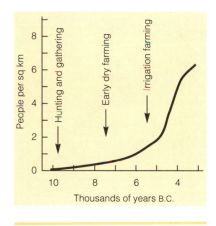

A graph of population densities associated with different subsistence strategies.

During the Pleistocene, human populations grew at a slow pace. If modern hunting-and-gathering populations are a reliable guide, a few individuals may have separated from parent groups when resources were exhausted or when disputes became common. In larger campsites, the latter could have been a potential problem, since as the population increases, the number of interactions between individuals expands even more rapidly. By the end of the Pleistocene with the peopling of most of the continents (albeit at low densities), fissioning would have become less an option for many groups. This pattern may partially account for observed late Pleistocene–early Holocene increases in local population densities, residential stability, greater reliance on lower quality foods, and decreases in social group territory sizes.

Following the end of the Pleistocene, the more rapid rates of demographic growth may relate in part to changing patterns of child rearing and diet. Recently settled hunters and gatherers often witness a reduction in the spacing between children. Mobile lifestyles limit the number of infants that a family group can transport and hence care for at any one time. Intensive exercise and prolonged breast feeding have been suggested as factors that temporarily diminish a woman's fertility. With increased sedentism, storage, and domestication, both the frequency of intensive female activity and the length of the nursing cycle may have decreased. Contemporary hunters and gatherers tend to breast-feed for two to six years because of the frequent absence or unreliability of soft weaning foods. The storable, staple cereal grains provide such an alternative "baby food" to mother's milk. In certain regions, animal milk also could be substituted.

More productive and storable food resources may have permitted larger communities and denser populations, yet a series of organizational changes often occurred at roughly the same time. For long-term maintenance and survival, larger communities would have required new mechanisms of integration, dispute resolution, and decision making. Kin relationships are severely tested when decisions must be made for groups of several hundred. Increased evidence for burials, ritual objects (e.g., figurines), non-residential structures, more formal patterns of exchange, and in cases more unequal access to goods and labor would seem to signal these very significant changes in social and political relations. Some of these new organizational forms were hierarchical, with more permanent, formal leadership roles instituted above the remainder of the population. Such leaders or decision makers in turn may have fostered greater concentrations of resources and labor, leading to intensified production and even larger communities.

The transition to agriculture and sedentism occurred at the onset of a rapid succession of changes that have culminated in our modern world. The pace of these recent changes is truly remarkable when viewed in the panorama of entire human history. While neither domestication nor sedentism alone is necessary and sufficient to explain the formation of early cities and ancient states, both permanent communities and food production are critical elements of those very significant, later developments.

SUGGESTED READINGS

Cohen, Mark. 1977. *The food crisis in prehistory*. New Haven: Yale University Press. A comprehensive indictment of global population increase as the cause of the domestication of plants and animals.

Flannery, Kent V., ed. 1986. *Guilá Naquitz: Archaic foraging and early agriculture in Oaxaca, Mexico*. New York: Academic Press. A detailed report on an important preceramic settlement in highland Oaxaca in the distinctive style of Flannery.

Gebauer, Anne B., and T. Douglas Price, eds. 1992. *Transitions to agriculture in prehistory*. Madison, WI: Prehistory Press. A series of technical papers dealing specifically with the question of cause in regard to the origins and spread of agriculture.

Gould, Stephen Jay. 1984. A short way to corn. *Natural History* 93(3):12–20. A nontechnical discussion of recent botanical research on the domestication of maize.

Harris, David R. and Gordon C. Hillman, eds. 1989. *Foraging and farming: The evolution of plant exploitation*. London: Unwin Hyman. A volume of papers on early agriculture, presenting evidence from around the world.

Hassan, Fekri A. 1981. *Demographic archaeology*. London: Academic Press. A balanced overview of long-term population change.

6

NATIVE NORTH AMERICANS

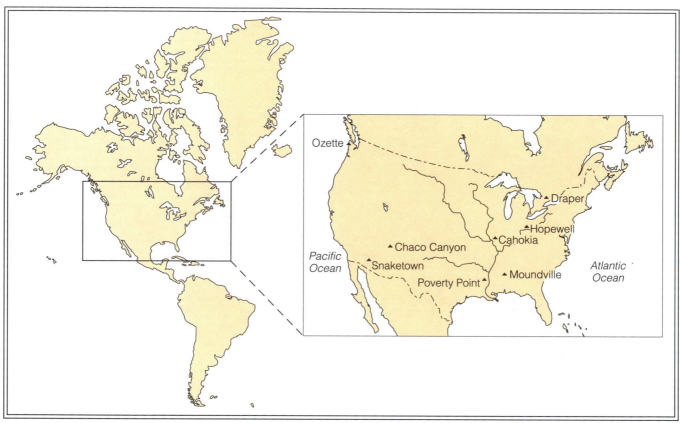

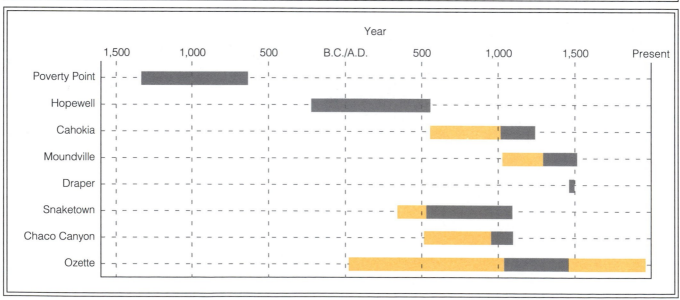

PROLOG
THE DIVERSITY OF NATIVE AMERICAN LIFE

Hunter-gatherers, farmers, and chiefs

On the twelfth of October in 1492, when Columbus landed on a small island in the Caribbean, roughly 40 million Native Americans resided in the Western Hemisphere. These peoples spoke about 400 mutually unintelligible languages, compared to the more than 2500 languages that were spoken in the Old World. Yet the diversity of the "spoken tongues" of Native Americans is impressive considering that the land mass of North and South America combined is less than half the size of Eurasia and Africa. One important factor that can promote linguistic divergence is time, and hominids have lived for only thousands of years in the New World compared to millions of years in the Old World. At the time of European contact, the populations of the Western Hemisphere were diverse in many ways other than language. Some peoples were incorporated into the great empire of the Inca in the Peruvian Andes; others paid tribute to the rulers of Aztec Tenochtitlan in the Basin of Mexico. Yet not all the Native American peoples were as socially and economically stratified as the Inca and the Aztec. Although some Mississippian chiefs in eastern North America may have received tribute from surrounding populations, the sociopolitical formations in what is now the eastern United States were not as complex as those further south. More egalitarian hunters and gatherers lived in the extreme north, Mexican deserts, and at the tip of South America.

The New World was first colonized by hunters and gatherers who crossed the broad Bering Land Bridge from Asia. Initially their way of life was highly mobile. In western North America, the colonists relied in large part on the hunting of large herd animals; the subsistence regime in eastern North America was generally more diversified. In much of the Americas, a long Archaic period followed the millennia (the Paleoindian period), during which several of the large herd animals that were important food sources became extinct. (See Chapter Three, "Beringia," for a discussion of Paleoindian, and Chapter Four, "Prolog," for a discussion of Archaic.)

During the Archaic, regional populations diversified their subsistence pursuits, each concentrating on a distinct set of local resources, hunting a wide range of small animals and gathering a variety of wild plants. Nevertheless, certain populations, such as those on the Great Plains, continued to hunt larger herd animals. Elsewhere, during the later Archaic, cultigens were added to the diet. In the Midwest, local seed plants were domesticated very late during the Archaic. In most other parts of what is now the United States, the earliest domesticated plants were imported from highland Mesoamerica. These plants—such as maize, certain varieties of squash, and gourds—were domesticated initially in the south, and then traded to the north in a down-the-line fashion, reaching first the American Southwest. Yet in most of North America, the introduction (or local domestication) of these agricultural plants generally did not promote immediate or drastic shifts in dietary composition or residential mobility. In certain areas, such as the coastal Southeast, the increasing exploitation of riverine and marine life, in conjunction with hunting and gathering, led to increasing residential stability even before cultigens were incorporated into the diet.

243

Native American ways of life also were diverse at the time of the European arrival, although no populations in the continental United States lived in urban communities as dense as those that we will see in the Basin of Mexico in Chapter Seven. In parts of the desert West, mobile hunting and gathering lifeways persisted until historic times. Yet in parts of the Southeast, the Midwest, the Northwest Coast, California, and the Southwest, a variety of more hierarchical political formations developed during the later precontact period. These institutions were diverse, distributed mosaically, and often were short-lived in any specific locality or region. Although an increasing reliance on maize was one key factor in the development of nonegalitarian social systems in the Southeast, the Midwest, and the Southwest, such institutions were established in portions of the West Coast in the context of sedentary hunting and gathering. Other late precontact populations incorporated maize into their diets but remained more egalitarian and mobile.

Up to now, in this book we have referred to **prehistory** in general terms as the time before the advent of written records. In North America, the prehistoric era extends into the second millennium A.D. and ends with the arrival of Old World populations, who carried a tradition of written records to the New World. The historic period begins between the sixteenth and eighteenth centuries A.D., with the specific timing varying by region depending on the pace of European conquest and expansion. The study of the fragmentary and/or scanty historic records written by both native peoples and Europeans is called **ethnohistory**.

In this chapter, eight North American sites are discussed. In time, they span from the late Archaic (Poverty Point) to the era of European contact (the Draper site and Ozette). These sites, ranging from the southern Arizona desert (Snaketown) to the floodplains of the middle Mississippi (Cahokia) to the arid lands of the Colorado Plateau (Chaco Canyon), capture some, but certainly not all, of the tremendous variability characteristic of the later prehistory of native North America. In fact, in focusing on the above sites, as well as Hopewell (Ohio) and Moundville (Alabama), we have selected elaborate ancient settlements, many of which have attracted archaeological attention for decades. Many of these sites are much larger and were occupied far longer than the average prehistoric North American settlement; hence, they are relatively well known.

Poverty Point (Louisiana) is atypical of the late Archaic north of Mexico, as it is one of the rare sites of its time that contains monumental earthworks. Yet Poverty Point does exemplify certain late Archaic trends in the southeastern United States—decreasing mobility, experimentation with fired clay, and the increasing role of cultivated plants in the diet. Over the next centuries, these trends became increasingly important in several areas outside the Southeast as well. For example, roughly coincident with the decline of Poverty Point in the middle of the last millennium B.C., the **Adena** complex developed in the Ohio River Valley. Adena sites tended to be associated with earthen burial mounds, greater grave-good assemblages, rudimentary cultivation (of food plants as well as tobacco), and friable (soft, porous) pottery. Mobile ways of life still may have been common, yet the presence of circular houses and/or ceremonial structures, as well as the increasing abundance of pottery, suggests greater residential stability at Adena sites relative to earlier occupations in the region. In many ways, the Adena complex was directly ancestral to the later Hopewell sites in southern Ohio (and surrounding states). The Hopewell site, one of the richest of these settlements, was excavated on the farm of M. C. Hopewell in the early 1890s to provide artifacts for an exhibit at the 1893 Chicago World's Fair.

The unequal distribution of grave goods at Hopewell sites may evidence social differentiation, yet it is not clear how marked those distinctions were or whether they were inherited. A similar debate concerns the nature of social organization at Poverty Point. However, by the end of the first millennium A.D., on the floodplains of the Mississippi, such inherited social distinctions appear well entrenched, at least at the Cahokia site in East St. Louis, Illinois. This ancient settlement, which contains the largest precontact pyramid built north of Mexico, includes ample indications of unequal access to wealth and power. Cahokia was one of the largest and most impressive **Mississippian** centers. Increasing reliance on corn farming at Cahokia is part of a trend found at later prehistoric sites across the eastern United States, although many Mississippian peoples retained some hunting, gathering, and fishing.

Moundville, overlooking the Black Warrior River in Alabama, was one of several important later Mississippian centers (along with Etowah in Georgia). Although these two centers are particularly well known, in part because of their monumental mound complexes and the elaborate artifacts recovered during excavations, they were not entirely typical of corn-farming peoples of later prehistory who resided in what is today the eastern United States. Archaeological findings, as well as the accounts from early European explorations into the Southeast, indicate that many indigenous peoples lived in smaller, more dispersed communities and were organized in less hierarchical social formations than are evident at great centers like Moundville and Etowah.

The late prehistoric groups of the Northeast and southern Canada also appear to have been organized less hierarchically. Their villages, which were comprised of multi-family **longhouses**, lacked the monumental constructions that were found at Moundville and Cahokia. The Draper site, a large Iroquoian village in southern Ontario, was almost completely excavated and thus provides a good picture of village plan and community organization in the Great Lakes region just prior to European contact.

One difference between the maize-farming peoples of the late prehistoric eastern United States and those of the West is the greater reliance on water control (irrigation) in the latter area. In the dry, changeable climate of the southwestern United States, rainfall farming would have been risky. This distinction is clearly indicated in the discussion of the Hohokam of the Sonoran Desert of southern Arizona. Snaketown, an early Hohokam community between Phoenix and Tucson, was for a long time the only example of an Arizona desert village. However, spurred by recent construction in the region, additional archaeological fieldwork at other Hohokam sites has broadened our understanding of these early villagers, documenting their evolution from local hunting-and-gathering peoples. Nevertheless, Snaketown remains a key site in the region. Early twentieth-century scholars postulated that the Hohokam migrated from Mexico; such explanations are no longer necessary to account for the transition to sedentary farming communities.

The emergence of the Hohokam tradition during the first millennium A.D. occurred with the rise of two other southwestern cultural traditions, the Mogollon and the Anasazi. While these traditions were not completely discrete, they do help to characterize the great cultural variation that marked the prehistoric southwestern United States. For the most part, the indigenous peoples of the Southwest lived in small dispersed communities, so it is not surprising to find so much diversity in diet, ceramic styles, and even residential and nonresidential construction. Despite this internal variation, the last few millennia B.C. and the first millennium A.D. were characterized by an increasing differentiation between the indigenous peoples of the Southwest and the generally less agriculturally dependent inhabitants of adjacent areas to the north and west.

Periodically the peoples of the American Southwest agglomerated into larger and more hierarchically organized multicommunity social networks. In general, these times of nucleation were short-lived and spatially localized. At Chaco Canyon on New Mexico's dry Colorado Plateau, the period around A.D. 900 witnessed the beginning of perhaps the most spectacular of such episodes. Although this relatively massive buildup of construction and nucleation was brief, it left an impressive record still evident.

Although the focus of this chapter is on the agricultural inhabitants of indigenous North America, we also examine the late prehistoric coastal village of Ozette in Washington. As early as 500 B.C., ranked social distinctions may have developed among certain hunter-gatherer populations in the Pacific Northwest. While Ozette dates much later, the village's destruction and burial by a mudslide resulted in unusually fine archaeological preservation. As a result, it provides a more complete picture of one group of Northwest Coast hunters and gatherers than can be gained from earlier sites in the area.

In the Epilog of this chapter, we briefly discuss the changing Euro-American perspective on native North American sites. The archaeology of North America is extremely important, because it provides a historical context for, and helps establish the rich heritage of, Native American peoples, the first inhabitants of the United States. In the concluding section we also raise the anthropologically important issue of ethnographic analogy, and the less-than-perfect fit that frequently is found between ethnohistorical accounts and the archaeological record.

POVERTY POINT

*Ancient earthworks in
southeastern North America*

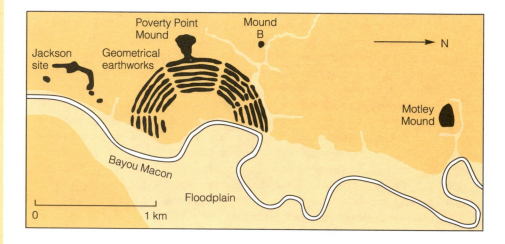

A plan of the earthworks and other
structures at Poverty Point.

The early Archaic hunter-gatherers of the southeastern United States lived in small, impermanent camps and followed a seasonal pattern of life based on a broad spectrum of plant and animal foods. The most important resources included nuts, acorns, berries, roots, deer, elk, bear, fox, wolf, squirrel, raccoon, opossum, beaver, otter, freshwater mussels, fish, turkey, and migratory waterfowl. By the middle of the Archaic, around 4000 B.C., population growth contributed to reduced residential mobility and the increasing differentiation of local cultural traditions. In coastal and riverine settings, the Archaic foragers often returned to the same location year after year in scheduled seasonal rounds to exploit localized and predictable resources. For example, deep Archaic shell middens that have been excavated along the lower Tennessee River represent the accumulated refuse of small communities that occupied these same sites on a recurrent basis at the time of the year when shellfish were abundant.

By 1000 B.C., prior to the end of the Archaic, several plant species were cultivated in the midwestern and southeastern United States, but foraging remained the dominant subsistence strategy. One of the first crops grown, gourds were used largely as containers. Their seeds are edible, and through time it appears that a reliance on this part of the plant increased. Other plants associated with domestication included sunflower, marshelder, and several varieties of squash. New tools, including heavy ground stone implements used to grind seeds, were added to the simple portable tool kits of earlier Archaic groups. There was also an increase in food storage, and at some sites, a fairly simple and friable fiber-tempered pottery, in which fibrous plant inclusions mixed with the clay, was made. Stone containers of carved **steatite** (soapstone) and sandstone are found as well.

Monumental constructions were not frequently built during the Archaic. Nevertheless, construction of a complex

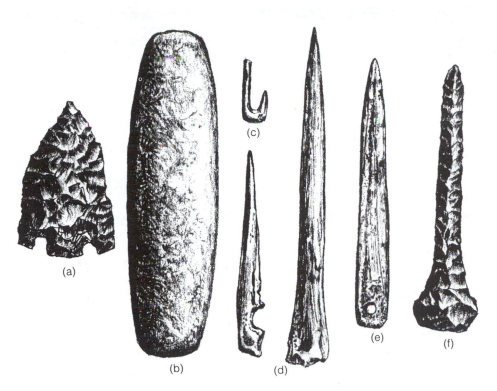

of great earthworks at Poverty Point in northeastern Louisiana was begun before 1200 B.C. Poverty Point contains some of the earliest large-scale construction in North America. The monumental construction at the site is evidence for a more sedentary residential pattern and the emergence of greater social differentiation than was present elsewhere in eastern North America at this time.

Poverty Point is located on a bluff above the Macon River, overlooking the floodplain of the Mississippi. A portion of the site has been eroded by recent stream action; nevertheless, what remains is impressive. The main complex at Poverty Point is a set of six concentric, earthen ridges that form a large semicircle, the outer one of which measures 1300 m (more than .75 mi) in diameter. Each of the ridges is spaced approximately 45 m (150 ft) apart. The earthen ridges, each of which is composed of a series of separate smaller ridges, average 2 m (6 ft) in height and 24 m (80 ft) in width. The presence of numerous **post molds,** hearths, and pits indicates that the ridgetops were used as living surfaces. The level area at the center of the earthen complex was close to 1 ha (or about 2.5 acres, larger than the size of four football fields) and contains habitation structures and associated debris.

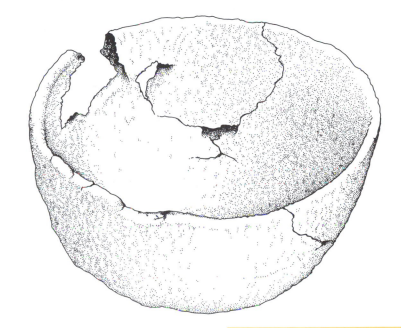

Fiber-tempered pottery bowl from the southeastern United States.

To the west of these earthworks sits a large mound more than 20 m (66 ft) high and 200 m (655 ft) long. A long ramp descends from the mound and faces the semicircular complex. From the mound, it is possible to sight the vernal and autumnal **equinoxes** across the center of the earthworks; however, it is not certain if this alignment was intentional. A small conical mound lies about 0.5 km (0.3 mi) north of the large mound. Another large

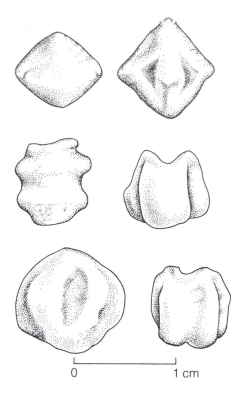

Examples of small baked clay objects found at Poverty Point and elsewhere in the lower Mississippi Valley.

0   1 cm

mound, similar in form to the tall ramped mound, is 2 km (1.2 mi) away. Gulley erosion down the sides of the large mounds has revealed that they were built with basketloads of clay fill. The irregular shape of the large mounds has led several scholars to suggest that the features resemble bird figures with extended wings.

The early population of Poverty Point is not well established, although the excavators of the site, James Ford and C. H. Webb, estimated that several hundred houses may have been occupied. Other estimates range as high as several thousand people. Smaller settlements, which lacked earthen mounds and contained fewer than sixty inhabitants, have been found up to 15 km (9 mi) away from the site. Similar settlement clusters, containing both large and small sites, also have been reported along tributary streams in other parts of the lower Mississippi Valley. Yet none of the associated earthworks were nearly as large as the impressive mounds at Poverty Point.

Most sites with artifacts similar to those at Poverty Point are found in locations where riverine resources were available. The presence of stone hoes suggests that cultivation may have been practiced on the floodplains, but probably not to a significant degree. The hoes also could

have served as digging tools for constructing the earthworks. Hunting, fishing, and gathering were important means of subsistence. Very little pottery, except for some nonlocal ware, has been found at Poverty Point. However, thousands of small fired clay objects were recovered. Most of these baked concretions are no larger than a baseball and were made in a variety of forms, including balls, cylinders, and odd finger-squeezed shapes. These baked clay forms are thought to have served as "boiling stones" for cooking in place of rocks, which are scarce in the alluvial areas of the lower Mississippi. In this method of cooking, stones (or the clay objects) were heated and then placed in containers to boil water and cook food.

Large quantities of such ornamental objects as polished beads, pendants, and effigies were manufactured at Poverty Point, even though very little stone is found on the marshy coastal plain where the site is situated. Flints and **cherts** (a dull-colored rock resembling flint) were imported from the north, and steatite from the Appalachians. Other imported stone included **galena** (lead ore), **hematite, slate**, and jasper (a high-quality flint). Poverty Point was strategically located between the sources of some of these materials and the more heavily inhabited areas to the south.

Poverty Point and its associated material culture began to decline around 700 B.C., just as mound building increased dramatically in the Ohio Valley to the northeast. In these northern woodland areas, the construction of burial mounds implies an increasing preoccupation with death and mortuary ritual. Common practices included cremation and the placement of exotic objects with the dead. Ornaments made of marine shell, copper, jasper, slate, and greenstone occurred with greater frequency in these contexts. Throughout the woodlands of the eastern United States, ceramic containers became more prevalent during the last centuries B.C. The cultivation of squash and local weedy plants, which were still not staples, also became more important. These developments were foreshadowed at Poverty Point, but centuries elapsed before northeastern Louisiana again saw the scale of monumental earthen construction evident in the region at the end of the Archaic.

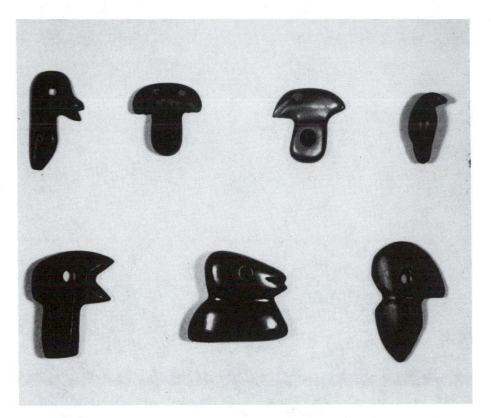

Hopewell

Prehistoric artisans and mound builders

SERPENT MOUND

In eastern North America, sunflower, marshelder, and chenopodium may have been domesticated as early as 2000 to 1000 B.C., but it was not until the end of the Archaic that some prehistoric peoples in the region increasingly relied on the harvesting of these and other native plants. At archaeological sites dating prior to 500 B.C., the scarcity of seeds of these early domesticates suggests that these plants mainly served to buffer temporary shortages and were not yet true staples; hunting and gathering continued to provide the major dietary resources. Nevertheless, many of these local cultigens, which produced a variety of seeds, had the advantage of being easily storable. Indigenous varieties of squash also may have been cultivated initially for their seeds rather than for the flesh.

These early Archaic experiments in cultivation laid the foundation for later developments, such as Hopewell in the Midwest (200 B.C. to A.D. 600). These developments depended to a much greater degree on cultigens. However, food production did not completely replace hunting-and-gathering economies. Foraging remained an important part of survival; Hopewell subsistence also included a wide variety of wild plants and animals, including seeds, nuts, deer, turkey, and fish. Before A.D. 200, maize was introduced into eastern North America from the west (possibly from the American Southwest, which in turn received the plant from highland Mexico, where it was originally domesticated). Yet maize remained a minor crop for hundreds of years in eastern North America.

About the time of the decline of Poverty Point in the lower Mississippi Valley, mound building and long-distance exchange intensified to the north in the Ohio River Valley. Elaborate earth-works — some as large as 100 m (330 ft) in diameter or larger — were constructed in the shape of circles, squares, and pentagons. These earthen features appear to have been sacred enclosures rather than defensive works, perhaps serving to affirm and strengthen group cohesion and to establish the link between a local group and its social territory. One mound that seems to have been constructed midway through the last millennium B.C. was in the shape of a snake with its tail in a tight coil. This feature, called Serpent Mound, was placed along a prominent hilltop in Ohio and probably served as a sacred **effigy**. Serpent (as well as bird) imagery remained important east of the Mississippi for 2000 years.

During the last centuries B.C., the construction of burial mounds became an important part of mortuary activities throughout the midwestern United States. Early burial mounds contained up to three individuals in a log tomb. Cremations often were found in simpler graves. The unequal distribution of grave goods suggests that social distinctions were marked at death in some (although not all) societies in the eastern United States. The more elaborate graves often contained greater quantities of highly crafted and exotic grave goods that possibly served as markers of rank. These items included **gorgets** (circular ornaments that were flat or convex on one side and concave on the other), axes, bracelets, beads, and rings made from copper imported from northern Michigan, carved tablets (some with abstract **zoomorphic** designs depicting birds of prey), and tubular pipes for smoking.

The Hopewell tradition first appeared in Illinois around 200 B.C. Material objects associated with this tradition quickly spread as far as upper Wisconsin, Louisiana, and New York, although the core of the phenomenon remained in the Midwest. The Hopewell tradition was not a single cultural group or society; rather, it was an exchange system for goods and information that connected distinct local populations. The complex trade network that defined this tradition has been referred to as the **Hopewell Interaction Sphere**. Goods that entered the network came from across the continent, including copper from the upper Great Lakes region and Georgia, obsidian and grizzly bear teeth from Yellowstone, chipped stone from Minnesota and North Dakota, galena from Illinois and Wisconsin, shell and shark teeth from the Gulf Coast, silver nuggets from Ontario, and mica and quartz crystals from the Appalachian Mountains.

Although goods entered the Hopewell Interaction Sphere from a wide area, the focus was the Scioto River Valley in the southcentral part of Ohio. Monumental mounds and extensive geometric earthworks were erected there between 100 B.C. and A.D. 600. House structures and village debris occur both within and outside the walls of these impressive earthworks. The Hopewell site in Ross County, Ohio, covered 45 ha (110 acres) and contained 38 burial mounds. Most of these mounds were small, dome-shaped structures, but one mound was 9 m (30 ft) high, 152 m (500 ft) long, and 55 m (180 ft) wide, and contained over 250 burials,

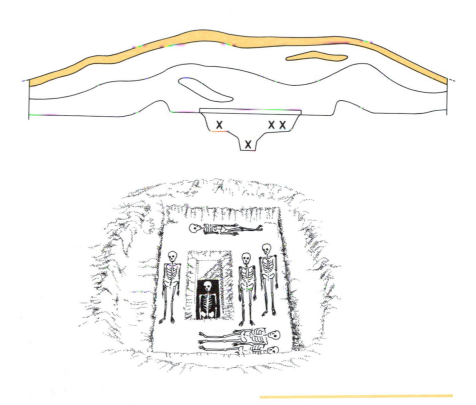

An artist's reconstruction of a burial mound and its central tomb.

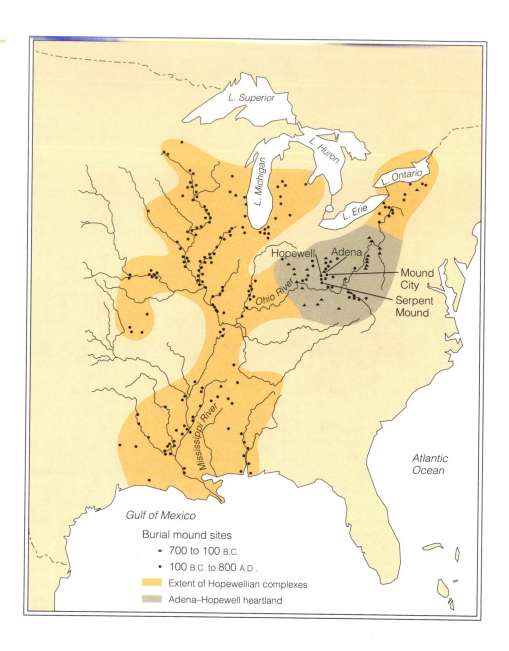

A map showing locations of Hopewell sites and other burial mound sites. Hopewell materials are found throughout the Midwest, but the focus was southern Ohio.

Burial mound sites
▲ 700 to 100 B.C.
• 100 B.C. to 800 A.D.
▮ Extent of Hopewellian complexes
▮ Adena–Hopewell heartland

L. Superior

L. Michigan

L. Huron

L. Ontario

L. Erie

Hopewell   Adena

Mound City

Serpent Mound

Ohio River

Mississippi River

Atlantic Ocean

Gulf of Mexico

as well as concentrations of grave goods. Another Hopewell burial mound complex at Mound City, Ohio, has at least twenty-four mounds inside a large enclosure. Not all the mounds at the Ohio Hopewell sites contain burials; some are effigy mounds alone.

Ohio Hopewell graves contain many objects made from copper, such as ear spools, gorgets, beads, pendants, and panpipes (primitive wind instruments). Heavy sheets of copper were used to make breastplates, and large copper nuggets were fashioned into axes, adzes, celts, and awls. Sheets of mica were cut into serpents, human hands, heads, swastikas, and bird talons. Other items found in the graves include flint tools, imported conch and other shells, teeth from alligators and sharks, turtle shells, and grizzly bear canines. A certain kind of fine pottery was created to be used only as grave goods. Charms were made from galena and quartz crystals. Carved stone pipes were one of the most important trade items. These pipes feature an animal effigy (beaver, frog, bird, bear, and even human) on top of a rectangular platform. The bowl of the pipe was positioned in the animal's back, and the smoke was drawn through a hole exiting at the end of the platform.

Many of the most elaborate Ohio Hopewell sites were excavated before this century, prior to the employment of modern equipment or contemporary standards of archaeological data recovery.

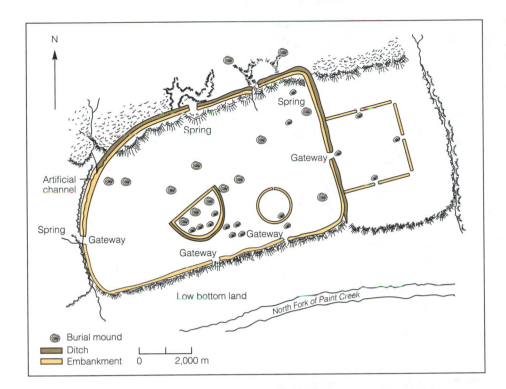

N

Spring
Spring
Gateway
Artificial channel
Spring
Gateway
Gateway
Gateway
Low bottom land
North Fork of Paint Creek

Burial mound
Ditch
Embankment

0   2,000 m

Consequently, few of these contexts are well dated. The early excavators concentrated on the mounds where "museum pieces" could be recovered. As a result, Hopewell is known largely from these features and their contents. Less is known about Hopewell community patterns. While many settlements were small and occupied seasonally, other sites probably were inhabited year-round.

Because most of the earlier excavations were in burial mounds, some archaeologists initially thought the elaborate artifacts that were recovered represented a ritual burial cult. Yet the subsequent discovery of some of these same items in domestic settings indicated that they were more likely status-specific objects that functioned in various civic-ceremonial contexts and eventually were deposited as personal belongings of the dead. The nature and quantities of burial goods may reflect the accomplishments and status of individuals during their lives. Only rarely were children interred with unusually large amounts of grave goods. The Hopewell groups appear to have been organized as socially differentiated societies in which people reached high status principally through their individual achievements, not through an established structure of inherited ranks.

In general, it is very difficult to reconstruct the religion, ideological beliefs, or ceremonial activities of prehistoric peoples when written records are unavailable. Yet Robert L. Hall, of the University of Illinois, Chicago, focusing on the symbolic importance of the famous Hopewell platform pipes, provides one potentially promising example. Drawing an analogy with postcontact customs of eastern native North Americans Hall argues that peace pipe ceremonialism served to mediate interaction over very great distances. European explorers and traders observed that violence was absolutely forbidden among the Native Americans when the pipe was being passed. Curiously, at the time of European contact, almost all smoking pipes were in the form of weapons, such as arrows. Thus the pipes were thought of as ritual weapons, and during peace pipe mediations the participants were sometimes considered to be "fighting with words."

Hall suggests that the Hopewell platform pipes also may have been ritual weapons. These earlier pipes were made in the form of the most common Hopewell weapon, the **atlatl**, or spearthrower (the bow and arrow were not in use in Ohio at this time). According to Hall's interpretation, these Hopewell effigy pipes were

simply not just one of many items that were exchanged; they were part of the mechanism of exchange itself. According to Hall, ritual "peace pipe diplomacy" served to reduce regional differences and to promote communication and friendly contact between the disparate groups involved in the Hopewell Interaction Sphere. The Hopewell pipes were prominent items in elaborate burials, most likely because of their importance to leaders who were involved in mediation, intergroup relations, and exchange.

The Hopewell Interaction Sphere began to decline after A.D. 400. Its demise undoubtedly was related to the disruption of the trade network, but we do not know exactly what factors prompted this breakdown. One explanation is that competition in rich river bottoms between emergent slash-and-burn horticulturalists, relying increasingly on maize, led to greater competition between communities. Such frictions may have engendered increasing closure of regional boundaries. In a few cases, dispersed settlements were replaced with small nucleated villages (enclosed by ditches or walls) that were situated in defensive positions on blufftops. The exchange of luxury goods linked the interaction sphere. Once the complex trade network was broken, either because artisans could not obtain the resources they needed or because warfare and competition disrupted alliances, the repercussions were felt throughout the regional system.

A sheet of mica that has been fashioned into a human profile, 18 cm high.

A platform pipe in the shape of a panther. The steatite pipe is 16 cm long. Smoke was drawn through the platform below the animal's hind legs.

Most — if not all — human societies engage in the exchange of goods and information, both within their own population and with other groups. Yet the volume and the mechanisms of these transactions vary greatly. Prehistorically many communities produced the great majority of items that they required for subsistence and survival, only occasionally exchanging an ornament or food with neighboring peoples. Other villages and societies included many specialist producers, who depended on trade for their livelihood.

Much ancient trade involved simple barter or **reciprocity,** face-to-face exchanges between known participants, such as kin or trading partners. In such small-scale reciprocal exchanges, the giver assumed that a return trade good or gift would be forthcoming at some time in the future. In the ancient Near East, pastoral herdsmen traded mutton to sedentary farmers in exchange for wheat and barley.

Other ancient trade networks were more centralized and included "nodal" individuals (like a Polynesian chief) or central institutions (such as the Inca state) that controlled the movement — or **redistribution** — of certain goods. Items were collected from peripheral communities by a central authority, who then redistributed all or part of what was collected. In certain cases, redistribution primarily served to balance out environmental or economic differences between participating communities. Often, such systems allowed central authorities to accumulate large surpluses, as they would only return part of what was initially collected. Centrally stored goods could be amassed for military campaigns, construction projects, or for the relief of local emergencies and natural disasters. Today, the federal income tax system of the United States acts as a very large and complex redistributive network.

Although reciprocity and redistribution were the most common mechanisms of exchange in the past, some ancient societies were involved in market transactions. For example, as we will see in Chapter Seven, the market was particularly important in prehispanic Mexico. The principles of supply and demand play a larger role in marketing than they do in either redistribution or reciprocity. In contrast to redistribution, which presumes the receipt and disbursement of goods by a central figure, marketing tends to involve more individualized transactions between buyers and sellers.

Trade or exchange is best documented archaeologically by the presence of foreign or exotic goods. In many cases this is obvious, such as when marine shell bracelets or beads are found at inland sites many kilometers from water. However, for materials like obsidian or turquoise, determination of the source requires laboratory analysis. The point of origin of these artifacts can be identified if the specific composition of the object matches the elemental "signature" of a known source. The amount and distribution of exotic goods in archaeological contexts helps to determine the means and the volume of exchange.

At the Hopewell site, one indication of a long-distance exchange network is the presence of ceremonial blades made of obsidian that probably came from the Yellowstone area of the Rocky Mountains. At Mound City, another Ohio Hopewell site, a bird effigy made with copper from an outcrop on Isle Royale in Lake Superior was found. Like the obsidian blades and the copper bird, most of the items that were traded long distances to the Hopewell sites were highly crafted and rare. In addition, many of the Hopewell goods were marked with a set of distinctive designs or motifs. Archaeologists generally assume that communities that share stylistic or ceremonial conventions are more likely to have been in contact with each other than contemporary communities that have adopted entirely different artistic conventions. Thus the relatively widespread distribution of these Hopewell motifs serves, albeit weakly, as an additional indicator for the long-distance interactions that characterized this ancient exchange sphere. Although archaeologists often have been able to document exchange, its relative volume, and its directionality, identifying the specific mechanisms generally is more difficult.

THE ARCHAEOLOGY OF EXCHANGE

A perspective on ancient economies

CAHOKIA

The largest prehistoric community north of Mexico

After the breakup of the Hopewell trade network in the middle of the first millennium A.D., a way of life dependent on maize agriculture, which archaeologists call Mississippian, developed along the lower Mississippi River bottomlands. While the spread of the Hopewell Interaction Sphere was largely ideological, the expansion of the Mississippian tradition probably involved some population movement into alluvial valleys with prime agricultural land, as well as the adoption of new symbols and subsistence systems by local populations. A key aspect of the Mississippian symbolic system was associated with warfare (another important focus was fertility). The atlatl had been the major weapon during Hopewell times. After the decline of the Hopewell phenomenon, the bow and arrow were introduced (around A.D. 700 to 800), becoming the dominant weapon in eastern North America by A.D. 1000.

The lush floodplains of the Mississippi River and its tributaries were ideal for cultivating maize. Yet it wasn't until around A.D. 800 that maize became a major crop. Beans, another imported domesticate, and squash (local and imported varieties) also were cultivated. Yet great dietary diversity continued. Excavations at several small communities in the Mississippi Valley have revealed that maize farming was added to a diet of wild game (deer, raccoon, turkey, and seasonally available waterfowl), fish, seasonal plants (nuts, tubers, fruits, and berries), and native domesticates.

Many changes in material culture that were adopted as part of the Mississippian way of life are associated with the increasing utilization and storage of maize. The number and size of storage pits increased significantly at emergent Mississippian sites. In addition, flint hoes were common artifacts at Cahokia and many other Mississippian sites. Population increased rapidly in some riverine areas, reflecting the more sedentary lifeways that had been adopted, the role of storable foods in easing people through lean seasons of the year, and/or changes in labor strategies that may have given selective advantages to larger households that could clear and cultivate more land. The latter would increase the economic value of children, thereby leading to larger households and regional population increase.

Cahokia (kah-ho'kee-uh), the largest Mississippian center, was established on the east bank of the Mississippi, in Illinois, across the river from St. Louis. This area, just south of the confluence of the Illinois, Missouri, and Mississippi rivers, is known as the American Bottom. The soils are extremely fertile, and there is a great diversity of biotic zones, including swamps, ponds, forests, and wet prairie grasslands. The major rivers provided avenues for communication and transport that enabled Cahokia to become the hub of an extensive exchange system. Black chert came from the Ozarks, sheet mica possibly from North Carolina, native copper from Lake Superior, lead from northern Illinois, and marine shells from the Gulf Coast. James B. Stoltman, of the University of Wisconsin–Madison, has suggested that deer hides or dried meat may have been traded south from southwestern Wisconsin.

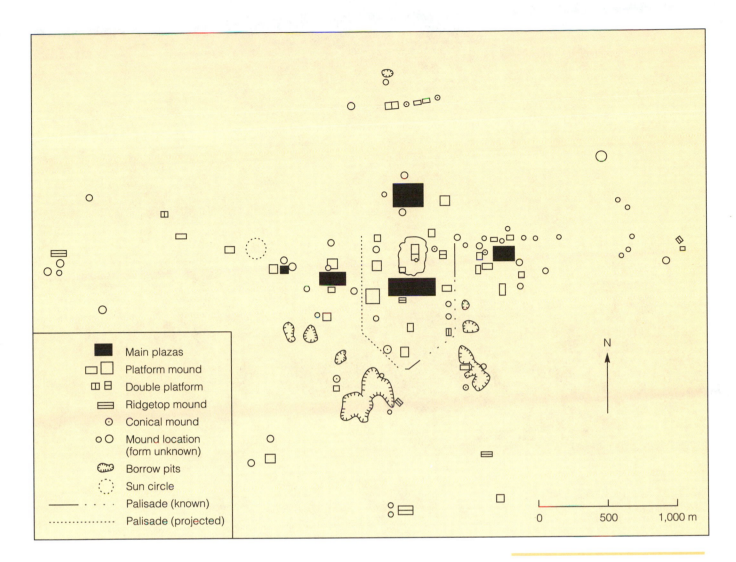

The plan of Cahokia, showing the dispersal and variety of mounds across the 13 sq km area covered by the site.

Legend:
- Main plazas
- Platform mound
- Double platform
- Ridgetop mound
- Conical mound
- Mound location (form unknown)
- Borrow pits
- Sun circle
- Palisade (known)
- Palisade (projected)

N

0   500   1,000 m

The name Cahokia was derived from an Indian group that lived in the area at the time of French colonization during the late seventeenth and early eighteenth centuries. However, the first intensive archaeological investigation of the site was not carried out until the 1920s, by Warren Moorehead under the auspices of the Illinois State Museum and the University of Illinois. This work confirmed that the mounds were manmade, rather than just erosional remnants. Also in the 1920s, the first aerial photographs of Cahokia, probably some of the earliest shot of an archaeological site in the United States, were taken. Today Cahokia is designated a National Historic Site, and the central part is protected, but each year the expansion of subdivisions and highways continues to destroy outlying portions of this ancient settlement. During the last decades, many of the archaeological projects at Cahokia have been salvage operations designed to recover as much information as possible prior to the destruction of a portion of the site.

Fully agricultural inhabitants first settled in the Cahokia area between A.D. 600 and 800. Small hamlets and villages consisted of houses constructed in shallow rectangular basins. Several distinct villages were dispersed on the terrain that later was to become Cahokia. By A.D. 900, the population in the region had expanded, and a hierarchy of settlements had emerged. The larger communities or towns contained 100 to 150 people. These sites often included a series of flat-topped platform mounds that served as the foundations for either temples, other public structures, or elite residences. Frequently the platform mounds were arranged around rectangular open plazas. Sites often were fortified with defensive palisades. These barricades enclosed the plazas and other nonresidential features;

An artist's reconstruction of Monks Mound and the central, walled part of Cahokia at its peak, around A.D. 1200.

houses generally were erected both inside and outside the palisades. Many of the towns were planned settlements, with rectangular single-family houses arranged in an orderly manner around the central plaza.

At its peak between A.D. 1050 and 1250, Cahokia was the largest prehistoric civic-ceremonial center north of Mexico. The site encompasses more than 100 earthen mounds in a 13 to 16 sq km area (5 to 6 sq mi) and may have had a population as high as 30,000 to 35,000. The central part of Cahokia consists of a large plaza surrounded by the giant Monks Mound and sixteen other earthen platforms. This entire "downtown" area covered more than 80 ha (200 acres) and was surrounded by an elaborate and massive wall. The wall served defensive purposes, as it included screened entrances and bastions. Yet it also may have been used to limit access to the central portion of the site. The people residing within the palisaded area undoubtedly were the highest ranked individuals in the community. People of lesser status had their own houses, public buildings, and burial mound areas outside this central portion of the site.

Monks Mound, the largest prehistoric structure in the United States, consisted of four platforms, with a large public structure and some related smaller structures and walls located on the summit. (See "Monumental Architecture," p. 260.) The other mounds at the site occur in a variety of shapes. Conical mounds were probably used as burial mounds. Linear "ridge-top marker" mounds situated at the edges of Cahokia may have served as markers, delineating the limits of the site. The most common mounds are large square platforms, several of which had two levels, such as Mound 42, a rectangular platform mound with a smaller mound on one corner. Excavations have revealed the presence of wood and post holes on top of several platforms, which are assumed to have served as sites for ceremonial structures. Also within the site area are features called **woodhenges**, demarcated by large upright timbers that once had been arranged in a circle. By sighting along certain marker posts, one can observe the annual sequence of the

solstices and the equinoxes. Woodhenge features may have served as solar observatories.

Excavations by Melvin Fowler, of the University of Wisconsin–Milwaukee, at Cahokia's Mound 72 have uncovered a series of burials from the 100-year period prior to A.D. 1050. In all, there were six burial episodes, involving at least 261 individuals (118 of which are thought to have been retainer sacrifices), and each episode resulted in the expansion of the mound as prior burials were covered over. During one of the first episodes, a **cache** of offerings, including pottery vessels, projectile points, and shell beads, was placed in a pit. In a subsequent episode, a pit containing more than fifty young women and a platform with four young men, who had been beheaded and behanded, were added. The closeness in age of the women argue against their having died from disease or some common disaster. Along with the four men, they appear to have been sacrificial victims who were dispatched to accompany powerful chiefs after death. One burial contained a possible chief who was laid out on a litter composed of thousands of drilled shell beads and surrounded by offerings. Near this figure were six individuals with elaborate grave goods, including rolled sheet copper, mica slabs, polished stones, and caches of arrowheads. The complexity of the Mound 72 burial sequence, the sacrifices, and the grave goods document elaborate burial ceremonialism and marked social differentiation at Cahokia.

Cahokia was a great center, dominating the floodplain for miles around, that contained a disproportionate amount of elaborate public architecture compared to the settlements in its surrounding hinterland. The craftsmanship and diversity of the goods present in burial and domestic contexts at Cahokia were unmatched at the smaller settlements. In addition, there is every reason to believe that Cahokia was well planned and that its construction required the control of a reasonably large, organized labor force. In sum, Cahokia appears to have been at the pinnacle of a hierarchically organized and complex social system that was centered on the rich American Bottom for several centuries.

After A.D. 1250, Cahokia continued to be occupied, but many of the site's mounds fell into disuse. Population at the site and throughout the American Bottom was greatly diminished, as people moved into surrounding uplands. The decline of Cahokia and some nearby settlements may have been related to the growing importance of other large Mississippian centers, such as Moundville in Alabama, that redirected channels of exchange, alliance, and communication. At the same time, the great buildup at Cahokia could have precipitated degradation of the local environment. Whatever led to the transition, the period after A.D. 1250 was dominated by a series of important Mississippian centers that were dispersed across the southeastern United States. Archaeological findings suggest that each of these sites was smaller and less monumental than Cahokia had been. The archaeological record dovetails on this point with early documentary accounts from the period of first white contact. The earliest European travelers in the southeastern United States encountered a number of chiefs, temple mounds, and hierarchically organized societies, but none of the reported centers matched the size or monumentality of Cahokia.

The skeleton of a man laying on a burial platform made of thousands of drilled shell beads. The burial is from Mound 72.

A Cahokia pottery vessel, with sophisticated spiral scroll design, 23 cm high.

Monumental Architecture

Monks Mound at Cahokia

Monumental construction is characteristic of complex societies. Some of the most famous structures of the ancient world are the Egyptian pyramids and the massive architecture and pyramids along the Street of the Dead in Teotihuacan, Mexico. Although large-scale constructions were erected by most ancient civilizations, the specific activities associated with these massive edifices vary from structure to structure and region to region. Some large-scale architecture served primarily to commemorate the dead, while other structures served as platforms for temples or high-status residences. Many other monumental buildings served multiple functions. For the archaeologist, the study of ancient architecture helps to identify the political and ceremonial activities carried out by peoples in the past. In some cases, the examination of ancient buildings also has allowed archaeologists to estimate the size of the labor force that was required to construct them.

The largest prehistoric structure in North America (north of Mexico) is Monks Mound at Cahokia. This immense earthen mound, located at the center of Cahokia, was 30 m high (or 98 ft, as tall as a ten-story building) and larger than a city block (316 m long by 241 m wide, or 1036 by 790 ft). Covering 6.5 ha (16 acres), it contained over 600,000 cu m (21,000,000 cu ft) of earth, or the equivalent of six modern oil tankers. Monks Mound was erected in as many as fourteen stages, beginning early in the tenth century A.D. The last level, the summit on which large public buildings were built, has been dated to the middle of the twelfth century.

In 1809, a land claim of 160 ha (400 acres), including Monks Mound, was assigned to Nicholas Jarrot, who donated this area to a group of Trappist monks. The monks, who established a monastery, gardened on the first terrace of the largest mound and built their settlement on a small mound nearby. They abandoned the site only four years later, due to disease and hardship, but it is from this brief oc-cupation that the largest mound at the site is now known as Monks Mound. In 1831, Amos Hill moved onto the property and built his house on the summit of Monks Mound. The area was under private ownership until 1923, when it was turned into a state park.

The form of Monks Mound is unique; it consists of four terraces or platforms. The lowest, or first, terrace extends across the south end of the structure and stands approximately 11 m (36 ft) above the surrounding ground surface. A projection that appears to have been a ramp leading to the ground is situated near the center of the southern end of the terrace. The southwest corner of this terrace is slightly higher than the rest. Excavations have shown that large public buildings were erected in this area; it likely was an important focal point for the Cahokia community around A.D. 1100. These public buildings were later covered over by another platform mound that also had a public structure on top of it. This platform mound was rebuilt several times. Later, a ridge was constructed connecting this platform with the main mass of Monks Mound to the northeast. Around A.D. 1700, Native Americans returned to the site and buried several individuals in this part of the mound.

The second terrace, extending from the first terrace back toward the northwest corner of the mound, actually consists of two flat-topped platforms at an elevation of 19 m (62 ft). These platforms were built sometime after A.D. 1250. The third and fourth terraces, situated in the northeast part of the structure, form the highest points of the mound.

The uniqueness and size of Monks Mound attest to its function as a symbol of civic-ceremonial power. Yet to many archaeologists, Monks Mound is more than a sacred place where annual ceremonies probably took place. The identification of ramps and stairways on the mound suggests that access to the apex of the mound, which stood far above the surrounding floodplain, was restricted, possibly lim-

ited to a small segment of Cahokia's population. Its monumentality provides an indication of the large numbers of people needed for its construction. Finally, Monks Mound, still visible today for miles around, also was the focal point of a powerful polity, a place where Cahokia's rulers surely must have displayed their great political influence for many to witness.

An aerial view of Monks Mound at Cahokia, looking northwest. The base is approximately 300 m north to south, more than 210 m east to west, and 30 m above the surrounding fields at the highest point.

MOUNDVILLE

A late Mississippian center in Alabama

Major changes in subsistence, material culture, and settlement patterns took place in the southeastern United States after A.D. 700. As with groups living on the Mississippi River bottomlands, corn became more important in the diet. Shell-tempered pottery appeared—a technological breakthrough that allowed for the construction of larger, more durable ceramic vessels. Although most settlements in the Southeast remained small, a few larger communities with several small pyramidal earthen mounds arranged around an open plaza were established. While none of these sites yet approached the size and complexity of Cahokia, the presence of residences on the tops of some of the mounds, which were continuously rebuilt, enlarged, and inhabited for generations, suggests that a more stable or institutionalized form of elite status (perhaps inherited leadership positions) had developed in portions of the Southeast.

Although the shift to maize did not occur simultaneously throughout the area, large quantities were grown in much of the Southeast by A.D. 1200. Wild plants and animals continued to be important sources of food, but maize agriculture (supplemented by beans and squash) was the economic foundation of these complex societies. The social and political hierarchies of this period were manifested in public architecture, as civic-ceremonial centers proliferated across the region. The largest of these centers was Moundville, a Mississippian community located on a bluff overlooking the Black Warrior River in westcentral Alabama.

Most Mississippian settlements were linked by political, economic, and social ties into larger regional polities (political organizations) that varied greatly in size and complexity. Some were small and simple, each consisting of a single center and its immediate hinterland. Others were much larger, consisting of major centers, minor centers, and villages. The larger polities, which may have had several levels of chiefs, did not emerge until after A.D. 1200. Many of the groups actually consisted of semiautonomous polities linked together by alliances. Such formations, or confederations, were constantly subject to fragmentation and realignment, especially as distance from the paramount center increased.

Relationships between communities also were maintained through exchange. Such materials as copper, marine shell, mica, galena, fluorite, and bauxite were moved over great distances in both raw and finished form. At Moundville, nonlocal materials were abundant, including marine shell from the Florida Gulf Coast, copper from the Great Lakes, pottery from many areas of the Southeast, galena from Missouri, and finished ceremonial objects from Tennessee and the Spiro site in Oklahoma. Most of the artifacts made from these exotic materials tend to be associated with rich burials at Moundville, suggesting they were traded through elite channels. Other more domestic items, such as salt and chipped stone, probably were traded through reciprocal transactions at the household level.

One of the more striking features at Moundville and other large Mississippian centers is the presence of an art style known as the **Southern Cult** (also called the Southeastern Ceremonial Complex). It

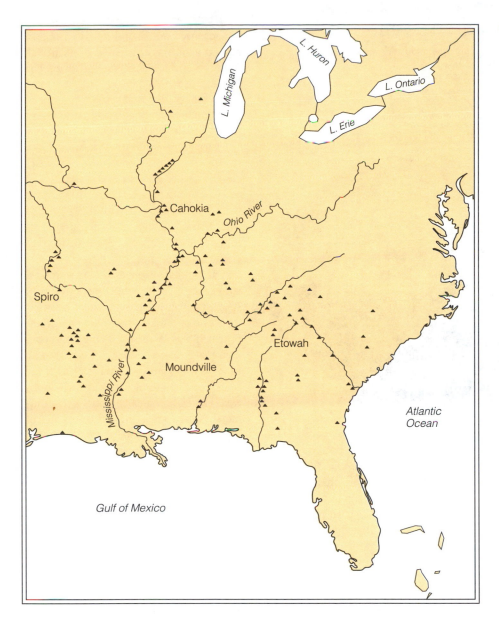

was not really a cult but a network of interaction, exchange, and shared information that crossed regional and subarea boundaries. So-called cult items have been found from Mississippi to Minnesota, and from Oklahoma to the Atlantic Coast, although they are most abundant at certain sites in the Southeast. Such motifs as human hands with an eye in the palms, sunbursts, weeping eyes, and human skull-and-bones characterize this style. They appear on polished black shell-tempered pottery, are embossed on pendants made from Lake Superior copper, and are incised on imported Gulf conch shells. The most famous Mississippian cult objects are the so-called effigy jars that are decorated with human faces,

some with signs of face painting or tatoos. Others represent sacrificial victims, with eyes closed and mouths sewn shut. Often the effigies are shown weeping, possibly denoting a connection between tears, rain, and water in Mississippian cosmology. Some of the common Southern Cult motifs — wind, fire, sun, and human sacrifice — seem to share certain thematic elements with Mesoamerica, although the basis for this similarity has not been established. The greatest concentrations of these Southern Cult objects occur in temple mounds at some of the major late Mississippian sites, suggesting that these goods had sacred importance.

Because of its large size (second only to Cahokia), Moundville has long at-

A black pottery vessel with bird effigy found at Moundville, 16 cm high.

A stone disk from Moundville, with the eye-in-palm motif (diameter about 31.5 cm).

tracted the attention of the public. In 1840, local planter and merchant Thomas Maxwell excavated in one mound, noted the stylistic similarities with Mesoamerica, and concluded that the site was an outpost of the Aztec empire. Several small-scale investigations of the site were made by the Smithsonian Institution during the latter part of the century, but the first large-scale excavations were not carried out until 1905–1906 by Clarence B. Moore. Excavating both platform mounds and village areas, Moore uncovered over 800 burials, many accompanied by pottery vessels and other artifacts of shell, copper, and stone. The second major episode of excavation was carried out by the Alabama Museum of Natural History during the Depression. From 1929 through 1941, 4.5 ha (11 acres) of the site surface was opened, and the excavations yielded over 2000 burials, 75 structures, and many other finds. More recent work has concentrated on understanding the chronological sequence at the site. In all, excavations at Moundville have yielded more than 3000 burials and over 1 million artifacts.

Moundville was occupied initially around A.D. 1050. At first the site con-

tained only one mound and was one of several small ceremonial centers in the drainage of the Black Warrior River. The burials from this period indicate some signs of marked, possibly inherited, social differentiation, although not to the extent found for later occupations.

Moundville flourished after A.D. 1300, when Cahokia was already in decline. The site grew to over 150 ha (370 acres). Twenty large platform mounds were built associated with a 30-ha (75-acre) plaza. The mounds were large, flat-topped earthen structures constructed to elevate temples or the dwellings of important individuals above the surrounding landscape. The mounds were built in stages, probably as part of community rituals. The two major mounds, the largest of which was 18 m (60 ft) high and covered more than 0.5 ha (1.25 acres) at its base, were situated within the plaza at the center of the site along the north-south axis. The eighteen earthworks surrounding the plaza are arranged into pairs of one large and one small mound. The small mounds usually include burials, while the larger earthen structures do not. Based on parallels with later Native American groups in the Southeast, each mound pair may represent the mortuary temple and elite residence of a particular kin group or clan.

In the northeast corner of the site, the dwellings were larger and more complex than in other parts of Moundville. Broken artifacts that correspond to items found in the higher status burials also are found in this probable elite residential area. **Charnel houses** (houses in which bones of the dead are placed) and a sweat house are located along the margins of the plaza. Commoner residential areas were placed at greater distances from the eastern, southern, and western sides of the plaza. At its height, Moundville is estimated to have been occupied by 3000 people.

Several craftworking areas have been identified away from the residential zones at Moundville. One contained a large quantity of finished shell beads, unworked shell, and beadworking tools, while another yielded hundreds of large bone awls and the stones that were used to sharpen them. The bone awls may have been employed to process hides. Large fire hearths, caches of shell (for temper), clay, and other items indicative of pottery production were found in a third area of craftworking.

Social differentiation was clearly expressed in mortuary goods from the later episode of occupation. The high-status segment of the society, which totaled approximately 5% of the population, was always buried in or near mounds. These individuals always were accompanied by rare and distinctive artifacts, including copper axes and gorgets, stone disks, Southern Cult items, and many shell beads. Each mound also contained lower-status individuals, who were accompanied only by a few ceramic vessels. The less elaborate burials could have been retainers who were positioned to accompany those of higher status. The largest proportion of Moundville's inhabitants were interred away from the civic-ceremonial part of the site. These graves generally included no more than a few ceramic vessels. The inclusion of individuals of both sexes and all ages in each class of burials suggests that the access to goods (at least at death) was determined partially through birthright.

While social status at Moundville appears to have been inherited, warfare may have provided one mechanism for certain individuals to enhance their status. Evidence of warfare is present in the archaeological record at Moundville, as well as elsewhere in the Southeast. Many communities, both large and small, were surrounded by fortification walls and ditches. In addition, skeletal studies have revealed numerous indications of scalping, the taking of trophy heads, and the burial of headless bodies. Warfare is also prominent in the **iconography** of the Southern Cult. One grave at Moundville contained eleven decapitated skeletons. This grave also included ceremonial flints and shell objects on which were engraved elaborately dressed individuals holding decapitated heads.

Mississippian culture persisted in parts of the Southeast until the sixteenth century. In the 1540s, Spanish **conquistador** (conquerer) Hernando de Soto encountered Creek Indian chiefs who still lived in fortified towns with temple mounds and plazas. With the European expeditions came smallpox, and other Old World diseases, for which the Indians

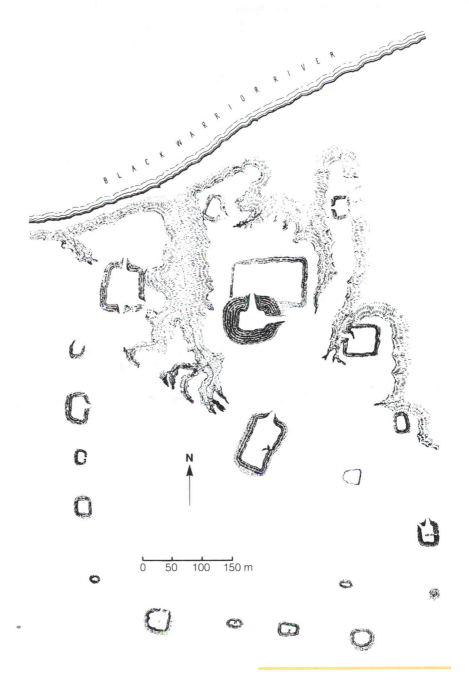

The plan of Moundville.

had developed no immunity. These communicable diseases quickly decimated the Native American population, and put an end to many facets of a way of life that had endured for centuries.

GRAVE GOODS

Indicators of social differences

Grave goods, the items buried with individuals at death, are an important source of information about the social organization of prehistoric groups. With other aspects of mortuary ritual, such as location of the burials and the "elaborateness" of tombs, grave goods inform archaeologists about the relative social position of the interred individuals. A person's status during life is generally reflected at death: elaborate burials and grave goods for people of high status, but few or no trappings for low-status individuals. Complex societies with marked social differentiation usually have a greater degree of mortuary variation than do less hierarchical societies. The distribtion of grave goods relative to age and sex also may indicate whether an individual had **achieved status** (earned through personal accomplishments) or **ascribed status** (inherited at birth). Some archaeologists have argued that graves of infants or children with an unusually rich array of grave goods are indicative of ascribed status, since these individuals would not have been able to achieve high status on their own.

In the Mississippian societies of the southeastern United States, social differentiation was expressed in mortuary ritual. Commoners were interred in simple graves, usually grouped in communal cemeteries or scattered near dwellings. Typical grave goods included simple shell ornaments, ceramic vessels, and domestic tools. In contrast, high-ranking people were buried in or near public buildings, often on mounds, and accompanied by elaborate grave goods.

The more than 3000 burials excavated at Moundville can be divided into several groups. Seven individuals had very high status; they were probably chiefs. All male, they were buried in large mounds and were accompanied by lavish grave goods, such as copper axes, copper-covered shell beads, and pearl beads. Sacrificial victims accompanied these burials (group A). A second group of elaborate burials (group B) included both children and male adults; these graves also were placed in or near the mounds. This group was interred with copper earspools, stone disks, bear-tooth pendants, oblong copper gorgets, and artifacts decorated with symbols associated with the Southern Cult. A third group of high-status interments (groups C and D) included individuals of both sexes and all ages, buried in cemeteries near the mounds, accompanied by shell beads, oblong copper gorgets, and galena clubs. Since rare and exotic items were buried with individuals of both sexes and all ages, it appears that status at Moundville must have been ascribed rather than achieved.

Less-elaborate burials at Moundville also were divisible into several groups (E through H), including a large number, mostly children and infants, that lacked any grave goods at all. Less ornate grave goods were distributed very differently than the goods associated with high-status burials. In the lower-status graves, the distribution of goods corresponded more closely with variation in age and sex. Graves of older adults generally contained pottery vessels, bone awls, flint projectile points, and stone pipes. Such other items as unworked deer, bird claws, and turtle bones were found exclusively with adults, while children and infants sometimes were accompanied by toy vessels and clay toys. Stone ceremonial celts (axe heads) were found only with adult males, while effigy vessels were found with adults of both sexes. The different grave goods indicate that status for commoners was determined according to sex and age. While high or low status in general was a result of birth, ranking within each group seems to have depended partially on individual achievement or role.

Similar burial patterns are found at other contemporaneous sites in the vicinity of Moundville. But there is one major difference: The most elaborate burials in the mounds of the minor ceremonial centers (those sites with only a single platform mound) did not contain the copper axes—the badge of office—that accompanied the highest-ranking burials at Moundville. The highest-ranking individuals in the social system apparently resided at the region's largest and most important ceremonial center.

Table 6.1 The Complexity of Mortuary Ritual at Moundville

Broad Groupings	Burial Group	Number of Individuals	Characteristic Grave Goods	Burial Context	Age	Infant Child Adults %	Sex
Highest-status graves	A	7	Copper axes	Central mound	I C A		? Male
	B	110	Copper earspools, Bear teeth, Stone disks, Red or white paint, Shell beads, Oblong copper gorgets, Galena	Mounds and cemeteries near mounds Mounds and cemeteries near mounds	I C A		Male No data
Other high-status graves	C	211	Effigy vessels, Shell gorgets, Animal bone, Fresh water shells	Cemeteries near mounds	I C A		Male and female
	D	50	Discoidals, Bone awls, Projectile points	Cemeteries near mounds	I C A		Male and female
Lower-status graves	E	125	Bowls and/or jars	Cemeteries near mounds and in village areas	I C A		No data
	F	146	Water bottles	Cemeteries near mounds and in village areas	I C A		Male and female
	G	70	Sherds	Village areas	I C A		Male
	H	1256	No grave goods	Retainers in mounds Isolated skulls with public buildings Cemeteries near mounds and in village areas	I C A		Male and female

Modified from Christopher Peebles and Susan Kus. 1977. "Some Archaeological Correlates of Ranked Society." *American Antiquity.* 42:421–448.

DRAPER

*A late prehistoric Iroquoian village
in southern Ontario*

When early European explorers and fur traders arrived in the northeastern United States and southeastern Canada, the native peoples they encountered differed in several important ways from the aboriginal populations further south. Corn-based agriculture was prevalent among most of the people east of the Mississippi River, yet the native peoples of the Northeast differed from those of the Southeast in village structure and social organization. Generally the Northeast groups were organized less hierarchically than were the societies of the Southeast. In the northeastern Iroquoian communities, leaders were chosen largely for their skills in settling disputes, organizing military expeditions, and for their ceremonial knowledge; leadership roles were based more on achievement than ascription, the latter pattern being more common among the southeastern groups. Also, northern villages were comprised of clusters of longhouses, often surrounded by **palisades** and lacking the platform mounds found at sites in the Midwest and Southeast, such as Cahokia and Moundville.

The historic Iroquoian tribal groups of the Northeast were the descendants of small, mobile bands of Archaic foragers. We have little evidence of their settlement patterns; however, a small circle of post molds at one Archaic site in Vermont suggests that they built temporary shelters framed with poles and possibly covered with bark or skins. Hunting, fishing, and collecting wild plants were the primary subsistence activities.

By the middle of the first millennium A.D., people in southern Ontario were living in semipermanent settlements during spring, summer, and early fall. These sites, usually positioned near good fishing locations, consisted of unfortified clusters of round or oblong houses. While limited amounts of squash may have been cultivated at this time, hunting, fishing, and collecting continued to be the principal subsistence activities.

After A.D. 700, major changes in settlement pattern, subsistence, and social organization occurred in the Great Lakes region. Villages were repositioned from major rivers and lakes to hilltop locations that were naturally defendable, and many settlements were surrounded by palisades. Most villages remained small (around 0.6 ha, or 1.5 acres), composed of small, multifamily, bark longhouses. These palisaded villages were occupied primarily in winter. By A.D. 1100, maize agriculture became a more significant part of the subsistence regime. This important dietary shift coincided with the evolution of heartier maize varieties that were better adapted to the colder, northern latitudes (where the growing season was relatively short). But even toward the end of the prehistoric era in the Northeast, maize farming did not completely supplant the hunting, fishing, and gathering of wild foods. Fishing remained an especially key part of the diet for many populations.

After A.D. 1300, the stockaded villages were occupied on a more permanent basis. Several archaeological indicators, including an increase in the complexity of village fortifications and a growing number of traumatic injuries found on skeletal remains, point to the intensification of warfare. The historically known patterns of Iroquoian internecine warfare and blood revenge may have been established by this time. Longhouse size expanded and village size increased. Some villages were as large as 6 ha (15 acres) and included 2000 people, although the average community was closer to 2.5 ha (6.25 acres) in size. In several areas, settlement pattern studies suggest that these larger villages apparently were formed through the nucleation of smaller communities. In these larger villages, the alignment of houses was usually much more formal than in the earlier, smaller settlements.

Excavations over the last twenty years at the Draper site in southern Ontario have provided a wealth of information on village organization in the late prehistoric period. Located 35 km (22 mi) northeast of Toronto, the site has a long research history; however, most of the settlement was excavated as part of a salvage operation initiated prior to the construction of a new Toronto airport. An unusually large village for late prehistoric Ontario, the site is particularly important because almost the entire settlement was excavated. The high cost of modern archaeological excavation makes it very rare for more than a small portion of most sites to be examined carefully. Yet in a few cases — Draper being one — the opportunity to excavate a large segment of the original village provides an unusually detailed picture of community plan, changes in settlement size over time, and house-to-house variation.

The Draper site is one of more than fifteen Iroquoian villages in the Duffin drainage, located in the white pine–hardwood forest region of southern Ontario. The settlement was inhabited between A.D. 1450 and 1500. This relatively short occupation is not unusual for southern Ontario, where most villages were resituated every twenty-five to fifty years, usually to new locations only 3 to 5 km (2 or 3 mi) away. Many factors have been proposed to account for these frequent relocations, including infestation of the wood-and-thatch longhouses by insects, soil exhaustion or weed competition (which would have prompted the clearing of forest for new agricultural fields), depletion of wood (for construction and firewood) and game around the settlement, and community realignments due to disputes and other social stresses.

The Draper site was composed of three spatially discrete areas of occupation: the main palisaded village, a small

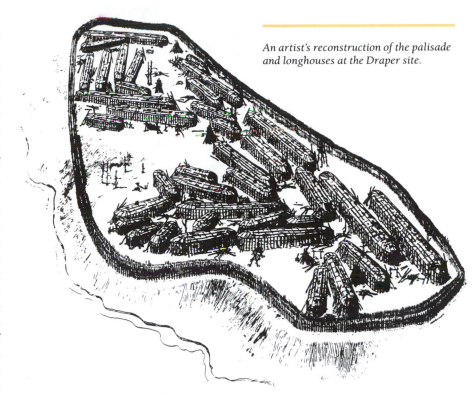

An artist's reconstruction of the palisade and longhouses at the Draper site.

group of seven houses located 50 m (160 ft) south of the main village, and a lone structure (Structure 42) located on a small knoll 80 m (260 ft) to the southwest. At different times in its occupation, the main village was surrounded by three or four palisade rows (each composed of wooden posts or beams). According to William Finlayson, who supervised the principal excavations in 1975 and 1978, the settlement appears to have been planned with defensive considerations in mind.

The site began as a 1.2 ha (3-acre) village of seven to nine longhouses (accommodating roughly 400 people). All the houses were built well back from the palisades. The first houses were arrayed in two clusters, with the houses in each cluster laid out according to similar compass orientations. Each set of houses may have represented a distinct social unit, perhaps a lineage or clan segment.

All the longhouses had a relatively similar set of internal features, including sweat baths, cooking hearths, pits (some of which were burials), storage cubicles, and benches (2 to 2.5 m or 6.5 to 8 ft wide), which were placed along the house walls. Each nuclear family within the longhouse is thought to have had its own cooking and sleeping area. The sweat baths were less abundant and were probably used in a more communal fashion. According to ethnohistoric accounts of the Huron — the Iroquoian tribal group considered to be descendants of the residents of the Draper site — sweat baths usually were taken by groups of men to prevent disease. Prior to the bath, the stones were heated in a large fire, then removed and put in a pile in the center of the lodge. Sticks were arranged at waist height around the pile, then bent at the top, leaving enough space between the sticks and the rocks for naked men sitting with their knees raised in front of their stomachs. When the men were in position, the whole bath was covered with large pieces of bark and skins to prevent air from escaping. While in the bath, the men often would sing. These sweat-bath rituals are thought to have had an important integrative function for a group of people who resided in very close quarters.

In the first Draper village, one of the longhouses had a number of characteristics suggesting a special function. This large structure had one of the highest densities of wall posts and sweat baths. It also had the greatest average distance between hearths, indicating that each family group had more space than other longhouse occupants. In addition, a special hearth was placed at one end of this somewhat unusual structure. Finlayson suggests that this longhouse may have been occupied by a community or kin-group leader or village chief. Such special structures may have been used for council meetings, community feasts, and ceremonies.

The Draper village underwent five expansions, eventually reaching a maximum population of 1800 to 2000 people. Prior to abandonment, the village was 3.4 ha (8.5 acres) in size. During each expansion episode, three to nine houses were built. The houses often were added in clusters, with the houses having similar orientations. The additions may represent new kin segments that moved into the site. Over time an increasing amount of space was devoted to nonhouse use; with each expansion the houses, or clusters of houses, were positioned to create new plazas. The plazas may have served as places for village ceremonies and social activities. Such integrative events may have increased in importance as the community

grew. Two of the houses that were added during these expansions are thought by Finlayson to have been leaders' houses.

Two rectangular structures that abutted the palisade also were added. These buildings have been interpreted as houses set aside for visitors. According to ethnohistoric accounts, visitors were assigned to special cabins so they could be closely monitored; they were not allowed to wander through the community.

The longhouses in the Draper site ranged from 14.5 to 75.1 m (48 to 247 ft) in length and 6.7 to 7.9 m (22 to 26 ft) in width. The narrow range of widths most likely was determined by the mechanical limitations of the construction procedures employed and the material available (wood). In contrast, the variation in length was probably related primarily to household or kin-group size.

The seven houses in the south field were smaller than those in the main village. They had a low density of pits and sweat baths, suggesting a shorter occupation. The presence of only a partial palisade, possibly used as a windbreak, suggests less concern for defense. Perhaps the occupants of this southern area moved inside the larger palisaded village when sieges occurred. Structure 42, also outside the main village, appears to have been a special-purpose structure, although its specific function remains little understood. Fragments of human bone were found on the surface prior to its excavation, but further study has not yet revealed additional signs of a burial area.

The late precontact Iroquoian villages in the Great Lakes region were not organized as hierarchically as were the larger, contemporaneous Mississippian polities in the Southeast. In the latter, labor was amassed to construct large pyramid mounds at central settlements. These focal settlements differed in size and function from the smaller villages that also comprised the settlement system. In contrast, the differences between the Draper site and surrounding settlements were not substantial. Although Draper was somewhat larger than its neighbors, the construction remains and material items at the site were basically similar to those found at surrounding communities.

Because of the tremendous changes that occurred in Native American ways of

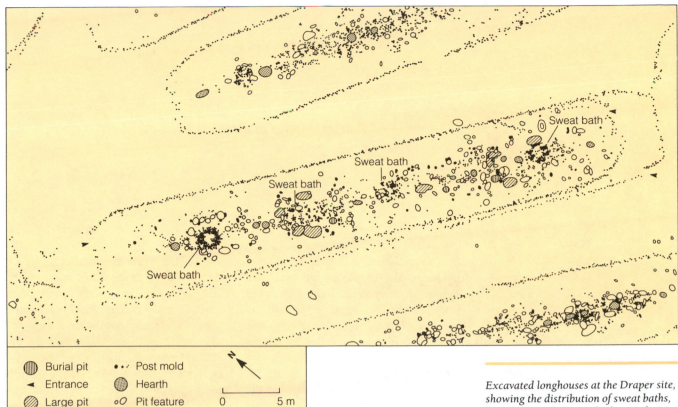

Burial pit
Entrance
Large pit
Post mold
Hearth
Pit feature

0   5 m

N

Excavated longhouses at the Draper site, showing the distribution of sweat baths, hearths, burial pits, and other pit features. The longhouses are clearly outlined by post molds. Other post molds are also present inside the houses.

life with direct European contact (and sometimes before, as the spread of disease and trade goods often preceded actual face-to-face relations), we cannot assume that the early European historical accounts (also called ethnohistoric records) present a full or completely accurate picture of the late precontact period. This potential disparity between archaeological and ethnohistoric records is especially troublesome in those areas where major settlements, such as the large Hohokam villages of the Arizona desert, were apparently abandoned sometime prior to European contact. (See "Snaketown," p. 272.) In such cases, the native people first encountered by the Europeans were not necessarily the direct descendants of earlier native populations, whose communities have been found by archaeologists. In other areas, the historical links between the historic and prehistoric peoples are somewhat clearer, such as for the Iroquoian groups of the Northeast. In these cases, ethnohistoric information can be more readily used to test and support interpretations derived from archaeological data. Nevertheless, the careful researcher must be prepared to recognize diversity and changes in the archaeological and ethnohistoric records.

For example, in the Great Lakes region, indirect contacts spread trade goods and disease vectors to most areas before direct meetings between native peoples and Europeans took place. In fact, some scholars have argued that the large-scale Iroquoian alliances and confederacies, which at times joined up to twenty-five villages and are well documented in the early historic accounts, may have been formed in response to contact-period processes. Such large linkages appear not to have been in place prehistorically. New trade demands and land pressures may have prompted the formation of new political structures. Warfare and trade certainly were important prehistorically in the Great Lakes region, but with European contact they took on new forms. Scholars, such as those studying the Iroquoian peoples, who can use and compare archaeological and historical sources as partially independent records stand the best chance of unraveling the complex, multifaceted, and often destructive processes that surrounded the arrival of the Europeans in the Americas and the effects of these processes on the native peoples.

SNAKETOWN

A desert village in the American Southwest

Despite its often arid and unforgiving landscape, the American Southwest has a rich archaeological past. The region was first populated around 9000 B.C. by hunter-gatherers who hunted big game species, such as mammoth and giant bison. These early inhabitants followed highly mobile food-collecting strategies and manufactured sophisticated tools for hunting and butchering game and for processing hides, wood, and bone. Their remains occur primarily as small, ephemeral kill and butchering sites characterized by animal bones and flaked stone implements. By 5500 B.C., big game hunting had declined in importance, and emphasis shifted to smaller animals and a variety of local plant resources. In southeastern Arizona and southwestern New Mexico, these wild foods included yucca, cactus leaves and fruits, and sunflower seeds.

By 1000 B.C., maize was introduced into the area from Mexico. Along with the other early southwestern cultigens (beans, squash, and bottle gourds), maize has a long history of cultivation in Mexico prior to its appearance in the Southwest. Eventually, maize became the most important cultivated crop in the Southwest. However, for at least 1000 years following its introduction, the peoples of the Southwest relied surprisingly little on maize or any other exotic domesticate and retained a primarily hunting-and-gathering subsistence regime.

After the year A.D. 1, villages appeared in various parts of the Southwest. This more sedentary existence, marked by the appearance of year-round dwellings, storage facilities, and ceramic containers, was related to an increased dependence on agriculture. In the colder, more northerly parts of the Southwest, farming was relatively risky. Perhaps that is part of the reason why many early villages were positioned defensively and generally included storage facilities. In the hot Sonoran Desert of southern Arizona, crop production was more secure (as long as sufficient water was available), villages were situated more in the open, and no specialized storerooms were constructed. The presence of basketry containers, and **metates** (grinding stones) and **manos** (companion handstones) for grinding corn or seeds, is indicative of a more settled existence in this area.

The early villages of the Southwest shared certain general characteristics. The earliest permanent dwellings were pithouses, structures in which the lower parts of the walls were actually the earthern sides of a shallow pit. The top part of the walls consisted of a framework of poles, interlaced with small twigs and then completely covered with mud on the exterior (a construction technique known as **wattle and daub**). Settlements often contained only two or three pithouses. In contrast, larger villages usually had one or more community, or special-function, structures in addition to pithouses.

Although the earliest ceramics in the Southwest were plainwares (without decoration), distinct regional variations soon developed. During the early centuries of the first millennium A.D., three major cultural traditions of the prehistoric Southwest began to emerge: **Hohokam** (ho-ho-kham′) in the deserts of southern Arizona, **Anasazi** (ah-na-sah′zee) on the high plateaus of the Four Corners region (northern Arizona and New Mexico, southwestern Colorado, and southeastern Utah), and **Mogollon** (muh-gē-yown') along the Mogollon Rim (in eastcentral Arizona) and in the mountains of southeastern Arizona and southwestern New Mexico. Each tradition eventually developed its own pattern of settlement and land use, architecture, community organization, and craft specialization. The discussion below of Snaketown (Hohokam) and the later section (p. 280) on Chaco Canyon (Anasazi) serve to highlight the diversity of Native American life in the prehistoric Southwest.

The Hohokam lived in the lower Sonoran Desert region of southern Arizona and adjacent Chihuahua and Sonora in northern Mexico. The area is basin and range country, composed of numerous more-or-less parallel mountain ranges rising 300 to 1070 m (1000 to 3500 ft) above the intervening basins. The desert area of southern Arizona receives less rain than the high plateaus of the Anasazi and is intensely hot in the summer. The land supports a rich natural flora of shrubs and cacti (saguaro, barrel, cholla, prickly pear); mesquite and other trees and shrubs grow in the washes. Yet because of the somewhat unpredictable rainfall, irrigation is necessary in many areas for reliable maize farming.

A sedentary way of life, based on agriculture, arose in the desert valleys of southern Arizona by A.D. 300. Snaketown, one of the earliest settled communities, is located in the Phoenix Basin, a broad, low alluvial region where southern Arizona's two major rivers, the Salt and the Gila, come together. Snaketown is situated on an upper river terrace about 1 km (0.6 mi) from the Gila River at an elevation of 360 m (1175 ft). According to Emil Haury, of the University of Arizona, who excavated at Snaketown in 1934–1935 and again in 1964–1965, good agricultural land, a river that could be tapped for irrigation, and a high water table were important features determining Snaketown's location.

Snaketown was the largest of the early Hohokam pithouse villages and may have had as many as 100 residents soon after its foundation. The early habitation levels included only residential pithouses; no public buildings were constructed. However, David Wilcox, of the Museum of Northern Arizona, has suggested that even early in its occupational history the

Snaketown during excavations in 1965.

site may have had a central plaza area. Corn was a dietary staple, although such wild plant foods as mesquite, saguaro, and cholla also were important.

By A.D. 600, the number of known Hohokam villages increased markedly, and the Phoenix Basin became the most densely populated area in southern Arizona. Many villages, including Snaketown, grew. At some sites **ball courts** and platform mounds were erected. (See "The Mesoamerican Ballgame," Chapter Seven, p. 323.) One of the most impressive of these oval Hohokam ball courts was constructed at Snaketown. Rubber balls, also found at Snaketown, suggest that certain aspects of the Hohokam ballgame may have been similar to the game played in Mexico. Hohokam platform mounds, usually low and rectangular, were made of

earth and **adobe** and topped with caliche (calcium carbonate) or adobe plaster. Ceremonial structures may have been positioned on the tops of these mounds. Both platform mounds and ball courts were generally erected at larger Hohokam sites, like Snaketown. These sites may have serviced the populations of smaller surrounding settlements that lacked such nondomestic structures.

The Hohokam cultural tradition, marked by its red-on-buff pottery, reached its greatest spatial extent after A.D. 900, spreading across much of central and southern Arizona. At about this time, Snaketown covered an area over 1 sq km (about 0.4 sq mi, or the size of the Indianapolis race track) and may have had a population of 500 to 1000 people. The plan of the village became more complex as well. At the site's core was a central plaza surrounded by an inner habitation zone. A series of mounds and two ball courts circled this area, with an outer habitation zone beyond. In all, sixty trash-filled mounds were constructed at the site, and as many as 125 pithouses may have been occupied at any one time.

At Snaketown, craftspeople specialized in the production of ceramics and developed elaborate shell- and stoneworking industries. Goods from all over the Southwest and northern Mexico were traded to the site. The shell was imported from the Gulf of California and was cut into bracelets, rings, pendants, beads, and ornaments decorated with designs etched with acid. Stone was fashioned into beads, earplugs, ornaments, carved paint palettes, axes with deep grooves for hafting, and vessels with animals in relief. Lizards were a common motif.

Other large Hohokam villages also were present in the region, especially in the Salt River Valley to the north. Although the residents of Snaketown dug several canals, it was along the lower Salt River of the Phoenix Basin that the Hohokam constructed the largest prehistoric irrigation system north of Mexico. At its largest extent, this irrigation network consisted of fourteen main canals, ranging from several kilometers up to 20 km (12.5 mi) in length, that drew water from the river, and hundreds of smaller canals that carried water to the fields. Canal irrigation required a large labor investment, first to dig the canals and then to maintain and repair them.

After A.D. 1150, the spatial extent of the Hohokam and their red-on-buff ceramic ware decreased. Snaketown was largely abandoned, and the surrounding Gila Basin was partially depopulated. Hohokam settlement then concentrated in the lower Salt River Valley, where several villages grew very large and the irrigation network reached environmental limitations on expansion. Pithouse villages were largely replaced by rectangular adobe enclosures built above ground, possibly for defensive purposes. Platform mounds continued to be constructed, while ball courts declined. In some instances, residential compounds, possibly associated with higher-status households, were

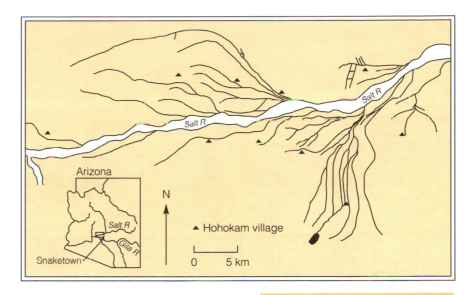

placed on the mounds. Multistory structures were built at some sites. Although an explanation for these changes is not well established, they do indicate that a political reorganization occurred.

When the first Spanish explorers entered the Phoenix Basin, the Hohokam were gone. The irrigation systems were abandoned, and the large villages, with their associated mounds and ball courts, lay in ruins. The Pima and Papago Indians, who consider the area to be their historic homeland, were the desert's only inhabitants and resided in small, scattered villages. Hohokam is their name for the people responsible for the ruins; the word can be translated as "those who have gone."

While archaeologists have postulated many reasons for the Hohokam demise — climatic change, invasion, flooding, political collapse — no single factor seems sufficient to explain this abandonment. Yet the Hohokam left a lasting imprint on the desert landscape. Their ability to master the desert is testimony to the sophistication of Hohokam engineering skills. This fact was not lost on the early European settlers, who reexcavated and used some of the long-abandoned Hohokam canals. Several canals still in use today in Phoenix follow the route and grade of the ancient waterways.

The network of Hohokam irrigation canals along the lower Salt River in the Phoenix Basin of central Arizona. Today Phoenix covers the area where these canals were situated; only a few of the ancient canals are still visible on the surface.

A shell with an etching of a horned toad (diameter 10.2 cm).

STUDYING COMMUNITY PLAN

Household clusters at Snaketown

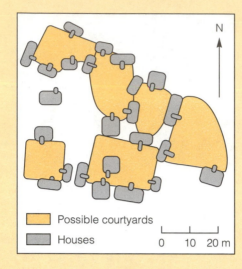

The distribution of pithouses and courtyards in one area of Snaketown, around A.D. 900 to 1100.

Possible courtyards
Houses
0   10   20 m

One objective of community studies is the examination of cohort groups at the residential level. Such units are important components (building blocks) within the social, settlement, and subsistence systems, and are for that reason a significant focus of archaeological research.

G. Rice (1987)

Over the last two decades, archaeologists have paid increasing attention to the analysis of village or site plans. These studies, which require the excavation of broad horizontal areas to expose sets of associated dwellings and features, are a means of examining settlement patterns at the scale of the community. The size and spacing of houses, as well as other archaeological features (storage facilities, cemetery areas, ritual structures, for instance), can provide the researcher with information about ancient household size, the nature and arrangement of social units above the level of the household, and the association of households with storage and other economic activities.

In the American Southwest, a long history of archaeological community pattern analysis extends back to the broad horizontal excavations conducted at pithouse villages along the Mogollon Rim by the late Paul Martin, of Chicago's Field Museum. In a classic study, James Hill, of the University of California, Los Angeles, used architectural and artifactual indicators to identify differences in room function at Broken K Pueblo, a late prehistoric Mogollon settlement in eastern Arizona.

More recently, David Wilcox and his associates have made a detailed study of ancient community structure at Snaketown. Wilcox began by identifying houses that were occupied contemporaneously. He then mapped the location and orientation of each set of houses that were inhabited during the same phase. Wilcox noted when the doorways of contemporaneous structures opened onto a shared courtyard. He found that house clusters from the early occupations at Snaketown usually consisted of only two associated structures. Later residential clusters at the site had as many as six houses around a plaza. Based on his analysis, Wilcox suggests that the people residing in each cluster of houses formed an extended family group and possibly shared certain domestic activities.

Most of the Snaketown houses have similar internal features, such as small hearths near the entrance. Other domestic activities were conducted in the shared outdoor space. Outside work areas included several types of hearths, as well as post holes that seem to mark the former position of windbreaks or brush kitchens. The inside hearths were too small to have held the large pieces of wood needed to produce adequate coals for cooking. Thus cooking may have been done outside on a cooperative basis.

Houses within each cluster were arranged at right angles to each other, defining rectangular courtyard areas. In general, clusters that contained the most houses also had the biggest courtyard areas. Over time, the location and orientation of the houses within a courtyard area showed considerable continuity, suggesting that residential placement was not random. Most larger household clusters included one structure that was square, as opposed to the usual oblong or rectangular shape. The square structures may have been used for special or ritual activities.

After A.D. 900, the largest clusters of houses at Snaketown were situated at the core of the site near major platforms and a central plaza. These larger house clusters contained more total floor area than the house clusters at the edge of the site. The emergence of these large clusters, possibly signifying increased differentiation between family groups, occurred in conjunction with a greater emphasis on civic-ceremonial construction. Some scholars suggest that these are indicators for increasing sociopolitical complexity.

PLATE 1: Three early hominid skulls and other remains found by Richard Leakey and coworkers in East Africa: *Homo habilis* (left), *Homo erectus* (center), and *Australopithecus robustus* (right). The discovery of these species in the same geological deposits suggests their contemporaneity.

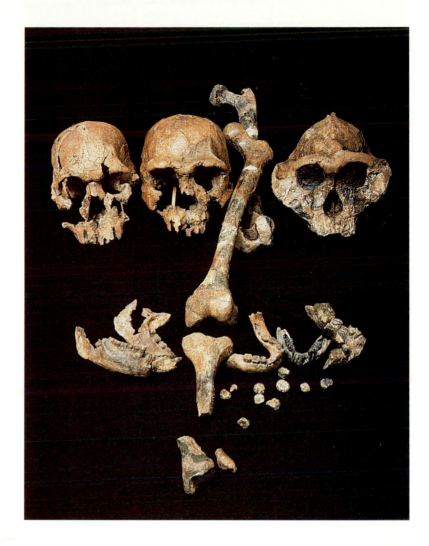

PLATE 2: The skull of "Zinj," a robust australopithecine, discovered at Olduvai Gorge in Tanzania by Mary Leakey in 1959. The background shows the walls of the gorge.

PLATE 3: The Neanderthal skeleton from La Chappelle-aux-Saints, France, was discovered early in this century. The femur and vertebrae are deformed by arthritis. These remains led Marcellin Boule to describe the Neanderthal as brutish and slow in wit, gait, and habit.

PLATE 4: The Upper Paleolithic cave of Lascaux in France contains many paintings of a variety of animals. This running horse appears with two feathered darts or plants beneath a rectilinear sign.

PLATE 5: The grave of a mother and child from a Mesolithic site at Vedbaek, Denmark. The mother's head rests on a bundle of teeth that would have decorated a hide blanket or piece of clothing. The newborn infant next to the mother is buried with a stone knife, as were all the males in the cemetery. The infant was buried on the wing of a swan.

PLATE 6: A painted statue and bust of plaster from the early Neolithic site of 'Ain Ghazal in Jordan after reconstruction. The eyes are cowrie shells set in bitumen. The statue is 90 cm high.

PLATE 7: The great diversity of modern maize is one indication of the tremendous adaptability and genetic plasticity of the plant. These varieties come from many regions of Mexico, and they prosper under different environmental and topographic conditions.

PLATE 8: A view of the Andes from Guitarrero Cave, a large natural rock shelter 2.5 kilometers above sea level in the mountains of northern Peru. The site was first used by Native Americans more than 10,000 years ago, and contains a valuable record of the beginnings of domestication in the South American highlands.

PLATE 9: Chetro Ketl, one of the great houses that was built on the floor of Chaco Canyon (New Mexico). For the most part, the large pueblo of Chetro Ketl was constructed during the late 10th and early 11th centuries A.D. The outer rooms, which faced the courtyard, were used primarily for residential activities, while the inner rooms served as storage.

PLATE 10: Mound 1 at San José Mogote in Oaxaca, Mexico. This natural rise was artifically enhanced, raising the top of the mound further above the rest of the site. Around 600 B.C., Mound 1 became the focus for public building at San José Mogote. The danzante found at San José Mogote was situated amidst a ceremonial building complex atop this mound.

PLATE 11: Part of the hilltop site of Monte Albán, Oaxaca, Mexico. The ruins of prehispanic structures are still visible at the summit, and residential terraces can be seen on the upper slopes. Monte Albán was the largest and most architecturally elaborate center in the Valley of Oaxaca for more than one thousand years.

PLATE 12: The Palace at Palenque, a Maya site situated at the foot of the Chiapas highlands in southern Mexico. The multi-room palace sits at the core of Palenque's complex of civic-ceremonial structures. The most distinguishing feature of the palace is a four-story tower, which provides a superb view of the city and the surrounding countryside.

PLATE 13: Recent excavations at Tenochtitlan's Templo Mayor. Today, this Aztec site lies at the center of downtown Mexico City. After the Spanish conquest, Mexico City rapidly grew up over the ancient Aztec center, and materials from the upper level of the Templo Mayor were used in the construction of Mexico City's main cathedral.

PLATE 14: An elaborate sacrificial knife that was used by the Aztec. The blade is made of chalcedony, a type of chert. The handle is made of wood that was inlaid with a mosaic of turquoise and shell.

PLATE 15: Aztec rulers of Mexico recorded the tribute they exacted from conquered peoples in books called codices. This page from the Codex Mendoza shows the name symbols of tributary towns and the kinds and amounts of tribute they owed.

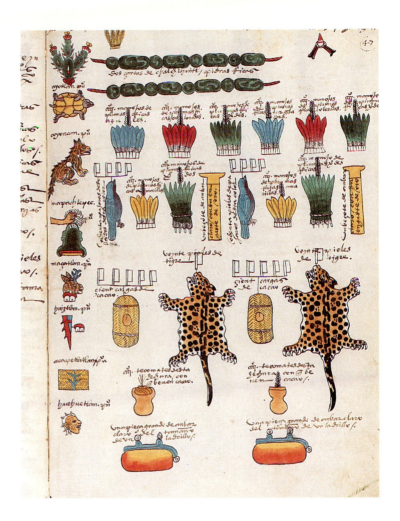

PLATE 16: A cloth mantle of the Paracas style. Images on ritual weavings played a key role in the visual communication of prehispanic Peruvian society, particularly at the south coast sites associated with this style. The "ecstatic shaman" shown in this weaving was a common image depicted on Paracas textiles.

PLATE 17: The north face of the fortress of Sacsahuaman at Inca Cuzco, Peru. This edifice was constructed of huge, stone blocks that were fitted together with great masonry skill. Some of these blocks weigh more than one hundred metric tons. The fortress was perched atop a high hill that has a commanding view of Cuzco below.

PLATE 18: The superbly preserved Inca administrative center of Machu Picchu, high in the Peruvian Andes, was discovered early in the 20th century by Hiram Bingham. The Machu Picchu ruins are a conglomerate of courtyards and stone stairways, as well as residential structures and public buildings.

PLATE 19: The Royal Standard of Ur was recovered by Sir Leonard Woolley from a complex of royal graves at Ur, an ancient city in southern Mesopotamia (Iraq). One side of the box portrays domestic activities, food production, and feasting (top). The reverse side depicts war-related images, including chariots, soldiers, and fallen enemies (bottom). In a society where most people could not read, the royal standard may have served to communicate socially approved modes of behavior.

PLATE 20: The ruins of ancient Mohenjo-daro, a well-preserved center situated in the Indus Valley of modern Pakistan. Much of the site was built on a massive mud-brick platform, which raised the settlement over the wet alluvial plain below. The balloon pictured over the site is the vehicle archaeologists used to view and to photograph the ruins from the air.

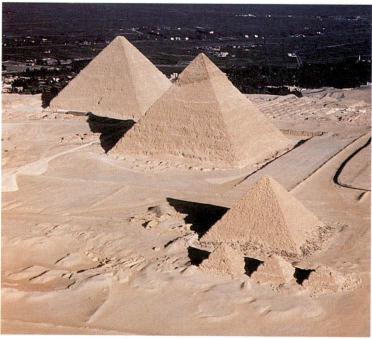

PLATE 21: Pharaohs of Old Kingdom Egypt (2686–2181 B.C.) built this enormous pyramid complex at Giza, near modern Cairo. The pyramids were built over a long period of time by a succession of pharaohs, each of whom had his own funerary monument constructed.

PLATE 22: The Great Enclosure and other stone ruins found at Great Zimbabwe. The Great Enclosure is the largest known prehistoric structure in sub-Saharan Africa. Inside the Great Enclosure were smaller stone structures, which are thought to have housed the site's ruling families.

PLATE 23: Excavations of the palisade area at the early Neolithic Bandkeramik site of Darion in Belgium. The lines of holes reveal the postholes of the palisade in the subsurface.

PLATE 24: The funeral mask of "Agamemnon" from the excavations in the shaft graves at Mycenae, Greece. Although this was determined not to be Agamemnon, it certainly was an important Mycenaean ruler.

PLATE 25: Early Celtic bronze mirror with engraved back from the Iron Age in England. It is 36 cm in diameter. The elaborate scrolling design on the mirror is typical of Celtic art.

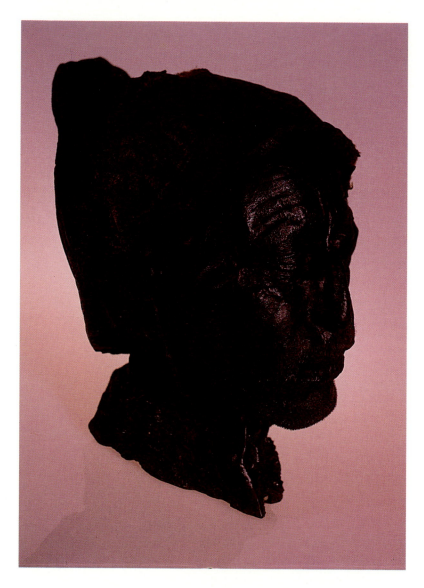

PLATE 26: The head of Tollund Man, a bog man from Iron Age Denmark. The corpse was preserved in bog deposits for almost 2000 years.

EMIL HAURY

A central figure in twentieth-century archaeology

Emil Haury with students on a field trip to Snaketown in 1974.

The youngest of four sons, Emil Haury was born in 1904 in Newton, Kansas, a small Mennonite community where his father taught Latin at Bethel College. Haury became interested in archaeology and spent the 1920s, 1930s, and 1940s traversing the backwoods and deserts of Arizona, often on horseback and living in the open, to visit the archaeological ruins.

At age 21, Haury joined Byron Cummings' excavation of Cuicuilco, a large site contemporary with early Teotihuacan, situated at the southern edge of Mexico City. In 1928 Haury returned to the University of Arizona, where he completed his Bachelor's and Master's degrees, and held his first teaching position in the Department of Archaeology. In 1929, Haury accompanied A. E. Douglass, an astronomer and the father of **dendrochronology** — the study of the annual growth rings of trees as a dating technique to build chronologies — on the Third National Geographic Society Beam Expedition to find datable tree-ring samples. Douglass discovered that certain trees produced distinctive ring sequences in response to shifts in precipitation and temperature. A long-term chronological sequence could be built by overlapping progressively older samples. Douglass already had recovered a sequence of tree-ring samples that formed one chronological continuum from the present back to roughly A.D. 1260. A second sequence of rings, 585 years long, was recovered from tree beams excavated at major southwestern ruins. Unfortunately the two chronologies did not connect, and the specific dates associated with the second chronology were unknown. At the time of the expedition, no consensus had been reached about the age of most of the prehistoric southwestern ruins. Finding tree-ring samples that would join the two chronologies (and date the prehistoric ruins) was the principal goal of the Third Beam Expedition.

The discovery of a tree-ring sample in Show Low, Arizona, ended Douglass' ten-year quest to bridge the gap between the historic and prehistoric tree-ring chronologies and permitted the first accurate dating of the major prehistoric ruins of the Southwest. Haury has de-

The large oval ball court at Snaketown.

scribed this discovery as the most dramatic event of his archaeological career. He said, "the experience was unforgettable. To be present at the instant of the celebrated break-through in science that set the chronological house in order for the southwestern United States was reward enough" (Haury, 1986, p. 60). Through his work with Douglass, Haury appreciated the importance of chronological concerns to prehistory. The importance of establishing archaeological chronologies pervades all of his subsequent research.

In 1930, Haury became the Assistant Director of the Gila Pueblo Archaeological Foundation in Globe, Arizona. This position provided him with ample opportunities for fieldwork. He excavated numerous sites in the Southwest, including Snaketown, and surveyed in the Grand Canyon and the mountains of central Arizona and New Mexico. During this time, he spent two years at Harvard University working on his Ph.D., which he received in 1934. In 1937, he returned to the University of Arizona to become Chairman of the Department of Anthropology, and a year later, the Director of the Arizona State Museum, positions he held until 1964.

By age 33, Haury had surveyed, excavated, and published widely. His many accomplishments helped establish a foundation for Arizona archaeology. He initiated a long-standing archaeological field school at Point of Pines in eastern Arizona. Although the field school occupied his summers, he found time to pursue other archaeological studies during the academic year, including the mammoth kill sites he uncovered in southeastern Arizona. In 1964, he stepped down from his administrative positions in both the Department of Anthropology and the Arizona State Museum to mount a major new Hohokam project. He returned to Snaketown, where he had excavated decades earlier, to resume work on the Hohokam chronology.

Haury's archaeological contributions have been recognized by his colleagues. He received the Viking Fund Annual Award in Anthropology (provided by the Wenner–Gren Foundation) in 1950 for distinguished research, publication, and contribution to science. In 1977, Haury was given the Alfred Vincent Kidder Award, which is presented every three years for eminence in American archaeology, particularly for research in the southwestern United States and Middle America. In 1985, he received the Distinguished Service Award, which the Society for American Archaeology presents annually for meritorious contributions to the discipline.

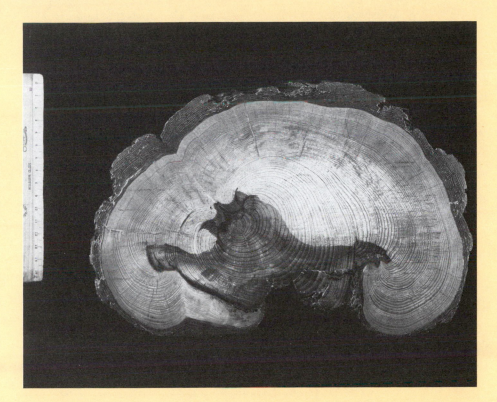

A cross section of ponderosa pine with a 108-year lifespan.

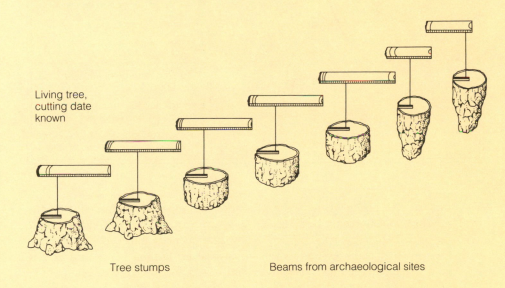

Living tree, cutting date known

Tree stumps

Beams from archaeological sites

Dendrochronology. The matching of tree rings from a modern tree with a known cutting date to those of progressively older tree samples results in a long sequence of distinctive tree-ring patterns that can be used to date beams from archaeological sites.

CHACO CANYON

A prehistoric regional center in the American Southwest

A map of Chaco Canyon, showing the principal towns and roads, and the early village of Shabik'eshchee.

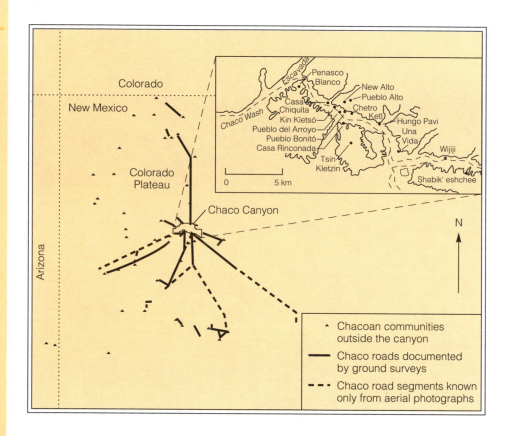

The Four Corners region of the Southwest — the junction of Arizona, New Mexico, Colorado, and Utah — is dominated by an extensive highland (elevation above 1500 m, or 5000 ft) called the Colorado Plateau. The plateau is drained by the Colorado River and its tributaries, which have cut a complex topography of mesas, buttes, valleys, and canyons into the landscape. Located in a remote part of northwestern New Mexico, Chaco Canyon is one of the largest of these erosion features.

Chaco (chah'ko) Canyon, 15 km (9 mi) long, has a sandy bottom and little permanent water. The bleak environment lacks trees and experiences dramatic temperature extremes. Rainfall, characterized by infrequent summer cloudbursts, is marginal for farming. Today the area is little used for agriculture, but once it was a center of prehistoric settlement and long-distance exchange. The Native Americans depended on rainfall for **floodwater farming,** in which they channeled seasonal runoff to agricultural fields, to supplement the water supply.

Several of the most spectacular ruins anywhere in the Southwest are located in Chaco Canyon. Although brief reports of these ruins extend back to the mid-seventeenth century when military forays from Spanish outposts entered the area, the first substantial accounts were not published until 1850. At that time, James Simpson, an officer in the Army Topographical Engineers, was sent to the canyon area to investigate claims that the Navajo were harassing isolated farms and ranchos (settlements consisting of only a few houses). Simpson was overwhelmed by the massive walls, which still stood three to four stories high and formed complexes of contiguous rooms. He described and measured many of the prehistoric structures, so that many other curious visitors soon followed. In 1906, Chaco Canyon was made a national monument to protect the ruins from destruction by treasure hunters and vandals.

The continuity of past and present Native American groups in the Southwest is most evident between the prehistoric Anasazi, a Navajo word meaning "ancient ones," and the contemporary Pueblo Indians. Many Pueblo peoples consider the Anasazi area of the Colorado Plateau to be their traditional homeland. Anasazi is one of the major prehistoric southwestern cultural traditions that developed out of the hunting-and-gathering adaptation around 2000 years ago. Prior to that time, temporary campsites and kill sites were present on the Chaco Plateau, but not in the canyon itself. The first sedentary Anasazi sites occurred around 100 A.D., located on mesas away from the bottomlands of the canyon, possibly for reasons of defense. Most of these sites contained five to ten shallow pithouses. Over the next several centuries, the diet at most Anasazi sites showed an increasing reliance on domesticated corn, beans, and squash. Yet the collecting of pine or piñon nuts and the hunting of cottontail and jackrabbit, deer, antelope, and Rocky Mountain bighorn sheep remained important.

By the middle of the first millennium A.D., villages, which may have been inhabited year-round, were located on the floor of Chaco Canyon. Once the canyon was occupied, its population grew, and although small sites remained common, some larger communities, with fifty to 100 pithouses, were established. **Kivas** (semisubterranean ceremonial rooms) were constructed at some sites, and the distinctive black-on-white Anasazi pottery first appeared.

Shabik'eshchee (shuh-bik'eh-she), an early village in the Chaco region, has been excavated. Occupied between A.D. 550 and 750, the settlement had as many as sixty-eight pit dwellings, a large kiva, numerous outdoor storage pits, and two large refuse heaps. Because roughly half of the excavated structures were intentionally dismantled to provide construction materials for later buildings, it seems unlikely that the entire village was inhabited simultaneously.

At Shabik'eshchee, the sides of the pithouses were lined with stone slabs and coated with mud plaster. The roofs were supported by four posts that were topped with crossbeams. The upper walls of the houses were formed by leaning poles and sticks against the crossbeams to the ground surface outside the excavated pit. The walls were then coated with a mixture of mud, twigs, and bark. The house was entered through a small antechamber. Inside the main chamber of the house was a centrally located hearth. The kiva, which was 3.7 m (12 ft) in diameter, was larger than the pithouses. Unlike the pithouses, the interior kiva walls were encircled by a low bench.

Sometime after A.D. 700, aboveground rectangular rooms of adobe or roughly layered masonry were constructed in the Anasazi area. At first these structures may have been used for storage, while pithouses continued to serve as dwellings. In later communities, pithouses were used largely as kivas, while most dwellings were of adobe bricks and placed aboveground. The Anasazi were the first in the Southwest to build compact villages of contiguous rectangular rooms, with different areas for habitation, storage, and ceremonial activities. For the most part, these later communities were situated at lower elevations, closer to the bottomlands, perhaps reflecting an increasing reliance on agricultural resources.

After A.D. 900, there was a considerable shift in settlement as population congregated in larger, apartmentlike **pueblos**, stone-masonry complexes of adjoining rooms. Clusters of rooms served as the residences for separate families

Black-on-white Anasazi pottery vessel.

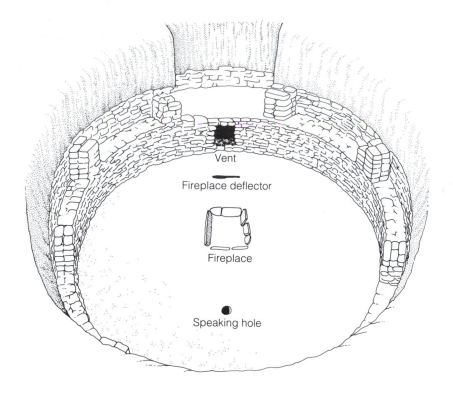

Vent

Fireplace deflector

Fireplace

Speaking hole

or lineages. Chaco Canyon supported at least nine large towns, or "great houses," of several hundred rooms each, plus hundreds of smaller villages of ten to twenty rooms each. The towns were large, multistory complexes, standing as high as four stories at the back wall, and averaging 288 rooms, some of which were large with high ceilings. The towns appear to have been built according to a preconceived plan, and there was a high degree of quality and uniformity in masonry styles. Each town also had at least one "great kiva." Placed in interior courtyards, these large kivas had a central ceremonial role in community activities. Many smaller kivas were located elsewhere in the towns and most likely served as ceremonial chambers for the various kin or family units that comprised the site population. These larger sites served as local centers for resource redistribution, long-distance trade, and ceremonial activities.

The largest and most impressive town, Pueblo Bonito, covers 160 by 100 m (525 by 325 ft, or the size of two soccer fields). It is a huge, D-shaped complex composed of over 800 apartment rooms arranged in several stories. At its height, Pueblo Bonito's population may have

been 1000 people. Situated at the base of a 30 m-high (100 ft) mesa on the north side of the canyon, the pueblo is protected by the steep cliffs of the canyon. Tree-ring dates obtained from preserved wooden beams at the site place the earliest building at Pueblo Bonito at A.D. 919; town construction apparently was finished by A.D. 1067.

The site's masonry consisted of layers of stone covering an interior core of rock and adobe rubble. The room walls were faced with adobe plaster. The rooms surrounded central courtyards. The outer rooms, which had doors and windows facing onto the courtyard, served as living quarters, and interior rooms were used for storage. The most elevated rooms were at the back of the complex along its outer rim. These back rooms included one great kiva and several smaller ones. This great kiva, the largest in the community, measured 20 m (65 ft) in diameter and was encircled by a wide masonry bench.

From A.D. 1020 to 1130, the Chacoan system peaked in population and spatial size. Much of the population of the northern Southwest participated in the regional trading network centered at Chaco Canyon. Throughout this network, which

Pueblo Bonito. The circular features are kivas. Interior rooms were used for storage, while outer rooms facing the courtyards served as living quarters.

covered over 53,000 sq km (20,500 sq mi), there were at least 125 planned towns with distinctive Chacoan architecture. Many of these settlements were linked by a complex of roads radiating from the canyon, built in straight lines, not contoured to topography, with ramps and stairways ascending the cliffs. Some were lined with masonry curbs, and some were up to 9 m (30 ft) wide, leading to sites up to 190 km (120 mi) away.

Chacoan towns evidently had the capability to mobilize large labor parties for construction. Timber was cut from forests up to 80 km (50 mi) away. Imported turquoise was worked in Chaco Canyon; some scholars have suggested that it functioned as a medium of exchange. Such exotic goods as **jet**, turquoise, shell bracelets, iron pyrite mosaics, conch shell trumpets, ornamental copper bells, and parrot and macaw feathers are found more frequently at the large central town sites than at smaller villages.

The Chaco regional system was disrupted in the mid-1100s. The population declined, although complete abandonment of the canyon did not occur for almost 200 years. The demographic collapse in the canyon coincided with population increases in other parts of the Colorado Plateau, including surrounding upland regions. In many areas, Anasazi villages shifted to well-protected, defensive locations, such as in sheltered cliffs at Mesa Verde in southwestern Colorado. Defense was a likely motive in the resettlement of some Anasazi villages, and this pattern may reflect an era of political instability that followed the collapse of the Chacoan centers.

By roughly A.D. 1300, the Anasazi region went through another major restructuring, and many Pueblo sites were again abandoned. Whether these episodes (first at Chaco and later in other parts of the Anasazi region) were triggered by climatic change, environmental degradation, shifting trade connections, changing political alliances, or a series of other factors remains a matter of conjecture and discussion. While the causes of these abandonments are still debated, the construction and maintenance of Pueblo Bonito, a structure that was the largest apartment building erected in the United States prior to the nineteenth century, in a dry, desolate canyon, remains a powerful testament to the ingenuity of the Native Americans who lived there.

The many questions that remain unanswered about the Chacoan regional system signify both the accomplishments and the challenges of Southwestern archaeologists interested in the problem of sociopolitical development. After nearly a century of survey and excavation throughout Chaco Canyon and the San Juan Basin, investigators have accumulated sufficient settlement pattern, burial, architectural, and artifactual data to conclude that the Chacoan regional system was hierarchically organized. This conclusion has prompted three major questions that will probably guide the next several decades of Chacoan research: How did this complex system develop? What kinds of relationships existed among its different components. . .? Why did the system collapse? These questions are challenging because they require that Chacoan archaeologists derive testable hypotheses from the various proposed explanatory models and that they then collect and analyze the data necessary for systematically evaluating these hypotheses.

J. Neitzel (1989)

OZETTE

*A prehistoric Northwest Coast
whaling village*

Ozette Village, located on the outer coast of the Olympic Peninsula. Cabins of the archaeologists are in the right foreground, with the excavated site just to their left.

The Pacific Coast of Oregon, Washington, and British Columbia is an environmentally rich area where land and sea hold a wealth of natural resources. The sea and the rivers contain mollusks and many species of fish, including salmon, halibut, cod, and herring. Sea mammals—such as seal, sea lion, otter, porpoise, and whale—thrive in the offshore waters. Waterfowl can be found along the shore, and further inland there are deer, elk, bear, and other smaller animals. The area has a heavy forest cover of fir, spruce, cedar, and some deciduous trees. Although vegetable foods are less plentiful, many species of berries abound.

The earliest known inhabitants of the Pacific Northwest were mobile hunters and gatherers, who moved into the area before 8000 B.C. At first, coastal foods did not comprise a major portion of the diet, but by 2000 to 3000 B.C., the accumulation of large shell middens at several sites indicates an increasing use of the readily available marine shellfish. Over the last 2000 years, subsistence patterns have continued to emphasize the exploitation of fish, shellfish, and sea mammals, supplemented by land mammals and birds. Such plant foods as berries, roots, and bulbs were not staples, but they were available for emergency at lean times of the year.

In later prehistory, the peoples of the Pacific Northwest were specialized hunter-gatherers who lived in permanent villages and developed large food surpluses by exploiting a variety of fish species. Although subsistence was based on wild resources, many of these societies had specialists in hunting, fishing, curing, and tool making. Large, permanent settlements of several hundred people appeared by A.D. 1000, despite the absence of agriculture. The abundance of giant cedar trees provided plentiful material for building houses and making dugout canoes. The natural wealth of the environment and the range of available foods allowed for the production of surplus goods and ornate material items, such as decorative wood carvings (including **totem poles**, carved boxes, canoes, and masks), cedar bark baskets, and textiles. Canoes made long-distance travel possible, facilitating the gathering of seasonal resources, the hunting of sea mammals, and the maintenance of far-reaching social networks.

Archaeological evidence indicates that social ranking appeared on the Northwest Coast by 500 B.C. At the time of European contact, all individuals in some Pacific Coast societies were ranked into a series of relatively higher and lower statuses, according to both heredity and wealth. There were chiefs and slaves, and in between, craftsmen, hunters, and fisherman. Most respected of all were the whale hunters. Whaling could be undertaken only by men from wealthy families; it was a hereditary right. Only chiefs possessed the necessary wealth to build whaling canoes, to outfit them, and to assemble the crew. Hunting whales in these large, oceangoing canoes was very dangerous. Bringing home one whale brought enormous prestige to a family, in addition to vast amounts of food.

One well-known Pacific Northwest settlement, Ozette, is located on the coast of Washington's Olympic Peninsula at Cape Alava, the westernmost point of the contiguous forty-eight states. Because the cape juts out into the Pacific Ocean, Ozette is close to the migration routes of a variety of whales, including gray, humpback, sperm whale, and others. The shoreline is a crescent-shaped beach protected by points of land, an offshore reef, and small islands. Abundant sea resources and a rich forest behind the beach made the cape an attractive location for prehistoric Native American groups. People settled in the area over 2000 years ago, and eventually Ozette grew into a major whaling village. Ozette is unique in that it was one of a few major whaling villages south of Alaska. Two other sites located south of Ozette on the coast are situated near quiet bays. Their long, straight beaches are washed by a rolling surf, making canoe travel much more difficult than at Ozette. In addition, sea mammals pass too far offshore to be worth hunting. As a consequence, these two sites show less reliance on ocean resources. Rather, the inhabitants focused on the bay and land resources, such as deer, elk, harbor seal, and salmon, in addition to oysters, mussels, and clams.

The village of Ozette stretched for almost a mile along the coast and had a maximum population of roughly 800 people. It is thought to have been a major settlement of the Makah Indians, who still reside on the Olympic Peninsula today. Although the population of Ozette declined after Europeans began to settle in the area in the mid-nineteenth century, it continued to be occupied until the late 1920s. Today, there are few surface remnants of the village left. Richard Daugherty, of Washington State University, began excavations at the site in the late 1960s when told of native accounts of mudslides that were believed to have periodically buried parts of the site. However, the actual discovery of the buried village area occurred accidentally after a violent winter storm in 1970. The harsh waves of the storm eroded sections of a bank and exposed a number of timbers, baskets, boxes, paddles, and other wooden artifacts, which were discovered by hikers. That spring, Daugherty began excavation of the buried houses.

Part of Ozette has been preserved by a massive mudslide that buried five houses around A.D. 1400 to 1500. Because

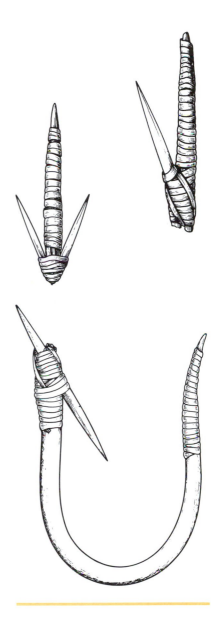

Examples of fishhooks made from bone and wrapped with bark.

A carved wooden bowl from Ozette.

A basket woven of cedar bark.

the heavy layer of clay sealed these houses and kept out oxygen, perishable artifacts of wood and fiber, which normally do not preserve well in the wet environment of the Northwest Coast, could be recovered. Since the village was occupied at the time of the mudslide, the excavated material represents the entire range of wooden artifacts that were used by a Northwest Coast household. In addition to the wooden planks and posts of the houses, the excavators recovered baskets, mats, hats, **tumplines** (carrying straps), halibut hook shanks, arrow shafts, harpoons, finely carved wooden clubs and combs, box fragments, bowls, wood wedges, a variety of fish hooks and barbed fish points (used on the end of a spear to stab fish in the water). In total, over 42,000 artifacts were recovered.

Due to the region's abundant rainfall and high groundwater, Ozette is water-saturated, like many other sites on the Northwest Coast. This condition has made normal excavation procedures difficult. When trowels and shovels were employed, as they are on most excavations, they sliced through and gouged the fragile wood and fiber. To deal with this problem, a method called **wet-site excavation** was developed. With this technique, water is pumped through garden hoses and sprayed onto the deposits to remove the dirt and expose the archaeological materials. High water pressure is used to remove the heavy clay deposits, and lower pressure is used to remove dirt from more fragile artifacts. This procedure works well because the water pressure can be adjusted continually to expose an artifact

without dislocating or destroying it. By using a very fine spray, even the remains of basketry and other fibers can be carefully revealed and removed.

The excavated houses at Ozette were very large, about 20 m (65 ft) long and 10 m (33 ft) wide, about the size of a tennis court. They were constructed of cedar planks, some up to 0.5 m (1.5 ft) wide, supported by upright wooden posts, and held in place with twisted cedar twigs. Roof boards were overlapped to keep out the rain. Raised platforms ringed the inside walls and were used for sleeping and storage. Most of the recovered artifacts were found in association with these platforms. The existence of several hearths in each house suggests that these large structures were occupied by more than one nuclear family. In one house, the highest-ranking family apparently lived in the left-rear quarter; ceremonial gear and whaling harpoons were found there. In this area, a woven cedar bark hat, traditionally worn by individuals of high status in later times, also was recovered. In another house, wood chips associated with woodworking activities were found.

Excavations at Ozette have provided ample evidence for the extensive hunting of sea mammals. Whale bones have been found in the earliest levels, indicating that the prestige and practice of whaling dates back at least 2000 years. Many whale bones also were found in later levels; some of the bone was used in house foundations, to shore up walls, or to divert water and mud from sliding down the hillside onto the backs of the structures. At low tide, a cleared strip through the offshore

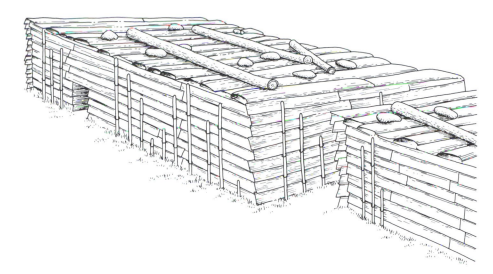

An artist's reconstruction of a house from Ozette.

rocks is still visible. Centuries ago, canoes could have taken this route to the open waters to encounter the migrating whales. Artifacts associated with whaling—parts of canoes, canoe paddles, and whaling harpoons—were plentiful at the site. The peoples of Ozette also hunted other sea mammals, including fur seal, porpoise, dolphin, and sea lion, which constituted the majority of mammal bones at the site. Elk and deer bones were present, but in small amounts. Although salmon bones were few at Ozette, halibut, ling cod, and shellfish were well represented.

The great importance of maritime resources is also evident 3 km (2 mi) south on the beach at Wedding Rock, where at least forty-four **petroglyphs**—drawings carved on rocks—have been found on beach boulders. Whale motifs are especially prevalent, including one of a pregnant whale. Although a rich ceremonialism on the Northwest Coast was associated with the hunting of sea mammals, especially whales, there is no definitive evidence that the petroglyphs were used as part of such ceremonies. One possible function of the carvings may have been to gain supernatural power over the inhabitants of the sea. Whale hunters may have made the petroglyphs to assure them good luck on whaling trips, or to commemorate other important events. No method of dating the petroglyphs is yet available. However, the Wedding Rock art may have been made at the same time that the excavated houses at Ozette were inhabited, because several of the carved motifs are also present on artifacts recovered from the site.

Petroglyphs of whales and human faces at Wedding Rock near Ozette.

Chiefs

Hereditary leadership among native North Americans

The first Europeans on the North American continent encountered a wide variety of social and political organization among Native Americans. Some groups were organized as bands or tribes, with little formal variation in the status or rank of individuals. People filled different roles according to their talents and achievements. At the other end of the spectrum were a number of groups in which positions of authority were inherited at birth. At the top of this hierarchy of social rank were "chiefs," who held political authority over individuals in the society. North American Indian chiefs engaged in a wide range of activities, including intersocietal politics, ceremonial leadership, and declarations of war. Yet none of these chiefly societies was as hierarchically organized or socially stratified as the largest polities of Mesoamerica and South America.

In the Americas before European contact, chiefs usually were associated with agricultural societies. Although food surpluses can be produced by most, if not all, economies, it often is easier to produce a storable surplus with agriculture. Domesticated plants are generally easier to store than wild resources, and they tend to produce greater returns for each unit of land. Chiefs can extract or control food surpluses; they also can encourage their kinsmen to work to produce beyond their immediate needs. In the southeastern United States, such large sites as Cahokia and Moundville were located in very fertile areas. The large mortuary mounds and burials, accompanied by elaborate grave goods, indicate the presence of powerful chiefs at these sites. But chiefs also were present in some societies that did not practice agriculture. Many of the societies on the Northwest Coast were based on hunting and gathering. Their economies focused on a rich and diverse base of marine resources, which permitted a surplus to be accumulated. These societies also had complex social organizations and hierarchies of social rank. Only individuals from the highest-ranking families could become chiefs.

Chiefs did not necessarily return all the produce they collected. This surplus provided the capital to obtain exotic and highly crafted goods through trade. Much chiefly exchange involved the acquisition of high-status items that were either traded to establish new allies or loaned to attract followers. Often a chief's power could be measured by the number of allies and dependents who could be mobilized for specific tasks.

Although the position of chief was largely acquired along hereditary lines, personal achievements also were important. Among Northwest Coast Native American groups, only high-ranking individuals could attain the position of chief. But one's role as chief had to be validated continually; failure to do so resulted in a loss of status. One way chiefs validated their position was by publicly displaying their wealth and distributing their accumulated property. At the time of European contact in the Northwest, an elaborate ceremonialism had developed, based on the **potlatch**, a large feast that included the display and dispersal of accumulated wealth to assembled guests. The mere possession of wealth did not confer prestige. But by distributing the wealth, the chief created social debts and obligations that could be called in and used to bolster his position at a later date. A potlatch gave the host far greater prestige than selling or trading, yet in economic terms the result was relatively similar: the redistribution of goods. Politically, the quest for prestige gave momentum to the whole system; the more a chief gave away, the greater his status.

To date, most archaeological interpretations have emphasized the functional or managerial advantages (especially the mitigation of food crises) associated with the emergence of chiefs. Yet such arguments are incomplete, because in many cases the likelihood of major crop failures—the kind requiring chiefly intervention—was low. The construction of more complete explanations requires that archaeologists extend their consideration beyond the benefits of chiefly societies to the political strategies of emergent leaders and the factors that allowed those strategies to work.

EPILOG
THE CLASH OF WORLDS

Changing perspectives on
Native North Americans

When the Europeans and Africans first penetrated the lands of the New World north of Mexico in the sixteenth, seventeenth, and eighteenth centuries, they observed huge earthen mounds at sites in the east that were no longer inhabited, as well as well-planned mud-brick ruins in the west. Yet blinded by the **ethnocentrism** of the era, many of the early explorers failed to recognize any of the obvious historical connections between the land's indigenous peoples and the impressive architectural features. Frequently, the Euro-American traders and adventurers speculated that the great earthworks and pueblos were remnants of earlier constructions built by Romans, Vikings, Celts, or people from imaginary lands, like Atlantis. Few early explorers were willing to accept the possibility that the ruins were part of the heritage of Native American peoples, whose lands and resources they coveted. Sadly, such migrationist views are still all-too-frequently advanced (and may even attract occasional popular attention today), although they remain entirely without solid empirical support. (Some authors have gone so far as to postulate extraterrestrial contacts!)

Fortunately, there were exceptions, like Thomas Jefferson, who held a serious interest in the origins of the Native North Americans. In the 1780s (before being elected President), Jefferson carefully excavated a burial mound on his property in order to address a series of questions that were posed in a French government questionnaire that was sent to him as Governor of Virginia. Some of the queries concerned the aboriginal population of the state. Jefferson's reasoned, stratigraphic analysis showed that the excavated mound represented several discrete interment episodes, with each burial group covered and separated by a layer of stones and earth. The absence of wounds on the bodies and the presence of children in the feature suggested to Jefferson that the burials were not related to warfare or militarism as others had surmised. He correctly concluded that the mound was constructed by the ancestors of the Native Americans who were encountered by early European colonists of Virginia.

In the nineteenth century, a principal focus of early North American anthropology was the Native American, in the past as well as in the present. Information was collected from archaeological evidence, early historic accounts, and contemporary observations. Continuities in language, ritual, and material culture were emphasized in an effort to confirm the historical relationships between living indigenous peoples, past documentary records that described the aboriginal inhabitants of North America, and artifactual inventories. While many of the associations between present and past were reasoned and justified (laying the foundation for twentieth-century archaeology and anthropology), the absence of an adequate time scale (no absolute dating techniques were yet invented) contributed to the occasional overreliance on contemporary or historical records to interpret the archaeological past. Archaeology depends on inspirations, clues, analogies, and models from more recent times to help flesh out the past. Yet archaeologists studying the prehistory of North America, as well as other areas, should be prepared to recognize changes that occurred during prehistory and immediately thereafter. Prehistoric peoples may have had a way of life and organizational formations that were markedly different from those recorded in written texts.

Many studies have documented that the contact period, the sixteenth through the eighteenth centuries, was a time of great change for most, if not all, native North American groups. In many areas, such as the Southeast, Native Americans not only were savaged in combat with the Euro-American invaders (such as the nine shiploads of *conquistadores,* led by Hernando de Soto, who landed on the coast of Florida in 1539), but were vanquished by the infectious, epidemic diseases (influenza, smallpox, measles, and whooping cough) that were introduced to the New World. Because the aboriginal peoples had no immunity to these diseases, their effect often was calamitous, decimating the native populations. In many regions, the impact of the diseases may have been further intensified by the social and economic dislocations that were occurring at the same time. Regardless of the specific causes involved, many Native American populations had been severely ravaged and disrupted in demographic size, subsistence, and sociopolitical organization when they were first encountered by more permanent settlers (and eventually anthropologists) in the seventeenth, eighteenth, and nineteenth centuries. As a consequence, anthropologists and archaeologists must be careful about relying too specifically on direct analogies between ethnohistoric, as well as early ethnographic, accounts and the deeper past that we see through archaeology.

When the Europeans first arrived in North America, no sites as large as Cahokia in the Midwest or the pueblos of Chaco Canyon in the Southwest appear to have been inhabited (or were described). Yet this fact should neither lead us to doubt the Native American heritage of these sites nor force us to inhibit our interpretation of the past by assuming that the archaeological settlements were organized in exactly the same manner as were the ethnographically observed inhabitants of the respective regions.

Such variation should not be surprising, because, as noted in the "Prolog," diversity in both space and time seems to have been a key feature of the Native American way of life. In part, the spatial variation may have been related to the great environmental differences that characterize the continent. At times, cultural changes may have been responses to documented episodes of climatic transitions. Yet such environmental factors alone cannot explain the range of prehistoric variability. Perhaps the smaller and less stratified social systems that inhabited North America were generally more flexible and organizationally (and demographically) fluid than were the more complex, hierarchical polities that developed in much of Middle and South America, as well as in a good portion of the Old World. Such flexibility and fluidity also may help account for the great cultural diversity of the prehistoric North American peoples.

Most people are interested in their past, their forebears, their roots. Where did they come from? How did they make their living? What were their ways of life? Our interest is generated by an almost innate understanding that our past has influenced and shaped our present. While some people show no concern with the past, others believe that the past is no different than the present, or that the only thing one needs to know about the past is written in holy scriptures. Still others may be afraid of the political or cultural realities that one may find by studying the past. Obviously, we as archaeologists agree with the English poet, G. K. Chesterton, who wrote:

> The disadvantage of men not knowing the past is that they do not know the present. History is a hill or a high point of vantage, from which alone men see the town in which they live or the age in which they are living.
>
> (Chesterton, 1933; p. 105)

As people tend to be most interested in their own ancestral roots, it is not surprising that Euro-American archaeology got off to an earlier start in Europe than did systematic archaeological research in North America. This circumstance may help account for the popularity of migrationist views in the history of the latter. European countries also enacted antiquity legislation, protecting archaeological resources from destruction, decades prior to the passing of such laws by North American governments. And even today, most European countries devote more resources per capita to studying local prehistory than do North American countries. At the same time, as Euro-American archaeologists investigate the prehistory of North America, they must remember that

> *The history of European colonial expansion following the late 15th century is riddled with a multitude of curious and seemingly inexplicable encounters between native cultures and Europeans, which demand the conjoining of historical and anthropological methods.*
>
> J. L. Hantman (1990)

they are helping establish the history of living peoples — Native Americans — who care just as much (if not more) about their ancestral heritage. Archaeologists should be sensitive to these realities. We should also remember that archaeological data have a significant role to play in liberating Native American history from an exclusive dependence on documentary sources, which are primarily products of Euro-American culture.

SUGGESTED READINGS

Coe, Michael, Dean Snow, and Elizabeth Benson. 1986. *Atlas of ancient America.* New York: Facts on File. An elaborately illustrated volume covering all of the Americas, with excellent maps.

Cordell, Linda S. 1984. *Prehistory of the Southwest.* Orlando, FL: Academic Press. The best current synthesis of archaeology in the American Southwest.

Crown, Patricia L., and W. James Judge, eds. 1991. *Chaco and Hohokam: Prehistoric regional systems in the American Southwest.* Santa Fe, NM: School of American Research. An up-to-date scholarly compendium of papers that compare and contrast regional variation in southwestern prehistory.

Fagan, Brian. 1991. *Ancient North America.* London: Thames & Hudson. A well-done and amply illustrated synthesis of North American archaeology.

Fowler, Melvin L. 1974. *Cahokia: Ancient capital of the Midwest.* Reading, MA: Addison-Wesley. A classic piece that describes the history of research at Cahokia.

Jennings, Jesse, ed. 1983. *Ancient North Americans.* San Francisco: Freeman. A collection of articles that summarizes North American prehistory, each one written by an expert in the region.

7

ANCIENT MESOAMERICA

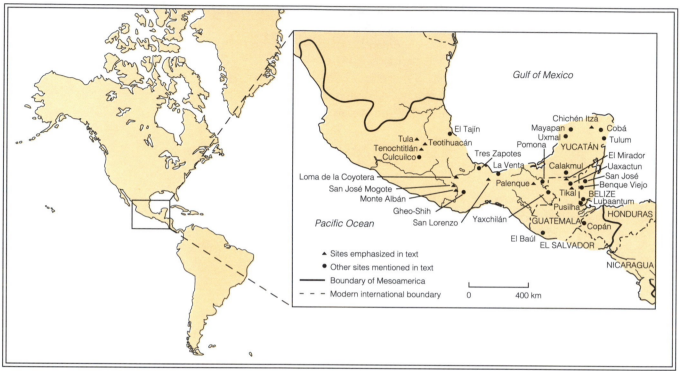

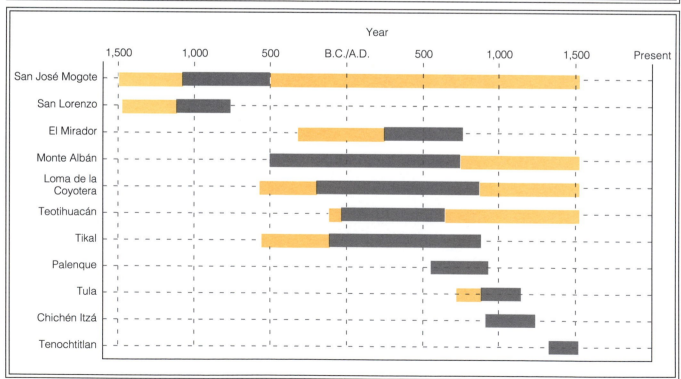

PROLOG
EARLY STATE DEVELOPMENT

Political developments in prehispanic Mesoamerica

Archaeologists and other social scientists define a **state** as an internally specialized and hierarchically organized political formation that administers large and complex polities. States are associated with populations that are socially and economically stratified. In these societies, wealth, social status, and political power are generally inherited, while in unstratified societies, such advantages are most often achieved through personal skills and experience. While some archaeologists have suggested that Cahokia, in the midwestern United States, was at the center of a short-lived state organization (see Chapter Six), most researchers argue that state formation in the New World did not occur north of Mexico before European contact.

Indigenous or pristine states, institutions that developed relatively free of significant external contact or outside influence, arose in Mesoamerica, South America, Southwest Asia, and China. The rise of these early polities, and several cases of secondary and tertiary state development, are presented in this chapter, as well as in Chapters Eight and Nine. In this chapter (Mesoamerica) and Chapter Eight (South America), we take a more historical approach in surveying the complex processes surrounding the rise of civilizations in two areas of the New World. Although comparisons are made throughout, we adopt a more consciously comparative perspective in Chapter Nine, where we discuss early civilizations from several parts of the Old World. Chapter Nine concludes with a discussion of some of the theories that have been advanced to explain state origins. (See also "Warfare and the Rise of the State," p. 315.)

The first indigenous states were established in the Near East during the fourth millennium B.C. For that reason, some of you may wish to read Chapter Nine before reading Chapters Seven and Eight. Because so many of the theories about state origins were constructed with the Near Eastern cases in mind, we thought it would be helpful to consider these different explanations in Chapter Nine in conjunction with the Old World examples. We also wanted to discuss these theoretical positions after we were able to consider the variability of early states. For that reason, we begin our discussion with Mesoamerica, drawing comparisons between the highland polities (such as Teotihuacan) and those of the Maya lowlands. We then move to Andean South America in Chapter Eight, where we consider some of the similarities and differences between the prehispanic Andean and Mesoamerican worlds. In Chapter Nine, we offer a more global, synthetic perspective.

When Hernán Cortés and his Spanish *conquistadores* landed on the eastern coast of Mexico in A.D. 1519, they encountered a remarkably diverse landscape of cultures and environments. The terrain is a complex vertical mosaic of snow-capped volcanic peaks, arid highland valleys, lush tropical forests, "scrubby" plains, swampy lowlands and estuaries, and beautiful sandy beaches. The climate ranges from the arctic cold of high mountain summits to sweltering heat at sea level, and climatic and topographic variability results in a rich mosaic of animal and plant life. Before the 1519 arrival of the Spanish, Mesoamerica — which includes central and southern Mexico, the Yucatán peninsula, and the northern parts of Central America — was also a world of enormous linguistic and

CONTENTS

293

ethnic differences. (See "Mesoamerica," p. 229.) The prehispanic inhabitants spoke many languages, employed a wide range of farming and water-control strategies, and inhabited towns and cities of varied form and function.

Yet the peoples of Mesoamerica also shared a great deal, including a reliance on similar staple foods, widespread trade, and related religious systems. This shared ceremonial realm included a calendar, stepped pyramids, ritual sacrifice of blood, writing systems, and specific styles of dress. The dietary "trinity" of corn, beans, and squash (supplemented by avocado and chili peppers) provided a remarkably nutritious diet. Maize (corn) provides most of the essential amino acids for building protein; lysine, a missing ingredient, is present in beans. An enzyme in squash contributes to the digestion of the protein in beans. Maize extracts nitrogen from the earth in which it grows; beans release nitrogen back to the soil. Corn and squash are rich in carbohydrates and calories. Beans and the avocado provide fat. The chili pepper, a regular condiment in Mesoamerican meals, is high in vitamins and aids in the digestion of high cellulose foods.

As discussed in Chapter Five, corn, beans, and squash were domesticated by 7000 years ago in the highlands of Mexico, where today the wild ancestors of these plants still grow side by side. These domesticated plants spread throughout Mesoamerica by 2000 B.C. At about the same time, perhaps a few centuries earlier, people began to make simple pottery in the shape of squashes and gourds. Yet it was not for another 500 years (around 1500 B.C.) that we find the first permanent farming villages in this region. This pattern differs from what we saw in eastern North America (Chapter Six), where some residential stability was present prior to dependence on domesticated plants. The sequence of development in highland Mesoamerica appears to be the domestication of plants, followed by the invention of ceramics, and then the emergence of village society. Once the indigenous peoples of Mesoamerica had adopted a sedentary farming lifeway, the advent of the region's earliest cities and states followed after roughly 1000 years. The Spanish conquest 2000 years later effectively terminated the indigenous rule of native Mesoamerican civilizations.

Information about those civilizations and their predecessors comes from a number of sources, including Spanish accounts, prehispanic texts, archaeology, and **ethnography**. The Spanish conquerors and priests kept diaries and descriptions of their impressions of this New World. These accounts often incorporated the remembrances of indigenous confidants as well. These ethnohistoric sources provide an invaluable record of ancient Mesoamerican customs, beliefs, and individual histories at the time of European contact. However, they also provide an incomplete and often ethnocentric picture of the prehispanic past. Scholars also derive information from the texts of the prehispanic peoples themselves. These records include both short accounts, written more than a millenium ago on stones, murals, and pottery, and a few later (and generally longer) books, or **codices** (singular **codex**). The surviving codices, written on bark paper or animal skins, date principally to the end of the prehispanic period. The religious zeal of the Spanish resulted in the destruction of much that was native, including the burning of many books, the razing of temples and palaces, and the destruction of the priesthood. Decipherment of the surviving written accounts, particularly those of the ancient Maya, has greatly improved our understanding of rituals, militarism, and rule in the prehispanic Mesoamerican civilizations. The native texts also are limited in scope and geographic coverage and reflect a bias toward the events in the lives of the literate elite and the rulers. Ethnographic studies of contemporary peoples in modern Mesoamerica provide information about the organization of agricultural systems and the survival of certain prehispanic customs. Nevertheless, the Spanish presence in Latin America effectively eliminated much of what was native through law, education, and religious doctrine.

Despite these historical and modern sources of information, archaeological research is essential for a basic understanding of the emergence of Mesoamerican cities and civilizations. More than a century of investigations in Mesoamerica has begun to yield significant findings. Major tomb and temple excavations have been conducted in lowland regions of Mesoamerica, where ancient Maya ruins sat virtually undisturbed from the time of their abandonment around A.D. 900 until their rediscovery in the last century. More recent studies have analyzed villages and the hinterland of ancient cities, temples, and tombs in order to understand the organization and operation of everyday life. In Mexico's Central and Southern Highlands, where archaeological preservation is generally good and ancient ruins are often visible on the present land surface, long-term, multistage archaeological excavation and settlement-pattern survey programs have been implemented.

In Mesoamerica, the beginnings of sedentary village life mark the start of the Formative (or Preclassic) period. Studies at San José Mogote document this early stage of village living in highland Mesoamerica. The rapid transformation from simple village society to the construction of impressive ceremonial centers occurred precociously on Mexico's Gulf Coast. San Lorenzo is the earliest of these lowland centers (and is roughly contemporaneous with Poverty Point in northeastern Louisiana, Chapter Six). Recently investigated, El Mirador is unusually large and spectacular for the Maya lowlands, considering its early date.

Late in the Formative period, major urban centers were established in the highlands; hilltop Monte Albán in the Valley of Oaxaca and giant Teotihuacan in central Mexico illustrate this episode of development. The small site of Loma de la Coyotera, situated part way between these two highland regions, marks an episode of Monte Albán militarism at the end of the Formative period. Following the onset of the Classic period in A.D. 200 to 300, Monte Albán and Teotihuacan grew significantly, with the latter city becoming one of the world's largest. Impressive centers, including Tikal and Palenque, also were built in the Maya lowlands during the Classic period. While the Classic Maya developed Mesoamerica's most sophisticated writing system, none of their centers achieved the size of Teotihuacan.

Between A.D. 700 and 900, the Mesoamerican world underwent a sequence of upheavals and transitions that included the decline and depopulation of most extant centers. The succeeding Postclassic period was characterized by somewhat greater political fragmentation and fewer architecturally massive centers. Yet places like Tula, on Mesoamerica's northern frontier, and Chichén Itzá, in northern Yucatán, did rise to power for several centuries. The greatest exception to this Postclassic pattern was Tenochtitlan, which during the last years before Spanish conquest became the largest city in the history of prehispanic Mesoamerica. Although the rulers of the latter center established a tributary domain that stretched as far as highland Guatemala, their armies were subdued by Cortés in less than two years.

Unlike most states in the Old World, Mesoamerican civilizations arose and flourished without beasts of burden, wheeled transportation, or metal tools. Yet during the thirty centuries that elapsed between the establishment of village farming communities and the Spanish conquest, this prehispanic world was the scene of highly developed statecraft, major urban centers, magnificent craftmanship, spectacular architecture, and large swamp and lakeshore reclamation projects. Thus Mesoamerica provides a physically diverse and scientifically important natural laboratory for joining historical and archaeological methods, in order to unravel and interpret societal continuity and change.

San José Mogote

A 3500-year-old community in Mexico's southern highlands

Carved stone (danzante) from San José Mogote.

The preceramic era in ancient Mesoamerica was long, and the pace of change was relatively slow. (See "Tehuacán" and "Guilá Naquitz Cave," Chapter Five.) However, this period was marked by the origin, and increasing dependence on, agriculture, as well as by steady but gradual increases in settlement size and occupational stability. The contrast with the subsequent episode of rapid change is pronounced. By the latter half of the third millenium B.C., the inhabitants of both coastal and highland settlements were making and using pottery. Within a few centuries, permanent villages were also established across much of the Mesoamerican landscape.

San José Mogote (san'ho-zay'mo-go'tay), one of the more thoroughly studied of these early settlements, was positioned on a low spur of land abutting the flat valley bottom in the Valley of Oaxaca (wah-ha'kah). This spot has been inhabited almost continuously to the present, and even today there is a small farming community at the site. First occupied before 1400 B.C., San José Mogote appears to be the oldest pottery-using village in the area.

A fairly complete archaeological record exists for the occupation of the site between 1500 and 1150 B.C. During this period, San José Mogote grew to become the largest — more than 2 ha (5 acres) — and most important of the more than twenty-five villages distributed across the Valley of Oaxaca. At this time, San José Mogote was the only settlement containing several public buildings. Most of the early villages were situated on or near to the valley bottom, the prime agricultural land. The inhabitants depended on maize, avocados, and other cultigens for subsistence, supplemented by wild plants from the piedmont and mountains; deer, cot-tontail rabbits, and other game were hunted. Small household units were equipped with braziers, earth ovens, and/or cooking hearths, as well as manos (grinding stones) and metates (ground stone basins) and blackened ceramic jars, for preparing and cooking food. Outside each household area were bell-shaped pits that were built for food storage and later used for trash disposal. Burials and other activity areas also were placed near the wattle-and-daub dwellings. In total, each house and its surrounding features encompassed about 300 sq m (3200 sq ft), an area about the size of a tennis court.

Clay figurines of humans and animals appear in association with ritual activities and burials in the first sedentary villages. Obsidian — a nonlocal stone obtained from volcanic sources elsewhere in Mesoamerica — also was found in varying quantities in each excavated residence. This evidence suggests that both trade and ritual were carried on at the level of the family during this period and that households were generally free of hierarchical control.

Household autonomy began to diminish after 1150 B.C. While most of the villages in Oaxaca remained small, San José Mogote continued to grow. Monumental architecture at the site was enhanced and enlarged. In the valley, certain craft activities were enacted only at San José Mogote. In one part of the town, magnetite (an iron ore) was polished into mirrors that were traded as far as the Gulf Coast, over 250 km (150 mi) away. At the same time, exotic equipment for ceremonial activities — such items as turtle shell drums, conch shell trumpets, and the bony, tail spines of sting-rays (used to draw blood in human autosacrificial rites) — were more abundant at San José Mogote than elsewhere. Obsidian also was more common here. Symbolic designs on pottery associated with the widespread connections of the Olmec Horizon, are prevalent in Oaxaca between 1150 and 800 B.C., particularly at this most important town. (See "Olmec Horizon," p. 304.)

After 700 B.C., differences between communities in the valley were even more pronounced. Major public buildings, incorporating adobe bricks and huge blocks of stone, were erected atop groups of earthen mounds. The valley's largest architectural complex prior to 500 B.C. was built on a natural rise (Mound 1) that was artificially enhanced so that it rose 15 m (50 ft) above the rest of San José Mogote. As part of this complex, a flat stone was laid on the ground as a kind of threshhold, in such a way that anyone passing through a corridor between ceremonially important structures would step on it. The body of an awkwardly sprawled naked individual with closed eyes, mouth ajar, and an open chest wound was carved on this slab. A similar theme, likely representing slain or sacrificed captives, appears slightly later with the carved stone *danzante* ("dancer") figures at the Oaxaca site of Monte Albán. (See "Monte Albán," p. 310.)

Slightly later at San José Mogote, the public buildings of Mound 1 were replaced by elite residential compounds, which could be reached only by the same stone stairway that had previously led to the public buildings. The importance of these residences also is suggested by the large storage areas associated with one of the compounds. A woman with three jade ornaments was buried in the same compound; the largest tomb at this time was situated in the central patio. Unlike the later palaces at Monte Albán, these elite compounds could have been built by the members of an extended family, without large labor gangs. Kent Flannery and Joyce Marcus, of the University of Michigan, who have worked for over two decades at San José Mogote, conclude that the community's highest-ranking family, however, did have sufficient power to direct the construction of a huge public building by corvée labor (physical work performed for little or no renumeration), and eventually even to preempt that platform as a site for personal residence.

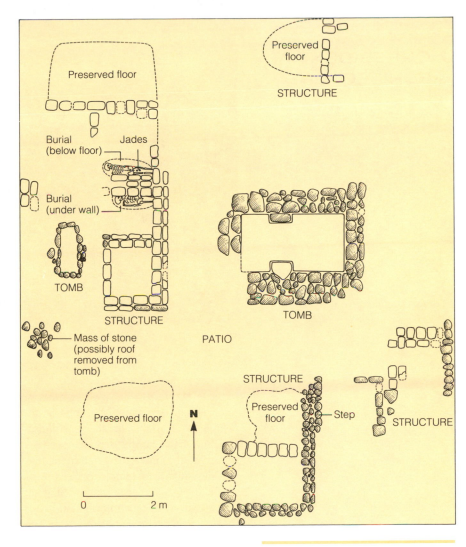

An elite residential complex with tombs on Mound 1.

Following the establishment of the city of Monte Albán (in 500 B.C.) on a hilltop, less than 10 km (6 mi) to the south, San José Mogote became one of several second-tier communities that were part of the expanding political entity that was to become the Zapotec (Valley of Oaxaca) state. San José Mogote never regained the regional and interregional importance that it had before 500 B.C. Yet for the roughly 1000 years prior, beginning with the transition from mobile hunting and gathering to a sedentary way of life, San José Mogote was the central community in the Valley of Oaxaca. In Mesoamerica, cultural change was rapid following the shift to village life. At San José Mogote, a small farming hamlet expanded into a town with special ceremonial and production functions encompassing more than 1000 people. These changes, which preceded the rise of Mesoamerica's first urban civilization, are captured in the site's archaeological record.

Nonresidential Architecture

Clues to changes in the use of space and the nature of ritual

Cut stone architecture at San José Mogote.

Anyone who has visited the archaeological sites of Mesoamerica remembers the massive pyramids, like the Pyramids of the Sun and the Moon at Teotihuacan, Temple I at Tikal, or the Castillo at Chichén Itzá. Nonresidential constructions, whether monumental, like the major Mesoamerican temple pyramids, or small, like Structure 6 at San José Mogote, can reveal significant information about the societies that built and used them. The size and complexity of construction can tell us about available labor and the power to organize and direct such projects. From the form or shape of public buildings, we can learn about the different kinds of communal activities that took place above the family level. Today such activities might include funerals, weddings, dances, sports, parades, political rallies, and the like. In prehispanic Mesoamerica, such activities included the ritual game played in formal ball courts (see "The Mesoamerican Ballgame," p. 323), the burial of elite individuals in ornate tombs, and various ritual sacrifices enacted in and around the temples. The use of nonresidential space also tells something about accessibility to ritual activities. For example, an open plaza, or "danceground," would have very different participants than the enclosed ritual space in the temples atop pyramid mounds.

Changing patterns in the use of public space have been documented in a series of excavations in the Valley of Oaxaca by Kent Flannery and Joyce Marcus. The earliest known communal area was identified at the center of Gheo-Shih, a preceramic temporary campsite. Excavations revealed an arrangement of boulders in two parallel rows, each roughly 20 m (65 ft) long. The 7-m (23-ft) wide space between the rows was swept clean and contained almost no artifacts, while outside the rock lines, artifacts were abundant. The space is thought to have been used for community rituals. Perhaps it was a kind of danceground that was similar to those used by the Native Americans of Nevada during the seventeenth and eighteenth centuries A.D.

A similar cleared feature also was found in the early levels of occupation at San José Mogote, the oldest known sedentary village in the Valley of Oaxaca. A new kind of construction appeared soon after the abandonment of this feature. A series of one-room structures, roughly 4 by 5 m (13 by 16 ft) in size, were constructed of pine posts, walled with cane and clay, and plastered with lime. The first was built around 1350 B.C. and was continuously repaired and rebuilt on the same spot for centuries. These structures included a pit, filled with powdered lime, and a low bench along the interior wall. The lime may have been combined with narcotics, like tobacco, and ritually smoked. Spanish chroniclers noted that the use of tobacco was prevalent among the Zapotec at the time of European contact. Although the specific rituals that took place in these early structures are unknown, only a limited number of the village's inhabitants could have participated in them. Compared to the dancegrounds, access to the sacred world may have been somewhat more restricted at this time. Furthermore, the continual upkeep and construction suggests that increasing care and energy were devoted to public buildings and group ritual.

Other elaborate public structures also were erected at San José Mogote and elsewhere in the Valley of Oaxaca during the Formative period. These buildings often were placed on flat-topped platforms of stone and adobe brick. By 600 B.C., this architecture was often faced with huge slabs of cut stone. Through time, the construction efforts in the Valley of Oaxaca reflected increased energy input and more restricted access to ceremonial activities. These two trends, along with the increasing diversity of Oaxacan public buildings, continued and intensified after 500 B.C. at the hilltop center of Monte Albán and elsewhere.

This sequence of nonresidential building in the Valley of Oaxaca reflects changes in a society that began as a small, mobile population. At that time, the entire population of an open-air camp could participate in ceremonies, dances, or other rituals. With sedentism, larger populations, and the development of greater social, political, and economic differences within the Zapotec population, ceremonial activities became somewhat more exclusive and restrictive. The most elaborate architectural constructions are found at larger sites, like San José Mogote and later at Monte Albán. At these sites, access to these important civic-ceremonial buildings (and the activities and rituals within) were limited to a small, favored segment of the overall population.

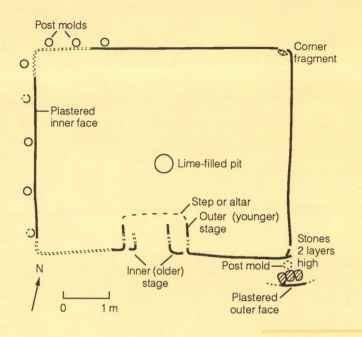

Structure 6, an early public building at San José Mogote.

The cleared area between the two rows of boulders, possibly used for communal rituals or dances, at Gheo-Shih.

SAN LORENZO

*The roots of Mesoamerican civilization on
the coastal plain of southern Veracruz*

In 1860, a workman in southern Veracruz was clearing the dense tropical forest for a sugar plantation, when he noticed a huge, round object on the ground. He reported it to his foreman, who dispatched a crew to unearth it. What they had believed to be a large iron pot was actually the top of a colossal human head, carved of volcanic stone, standing 1.5 m (5 ft) tall. More than fifty years later, the place of discovery was recognized as the archaeological site of Tres Zapotes (tray'zah-po'tays).

In the decades following this discovery, many other artifacts and artificial mounds were noted along the Gulf coastal plain in the states of Veracruz and Tabasco in Mexico. Yet archaeologists could not determine the age of these finds. The unique style of the monumental carved stone heads did not match the known archaeological traditions of the Maya, the Aztec, or even pre-Aztec Teotihuacan. Few archaeologists suspected that these magnificent coastal materials were much earlier than those of the later, better known traditions.

The age of the great basalt heads was not determined until the 1930s, when Matthew Stirling and his associates, of the Smithsonian Institution, began a twenty-year project of mapping and excavation at the sites of San Lorenzo, La Venta, and Tres Zapotes. These sites were located in dense, often swampy, tropical vegetation on broad river plains along the Gulf Coast. Stirling's discoveries of carved basalt, extensive earthen mound groups, and caches of jade captured broad public and archaeological attention. Of great importance was the recovery of actual dates

(circa 31 B.C.) in the Mesoamerican calendar on carved stones at Tres Zapotes. These dates were older than any identified for the Maya and confirmed the antiquity of these materials, which are referred to as **Olmec**. (See "The Olmec Horizon," p. 304.)

Stirling's pioneering work prompted more extensive studies at both La Venta and San Lorenzo. In the late 1950s, a University of California, Berkeley, project used the radiocarbon method to date the principal Olmec occupation at La Venta to between 900 and 400 B.C. During that period, a series of clay and earthen pyramids were constructed on a low island in the middle of a swamp near the Tonalá River. The linear complex of structures, oriented 8° west of true north, covered an area more than 1.6 km (1 mi) long. One of the structures was more than 30 m (100 ft) high. North of that high mound, a series of smaller platforms, plazas, and mounds were arranged symmetrically. Several platforms were built over mosaic pavements, each made of hundreds of blocks of greenstone. One mosaic depicts the symbolic mask or face of a jaguar. Other offerings of greenstone, jade, and magnetite objects were found in the excavations. The most spectacular of these lay under the center line of the architectural complex and included sixteen greenstone human figures and six jade celts. These polished green objects (30 cm or 12 in. tall) had been placed upright in a ceremonial arrangement.

At its peak, La Venta was a very impressive center. The pyramids were built of clays of different colors, and the platforms were painted in various hues.

A colossal human head from San Lorenzo.

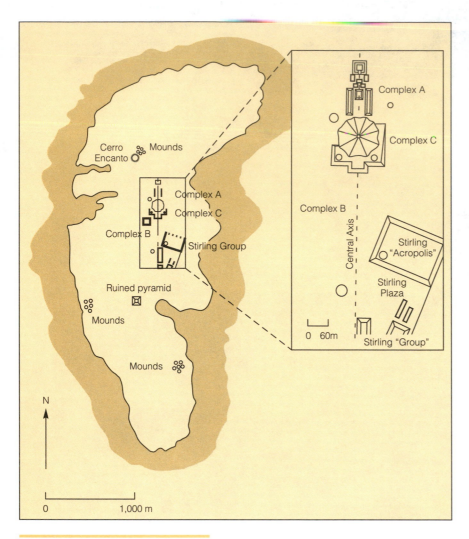

The plan of La Venta.

Sculpted monuments, including four massive stone heads, were carved from volcanic basalt brought from about 100 km (60 mi) away. The work at La Venta made clear the antiquity of this early Gulf Coast occupation, as well as the labor, calendrical, and craft skills that may have been controlled by the Olmec rulers. These rulers were probably the individuals portrayed in the massive stone heads.

A more recent project, conducted by Michael Coe, of Yale University, and Richard Diehl, of the University of Alabama, has provided significant information about the beginnings of the Olmec. At San Lorenzo, the Yale project mapped hundreds of monuments, mounds, and other features visible on the surface. These included twenty **lagunas,** manmade depressions that may have begun as borrow pits where dirt was removed for the construction of earthen mounds; later

they were lined with waterproof bentonite (shalelike) blocks. The *lagunas* may have been used for ritual bathing. Part of the site was located on top of an artificially enhanced natural rise that stands 50 m (164 ft) above the surrounding countryside. Excavations revealed that San Lorenzo had a long and complex occupational history, reaching its peak between 1150 and 900 B.C., somewhat earlier than the major construction phase at La Venta.

Significantly, the peak Olmec occupation at San Lorenzo was preceded by earlier village habitation. The first inhabitants settled only a small part of San Lorenzo, perhaps as early as 1500 B.C. By 1250 B.C. ceramic designs clearly related to the Olmec occupation were in use, and the villagers began to raise the natural mesa on which their houses were located. Deposits from 1250 and 1150 B.C. included basalt chips and lumps, discarded during monument carving, as well as Olmec black-and-white pottery.

The Yale project established antecedents to the major occupation at San Lorenzo. This latter period was characterized by a major building episode that included massive mound and plaza construction, the carving of at least eight basalt heads and other monuments, and the layout of a drainage system to take water from the artificial *lagunas.* It was also during this time that San Lorenzo developed ties with other areas throughout Mesoamerica. These connections are evident in the foreign goods found both at San Lorenzo and at sites in the highlands of Mexico, as well as in the widespread presence of the shared motifs of the Olmec Horizon. These designs probably had sacred or ritual importance throughout much of ancient Mesoamerica. For unknown reasons, building activities at San Lorenzo ceased after 900 B.C. The site was replaced, probably by La Venta, as the principal Olmec center.

Michael Coe refers to the Olmec as Mesoamerica's first civilization. Other archaeologists, like William Sanders, of Pennsylvania State University, and Kent Flannery, suggest that San Lorenzo and La Venta were chiefly centers associated with social inequality and permanent leaders, but not with urbanism or state govern-

North
Court

Central
Court

South
Court

Lagunas
Mounds

A map of the central part of San Lorenzo, showing the locations of mounds and lagunas.

ment. Clearly the Olmec centers were occupied by elites as well as by lower-status people. The former wore greenstone earplugs, hung iron-ore mirrors as **pectorals** (large chest ornaments), sat on sculpted thrones of basalt, and probably planned the ceremonial architectural precincts at the major centers. The lower-status people must have farmed and helped transport the construction materials of earth and basalt. Most of our information about the ancient Olmec comes from the ceremonial centers of a few key sites and the artifacts and sculptures associated with those high-status areas. Until we have more in-formation about the size and layout of the Olmec polities and more excavations of villages and simple residences, it will be difficult to paint a more complete picture of this ancient social system.

THE OLMEC HORIZON

Exchange and interaction in Formative Mesoamerica

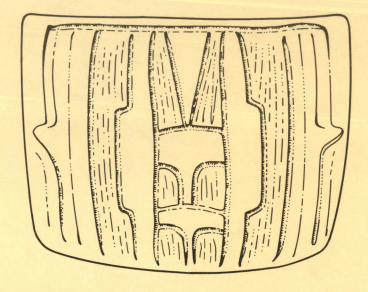

A stylized were-jaguar on a ceramic vessel.

On the Gulf Coast, the period dating between 1150 and 700 B.C. is distinguished by specific styles of monuments and art including the massive basalt heads, large flat-topped mounds, rectangular carved stone thrones, an abundance of greenstone, slant-eyed clay figurines, the half-jaguar/half-human or **"were-jaguar"** figure, black-and-white pottery, and the repeated use of certain stylized designs on ceramic vessels. While some of these elements, such as the huge stone heads, are known only from the Gulf Coast heartland, other traits, like the ceramic paw-wing and crossed-bands motifs on pottery, are found both locally in the Gulf Coast and at early sedentary settlements across Mesoamerica. These widespread Olmec stylistic motifs have become recognized as elements of what archaeologists refer to as a horizon, a broadly distributed array of archaeological traits that appears to have spread rapidly and may have been associated with a shared symbolic or ritual system.

The Olmec Horizon is not evenly distributed across Mesoamerica. Kent Flannery has noted that several Olmec designs are more common in the Valley of Oaxaca than along the Gulf Coast. Archaeologists have puzzled over the meaning of the Olmec Horizon. Some have suggested that it reflects Olmec conquests in the highlands or even an early empire, but this explanation seems doubtful, given the scale of the heartland Olmec sites and the wide distribution of the stylistic elements. The Gulf Coast Olmec were not powerful or numerous enough to stake out and rule such far-reaching localities. Even the later and much larger Aztec state (with a large core population and a strong military) had great trouble maintaining its broad tributary domain (the area from which it demanded tribute from local populations).

Others have proposed Olmec colonization of those areas where elements associated with the horizon have been found. But this explanation also seems unlikely; most of the participating regions had distinctive local traditions that existed before, and continued after, the adoption of horizon motifs. For example, in the highlands, local ceramic traditions generally were retained, incorporating the Olmec motifs into local ceramic complexes.

Perhaps the most reasonable interpretation of the Olmec Horizon is that it represents an important symbolic component in a network of interaction that linked sites on the Gulf Coast with those elsewhere in Mesoamerica. Highland resources like obsidian, jade, and magnetite

were found at the Gulf heartland centers, while mollusk and turtle shell, stingray spines, shark teeth, and Gulf Coast pottery were recovered in upland sites. In general, these exotic goods are found in ritual or high-status contexts, as are the items carrying the Olmec symbols. The exotic goods and shared pottery designs may have served to enhance or affirm the social positions of certain individuals in both the Gulf Coast and the highlands. These social systems were characterized by increasing societal differentiation and the development of more formal leadership roles during this early village era.

Clearly, the shared Olmec Horizon elements had a strong ritual aspect, certain motifs serving as symbolic representations (icons) for specific mythic creatures, deities, or kin-group totems, like the were-jaguar. The sharing of rare materials and the ritual symbols also may have helped to solidify communication and marriage alliances between groups of high-status individuals. The relative elaboration and abundance of the Olmec symbols in the heartland may signal the greater importance (and hence the expanded involvement in ritual, rule, and exchange) of the leaders at San Lorenzo compared to those at the smaller centers in other regions of Mesoamerica.

EL MIRADOR

*New perspectives on the beginnings of
ancient Maya civilization*

The Maya civilization flourished in the tropical forests of the Petén lowlands of northern Guatemala between A.D. 250 and 900. Speculations about its beginnings have focused outside the region, in part due to the notion that the tropical forest was not suitable for large-scale agriculture. Some archaeologists saw the origin of the Maya as a direct extension of the Gulf Coast Olmec tradition, fostered by a belief that the Olmec were the "mother culture" of Mesoamerica, giving rise, like a pulsating beacon, to all later civilizations in the area. However, new interpretations of the Olmec Horizon have questioned this beacon model and have envisioned a network arrangement, in which certain concepts, knowledge, and symbols were shared by an emergent elite at a number of centers across Mesoamerica. With the recent discovery of early preceramic and ceramic sites in the tropical forest of Guatemala and Belize, the origins of the Maya can now be traced locally. Outside influences or introductions from elsewhere in Mesoamerica, or even farther afield, are not essential to explain the rise of this important civilization.

Recent investigations at El Mirador (el-mere-a-dor′, "the lookout") in the dense Petén forest of Guatemala have yielded new insights into the beginnings of Maya civilization. Surrounded by dense vegetation, more than 60 km (37 mi) from the nearest modern road or town, El Mirador is almost inaccessible today. Although there have been sporadic reports of these massive colossal ruins for more than sixty years, the first scientific visit took place in 1967, when Ian Graham, of Harvard University, made a preliminary map. Investigation of such a remote site is extremely difficult. Research teams in the 1980s had to transport food, mail, and supplies to the site by weekly mule trains; a landing strip had to be cleared to fly in equipment and personnel.

Nevertheless, the preliminary findings are extraordinary. Ceramic and architectural clues, as well as a few radiocarbon assays, date most of the occupation that has been found thus far to between 300 B.C. and A.D. 250, prior to the Maya Classic period. Thus, at a time when most Maya settlements are thought to have been small, containing only a few nonresidential structures, El Mirador was huge and architecturally astounding. The site includes several hundred structures, some of which were as large as any built during the Maya Classic period. El Mirador is particularly important because there apparently was little building activity at the site during the later Classic period. Thus, unlike Tikal and most other Maya sites, the site's Preclassic structures remain relatively undisturbed by later occupations.

El Mirador lies on a limestone plain dotted with broad, flat, clay-lined depressions, or **bajos,** which are filled with water for several months each year. The site is not arranged according to a grid plan and appears to have been built in accordance with local topography. The structures at the site are distributed over 16 sq km (6 sq mi), with large, open spaces between buildings. The architectural core covers at least 2 sq km (0.8 sq mi) and is composed of a series of complexes: groups of plazas, platforms, buildings, causeways (raised roads), and other constructions. This core of the site is di-

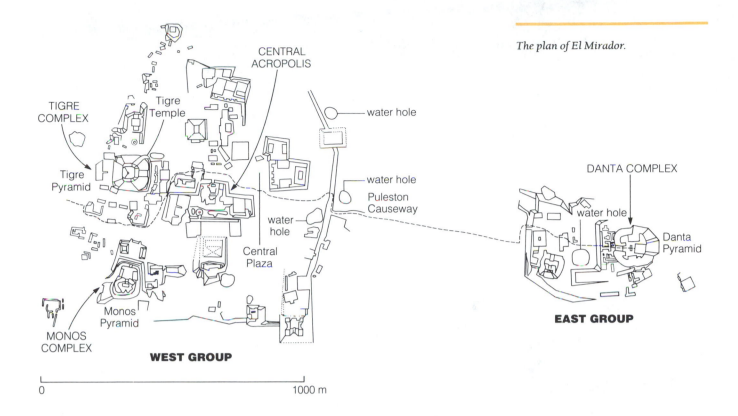

CENTRAL ACROPOLIS

TIGRE COMPLEX

Tigre Temple

Tigre Pyramid

water hole

water hole

Puleston Causeway

water hole

Central Plaza

Monos Pyramid

MONOS COMPLEX

WEST GROUP

DANTA COMPLEX

water hole

Danta Pyramid

EAST GROUP

0   1000 m

A helicopter bringing supplies to El Mirador.

vided into two major building groups almost 2 km (1.2 mi) apart. The West Group is defined by a stone wall and ditch to the south and east and by steep escarpments to the north and west. Access to this area was controlled by a series of gates in the walls. These barriers may symbolically delimit the West Group as the sacred core of the site.

Three features dominate the West Group: a Great Acropolis and two enormous pyramids, called the Tigre and Monos complexes. The Tigre Complex, with an enormous pyramid 55 m (180 ft) high, apparently was constructed primarily during the last centuries B.C. This complex forms what Mayanists refer to as an **E Group**, an arrangement of buildings designed to mark the position of the rising sun during important solar events, such as equinoxes and solstices. Structure 34, a small temple included within the Tigre Complex, had large **stucco** sculptures on its **facade**. The sculpted stucco masks, which incorporate both human and jaguar features, are very similar in style and context to those at other sites in the Maya lowlands. The messages transmitted through these symbols may convey divine sanction for the right to rule.

Archaeologists uncovering a stucco mask on the Tigre Temple.

Although the huge Monos Complex is still not fully explored, the Central Acropolis has been mapped and appears to be the nucleus of the site. Measuring 330 m (1080 ft) long by roughly 100 m (325 ft) wide (the area of twelve football fields), this structure supports a number of buildings, including several possible "palaces" or high-status residences.

A causeway leads from the east gate of the West Group to the East Group, 2 km (1.2 mi) away. This group is known largely for the Danta Complex, a massive series of sculpted terraces and platforms, built on a natural elevation that was leveled and modified to accommodate the monumental construction. From the top of the highest building in the Danta Complex, one can see above the forest canopy for 40 km (25 mi) in all directions.

El Mirador could not have existed in a vacuum. Food and labor for construc-tion almost certainly had to come to the site from the surrounding countryside. The movement of people and materials followed a series of six long causeways built like the spokes of a wheel from the site's hub. These impressive causeways would have been especially useful during the summer rainy season, when the *bajos* and low ground turns to heavy and sticky mud, becoming impassable.

Much of El Mirador is still unex-plored, hidden under thick tropical vege-tation. Some questions remain about the actual size of the site and exactly how much of it was built prior to A.D. 250, the start of the Maya Classic period. Yet there seems little question that El Mirador and other recently discovered early Maya sites have revolutionized archaeological views of both the Preclassic in the Petén lowlands and the origins of Maya civili-zation.

From the carved heads and thrones of the Olmec to the circular calendar stone of the Aztecs, stone was a primary medium of prehispanic Mesoamerican art. At almost every major site, archaeologists have recovered sculpted stone monuments. Such stones were used as architectural elements, for the facades of earthen or rubble-filled structures, or as free-standing monuments, such as the thrones and giant heads of the Olmec, or the upright stone shafts or **stelae**, from later periods. Such stelae often glorified the ancestries and accomplishments of specific rulers or elites.

Free-standing stelae are particularly important because they contain examples of the earliest Mesoamerican writing. The first carved stones with **hieroglyphs**, found in the Valley of Oaxaca and at the Gulf Coast site of La Venta, date to between 600 and 400 B.C. The inscription from Oaxaca contains two **glyphs** (conventionalized symbols) that indicate "1 Earthquake." This inscription represents a date in the Mesoamerican calendar. (See "Writing and Calendars," p. 336.) It is the first documented use of that sacred system. These glyphs were carved between the feet of an individual who was a probable captive or sacrificial victim. In Mesoamerica, individuals often were named by their birth date, and Joyce Marcus has suggested that 1 Earthquake may be the name of the prisoner depicted. The La Venta stone, the so-called Ambassador Monument, includes three glyphs, a central figure, and an isolated footprint. Later in prehispanic Mesoamerica, the footprint was a conventional symbol for travel or journey.

Writing, calendrics, and the use of stelae were developed to their greatest extent by the Maya of the Petén lowlands between A.D. 250 and 900. The earliest Maya stelae with written inscriptions, however, do not appear in the Petén lowlands but in the Maya highlands and at sites along the Pacific Coast. Some of these monuments include calendar dates in the Long Count, a cycle with a fixed zero date that is capable of recording very large blocks of time. (See "Writing and Calendars," p. 336.) The earliest Long Count

dates fall in the last century B.C. and the first century A.D., years before the first Petén stela, which was erected during the third century A.D. (See "Tikal's Monument Record," p. 330.)

These carved stones must have carried great importance for prehispanic Mesoamericans. Significant labor was devoted to both their construction and, at times, their destruction. At many Olmec and later Maya sites, there is evidence for the intentional mutilation and defacement of these stone monuments, possibly to diminish the importance of the individuals who were represented (perhaps after their deaths), just as statues may be toppled in a revolution today. Yet despite the destruction, the carved stones are durable and provide an important record for archaeologists. Unfortunately, the many later Mesoamerican documents on bark paper and deer skin did not fare as well.

CARVED STONE

A medium for important prehispanic Mesoamerican messages

Stela 1 from Monte Albán in the Valley of Oaxaca.

Inscriptions on the Ambassador Monument from La Venta.

Monte Albán

A hilltop city in the Valley of Oaxaca

Danzantes *on an early public building at Monte Albán.*

The Valley of Oaxaca is divided into three major arms by the Atoyac River and its tributary, the Salado. The northern arm was the primary focus of early settlement between 1500 and 500 B.C., particularly around San José Mogote. Although several large villages were established in the valley's southern and eastern arms after 700 B.C., San José Mogote continued as the region's largest and architecturally most impressive locality. Around 500 B.C., the pattern of settlement shifted, following the establishment of the hilltop center of Monte Albán at the hub of the valley's three arms.

The monumental hilltop ruins of Monte Albán (moan′tay-al-bahn′) have attracted explorers, antiquarians, and archaeologists for well over a century. Systematic excavations were begun at the site in 1931. These studies were enacted over eighteen field seasons by Mexican archaeologist Alfonso Caso and his associates, Ignacio Bernal and Jorge Acosta. Their research involved the opening of more than

170 tombs, a series of stratigraphic excavations, and the clearing and reconstruction of a number of buildings. Much of their work focused on the Main Plaza at Monte Albán, an impressive concentration of architecture erected on the artificially flattened summit of the hill.

In 1971, Richard Blanton, of Purdue University, initiated a survey to map the ruins of Monte Albán and to define changes through time in the size and organization of the site. From its foundation, Monte Albán was unique in the Valley of Oaxaca. While earlier settlements were on or next to the valley bottom, Monte Albán was situated above and at some distance from good farmland. Blanton's survey indicates that the city also grew very rapidly to a size of more than 1 sq km (0.4 sq mi). During the last centuries B.C., it had an estimated population of roughly 15,000 people and, after its foundation, quickly surpassed San José Mogote in size and architectural elaboration. Soon after the establishment of Monte Albán, major build-

Building J on the Main Plaza of Monte Albán.

ing activities ceased at San José Mogote for several centuries.

During the phase known as Monte Albán I, from 500 to 200 B.C., more than 300 stone monuments were carved and displayed in one of Monte Albán's first public buildings. Although the figures on these stones have been named the **danzantes** ("dancers"), most of them are similar to an earlier monument with a military theme at San José Mogote. Naked, sprawled in grotesque, rubbery positions with closed eyes and blood running from one or more wounds, the *danzantes* probably represent captives or prisoners of war. Although the specific meaning of these carved stones remains uncertain, their date corresponds in time to the consolidation of power at Monte Albán and the political unification of the Valley of Oaxaca.

Many other changes took place in the Valley of Oaxaca with the rapid growth of Monte Albán. Monumental construction increased. Greater concern with the dead (and with their ties to the living) was reflected in the construction of elaborate subterranean tombs. Domestic architecture evolved from simple, wattle-and-daub structures to more permanent adobe constructions. Greater regional similarities in pottery styles also were noted. New ceramic forms, including the tortilla griddle, or **comal,** and the incense burner, or **incensario,** suggest changes in both cooking technology and ritual activities at this time. The rapid growth in the number and size of settlements in Valley of Oaxaca is further indication that this was a period of dynamic transition.

During the second phase of Monte Albán (Monte Albán II), from 200 B.C. to

Building J on the Main Plaza of Monte Albán.

The Main Plaza at Monte Albán.

Building Over
Tomb 104

NORTH PLATFORM

Sunken
patio

Ball court

Danzantes
Gallery

Tunnel

Building J

SOUTH
PLATFORM

N

0   100 m

A.D. 200, the site expanded its political, economic, and military influence beyond the Valley of Oaxaca. At the same time, a 3-km (2-mi) defensive wall was erected at the site. An unusual building with an arrowhead-shaped groundplan (Building J) was erected in the Main Plaza. Set into the walls of this structure were more than forty carved stone panels. Each panel included a set of glyphs with a "place" name (emblem glyph), probably identifying a location, along with an upside-down human head, that likely signified military defeat. Caso identified these slabs as the documentation of Monte Albán's conquests, and Joyce Marcus has suggested identifications for several of the localities represented on the stone slabs.

Monte Albán's dominance over the Valley of Oaxaca continued during the third phase of its history (Monte Albán III), from A.D. 200 to 700. However, during this phase, its influence outside the Valley diminished, perhaps due to the increasing importance of Teotihuacan, the great urban center in the Valley of Mexico. (See "Teotihuacan," p. 318.) Late in Monte Albán III, Monte Albán itself reached its greatest physical size, with a population of 25,000 to 30,000 people. Sometime around A.D. 700, major construction at Monte Albán ceased, and the city began to decline in size and importance. Although a remnant population occupied the hilltop for much of the rest of the prehispanic era, the city never again achieved its former glory. Toward the end of this phase, a very powerful ruler was buried in a tomb originally built earlier at Monte Albán. This subsurface feature (Tomb 7) contains ancient Mesoamerica's greatest treasure, a tomb stuffed with gold, carved jaguar bones, shell, turquoise, **jet**, crystal, and numerous other exotic items.

Monte Albán was quite different in plan, size, and function from the contemporaneous Mesoamerican centers of Teotihuacan or Tikal or the later Aztec city of Tenochtitlan. Monte Albán's hilltop location is not typical of Mesoamerican sites as a whole. With its monumental Main Plaza, dwarfing the architecture found at contemporary sites on the valley floor, Monte Albán's politico-religious functions always surpassed its regional commercial role. In general, archaeological indicators for craft activities are surprisingly few at the hilltop city, and no central market area has yet been identified. The site was not laid out according to a grid plan. Few major roads were constructed, and access to the Main Plaza was restricted to several narrow entryways. The bulk of the population lived on the more than 2000 residential terraces carved out of the hillside beneath the Main Plaza, and on adjacent hills. Held in place by stone retaining walls, each terrace contained no more than a few households.

By 200 B.C., Monte Albán was the capital of a Zapotec state whose limits stretched beyond the Valley of Oaxaca. While archaeologists have yet to unravel all the factors responsible for either the foundation of this hilltop center or the rise of the Zapotec state, these changes seem in part tied to the increasing role of militarism in Oaxaca. The *danzantes,* the conquest slabs, Monte Albán's hilltop location, and its defensive wall all point to the importance that warfare may have had. Yet the emergence of Monte Albán also coincided with marked regional population growth, as well as changes in the local systems of exchange and production, and these factors also may have had key roles in these important societal transitions.

Settlement Pattern Surveys

Examining ancient demography and the distribution of sites on regional landscapes

Traditionally archaeologists have depended on excavation as the primary means for obtaining information. Paradoxically, however, when archaeologists excavate sites, they also destroy the buried deposits of material. Unlike physics or chemistry, in which experiments can be repeated numerous times under the same conditions, archaeologists can only dig a particular area once. Excavations, therefore, proceed slowly and carefully, in order to record as much detailed information as possible. Because of limited time and money, we are lucky to investigate more than a small part of any one site, or more than a few sites in a given area.

Sociologists would be uncomfortable describing a modern city from only a few interviews and often supplement detailed accounts with broad urban surveys or censuses. For similar reasons, geologists and geographers often combine very specific information gathered from soil probes or individual field studies with the larger-scale perspective provided by satellite imagery. Over the last fifty years, archaeologists have developed a technique — systematic settlement pattern survey — for studying areas larger than one or a few sites.

Archaeologists have for a long time used surface survey procedures to locate sites based on the presense of artifactual or architectural debris on the ground. Frequently, unsystematic surveys, or reconnaissances, are utilized to find sites to excavate. Over the last several decades, archaeologists have refined regional archaeological survey procedures. In systematic surveys, large blocks of land are thoroughly and carefully walked over in an effort to locate surface evidence of past occupations. These occupations, which are dated by the artifactual scatters associated with them, are placed on aerial photographs or topographic maps. The entire distribution of sites known for each particular period represents that era's settlement pattern.

The first systematic settlement pattern survey was carried out in the Virú Valley on the coast of Peru soon after World War II by Gordon Willey, of Harvard University. Willey designed this study to determine the geographic and chronological position of sites, to outline the developmental history of settlement, and to reconstruct cultural institutions as far as they were reflected in the settlement data. To achieve these ends, Willey and his assistants walked over the valley, mapping a total of 315 archaeological sites. These sites were dated and classified according to estimated function, determined primarily by site size, location, and the kind of architecture visible on the surface. Pieces of pottery on the ground surface were used to date the sites. Through this extensive surface survey, Willey obtained a regional overview of changing patterns of settlement that he could supplement with detailed excavations at a few sites.

Since Willey's pioneering study, systematic settlement pattern surveys have been undertaken in many areas, including the highlands of Oaxaca and central Mexico, the rivers and foothills of Southwest Asia, the mountain valleys of the Andes, and the deserts and plateaus of the southwestern United States. Surveys are most successful where artifacts are readily visible on the surface of the ground. Such conditions are found frequently in semi-arid climates, where vegetation is limited and soil formation is slow.

Archaeological surveys provide a variety of information about the past. The number and sizes of sites allow the archaeologist to estimate ancient population size and changes in demography over time. Archaeologists also can examine the distribution of sites on the landscape in relation to different kinds of soil, topographic features, and resources.

Like household interviews and censuses, soil probes and satellite images, excavations and surveys provide complementary insights. Excavations yield detailed, specific, precise observations at a small scale. Surveys provide broader, less fine-grained information at a larger scale. When used alone, each method can provide misleading results because of small sample size (excavation) and the reliance on surface materials no longer in their primary context (survey). The most complete descriptions are achieved when both kinds of information are used jointly.

The state is a form of government with an internally specialized decision-making apparatus. Usually a state has three or more administrative levels. Anthropologists have recognized that societies with state governments tend to have other features, including large and often urban populations, systems of tribute or taxation, and a military force with the power to coerce. The inhabitants of state societies are generally stratified into a series of socially defined classes, and they usually use writing systems, although the ancient Inca of Peru seem to be an exception.

In a day of sprawling metropolises and superpower nations, it is difficult for us to perceive a world without cities and states. Yet these institutions are relatively recent, appearing initially in Mesopotamia shortly after 4000 B.C. (See "Uruk," Chapter Nine, p. 404.) The places where such early states developed independently, without influence from more powerful outside groups, are few and far between. These first pristine states emerged prior to written history, so we must rely on archaeology to understand their rise and the factors responsible.

Numerous reasons have been invoked to account for the development of the state. One general model for state development was proposed by Robert Carneiro, of the American Museum of Natural History. Stimulated by his ethnographic work among tribal groups in the Amazon Basin of South America, Carneiro suggested that environmental and social boundaries, in conjunction with warfare, may account for the origin of states. Carneiro recognized that warfare alone does not account for the rise of the state. Warfare was present (even endemic) in many places, yet the state never formed in those areas. In Carneiro's scenario, a population first must have increased in size beyond the capacity of its local resources. **Circumscription** by either environmental boundaries (mountains, oceans, rivers) or social boundaries (neighboring groups) would then require warfare and conquest to obtain more food.

While warfare does appear to have been an important factor in some cases, such as the rise of Monte Albán, Carneiro's formulation has not met with unanimous support. In the Valley of Oaxaca, the connection between political power and militarism began during a period when the regional population was small. During the early phases at Monte Albán, when military exploits were commemorated with *danzantes* and the conquest slabs, the populations of the valley, as well as areas like the Cañada (see next page for discussion and location of this area), were still well below the number of people that potentially could have been fed by locally grown foods. In addition, at least some of Monte Albán's conquests were not carried out to obtain necessities (like basic high-calorie staple foods), as Carneiro's model predicts, but to acquire luxury goods and other desirable items (tropical fruits, intoxicants) for the elite. As a later parallel, much of the tribute collected by the Aztecs was in the form of rare materials and finished products that were used or distributed by the wealthy members of Aztec society. (See "Tenochtitlan," p. 344.)

Given the range of ancient states and the diversity of their environmental and historical settings, it is unlikely that any one factor or set of factors can explain the development of all state societies. As Carneiro recognized, warfare and imbalances between food and people are two factors that can stress human political organizations and their decision-making structures. But we also know that population growth, changing trade patterns, the management of water-control systems, environmental shifts, natural disasters, and other factors may promote the administrative changes that lead to increasing political complexity and the rise of states.

WARFARE AND THE RISE OF THE STATE

Carneiro's circumscription theory

LOMA DE LA COYOTERA

Zapotec militarism in southern Mexico

The Cuicatlán Cañada, a low-lying valley between the highlands of Tehuacán and Oaxaca.

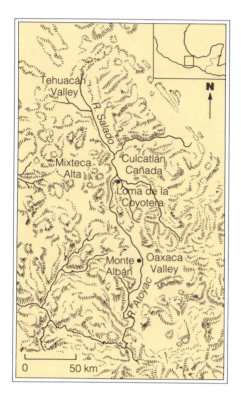

Antiquarians and archaeologists working in Mesoamerica have mainly focused their attention on major sites. These ancient settlements contain the most spectacular architecture, the grandest art, and the largest concentrations of artifacts. Yet during the last two decades, new questions have emerged that require information about small and middle-sized sites, often located in more peripheral regions.

An example of recent problem-oriented research was conducted by Charles Spencer and Elsa Redmond, of the American Museum of Natural History, in a small, low-lying valley called the Cuicatlán Cañada (kwee-kaht-lahn'kahn-yah'dah), on a strategic communication corridor between the highlands of Oaxaca and Tehuacán in central Mexico. Spencer and Redmond studied the relationship between the Cuicatlán Cañada, where trop-

ical foods can be grown, and the Valley of Oaxaca during the period when Monte Albán emerged and expanded its political influence.

Between 200 B.C. and A.D. 200, some forty inscribed stone slabs were erected on Building J at Monte Albán. These slabs identified geographic localities that were either conquered by, or in tributary relationship to, that hilltop site. Comparison of these place signs with known locations shown in a sixteenth-century codex suggested to Joyce Marcus that one of the slabs referred to the Cuicatlán Cañada. Spencer and Redmond reasoned that if the Cañada was indeed subjugated by Monte Albán, then major changes should have taken place. A significant shift in settlement was noted in the Cañada at that time. Prior to Monte Albán's conquest of the area, there were two important centers, distinguished by their larger size and architecture and greater quantity of foreign trade goods (including small amounts of pottery from the Valley of Oaxaca).

Most settlements were abandoned following Monte Albán's conquest, particularly those in low-lying areas. New sites were established in higher, more defensible locations. Settlements with fortification walls were strategically placed to seal off the northern end of the Cañada. Only these border sites contained Monte Albán-style pottery, and further to the north in the adjacent Tehuacán Valley, local pottery was markedly different. Redmond has suggested that these sites at the northern edge of the Cañada marked the limits of Oaxacan power. Communities in the central and southern Cañada were small, relatively undifferentiated, and located on hills and ridges. Loma de la Coyotera (low'ma-day-la-koy-a-tare'a), a roughly 3-ha (7.5-acre) site excavated by Spencer, was situated on a natural ridge directly

One of the conquest slabs erected on Building J at Monte Albán.

above an earlier site on the valley floor. Irrigation canals were created to bring water to the fields. Midden deposits at Loma de la Coyotera document a tremendous density of tropical fruits and nuts, suggesting an emphasis on these plants. This emphasis may have related to newly instituted tribute demands from Monte Albán. While tropical products may have been sent south to the Valley of Oaxaca, maize surpluses could have been used to sustain the defensive garrisons to the north.

Spencer's excavations at Loma de la Coyotera also provide the best indication for the intrusion of Monte Albán into local affairs in the southern Cañada. Excavations in front of small civic-ceremonial mounds at the site uncovered sixty-one human skulls, laid out in rows. Spencer interpreted these as the remains of a collapsed skull rack, what the Aztec called a *tzompantli*, where the heads of war captives were placed. Such constructions were in common use by conquering groups in later prehispanic Mesoamerica.

After A.D. 200, the occupation of the Cañada changed again. With one exception, the defensive sites in the north decreased in size or were abandoned. In the central and southern Cañada, the number of communities increased, and some became significantly larger than others. Spencer and Redmond argue that the Cañada was no longer under the control of Monte Albán. At Loma de la Coyotera, the occupation expanded from just over 3 ha (7.5 acres) to more than 9 ha (22 acres), with a concommitant growth in public architecture. A new, larger civic-ceremonial complex was erected about 200 m (655 ft) from the small plaza where the skull rack had previously been located.

The withdrawal of Monte Albán influence from the Cuicatlán Cañada and the changes in the settlements there may relate to the increasing power of the rapidly growing central Mexican urban center of Teotihuacan. Teotihuacan established a series of promontory settlements, which could have easily guarded the direct trade route through the Valley of Tehuacán. Under such circumstances, the presence of the Monte Albán state in the neighboring Cañada may have proven unacceptable to the rulers of the giant central Mexican city.

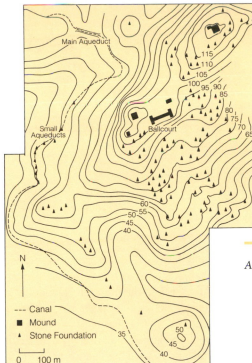

A general plan of Loma de la Coyotera.

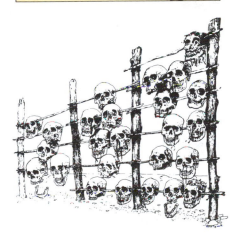

An artist's reconstruction of the skull rack (tzompantli) at Loma de la Coyotera.

Spencer's and Redmond's research supports Marcus' hypothesis that Monte Albán held tributary domination over the Cuicatlán Cañada. The palm frond depicted as the place name on a conquest slab at Monte Albán bears a strong similarity to the coyol palm, which is grown in the Cañada and not in the Valley of Oaxaca. The coyol produces a nut that can be eaten or processed to make a valuable cooking oil. Sap from the palm also was brewed into an intoxicating beverage. Carbonized remains of the coyol palm were one of the common species in the deposits at Loma de la Coyotera. The many products of the coyol palm may have been one of the key items sought as tribute from Cuicatlán by the elite at Monte Albán.

An inscription from a conquest slab on Mound J at Monte Albán. The place-name glyph, represented by palm fronds, refers to the "Place of the Palms."

TEOTIHUACAN

One of the world's largest cities in A.D. *500*

Today Mexico City, with over 12 million inhabitants, covers most of a huge geological basin in the Central Highlands of Mexico. Before the enormous growth of Mexico City, the Basin of Mexico contained the largest expanse of flat, agricultural land in all of highland Mesoamerica. The basin lies at an elevation of 2100 m (7000 ft) and is ringed by a series of dormant, snow-capped volcanoes forming a palisade around its perimeter. The outlet for the basin was dammed by a number of volcanic eruptions several million years ago, forming a series of lakes. The floor of the basin originally held five shallow lakes, brackish in the north and fresher to the south. These lakes, of particular importance for the Aztec civilization, were drained by the Spanish during the Colonial period, when Mexico was ruled by the Spanish crown (A.D. 1521 to 1821), and only small remnants of them remain.

The Basin of Mexico was the center of at least two major prehispanic civilizations. Systematic archaeological surveys of more than half the floor of the basin, made during the past thirty years, have shown that the first sedentary villages were concentrated in the southern half. This area receives more rainfall than the northern portion of the basin and is better for farming. Prior to 500 B.C., occupation was established at a site called Cuicuilco (kwee-kwil'co) in the southwestern part of the basin. Relatively little is known archaeologically about this site. It was buried by at least two prehispanic lava flows and then covered by the urban sprawl of modern Mexico City. Only the tops of a few small pyramids rise above the mantle of volcanic stone. Yet the scale of Cuicuil-

co's distinctive structures, and the large area of its occupation, suggest that the site was the basin's first major town.

The volcanic eruptions may have helped end Cuicuilco's preeminence and may have contributed to a shift in the balance of power in the basin. By the end of the second century B.C., the site of Teotihuacan (tay-o-tee-wa-kahn') had been established in the northeastern corner of the basin, about 20 km (12 mi) from the lakeshore. Situated in low hills adjacent to a series of natural springs, Teotihuacan grew rapidly, becoming one of the region's two primary centers, along with Cuicuilco. Based on his urban survey of Teotihuacan, René Millon, of the University of Rochester, estimates that the site may have reached 6 to 8 sq km (2.5 to 3 sq mi) in area, with a population of at least 20,000 by this time. The population of the basin became increasingly nucleated during this period, particularly around the major centers. At the same time, areas of little habitation formed between the population clusters, suggesting the emergence of buffer zones between hostile groups.

By the first century A.D., Teotihuacan had become the primary settlement in the Basin of Mexico. While the urban center sprawled to almost 20 sq km (7.5 sq mi), encompassing roughly 90,000 people, other centers in the basin declined in size and importance. In fact, the next largest communities had populations of less than 5000 people and comparatively little non-residential construction. This tremendous nucleation of population and power continued over subsequent centuries, signaling the dramatic political and economic

The Basin of Mexico, showing the pre-hispanic lakes, volcanoes, and major early centers.

reorganization that took place during the hegemony (or predominance) of Teotihuacan.

Several hypotheses have been advanced to account for the rapid growth and development of this great city. We will likely never know just how closely the growth of Teotihuacan was related to the natural disaster that buried a portion of the contemporary center of Cuicuilco in the last centuries B.C. Alternatively, William Sanders, of Pennsylvania State University, has emphasized the importance of Teotihuacan's location, positioned to tap springs for a series of irrigation canals. For decades, Sanders and other archaeologists have been influenced by the writings of Karl Wittfogel, who emphasized the managerial costs of water control and the possible role such management had in stimulating political change. While canals were built to harness the water from these springs, the specific timing of this construction has not been verified. Sanders and others have suggested that canal construction and agricultural intensification would have been required to feed the burgeoning population of this ancient city and the basin as a whole.

Noting the abundance of obsidian at Teotihuacan, Michael Spence, of the Uni-versity of Western Ontario, has suggested that the manufacture of obsidian artifacts may have played a role in the growth of the city, something like the relationship between the atuomobile and Detroit. In the ancient Mesoamerican world, obsidian provided the best cutting edge available. It was used economically for knives and other tools, ritually to extract blood in autosacrifice (the drawing of blood from the fleshy parts of one's own body), ornamentally as part of masks and necklaces, and militarily for weapons. Raw obsidian nodules can be taken from the San Juan River, which cuts directly through the site of Teotihuacan, as well as from a large source of grey obsidian only 16 km (10 mi) away. Teotihuacan is also close to a source of green obsidian at Pachuca, roughly 50 km (30 mi) to the northeast. Pachuca obsidian, present in great quantity at Teotihuacan, was valued both for workability and for the symbolic importance of its color. While Spence has emphasized the role of obsidian production and export in Teotihuacan's rise, John Clark, of the New World Archaeological Foundation, has suggested that most of the surface obsidian debris could reflect production for local use. Regardless of its eventual destination, there is little doubt

It has mainly been the humanists who have studied the informational aspects of complex societies — art, religion, ritual, writing systems, and so on. The "ecologists" have largely contented themselves with studying exchanges of matter and energy — the "techno-environmental" factors. . . . To read what the "ecologists" write, one would often think that civilized peoples only ate, excreted, and re-produced; to read what the humanists write, one would think civilizations were above all three, and devoted all their energy to the arts. . . . I will argue that humanists must cease thinking that ecology "dehumanizes" history, and ecologists must cease to regard art, religion, and ideology as mere "epi-phenomena" without causal significance.

Kent V. Flannery (1972)

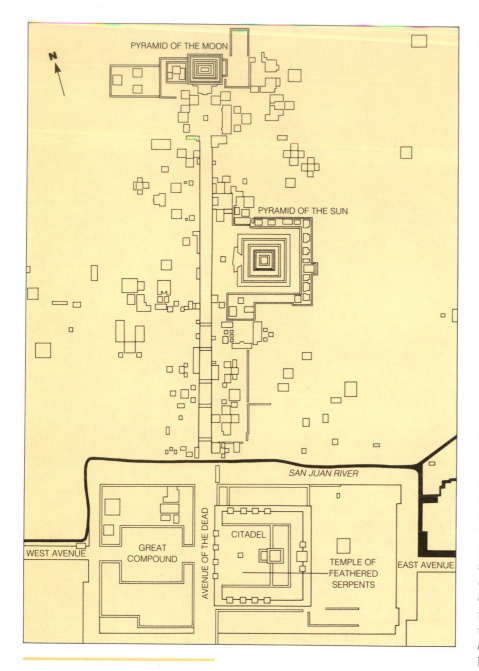

The central core of Teotihuacan.

axis, the Avenue of the Dead, intersected with lesser East Avenue and West Avenue. Together these avenues divided the city into quadrants. At their intersection were the distinctive Cuidadela ("citadel") and the Great Compound, which formed a massive architectural unit. The Great Compound is thought to have been the city's central marketplace. The Cuidadela was a huge political and religious precinct, enclosing a sunken courtyard and the imposing Temple of the Feathered Serpent. The Ciudadela, together with all the buildings along the Avenue of the Dead, was constructed with cut-stone facing known as **talud-tablero**. This style, composed of framed panels and sloping basal elements, is recognized as a symbol of Teotihuacan temples. Its presence on the entire 2 km (1.25 mi) of structures from the Ciudadela to the Pyramid of the Moon would seem to denote the sacred aspect of the central city.

The largest of the city's more than 5000 known structures, the Pyramid of the Sun and the Pyramid of the Moon, dominate the surrounding landscape. The monumental Pyramid of the Sun was the largest structure ever built during a single construction episode in the ancient Americas. This structure stands 61 m (200 ft) high and measures roughly 213 m (700 ft) on a side. It contains 1 million cu m of adobe and rubble fill (35,000,000 cu ft, or equivalent to the volume of ten modern oil tankers), which was carried to the site in basketloads. The cut-stone exteriors of these massive structures (as well as most other site platforms) are believed to have been faced with a thick, white plaster and painted red to enhance their visibility. The pyramid was built directly over a natural underground cave, with an entrance at the front of the main staircase of the pyramid. The cave was used for ceremonies during the first centuries A.D., when the first stage of the pyramid was constructed over it. Caves were sacred in Mesoamerican religion, associated with the creation of the sun and the moon. The Pyramid of the Sun was probably placed where it was because of the cave. In fact, Teotihuacan itself sat above a series of caves and caverns, and the city's location may have been related to those features.

The residential pattern for earliest Teotihuacan is not well known. However,

that the quantity of obsidian at Teotihuacan far exceeds what is typical in Mesoamerican sites.

Millon has stressed the importance of ideological, as well as economic, factors in the developmental history of Teotihuacan. It was a sacred city with more temples than any other prehispanic Mesoamerican site, before or after. At its maximum size, between the fifth and seventh centuries A.D., Teotihuacan covered an enormous area of 22 sq km (8.5 sq mi), with an estimated population of at least 125,000 people. The city was planned and laid out along a rectilinear network of roads and paths. The major north–south beginning in the third century A.D., a series of distinctive, multihousehold residential units can be recognized. Some 2200 of these well-planned, single-story apartment compounds were eventually built. During the site's later history, these compounds were the principal kind of residential structure. The interiors of the compounds were divided into different apartments, each with rooms, patios, and passageways. The exteriors were surrounded by tall, windowless stone walls of cement and plaster. The compounds varied significantly in size. Millon estimates that the average structure housed about sixty people, while the larger ones held 100 or more.

From size, architectural differences, and the kinds of artifacts and wastes found at the compounds, it is clear that the occupants of these units varied in socioeconomic position. The groups that lived in the compounds were enduring. Many of the structures were rebuilt several times over several centuries, with little change in plan. The specific relationships that

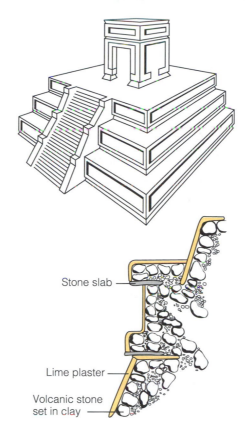

A drawing of talud-tablero *architecture.*

Stone slab

Lime plaster

Volcanic stone set in clay

Pyramid of the Sun at Teotihuacan.

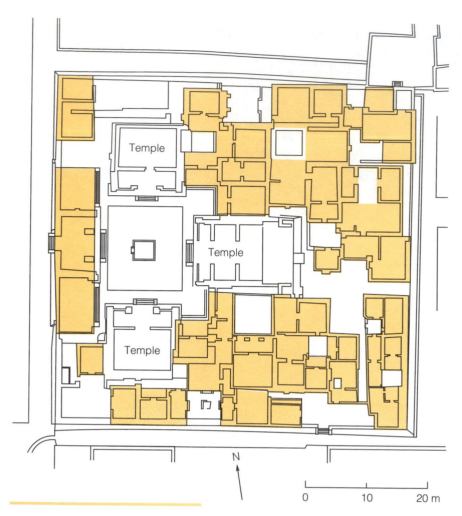

The plan of an apartment compound at Teotihuacan. The shaded areas are roofed; the unshaded areas are open plazas or temples.

pottery vessels were made from local basin clays in the Oaxacan style. At least some of the foreign residents are assumed to have been merchants or traders. Teotihuacan was involved in trade relations that extended as far as the Gulf Coast of Mexico, the Maya lowlands, the Guatemalan highlands, and the deserts of northern Mexico. On Monte Albán's Main Plaza, carved stone monuments depict an important, yet apparently peaceful, meeting between an emissary wearing a costume from Teotihuacan and a Zapotec lord. Figures bearing symbols associated with central Mexico also are portrayed on stelae from Maya Tikal. Yet despite these long-distance exchange and diplomatic contacts, there is little evidence that Teotihuacan directly controlled much territory outside the Basin of Mexico.

Little is known about the decline of Teotihuacan in the seventh through tenth centuries A.D. The site was not abandoned, but its size decreased by more than half during this period. Militarism is a prominent theme in the art between A.D. 650 and 750, although perimeter defensive walls were never constructed. Part of the city was burned in the seventh and eighth centuries; the fires appear to have started intermittently. The core of the city—the buildings along the Avenue of the Dead—was burned, as were temples, pyramids, and public buildings throughout the site. Millon has suggested that the conflagration was deliberate and ritually inspired, similar to the earlier desecration of the Olmec stone sculptures. In ancient Mesoamerica, the symbolic destruction of selected monuments or sacred structures was repeatedly associated with decline and the loss of power.

After A.D. 750, the enormous pyramids, the magnificent palaces, the avenues and markets, and the memory of the Classic civilization were in decline. The Aztecs, centuries later, referred to the mounds of stone and broken walls as "the place of the gods." Today Teotihuacan is one of the most important tourist sites in Mexico. The magnificent Avenue of the Dead has been reopened and leads past the Pyramid of the Sun to the plaza and the Pyramid of the Moon. The pyramids have been restored, and each year thousands climb them in awe and admiration for the creations of the ancient Mexicans.

linked households in a compound remain unknown. Spence's preliminary study of the skeletal materials led him to speculate that the males within compounds generally had fairly close biological ties, while compound females were more diverse. Such a pattern suggests a lineage or extended-family residence pattern, called **patrilocal**, in which females moved in with the family of the groom after marriage. Spence also has suggested that individuals within apartment compounds may have shared certain economic skills, such as working obsidian. Each compound had at least one temple or shrine, suggesting joint participation in ritual by the residents.

Particular neighborhoods at Teotihuacan were associated with foreign residents. The compound occupied by people from Oaxaca included a tomb with an inscribed stela bearing a glyph and number in the distinctive Oaxacan style. One ceramic urn in the compound came directly from the Valley of Oaxaca, while other

322   ANCIENT MESOAMERICA

Among the traits that the late art historian Paul Kirchhoff used to define the boundaries of prehispanic Mesoamerica was the game played with a solid rubber ball. First reported in sixteenth-century Spanish accounts, the ballgame, called **tlachtli** by the Aztecs, was a team game played by somewhat different rules from place to place. Ceramic evidence suggests that some form of the ballgame was played in Mesoamerica as early as 1000 B.C., soon after the transition to village life. Ballplayers are depicted in clay figurines from central and western Mexico, as well as from sites along the Gulf Coast. The pottery figures are shown wearing such playing gear as knee guards.

Archaeological evidence also suggests that the ballgame was played in different ways during its history. For example, the Spanish chroniclers witnessed a game played on a court where stone rings were used as goals. Most ball courts from before A.D. 700 do not have such rings of stone. Small, shallow pits enclosed by four earthen retaining walls, known from San Lorenzo Tenochtitlan, may have served as early playing fields in the Olmec period. The earliest I-shaped ball courts with stone walls were not built until several centuries later. This more traditional form, often with sloping playing surfaces, has been found throughout Mesoamerica. (Compare the oval ball court of the U.S. Southwest; see p. 278.) The absence of a ball court at Teotihuacan is a mystery, since ballplaying is depicted on polychrome murals in one of the compounds. Ballplayer figurines also have been found at the site.

The Mesoamerican ballgame was not just for the sake of sport. Spanish chroniclers describe the sixteenth-century version as very rough, played with a ball weighing up to 11 kg (5 lb). In one version, the ball had to be kept in motion and could not be hit with hands or feet. Hips, knees, and elbows were used, and injuries were frequent. In prehispanic times, the game was associated with fertility, death, militarism, and sacrifice. At the site of El Tajín in Veracruz, a stone relief panel in the ball court graphically shows one player stretched over a sacrificial stone, while another is poised with a stone knife ready to be plunged into the chest of the victim. Sixteenth-century accounts also detail the sacrifice of defeated team members. Interestingly, the ball courts at the Maya site of Chichén Itzá and at the Aztec capital of Tenochtitlan were directly adjacent to the *tzompantli,* the skull rack.

THE MESOAMERICAN BALLGAME

A ritual game with symbolic and political importance

The ball court at Monte Albán.

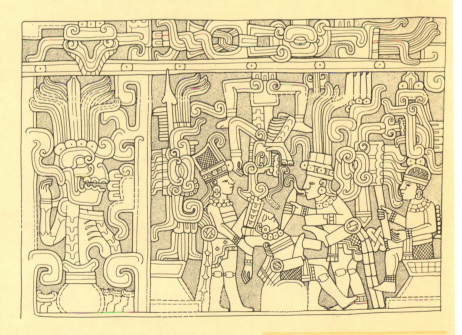

A stone relief panel from the ball court at El Tajín.

TIKAL

A Maya city in the rain forest of Guatemala

The first adventurers and antiquarians who discovered the overgrown ruins of Maya sites in the rain forests of the Petén assumed them to be the remains of ancient cities with large populations. Yet by the first decades of this century, opinion shifted to the belief that the ancient Maya resided in vacant ceremonial centers inhabited by small groups of priests. These individuals were purported to direct rural, peasant populations through periodic rituals at the centers. This shift in perspective, from urban to ceremonial, was the result of the concentration of archaeological investigations at the ceremonial cores of these sites and preconceived notions that tropical forests could not support urban centers. The researchers failed to recognize residential architecture, and they often neglected to look in the less developed areas for houses. Moreover, since the present Maya practice slash-and-burn cultivation, it was assumed that the ancient Maya used the same technique. **Slash and burn** is a simple strategy that involves a cyclical process of field clearing, cultivation, and abandonment. Such extensive agriculture was not thought capable of supporting large urban enclaves or high population densities.

During the last three decades, however, new information has revived an interpretation similar to the original one. Fifteen years of investigations at the site of Tikal (tee-cahl′) by researchers at the University Museum of the University of Pennsylvania included survey and mapping, excavation in selected areas, and the recording of carved stone monuments. The Tikal survey recorded thousands of small mounds in the thick, forest vegetation. More common near the center of the site, the mounds decreased in number toward the periphery. A few of the mounds were excavated and found to be residential structures. At Tikal, the quantity of these residential structures demonstrated that the site had held a sizable population. Subsequent mapping of other Maya centers has indicated that the lowland population during the period of the Classic Maya, from A.D. 250 to 900, was much larger than anyone suspected, considerably larger than it is today.

Once the population density of the ancient Maya was recognized, new questions were raised about agricultural subsistence, craft production, and sociopolitical organization. It is now clear that the ancient farmers of the lowlands employed several different strategies, such as terracing and ridged fields, for more intensive agricultural production. (See "Raised Fields," p. 328.) Classic Maya communities also were shown to have had specific occupational groups, like craftsmen, in addition to the groups of peasants and ruler-priests envisioned in the ceremonial center model.

The core of Tikal is situated on a series of low ridges standing roughly 50 m (165 ft) above two swampy areas (*bajos*). Most of the great sructures presently visible, clustered on the rises, date to the later part of the Classic, the period of most pronounced construction activity at Tikal and in the Maya lowlands in general. Yet excavations have revealed that many earlier buildings, some contemporaneous with the major Formative period occupation at El Mirador, were encased within the later structures.

A view of Tikal.

For most of its history, the core of Tikal was the Great Plaza, although it did not dominate Tikal to the extent that the Main Plaza did at Monte Albán. In Tikal, this central open area, laid out prior to 100 B.C., stretches for roughly a hectare and was replastered four times. At the eastern end of the plaza, the Temple of the Great Jaguar (Temple I) rises to 45 m (150 ft), with its crowning roof comb peaking out above the tropical canopy of mahogany, cedar, and chicle (gum) trees. A large seated lord was originally painted in an array of colors on the face of the hollow comb. Temple I itself has three high, narrow rooms with carved wooden beams spanning its door frames. The innermost of these beams, or **lintels**, portrays a Maya lord towered over by a jaguar, which may serve as his protector. Temple I was dedicated in the Late Classic period to Lord Ah Cacau, whose sumptuous grave was found beneath its base, and whose portrait is found on the lintels and roof comb. Directly across the plaza from Temple I lies the slightly shorter Temple II, probably dedicated to Ah Cacau's wife.

The north side of the plaza is framed by the North Acropolis, a huge, 100 by 80 m (325 by 260 ft) platform that was continually expanded between 200 B.C. and A.D. 550. The University of Pennsylvania

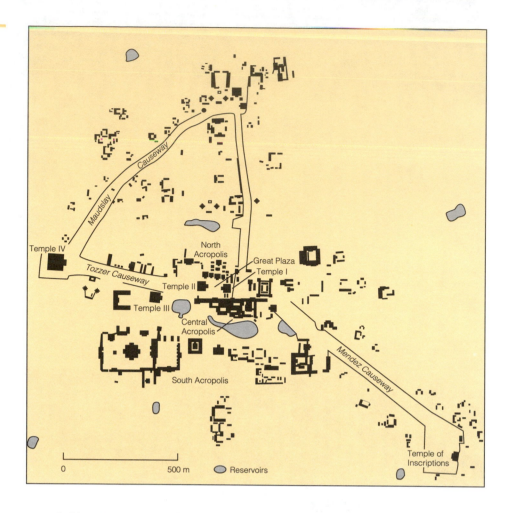

A map of Tikal.

team, led by William Coe, intensively excavated this structure, discovering a rich succession of elaborate, elite tombs. Based on their findings, the North Acropolis appears to have been a burial place for a long sequence of Tikal's rulers.

South of the Great Plaza sits Tikal's greatest palace complex, the Central Acropolis. In total this complex spreads over more than 1.6 ha (4 acres) and contains a maze of forty-two multistory buildings with multiple rooms interspersed with internal courtyards. The elaboration of the room decorations, which included thronelike seats with armrests, implies that Tikal's lords and their retainers lived and conducted their activities here.

Other monumental buildings and important plazas are linked to the Great Plaza by broad, raised causeways called **sacbes,** or rainforest paths. The Tozzer Causeway (named for a renowned Mayanist) runs west from Temple II to one of the two tallest structures in the pre-Columbian world, Temple IV. Temple IV, some 70 m (230 ft) tall, was built in the

middle of the eighth century A.D. to commemorate one of Tikal's last known rulers, Ah Cacau's son and successor, Yax Kin.

The final pyramid temple, Temple III, was built as a funerary monument to Chitam, the last well-known Tikal ruler. Temple III is significantly taller than either Temple I or II, attesting to the labor power that Chitam or his immediate successor could still amass. In the summit shrine, the wooden lintel framing the doorway covers 1.3 sq m (14 sq ft) and depicts a central figure carved in **bas-relief** (low relief). This corpulent person, believed to be Chitam, is flanked by two attendants. The central figure is dressed in lordly finery, including jaguar skins; he wears a jaguar headdress plumed with feathers from the **quetzal,** a native bird, and sports adornments made of jade and shell. There is little question that Chitam's reign marked the final "glory days" of prehispanic Tikal. After Chitam, little construction was carried out, and few stelae were erected. A century or two later, this giant city was abandoned by humans and eventually reverted to forest.

The Temple of the Great Jaguar (Temple I).

The Central Acropolis at Tikal.

RAISED FIELDS

Intensive agriculture in the Maya lowlands

Thirty years ago, most Mayanists believed that the ancient Maya relied entirely on the slash-and-burn farming practices employed in the Yucatán today. For example, in 1956, Sylvanus Morley and George Brainerd summarized the prevailing viewpoint as follows:

> Modern Maya agricultural practices are the same as they were three thousand years ago or more — a simple process of felling the forest, burning the dried trees and bush, planting, and changing the locations of the cornfields every few years.
>
> (Morley and Brainerd, 1956, p. 128)

Yet during the last decades, with the completion of archaeological settlement surveys, a large number of sites have been mapped. Often these sites were found to have contained a greater residential population than had been expected, raising questions concerning Maya subsistence and population. Most notably, given the long fallow cycles required by slash-and-burn farming, how did the large Classic Maya populations sustain themselves?

The late Dennis Puleston, who surveyed outlying portions of Tikal, provided an alternative hypothesis. Noting the high spatial association between the ruins of Tikal house mounds and the distribution of ramón trees (local trees bearing edible fruits), Puleston suggested that the fruit of the ramón, eaten today as a dietary supplement, may have been a food staple in the past. Although Puleston may have overestimated the ancient dietary significance of ramón, more recent findings have supported his view that the ramón and other fruit trees were tended by the prehispanic Maya and probably contributed to their diet.

In 1969, Puleston, collaborating with geographer Alfred Siemens, discovered raised-field complexes during an aerial reconnaissance in the vicinity of a series of Maya sites along the Candelaria River in the state of Campeche. Subsequent aerial photographs, on-the-ground checks, and archaeological excavations confirmed that the observed patterns of raised fields and interdigitated canals were constructed prior to the Spanish conquest. Since the initial work of Siemens and Puleston, these agricultural features, which are similar in function to the prehispanic central Mexican *chinampas,* also have been noted in other parts of the Maya lowlands. (See "Tenochtitlan," p. 344.)

Along the Hondo River in Belize, Puleston's excavations suggested that the prehispanic raised features were built up by piling floodplain sediments above the natural terrain. In the swampy domains where they frequently were constructed, the cultivated fields were elevated above the floodplain during the rainy season, but if necessary they could receive water supplements from the intervening canals in the dry season. In addition, the periodic cleaning of the canals further raised and naturally fertilized the fields. While these features were laborious to construct, the returns also were significant, allowing for a much more continuous output than that afforded by slash and burn. The canals within the raised-field systems also could have promoted fish cultivation and facilitated transport and communication. The Maya glyph signifying abundance was the water lily, a key natural floral component of the artificially constructed aquatic raised-field/canal environment.

Pollen samples from the silt of the ancient Hondo River canals have identified maize and cotton as crops grown in the raised-field complexes. Thus, subsistence foods as well as nonfood plants were grown. Significantly, radiocarbon dates from the Hondo River fields place the initial construction of this artificial landscape in the first millennium B.C., prior to significant population expansion in the Maya lowlands.

In the last decade, Side-Looking Airborne Radar (SLAR) has been used to locate huge areas of suspected raised-field complexes in a large portion of the Maya region. Yet most of these proposed field systems have not been checked on the ground. Several other linear patterns observed by radar apparently reflect no more than natural soil formations. Thus the geographic extent of ancient Maya raised-field complexes remains unknown.

A raised-field complex in Pulltrouser Swamp, Belize.

In several areas, the ancient Maya supplemented extensive swidden farming (slash and burn) with the construction of artificial terrace systems. Evidence for these agricultural features, which converted otherwise unfarmable slopes into a patchwork of level plots, has been found in both western Belize and the vicinity of the River Bec. While doubts persist about the dating and distribution of Classic Maya agricultural systems, there is no longer any question that they employed a great diversity of subsistence strategies, including a series of intensive-farming techniques.

TIKAL'S MONUMENT RECORD

The rulers of Tikal

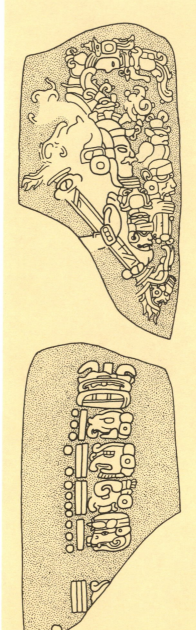

Stela 29, with a richly dressed noble on one side of the monument and glyphs arranged in a single column on the other.

Just as the ancient Maya economy was more complex than expected, recent studies in Maya archaeology and **epigraphy** (the study of inscriptions) have demonstrated that Classic Maya society was not egalitarian, but was hierarchically organized. The commemoration of the births, accessions, conquests, and deaths of important rulers was a major theme of their carved stone monuments.

One of the most important monuments at Tikal, known as Stela 29, exhibits the earliest known and well-**provenienced** inscriptions in the Maya lowlands with a Long Count date of A.D. 292. (See "Writing and Calendars," p. 336.) For archaeologists, Stela 29 is a marker for the beginning of the Maya Classic period, an era during which the Long Count was used on numerous Maya inscriptions. The end of the Classic period (A.D. 900) roughly coincides with the cessation of Long Count inscriptions. Stela 29 also includes the earliest emblem glyph (place name), a distinctive sign that identifies either a specific Maya center or the ruling lineage associated with that location.

In the Early Classic period, the importance of Tikal and its ruling lineage is indicated by the numerous dated monuments at the site. While other Maya centers in the immediate vicinity of Tikal also asserted their importance and autonomy by erecting fourth-century A.D. monuments, Tikal and its neighbor Uaxactún (wah-shak-toon′) raised almost half of these early stelae. Stela 5 at Uaxactún, dating to A.D. 358, includes Tikal's emblem glyph, an indicator that the former site by that time may have been under Tikal's jurisdiction. Soon thereafter, several other Petén sites ceased erecting stelae, another signal that Tikal may have expanded its sovereignty early in the Classic period.

Precocious political development at Tikal and Uaxactún may have been related to the close ties that these centers developed with foreign elite. A stela erected in A.D. 377 at Uaxactún portrays a figure in non-Maya attire. Less than two years later, Tikal Stela 4 records the accession of a new ruler, Curl Nose, who is posed facing front rather than in profile, as was typical of earlier Maya rulers. In pose and costume, Curl Nose resembles Teotihuacan nobles, and the excavation of the tomb, thought to have been his, included objects suggesting a Teotihuacan connection.

This foreign link continued, although perhaps somewhat diminished, during the reign of Curl Nose's heir, Stormy Sky. The latter figure is portrayed on Tikal Stela 31, which commemorates the twentieth year of his rule. On the stela, Stormy Sky appears in Maya regalia, flanked by two subordinate figures wearing outfits more indicative of the highlands. Their shields are adorned with the face of the central Mexican rain deity, prominent at Teotihuacan. During and immediately after the reign of Stormy Sky, Tikal's influence spread even further in the lowlands, possibly stretching to distant Yaxchilán (yah-chee-lahn′), a Maya center on the Usumacinta River. Tikal's broad foreign ties and political importance may have stemmed mainly from the site's location on land that lies between two major drainage systems, which linked the Gulf of Mexico with the Caribbean Sea, and interconnecting the Maya lowlands.

Early in the sixth century A.D., a stela at Yaxchilán displayed the site's own emblem glyph, which may imply that independence from Tikal had been secured. Tikal's declining influence was signaled by a construction slowdown and a long break, from A.D. 534 to 692, in the carving of dated stelae. During the first fifty-nine years of this period, called the hiatus, monument erection practically ceased at many sites in the central Maya lowlands. Just prior to the hiatus, a Tikal ruler, Double Bird, was apparently defeated in battle by a ruler from Caracol. During the hiatus, even the tombs of the elite contained meager offerings compared to the exotic and sumptuous items found earlier. Gordon Willey has proposed that the hiatus may have been due to the long-distance repercussions of the declining importance of Teotihuacan in regional trade and alliance networks.

The construction slowdown abruptly ended after A.D. 600. Monumental architecture and stelae were erected at new and rejuvenated centers across the Maya region. Late in the seventh century, the most massive construction episode was begun at Tikal under the ruler Ah Cacau, who deliberately harkened back to powerful Stormy Sky. Clemency Coggins, of the Peabody Museum at Harvard University, has proposed that Ah Cacau's accession was timed to occur exactly 256 years after the inauguration of Stormy Sky. Under Ah Cacau and his immediate successors, Tikal's central Twin Pyramid groups, and the most massive **acropoli** (singular **acropolis**) (mazelike complexes of palaces and courtyards), were built, and the site grew to more than 120 sq km (45 sq mi). At its maximum size, bounded by the swampy *bajos* to the east and west and defensive earthworks to the north and south, the site is thought to have been occupied by 50,000 to 80,000 people.

While the later Classic period was characterized by a series of politically autonomous centers, including Tikal in the central Petén, Palenque in the southwest, Yaxchilán along the Usumacinta, and Copán in the southeast, stylistic and **iconographic** conventions were shared across the southern Maya lowlands. A standardized lunar calendar was employed throughout the region for almost a century (A.D. 672 to 751). Monuments from various centers indicate that communications between the sites was fostered by elite intermarriage, as well as by military alliances. Archaeological findings suggest that exchange also was an extremely important means of regional integration.

During the Late Classic, the ruling lineage at Tikal never developed the far-flung influence that Curl Nose and Stormy Sky apparently had achieved earlier. Yet epigraphic findings indicate that the later rulers did extend their political connections to a network of smaller, adjacent central Petén sites. By the end of the eighth century A.D., construction at Tikal, and at many other major Maya centers,

began to wane. A large percentage of Tikal's excavated house mounds were occupied during the major episode of building, yet most of the habitation after A.D. 830 was restricted to the site core, and the total site population may have only been one-tenth of what it was a century before. In A.D. 889, the latest monument was erected at Tikal, and the last known Long Count date anywhere was carved in A.D. 909. Tikal's fate was only part of the significant demographic decline and political breakdown, the so-called Maya collapse, which characterized almost the entire central and southern lowlands during the ninth and tenth centuries.

Stela 31, showing Stormy Sky flanked by two subordinate figures.

PALENQUE

*A Classic center at the edge of
the Maya lowlands*

*The plan of the central part of
Palenque.*

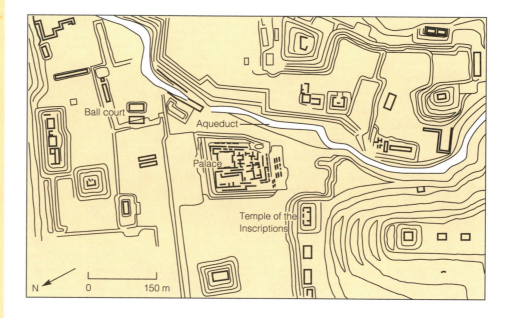

The Maya and other native groups in the New World divided their physical realms into four quarters, with each quarter associated with specific colors, living things, and supernatural forces. Original Maya maps consistently place east at the top, suggesting that east was viewed as the dominant direction.

In A.D. 731, a stela was erected at the site of Copán, a large center in the southeastern part of the Maya lowlands. This monument lists the place names of four major Maya centers, each associated with one of the four cardinal directions. Preceding this list is a clause that Joyce Marcus interprets as "four on high," or "divided into four quarters." It appears that the Maya associated each section of their world with an important place or center. Not surprisingly, the monument carvers at Copán associated their site with the fore-

most direction, east. Tikal was associated with the west, while Marcus has suggested that the emblem glyph associated with the south belonged to a site called Calakmul. Palenque (pa-len'kay), a center at the western edge of the lowlands, was linked with the direction north. Although these directions did not correspond closely to the actual geography, the cosmological model, dividing the Maya world between a series of centers, did reflect the political diversity of the Late Classic Maya realm. This is not to say that the lowland Maya world only contained four autonomous centers in A.D. 731. There were many more. Rather, some authority at Copán perceived these four centers to be of the greatest importance.

Palenque is situated on a series of rolling hills approximately 50 km (30 mi) from the Usumacinta River, in the state of

Chiapas, Mexico. The site was occupied early in the Classic period but remained relatively small until the seventh century A.D., when a major building boom was started following the hiatus. The new structures at the site were built by a powerful lord who, inscriptions indicate, came to power in A.D. 615, and may have been named Pacal ("shield"). During Pacal's rule, Palenque also grew in size, expanded its authority over the neighboring region, and the site's emblem glyph appeared. The major structures at the site today were begun after Pacal's accession.

Lord Pacal was buried in an elaborate tomb beneath the pyramid that supports the Temple of the Inscriptions. The tomb was discovered by Alberto Ruz Lhuiller. Several years later, after clearing a staircase that led deep under the pyramid, Ruz found a large stuccoed crypt. The huge stone coffin (**sarcophagus**) was topped with a superbly carved lid, depicting the dead ruler falling into the underworld. Beneath the lid were the remains of Pacal,

wearing beads and a mosaic mask of jade, surrounded by other treasures.

Epigraphic studies of the stone lid of the sarcophagus and other inscriptions at Palenque have led to the reconstruction of the long dynastic history of the site. Pacal was succeeded directly by his son, Chan-Bahlum, who in a relatively short reign continued the massive construction at the core of the site. Following Chan-Bahlum's death early in the eighth century, his brother, Kan-Xul, replaced him. During his rule, Palenque's realm reached its greatest extent. Kan-Xul also expanded Palenque's so-called Palace structure by erecting an unusual four-story tower in veneration of his father. During winter solstices, the sun seems to set directly behind the Temple of the Inscriptions when viewed from the top of the Palace tower.

After the death of Kan-Xul, the site and its inscriptions began to wane. A series of three rulers with brief and possibly broken reigns followed. Two of Lord Pacal's later successors apparently were

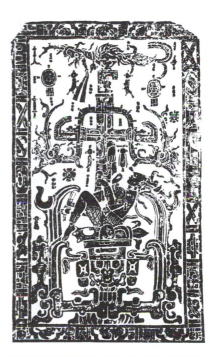

Inscriptions on the lid of Lord Pacal's coffin.

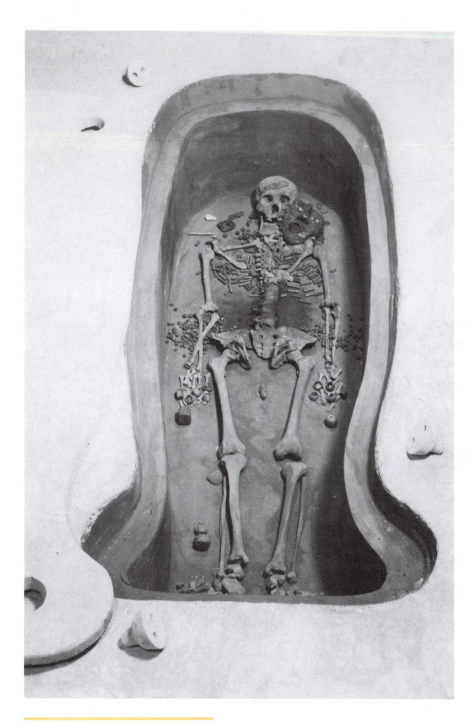

Lord Pacal's sarcophagus in the tomb.

women. The last recorded accession date of a ruler in Pacal's lineage was A.D. 764. The last Long Count date known from Palenque (corresponding to A.D. 799) occurs on an inscribed pottery vessel and records the accession of a ruler with a central Mexican style name (non-Mayan), 6 Cimi, suggesting that the site may have been taken over or influenced by foreigners late in the eighth century.

Palenque was one of the earliest Maya centers to experience collapse. Monumental construction and the textual record waned during the latter half of the eighth century and ceased early in the ninth century. Pomona, a small former dependency of Palenque, displayed its own emblem glyph in 771 A.D., suggesting that it had achieved independence. Palenque was also one of the first sites to show an increasing tie to Gulf Coast or central Mexican elements. In parts of the Classic Maya world, this external bond often was associated with the cessation of monumental building and the erection of stelae. On a stela that was raised at the site of Seibal in A.D. 889, Palenque and Copán were no longer considered among the four primary centers of the Maya region. By then, the realm of the Classic Maya had shrunk to little more than its former core around Tikal.

While Palenque at its height was clearly part of the Classic Maya cultural realm, the site's distinctive layout and architecture reflected its location at the western periphery of the lowlands. Compared to the imposing appearance and vertical thrust of the architecture at Tikal and other Classic Maya centers, Palenque's major structures were broader and more dispersed, giving the site's civic-ceremonial center a more horizontal flow. Palenque also lacked a corpus of freestanding sculptured monuments (stelae and altars). Instead, hieroglyphic inscriptions generally were written on stone panels or plaster and incorporated directly into buildings.

Son of a wealthy New York City merchant, John Lloyd Stephens graduated from Columbia College in 1822. By the time he was 34, when he boarded a British brig in New York for Belize, he was already one of America's best-known travel writers. On this trip, Stephens teamed up with Frederick Catherwood, a British architect, whose drawings of Old World antiquities were highly esteemed by Stephens. While Stephens knew he was not the first person to visit the ruins of the ancient civilizations of Mesoamerica, he also was aware that most people in New York, Boston, and London were still unfamiliar with the magnificent archaeology of this tropical region.

Stephens and Catherwood set off for the site of Copán in Honduras. Stephens first purchased the site from the local landowner for the equivalent of about $50, and then mapped the overgrown ruins in the jungle. Catherwood frequently drew the monuments while standing in deep mud, wearing gloves to shield his hands from hungry mosquitoes. During their two weeks at the site, Stephens described the ruins in a thoughtful manner. Most notably, he interpreted the carved monuments as having historical themes, a view that has been confirmed in recent years. On the question of Maya origins, Stephens concurred more with the early Colonial period interpretations, such as those offered by Franciscan friar Diego de Landa, than with the fanciful ideas advanced by many of his nineteenth-century contemporaries. He recognized that the ancient center was built by native peoples and rejected the then-popular notion of transoceanic migrations.

After Copán, Stephens and Catherwood set off for their primary destination of Palenque, the best-known Maya site of their day. Stephens soberly described the ruins in print, while Catherwood's illustrations provided architectural detail and wonder. With the arrival of the spring rains in 1840, the pair left Palenque, sailed down the Usumacinta River and around the coast of the Gulf of Mexico, and visited the site of Uxmal in the northern Yucatán. When Catherwood fell ill, the exploration was halted, and the two returned to New York.

Stephens spent less than two months at the sites. His 1841 publication, *Incidents of Travel in Central America, Chiapas, and Yucatán,* devoted only 25% of its pages to the ruins. Yet this two-volume collection was an important watershed in Maya studies. Stephens' compelling text, supplemented by Catherwood's superb illustrations, captured the public interest, necessitating a dozen printings of the volumes within three months. In addition to drawing public attention to the importance and magnificence of ancient Mesoamerican ruins, Stephens' work opened a new chapter in Maya research, through his careful descriptions and his dismissal of exotic origins.

Stephens and Catherwood set sail on a second expedition in 1841. This trip took them back to Uxmal and then to most of the other large sites then known in the northern Yucatán, including Chichén Itzá and Tulum. This journey was devoted solely to archaeology and was published (again in two volumes) in 1843 as *Incidents of Travel in Yucatán,* a more scholarly, but still popular, account. The second trip was the first intentional archaeological reconnaissance into the Maya region. Stephens and Catherwood's work was truly a landmark. These two individuals embarked on some of the last truly romantic explorations of Maya sites and completed one of the first objective studies of the ruins and civilization of prehispanic Yucatán.

JOHN LLOYD STEPHENS, 1805–1852, AND FREDERICK CATHERWOOD, 1799–1854

Early reconnaissances in the land of the Maya

WRITING AND CALENDARS

The Maya numerical system and calendar round

The earliest Mesoamerican writing appeared more than 2500 years ago, prior to the rise of the state or the existence of urban centers. Four different prehispanic Mesoamerican writing systems are known: the Maya, Zapotec, Mixtec, and Aztec. Each appears to include a mixture of **pictographic**, **ideographic**, and **phonetic** elements. The latter two are known from late prehispanic texts written on prepared bark paper or deerskin; the older Zapotec system is preserved on inscriptions carved in stone. The Maya writing system has been preserved in late prehispanic folding books, as well as in a very large body of texts on stone, pottery, and wall paintings from the Classic period. The Maya writing system is the best known of the four, and several major breakthroughs in decipherment have come in the last decade.

At first, the Classic Maya inscriptions were thought to relate exclusively to astronomy and calendrics, because these subjects comprised the first portions of the texts to be deciphered. Today epigraphers recognize that the principal theme of Maya inscriptions is a political or dynastic one. Carved stones commemorate significant events — birth, autosacrifice, accession to rule, marriage, military victory, death — in the lives of the Maya lords and their kin. Often the text helps frame a stylized picture of a commemorated event. The blocky hieroglyphs are presented in double columns that are intended to be read from left to right and top to bottom. As with ancient Egyptian monuments, the messages are generally brief and composed largely of nouns and verbs.

Prehispanic texts are closely linked to the pre-Columbian calendar. Classic Maya inscriptions are distinguished by their frequent use of the **Long Count** calendar, a system capable of tracking extended cycles of time. Although the Maya did not invent the Long Count, they refined and used it to the greatest degree. The smallest Long Count unit is the day, or *kin*. The second Long Count unit, composed of 20 *kins,* is the *uinal*. The third unit, the *tun*, consists of 18 *uinals,* or 360 *kins*. Above this third cycle are the *katun* and the *baktun,* consisting of 20 and 400 *tuns,* respectively. In accord with all prehispanic Mesoamerican numeration systems, the Long Count had a vigesimal structure, one based on multiples of 20. The only adjustment necessary to approximate the solar year was a change in the third unit, or *tun,* from 20 to 18 *uinals*.

The Long Count system allows scholars to date precisely many of the Classic Maya inscriptions. Long Count dates were calculated by the Classic Maya and their Mesoamerican forebears, who established the system by adding the total amount of elapsed time to a base date to begin their calendar. Until this starting point was calculated, Long Count dates could not be

An example of Maya hieroglyphs.

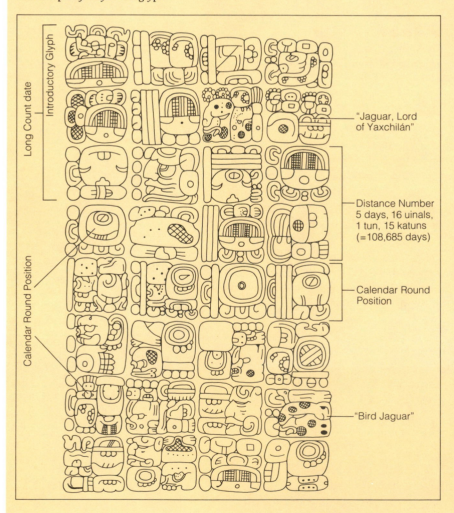

Long Count date

Introductory Glyph

Calendar Round Position

"Jaguar, Lord of Yaxchilán"

Distance Number 5 days, 16 uinals, 1 tun, 15 katuns (=108,685 days)

Calendar Round Position

"Bird Jaguar"

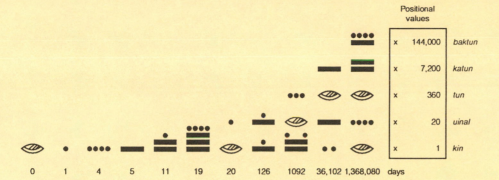

Positional values

	x	144,000	baktun
	x	7,200	katun
	x	360	tun
	x	20	uinal
	x	1	kin

0   1   4   5   11   19   20   126   1092   36,102   1,368,080   days

The Maya numbering system and Long Count units. The base-20 system used only three symbols, the stylized shell for zero, a dot for one, and a bar for five. The numbers were arranged vertically (rather than horizontally, as in our Arabic numeration), with the lowest values at the bottom.

equated with our calendric system. Some scholarly disagreement still exists, yet the great majority of researchers place the base date for the Long Count near the end of the fourth millennium B.C. (with 3114 B.C. the most widely accepted figure).

In addition to the Long Count, the Maya and other Mesoamerican peoples used the Calendar Round. The main element of this calendar was the Sacred Almanac, or 260-day count. Primarily religious and divinatory in function, the almanac can be visualized as having been composed of two integrated "cogged wheels" or cycles of numbers; one cycle of numbers ran from 1 to 13, while the other cycle consisted of twenty named days. In general, these named days were similar across Mesoamerica; however, some differences did occur from group to group. The combination of a number and a day name formed a unit that would not reoccur until 260 days had elapsed, at which point the cycle began again. The numbers were usually expressed in typical Mesoamerican bar-and-dot fashion, with a dot equivalent to one and a bar equivalent to five.

A second element of the Calendar Round was the 365-day Vague Year. This year was divided into eighteen "months" of twenty days each. An extra period of five days (Uayeb) was added at the end of the year. While the Classic Maya were aware that the tropical year actually was 365.25 days, they did not employ a leap-year correction. The permutation of the Sacred Almanac and the Vague Year pro-

duced a 18,980-day Calendar Round that cycled back to its original start every fifty-two solar years.

The Maya believed that significant moments in time had their links with divinities and astrologically based auguries, and these associations were known and recorded. The Maya viewed time in a cyclical fashion. Points in time and the events assigned to them were not thought to be unique; the past, present, and future often could be woven together in prophecy and divination. Given the intricacy of Classic Maya writing and calendrics and their importance in the politico-religious sphere, it appears that this special knowledge was generally held by only a relatively small segment of the population.

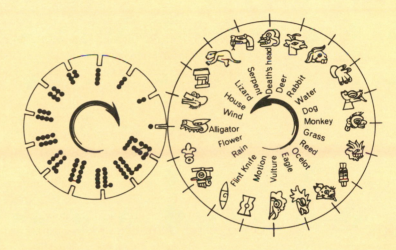

The 260-day Sacred Almanac for the Aztec. The twenty named days intermesh with the numbers 1 to 13.

Of all the New World states, it is perhaps the Maya that afford us the greatest opportunity for understanding the evolution, operation, and demise of a complex society. No other New World state offers us such a variety of complementary data sets, including eye-witness reports preserved as ethnohistorical documents, hieroglyphic texts that span some 600 years, regional settlement pattern data, linguistic reconstructions, subsistence data, and architectural evolution. The challenge remains for us to integrate all these lines of evidence, to highlight the differences and similarities among them, and to understand the Maya better by learning more about other Mesoamerican states.

Joyce Marcus (1983b)

TULA

Capital city of the Toltec empire

When the fifteenth-century Aztec ruler Itzcoatl purged the state archives, burning older documentary records, he greatly limited our ability to reconstruct the late prehispanic history of central Mexico. Fortunately, some lists of rulers (king lists) and other fragmentary accounts of the previous periods survived. In conjunction with archaeological discoveries, these records enable us to begin to understand the events in the Central Highlands between the decline of Teotihuacan, around A.D. 700 to 800, and the establishment of the Aztec city Tenochtitlan, in A.D. 1325.

Sixteenth-century Spanish clerics and men of letters, curious about prehispanic civilization, inquired about the native history of Mexico. Repeatedly their Aztec informants attributed the origins of their society to a semilegendary race known as the Toltecs. According to these part-historical, part-mythical accounts, the Toltecs were great warriors, but also peace-loving people. These mythic histories also described the Toltecs as innovators, builders, and craftspeople, who cultivated giant ears of corn and colored cotton that did not have to be dyed. Their capital was supposedly an architectural masterpiece known as Tollan. The Aztecs traced their right to rule directly to their Toltec ancestry.

Like many such accounts, the origin myths of the Aztec blended historical reality with fiction and distortion. Some of the stories did contain elements of truth, which enabled Mexican ethnohistorian Wigberto Jiménez Moreno to persuasively suggest that the Toltec capital was an actual place near the modern town of Tula de Allende, in the state of Hidalgo.

Over the last decades, several archaeological projects at Tula have substantiated Jiménez Moreno's identification.

Tula (too'la) is situated at the northern fringe of Mesoamerica, about 65 km (40 mi) northwest of modern Mexico City. The site had little significant occupation when Teotihuacan was partially burned and abandoned. The collapse of that great city, nearly coincident with the demise of monumental building at Monte Albán, marked a major transition in the highlands of Mexico. Following the fall of Teotihuacan, no single dominant community emerged in the Central Highlands to control the Basin of Mexico. Tula rose rapidly in this politically fragmented landscape.

Soon after A.D. 800, a substantial occupation was present at the site. Even at its height, Tula was considerably smaller than Teotihuacan or the later Aztec city of Tenochtitlan. Tula also lacks any evidence of urban planning outside its civic-ceremonial core. It reached its maximum size and its greatest influence between A.D. 950 and 1150: 13 sq km (5 sq mi) and about 40,000 people. The major structures at the site, including two large ball courts, were built during this period. While the monumental architecture at Tula was far less grandiose than at Teotihuacan, a series of squat but substantial temple pyramids were erected. The most impressive and well-known remains at Tula are the sculpted **Atlantean columns**, which stand 4.6 m (15 ft) high. The military theme depicted by these giant basalt figures is also evident in a series of carved-stone relief panels showing jaguars, eagles eating hearts, and coyotes, all creatures perhaps associated with specific warrior groups in the city.

Raw-material procurement, trade, and craft production were very important economic activities at Tula, as they were at Teotihuacan and Tenochtitlan. Containers of travertine, a white sedimentary stone, were made at the site, and sixteenth-century accounts describe many other fine, high-status goods produced by the Toltec craftspeople. As at Teotihuacan, areas of heavy obsidian use and/or production have been recorded at Tula. Most of the obsidian was derived from the same source that furnished workshops at Teotihuacan. Tula borders on arid regions to the north, where little can be grown except maguey. This plant is an important source of fiber, needles, sap, and other products. In ancient Mesoamerica, maguey fibers were raw material for cloth, clothing, nets, and bags. The abundance of spindle whorls at Tula indicates that the spinning of these fibers into twine also was an important economic activity. The presence of pottery and marine shells from the Pacific Coast further documents the extent of exchange with peoples in northern and western Mexico.

Both historical and archaeological sources agree that Tula had lost much of its influence before A.D. 1200. Excavations by Mexican archaeologist Jorge Acosta revealed evidence of burning and disruption at all the major structures; however, the specific date of this destruction was not determined. A recent project by Richard Diehl found that Tula was at least partially abandoned by A.D. 1200, although the extent of the collapse is unknown. Diehl's study also recorded a sizable Aztec occupation at Tula. Acosta found extensive evidence for late prehispanic looting in earlier monumental structures and even in the residential compounds. Colonial era texts of the Spanish friar Bernardo de Sahagún allude to this looting, citing the removal of Toltec artifacts from the earth.

Various written accounts provide a more intriguing depiction of Tula's end, yet their accuracy is unconfirmed. Although the accounts themselves are somewhat contradictory, the story ties the fall of Tula to a conflict between cosmic forces. The Mesoamerican cosmos was

One of the Atlantean columns at Tula.

frequently symbolized as a duality. Quetzalcoatl, the representative of day, light, traditional religion, and good, was opposed to Tezcatlipoca, the embodiment of night, darkness, chicanery, and evil. In these accounts, Quetzalcoatl ("the feathered serpent"), or a ruler associated with him, is tricked, disgraced, and forced to leave the city, an event resulting in Tula's downfall.

Archaeological and historical sources both indicate that following the collapse, the Basin of Mexico and its northern fringes once again fragmented into a series of small polities, each controlling only their immediate vicinity. It was during this era of political decentralization that the Aztecs began their ascent to power.

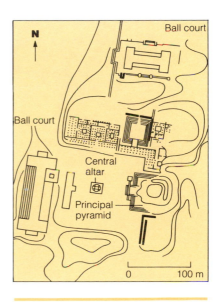

The plan of Tula.

CHICHÉN ITZÁ

*The most magnificent late Maya center in
the Yucatán*

*Puuc-style architecture at Chichén
Itzá.*

The collapse of major centers in the central and southern Maya lowlands during the ninth and tenth centuries A.D. coincided with an episode of development and population increase in the drier northern fringe of the Yucatán Peninsula. Several clusters of larger centers were established in the northern lowlands, each marked by its own distinct architectural style.

The most widespread of these, the Puuc style is identifiable by a mosaic of limestone masonry covering a rubble core. The earliest construction at the site of Chichén Itzá (chee-chen'eet-zah') is characterized by this style. Chichén Itzá, one of the easternmost of the Puuc sites, was strategically situated toward the center of the Yucatán Peninsula, near two large natural sinkhole wells, or **cenotes**. The limestone bedrock of northern Yucatán is very porous, and rainfall soaks immediately into the ground. There are no rivers and very little surface water in this area. The cenotes in the limestone landscape are a very important source of drinking water.

The flowering of the Puuc centers is associated with ceramic and architectural elements from the non-Maya areas of Mexico, perhaps the Gulf Coast. The archaeological indications of these exotic connections fit well with later written accounts suggesting the role of "Mexicanized" Maya traders in the rise of the northern Yucatán centers during the Late Classic period. Their influence was related to a shift in long-distance trade routes and involved an expansion of circum-Yucatán sea transport at the expense of the old Petén River route across the Petén lowlands.

Late in the tenth century A.D., a second, more opulent construction boom led to the rebuilding of the center of Chichén Itzá in an architectural style more similar to that found at Toltec Tula. During this later construction phase, Chichén Itzá grew to its maximum size, more than 5 sq km (2 sq mi). The new architecture in-

A map of the central area of Chichén Itzá.

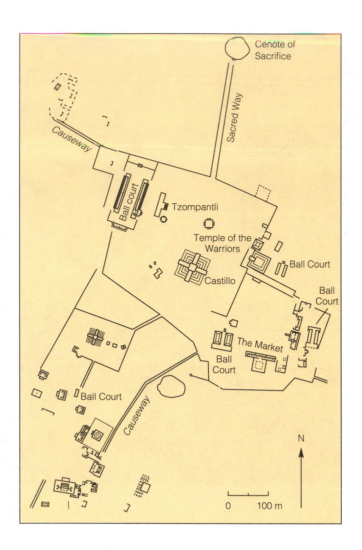

A carved tzompantli *(skull rack) at Chichén Itzá.*

cluded colonnades, extensive I-shaped ball courts (the largest in Mesoamerica), relief carvings of prowling jaguars, carved warrior figures, carved *tzompantlis* (skull racks), and fascinating, sculpted *chac mools*. A **chac mool** is an altar in the form of a reclining figure with head and knees raised. The hands surround a bowl-shaped impression at the navel, where sacrifices or offerings were placed.

Some archaeologists have suggested an actual central Mexican Toltec presence at Chichén Itzá on the basis of ancient legends that tell of the god Quetzalcoatl from Tula arriving in the Yucatán in A.D. 987. This interpretation is supported by murals in a temple at Chichén Itzá depicting warriors (assumed to be Toltecs) arriving in canoes and doing battle with the local populace. Yet the same textual sources that tell of foreign invaders in the Postclassic Yucatán note that they spoke a Maya language, suggesting that they were not actually central Mexican Toltecs. The nature of the relationship between the two centers remains uncertain and under debate.

The later construction at Chichén Itzá reflects a strong Maya influence, with veneer masonry, mosaic facades, and the use of vaults, and they are generally more finely made and larger than similar buildings at Tula. The focus of the new construction was a huge 12-ha (30-acre) plaza area. For almost two centuries, Chichén Itzá was the primary locus of truly monumental construction in the northern Yucatán. The scale of building at the site, including fifteen large plaza groups and numerous ball courts, is not found elsewhere. Yet excavations indicate that construction slowed by the middle of the thirteenth century, conforming with documentary accounts that imply that Chichén Itzá's rule was broken by A.D. 1221.

During Chichén Itzá's ascendancy, and even after its demise, the cenotes remained important sites of sacred offerings. A *sacbe* (stone causeway) ran directly from the site's main plaza to one of the cenotes. Offerings of all kinds from across the Maya region, including Classic period items that may have been looted, were cast into this sacred natural well, appropriately named the Cenote of Sacrifice. According to Bishop Diego de Landa, a Spanish cleric who chronicled life in sixteenth-century Yucatán, men were thrown alive into the well as a sacrifice to the gods during times of drought. Indeed, the dredging of the sacred cenote turned up human bone as well as prehispanic copper, gold, and jade.

A chac mool *at Chichén Itzá.*

TENOCHTITLAN

*The capital city of the Aztecs: the Venice of
the New World*

The Aztec civilization, the best known of any indigenous Native American society, has aroused scholarly interest since the discovery and conquest of Mexico by the Spanish in the early sixteenth century. Although written accounts of Aztec society are rich and full of descriptive detail, the archaeological record is somewhat impoverished, in part because the Aztec capital of Tenochtitlan (ten-noch-teet-lan') is buried under the bustling metropolis of Mexico City.

In February 1978, electric workers were digging trenches for cables in Mexico City when they found a large stone sculpture. Located 2 m (6.5 ft) below the surface, this sculpture depicted the Aztec female lunar deity Coyolxauhqui, who according to myth was slain and dismembered by her very important brother Huitzilopochtli, the war god. This discovery revived national interest in the great temple of the Aztecs, the Templo Mayor: a twin temple dedicated to Huitzilopochtli and Tlaloc, the rain deity. The accidental discovery initiated a long-term research project that has added greatly to our information about this city and the temple that was the physical and psychic heart of the Aztec world.

The Aztecs, who referred to themselves as Mexica, had humble origins. The Mexica were Chichimecs from the northern desert who did not arrive in the Basin of Mexico until the middle of the thirteenth century A.D. Although the specific cause of this population movement is not known, it appears to have coincided with an episode of drought in the north, which may have made that already dry area particularly unsuitable for agriculture. Alternatively, the Mexica and other northern groups may have been attracted to the economic and military opportunities afforded by the rise of Tula on Mesoamerica's northern frontier.

When the Mexica arrived, more than fifty small, autonomous **petty states** were present in the Basin of Mexico. At first, the Mexica had little choice but to settle on lands controlled by others. The established basin populations viewed the Mexica as barbarian heathen, yet they also recognized their military prowess, important during a period characterized by military conflicts and competition.

The Mexica's migrations did not end after their arrival in the basin. Feared and despised by more powerful and urban groups, they were repeatedly driven away. They took asylum on lands owned by Culhuacan, a relatively powerful petty state with ancestral ties to the ruling families at Tula. According to legend, the Mexica served the Culhua well as mercenaries. Eventually they asked for the hand of the daughter of the ruler of Culhuacan to strengthen their bloodlines through marriage. Unfortunately one of their gods, Huitzilopochtli, spoke to the Mexica priests and asked them to kill and sacrifice the girl. The Culhua ruler, invited to a ceremony to dedicate his daughter as a goddess, instead found a Mexica priest dressed in the flayed skin of his offspring. His wrath again forced the Mexica to retreat.

At the start of their journey, the Mexica had been told by the same god that they would find an eagle perched atop a

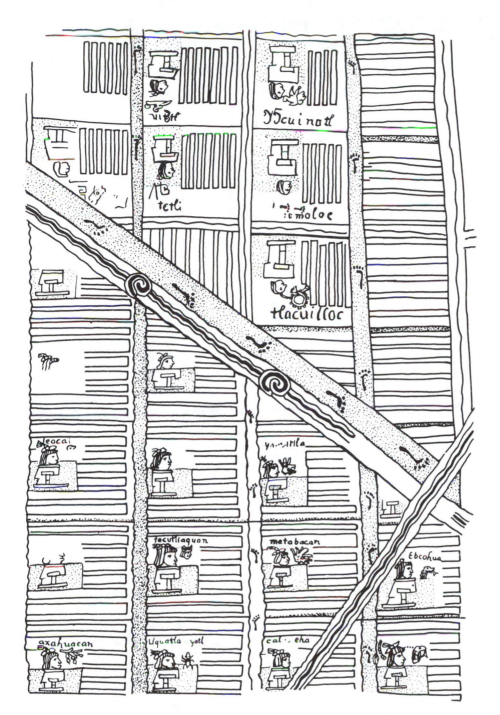

cactus plant to mark the end of their wanderings. Fleeing into the swamps of Lake Texcoco, one of the principal lakes of the basin, they found the eagle and cactus (a scene now immortalized on the flag of Mexico) on a nearby small, marshy island. The Mexica settled here and erected a temple for Huitzilopochtli. They named the settlement Tenochtitlan ("place of the fruit of the prickly pear cactus").

When Tenochtitlan was founded in A.D. 1325, the island lacked most construction materials (such as wood and stone), suffered periodic flooding, and was abundant only in insects. But the location offered several advantages. Waterfowl and fish were plentiful, and the freshwater lakeshore was amenable to intensive *chinampa* agriculture. These farm plots, created by draining standing water and raising the surface of the swamp with soil and vegetation mats, became a major source of food production for the Aztec. The little island was also in a prime location for controlling transportation in the basin. In ancient Mesoamerica, trans-

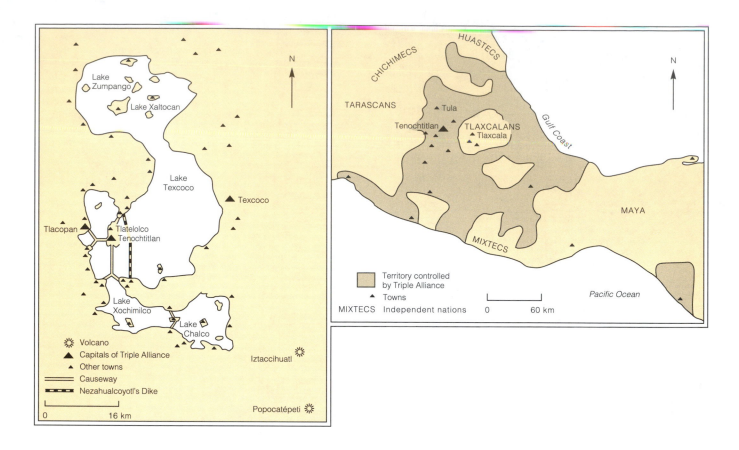

Map of the Basin of Mexico during Aztec times and the domain controlled by the Triple Alliance.

port was exclusively by foot or canoe; there were neither beasts of burden nor wheeled vehicles (although toys with wheels were made). Water transport saved time and energy, especially when heavy loads were involved. Canoes plied the waters of the lake as the most efficient means of moving goods and materials between communities.

In the less than two centuries between its founding and the Spanish conquest, Tenochtitlan developed from a small island town to the largest and most powerful city in all of Mesoamerica. During its first century of existence (A.D. 1325 to 1428), the settlement was subordinate to more important basin centers. During this phase, the Aztecs constructed *chinampas,* encouraged immigration to Tenochtitlan, and continued to gain renown for their mercenary skills. Their rulers strategically intermarried and allied themselves with more established elite in the region.

By 1428, Tenochtitlan was powerful enough to join with the petty states of Texcoco and Tlacopan, forming a Triple Alliance that soon vaulted the Aztec capital to a supreme political position in the

Basin of Mexico. In the years before the Spanish conquest, Tenochtitlan consolidated this political dominion, while its armies defeated and demanded tribute from foreign polities across western Mesoamerica and as far away as Guatemala.

In 1473, Tenochtitlan defeated its neighbor city of Tlatelolco and incorporated the latter, including its giant marketplace, into the metropolis. The dual city was linked to the mainland by three large, manmade causeways that ran from the lakeshore to the central ceremonial district of the capital. When the Spanish arrived, Tenochtitlan was a city of roughly 150,000 to 200,000 people. The Spanish leader Cortés was greatly impressed by the size and grandeur of Tenochtitlan, calling the Aztec city "another Venice."

Early Colonial period maps and accounts indicate that the basic residential unit at Tenochtitlan was smaller than the apartment compounds at Teotihuacan. Most household compounds at Tenochtitlan were occupied by nuclear or joint families, each with its own direct access to the streets and canals of the city. Individual compounds were more easily differentiated, permitting public displays

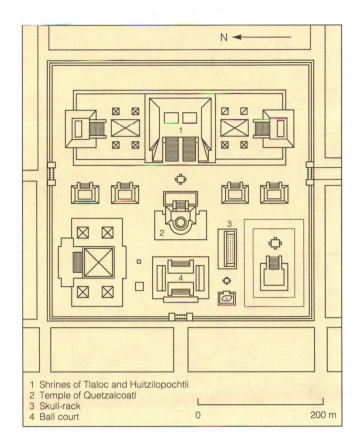

1 Shrines of Tlaloc and Huitzilopochtli
2 Temple of Quetzalcoatl
3 Skull-rack
4 Ball court

0   200 m

The plan of the ceremonial core of Tenochtitlan.

of status and wealth. In Aztec society, advances in social position could be achieved through military or economic successes.

Numerous craftspeople (including featherworkers, lapidaries, and reed mat-makers) were encouraged to settle in the city, adding to its importance as a commercial center. Finished goods from Tenochtitlan may have undermined local craft production in some of the communities in outlying parts of the basin. Tenochtitlan also obtained large quantities of exotic resources and finished goods as tribute payments from defeated polities. In general, nearby polities gave foodstuffs, wood, woven mats, and other heavier, more utilitarian items; more distant states sent rarer, more valuable goods. Captive states were typically instructed to send local materials. Other exotic goods were brought back to the city by the **pochteca,** a hereditary guild of long-distance traders. The *pochteca* also returned to Tenochtitlan with valuable military or political information.

The Aztec tribute demands were heavy, and noncompliance was dealt with harshly. It is not surprising that Cortés' small band of adventurers received invaluable military and logistic support from Indian groups that despised the Aztec. Obviously Cortés and his few hundred men would not have defeated the Aztec armies as quickly and easily without this native assistance. Once victorious, the Spanish razed the ceremonial core of Tenochtitlan, replacing the temples and shrines with churches, governmental buildings, and palatial residences. Mexico City rapidly grew up over the ancient Aztec center. The upper level of the Templo Mayor was dismantled, and the materials were used to build Mexico City's Main Cathedral.

During the Colonial era, Spanish power in Mesoamerica was strengthened by occupation of the same place as the prior Aztec civic and sacred authority. Eventually in response to several destructive floods, the once-productive lakes were largely drained by the Spanish. The Colonial authorities could not adequately manipulate the complex networks of dikes and canals that had been built and used by the Aztecs. The dry lake bottom now serves as the soft foundation of Mexico's earthquake-prone capital.

Reconstruction of the Templo Mayor, superimposed over recent excavations. The main Spanish cathedral (still in place) was situated adjacent to the prehispanic temple.

Aztec market scenes from the Codex Florentino. Top left: a produce market with neatly arranged wares; top right: King Ahuitzotl receiving shells, jaguar skins, plumage, jade, and cacao from the coast; bottom left: members of a slave family wearing bars across their necks as a sign of bondage; bottom right: a merchant from the coast bartering for cloth, gold ornaments, copper, obsidian tools, and maguey-fiber rope from the highlands.

In today's market economies, people try to minimize costs and maximize returns in order to make a profit. Anthropologists distinguish this type of market endeavor from reciprocal and redistributive exchange networks. (See "The Archaeology of Exchange," Chapter Six, p. 255.) Reciprocity refers to face-to-face exchanges between known participants, such as relatives or trading partners, in which the specific return is not predefined (gift giving, for example). Redistribution is the accumulation and later dispersal of goods from a central place or by a central person (the income-tax system, for example).

Aztec **marketing**, with its network of marketplaces, various currencies, and numerous participants, clearly fits within the conventional definition of a market system. The *conquistador* Bernal Díaz del Castillo wrote, in awe of the size and variety of goods offered at the main Tlatelolco marketplace in Tenochtitlan:

> After having examined and considered all that we had seen we turned to look at the great market place and the crowds of people that were in it, some buying and others selling, so that the murmur and hum of their voices and words that they used could be heard more than a league off. Some of the soldiers among us who had been in many parts of the world, in Constantinople, and all over Italy, and in Rome, said that so large a market place and so full of people, and so well regulated and arranged, they had never beheld before.

(Bernal Díaz del Castillo, 1956, pp. 218–219)

This market alone served 20,000 to 25,000 people on a normal day, and twice as many every fifth day when it was the focus of a cycle of changing regional markets. Many exchanges were made by bartering. Others were facilitated by accepted currencies. **Cacao** beans, used to make a favorite drink of the nobility, were the most common form of money, but large cotton cloaks, quills filled with gold dust, stone and shell beads, copper beads, and axes were also employed. Cacao beans, which in fact did grow on trees, was accepted in payment for either goods or labor. Its importance was such that the dishonest buyers and sellers tried to counterfeit cacao by filling the bark or skin of the beans with earth. These fake cacao beans were then adeptly sealed and mixed into piles with true beans, where they could be passed off as genuine. The presence of the counterfeit beans and the presence of market judges to catch and punish dishonest merchants emphasize the importance of profit as a motive in this precapitalist society.

HUMAN SACRIFICE AND CANNIBALISM

Divergent interpretations of ancient rites

A depiction of an Aztec ritual heart sacrifice from a sixteenth-century codex.

No issue concerning ancient Mexico has attracted more attention and biting scholarly debate than human sacrifice and **cannibalism**. The Aztecs have frequently been portrayed in the popular press as violent, insatiable cannibals, practicing blood-thirsty and ghoulish acts. Ritual sacrifices have been documented archaeologically in early Mesopotamia, as well as in dynastic Egypt and ancient China. Human sacrifice has a very long history in prehispanic Mesoamerica, perhaps even back to the preceramic era in the Tehuacán Valley. Human sacrifice is depicted graphically in Classic Maya inscriptions and is strongly suggested by the Oaxacan *danzante* stones. Ancient Mesoamerican societies also gave great ritual importance to blood. Both autosacrifice, as well as the ritual offerings of blood, are present in the archaeological and epigraphic evidence.

Why, then, are the Aztecs so closely linked to the practice of human sacrifice? Most likely it is because the custom was featured so prominently in Spanish descriptions of central Mexico. While the Aztecs believed human sacrifice was a deeply religious practice, necessary to preserve the continuity of the universe, the Spanish Catholics saw it as the devil's work. Furthermore, the Europeans believed it to be their duty to abolish this behavior through conquest, conversion, and whatever means possible. Thus the elimination of these customs, which horrified the Spaniards, became a rationale for achieving their envisioned destiny to rule New Spain. (It should be noted that at the time the Spanish themselves were not above ghoulish behavior; in Spain, people were burned at the stake, while in Mexico, many Indians were mistreated and massacred.)

Anthropologist William Arens, of the State University of New York, Stony Brook, argues that the Spanish were so interested in defaming the native inhabitants and justifying their conquests that their sixteenth-century accounts cannot be trusted. Arens questions whether cannibalism even existed among the Aztecs. While the evidence for cannibalism is not as overwhelming as it is for large-scale sacrifice, independent accounts describe the consumption of sacrificed prisoners, particularly by warriors and members of the elite.

An alternative to Arens' explanation has been advanced by Michael Harner, of the New School for Social Research, who argues that the absence of domesticated animals and the large number of people in late prehispanic central Mexico necessitated massive Aztec sacrifices to alleviate a dietary shortage of meat protein and fat through cannibalism. Harner's ecological interpretation, which lists cannibalism as the reasons for massive sacrifices, has met with little nutritional, economic, or historical support. Harner argues that some 250,000 people were sacrificed each year in central Mexico, while most scholars place the yearly figure in the tens of thousands. He ignores the religious context of Mesoamerican sacrifice and symbolic blood offerings, which often occurred without cannibalism. Many of the Aztec sacrificial events, which elaborated and embellished these prior customs, were dedicatory, carried out as thanksgiving rituals, and involved no cannibalism.

It is doubtful that the population of prehispanic Mexico was protein- or fat-deficient. In combination, the dietary staples of maize and beans provide a complete protein source. Such staples were sent in tribute to Tenochtitlan from surrounding polities and distributed through the market system. In one sixteenth-century account, thirty-two different types of wild fowl, many of which were very fatty, were described as edible; several of these were noted as abundant. Fish and other lake flora and fauna, including high-protein algae that was made into a cheeselike delicacy, were also available, as were domesticated dog and turkey. Many of these foods were stored. Some agricultural fields, like the *chinampas,* produced two or three crops annually.

If, as Harner implies, cannibalism provided the Aztecs with a major source of food, why were most sacrifices held immediately following the major harvest when food was abundant? In addition, why was human flesh restricted to the warriors and elite, groups likely to have the most to eat anyway? During Cortés' long siege of Tenochtitlan, the inhabitants were starving, eating almost anything, even adobe and leather. Yet human bodies lay all around, untouched.

Aztec human sacrifice is more convincingly interpreted in its historical and symbolic context. The Aztec traditions are connected with earlier Mesoamerican customs of blood-letting, dedicatory offerings, and the sacrifice of war captives in ritual events. The embellishment of the practice of human sacrifice by the Aztecs would seem to be associated with their distinctly militaristic background. According to Aztec ideology, they were the people chosen to nourish the deities through human sacrifice, as a hedge against uncertainty and to maintain order in the universe. As sacrificial victims were frequently (though not exclusively) prisoners or slaves, these beliefs may have motivated and fanaticized the Aztec military. The Aztecs conducted several kinds of sacrificial rituals — to bring rain, to commemorate temples, and as a kind of thanksgiving. Large sacrificial events also must have conveyed a powerful message about the strength and sanctity of Tenochtitlan to individuals both inside and outside the city.

EPILOG
THE END OF PREHISPANIC CIVILIZATIONS IN MEXICO

The legacy of Middle America's past

People first set foot in Mesoamerica approximately 10,000 to 15,000 years ago. From their arrival until A.D. 1519, when the Spanish arrived, Mesoamerican societies developed and diversified independently of contacts with non-native peoples. Over that period, a Mesoamerican world evolved, composed of diverse groups and polities connected through trade, warfare, intermarriage, and other long-distance contacts and communication. These peoples shared a common cultural background that was distinctively Mesoamerican.

The study of ancient Mesoamerica enables archaeologists to examine both agricultural origins and the rise and fall of early civilizations. It also permits the investigation of a large macroregion that, unlike portions of the Old World, was never politically controlled by a single empire. Even the powerful Aztec armies were unable to defeat and consolidate the nearby peoples of Tlaxcala or the west Mexican Tarrascans. While long-term change in Mesoamerica did not follow the same exact course in Mesopotamia and China (Chapter Nine), Europe (Chapter Ten), or even neighboring South America (Chapter Eight), there are numerous features of these sequences of change and transition that can be compared and analyzed.

The prehistory of Mesoamerica is documented by a variety of sources of information, including both indigenous and sixteenth-century Spanish texts and archaeological studies. The Mesoamerican highlands are well suited to archaeological surveys. In the valleys of Tehuacán, Mexico, and Oaxaca, as well as in several other highland Mesoamerican zones, the regional perspective from such surveys supplements the more specific findings from careful excavations at individual sites. We have learned that the size and number of prehispanic settlements did not increase at a uniform rate during the prehispanic era, and that the pattern of population change was somewhat different in each of the regions.

The diversity of available information has spurred long-term research programs in Mesoamerica. These multidisciplinary projects, such as the one implemented in Tehuacán by Richard MacNeish or by Kent Flannery in the Valley of Oaxaca, have greatly expanded our knowledge of the past in this part of the world. Just as modern societies operate at a variety of spatial scales, from the individual to the household, to the community, to the region and beyond, so, too, did ancient peoples. It is not surprising that we get a more complete picture of past human behavior and its complexity when we look at several spatial scales simultaneously.

The art and architectural ruins of ancient Mesoamerican societies have captured attention for centuries. Now, as we collect more information about their makers, scholars have become fascinated with economies, statecraft, religious systems, and other aspects of their lifeways. The diversity of Mesoamerican cities is truly astounding in size and function. Thus Mesoamerica has become a fruitful domain for the study of early urbanism and the processes associated with the rise of ancient cities. Some Mesoamerican cities, like Teotihuacan, were compact and laid out on a grid plan. Others were dispersed and positioned according to local topography, as in the Maya region during the Classic period. In Classic Maya cities and at Monte Albán, for example, the major thoroughfares were not planned to be strictly perpendicular to one another. Residential architecture also was far from uniform at major Mesoamerican cities. Craft manufacturing was central to ancient Teotihuacan, yet it played a smaller role in most other cities. Although exchange was an integrative mechanism that linked most Mesoamerican cities with their hinterlands, marketing may have had an especially crucial role at Tenochtitlan.

Even though exchange and economic production helped integrate the landscape, the volume and magnitude of trade was almost certainly limited by prehispanic transport. One can only marvel at the mechanisms that allowed for the organization of tens (and even hundreds) of thousands of people. The longevity of cities like Teotihuacan or rain forest Tikal point to the effectiveness of the kin, ceremonial, and stately ties that integrated Mesoamerican polities. In prehispanic Mesoamerica, such features as the calendar, the ballgame, symbolic and written symbols, sacrificial (blood) rituals, public architectural conventions, and astronomical knowledge were all part of key informational systems that were shared and communicated primarily by the elite, and seemingly central to the maintenance of both their position and societal continuity.

Although the autonomy of ancient Mesoamerican societies ended in the sixteenth century with the arrival of the Spaniards, the ancestry and culture of the indigenous people has in part survived, helping to meld the contemporary lifeways of Mexico and Central America. The foods, craftsmanship, music, religion, and languages of these areas owe much to their prehispanic heritage. The demise of Aztec society, as well as that of their allies and enemies, has remarkable parallels to similar events further south. In the northwestern quadrant of South America, the sixteenth-century Spanish clashed with a powerful indigenous Andean society, the Inca. Inca administration also had come to dominate a large cultural area, even bigger than that dominated by the Aztec. But they, too, were conquered by the arriving *conquistadores*. In the next chapter, we examine these Andean societies and the series of processes and events that culminated in the empire of the Inca.

> *I'm not particularly interested in ancient objects. This seemingly heretical statement for an archaeologist usually takes aback friends who believe that the best way to entertain me is to show me the local museum. On more than one occasion, I have had to explain that beautiful Classic Maya vases or finely carved jade pendants hold less interest to me — and to many of my colleagues — than the scientific investigation of ideas about why and how ancient cultures like the Maya developed.*
>
> J. A. Sabloff (1990)

SUGGESTED READINGS

Adams, Richard E. W. 1991. *Prehistoric Mesoamerica,* rev. ed. Norman: University of Oklahoma Press. A current overview of Mesoamerican cultural history.

Berdan, Francis. 1982. *The Aztecs of central Mexico: An imperial society.* New York: Holt, Rinehart & Winston. A valuable synthesis of Aztec life and society.

Blanton, Richard E., Stephen A. Kowalewski, Gary Feinman, and Jill Appel. 1981. *Ancient Mesoamerica: A comparison of change in three regions.* Cambridge: Cambridge University Press. An interpretive analysis of long-term change in three important Mesoamerican regions.

Flannery, Kent V., ed. 1976. *The early Mesoamerican village.* New York: Academic Press. A humorous, yet highly instructive, volume on ancient Mesoamerica that illustrates how archaeology should proceed at various scales of analysis to interpret the past.

Flannery, Kent V., and Joyce Marcus, eds. 1983. *The cloud people: Divergent evolution of the Zapotec and Mixtec civilizations.* New York: Academic Press. The synthetic overview for prehispanic Oaxaca.

Henderson, John S. 1981. *The world of the ancient Maya.* Ithaca, NY: Cornell University Press. A basic, easily readable text on the ancient Maya.

Morley, Sylvanus G., George W. Brainerd, and Robert J. Sharer. 1983. *The ancient Maya,* 4th ed. Palo Alto, CA: Stanford University Press. The most recent revision of a classic text on the Maya. The book is encyclopedic in its coverage and includes an ample bibliography.

SOUTH AMERICA: THE INCA AND THEIR PREDECESSORS

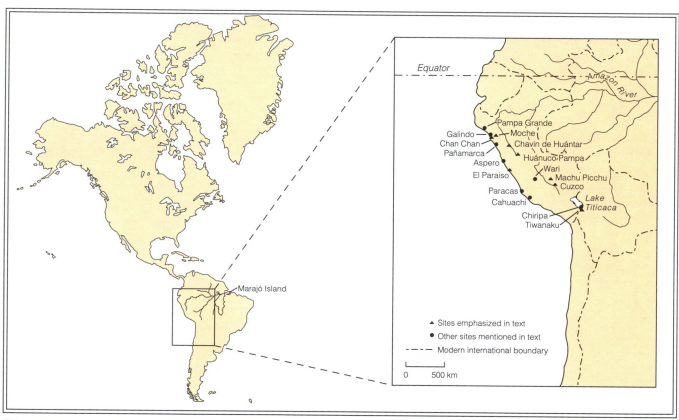

Marajó Island

Equator

Amazon River

Pampa Grande
Galindo
Moche
Chan Chan
Chavin de Huántar
Pañamarca
Huánuco Pampa
Aspero
Wari
El Paraíso
Machu Picchu
Cuzco
Paracas
Cahuachi
Lake Titicaca
Chiripa
Tiwanaku

▲ Sites emphasized in text
● Other sites mentioned in text
--- Modern international boundary

0   500 km

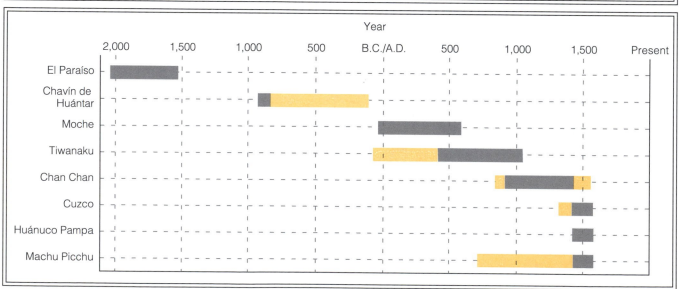

Year

| | 2,000 | 1,500 | 1,000 | 500 | B.C./A.D. | 500 | 1,000 | 1,500 | Present |

El Paraíso
Chavín de Huántar
Moche
Tiwanaku
Chan Chan
Cuzco
Huánuco Pampa
Machu Picchu

PREHISPANIC SOUTH AMERICA

Early coastal villages and large mountain states

When Christopher Columbus left Spain on the voyage that brought him to America, the largest empire in the world was Tawantinsuyu, the Inca empire. Much greater in size than any fifteenth- or twentieth-century European state, Tawantinsuyu ("land of four quarters") stretched over 984,000 sq km (380,000 sq mi) (about the combined size of Washington, Oregon, Idaho, and Montana). The Inca controlled the most extensive political domain that ever has existed in the Southern Hemisphere. Cuzco, the capital of the realm, governed roughly eighty provinces that sprawled from Columbia in the north across the Andean highlands of Argentina, Bolivia, Peru, and Ecuador to Chile in the south.

From the Pacific Ocean, the Andes Mountains rise so abruptly that a mere sliver of flat coastal land separates the high mountains from the water. This coastal strip is one of the world's driest deserts. In the high Andes, where peaks rise to more than 6100 m (20,000 ft) above sea level (the highest peaks in North or South America), humans occupied the relatively flat basins and valleys, as well as the high grassland plateaus (*punas*). The eastern side of the mountains, called the *montaña*, is wet and heavily vegetated. Further east lies the enormous drainage basin of the Amazon, composed of tropical forests and savannas. Feathers and many tropical plants were brought from the forest into the Andean and coastal zones.

Our focus in this chapter is Andean South America. The people of the Amazon rain forests and savannas also had a unique and important prehistory as well. Yet because of the impenetrability of the lush environment, archaeologists and ethnohistorians still know much less about the latter area than about the more accessible coastal and mountain zones.

In 1948 and 1949, Betty Meggers and Clifford Evans, of the Smithsonian Institution, began preliminary investigations on Marajó Island at the mouth of the Amazon River. On this large island, 39,000 sq km (15,000 sq mi), huge earthworks were found, which Meggers and Evans intrepreted as the remnants of a complex society that had moved to the island from the Andes only to meet a rapid demise. At the time, this interpretation was well-reasoned because the large scale of the earthworks was unexpected, given their absence in small, egalitarian, contemporary Amazonian Indian villages. Recent archaeological work on Marajó Island by Anna Roosevelt, of the Field Museum of Natural History, and her colleagues has revised our perspective on Marajoara origins. They have illustrated the numerous continuities between modern Amazonian people and the earlier Marajoara occupation, and documented a more than 1000-year habitation sequence (400 B.C. to 1300 A.D.) on the island. For example, Roosevelt found large, globular burial urns that were painted to represent crouching humans, decorated with multicolored, geometric patterns similar to the abstract drug visions illustrated by contemporary Amazonians. Marajoara art also has antecedents in earlier lowland styles, and the painting method is Amazonian (not Andean) in character. The physical affiliation of Marajoara skeletons is closer to Amazonian than to Andean people.

At the same time, reanalysis of written accounts of sixteenth-century Spanish penetration into the Amazon has led researchers to argue that many of the late prehistoric populations of this region may have been more hierarchically organized and densely distributed than Amazonian populations today. Differences, such as the cessation of inherited positions of leadership, between pre-Columbian inhabitants and contemporary groups may owe much to the diseases and excesses brought by the Europeans.

Western South America contained the continent's first agricultural settlements (e.g., Guitarrero Cave) as well as its earliest sedentary communities. We examine the prehispanic peoples of this area, beginning with the early site of El Paraíso, a sedentary coastal community dating prior to 2000 B.C., and concluding with the late prehispanic Inca sites of Cuzco, Huánuco Pampa, and Machu Picchu.

The prehistory of this part of South America is, in a general way, similar to that of Mesoamerica. In both areas, the earliest experiments with food production preceded the transition to sedentary village life. In South America, the first villages date prior to 3500 B.C., much earlier than in Mesoamerica. In both regions, however, these first sedentary communities were situated on the coast. Soon thereafter, greater social differences and the first positions of leadership become evident in the archaeological record. In Mesoamerica, these changes occurred along with the development of an interregional style, the Olmec Horizon, represented in exotic and highly crafted items found in both the highlands and the lowlands. Between 900 and 200 B.C., a similar phenomenon, the Chavín style, was shared from the edges of the Amazon to the Pacific Coast. This style is named for the carvings found on a temple in the uplands of central Peru at Chavín de Huántar. In Peru, however, the spread of the Chavín style appears to postdate the construction of truly monumental public architecture, and the emergence of social differences at coastal sites that were contemporary with earlier El Paraíso.

In South America, the last centuries B.C. were marked by the rise of major centers that became the core of states administering regional populations. We discuss Moche, on the north coast, and refer to the fantastic line drawings constructed by the Nazca in the south. Later Tiwanaku, a giant economic and religious center near the southern end of Lake Titicaca in Bolivia, began to incorporate larger areas outside its local region.

As with the Aztecs in the highlands of central Mexico, the end of the prehispanic era in South America was characterized by a powerful people, the Inca, whose rulers exacted tribute from a wide domain. Yet this much larger South American empire had clearer imperial predecessors, such as the Tiwanaku polity and the Chimú kingdom. After A.D. 1000, the latter, which was centered on the north coast at Chan Chan, consolidated a large, primarily coastal domain. This political sphere was eventually engulfed by the expansive Inca, who conquered the Chimú between A.D. 1462 and 1470. We examine the nature and organization of this New World empire by looking at Cuzco, the Inca capital, the famous high mountain settlement of Machu Picchu, and the provincial administrative center of Huánaco Pampa.

While parallels can be drawn between the long prehispanic sequences in Mexico and Peru, there also were important differences. Most of the major Peruvian centers were shorter-lived than Mesoamerican sites, like San José Mogote, Monte Albán, and Teotihuacan, which were inhabited almost continuously for a millennium or more. The Andean world also seems to have lacked a core region, like the Basin of Mexico, which dominated the larger landscape for much of the prehispanic era. In South America, the balance of power seems to have shifted repeatedly between the Pacific Coast and the rugged uplands.

Animal domestication was more important in South America, where a variety of camelids, in addition to guinea pigs, were tamed. Since only the turkey, the dog, and the honeybee were domesticated in Mesoamerica, long-distance land transport was conducted entirely by human bearers. In South America, the llama (a camelid), used also for wool and meat, served as a pack animal for loads up to 45 kg (100 lb), making land transportation considerably less costly than it was in Mesoamerica. Llamas, like the more efficient Old World beasts of burden, subsist on grasses and other foods that humans cannot digest.

The Inca built and maintained an extensive, often paved road system, with suspension cables, stone bridges, and a system of relay runners, that crossed almost the entire empire and was unmatched in Mesoamerica. Alternatively, water crafts, including giant trading canoes, were more developed in Middle America.

In Mesoamerica, a writing system developed more than 2000 years ago, diversifying into several systems, particularly that of the Maya, and becoming more complex (with relatively long texts). In contrast, no archaeological evidence for prehispanic Andean writing has been found to date. The Inca did possess an ingenious numerical apparatus, the **quipu** ("knot"), which was composed of a main horizontal rope from which a series of smaller cords hung. The *quipu* was used to record numbers by tying knots at various intervals on the strings, the knots farthest from the main string representing the smallest numbers. Although the *quipu* makes an excellent system for recording numbers, it would have been somewhat more cumbersome to use in calculations. Nevertheless, even without a system of writing, the Inca were able to establish a larger and better-integrated political system than ever existed in prehispanic Mesoamerica.

Although the written words left by the Maya and other Mesoamerican peoples are absent in the Andes, archaeologists working along the arid coast of Peru have the advantage of a quality of preservation unknown almost anywhere else. Standing adobe architecture frequently sits almost unscathed by the elements for centuries, even millennia. The recovery of large woven textiles is not unusual. Preservation can be so good that even fingernail clippings and human hair were found by Joyce Marcus using careful excavation procedures at coastal Cerro Azul, a site that postdates A.D. 1100. Marcus also found a series of mummified burials at Cerro Azul. While the men generally were buried with fishing nets or slings (for hunting), the women were interred with an array of different weaving implements (including camelid bone tools, bobbins made of thorn, needles, and balls of various colored yarns).

South America provides a second fascinating area for studying the emergence of an indigenous civilization. Only through archaeology can we hope to discover the remarkable similarities — as well as the all-important differences — that characterized these long cultural processes in various regions of the globe.

EL PARAÍSO

*An early sedentary village on
the coast of Peru*

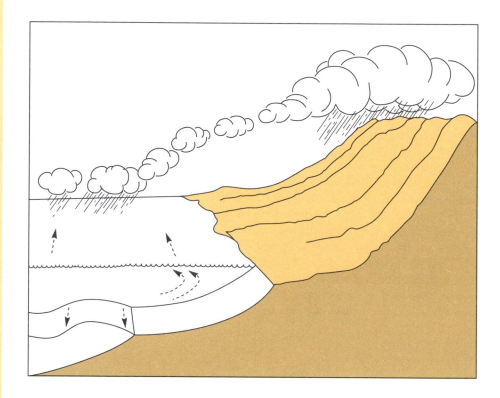

The waters off the west coast of Peru are one of the world's richest fishing areas. A complex mixing of ocean currents provides an extraordinary source of marine foods. The shore of these abundant waters, however, is one of the world's driest deserts. The same cold waters that foster rich plankton and fish life also inhibit rainfall on the coast. This coastal zone, stretching from the shoreline to the foothills of the Andes, only rarely receives measurable quantities of precipitation. Short-lived torrential downpours occur only once or twice a decade. Streams carrying the snowmelt and rainfall from the Andes provide most of the surface water, cross-cutting the bleak coastal desert in an east-west direction. These rivers and streams are in essence isolated, verdant pockets along the arid coastline.

The desert coast of central Peru was first settled after 7000 B.C. by mobile groups who exploited a wide range of ecological zones. The Pacific Ocean was a source of fish and shellfish; while deer, small mammals, and birds were hunted and wild plants collected in the coastal river valleys. The dry foothills of the western Andes become virtual oases of scattered communities of fog vegetation (**lomas**) between June and October (winter in the Southern Hemisphere). Here the early inhabitants ate deer and the edible seeds of grasses or sagelike plants. Grinding stones necessary for the preparation of these plants have been found in these areas.

After 5000 B.C., these coastal peoples relied increasingly on marine and plant products, including cultivated squash and tubers that had been introduced to the

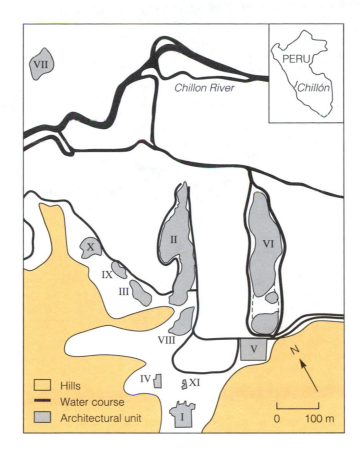

desert coast from the highlands. Settlements clustered closer to the ocean than they had previously, and Peru's first permanent, year-round villages were established shortly after 4000 B.C., more than 1000 years before the first Peruvian evidence for pottery. These early villagers wove nets of cotton; net fragments, cotton twine, cordage pieces, and various remnants of cotton plants have been recovered from dry midden deposits at the early oceanside sites.

Around 2000 B.C., several larger settlements were established. El Paraíso (el'-par-a-ease'o), the most extensive of these preceramic settlements, was situated about 2 km (1.2 mi) from the coast along a permanent stream, next to a wide area of irrigable land. El Paraíso contains eight or nine large stone structures that, in total, cover over 58 ha (140 acres). The structures range in size from three or four rooms to massive complexes 300 m (980 ft) long by 100 m (325 ft) wide. The site represents one of the New World's earliest examples of monumental construction and nucleated population.

Although El Paraíso has been known to archaeologists for decades, it was not excavated until 1965 by Frederic Engel. The first excavations indicated an early preceramic date and revealed that one of the stone structures (Unit I) consisted of a series of rectangular rooms, courts, and passageways delineated by walls of 1.5 to 2.5 m in height (5 to 8 feet). The walls were built of large stone blocks cemented together with clay. The blocks also were faced with a mud plaster painted with black, red, ochre, and white. The compound was filled in with rock rubble and then rebuilt several times during the occupation of the site. Recent excavations by Jeffrey Quilter, of Ripon College, and his colleagues, have confirmed that two of the other compounds also were preceramic. Radiocarbon dates from the three compounds also indicate a short, possibly 300-year contemporaneous occupation that ended by 1500 B.C.

Despite the recent findings, many questions remain. How were these masonry compounds utilized? Although some of the rooms in Unit I contain possible offerings and may have been used for ceremonies, the diversity of artifacts (grinding stones, a wooden sling, stone and wooden tools) from the compound

The north face of Unit I at El Paraíso.

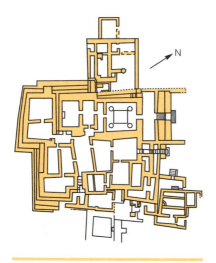

Plan of Unit I, a partially restored architectural complex at El Paraíso.

suggests it was not simply a religious structure. Quilter found domesticated cotton, wool, and needles in one room in Unit II, suggesting that this area may have been used for making textiles. Large quantities of bird **guano**, a bird offering, and colorful bird feathers also were found in the same room, likely evidence for the ancient practice of weaving colored feathers into high-status cloths. Other cotton was woven into the nets and lines that were used in fishing. Although there is little consensus about the kind of socio-political organization at El Paraíso, large quantities of labor clearly were required to quarry and shape the stone blocks used to build the compounds. Additional co-ordination, planning, and muscle power were needed to repeatedly rebuild the structures.

Yet the biggest mystery concerns the diet of the inhabitants of El Paraíso and the other preceramic inhabitants of coastal Peru. In 1975, Michael Moseley, of the University of Florida, proposed that the foundations of later Andean civilization were established during the preceramic era at such places as El Paraíso. He believed the inhabitants depended largely on marine foods. Although no one disputes the important role of foods from the sea (shellfish, marine mammals, and fish), various plants, including the starchy trop-ical tubers (jiquima and achira), culti-vated common beans and lima beans, and domesticated chile pepper, gourds, and squash, have all been recoved at El Pa-raíso, along with the remains of birds and small quantities of land mammals. More than 90% of the faunal remains identified by Quilter and his team belonged to bony fish and mollusks. However, the site's lo-cation, adjacent to an unusually large patch of arable land near the mouth of the Chillon River and 2 km (1.2 mi) from the Pacific, also indicates a terrestrial compo-nent important to the preceramic econ-omy (cotton production) and diet. This inference is supported by the analysis of ten human coprolites from El Paraíso, which revealed that both squash and a variety of wild plant foods (including grasses, seeds, and tree fruits) comprised a significant portion of the human diet.

Many questions remain to be an-swered about the early inhabitants of El Paraíso. Yet there is no doubt that the ar-chaeological work at this site and others along the dry Pacific Coast has revolution-ized our knowledge of ancient South America and its early sedentary begin-nings, thousands of years ago.

In 1975, Michael Moseley proposed that complex societies with monumental architecture emerged during the preceramic period on the Pacific Coast of South America. Subsistence activities at these sites appears to have focused on marine resources. Moseley intended to refute "the widely accepted maxim that only an agricultural economy can support the foundations of civilization." He bolstered his argument (called the Maritime Hypothesis) by noting the abundance of shellfish middens and fishing nets at many coastal settlements, particularly at several sites that were closer to the coast and somewhat earlier in time than El Paraíso.

Although there is little doubt that marine foods were an essential component in the diet of the prehispanic coastal dwellers, several recent studies have suggested that both wild and agricultural plants also were a significant part of ancient Peruvian subsistence. Root and seed crops have been recovered in relatively small quantities in midden deposits at El Paraíso, as well as at other preceramic coastal sites. However, the quantity of plant remains, compared to the abundance of shell, may not provide an accurate reflection of the relative importance of these foods in the ancient diet. Plant remains generally do not preserve in the archaeological record nearly as well as harder materials, such as mollusk shell. Poor preservation is a particular problem for detecting the root crops that were important in ancient Peru, because they lack the harder parts that make seed crops somewhat easier to find. The problems of preservation were aggravated in many early coastal excavations where fine screening and other meticulous recovery techniques were not employed.

Several critics of the Maritime Hypothesis have noted that a subsistence regime largely dependent on the abundant marine resources of the Peruvian Pacific would have left the coastal inhabitants at the mercy of the warm countercurrents that periodically disrupt the bounty of the ocean environment. Five to ten times each century, a countercurrent, referred to as **El Niño** ("the Christ Child") moves in from the north soon after Christmas, altering the normal patterns of water temperature, flow, and salinity, and diminishing the availability of nutrients. El Niños generally last two to twelve months and cause severe disturbances to marine life. Bountiful schools of fish and flocks of sea birds either migrate or die. Because of the irregularity of these maritime disruptions and the difficulty of storing large quantities of marine products in a warm climate, it seems likely that plant foods provided a significant portion of the ancient diet. In fact, this suggestion has been supported by Jeffrey Quilter's recovery at El Paraíso of a diversity of wild and domesticated plant foods, through both coprolite analysis and the sifting of excavated trash deposits through ¼-inch hardware cloth and ¹⁄₁₆-inch mesh. As Quilter recently noted: "It was not simply the adoption of domesticated plants or the importance of seafood that led to complex societies in Peru but the roles of a variety of subsistence and other resources within the context of social interactions" (Quilter and Stocker, 1983, p. 554).

THE MARITIME HYPOTHESIS

Preceramic subsistence on the Pacific Coast

CHAVÍN DE HUÁNTAR

An early Andean center

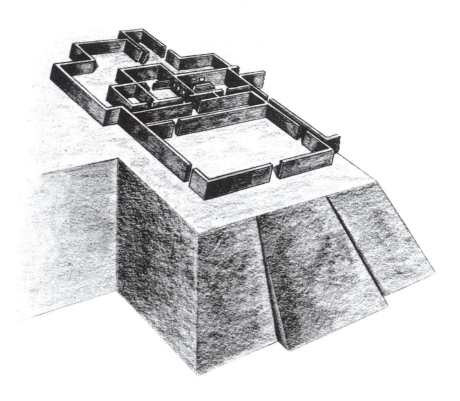

The Peruvian coast, homeland for such late prehispanic polities as the Nazca, Moche, and Chimú, also gave rise (prior to 2000 B.C.) to the first complex political systems in western South America. Centralized polities, which were focused on large sites that contained monumental architecture, including ceremonial mounds and plazas, developed in a number of valleys along the north and central coasts.

Excavations at the coastal site of Aspero by Robert Feldman, of the Field Museum of Natural History, have revealed interconnected rooms of various sizes that were divided by stone walls. The outer rooms were usually the largest and had the widest doorways. The inner rooms, which contained cached artifacts and wall niches, were small. These central rooms, the walls of which were elaborately deco-rated, could be entered only by winding through the more open larger rooms and then stepping through narrow entryways. Thus access to the inner cores of these nonresidential structures probably was restricted to a small segment of the population.

As with many ancient Native American ceremonial structures, these multi-room compounds were repeatedly re-floored and rebuilt. In some instances, old rooms were filled with **shicra** (meshed bags containing rocks) to provide a new base for further reconstruction. At about the same time, early villages in the highlands contained more modest nonres-idential structures, usually one-room, free-standing buildings. The highland structures included ceremonial hearths, wall niches, and colored plaster, features also found in the coastal compounds. Some communication and exchange of foods, shells, and colored stones occurred between the upland and coastal environments, although for more than a millennium the coast contained the larger, more socially differentiated polities.

After 1000 B.C., the balance of power began to shift upward as larger centers developed in the Andean highlands. Perhaps the best known of these sites is Chavín de Huántar (cha-veen′day-whan′-tar), situated at the confluence of two rivers, more than 3000 m (10,000 ft) above sea level in what is today a typical Peruvian valley. The site is surrounded by steep slopes, including the snow-capped Cordillera Blanca, whose highest peaks rise above 5500 m (18,000 ft).

In the early years of the Colonial era, Spanish chroniclers noted the grandeur of the ruins and the beautiful decoration visible in the finely cut stones at Chavín de Huántar. Yet the historical placement of the ruins and their importance to Andean prehistory only were established about fifty years ago through the works of the late Peruvian archaeologist Julio Tello. Tello correctly recognized the important artistic similarities between the stone carvings at Chavín de Huántar and the decorative items of pottery, stone, and metal found at other sites in the highlands and on the coast. These similar motifs define a stylistic pattern that has become known as the Chavín Horizon. Typically, Chavín carvings interweave figures that combine the natural features of people, snakes, jaguars, **caymans** (alligators), and birds with intricate geometric and curvilinear designs.

Recent radiocarbon dates from Chavín de Huántar by Richard Burger, of Yale University, place the major occupation of the site between 850 and 200 B.C. It appears that construction of the civic-ceremonial architecture began early in the occupation but did not reach its largest (over 40 ha, or 100 acres) and most monumental extent until after 390 B.C. By 200 B.C., the central core of the site included a complex of rectangular, stone masonry platforms covering an area greater than 4000 sq m (about 1 acre). Although the height of this construction is difficult to assess because the main structures were on a slope, the largest platform (the Castillo, or New Temple) rises about 13 m (45 ft) above the surrounding terrace.

The Castillo platform was not solid masonry, but was composed of three superimposed levels of small, interlocking galleries and rooms, which were covered by flat slabs and separated by adobe and stone walls. The interior walls were sometimes painted, and the inside rooms were ventilated by a complex network of shafts. The platform exterior was faced with dressed granite, and at one time these outer walls were adorned with sculpted human and animal heads.

The so-called Old Temple at Chavín was U-shaped and consisted of a main building with two wings that enclosed three sides of a rectangular plaza. Deep inside the Old Temple stands a carved, prismlike shaft of white granite. This 4-m (13 ft) high pillar, named the Great Image or the Lanzón, was pointed at both ends and was fastened to both the floor and the ceiling of the interior gallery in which it stood. Each side of the Great Image was

Finely carved stone from Chavín de Huántar.

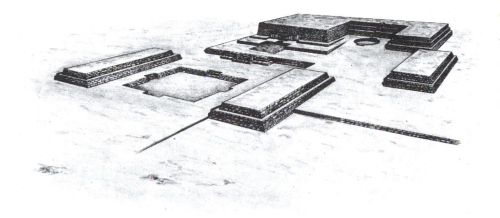

An artist's reconstruction of the Temple of Chavín. The Old Temple is in the upper right; the New Temple and its sunken plaza complex are at left and center. The sunken plaza measures approximately 500 by 500 m.

carved in bas-relief, depicting a standing human figure with feline teeth and nostrils. The anthropomorphic figure was wearing earplugs, a necklace, and a belt that contained serpent-jaguar faces. The latter images also adorned the upper portion of the monolith, as a kind of headpiece perched on the serpent hair of the main figure. The Great Image was just one of a number of large stelae found at the site.

By the last centuries of the Early Horizon (900 to 200 B.C.), several thousand people lived at Chavín de Huántar, with residential areas surrounding the ceremonial complex. In size and scale of construction, the site far surpassed any other occupation in the narrow Mosna Valley in which it was situated. During this period, Chavín de Huántar also became much more interconnected with large settlements in other highlands, as well as on the coast. Although some archaeologists have proposed that the sharing of the Chavín style reflects some kind of broad, centralized religious or economic control, this now seems highly improbable. Rather, this wide distribution of certain ideological and stylistic conventions may mark an intensified level of exchange, communication, and militaristic competition between highland and coastal settlements. In certain ways, the Chavín Horizon is similar to the Olmec phenomenon in Mesoamerica, although in contrast to the latter, sociopolitical differences were present in certain South American polities for centuries prior to the spread of the Chavín style.

The Lanzón in the Old Temple of Chavín.

THE TEXTILES OF PARACAS

Clues to visual communication in ancient South America

A close-up view of a Paracas mantle with the embroidered image of an elite figure and the Ecstatic Shaman (lower right).

In ancient Peru, textiles were an important means of visual communication. The use of woven cloth to convey ritual images is perhaps best exemplified on the south coast of Peru by the Paracas culture (about 600 to 150 B.C.). Paracas elite wore lavish costumes of mantles, ponchos, skirts, tunics, loincloths, and woven headgear. Even after death, these individuals were covered with many fine weavings. On the dry south coast, careful excavations have uncovered mummified burials still wrapped with brightly colored, embroidered ritual cloths, providing a vivid picture of the symbolic life of these ancient Peruvians.

Although the Paracas textiles have their own distinctive style, they do share certain artistic features with contemporary Chavín cloths. Both portray anthropomorphic and composite zoomorphic figures. Yet on the brightly colored Paracas textiles, these figures have a less somber presence than do the supernatural creatures depicted in stone and pottery at Chavín de Huántar.

One of the most frequent images found on the Paracas textiles is a human figure called the Ecstatic Shaman. Arched sharply backward with outstretched arms, head askew, and flailing hair, these figures seem frozen in the midst of rapid movement, perhaps magical flight. The symbolism of the long, untamed hair may have greater significance than simply conveying action, because in the Paracas textiles only these figures and trophy heads are depicted with unbound locks. The Spanish chroniclers tell us that among the later Inca long hair was considered an important attribute for shamans and certain sorcerors.

The Paracas textiles provide a dramatic record of ancient Peruvian weaving skills. Copper and gold ornaments attest to the metallurgical proficiency of other South American peoples during the same period. Small copper tools and ornaments have been recovered in northern Bolivia, where the cold metal was worked by hammering and shaping. In the north, gold was made into earspools, as well as nose, chest, and other head adornments. The latter were crafted by working the metal into thin sheets and then hammering it over a mold, a process referred to as **repoussé**. These gold ornaments, which also frequently were soldered or welded, often bore the composite figures characteristic of the Chavín Horizon.

MOCHE

Giant pyramids on Peru's north coast

The end of the Chavín phenomenon marked the advent of the First Intermediate period (200 B.C. to A.D. 600), an era that for the most part was characterized by the development of many small local polities with their associated distinct regional ceramic traditions. Around the time of Christ, the site of Moche (mo'chay) was established about 6 km (3.5 mi) from the ocean near the modern city of Trujillo, in the Moche Valley, on the north coast of Peru. The site was situated 600 m (2000 ft) from the Moche River, close to the center of the Moche Valley, and up against Cerro Blanco, a large hill that rises abruptly to a height more than 500 m (1650 ft) above sea level. In its day, Moche was the largest settlement on the north coast of Peru. Unlike most other First Intermediate period centers, it controlled not only the rest of the Moche Valley but also other adjacent coastal valleys for centuries.

The Moche site is dominated by two major pyramids, or **huacas,** the Huaca del Sol and the Huaca de la Luna. The two structures are separated by a 500-m (1650-ft) wide plaza or level area. The Huaca del Sol towers 40 m (130 ft) above the surrounding plain and measures at least 340 by 160 m (1100 by 525 ft, larger than a city block). It was one of the largest, if not the most massive, solid adobe structure ever built in the New World. The Huaca de la Luna, which rests on the lower slopes of Cerro Blanco, is a 30-m (100-ft) high complex of platforms, walls, and courtyards. Made of adobe, it was formed by three mounds connected by courts, and was constructed in at least three stages.

The two pyramids were used differently. Activities on top of the Huaca del Sol were associated with the accumulation of domestic refuse, while the summit of the Huaca de la Luna was swept clean, and the uppermost structures were decorated with painted murals. The murals were found in 1899 by the late archaeologist Max Uhle, who also discovered a cemetery area between the two pyramids.

More recently, Michael Moseley and his associates have studied the adobe bricks from the two *huacas,* and found more than 100 different symbols impressed on their top surfaces. Because these symbols were applied during production, Moseley reasoned that they were makers' marks, used to distinguish the bricks manufactured by different groups. The two *huacas,* which required hundreds of millions of adobe bricks, were constructed segmentally, in similar, discrete rectangular units composed of stacked bricks. Moseley found that these adobe segments, or columns, generally included only bricks marked by a single maker's symbol. While some symbols marked the bricks in numerous construction segments, others appeared less frequently. Thus Moseley suggested that segments of the two pyramids were built by groups of associated laborers, with some work parties involved in the construction more often than others. The use of conscripted laborers to complete discrete organizational tasks — the **mit'a system** — was a familiar means of tribute employed more than a millennium later by the Inca state.

By A.D. 300 to 400, Moche influence dominated not only the larger Chicama

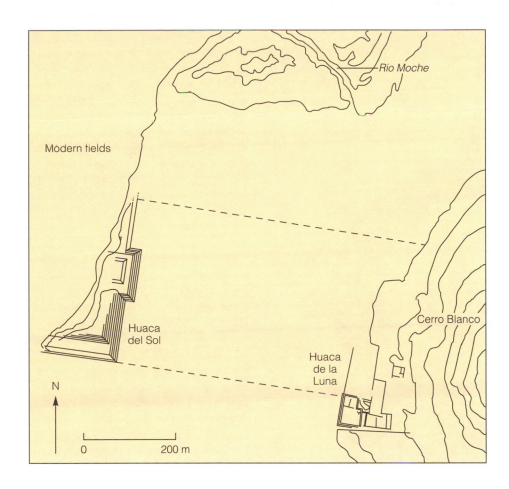

The plan of Moche.

Huaca del Sol.

A Moche stirrup-spout jar with a scene of a ruler receiving a messenger.

approach the Huaca del Sol in size, each was generally the largest structure of its time in its region, and each was associated with Moche pottery or mural art. Further south in the Nepeña Valley, Moche pottery appeared somewhat later but is limited to settlements in a small area around the site of Pañamarca, a large community that may have guarded the southern limits of Moche hegemony. In each of these valleys, Moche influence ceased by A.D. 600, at roughly the same time that the Moche site was abandoned.

Prior to the decline, the Moche people grew cotton, maize, potatoes, peanuts, and peppers by irrigating the coastal desert. Complex canal systems were built to transport water to flat desert lands located kilometers away. The building and maintenance of these water-control systems also may have required labor recruitment practices similar to those employed in the building of the *huacas*. Fishing and the hunting of sea mammals provided important dietary resources. To date, large public food storage complexes, similar to those associated with the later Chimú and Inca polities, have not been found at Moche.

Moche society was highly stratified. There were great, and probably inherited, differences in the access to wealth and power. Marked disparities have been noted in the quantity and quality of grave goods found with burials. Graves that were incorporated into or found near the two Moche pyramids tended to be more lavish. Status variation also can be inferred from variability in domestic architecture. Residential structures that were more solidly built were also architecturally more elaborate than other domestic constructions. The former also tended to be associated with more highly decorated ceramic forms, such as ornate stirrup-spout vessels, and other objects of value, such as copper implements.

Moche artisans are recognized for their accomplishments in metal smithing, making objects of silver and various alloys. They not only used the known techniques of hammering, annealing, embossing, repoussé, and soldering, but began to use turquoise mosiac inlay and simple casting. They also developed **lost wax casting**, in which a hollow cast was made

Valley to the north but also the adjacent Virú and Santa valleys to the south. In Virú and Santa, Moche pottery appeared suddenly and rapidly displaced the local pottery traditions. This ceramic shift coincided with dramatic changes in settlement pattern, in which the local populations congregated at a few, large settlements. In each valley, a sizable monument was built following the architectural canons used in the two Moche Valley *huacas*. Although these pyramids do not

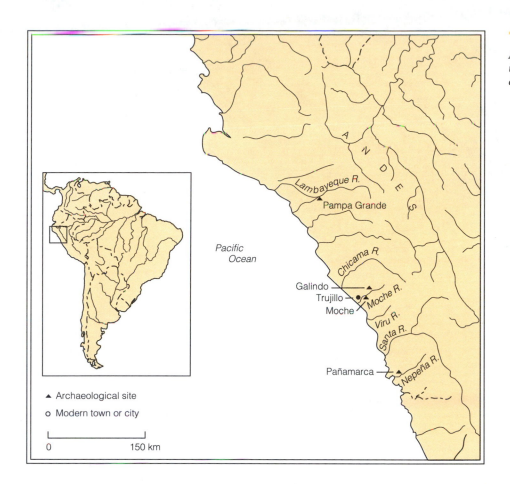

A map of north coastal Peru, showing the location of Moche and other valleys dominated by Moche influence.

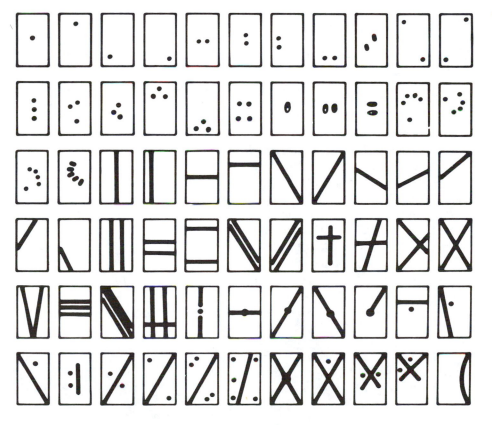

Makers' marks on adobe bricks at Moche.

A representation of the Presentation Theme.

by allowing the molten metal to replace a wax lining in the cast. While the bulk of the metal was used for ornaments, copper ingots were smelted for storage. In addition, the Moche smiths made chisels, spearpoints, digging stick tips, spearthrower hooks, tweezers, and fishhooks.

The most renowned craftsmen were the potters, who, through a wide array of painted ceramic vessel forms and high relief sculptures, have left an unsurpassed portrayal of Moche mythology, ritual, and everyday life. Scenes showing deer being hunted with spearthrowers, as well as fishermen at sea in one-man canoes made of bundles of rushes, are common. Other figures often portrayed include warriors, weavers, prisoners, mothers with children, messengers, and rulers carried in litters or sitting on platforms. Battles also are frequently shown, as are scenes in which victorious soldiers accompany naked prisoners, with ropes tied around their necks. The pottery also provides further evidence for social stratification. In general, men wore a loincloth and a sleeveless shirt beneath a belted tunic that stopped above the knee. However, more important people also wore a large cloth mantle. While all men wore headgear, only a few important individuals had animal skin headdresses decorated with feathers and small pieces of metal.

Moche potters were explicit in their depiction of sexuality. A range of erotic practices was displayed. Some of the more graphic depictions are scenes of masturbation and male–female couples engaged in fellatio. Historical data from the time of Spanish contact indicate that the native people on the north coast of Peru practiced sodomy, and that some of their ceremonies included orgies.

Traditionally, archaeologists and art historians have implied that the Moche ceramicists depicted all aspects of life. Yet recently, Christopher Donnan, of the University of California, Los Angeles, noted that certain scenes, such as the presentation of a goblet to an important person, tended to recur on Moche pottery. This Presentation Theme usually included a series of associated symbolic elements, such as rays surrounding the important individual, a warrior extracting blood from a naked captive, a composite human-feline who often held the captive, animated weapons, and a dog near the rayed figure. Elements of this scene were illustrated individually on other Moche vessels. Donnan proposed that rather than depicting all facets of Moche life, the pottery focused primarily on a few ritually important mythic, or nonsecular, themes. Whatever the specific meaning of these modeled and painted vessels, their visual record, in conjunction with excavations and settlement pattern studies, provides a more complete picture of the Moche than we have for most other ancient South American peoples.

On the south coast of Peru, the Nazca style developed from the earlier Paracas art around 200 B.C. Most Nazca ceramic art, renowned for brilliantly painted **polychrome** vessels with six or seven colors, comes from looted cemeteries, although a few large Nazca sites have been studied more systematically. Most notable is the site of Cahuachi in the Nazca Valley, a large aggregation of adobe platforms, courts, and associated buildings that covers roughly 1 sq km (0.4 sq mi). Cahuachi, with a large 20-m (65-ft) high stepped pyramid, was the largest center of its day in the Nazca region and may have had a role in the dispersal of the Nazca style to other valleys along the south coast.

Perhaps the most astonishing feature in the Nazca region of southern Peru is spread out over several hundred square kilometers (an area three to four times larger than Manhattan Island) in the desert between the Ingenio and Nazca river valleys. More than 1000 years ago, lines, geometric forms, and various figures were drawn on the desert surface by removing dark rock fragments to expose a light-colored underlying soil. The geometric shapes, mostly triangles and trapezoids, alone cover an amazing 360 ha (900 acres). The majority of the several dozen figures, the most famous of the Nazca lines, are animals, although several are plants and others are humanlike. The animals include birds, lizards, and fish, as well as a spider and a monkey. The latter, an inhabitant of the Amazon forest and not of the dry coast, is known to have been important in coastal religion and symbolism.

One of the myths about the Nazca lines is that they must be seen from the air to be appreciated. Recent studies indicate that they were meant to be viewed by people on the ground. Most of the lines and drawings are visible from the desert floor, and they can be seen even more clearly from either the low hills or the huge sand dunes that border the dry plain. While it has been suggested that the desert drawings relate to calendrics and astronomy as well as to ritual or ceremonial pathways, the specific intentions of the original makers remain a matter of debate.

THE NAZCA LINES

Desert images

An aerial photograph of a monkey at Nazca.

TIWANAKU

Bolivia's high altitude ancient city

When the Spanish chroniclers asked the Inca rulers about their origins, they were told that the genesis of the first Inca took place in the part of the realm called Collasuyu. This Inca origin myth may have developed from the belief in the sacred nature of Collasuyu's Lake Titicaca, the largest lake in South America. When King Pachakuti (A.D. 1438–1470) began the Inca imperial conquests, it is no coincidence that he moved first against polities on the shores of Lake Titicaca.

The first sedentary settlements south of Lake Titicaca, in what is today Bolivia, were established during the second millennium B.C. The inhabitants of these early communities on the windswept high-altitude steppe, or **altiplano,** depended on a mixed agrarian economy in a zone that most North Americans would consider to be too elevated for agriculture. In the cold *altiplano,* the early villagers subsisted on a range of domesticated species adapted to the torrential rains of the wet season (November through May), as well as to an extended dry season (April through October). The most important food resources included hardy tuberous plants like the potato, cold-adapted grains like quinoa, and such domesticated camelids as alpaca and llama.

One of the early villages on the southern shores of Lake Titicaca was Chiripa. At the center of this site was a large, artificial mound that was first constructed around 1300 to 1200 B.C. Between 900 and 100 B.C., the mound was expanded, and stone retaining walls were built along three sides. At that time a series of subterranean houses was arranged around the mound. Later a sunken court (measuring roughly 23 m, or 75 ft, per side) was built at the apex of the mound. The Chiripa court, a prototype for later ceremonial precincts at the site of Tiwanaku (tee-wah-nok'u), was embellished with carved plaques and limestone columns.

During the last centuries of the first millennium B.C., a small settlement was founded 20 km (12 mi) south of Lake Titicaca, on the site that was to become the great city of Tiwanaku. Situated 3850 m (12,600 ft) above sea level in a small valley in the Bolivian *altiplano,* at more than twice the altitude of Denver, Colorado, Tiwanaku was one of the highest urban centers ever established. Monumental architectural construction began during the first centuries A.D., when the site rose to importance in the southern basin of Lake Titicaca. Tiwanaku grew to its greatest geographic size (more than 4 sq km, or 1.5 sq mi) and demographic extent (an estimated 25,000 to 40,000 people) around A.D. 400. For the next 600 to 800 years, the city dominated the entire Lake Titicaca region, and ceremonial art styles associated with the capital spread over a far wider area.

The civic-ceremonial core of Tiwanaku was a 20-ha (50-acre) area at the center of the site. This precinct, laid out according to a grid oriented in the cardinal directions, included a series of truly impressive architectural features. Akapana, an enormous stone-faced, stepped platform mound, 200 m (655 ft) on a side and 15 m (50 ft) high, was the most massive construction. It included huge blocks of stone, some of which weighed as much as 10,000 kg (11 tons) and had to be brought over land and water to Tiwanaku

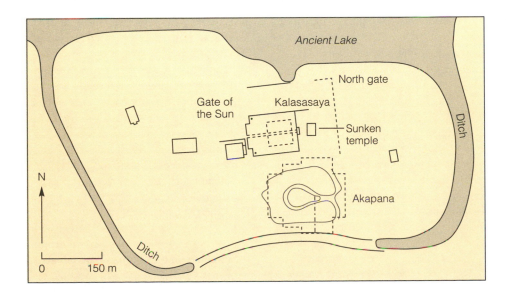

A map of Lake Titicaca and the domain of Tiwanaku.

The plan of the civic-ceremonial core of Tiwanaku.

The Gateway to the Sun.

from quarries more than 100 km (62 mi) away. A second platform, Pumapunku, measured more than 5 m (16 ft) high, with walls 150 m (500 ft) long. Tiwanaku's ceremonial core also included a complex of buildings, with a stone drainage system, that is thought to have been a palace.

The most famous stone sculpture at Tiwanaku, the Gateway of the Sun, was incorporated into a large rectangular precinct known as the Kalasasaya. The Gateway of the Sun, carved from a single huge stone block, portrays a central figure holding two scepters that end in the heads of condors. This individual is flanked by rows of winged attendants who each carry a condor scepter. The central character recalls a figure with two staffs, frequently shown in Chavín iconography. Inside the Kalasasaya were rectangular sunken courts. These architectural features, which may have been temple precincts, have a precedent at earlier Chiripa.

At Tiwanaku, the local *altiplano* economy of camelid pastoralism and the cultivation of hardy grains and tubers was supplemented by the reclamation for agriculture of waterlogged lands adjacent to Lake Titicaca. In addition, Tiwanaku maintained long-distance trade connections, establishing economic colonies in both the Pacific Coast zone to the west and the more tropical forested zones to the east, thereby enabling the Inca to link the diverse and vertically separated reaches of the Andean realm. Warm-region crops, such as maize and coca (a native Andean shrub whose dried leaves are chewed as stimulants), were obtained, as well as birds and medicinal herbs from the east, and obsidian and coastal products, like shell and dried fish, from the west. Trade connections were maintained by large llama caravans, which traveled throughout the Bolivian *altiplano* and to southern Peru and the Chilean coast.

Recently, Alan Kolata of the University of Chicago, has studied agrarian reclamation on the Pampa Koani, an area subject to frequent natural flooding on the southern border of Lake Titicaca. Dur-

ing the first millennium A.D., the water-logged land was reclaimed through the construction of raised fields near the lake, by excavating the heavy Pampa soils on either side of the field surface and mounding the dirt in the center to form an earthen platform elevated above the seasonally high waters. Kolata found that some raised platforms were constructed more elaborately to enhance plant growth. In one field at the lakeshore, the platform consisted of a cobblestone base, covered by a thick clay layer, superceded by three gravel layers and a rich layer of topsoil. In this ingenious structure, the clay, held in place by the cobblestones, prevented the brackish lake water from penetrating into the field from below, while fresh rainwater could percolate down to the roots of the crops from above.

During the latter half of the first millennium A.D., while Tiwanaku was the principal center in the South Andes, the Peruvian highland site of Wari dominated more northerly highland and coastal reaches. Andean archaeologists suggest that while Tiwanaku developed economic ties with its hinterlands, Wari's control over the surrounding area was more militaristic. Wari's regional domination also was shorter-lived, as that site lost its influence and was largely abandoned prior to the tenth century A.D. While the artistic styles associated with Tiwanaku and Wari were similar, both featuring jaguars and raptorial birds, the specific relationship between the two centers remains unknown.

Soon after A.D. 1000, Tiwanaku's domination over the basin of Lake Titicaca began to wane. A number of smaller competing states emerged, each maintaining its own local sphere of influence until the middle of the fifteenth century A.D., when the Titicaca basin was unified under Inca domination. The decline of Tiwanaku coincided with the abandonment of the raised fields of the Pampa Koani. The vast landscape of once-productive fields reverted to pasturage, a function they still serve today. Even the Inca did not reclaim the seasonally waterlogged Pampa lands that had once helped feed the population of Tiwanaku, focusing instead on the rocky mountain slopes above the plain. There, the Inca expanded the region's agricultural productivity by constructing terraces that transformed steep hillsides into arable farmland.

Although the specific causes of Tiwanaku's collapse have not been determined, we do know that several of the important organizational features associated with the later Inca empire can be traced to this earlier *altiplano* center. The widespread Tiwanaku iconographic style seems to presage the broad dissemination of Inca state art. Likewise, Tiwanaku's establishment of small economic colonies in diverse environmental settings augurs an Inca practice. Perhaps the Inca kings recognized the powerful influence of Tiwanaku on the later prehispanic Andean world when they traced their ancestry to the basin of Lake Titicaca. In so doing, the Inca rulers also were invoking the mystique of Tiwanaku's past to bolster their own efforts to reestablish a far-reaching Andean domain.

A Tiwanaku pottery vessel decorated with a figure holding two condor scepters.

CHAN CHAN

Desert city of the Chimú

On the north coast of Peru, the seventh-century collapse of Moche coincided with a shift in political power. In the Moche Valley, occupation focused on the large settlement of Galindo. Yet unlike the Moche site with its huge adobe *huacas*, the nondomestic construction at Galindo was small. At the same time, a much larger settlement, Pampa Grande, with more elaborate architecture, was established in the Lambayeque Valley to the north. Both Pampa Grande and Galindo were positioned in easily defendable locations from which they could control local irrigation systems. Thus although the north coast was not conquered by Wari invaders from the south, that expansionist polity may have caused sufficient unrest to effect major shifts in population and power.

By approximately A.D. 800 to 900, a small settlement was founded at the mouth of the Moche Valley at Chan Chan. Although the exact extent of this early occupation has not been determined, it is clear that the site grew rapidly in size and importance. By the middle of the fifteenth century, Chan Chan had become a sprawling coastal city covering more than 20 sq km (8 sq mi). Chan Chan was also the capital of the Chimor state, which stretched 1000 km (620 mi) from southernmost Ecuador to central Peru.

At its height (mid-fifteenth century), the civic-ceremonial core of Chan Chan covered roughly 6 sq km (2.3 sq mi, roughly twice the size of New York's Central Park). This central area was dominated by ten rectilinear compounds, or *ciudadelas* (literally, "little cities"), each surrounded by high adobe walls. The nucleus of Chan Chan also included a large platform-court complex, as well as flat-topped mounds and numerous smaller monuments and structures, yet the most striking and massive features were the *ciudadelas*, many of which measured 200 to 600 m (650 to 1950 ft) on a side.

The *ciudadelas*, oriented roughly north–south, each had a single entrance through the north wall that opened onto a corridor leading to a broad court. A ramp sloped up to a long bench along the south wall of the court. Human corpses, probably buried when the compounds were constructed, were uncovered during excavations of these ramps. Each compound also included a multitude of storerooms, smaller courts, and living quarters. Usually the last structure built in each *ciudadela* was a burial platform, which presumably held the bodies of the family that occupied each of these mazelike compounds. Later records name ten Chimú kings, corresponding to the ten palatial compounds at Chan Chan. Geoffrey Conrad, of Indiana University, believes that each *ciudadela* was a particular king's residence and the administrative center for the kingdom of Chimor. Following the death of the ruler, the compound became the mausoleum for the king, maintained by his living kinsmen. Conrad argues that the maintenance of a dead Chimú ruler's personal property by his heirs, who did not succeed him in office, was derived from a broader pan-Andean custom of ancestor worship. On succession, each new ruler built his own *ciudadela* to serve as headquarters and royal treasury.

Most of the inhabitants of Chan Chan resided outside these massive compounds in small structures composed of six to

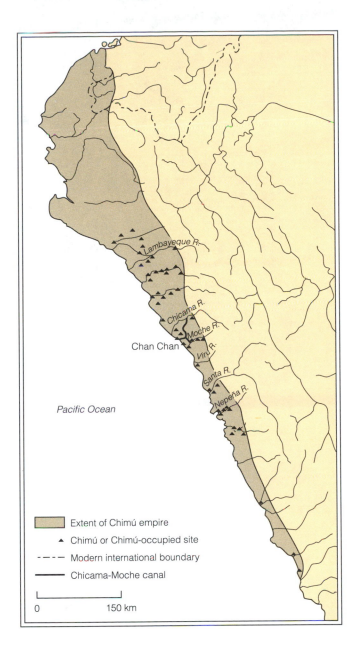

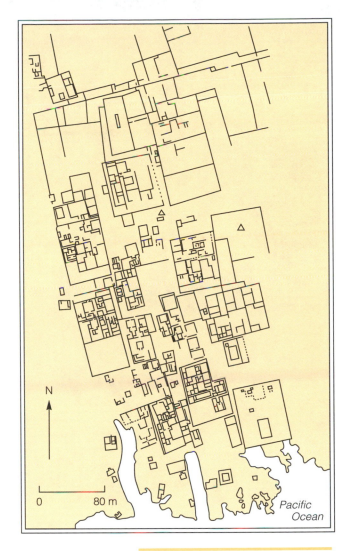

A map of the Chimú area (left), and the plan of Chan Chan (above).

eight small rooms. During excavations in these quarters, few farming or fishing implements were found. Instead the evidence for craft manufacture was abundant, including lapidary and woodworking tools, spinning and weaving implements, and the equipment for metalworking.

As at earlier Moche, most of the monumental construction at Chan Chan was built by a labor force from outside the center. Michael Moseley, of the University of Florida, estimates that the population at Chan Chan remained relatively small, perhaps 25,000 people. In the city's hinterland, massive labor investments were made in agricultural intensification. Sophisticated hydraulic systems brought water to the land surrounding Chan Chan. The Chimú even constructed an intervalley canal designed to carry water to the Moche Valley from the Chicama River, 65 km (40 mi) away.

The development of the large irrigation networks around Chan Chan would seem to relate to the Andean practice of labor tribute (the *mit'a* system), as well as to the Chimú pattern of succession. According to one hypothesis, the Chimú, like the Inca, practiced a policy of **split inheritance**, by which the successor to the throne received the inherited office of

An aerial view of Chan Chan.

the supreme leader. The lands, the palace, and the personal wealth of the dead ruler were left to a corporate group of other junior kinsmen. As a consequence, each new ruler had to raise his own revenues to erect his residential compound and finance his reign. His principal resource was a large labor force that could be employed in monumental construction, agricultural intensification, road building, and militaristic ventures.

Between 1462 and 1470, the Chimú were in competition with the increasingly powerful Inca. By the end of that decade, this conflict ended with the incorporation of the kingdom of Chimor into the rapidly growing Inca empire. In this manner, the Inca were able to link their lands and road systems with those previously controlled by the Chimú. Curiously, Chimú artifacts

were found more widely distributed after the Inca conquest than before, perhaps as the result of the emergence of new patterns of trade and taxation, or possibly because of the great admiration the Inca had for Chimú craftsmen. For example, Chimú metalworkers were brought to the capital of Cuzco to work for the Inca state.

Today the quiet desolation of the dry coastal environment is broken only by the nearly continuous howl of onshore winds. No one lives at Chan Chan, but the site is covered by a series of trails and paths that skirt the undulating tops of collapsed adobe ruins that were once the palaces of the Chimú kings. At dawn from a distance, the diffused, weak daylight makes it difficult even to distinguish the massive earthen walls of this once important city from the sky at the horizon.

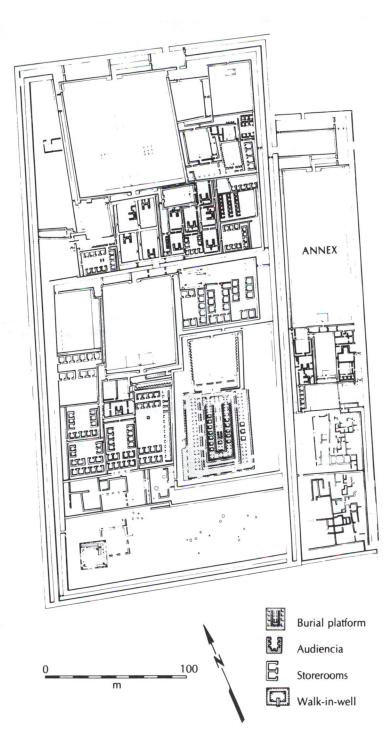

ANNEX

0   100
m

N

Burial platform

Audiencia

Storerooms

Walk-in-well

The plan of one of the ciudadelas *at Chan Chan. The* audencias *are U-shaped structures that may have been used by nobles holding audience with lower-status people. Each structure holds only one seated person, and each has its own court.*

Cuzco

Capital of the Inca

As with the Aztecs of Mesoamerica, much of what we know about the Inca comes to us not from archaeology but through written documents, filtered through the eyes of European chroniclers, whose goals and experiences differed greatly from those of the Inca themselves. In 1532, a small band of Spaniards led by Francisco Pizarro came into contact with populations in the northern coastal valleys of Peru that were part of a giant centralized political domain called Tawantinsuyu. The capital of this great polity was Cuzco (kuse'co), a city in the southern highlands. The highest-ranked leader was called Inca, son of the diety Inti (the Sun God) and descendant of a long line of heroic dynasties. At that time the empire was in the midst of a severe crisis, provoked by a bitter rivalry between two brothers, Huascar and Atauhualpa. Although Atauhualpa eventually won the power struggle, his costly victory may have lost the empire, as control of the Inca domain was soon in the hands of the Spanish.

According to legend, the rapid rise of the Inca began with hostilities between the inhabitants of Cuzco and the Chanca (a neighboring people). The Chanca, fresh from military victories over several adjacent polities, laid siege to Cuzco, forcing many of the inhabitants, including the reigning Inca, to flee to the surrounding hills. At Cuzco, a son of the Inca ruler named Cusi Inca Yupanqui was left to spearhead the final defense of the city. While waiting for the final Chanca onslaught, Cusi Inca Yupanqui had a vision in which he was told by a supernatural being that he would eventually rise to power and conquer many nations. Inspired by the apparition and buoyed by the support of new allies, Cuzco's defenders rallied to defeat the Chanca and drive them far from the Inca homeland. Cusi Inca Yupanqui was crowned Inca and renamed Pachakuti, "he who remakes the world." From that date, generally placed around A.D. 1440, Pachakuti is said to have initiated the dramatic series of conquests that culminated less than a century later in the huge empire stretching over 4300 km (2700 mi) from north to south.

Inca imperial propaganda proclaimed that the Andean world was in a state of savagery prior to their rise. This claim was obviously ethnocentric and fallacious. Clearly the royal families at Cuzco inherited administrative strategies and systems of legitimization from the rulers of earlier states, centered at Chan Chan and Tiwanaku. Archaeology has shown us that at the outset of the second millennium A.D., following the fall of Tiwanaku, the southern highlands around Lake Titicaca did undergo an episode of decentralization in which many small polities fragmented a landscape that had previously been unified by the earlier *altiplano* center. Supporting the legendary accounts, archaeological analyses indicate that by A.D. 1450, these autonomous competing polities of the Titicaca basin began to come under Inca hegemony. Centered at Cuzco, the Inca rapidly established major ceremonial centers on islands in Lake Titicaca, to solidify their control of this important geographic resource and legitimize their ancestral link to earlier Tiwanaku.

Cuzco was established by Manco Capac, the first Inca ruler, in a mountain valley nearly 3500 m (11,500 ft) above sea level. Because the site is situated relatively close to the equator, its climate is reasonably mild in spite of the high elevation. Cuzco remained a small community until it was rebuilt by the victorious Pachakuti. The Inca canalized and straightened several small rivers that cut through the settlement. Cuzco's most elaborate buildings, many of which were built entirely of finely hewn stone, were erected in the area between these rivers. An imposing fortress with massive masonry walls was placed on a steep hill above this center area, which was not fortified. Drawing on Inca sources, John Rowe, of the University of California, Berkeley, has suggested that Cuzco was intentionally laid out in the shape of a puma, with the fortress representing the animal's head and the intersection of the rivers serving as its tail. The area between the puma's front and back legs was paved with pebbles and served as a central ceremonial square.

The magnificent Temple of the Sun, the most important Inca structure in Cuzco, was built by Pachakuti at the site's center. The building's exterior walls, which measured more than 50 m (160 ft) per side, were decorated with a thick gold **frieze**. Entrances to the structure were covered with heavy gold plates. The interior walls also were coated with the metal. Early Spanish accounts describe a central patio or garden that included both natural and gold-crafted vegetation, including maize plants in which the ears, stalks, and leaves were all made of metal. The temple's principal sanctuary was dedicated to Inti. Inside the room were idols of gold and silver, as well as mummies of former Inca rulers and their wives.

Cuzco also contained other smaller temples, in addition to public buildings and elite residences. Public structures generally were built of cut stone, finished with such care and precision that the joints matched perfectly, and mortar was not required. These architectural monu-

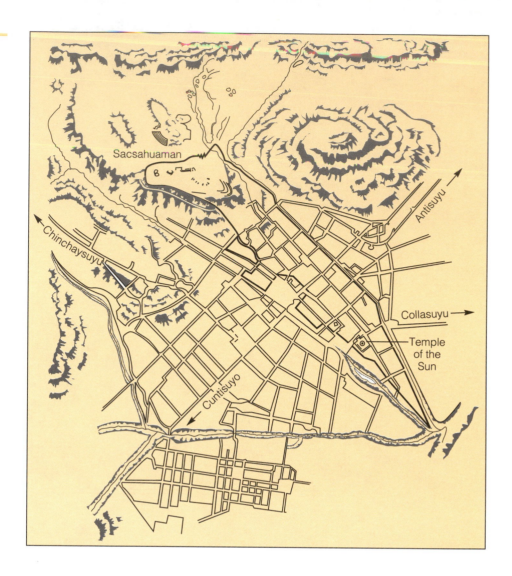

The plan of colonial Cuzco, which was built on Inca remains. The fortress and walls of the Inca city are outlined as a stylized puma.

ments, which required both great skill and significant labor power, were erected by commoners as part of the *mit'a* system. Pachakuti also erected a special public building that served as a convent for Chosen Women, brought to the capital to weave the finest cloth and to participate in specific religious rituals.

As the nucleus of an empire, Cuzco was not a typical Inca city. Its principal function was administration, and many of its inhabitants were involved in civic-ceremonial activities: priests, nobles, military officers, architects, and servants. Most of the supporting commoner population resided in smaller communities in the surrounding valley. In these settlements, the structures were built of field stone and adobe rather than cut-stone blocks. A network of state storehouses and religious shrines also marked the well-

planned terrain in the immediate vicinity of Cuzco.

The market in Cuzco was small and outside the center of the city. The peripheral nature of commercial activities at Cuzco reflects the administrative-elite character of the capital. However, it also indicates the nature of Inca economy, in which the state had a central role in the collection and redistribution of goods. Craftspeople and other specialists contributed labor to the imperial government, which thus took control of a wide range of craft items. Compared to the contemporary Aztec polity, private trade and marketing occurred at a very low level in the empire of the Inca.

The Spanish were greatly impressed by Cuzco, its stone architecture, and its treasure of precious metals. Before the arrival of the Europeans in 1532, the accu-

The Fortress of Sacsahuaman.

mulation of wealth was fostered by an Inca regulation that forbade anyone from removing gold, silver, or fine cloth from the city, once it was inside. In 1535, Cuzco was systematically burned and largely destroyed by the Inca themselves, when they besieged a Spanish garrison. But because the conquering Spaniards reconstructed the city promptly, often using Inca builders, much of the prehispanic plan has endured. Solid Inca walls still provide the stone foundation for many later buildings. Even the remnants of the once-spectacular Temple of the Sun now stand as the base for the Church of Santo Domingo. Like modern Mexico City, lying above the ruins of ancient Aztec Tenochtitlan, Cuzco is undoubtedly one of the longest continuously occupied cities in the New World.

Fitted-stone architecture at Cuzco.

INCA HIGHWAYS

Lifeline of the Inca empire

The movement of goods and information between the Pacific Coast, the Andean highlands, and the Amazonian *montaña* has been an important aspect of the South American world since at least the first millennium B.C. John Murra, of Cornell University, has shown that many Andean ethnic groups established colonies and devised other strategies to gain access to the products from these diverse ecological niches. As in Mesoamerica, much of this long-distance traffic was accomplished by foot. Yet in prehispanic South America, light loads (up to 45 kg, or 100 lb) also were carried by the domesticated llama, slightly easing the cost of long-distance transport.

Archaeologists do not know when the first Andean roads were built. Some scholars have suggested that they may date to the time of Chavín de Huántar. By the time when Tiwanaku and Wari dominated the Andean landscape, roads were in use. Well-built roads cross right through major Wari centers. Later the Inca linked existing roads into their own extensive system, creating South America's largest contiguous archaeological remain.

The Inca road system.

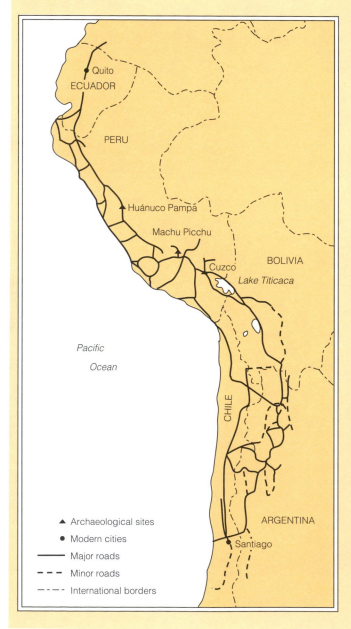

Key:
- ▲ Archaeological sites
- ● Modern cities
- —— Major roads
- – – – Minor roads
- –·–·– International borders

A woven Inca bridge over the Apurimac River in Peru, spanning a gap of about 45 m. This engraving was published by E. George Squier, one of the last travelers to see the bridge, in 1877.

Not surprisingly, Cuzco was the hub of the Inca road system. The principal road ran through the highlands from the capital to Quito (in Ecuador) and into present-day Columbia. A second mountain segment ran south through Bolivia to Santiago (in Chile) and northwest Argentina. There was also a long coastal road that was connected to the highland network at more than a dozen points. The total extent of this road system spanned more than 40,000 km (25,000 mi).

Wheeled transport did not exist, and the Inca roads generally were narrow, ranging from 1 to 16 m (3 to 52 ft) in width. For the most part, the mountain roadways were more winding and not as wide as those along the coast, as the road builders had to make concessions to terrain. In some places, the road was little more than a well-beaten path. Deserts, very high altitudes, and swamps were avoided when possible, although the Inca had means for coping with all of these situations. Across the desert, roads were lined with walls of posts, adobes, or stone to block wind-blown sands. Mountain roads were built to follow topographic contours, often narrowing along cliff facings. In wet areas, stone pavements were laid over the road, and drainage canals were built.

The Inca are renowned for their bridges over deep chasms and water courses, and they constructed several types of bridges. The rope suspension bridges, derived from the ancient Andean weaving tradition, greatly impressed the early Spanish chroniclers. Some of these bridges, where cables were hung from supporting masonry towers, continued in use into this century. Other Inca bridges were constructed with superstructures of wood, stone, or even floating reeds. In Inca times, most natives of the Andean highlands could not swim. Therefore, when a bridge could not be built or was being repaired, the Inca generally used ferries of balsa wood or reed.

The Inca road system was the lifeline of the Inca state and could not be traveled without an imperial directive. Most frequently, the roads were used to move gov-

A 10-m-wide Inca road.

ernment messengers, Inca armies, royal litters, or state trade caravans. Sometimes conquered populations were forcibly moved along the road system.

To service road traffic, the Inca built a network of roughly 1000 to 2000 *tampu*, roadside lodgings and storage places (primarily for food, fodder, firewood, and other commodities). The *tampus*, which tended to be situated roughly a day's walk apart, also served as seats of local government. Archaeological studies also have found evidence of mining, spinning, pottery manufacture, coca exploitation, and ceremonial activities associated with specific *tampu* sites. On the eastern Andean slopes of Bolivia, certain fortified sites may have served *tampu* as well as military functions.

Francisco Pizarro's conquest expedition traveled through Tawantinsuyu along Inca roads and robbed the stored food of the Inca *tampus*. Ironically, the great road system, which allowed the Inca to control their widespread empire, also may have contributed to their downfall.

Communications and their maintenance have been a major concern of Andean peoples from Inca times and probably earlier. In Andean conditions, roads, trails, and bridges were probably as essential to the political cohesion of the Inca state and to the redistribution of goods within it, as they are today to political integration or economic development.

D. E. Thompson and J. V. Murra (1966)

HUÁNUCO PAMPA

A provincial outpost of the Inca

An official (right) uses a quipu to relate accounting information to the Inca
emperor (left).

Following his conquest of the Lake Titicaca basin, the Inca Pachakuti began what
was to be almost a century of expansion.
When possible, Inca ambassadors tried to
negotiate a peaceful submission, a strategy that proved successful among smaller
polities too weak to defend themselves.
Some leaders may have been more willing
to join than fight because of the Inca policy allowing local rulers to retain power
as long as they gave their primary alle-
giance to the Inca. When military action
was necessary, the Inca had a large, effective fighting force supplied in part
through their road network.

Tawantinsuyu, the Inca empire, was
divided into four quarters that, according
to Spanish chroniclers, were subdivided
for administrative purposes into smaller
population units. The latter subdivisions
were based on multiples of ten; the **waranqa** of 1000 taxpayers was the unit most
frequently used. The decimal system of
administrative divisions was probably coordinated with the *quipu,* an Andean recording device that uses knotted strings
in a positional decimal system. As far as
we know, neither the Inca nor any of the
other prehispanic South American people
devised a formal system of writing.

To minimize provincial rebellion, the
Inca used a system of colonization, the
mitmaq. Populations were shifted from
one part of the empire to another to break
up dissident groups or to improve the exploitation of certain resources. Yet the Inca's effect on the Andean political landscape was less dramatic than it might
seem. A common misconception in popular accounts is of the Inca having ruled a
monolithic and uniform state. In actuality,
the empire was an amalgam of many
units, which differed in ethnicity, political
structure, size, and often language. Inca
imperial administration was variable, depending on the economic and political
significance of the conquered domain.
The Inca tended to make substantial
governmental changes only when a region's pre-Inca organization was fragmentary, or where resistance to Inca rule was
persistent.

Spanish chronicles from the sixteenth century emphasize the military
and administrative strategies used by the
Inca to control their empire. Yet the Inca
also established and maintained the authority of the state through a series
of civic-ceremonial rituals, as well as
through the economic activities on which
these ritual events were centered.

An archaeological perspective on Inca provincial rule has been illustrated most clearly at the site of Huánuco Pampa (wan'a-ko-pam'pa), a late prehispanic administrative center located in central Peru. In this highland region, Craig Morris, of the American Museum of Natural History, and Donald Thompson, of the University of Wisconsin, studied the civic-ceremonial center, as well as the surrounding communities. The Inca rapidly built Huánuco Pampa during the middle of the second half of the fifteenth century A.D. The site was placed on an inhospitable high plain at 3800 m (12,500 ft), an area previously uninhabited and relatively isolated from other settlements. Significantly, Huánuco Pampa lies directly on the main Inca road between Cuzco and Quito.

The ruins of the settlement cover roughly 2 sq km (0.8 sq mi). By the time of the Spanish invasion in 1532, Huánuco Pampa included more than 4000 stone buildings. Much of this construction is remarkably different from that found at outlying communities. Both the architectural and ceramic remains at Huánuco

A giant stone platform at Huánuco Pampa.

Pampa mimic the imperial Inca tradition found at Cuzco, while smaller towns and villages retained customary local practices.

The Inca stone masonry was finest at the core of the site. An enormous central plaza (550 by 350 m, or 1800 by 1100 ft, larger than four city blocks) included a giant stone platform and was flanked by several smaller plazas and large stone compounds. The stonework in the platform and central compounds was a good imitation of the Inca style, even though it lacked the precise joining of intricately shaped stone blocks seen at Cuzco itself.

The extensive storage facilities associated with Huánuco Pampa are indicative of the dependence of the site on its supporting hinterland, as well as the great power of the Inca administration. Although Huánuco Pampa's immediate agricultural hinterland could have supplied small quantities of potatoes, it could not have produced sufficient amounts to feed the site's 10,000 to 15,000 inhabitants. Maize found in storage facilities had to have been imported from fields at lower elevations. Food supplies and the labor to construct the center must have been drawn from a wide hinterland.

Huánuco Pampa was not a manufacturing center and lacked a major market. Much of its populace was an administrative elite, along with their retainers and record keepers. However, in Huánuco Pampa's central state compounds, Morris and Thompson found unusual concentrations of both the giant storage vessels as-

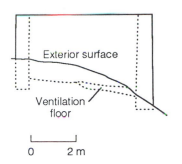

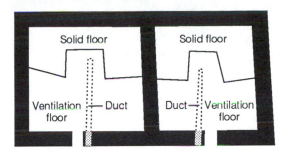

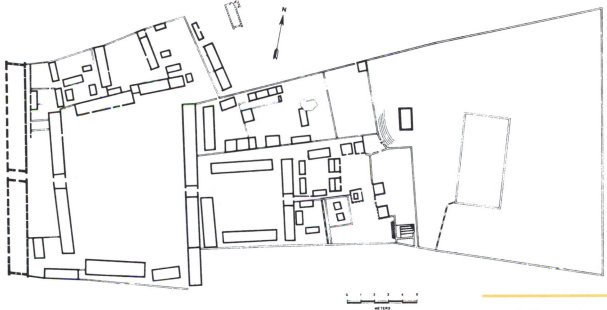

A set of architectural compounds connected by gateways at Huánuco Pampa.

sociated with the production of maize beer (**chicha**), and spindle whorls and other artifacts linked to the manufacture of textiles. Since *chicha* is neither easy to store nor to transport, it probably was distributed at Huánuco Pampa during feasts and state rituals. The unusual abundance of large food preparation vessels and serving platters in the ruins of the central compounds at Huánuco Pampa further suggests the importance of such activities. State-sponsored feasts could have been held in the huge open plaza at the core of the preplanned site, adjacent to the food-preparation and serving areas.

Traditionally the sharing of food and drink was a central feature of prehispanic Andean social relationships. At Huánuco Pampa, customary modes of sharing food and drink probably were used by the Inca state to establish loyalties and encourage the help of the local population in military, political, and economic activities. The state control and centralization of cloth production also may have played a part. As John Murra has noted, textiles had an unusual sociopolitical significance in the prehispanic Andes. Cloth was exchanged at most of life's major turning points, such as marriage, as well as during major political events, like conquest and incorporation. The more textiles the Inca state had, the more effectively it could raise and control armies and workers, and the more successfully it could consolidate conquered domains.

Through the control and manipulation of cloth and administration-sponsored feasting and hospitality, the state was able to cement the symbolic ties between the Inca and the conquered people. The extensive roadways, military strength, and innovative bureaucratic technology clearly were critical to the growth and maintenance of the Inca empire. Perhaps, too, were the rituals that helped to build a giant platform, or fighting in a remote war; it included shaping ideological perspectives as well.

MACHU PICCHU

Mountain settlement of the Inca

The most famous site in Peru and perhaps all of South America is Machu Picchu (ma'chew-pee'chew). This site is dramatically situated on the eastern frontier of the Inca empire, and the ruins lie on a saddle between two mountain peaks, which tower over the site and overlook a large bend in the Urubamba River. Machu Picchu is a graphic reminder of the architectural grandeur of the Inca. Yet in spite of its international popularity as a tourist attraction, archaeologists know relatively little about this magnificent ruin.

During the early part of this century, excavations were conducted at Machu Picchu by the late Hiram Bingham, then of Yale University. Bingham found a wealth of highly crafted artifacts, including silver rings, bronze ornaments, carved stone animal figures, and a variety of polychrome ceramic vessels. Burials at the site included both males and females, suggesting that, despite its remote location, Machu Picchu was not simply a military garrison or a fortified citadel. Nevertheless, access to the site was limited by gates and removable rope bridges. The ceremonial core of Machu Picchu could only be entered through a stone gateway, making access to this part of the site especially difficult.

The architecture that is visible today at Machu Picchu reflects its Inca heritage, although an earlier occupation appears to have been covered by this later construction. Recent excavations by Rainer Berger, of the University of California, Los Angeles, and his colleagues indicate that Machu Picchu may have had a long history prior to Inca times. In test excavations

they recovered charcoal from one hearth dating to the seventh century A.D. Nevertheless, most of what we know of the site pertains to the later Inca occupation.

The Machu Picchu ruins are a conglomerate of courtyards and stone stairways, as well as residential structures and public buildings. Constructed as a planned settlement, structures at the site were built almost entirely in the cut-stone architectural style characteristic of the Inca. The most important Inca structures, such as the site's principal temple, were built with great care and precision, using finely cut and fitted stone blocks. The largest stones were positioned at the base, with the other blocks diminishing in size from bottom to top. This architectural design gives an impression of strength at the base, lightness above, and grace throughout. Houses at the site were built of more roughly hewn stones covered with clay plaster. Some of the larger and better-made stone houses had both windows and carefully built wall niches.

Hundreds of agricultural terraces line the mountain slopes around Machu Picchu and supplied food to the inhabitants. Such farming features were constructed across the Andean highlands, especially late in the prehispanic era. By transforming jagged uncultivable slopes to flat, farmable terraces, the ancient Peruvians greatly expanded the land available for cultivation.

In the Andes, the size of the agricultural terraces depended largely on the steepness of the slope. While most terraces ranged from 2 to 4.5 m (6 to 15 ft) wide, terraces on very steep slopes were narrower, sometimes only 1 to 1.2 m (3 to

4 ft) wide. Often 100 terraces, each 2.5 to 4.25 m (8 to 14 ft) high were stacked one above the other on hillslopes. In many areas, modern farmers grow wheat and barley on these prehispanic agricultural features, which originally were cultivated in maize and coca. In other areas, prehispanic agricultural terraces are no longer used.

According to Spanish legal documents analyzed and synthesized by John Rowe, at the time of conquest Machu Picchu was the property of the descendants of the Inca ruler Pachakuti. Machu Picchu was one of several royal estates built by Pachakuti, as commemorative memorials to his various military/political exploits, and it was passed to his kin at his death.

The ruins of Machu Picchu.

Cut-stone architecture of the Inca.

Commoners' houses, with roughly hewn stones and windows.

The intihuatana *recovered at Machu Picchu.*

Elaborate dwellings at the site housed the king and his court when they were in residence, usually during the dry season. Rowe suggests that a smaller permanent population, responsible for maintaining the estate, resided at the site during the rest of the year. The site's large number of sacred features, as well as its location, reflect Pachakuti's concern with religion. The topography of the area — an impressive canyon surrounded by large rocks, conical peaks, and snowy vistas — combines many features that were important to Inca religion and cosmology.

At the site, Bingham found an intact *intihuatana,* a large stone pillar that is thought to have had a ceremonial function. Usually when the conquering Spanish found such features at other Inca sites, they destroyed them because of their suspected association with the native religion. Some researchers, including Bingham, have proposed that the *intihuatana* at Machu Picchu was used by Inca priests as a sundial to read the length of the shadows cast by the sun. However, recent **archaeoastronomical** work at the site has found that the pillar has no obvious astronomical function. Nevertheless, this study suggests that other features at Machu Picchu did have astronomical functions. A cave just below the site is thought to have been an observatory for the December solstice, and from the Torreón, a large masonry tower built on a rock promontory with a clear view to the east, the Inca could record the path of the rising sun during the June solstice.

Although Machu Picchu was inhabited by the Inca late in the prehispanic era, it may not have been visited by the Spanish *conquistadores*. In fact, Machu Picchu was largely unknown to the Euro-American world until it was publicized by Bingham's expedition in 1911. Today, amid the clouds and the snow-capped mountain peaks, Machu Picchu remains a magnificent remnant of a once great and powerful civilization that ruled the prehispanic Andean world.

EPILOG
THE ORGANIZATION
OF STATE SOCIETY

Similarities and differences in
two prehispanic worlds

The Prolog of this chapter outlined some of the key similarities and differences between the early civilizations of Mesoamerica and the Andean region of South America. The market, an important institution in prehispanic Mesoamerica, was not nearly as important in the ancient South American world. While the Cortes-led conquerors of the Aztecs were amazed by the size and splendor of the central Mexican market, the sixteenth-century Spaniards in Peru were impressed, not by markets, but by the incredible number of giant storage areas that were controlled by the Inca state. The young Spanish soldier, Pedro Cieza de León, writing less than two decades after the fall of the Inca, noted that:

> In more than 1200 leagues of coast they ruled they have their representatives and governors, and many lodgings and great storehouses filled with all necessary supplies. This was to provide for their soldiers, for in one of these storehouses there were lances, and in another, darts, and in others, sandals, and in others, the different arms they employed. Likewise, certain buildings were filled with fine clothing, and others, with coarser garments, and others with food and every kind of victuals. When the lord was lodged in his dwellings and his soldiers garrisoned there, nothing from the most important to the most trifling, but could be provided.

(Cieza de León, 1959, pp. 68–69)

The impressive storage facilities, described in the historical accounts, correspond closely to the large storage features associated with such Inca sites as Huánuco Pampa. Written and archaeological evidence suggests that state-imposed tribute and labor drafts were clearly central to the organization of the Inca, as well as their antecedent South America, states.

Despite the obvious differences between the ancient urban civilizations that arose in Middle and South America, the later prehispanic societies that developed in both regions share a number of important organizational features. We know that even before the beginning of the modern era, the populations of both areas were characterized by differences in wealth and power, which generally became more apparent later in the prehispanic era. These distinctions were manifest in the clothes and ornaments people wore, the food they ate, the variety of goods they had, and the houses in which they lived.

For example, in Mesoamerica, Aztec lords, most of whom inherited their social status, dressed in cotton, ate venison, and lived in elaborate residences with retainers and servants. Alternatively, the commoners wore clothes made of coarser maguey fibers, ate relatively little animal protein, and lived in small adobe and stone houses. Inca lords ate, dressed, and resided very differently from Andean commoners. Thus, in both regions, these peoples, with powerful governmental institutions and large population centers, were also characterized by a marked degree of social stratification.

Nevertheless, we know that personal attributes could be important even in highly stratified societies, such as the Inca, where great warriors or able administrators could achieve noble status. In the Inca case, such social mobility was most evident because the

Inca expanded their empire so rapidly that there was a nearly constant need to fill administrative posts. Despite the social mobility, the most powerful ruling positions were in principle only to be filled by members of noble lineages. Inca emperors were believed to have ruled by divine right, claiming descent from the sun. Their power was absolute, checked only by the fear of revolt and past custom. Bloodlines were so important in later Inca times that the primary wife of the Inca emperor was his full sister, the Coya. However, each emperor kept a large harem of secondary wives, some of whom were the daughters of neighboring rulers.

If we are to understand how the state and inherited social differences first emerged in human societies, the answers are apt to come largely through archaeology. These sociopolitical features were not part of the earliest human behavior, and they seem uncharacteristic of human populations with extensive hunting-and-gathering economies. Yet as we have seen in the Andes, social stratification and the state developed long before European contact. Even in Mesoamerica, where written records have survived the ravages of time, the beginnings of social and political inequality predate the advent of writing. Many answers may lie at sites like El Paraíso and Chavín de Huántar, which were not the capitals of urban states yet show indications of emergent inequities in power and wealth.

While ultimately the answers lie in the archaeological record, they will not be achieved quickly. The questions posed are the kind of big, messy research issues that require mountains of carefully collected information, as well as brilliant, yet measured, inferences and ideas. Even then, each question probably has more than one answer, or at least complex answers that interdigitate a multiplicity of factors. We can only hope to continue to make the kind of rapid progress in understanding our past that we have seen during the last few decades.

SUGGESTED READINGS

Burger, Richard L. 1989. An overview of Peruvian archaeology (1976–1986). *Annual Review of Anthropology* 18:37–69. A scholarly overview of recent Peruvian archaeological research.

Coe, Michael, Dean Snow, and Elizabeth Benson. 1986. *Atlas of ancient America.* New York: Facts on File. An elaborately illustrated volume covering all of the Americas, including excellent maps.

Hyslop, John. 1984. *The Inka road system.* New York: Academic Press. A descriptive account of the Inca road network.

Jennings, Jesse, ed. 1983. *Ancient South Americans.* San Francisco: Freeman. A volume of synthetic readings on ancient South America.

Keatinge, Richard W., ed. 1988. *Peruvian prehistory.* Cambridge: Cambridge University Press. A collection of recent overviews on prehispanic South America.

Morris, Craig, and Donald E. Thompson. 1985. *Huánuco Pampa: An Inca city and its hinterland.* London: Thames & Hudson. A well-written description of a late prehispanic administrative center.

Roosevelt, Anna C. 1989. Lost civilizations of the lower Amazon. *Natural History* 98:74–82. An overview of recent developments concerning the prehispanic lowlands of South America.

OLD WORLD STATES AND EMPIRES

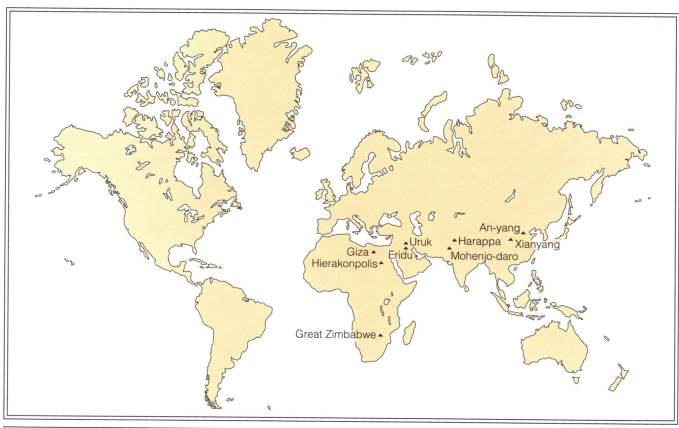

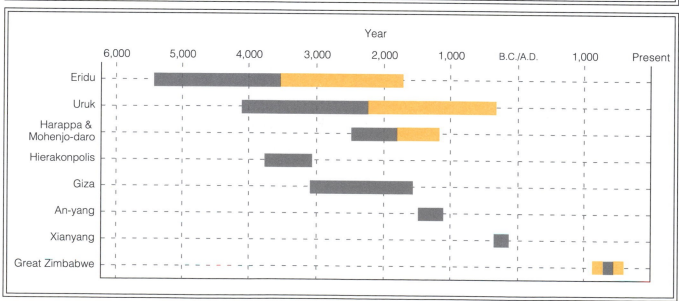

PROLOG
THE OLD WORLD AFTER THE ORIGIN OF AGRICULTURE

The rise of early states and urban centers

The study of man and civilization is not only a matter of scientific interest, but at once passes into the practical business of life. We have in it the means of understanding our own lives and our place in the world, vaguely and imperfectly it is true, but at any rate more clearly than any former generation. The knowledge of man's course of life, from the remote past to the present, will not only help us to forecast the future, but may guide us in our duty of leaving the world better than we found it.

(Tylor, 1960, p. 275)

In many ways, E. B. Tylor's words are as meaningful today as they were when first published in 1881. With more than a century of archaeology behind us, we can describe the trajectories of long-term change for a number of world regions, as well as compare and contrast the sequences from these areas. Although a thorough understanding of these differences and similarities remains ahead of us, today we know much more and therefore can ask research questions that are more specific than was possible in Tylor's day.

In Chapter Five, we examined the transition from hunting and gathering to agriculture and the adoption of more sedentary lifeways in a number of world regions. In Chapters Seven and Eight, we began with early sedentary communities in Mesoamerica and South America and examined the various paths of change that led to the rise of the complex polities centered at Tenochtitlan (Aztec) and Cuzco (Inca). In this chapter, we will review the transitions from early farming villages to more hierarchical polities in five regions of the Old World: Mesopotamia, South Asia (the Indian subcontinent), Egypt, North China, and southern Africa. We will examine the beginnings of agriculture and the development of early states in Europe in Chapter Ten.

Although the apparent causes of the changes we describe often varied greatly, long-term shifts resulted in the rise of polities and institutions that were hierarchically organized. Such institutions emerge in conjunction with larger, denser populations, where consensual methods of decision making can no longer work effectively. At the same time, hierarchical institutions, characterized by differential power and authority, tend to become self-serving as well as system-serving. They work to perpetuate and enhance the extant structure (and its inequalities), so that those who are already advantaged remain the privileged class. Increasing inequality in wealth and power is a hallmark of so-called civilized societies. Such stratification also may be related to the problem of succession that characterizes all hierarchical institutions. By specially marking and treating the offspring of the privileged from birth, society can expose them to the knowledge, personal connections, and traditions necessary to assume power. At the same time, such marking can limit the number of rightful heirs, thereby minimizing (if not eliminating) the disruptive consequences of succession disputes. Of course, wealth differentials and stratification are associated with the unequal control of power, land, and resources.

As we will see in this chapter, the rise of hierarchical polities is generally linked with economic transitions in exchange and production. Particularly in the Old World, where beasts of burden and wheeled vehicles could distribute goods relatively inexpensively, we see the development of increasingly large-scale and specialized craft industries.

CONTENTS

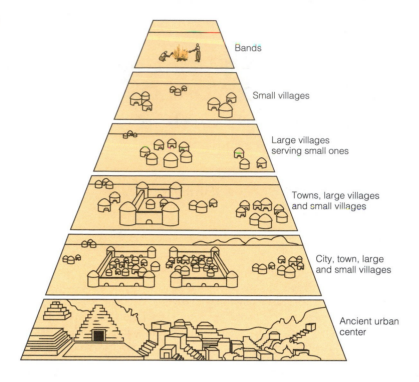

A schematic representation of the changes in social systems from bands to urban societies.

Bands

Small villages

Large villages serving small ones

Towns, large villages and small villages

City, town, large and small villages

Ancient urban center

Although such industries frequently were controlled by independent entrepreneurs, over time they offer central political institutions greater opportunities to limit access and concentrate wealth. As societies increase in size and organizational complexity, the mechanisms of exchange also shift from face-to-face contacts to tribute and marketing.

Although these general trends are evident in many of the regions discussed in this chapter, the specific sequences of transition and the rates of change were not uniform. The world's first states evolved in Mesopotamia, where the temple institution became a central focus. We will begin our discussion with Eridu, the site with perhaps the earliest Mesopotamian temple, established by the end of the sixth millennium B.C. The Mesopotamian temple was different in function than the Mesoamerican temple. The former had a central economic role (not seen in the Mesoamerican institution) in that it received goods through tribute and then redistributed a portion during feasts and other activities. We will next examine the early Mesopotamian urban center of Uruk, situated amid a network of ancient canals not far from the Euphrates River. Scholars agree that large-scale canal irrigation was a key feature of early Mesopotamian civilization, and the remnants of the ancient waterways are still evident on the desiccated landscape. However, the specific causal relationship between water management and state development in Southwest Asia, also known colloquially as the Near East, remains a matter for debate. While some argue that the allocation of water and the maintenance of the canals necessitated some kind of central authority, others have suggested that the monumental water-control systems were built only after the rise of powerful states. Whichever scenario is eventually supported, the later Near Eastern states and empires capitalized on the great grain-producing potentials afforded by large-scale canal irrigation systems.

Slightly later, during the third millennium B.C., major centers arose along the Indus River and its tributaries in what are today Pakistan and India. Here we focus on the best known of those Indus civilization sites, Harappa and Mohenjo-daro. Although these South Asian sites have not yielded rich tombs, like those in Mesopotamia, they are known for their highly developed craft industries. Indus centers generally were not as large as those in Mesopotamia, but they appear to have been more systematically planned, with centralized drainage networks for individual houses.

To a degree, the rise of civilization in Egypt was inspired by political and economic ties with the Near East. Yet the course of development was different. Large-scale political centralization was much more in evidence in Egypt than in Mesopotamia. We begin with the center of Hierakonpolis, a major settlement along the Nile whose occupation largely

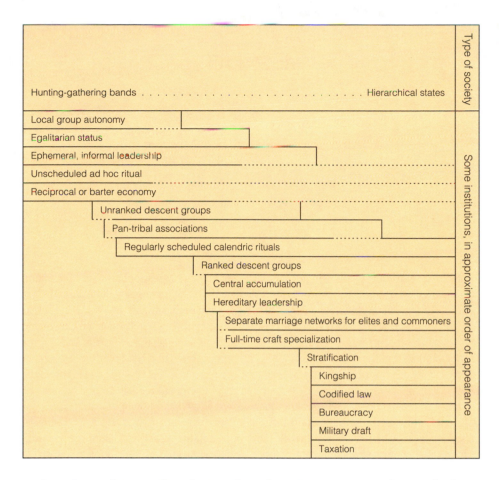

Type of society	
Hunting-gathering bands . . . . Hierarchical states	

Some institutions, in approximate order of appearance

- Local group autonomy
- Egalitarian status
- Ephemeral, informal leadership
- Unscheduled ad hoc ritual
- Reciprocal or barter economy
- Unranked descent groups
- Pan-tribal associations
- Regularly scheduled calendric rituals
- Ranked descent groups
- Central accumulation
- Hereditary leadership
- Separate marriage networks for elites and commoners
- Full-time craft specialization
- Stratification
- Kingship
- Codified law
- Bureaucracy
- Military draft
- Taxation

Types of societies, and the appearance of institutions.

predates the unification of northern and southern Egypt. We next discuss the later funerary complex at Giza, which was situated close to the ancient capital at Memphis. Both were important places in Dynastic Egypt. At Giza, several centuries after unification, powerful pharaohs constructed some of the world's largest pyramids.

By early in the second millennium B.C., states developed indigenously in North China. An-Yang, the last capital of the Shang dynasty, was excavated initially in the late 1920s and remains one of the best-known early Chinese cities. Although early Chinese centers were somewhat less urban than those in early Mesopotamia, they became some of the largest in the world by A.D. 1. During the last centuries B.C., in the short reign of the Qin dynasty, a magnificent tomb was built near the capital of Xianyang. The mausoleum included a huge army of life-size **terracotta** (a hard earthenware) foot soldiers and cavalrymen, and illustrates the extreme stratification of ancient imperial China.

Finally we discuss sub-Saharan state development in southern Africa at Great Zimbabwe. Great Zimbabwe was not the earliest sub-Saharan state, but it is a spectacular site with large brick structures erected early in the second millennium A.D. Long-distance exchange with Indian Ocean sites appears to have been important here.

The Epilog of this chapter returns to some of the key models and ideas that have been advanced to account for early state development. In a world that often seems to be dominated by powerful presidents, despots, kings, legislatures, bureaucracies, and tax collectors, one wonders how such hierarchical systems arose in the first place and why individual households lost their autonomy. To answer such questions about the beginnings of inequality and the rise of the first hierarchical decision-making institutions, we must turn to archaeology. In most parts of the globe, the processes that culminated in unequal access to power and wealth began centuries before the advent of written records. As a consequence, written histories alone cannot answer these evolutionary questions. Archaeology must continue to focus on the dramatic changes that occurred between the advent of agriculture and the rise of urbanism in many areas of the world. Unraveling the processes and causal connections surrounding these episodes may help explain the course of recent human history.

ERIDU

An early ceremonial center in Mesopotamia

For close to 10,000 years, the people of Southwest Asia have lived in farming communities. Their settlements, consisting of small, closely packed mud or clay rectangular structures, are ideally suited to the climate and the resources available. But mud-brick dwellings deteriorate rapidly. They must be rebuilt every fifty to seventy-five years (after a few generations of use). Over millennia, mud-brick abodes have been rebuilt repeatedly on top of earlier structures. As this recurs across an entire community, large mounds of accumulated mud and clay, known as tells, are formed. Thousands of such mounds rise above the landscape of the Near East, some standing as much as 50 m (165 ft) above the surrounding terrain. These tells contain debris from thousands of years of habitation. Ancient irrigation canals also cover the landscape of Southwest Asia. For the last 7000 years, irrigation has been practiced in this part of the world, and remnants of canals remain a visible reminder of the region's rich archaeological past.

The soils of the alluvial plain were deposited by the annual floods of the Tigris and Euphrates rivers. The rivers also provide the water that makes irrigation (and hence agriculture) possible in this region, where rainfall is inadequate for farming. Today Mesopotamian farmers using irrigation are able to cultivate a variety of crops, including wheat, barley, dates, olives, lentils, oranges, and onions. Along the swamps formed by the rivers, a variety of usable plants, such as flax for textiles and rushes for basketry, can be collected. While scrub forests along the rivers do not support much game, fish are abundant in the rivers. However, the soft

sediments of Mesopotamia do not contain much in the way of raw materials.

No early agricultural villages, such as those established in the coastal Levant and in the foothills of the Taurus and Zagros mountains (Chapter Five), have been recorded on the flat plain between the Tigris and Euphrates rivers in southern Iraq, the area known as Mesopotamia (Greek for "land between two rivers"). The alluvial floodplains and deltas here are hot and dry, composed primarily of inhospitable sand, swamp, and dry mud flats. Yet it was in Mesopotamia that the world's first civilization developed.

By 6000 B.C., the first scattered farming villages were settled on the northern fringe of the Tigris and Euphrates floodplain, an area where seasonal rainfall can sustain agriculture. These communities were generally composed of several houses, entered through the roof, containing two or three rooms. Ovens and chimneys were common features. By 5500 B.C., a new style of painted pottery, called Halafian, spread throughout a wide area of northern Mesopotamia, replacing the monochrome wares that had been made previously. The remarkable similarity of Halafian pottery over a wide area suggests that small villages were linked into far-reaching networks.

Shortly after the appearance of Halafian ceramics in the north, the focus of Mesopotamian settlement shifted to the southern alluvial plain of the Tigris and Euphrates rivers, an area known as Sumer. No sedentary villages prior to the sixth millennium B.C. have yet been recorded in this area. This is not surprising, because the area lacks wild game animals, edible plants, and even usable stone. In

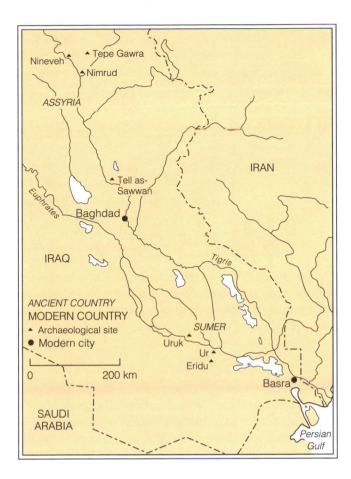

most years, the region receives insufficient precipitation for dry farming. Yet with an economy based on fish, irrigation agriculture, and domestic cattle, Sumer became the demographic and political core of Southwest Asia for most of the next 4000 years. The 'Ubaid period (5300 to 3600 B.C.), which begins this sequence, is marked by an increasing reliance on canal irrigation and the establishment of the temple. (See "Temples," p. 403.)

The first villages in southern Mesopotamia were small, 1 to 2 ha (2.5 to 5 acres). Yet relatively rapidly, a few of the settlements, such as Eridu, grew in size and importance. Eridu (air′ih-dew), the earliest known settlement on the southern Mesopotamian alluvium, was established around 5400 B.C. Ancient Sumerian accounts of creation (written in 3000 B.C.) name Eridu as one of the first communities to emerge from the primeval sea.

While most of the structures at Eridu were houses, the initial occupational levels feature a significant nonresidential structure. The architectural plan of this public building bears sufficient similarity to later Sumerian temples (depicted in written texts) to suggest that it may have served as an early temple. The building, constructed of mud-bricks, measured 3.5 by 4.5 m (11.5 to 15 ft), with a possible altar facing the entrance and a pedestal in the center of the room. Signs of burning on the pedestal indicate that it may have been used for offerings. This possible temple suggests that the organizational capacity for the construction of minor public architecture was present; however, its small size reflects a much lower level of social complexity than in later times.

Yet the temple institution may have had antecedents that preceded the movement of populations into Mesopotamia's southern alluvium. An earlier T-shaped structure at Tell as-Sawwan, on the border between the northern plain and the southern alluvium, may have served as a public building with functions similar to the later temple. In addition, a circular domed structure at Tepe Gawra, on the fringes of the northern plain, was found below a sequence of superimposed temples. At other northern Mesopotamian sites, similar circular structures, often joined to a rectangular entryway and thereby making a keyhole shape, have been found. These structures, or *tholoi*, were distinct from

An artist's reconstruction of the Uruk period temple at Eridu.

the traditional rectangular dwellings and seem to have had a nonresidential purpose, perhaps related to ritual and storage.

Because the temple institution was a focal point of early civilizations in Southwest Asia, questions concerning its origin and antecedents are important for Near Eastern prehistory. Yet there are also more general implications. If the temple only emerged in Sumer, then its development may be linked to the increasing and necessary reliance on canal irrigation. Social theorists have long argued that the management of irrigation systems necessitates the cooperation among farming populations to allocate water and maintain canals—a particular problem in Sumer, where the rivers carry and deposit great quantities of silt. Alternatively, if antecedents of the temple were established prior to the occupation of the southern Mesopotamian alluvium, it could be suggested that the movement into Sumer only became possible once a central redistributive institution, like the temple, was in place. Without such an integrative institution, the agricultural hazards of flooding, drought, and dust storms could not have been overcome. In this later scenario, the irrigation management may be responsible for the expansion and elaboration of the temple institution, but not its initiation. Likewise, an additional consequence of irrigation is that it tends to enhance disparities in agricultural productivity and hence land value. In Sumer, emerging inequalities in agrarian production may have fostered increasing economic stratification. Much additional archaeological research is necessary if such issues are to be adequately addressed.

By 4500 B.C. the southern Mesopotamian alluvium was dotted with full-fledged towns and public buildings. Based on irrigation farming, the economy produced enough food to support a growing population, yielding a surplus that supported craft producers and decision makers. Eridu may have covered 10 ha (25 acres) by this time and had a population as large as several thousand people. The temple at Eridu was rebuilt numerous times and expanded so that it contained multiple altars and offering places. The most elaborate residential dwellings were situated immediately around the temple at the center of the community; craftspeople and peasants lived at ever-increasing distances from the core of the settlement.

The development of the temple institution and the spread of canal irrigation were key features of the 'Ubaid period in southern Mesopotamia. This period was identified by a widespread monochrome pottery decorated with geometric designs. The 'Ubaid time also was characterized by population growth, as well as by increases in craft work. 'Ubaid pottery was made in a wider range of forms than was the earlier Halafian ware. Yet it tended to be somewhat less decorated, and the different ceramic varieties were generally more uniformly distributed over space. Most of the 'Ubaid ceramics appear to have been made on a slow-turning potter's wheel, in use for the first time. Because of the absence of suitable sources of stone, hard-fired clay was used to make sickles, mullers (implements used to grind paints, powders, etc.), hammers, and axes.

The complex processes that led to the growth of later civilization in Mesopotamia clearly had begun during the 'Ubaid period. But it was not until the subsequent Uruk period (3600 to 3100 B.C.) that monumental urban centers arose. Eridu remained an important place for more than a thousand years following the end of the 'Ubaid period. Yet early in the fourth millennium, other centers, such as Uruk (also known as Warka), rapidly surpassed it in size, monumentality, and political significance. Although for much of its early history the centers and polities of Mesopotamia shared a common cultural tradition, rarely was this region dominated politically by a single ruler or core state.

Temples were established in southern Mesopotamia no later than the 'Ubaid period (5300 to 3600 B.C.), and by the end of the 'Ubaid, the Sumerian pattern of towns with temples was well entrenched. In later Mesopotamian cities, the temple was always the largest and most impressive building, and it served both economic and religious functions. The temple institution became the focal point for the powerful religion and statecraft that integrated and maintained the complex polities that arose in ancient Mesopotamia.

At Eridu, a series of around twenty superimposed temples, spanning 3500 years, was excavated. Built atop earlier ruins, the later temples were raised above the land. The remains of earlier shrines are preserved within the foundations of later buildings. Each structure was separated from the others by deposits of debris, including small animal bones and fishbones, that may have been offerings.

Although not all temples are associated with **ziggurats** (great stepped towers), many are. How significant the ziggurats were is evident in the names by which they are known — House of the Mountain, for example. In Mesopotamia, the word *mountain* has great religious significance, as the place where the power of all natural life is concentrated. In a terracotta relief found in a temple from the second millennium B.C., the body of the deity issues from a mountain.

In Mesopotamia, religious order centering on the temple assumed much of the burden for structuring society. Third-millennium texts tell us that the laws of the gods were unchanging and people were governed by the gods' decisions. However, the rapid rise in the importance of the temple cannot be explained fully by religion. The growth of the temple and of the early cities that developed around them also was closely related to the economy. The temple, which generally was associated with storage facilities, became a redistributive center for both agricultural produce and craft goods. It also provided disaster relief in times of flooding, dust storms, and scorching winds when agricultural crops failed.

Temple administrators organized the cooperative projects necessary to construct and maintain irrigation channels, and likely decided who received how much water. The construction of the irrigation canals created unequal land values and inequities in land holdings. The temple elite became managers of large sectors of the economy. They owned land, employed people directly, and were extensively involved in farming and manufacturing activities. Because they controlled large amounts of foodstuff, they supported full-time craft specialists, including stonemasons, copperworkers, and weavers. The temple also directed the long-distance trade that provided raw materials to the craft specialists. Status goods were received in return, reinforcing the position of the temple elite. Although other private and royal estates also were important, it was the temple that became the central economic force in early Mesopotamian cities.

The building of ziggurats required huge amounts of labor and materials. The fact that so much energy was diverted to nonutilitarian tasks attests to the power of the temple elite. The construction of monumental architecture served to reinforce social and political hierarchies. The temples may have been objects of civic pride, proclaiming the well-being of the communities that built them and the majesty of the gods to whom they were dedicated, while at the same time, through rituals and religious sanctions, validating the power and authority of the ruling elite.

The role of the temple institution in Mesopotamia

The long sequence of temples excavated at Eridu.

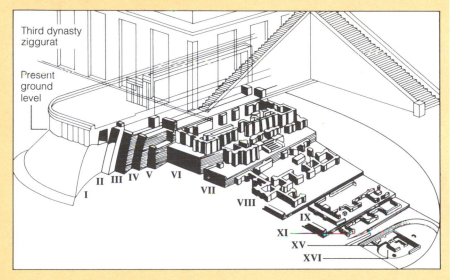

Third dynasty ziggurat

Present ground level

II III IV V VI

I

VII

VIII

IX

XI

XV

XVI

URUK

The world's first city

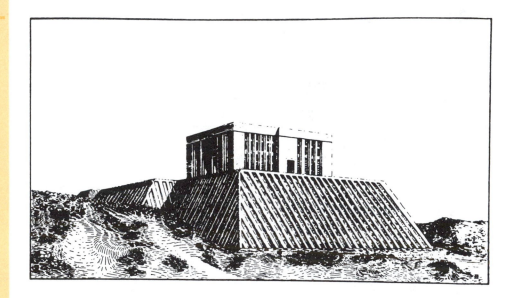

The complex processes that fostered the growth of urban civilization were clearly evident in Sumer during the 'Ubaid period. Yet it was during the succeeding Uruk (3600 to 3100 B.C.) and Early Dynastic (3100 to 2370 B.C.) periods that urban settlements and the earliest states were first established. Based on the great surplus potentials of intensive irrigation agriculture, the power of cities and their rulers increased. In Mesopotamia, the site of Uruk (oo-rook'), with its giant stepped pyramid, the Anu Ziggurat, was the largest and most impressive. During the fourth millennium B.C., Mesopotamia also entered the era of history, as a system of writing on clay tablets was employed.

Located on the banks of the Euphrates River less than 160 km (100 mi) north of Eridu, Uruk was settled prior to 4000 B.C. during the 'Ubaid period and became a major city of more than 10,000 people (covering 100 ha, 250 acres) by 3100 B.C. Residential architecture at Uruk was made of whitewashed mud-brick. Houses were rectangular in shape and were built along narrow, winding streets.

Most outlying sites were small, only 1 to 3 ha (2.5 to 7.5 acres) in size (smaller than a city block), although several settlements of intermediate size also were established. Population growth during the Uruk period was so rapid that it was probably due to in-migration and perhaps the settling down of nomadic peoples, in addition to natural increases in population resulting from changes in rates of fertility and mortality.

The earliest monumental architecture at Uruk, the Anu Ziggurat, is comprised of a series of building levels, the earliest going back to 'Ubaid times. This stepped pyramid, named for the primary god (Anu) in the Sumerian pantheon, attained its maximum size at the end of the Uruk period. At this time, the White Tem-

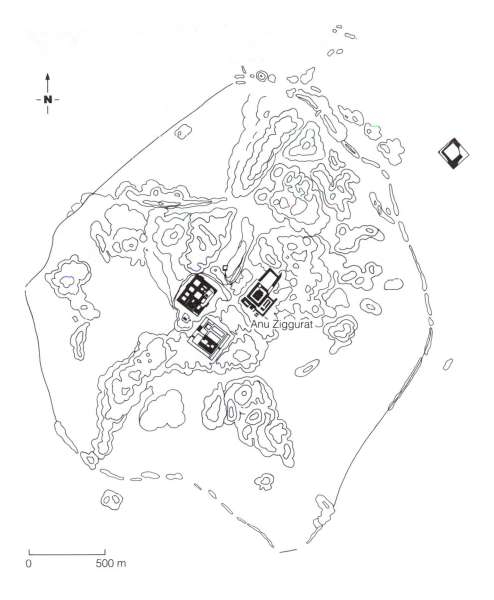

Anu Ziggurat

0   500 m

ple was built on top of the Anu Ziggurat, 12 m (40 ft) above the ground. The temple measured 17.5 by 22.3 m (57.5 by 73 ft), was made of whitewashed mud-brick and decorated with elaborate recesses, columns, and buttresses. Inside, the pattern followed the tripartite temple plan described for Eridu centuries earlier, which consisted of a long central room with a row of smaller rooms on each side.

The Anu Ziggurat and the White Temple mark a transition that was occurring in Mesopotamian society. The earlier Eridu temples were small compared to Uruk temples, and probably were administered by civic-ceremonial functionaries who had only limited influence over the populace. However, the economic and political power of the temple expanded as the size of its buildings increased. The

Anu complex, estimated to have taken 7500 man-years to build, represents the control of a large, organized labor force. As has been argued for Medieval Europe: "What constituted the real basis of wealth . . . was not ownership of land but power over men, however wretched their condition" (Duby, 1974, p. 13).

As temples became more elaborate, the structures, as well as the individuals associated with the institution, were separated from the general populace. Platforms and ziggurats elevated the temples above the remainder of the community. In the Early Dynastic period, temples and the associated priestly residences were often enclosed by high walls that further divided and protected this increasingly wealthy precinct from the lower socioeconomic strata below.

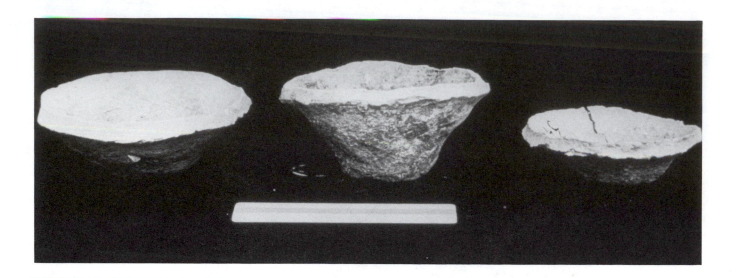

Undecorated crudely made beveled-rim bowls.

By the middle of the fourth millennium B.C., economic specialization in a wide variety of arts and crafts was evident, including stone cutting, metallurgy, and pottery production. Earlier Halafian and 'Ubaid potters had crafted beautifully painted vessels, but during Uruk times these wares were largely replaced by unpainted pottery (a trend that may have begun earlier in the 'Ubaid period). An important Uruk development was the introduction of the potter's wheel, which allowed for the more rapid production of fired-clay containers. Using the wheel and molds, potters began to produce mostly undecorated utilitarian vessels in great volumes, including crudely made beveled-rim bowls that may have been used for rations. In earlier Halafian and 'Ubaid times, highly decorated pottery vessels may have served as wealth or status items that also marked or defined certain social, territorial, or kin groups. By the Uruk period, ceramic items appear not to have played these roles, as they were even plainer and more uniformly distributed over space. Perhaps textiles and metal items largely replaced pottery as wealth items and markers of social identity.

As craft specialization and the demand for raw materials increased, trade flourished along major waterways, especially on the slow-moving Euphrates. Ships sailed up the rivers from the Persian Gulf, carrying food and raw materials including shell, carnelian, silver, gold, lapis lazuli, onyx, alabaster, ivory, textiles, tim-

ber, and skins. Copper, which first appeared on the plateau to the north as early as the fifth or sixth millennium B.C., was imported into lower Mesopotamia around 3500 B.C. Metal implements soon took on an important role in agriculture and warfare. Coppersmiths were present in most Mesopotamian cities by 3000 B.C. The wheel also was introduced during the fourth millennium B.C., and wheeled vehicles, drawn by horses, asses, and oxen, became vital in trade and warfare.

Another important development during the fourth millennium B.C. was the invention of the plow, which resulted in increased agricultural yield. In large part, Uruk's power depended on the city's ability to extract agricultural surplus from the hinterlands. In the southern Mesopotamian alluvium, agricultural surplus was vital, as the region lacks mineral and stone resources. The major crops were wheat, barley, flax, and dates; cattle raising and fishing also were important.

The world's earliest known written documents, clay tablets dating to 3400 B.C., came from Uruk. The principal function of this earliest Mesopotamian writing appears to have been economic, as the clay tablets record lists of commodities and business transactions. Over 1500 pictographic symbols have been identified in these early texts. Signs for carpenter, smith, chariot, copper (in the form of an ingot), plow, and harp have been recognized. Lists of commodities include dairy products, cattle, wheat, barley, bread, beer, clothing, and flocks of sheep. The pictographic elements of the early Uruk writing system have been shown to be the forerunners of later Sumerian cuneiform. (See "Early Writing Systems," p. 409.)

By the beginning of the Early Dynastic period (ca. 3000 B.C.), Near Eastern civilization was well entrenched. Metal tools, which were far more efficient than earlier tools, became much more common. Smiths began to alloy copper with tin to produce bronze, which is much harder than copper. The development of bronze weapons was directly linked to the increasing role of warfare as the means of attaining political ends. Armies were equipped with wheeled chariots and wagons. Rulers became more despotic, concentrating wealth and controlling subjects by military strength, religious sanction, and taxation.

During the Early Dynastic, Sumer was divided into ten to fifteen contemporaneous city-states, which were largely politically autonomous. Uruk grew to 400 ha (1000 acres) and may have contained as many as 50,000 people. This demographic growth was indicative of the great nucleation (in cities) that characterized Early Dynastic Mesopotamia. As the wealth and power of these closely packed cities increased, so did the competition between them. Great defensive walls were constructed around the major urban centers, including Uruk. This period also was characterized by dynastic rule, as individual monarchs and their courts gained independence from long-powerful temple institutions.

After its peak around 2700 B.C., Uruk's supremacy was challenged by other early cities, and its political importance eventually declined. Yet no single city-state dominated the Mesopotamian landscape for long during the Early Dynastic. Ur, a smaller center situated just 120 km (75 mi) away, became Uruk's economic and military rival. Ur was inhabited as early as the Uruk period, but the settlement only rose to great prominence in the subsequent millennium.

Early Dynastic Ur is renowned for the Royal Cemetery, which was excavated in the late 1920s by British archaeologist Sir Leonard Woolley. More than 2500 burials were unearthed, providing graphic evidence for superb craftsmanship, opulent wealth, and developed social stratification. Fewer than twenty graves actually contained "royal" individuals, who were placed in private chambers made of stone blocks and mud-brick. The contents of these graves indicated great concentrations of wealth and the trappings of earthly power.

Perhaps the best-known vault is thought to contain the body of queen Shub-ad. She was lying on her back upon a bed, accompanied by female attendants. Two wagons drawn by oxen and attended by male servants had been backed down the entry ramp where fifty-nine bodies, mostly female, were on the ground near the tomb chambers. All retainers were lavishly bedecked with crafted ornaments made of gold, silver, carnelian, lapis lazuli, and turquoise. Woolley believed that all the people and animals buried with the queen entered the vault alive. After the queen and her possessions were placed in the pit, the animals were dispatched by their keepers, who then consumed poison that was ready for them in the shafts. No violence or confrontation is evident in the arrangement of the corpses. Although royal interments are few at Ur, numerous graves contain modest quantities of goods, and an even larger number include little or no material wealth. Great disparities in an individual's treatment at death are evident at Ur, suggesting that social stratification was marked.

By the end of the Early Dynastic period, bureaucratic organization, social stratification, trade, crafts, and writing were all highly developed. Yet if anything, the pace of military conflict and political upheaval was intensified. For Sumer, the history of the third and second millennia B.C. (and beyond) is extremely complicated, with political realignments, military conquests, and dynastic replacements occurring frequently. Although increasingly large territorial units and empires were formed periodically, these large polities frequently were short-lived. In other instances, expansive polities came into contact and conflict with each other, leading to the collapse of at least one of them. The political fluidity that has characterized this part of the world in recent decades may have roots in the distant past.

A clay tablet from Uruk.

MAX MALLOWAN, 1904—1978

Archaeologist and companion of mystery writer Agatha Christie

Max Mallowan was born in London in 1904. At Oxford University from 1921 to 1925, he studied archaeology. One of his professors recommended Max to Leonard Woolley when Woolley was looking for an assistant to help with excavations at Ur. Woolley took Max on, and in October 1925, after twelve-hours by rail from Baghdad across desert and steppe, Max arrived at Ur. The next morning he got his first view of the great tell of Ur, standing 18 m (60 ft) above the plain.

The work at Ur employed 200 to 250 local tribesmen each season; over the twelve years of the project, hundreds of thousands of tons of dirt were moved. In 1930, Max's fifth year at Ur, he met Agatha Christie. Christie had visited Baghdad and become friendly with the Woolleys, who had read several of her mystery novels. At Katherine Woolley's request, Max accompanied Agatha on a journey to Baghdad to see the desert and other places of interest. They then traveled partway home together on the Orient Express. The trip was so enjoyable that Max and Agatha were married after they reached Britain. He returned to Ur without Agatha for another season, but he missed her and decided to seek work at another site where his wife would be allowed to accompany him. When invited to work at Nineveh, several hundred miles to the north, Max gladly accepted.

In 1932, Max conducted a dig of his own at the site of Arpachiyah, Iraq (6.5 km, or 4 mi, east of Nineveh). Mallowan's staff consisted of himself, Agatha, and a good friend, John Rose. In his memoirs, Max looks back on this dig as one of the happiest and most rewarding of his career. Agatha accompanied Max on all his subsequent expeditions, serving as hostess, photographer, and helping with the cleaning and recording of small finds.

Mallowan next worked in Syria, where his archaeological career was disrupted by World War II. After the war, Mallowan was appointed as the first Chair of Western Asiatic Archaeology at the University of London, a position he held until 1960. His time was divided between home and abroad, with several months each year spent at Nimrud in Iraq, one of four ancient Assyrian capitals. He spent almost ten years excavating the acropolis at Nimrud, which covered 26 ha (65 acres). At Nimrud, he built a room for Agatha, and there, season after season, she sat and wrote her mystery novels on a typewriter. Agatha wrote six books while on archaeological projects.

By age 85, Agatha had written eighty-five books, some of which drew on her experiences with Max. *Come Tell Me How You Live* is an account of the daily life on an archaeological expedition to North Syria between 1935 and 1938. Two other novels, set in Egypt — *Death on the Nile* (1937) and *Death Comes as the End* (1945) — have no particular reference to archaeology, but they do mention some of the places where Max and Agatha stayed. *Murder in Mesopotamia* (1963) is more closely related to their work, and could not have been written without knowledge of Ur. Leonard and Katherine Woolley had parts in the book (Katherine was the murder victim), as did Max in the role of Emmott, a minor character. Agatha dedicated *Murder on the Orient Express* to Max because of his enjoyment of the Orient Express.

In 1962, Mallowan received a fellowship at All Souls College, Oxford. This appointment released him from administrative duties and enabled him to finish writing about his work at Nimrud. He also received many other honors, including election to the British Academy, the Académie des Inscriptions et Belles Lettres, and the Royal Danish Academy, and he was knighted in 1968. He received the Lucy Wharton Drexel Gold Medal from the University of Pennsylvania, the Lawrence of Arabia Memorial Medal from the Royal Central Asian Society, and in 1976, the first Gertrude Bell Memorial Medal of the British School of Archaeology in Iraq "for outstanding services to Mesopotamian Archaeology." Mallowan was elected an Honorary Fellow of New College (Oxford), his old college, and an Emiritus Fellow of All Souls upon his retirement. He was also made a Trustee of the British Museum.

Early civilizations employed different systems of communication, information storage, and accounting. In the Andes, the *quipu* was used by Inca bureaucrats to keep accounts; no system of writing was developed. Some of the first writing in China was on animal bones and turtle shells. Scapulas (shoulder blades) and other bones were heated until cracks formed. The patterning of the cracks in relation to the written characters was used ritually by diviners to foretell the future—a practice referred to as **scapulimancy**. In the Indus Valley, evidence for early indigenous script is found primarily on soapstone seals that apparently were used to mark ownership. In Egypt, many early texts recorded dynastic and kinship themes. In prehispanic Mesoamerica, writing was frequently used to record dynastic records (births, marriages, accessions, and deaths), to announce military victories, and to document political events. Calendrical inscriptions often were incorporated by the Maya and other Mesoamerican peoples to track historical themes. In Mesopotamia, the principal function of the world's first writing system was similar to that described for the Indus Valley; however, the particular conventions of the Mesopotamian writing system and the actual script and symbols employed were markedly different.

In 1929, a team of German archaeologists discovered written inscriptions on clay tablets at the site of Uruk. These earliest Mesopotamian texts, dating to the late fourth millennium B.C., revealed an already developed writing system that included as many as 1500 different symbols and fairly consistent conventions for the presentation of information. By 3000 B.C., this writing system was in use across southern Mesopotamia. The written symbols were primarily ideographs (abstract signs), although a few of the signs were pictographs that more or less portrayed the represented object.

In the mid-1960s, French excavations at Susa, on the Susiana Plain east of Uruk, discovered hollow clay spheres or envelopes, called **bullae**, that enclosed modeled clay tokens or geometric forms. Dating to the end of the fourth millennium B.C., these bullae are impressed on the outside, thus providing evidence for writing that is approximately as old as the Uruk tablets. They resemble the hollow clay tablets containing clay tokens that were used for accounting as late as 1500 B.C. in parts of Southwest Asia.

In 1969, Denise Schmandt-Besserat, of the University of Texas, Austin, initiated a study on the earliest uses of clay in the Near East. Traveling to museums around the world, she recorded collec-

The economic basis of Mesopotamian written symbols

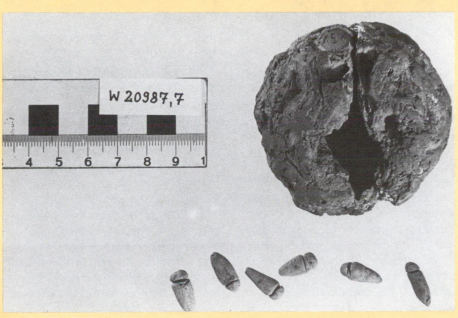

A clay envelope (bulla).

Clay tokens from the ancient Near East.

tions of early pottery, bricks, and figurines. Yet in addition to those expected objects, she noted that most of the collections (made from Turkey to Pakistan) also included hand-modeled clay tokens dating to as early as the ninth millennium B.C. Schmandt-Besserat recognized the similarity between these tokens, which generally had been catalogued as "toys," "gaming pieces," or "ritual objects," and the tokens associated with the later bullae and the hollow tablets. She also noted more than thirty formal correspondences between three-dimensional geometric tokens and the two-dimensional ideographic symbols that were inscribed on the early tablets.

Based on these correspondences, Schmandt-Besserat reasoned that Neolithic clay tokens, like the later bulla-enclosed counterparts, may have been used to record or keep track of economic transactions. The earliest token shapes that could be associated with later written characters referred to quantities of various agricultural products. Other common token forms were linked formally with the two-dimensional symbols for numerals and key commodities, like cloth, bread, animals, and oil. Not surprisingly, the variety of tokens increased through time, generally becoming more elaborate. Overall, more than 200 different kinds of tokens have been identified at sites dating to between 9000 and 1500 B.C. If Schmandt-Besserat's interpretation is correct, the first communication revolution — the advent of the clay tokens — was associated with the transition to village sedentism, farming, and an increased volume of economic transactions and long-distance trade.

Relatively little change in this recording system is evident prior to the emergence of urbanism and the state during the fourth millennium B.C. Sometime after 3500 B.C., a sizable proportion of the tokens were perforated, as if for stringing. Schmandt-Besserat reasons that tokens may have been strung together to signify that the objects represented were part of a single transaction. By the end of the fourth millennium B.C., tokens also began to be placed in bullae. Sealing the tokens within a single bulla also could have served to segregate a specific transaction. Seals of the individuals involved were placed on the outside of the bulla, perhaps validating the event. A bulla may have been used as a bill of sale would be today. The honesty of the deliverer could be checked by matching the goods received with the tokens enclosed in the accompanying bulla. But there was one major drawback to this innovation: Checking the tokens required that a bulla be broken, but to preserve the record, the bulla had to remain intact. The solution was to press the tokens on the exterior of the clay envelope before enclosing the tokens and firing the bulla. In this way, the contents of the load could be checked by the receiver while the validating inscriptions remained intact. In some instances, a finger or a stylus was used to impress the image of the token on the bulla surface.

By the outset of the third millennium B.C., hollow bullae with tokens inside were generally replaced by clay tablets. Anyone could check the outside of a bulla without destroying the record. An inscribed bulla or tablet was much easier to make and store than clay tokens. Such economizing measures would have become more important as the development of tribute-collecting institutions (the temple) and urban centers fostered an intensified volume of economic transactions. Thus it is not really surprising that the earliest tablets were convex and made of clay, mirroring the shape and material composition of the spherical bullae. Likewise, it is easier to understand the early reliance on ideographs on the tablets, because the earliest written signs followed the shapes of the geometrical tokens. The use of Mesopotamian writing to record economic transactions also seems a logical development from the function of the earlier token system. Mesopotamian writing clearly did not emerge in a vacuum; it evolved from an old and widespread system of communication and accounting.

Mesopotamian writing was simplified and made more efficient through time. To simplify writing, Sumerian scribes reduced the number of symbols and substituted wedge-shaped marks for the signs, giving rise to **cuneiform,** the name given to subsequent Mesopotamian scripts. This was just the opposite of what occurred in Egypt, where the hieroglyphic symbols were made increasingly difficult to execute. In Egypt, writing served a more limited purpose for a relatively small segment of the population.

The most significant contribution of writing was expediting the flow of information in increasingly large and stratified societies. It facilitated administrative activities and enabled the further growth and centralization of Mesopotamian cities. Writing also may have crystallized and preserved Mesopotamian cultural and bureaucratic traditions so that they outlived the hegemony of single rulers or dominant city-states. Yet an alphabetic system was not invented in Mesopotamia, and in 1900 B.C., Sumerian written language still contained between 600 and 700 unique elements, with an organizational structure somewhat analogous to traditional Chinese. The first truly alphabetic written languages developed toward the end of the second millennium B.C. By 1000 B.C., the Greeks adapted the Syrian alphabet to their own language and reduced the number of written signs to twenty-five. The Greek alphabet then became the foundation for all contemporary European language systems.

HARAPPA AND MOHENJO-DARO

Urbanism and the rise of civilization in the Indus Valley

The broad fertile floodplain of the Indus River and its tributaries, in what is now Pakistan, was the principal focus of the Indus Valley civilization (mid-third millennium to 1800 B.C.). Covering 300,000 sq km (117,000 sq mi, or about the size of Arizona), this area is bordered by the Baluchistan Hills to the west, the Arabian Sea to the south, the Great Indian Desert to the east, and the majestic Himalaya Mountains to the north.

The earliest known sites in the riverine heartland of the Indus civilization date to the late fifth and early fourth millennia B.C., postdating earlier occupations like Mehrgarh 200 km (125 mi) to the west. These settlements, referred to as Early Harappan, were scattered across the plains in major agricultural areas or along important trade routes. Many of them exhibit artifacts and organizational features that are directly antecedent to the later sites, suggesting that the Indus Valley civilization had a long, local path of development. The Indus development does not appear to have been a simple consequence of stimuli from the ancient civilizations of Mesopotamia, a view held by previous generations of scholars. The early Indus Valley settlements consisted of small, contiguous, rectangular mud-brick houses, some of which contained multiple rooms. The size of settlements varied, and a few included monumental construction. Several settlements were walled and laid out on a grid plan. Plow-based agriculture was practiced. Cattle, sheep, and goats were kept, but hunting and fishing also remained important subsistence activities.

Craft technologies associated with later Indus civilization developed to a high degree at these pre-Indus settlements. Rings, bangles, beads, pins, axes, and celts were manufactured from copper and bronze. Fine stones were ground and polished into beads. Using kilns, potters produced a variety of vessel forms, some of which were elaborate, such as serving dishes on stands. Much of the pottery was finely painted. Other important crafted items included terracotta figurines. By the late fourth millennium B.C. writing was present, and seals were inscribed with various symbols.

The Indus Valley civilization (also called the Harappan civilization) was first identified by Sir John Marshall in 1921 at the site of Harappa in the Punjab highlands in the upper Indus Valley. Although few systematic settlement pattern studies have been undertaken, 250 to 300 Harappan sites have been reported in the Indus Valley. Few villages have been excavated, but most appear to be between 1 and 5 ha (2.5 to 12.5 acres), and are located near rivers or streams. There are at least four large urban centers, the best known of which are Harappa and Mohenjo-daro, 460 km (290 miles) to the south in the Indus lowlands. The two sites, both of which have been the foci for major archaeological field studies, are surprisingly similar. Both towns are estimated to have covered approximately 85 ha (210 acres) and to have contained populations of roughly 30,000 to 40,000 people at their respective heights. Both Mohenjo-daro and Harappa were built on massive mud-brick platforms (Mohenjo-

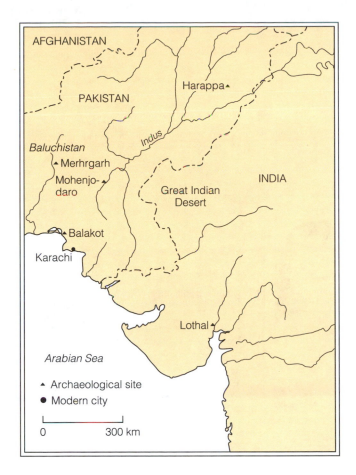

daro was rebuilt at least nine times) that raised the towns above the surrounding floodplains.

Harappa (ha-rap′ah) and Mohenjo-daro (mo-henge′o-dah′ro) consisted of two sections, both of which were walled. The eastern section was largely residential, while the higher fortified western mound, or "citadel," contained many non-residential, public structures. The western mound at Mohenjo-daro consists of a platform raised 12 m (39 ft) above the plain. Buildings were constructed on the platform and enclosed by a vast wall with towers. The major structures included a possible granary, a Great Bath, and a great hall almost 730 sq m (8100 sq ft). Some scholars have argued that the granary (1000 sq m, or 11,000 sq ft, equivalent to an Olympic-size swimming pool) was erected over brick supports so air could circulate under the stored grain. Its spatial proximity to several threshing floors has been used to support the contention that this structure was indeed used to store grain. The Great Bath — 12 by 7 m (39 by 23 ft), and 3 m (10 ft) deep, which may have been used for ceremonial ritual bathing — included eight small private bathrooms or changing cubicles. The bath itself was fed by a well, and its brickwork was sealed with bitumen, tar that is waterproof.

Mohenjo-daro's eastern part was divided into blocks by streets, the broadest of which were about 10 m (33 ft) wide. Hundreds of houses lined the streets and alleys, some of which were paved with stone. Some of these structures had two stories and were made of baked mud-bricks (at smaller settlements, houses generally were built of sun-dried mud-bricks). At Mohenjo-daro, more spacious dwellings, perhaps for high-status individuals and merchants, were laid out around central courtyards. These residences had private showers and toilets connected to a central drainage system built partially underground. Small temples or shrines also were present, as were buildings like barracks, which may have housed slaves.

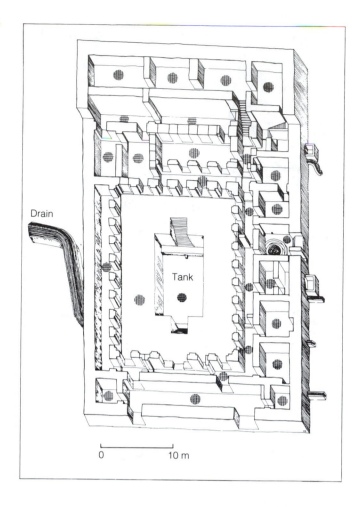

Drain

Tank

0   10 m

A striking feature of Harappan society is the extent of standardization, including a system of weights and measures. Precisely cut pieces of chert were used as counterweights in balances. Shell surveying tools and measuring sticks of 33.5 cm (about 1 ft) were used, similar to those used in later Indian systems. Dwellings had standard dimensions, and most building bricks were made in uniform sizes. Ceramic forms and ornamentation were remarkably similar at sites throughout the Indus system.

A considerable degree of occupational specialization was present in Indus society, and one's profession was probably an important factor in social differentiation. At the major urban centers, there were designated living and working quarters for beadmakers, coppersmiths, and weavers. Certain smaller sites were devoted almost entirely to a specific industry, craft, or trade, including brickmaking, ceramic production, and coppersmithing. Metallurgy was well developed, and copper and bronze were used for a variety of tools and weapons. The availability of copper, lead, and silver within or close to Indus territory contributed to a greater use of metal tools than was evident in Mesopotamia.

There were significant differences between the Indus Valley and Mesopotamian civilizations. The Indus civilization covered a larger geographic area — over 1,000,000 sq km (425,000 sq mi) — yet had a smaller number of major centers. Mesopotamia was composed of many city-states. The similarities between Harappa and Mohenjo-daro suggest that Indus centers were closely linked economically and culturally (although probably not politically). The Indus civilization may have had a more equitable distribution of wealth than was the case in other early Old World societies. Little evidence exists that exotic stones or metal were restricted to Indus elite contexts; considerable quantities of wealth have been recovered at even modest settlements. Indus material culture was simple in comparison to that of Mesopotamia; there was little representational or lavish art. Instead, one finds figurines, small sculptures, carvings on bone and ivory, decorated pottery, and intaglio figures on seals. The Indus elite also engaged in fewer lavish public displays; they built fewer rich tombs, elaborate palaces, or fancy temples. But there were some brick-lined tombs that yielded far more grave offerings than the average burial. Nevertheless, nothing approaching the royal graves at Ur or the Egyptian tombs has yet been found in the Indus region. In fact, whatever rulers and elite the Harappans had remain anonymous. Individual conquests and accomplishments are not enumerated, and few portraits have been found. A steatite (soapstone) figure from Mohenjo-daro depicting a bearded man in an embroidered robe is a rare exception.

Indus settlements were closer to natural resources than were Sumer sites. The large Harappan centers were connected with outlying rural communities and resource areas through complex internal trade networks. Both maritime and overland routes were used. Wheeled carts were drawn along regular caravan routes, and deep-sea vessels traveled the Indian Ocean. Long-distance exchanges moved seals, carnelian beads, and other miscellaneous items from the Indus region to the Persian Gulf, northern and southern Mesopotamia, Iran, and Afghanistan. Imports included lapis lazuli from Afghanistan, shank shells from southern India, turquoise from northeastern Iran, carved chlorite (a kind of green stone) bowls from the Iranian Plateau, and jade from central Asia. Few Mesopotamian items have been found in the Indus area. A possible explanation is that Mesopotamia exported mostly perishables, such as barley, fruits, oil, and textiles.

A system of writing that was very different from the early Mesopotamian script developed in the Indus Valley. Over 4000 seals with Indus script have been found. Most inscriptions are short; no known inscription is longer than twenty-one signs, and the average text is only five or six signs. The lack of long texts has added to the difficulty of interpreting the Indus script. Over 400 different symbols have been identified, yet few have been deciphered. Inscriptions, including both writing and pictures, are found on small copper tablets and postherds, but most are found on square seals of soapstone, a material that is easy to carve. Most seals had holes that allowed them to be strung and worn around the neck. The script seems to identify the owner of the seal.

Many animals are depicted on the seals, including elephant, unicorn, water buffalo, rhinoceros, tiger, crocodile, antelope, bull, tiger, and goat. Walter Fairservis, Jr., of the American Museum of Nat-

A Harappan seal with a unicorn.

A collection of stone cubical weights from Harappa.

ural History, suggests these animals may be totems or symbols representing specific kin groupings; some seals depict processions with animal effigies being carried as standards. Thus each seal may identify its owner to a social grouping. This might help to explain why similar scenes are repeated on multiple seals. Two different themes that are very common in Indus scripts may represent larger groupings known as **moieties**. One theme reveals a cross-legged figure (the lotus position) wearing a water buffalo-horned headdress, surrounded by various animals; the other represents a pipal tree (a species of fig tree) with various anthropomorphic and human figures. Some archaeologists have suggested that the figure with the headdress may be an early incantation of the later Hindu deity Shiva, in his role as Lord of the Beasts.

The Indus civilization began to decline around 1800 B.C. The major Harappan centers were eventually abandoned, and the center of power shifted from the Indus to the Ganges River Valley to the east where, after 1100 B.C., large cities were built and state-level organizations were formed. Archaeologists now think that the changes in the early part of the second millennium B.C. were not a complete collapse or population replacement, but rather the beginning of an episode of decentralization. Many elements of the earlier Harappan civilization were retained in these new settlements. As with the rise of the Indus civilization, we really do not know why these ancient centers collapsed. Traditional views emphasize an Aryan invasion from the northwest, but this interpretation has received little support in recent years. Another hypothesis postulates that a great tectonic uplift blocked river flow and caused major, destructive flooding. The ultimate answer may entail more than one cause.

The persistence of many aspects and traditions of the Indus civilization into more recent times is startling. Ceremonial bathing, ritual burning, specific body positions (such as the lotus position) on seals, the important symbolic roles of bulls and elephants, decorative arrangements of multiple bangles and necklaces (evident from graves and realistic figurines), and certain distinctive headgear — all are important attributes of ancient Harappan society that remain at the heart of contemporary Hinduism. In addition, the Indus script bears many similarities to later South Asian writing. Many of the specific signs can be found on documents associated with the subsequent Ganges sites. Both were written in the **boustrophedon** format, in which text flows from right to left on one line and then from left to right on the next. Even the standard Harappan unit of weight, equivalent to roughly 0.5 oz (14 g) continued in use at South Asian bazaars and markets into the last century. Although ancient Harappa and Mohenjo-daro lie in ruins today, the civilization of which they were a part has left an extremely important legacy.

With population growth, more densely packed communities, and increasing political complexity, household self-sufficiency becomes difficult, if not impossible, to sustain. Gaining access to all the resources a family needs requires new mechanisms of acquisition. As more tasks become specialized, people exchange what they produce for other goods and services through markets and trade networks. In some societies, the control of markets or exchange networks is an important source of power.

Trade and craft production appear to have been key features of Indus Valley society. Complex internal trade networks connected the major urban centers of the Indus civilization with rural agricultural and resource areas. Evidence from Mohenjo-daro suggests that the large Indus cities included craft areas that served as the living and working quarters for specialists. Some crafts, like the working of shell, stone, pottery, and metal, may have developed into hereditary occupations.

Shellworking, an important Indus craft, was undertaken by specialists. The earliest use of shell was limited to simple ornaments made by perforating natural shells. Later, during the time of the Indus civilization, shell use increased to include a variety of decorative, utilitarian, and ritual objects, including ornaments (bangles, rings, beads, pendants, and large perforated discs), utensils (ladles), inlay pieces, and other special objects.

According to J. Mark Kenoyer, of the University of Wisconsin, Madison, each of the workshops at Mohenjo-daro specialized in producing different shell items. For example, one area appears to have produced mostly inlay pieces. Shell workshops similar to those at Mohenjo-daro were present at Harappa and other urban centers. But at Harappa there was less variety in shell species and a lower frequency of shell artifacts in general, because of its location further inland. At the site of Lothal, on the coast of the Arabian Sea, shell workshops also produced a variety of objects.

Another major shell site, Balakot, on the coast near Karachi, Pakistan, specialized in shell bangles, beads, and smaller objects. The site has workshop areas with stone grinders and hammers, bangles in various stages of manufacture, and unworked shell. One type of shell was cut with a specialized bronze saw. Metal tools were expensive, and at most sites, only craftworkers who were supported or controlled by more affluent individuals had access to metal tools. Most of the bangles were made by an alternative chipping and grinding process that used stone tools. Regardless of the method of manufacture, the resulting bangles at Balakot were almost identical. Even though Indus sites specialized in different types of finished products, a single standardized manufacturing technology and certain decorative conventions were often employed across the region.

While certain shell items were decorative, the function of other Indus shell artifacts remains a mystery. Historical and ethnographic data show that shell bangles are still used for various social and ritual functions. Through historical accounts, the antiquity of finely crafted shell objects (and their ritual functions) can be traced back to 600 B.C. It seems reasonable to deduce that some of these socioritual uses may have their ultimate roots in the practices of the Indus civilization.

ECONOMIC SPECIALIZATION

Shellworking in the Indus civilization

HIERAKONPOLIS

The emergence of the Egyptian civilization

In spite of the general popularity of Egyptian archaeology, we know surprising little about early Egypt, particularly prior to the rise of early states and the first written documents. What we do know about Egypt suggests that this civilization along the Nile River was different in its long-term history from the ancient civilizations that developed in other parts of the world. For example, Egypt was relatively centralized for almost 2500 years, with only one major episode of political fragmentation (2200 to 2000 B.C.).

Egyptian civilization was focused on the Nile Valley, which is a long oasis surrounded by desert. The Nile flows to the north and the Mediterranean Sea, more than 6400 km (4000 mi) from its source in the swamps and lakes of equatorial Africa. Its final 1300 km (800 mi) cut through Egypt before fanning out into an enormous delta. In Lower Egypt, an area of rich, cultivable floodplains to the north, the river valley is up to 20 km (12.5 mi) wide. The south, known as Upper Egypt, has less alluvial land (only several kilometers wide), forming a narrow strip surrounded by jagged rock escarpments.

Prior to the construction of the Aswan Dam in the 1960s, annual flooding along the Nile was common, and tons of rich soil were deposited. As a result, the floodplain of the Nile is extremely fertile. Because of sparse rainfall today, irrigation is necessary for farming, but the annual temperature regime is perfect for the cultivation of a wide range of crops. Staple crops have been legumes, barley, onions, cucumber, melons, and figs. Other plants include rushes and reeds used for making baskets, flax for linens, and papyrus for

cordage and paper. As it did in the past, today the area supports sheep, goat, pig, cattle, duck, geese, fish, turtle, crocodile, hippopotamus, and other game animals. Although the surrounding deserts provide very little in the way of food, they are rich in building stone and minerals, including copper, gold, and silver.

The floods along the Nile were more predictable and easier to control than those of the Tigris and Euphrates rivers in Mesopotamia. The Egyptians could very easily modify natural basins on the floor of the Nile Valley to retain floodwater for their crops. Higher levees along the river provided dry locations for settlements.

No definite sedentary villages have been found in the Nile Valley prior to the sixth millennium B.C., when nomadic cattle herders and farmers began to settle in the area. Prior to 6000 B.C., the Nile Valley was occupied by groups of hunter-gatherers who followed an annual round in which they hunted along the margins of the desert for wild cattle, gazelle, and birds during part of the year, and took fowl and fish at other times. The presence of grinding stones indicates that wild grains also were an important food item.

Soon after 5000 B.C., food production was established in the Nile Valley. The early farming settlements raised Near Eastern domesticates: wheat, barley, sheep, and goats. Most of what is known about predynastic Egypt comes from the south, where there has been less deposition to bury sites. Yet it is possible that sedentism actually may have occurred earlier in the more fertile north. One floodplain settlement near the Nile Delta, Merimde, dating to as early as 4900 B.C.,

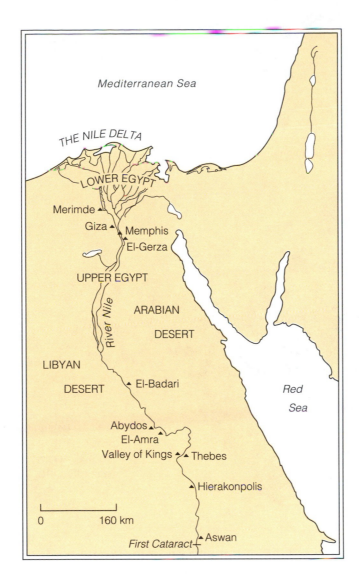

Map labels: Mediterranean Sea · THE NILE DELTA · LOWER EGYPT · Merimde · Giza · Memphis · El-Gerza · UPPER EGYPT · ARABIAN DESERT · River Nile · LIBYAN DESERT · El-Badari · Red Sea · Abydos · El-Amra · Valley of Kings · Thebes · Hierakonpolis · 0 160 km · First Cataract · Aswan

consisted of a cluster of semisubterranean, oval houses with roofs made of sticks and mud. The inhabitants used stone axes, knives, and flint arrowheads. Grains were stored in ceramic jars, baskets, and pits. Circular clay-lined threshing floors also have been reported.

The earliest occupations in the south (roughly contemporary with those in the north) are called Badarian, after the best known settlement of El-Badari in Upper Egypt. Badarian settlements consisted of clusters of skin tents or small huts. Many of the dead were buried carefully in oval or rectangular pits that were roofed over with sticks or mats. Utensils and food were commonly placed in the burials. Other grave offerings included rectangular stone palettes, ivory spoons, and small ivory or stone vases, all of which may have been associated with the preparation and use of green face paint. These items are all common components of predynastic burial assemblages. The Badarian focus on grave features and the accompanying goods may have been at the root of the later Egyptian emphasis on burial custom.

In the south, materials associated with the Amratian tradition (3800 to 3500 B.C.) are frequently found directly above Badarian levels. The name Amratian was derived from the site of El Amra near Abydos in Upper Egypt. The Amratian materials seem to reflect direct continuity with the earlier Badarian, yet the latter period is characterized by the appearance of more developed craft industries (particularly in pottery, alabaster, and basalt), and a larger number and more widespread distribution of settlements. Copperworking, which may have been

The ceremonial macehead of King Scorpion.

of a dry streambed. The size and contents of the tombs varied, perhaps reflecting status and prestige. One grave, measuring 2.4 by 1.5 m (8 by 5 ft) and 1.8 m (6 ft) deep, contained baskets, fine pottery, rope, flint arrowheads, and wooden arrow shafts. Unfortunately the grave was looted in later times, and the most valuable goods may have been stolen. A second grave contained scraps of **papyrus** (an ancient type of paper) and a disk-shaped macehead made of polished green-and-white stone, called porphyry. Maceheads, which were mounted on wooden staffs (called maces), were recognized in Egypt as a sign of authority. The presence of the macehead at Hierakonpolis indicates that the process of political development already may have been well underway. Similar polished, hard-stone maceheads have been found at several other contemporaneous sites, possibly indicating the presence of several small competing political units.

Hierakonpolis also was the center of a very large pottery industry. At least fifteen Amratian pottery kilns have been identified, the largest of which were massive features covering over 1000 sq m (0.25 acre). Two distinct types of pottery were made: a coarse ware for everyday household or industrial use, and a fine, untempered ware for grave offerings. The kilns appear to have been part of one well-organized complex, in that each kiln was used for the manufacture of a different kind of pottery. The large kilns must have produced far more than was needed locally. The late Michael Hoffman postulated that the people in charge of pottery production acquired considerable economic power.

During the subsequent Gerzean period (3500 to 3100 B.C.), craft activities, including pottery production, metallurgy, and the manufacture of stone bowls from very hard materials such as diorite and basalt, appear to have been carried out at a still larger scale. Copper artifacts, which were now cast as well as hammered, increased in frequency. Gold also was worked at this time, and some luxury items were wrapped in gold foil. Trade with the Near East intensified in volume. Some of the pottery of this time was painted in Southwest Asian style, with

initiated in the Badarian, also gained in importance. Amratian metalworkers used copper to make pins, flat axes, awls, and daggers. Scholars do not agree on the origins of Egyptian metallurgy. Many have argued that it was introduced from Southwest Asia, while others, pointing to earlier metalworking in Upper than Lower Egypt, suggest that it may have been an indigenous accomplishment.

The best-known Amratian center, Hierakonpolis (heer-ra-kon′po-lis) ("city of the falcon"), had a population of several thousand people. Most inhabitants lived in rectangular, semisubterranean houses of mud-brick and thatch. The more important artisans and traders lived in larger houses in separate compounds. Near the site was a large cemetery with part of the burial area reserved for elaborate tombs. These tombs were not as spectacular as later ones in Egypt, but they were impressive. The early tombs were constructed by cutting rectangular holes into the terrace

Narmer's carved stone palette.

dark red colors painted on a buff background. Foreign motifs also were incorporated into the local decorative tradition.

Gerzean remains have been found in Upper and Lower Egypt, possibly indicating greater integration between the two areas. Yet important differences in ceramic styles and burial customs continued to distinguish Upper and Lower Egypt. On carved palettes and other art, key individuals are depicted wearing distinctive headgear or crowns. These crowns vary from one area of Egypt to another, suggesting that several different polities may have developed along the Nile.

During Gerzean times, social and economic inequalities, as evidenced from tomb size, grave design, and burial inclusions, increased markedly. One macehead found at Hierakonpolis, with a scorpion on it, has been identified as belonging to King Scorpion, the predecessor of Egypt's first pharaoh. Hierakonpolis, whose loca-

tion shifted slightly closer to the Nile, was the largest known settlement, with 5 ha (12.5 acres) of occupation, including large, nonresidential structures, such as palaces and temples.

Written records and stone monuments indicate that the incidence of warfare increased at this time, with local kings trying to gain control over adjacent kingdoms. Among the competing kings, it is thought to have been Narmer from Hierakonpolis who finally succeeded in unifying Egypt into one kingdom around 3100 B.C. As Egypt's first pharaoh, Narmer founded a dynasty (3100 to 2890 B.C.) and a political structure that lasted for nearly 3000 years.

Unification of Upper and Lower Egypt was recorded for posterity on a 64-cm (25-in.) carved stone palette that was discovered by English archaeologists in 1898 at Hierakonpolis. One side of the tablet depicts Narmer, the leader of Upper Egypt, wearing the white crown of Upper

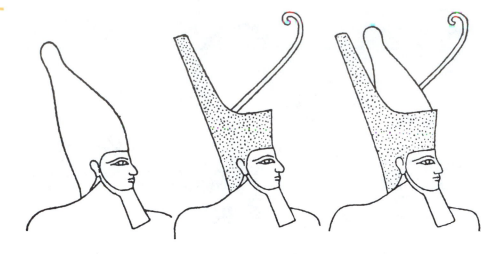

The Egyptian crowns: the white crown of Upper Egypt (left), the red crown of Lower Egypt (center), and the double crown of unified Egypt (right).

Egypt, and holding his symbolic mace. The other side shows him wearing the red crown of Lower Egypt. On both sides are scenes of the king involved in battle.

The Egyptian state was far larger and more complex than any city-state in Mesopotamia. The nature of rule also was much different in Egypt than in Mesopotamia. In Egypt, the royal court centralized power and wealth, and this consolidation is evident in the concentration of resources in the mortuary complexes of the kings. The relative stability of Egyptian rule diminished some of the insecurity that in Mesopotamia led to the construction of great walled complexes around nucleated urban centers. In Egypt, much continuity can be seen with earlier occupations, in such areas as stoneworking, death ritual, and the use of the mace-head as a symbol of rule.

The unification of Egypt is closely timed with the earliest hieroglyphic writing. Although writing first developed in Mesopotamia, the Egyptians devised their own script, which is very different from Near Eastern writing. Egyptian hieroglyphs consist of both pictographic and phonetic scripts, written on papyrus and carved into public buildings. Egyptian writing was more concerned with rule and kinship than with economic transactions. The deeds and accomplishments of leaders were recorded, and this may have had a role in the consolidation of power in the hands of a limited few. The widespread adoption of irrigation agriculture also coincided with the unification of Egypt. Ancient Egyptian irrigation prac-

tices were very simple, such as modifying natural basins to serve as reservoirs for floodwater. Yet the large surpluses that these techniques permitted clearly were necessary to support the opulent lifestyles and mortuary rituals of the emergent pharaohs.

The earliest tombs in Egypt were small wooden graves in which the dead were buried with utensils and food to sustain them in the afterworld. In late predynastic Egypt (the fourth millennium B.C.), more elaborate tombs were constructed for the burial of elite members of society. These graves contained a variety of goods, including beautiful pottery, baskets, braided leather rope, painted reed arrow shafts, flint arrowheads, pieces of papyrus, and maceheads.

The architectural styles of tomb construction differed in Lower Egypt and Upper Egypt. In the royal **necropolis** (cemetery) at Hierakonpolis, these differences were utilized symbolically by Narmer or his immediate predecessors. Constructed at the end of the fourth millennium B.C., the cemetery was arranged (according to Michael Hoffman, who excavated at the site) to represent the union of Upper and Lower Egypt, perhaps to legitimize the military conquest of Lower Egypt by the Upper Egyptian rulers.

Tombs in the style of Lower Egypt were constructed at the downstream end of a **wadi** (dry streambed), which represented the downstream end of the Nile, or Lower Egypt. These tombs were lined with mud-bricks, and large, painted wood and reed structures were placed over them. Low reed fences surrounded these tombs. The burials occurred in groups of three, four, and five, suggesting that rulers were buried with other family members or members of their court. A fragmented wooden bed was found in one tomb. It was finely carved, with two legs crafted to resemble a bull's legs — a forerunner of the furniture in King Tutankhamen's tomb.

At the opposite end of the cemetery, or upstream with respect to the wadi, was a stone tomb in the architectural style of Upper Egypt. This stone feature is surrounded by apparently similar tombs that are still to be excavated. Cut into subsoil bedrock, the excavated tomb was a long, narrow trench with an L-shaped hole cut into the middle of the floor. There was no superstructure associated with it. Surrounding this stone tomb was a precinct of animal burials, including the remains of hippopotamus, elephant, crocodile, baboon, cattle, goat, sheep, and dogs. Some of the animals were mummified and probably had civic-ceremonial significance. In Dynastic times, the Egyptians used various animals as godlike symbols of the different **nomes**, or geographical provinces, that comprised the Egyptian state. Some of these same animal symbols are portrayed atop standards on Narmer's tablet. In accordance with the rest of the necropolis, it seems possible that the animal burials also followed a symbolic orientation. For example, the easternmost tomb had six baboons, an animal that ancient Egyptians associated with the rising sun.

Hoffman proposed that this desert cemetery presages key attributes of the Egyptian state. These features include the use of the royal death cult and an associated cemetery area as national symbols, the division of the state into the symbolic halves of Upper and Lower Egypt, and the incorporation of conquered polities and people through ritual as well as military means. In contrast to the neighboring polities of Southwest Asia, political integration in Dynastic Egypt was tied less directly to specific fortified towns and was linked more closely to elite lineages and cemetery and temple complexes. The roots of that civic-ceremonial organization appear to extend to Hierakonpolis.

THE CEMETERY AT HIERAKONPOLIS

Steps toward the unification of Egypt

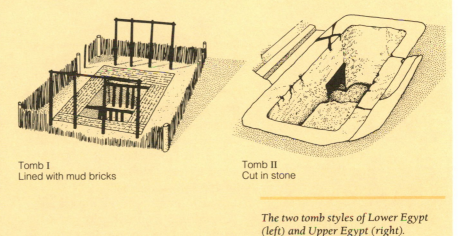

Tomb I
Lined with mud bricks

Tomb II
Cut in stone

The two tomb styles of Lower Egypt (left) and Upper Egypt (right).

GIZA AND DYNASTIC EGYPT

Pyramids and pharaohs

An aerial view of the pyramids at Giza.

By 3100 B.C., Upper and Lower Egypt were unified into one state when Narmer, Egypt's first pharaoh, conquered the northern delta. Narmer moved the capital from Hierakonpolis, in Upper Egypt, to Memphis, at the junction of Upper and Lower Egypt, where the Nile Valley spreads out into the broad delta. Memphis remained the political center of Egypt for 1500 years. Although the Nile Valley around Memphis was not a particularly rich agricultural area, the city was strategically positioned for riverine communication between southern and northern Egypt.

The symbol of the pharaoh was the double crown of Upper and Lower Egypt. A series of pharaohs during the first (3100 to 2890 B.C.) and second (2890 to 2686 B.C.) dynasties ruled under the double crown, but consolidation of the two disparate regions was not a steady or easy process. The Egyptian kings adopted the strategy of establishing outposts, temples, and shrines throughout their domains, maintaining integration and preventing the monopoly of functions or power in any single place or capital. Intermarriage of the elite from north and south may have been used to solidify the unification.

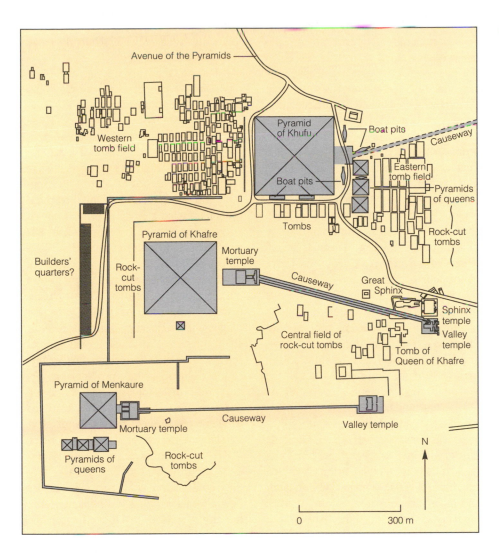

Within the map:

Avenue of the Pyramids

Boat pits

Pyramid of Khufu

Causeway

Western tomb field

Eastern tomb field

Boat pits

Pyramids of queens

Tombs

Rock-cut tombs

Builders' quarters?

Pyramid of Khafre

Rock-cut tombs

Mortuary temple

Causeway

Great Sphinx

Sphinx temple

Valley temple

Central field of rock-cut tombs

Tomb of Queen of Khafre

Pyramid of Menkaure

Mortuary temple

Causeway

Valley temple

Pyramids of queens

Rock-cut tombs

N

0   300 m

The Egyptian population was less urban than in Near Eastern societies, which generally had larger centers. Apart from a few large sites, most of the Egyptian population continued to live in unwalled, largely self-sufficient villages. This may account for the preoccupation of the Egyptian elite with rural lifeways. Despite this preoccupation, a massive, hereditary bureaucracy developed, devoting official energy to tax collection, harvest yields, and the administration of irrigation. Each nome (or province), administered by a local governor, was under overall central control. During the first dynasty, the Egyptian kings also supported an increasing number of craft specialists. Trade links were extended to what is now Sudan (Nubia) and Libya. With the elaboration of the court during the early dynasties, the demand for sub-Saharan products like ivory and ebony intensified, thereby heightening interest in areas to the south.

Between the third dynasty in 2686 B.C. and the Persian conquest in 525 B.C., Egypt was ruled by no fewer than twenty-three dynasties. The third through sixth dynasties comprise what is known as the Old Kingdom (2686 to 2181 B.C.), a time of despotic pharaohs and grandiose pyramid construction. The largest Egyptian pyramids were constructed by these early dynasties. The first pyramid was a stepped-stone structure constructed by the pharaoh Zozer, as the centerpiece of his funeral complex. The step pyramids were soon followed by the more familiar pyramids with smooth faces. Like all royal tombs until 1000 B.C., the pyramids were constructed in the desert on the west side of the Nile River and were surrounded by the tombs of contemporary officials.

Although few written records have survived from the Old Kingdom, sketchy accounts provide a perspective largely unavailable for earlier periods. Scribes were

The double statue of Menkaure and his sister, Khamerernebti II.

an important part of the government. Special schools trained writers for careers in the palace and the treasury. Contemporary documents on papyrus show that Egyptians were skilled in architecture, surgery, accounting, geometry, and astronomy. But most of the population, as in other early civilizations, consisted of illiterate peasant farmers who maintained the Egyptian agricultural base.

One major site of the Old Kingdom is Giza, located near modern Cairo. Just a short distance from the ancient capital city of Memphis, the Giza Plateau is where King Khufu (known as Cheops in Greek), of the fourth dynasty, built his massive pyramid. Called the Great Pyramid, this monumental edifice required precise planning and complex engineering, and serves as a clear reflection of state power and labor control. The pyramid is 150 m high (500 ft, or not quite as tall as the Washington Monument), covers 5.3 ha (13.1 acres), and contains a series of internal passages and chambers. Khufu's pyramid was constructed of 2,300,000 stone blocks with an average weight of 2275 kg (2.5 tons). Its construction involved roughly 13,440,000 man-days of labor and incorporated materials from areas as far away as Lebanon, Sinai, Aswan, and Nubia.

Surrounding the Great Pyramid were the much smaller pyramids of three queens and the rectangular tombs of Khufu's closest royal relatives and high officials. Nearby was the king's palace complex and villages for the administrators and workmen. Two other large pyramids were constructed by his successors Khafre (known as Cephren in Greek) and Menkaure (Mycerinus in Greek). Khafre's pyramid is almost as large as Khufu's, but its internal structure is much simpler, with a single tomb chamber at the base of the structure. One of the most famous ancient Egyptian structures, the king-headed lion or Sphinx, bears Khafre's features. It was constructed to guard the sacred realm of the dead kings. The power that emanated from these kings was believed to have continued to activate the universe in which their successors ruled. While of the same design, Menkaure's pyramid is much smaller, and its construction marks the end of the era of massive pyramid construction. The pyramids built during the following dynasty were relatively small and poorly constructed.

During the early dynasties, these pharaohs were central to the Egyptian state. They were considered divine, sometimes referred to as "the good god." These paramount rulers controlled economic exchange, served at the top of a great bureaucracy, and acted as the heads of state religion. Toward the end of the Old Kingdom, the construction of smaller pyramids paralleled a decline in royal power. Following the pattern often seen in ancient states and empires, the Old Kingdom collapsed after five centuries of strong central rule, and was followed by a period of decentralization. The provinces became competitive petty kingdoms that fought with each other, either alone or in small alliances. With the fragmentation of the Egyptian state into these smaller territorial political groups, provincial governors and bureaucrats gained more power. Comparatively large mud-brick tombs were erected in these provinces, displaying the growing power of local authorities.

The beginning of the Middle Kingdom, around 2000 B.C., was marked by the reunification of Upper and Lower Egypt under a dynastic line centered at the city of Thebes in Upper Egypt. The rulers pacified southern Egypt and then overthrew the dynasty in power to the north. The capital was brought back to Memphis, and the fortified towns of the earlier decentralized period disappeared. With increased administrative centralization, a second era of ostentatious pyramid building began. Yet the Middle Kingdom pharaohs were less despotic. Trading contacts were extended, and parts of Nubia, just to the south of Egypt, were conquered. Huge fortresses were erected to solidify control of this frontier along the Nile.

During the first half of the second millennium B.C., central administrative authority again weakened, and a period of short-lived dynasties and regionalization followed. In the sixteenth century B.C., a later Thebean dynasty began a third era of unification and centralization, called the New Kingdom. The dynasties of this period are richly documented in historical texts. The kings of the New Kingdom reasserted control from the Nile Delta to Nubia and conquered parts of Lebanon,

Palestine, and southern Syria. No earlier Egyptian polity had established such far-ranging external contacts. The highly centralized government of the New Kingdom depended on large external tribute levees for its maintenance and support.

During the New Kingdom, kings were considered quasi-divine, the mediators between humans and the gods. These rulers often married their own sisters to concentrate status and divinity in a dynastic line. The kings lived in elaborate complexes that contained throne rooms and extensive private chambers for the royal family, harems, court officials, and servants. The pharaohs adopted new burial customs; their mummies were buried in rock-cut tombs in the Valley of Kings near Thebes. Among the New Kingdom pharaohs were a number of historically renowned figures: Tuthmosis III, Ahkenaten, Tutankhamen (better known as King Tut), and Ramses II.

During the New Kingdom, an important innovation in irrigation permitted the agricultural development of the broad Nile Delta. The **shaduf**, a labor-saving bucket-and-lever lifting device, allowed water to be raised a few feet from wells or ditches into gardens and fields. This innovation, still in use today, may have contributed to the demographic buildup in the delta during the New Kingdom. The kings of the nineteenth dynasty divided their residence between the traditional centers of power, Thebes and Memphis, and a new royal residence that was established in the eastern delta.

The administrative centralization and stability that characterized the New Kingdom came to a halt around 1000 B.C. Hostilities erupted when strong provincial leaders and local army commanders increased their regional power. A period of foreign intervention followed, and for millennia, Egypt did not regain its autonomy for anything but a brief interlude. The Nile Valley was ruled in succession by Assyrians, the Persians, and then Alexander the Great, king of the Macedonians (northern Greece). The almost 3000-year succession of pharaohs ended when Alexander appointed one of his generals as ruler of Egypt.

Several hypotheses have been advanced to account for the highly centralized nature of the early Egyptian state. The constricted distribution and relatively small proportion of usable land (along the Nile) may have fostered the concentration and monopolization of wealth. Commoners and peasants would have had relatively few options when they were heavily taxed or asked to contribute to labor gangs. In an environment such as the fertile Nile Valley, surrounded by desert, it would be very difficult for people to move away, and yet maintain access to cultivable land. The critical nature of water control (often requiring centralized maintenance and adjudication) also may have been a factor; however, according to Karl Butzer, of the University of Texas, Austin, early Egyptian irrigation systems were not highly centralized and were largely under local control. Nevertheless, the disastrous potential of Nile flooding may have encouraged the establishment of a central agency to help alleviate periodic local disasters. Finally, Egypt had a number of military-political threats on its borders throughout much of its history, and this, too, may have encouraged the centralization of power in the hands of a few to coordinate a strong defense. While none of these interpretations is convincing on its own, they do suggest questions and directions for future research.

PYRAMIDS

Ancient monuments in the Old and New Worlds.

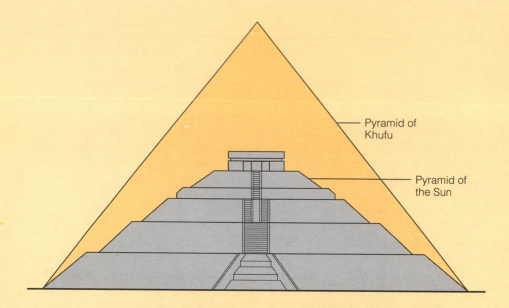

Pyramid of Khufu

Pyramid of the Sun

A comparison of the Pyramid of the Sun at Teotihuacan and the Great Pyramid at Giza, which is approximately 146 m high.

Pyramid-shaped structures were built by ancient civilizations in both the Old and New Worlds, representing the wealth and power of those who erected them. Yet the building techniques employed and the specific uses of these constructions varied greatly from one ancient civilization to another.

The best-known pyramids in the Old World were erected by the ancient Egyptians during the third millennium B.C. The Egyptian pyramids were constructed of cut-stone blocks, with internal passageways and tombs. The first royal pyramid, built around 2680 B.C. at Saqqarah, was a six-step pyramid. Over the next century, the pyramid shape was perfected, culminating in the magnificent pyramids at Giza. The construction of these Old Kingdom pyramids required an enormous expenditure of energy and labor, involving both unskilled labor to quarry and transport the stones, and skilled masons who would cut, fit, and smooth the stones. Given the construction techniques known at the time, such large structures had to be in the shape of a pyramid to support their weight.

Constructed as monuments for kings, the Egyptian pyramids have as their origin the tomb architecture of predynastic Egypt. They were built in one episode of construction, without outside stairways, and were not meant to be climbed once they were completed. They served not only as tombs for the pharaohs, but also as their houses for eternity. As such, the pyramids reflect the importance Egyptians placed on life in the afterworld.

Kurt Mendelssohn argues that the construction of monumental tombs for the pharaohs, who could have been interred at much less cost, was not the only goal. It was the erection of the pyramid itself that was important. He suggests that pyramid construction was an administrative strategy used by the pharaohs to institutionalize the state. The thousands of peasants who worked on the pyramids depended on the central government for food during three months of the year. They were fed from food surpluses obtained from villages through taxation. One consequence was that the population became reliant on the state bureaucracy to redistribute food and organize labor.

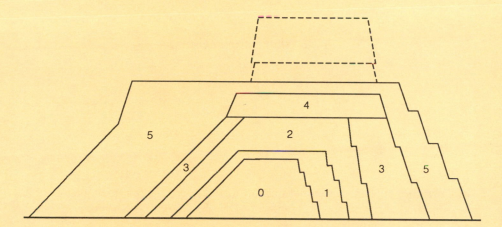

The building episodes of a Late Post-classic pyramid in the Basin of Mexico. The earliest pyramid is represented by 0 and the latest by 5.

Whether this outcome was planned is unclear. Nevertheless, Old Kingdom pyramid construction may have had some of the consequences outlined by Mendelssohn.

Monumental structures in the New World were very different in form from their Egyptian counterparts. For example, in western Mexico, such buildings could be circular as well as square and rectangular. Throughout the New World, most large structures were actually truncated pyramids, with flat tops. Most Mesoamerican pyramids were rubble-filled, with a cut-stone facing. However, some central Mexican pyramids have a core of adobe bricks with a stone facing held together by mortar. Other North American pyramids, such as Monks Mound at Cahokia, were built almost entirely of earthen fill.

The Mesoamerican pyramids were smaller than the earlier Old Kingdom pyramids at Giza. Two of the most massive Mesoamerican pyramids—the Pyramid of the Sun and the Pyramid of the Moon—were constructed at Teotihuacan in central Mexico around 100 B.C. At its base,

the Pyramid of the Sun is about the size of the Pyramid of Cheops at Giza but only about half as high. In contrast to the Egyptian pyramids, Mesoamerican structures often were built in a series of construction episodes, in which they were enlarged and often changed drastically in appearance. The largest Mesoamerican pyramid, the Great Pyramid at Cholula (in the state of Puebla), was enlarged many times over hundreds of years.

New World pyramids generally served as foundations for other public buildings, such as temples, shrines, palaces, or elite residences. Stairways provided access to the structures above. The truncated pyramids emulated natural features, such as hills and mountains, raising structures above the ground level. The platforms increased the "visibility" of the public buildings, while making direct access to them more difficult. While many New World pyramids include burial features, few were designed or used (as were the Egyptian pyramids) exclusively as the final resting place for a particular ruler or elite figure.

An-Yang

A late Shang city in China

The emergence of Shang civilization initially appeared to be without direct antecedents; it was formerly thought that early Chinese cities and states arose due to Mesopotamian contact. But as with Egypt and the Indus Valley, recent archaeological fieldwork has demonstrated that the trajectory from the diversity of the Chinese Neolithic to the rise of early civilizations was more continuous, with outside influences playing a small role. The development of civilization in China was largely indigenous, with its own character and its own writing system. Wheat, barley, and the horse-drawn chariot were significant western introductions into early China; however, these innovations were not the principal stimuli for the rise of Chinese civilization.

During the Yang-shao period (5000 to 3000 B.C.) of the North Chinese Neolithic, the Huang Ho (Yellow River) region was settled by millet and pig farmers who resided in large villages of up to 100 houses. One such village was Ban-pots'un. (See Chapter Five.) The community included large central structures that may have served as clan meeting houses or the residences of certain influential villagers. Marks found on some Yang-shao ceramic vessels resemble written Shang characters dating to more than several thousand years later. During the subsequent Longshan period (3000 to 2205 B.C.), significant changes took place in North Chinese social organization, including increased social ranking. Compared to earlier Yang-shao burials, Longshan mortuary assemblages exhibit more variation; some include jade ornaments and ceremonial weapons. For the first time, many of the Longshan period settlements were walled.

During Longshan times, scapulimancy, the interpretation of cracking patterns on heated bone, was practiced. Although no written inscriptions are found on Longshan bones, Chinese written characters have been found on numerous bones at later sites. In later times, divination rituals involving **oracle bones** were addressed to royal ancestors and were carried out by religious specialists. In addition to scapulimancy, the manifestations of ritual were prevalent in many other ways during the Longshan period. Fantastic or mythical animals were crafted on objects of pottery, wood, and jade. Many of these objects were likely associated with shamanistic rituals that we know were important in the later Three Dynasty and Shang times.

The era following Longshan in North China is known as the San dai, or Three Dynasties: Xia, Shang, and Zhou. The Xia dynasty (2205 to 1766 B.C.) is the first hereditary dynasty in recorded Chinese history. Although later historical texts suggest that there were seventeen rulers in 471 years, the period is still somewhat of a mystery archaeologically. K. C. Chang, of Harvard University, has suggested that the archaeologically known Erlitou culture, with a spatial and temporal distribution that fits the historical accounts of the Xia dynasty, is the archaeological manifestation of that dynasty.

The Xia dynasty was transitional between the late Neolithic and the Shang dynasty. Scapulimancy continued to be practiced. Although there are no known

inscriptions on oracle bones, signs and symbols have been found on pottery vessels. Bronzeworking, which was in evidence by the end of Longshan, became an increasingly important craft. According to a first-millennium B.C. text, the two principal affairs of the Chinese state were ritual and warfare. Most of the bronze was used to make ritual food and drink vessels, musical instruments, and weapons. Other valuable objects were crafted from jade, turquoise, and lacquer. A few basic bronze implements were fashioned, but most utilitarian tools, including knives, sickles, and hoes, were made in stone, shell, wood, antler, or bone. Wheel-thrown ceramic ware, first manufactured toward the end of the Neolithic, increased in abundance, although handmade pottery also continued to be used.

Two palatial house foundations of stamped earth, found in later strata at the site of Erlitou, also indicate a possible break with Longshan. Both palace foundations are much larger than the other houses at the site. The largest foundation was 108 by 100 m (350 by 330 ft), and was associated with ritual burials (including one individual with bound hands).

The decline of the Xia dynasty coincided roughly with the rise of the Shang dynasty (1766 to 1122 B.C.). The Shang period is known from archaeological excavations at its last capital, An-yang, information from other ancient sites, and written records. The Chinese state had developed by Shang times. The major Shang centers were Ao (an early capital located underneath the modern industrial city of Zhengzhou), Lo-yang, and An-yang. Each had a clearly defined ceremonial core, inhabited by a royal household and also containing a series of nonresidential buildings (meeting halls and ancestral temples). The ceremonial core was surrounded by a service area and the pit-house residences of the commoners.

Ao is partially hidden by contemporary building; however, at its height it is thought to have covered 3.4 sq km (1.3 sq mi). The central precinct was enclosed by a huge earthen wall 9 m (30 ft) high and 36 m (118 ft) wide at the base. The quantity and quality of artifacts indicate the presence of hundreds of skilled craftspeople. One area contained more than a dozen high-temperature pottery kilns, each associated with dense concentrations of oven-fired and broken pottery. In another area, human and animal bones were worked into fish hooks, awls, axes, and hairpins. Bronzeworking was one of

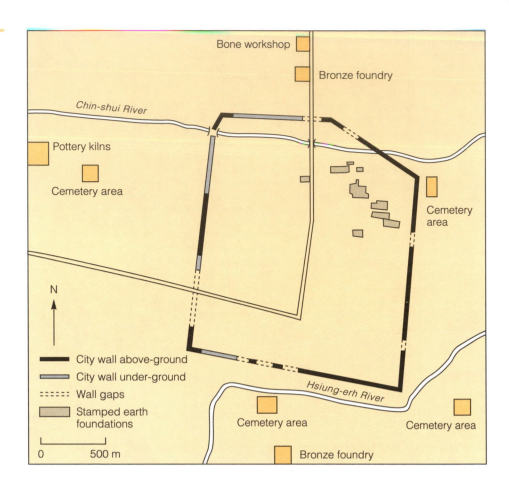

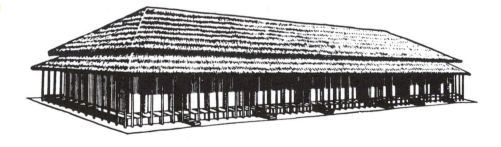

An artist's reconstruction of a Shang palace at Ao.

the most highly developed crafts. The metal was fashioned into ornaments as well as tools. In one workshop, molds were used to mass-produce bronze arrow points. As yet, the Shang materials contemporaneous with Zhengzhou have yielded no definitive indications of writing, chariots, or royal mausoleums, all features well linked with An-yang and its late Shang materials. However, the construction technology and the basic layout of the palace structure at Zhengzhou were nearly identical to that at subsequent An-yang.

Toward the end of the Shang dynasty, the capital was moved north to An-yang (ahn′yong′). As with the earlier capital, An-yang was a large ceremonial and administrative center with monumental architecture surrounded by craft areas (including bronze foundries, stone and bone workshops, and pottery kilns). Circling the center were residential hamlets (small concentrations of wooden houses with thatched roofs), a royal cemetery area at Hsi-pei-kang, and more workshops.

An-yang consisted of three groups of buildings with a total of fifty-three rectan-

gular structures built on top of stamped-earth platforms. The largest structure was 60 m (195 ft) long and is presumed to have been a royal palace. Between two of the building groups is a square, earthen foundation that is thought to have been a ceremonial altar. As a whole, this building complex appears to have been well planned, although it almost certainly was implemented in several construction stages.

Late Shang society was highly stratified into upper and lower classes. The extent of social distinctions, present as early as the Longshan period, were exaggerated by the establishment of An-yang. The king, his family, and officials were at the top. Kings were considered divine, with power flowing from the king to the nobility to the court, and lastly to the commoners. Only those of high status possessed the spectacular Shang bronzes, used the Chinese script, and controlled the archives. The king and his court received grain and other forms of tribute, which they used to support a lavish style in life as well as death. In the eleven large "royal" tombs at Hsi-pei-kang, Shang kings were

Sacrificial burials at An-yang.

A chariot burial at An-yang.

An inscribed oracle bone from the Shang period.

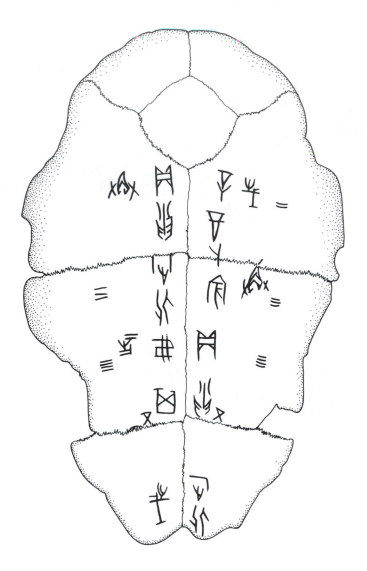

buried with sacrificed retainers, horse-drawn chariots, and large quantities of luxury items, including bronze vessels, shell and bone ornaments, jade, and pottery. For each of these graves, the earth moving alone would have required thousands of working days. The royal tombs were surrounded by 1200 smaller and simpler graves, most of which lack any grave goods.

The lower class was comprised of farmers and craftspeople. Some of the more skillful and highly specialized ones (bronzesmiths, lacquerwarers, and wood carvers) may have had some of the privileges of the upper class; yet overall the farmers and craftspeople used stone and bone implements, coarse gray pottery, and lived in semisubterranean pithouses. The commoners labored for public works and military campaigns. At the bottom of the

lower class were the war captives, who were kept as slaves or served as sacrificial victims for rituals and dedications of temples.

Shang civilization is famous for its bronzework. Food and drinking vessels are the most common bronze items, but some weapons, chariot and cavalry fittings, and musical instruments also were made of bronze. Small objects, such as spearpoints, were made by pouring a molten mix of copper and tin into molds. Large ceremonial vessels were made by a more complex process involving clay prototypes. During the first half of the twentieth century, western scholars familiar with the An-yang bronzes presumed that the metalworking technology was introduced from Europe or Southwest Asia. Yet the absence of such western techniques as annealing, hammering, and lost wax casting, and the presence of complex mold-casting technologies, point to an indigenous origin for Shang bronzeworking. The roots of late Shang metallurgy may lie in the sophisticated pottery kilns that were employed as early as the late Neolithic.

At An-yang, scapulimancy became more complex and sophisticated. In addition to the shoulder blades of cattle and water buffalo, diviners also used the carpaces of turtles. Once an answer was obtained, by consulting ancestral spirits and interpreting the cracks on the oracle bones, both the question and the answer were sometimes recorded on the surface of the bone. A symbol similar to the later written character for "book" is found on one bone, indicating the presence of scribes. The earliest Chinese writing may have been expressed on silk, bamboo, or wooden tablets. These surfaces commonly were used for written inscriptions in the last half of the first millennium B.C.; however, no texts on these highly perishable materials yet have been found for Shang. By late Shang times, Chinese written language developed to the point where over 3000 phonetic, ideographic, and pictographic symbols were employed. Based on more than 150,000 inscribed turtle shells, in addition to inscriptions made in bronze, pottery, and stone, it is clear that early Chinese writing was related closely to the political, military, and ritual activities of the upper class and had little to do with mercantile matters.

The borders of the Shang state are unknown; however, late Shang rulers had at least some control over a fairly large area in northern China. The extent of their influence varied according to distance from the capital. Shang rulers traveled widely across their domain, and the extent of their influence was related in part to their actual physical presence. The rulers were assisted by a complex hierarchy of local nobles, who had considerable autonomy in their own territories. These local lords were responsible for collecting taxes and supplying men for public projects and military campaigns. On occasion, armies as large as 30,000 men were amassed to wage war against "barbarians" at the edge of the Shang domain. Military success depended on the horse-drawn chariot. War was waged more for people than for land.

In these campaigns, thousands of prisoners were taken, most of whom were sacrificed or used as slaves.

Despite major changes in political organization, written communication, and social stratification, the basic subsistence technology of the late Shang period changed little from earlier times. Millet remained the principal food crop in North China, supplemented by rice and wheat. Stone hoes, harvesting knives, and wooden digging sticks remained the primary cultivation implements. In some areas, two crops a year were grown, suggesting irrigation; yet large-scale water control was not implemented until the last centuries B.C. Changes in labor practices may have constituted the most dramatic shift in the Shang economy. Larger numbers of people were employed in farming, thereby increasing production per unit of land as well as the amount of cultivated terrain. The reliance on human energy may help account for the kind of military campaigns that were waged, as well as the rapid demographic increases that occurred in China during this period. The importance of agricultural labor may have encouraged rural families to grow, since children could be used in the fields at an early age. One consequence would have been large-scale population growth.

The Shang dynasty was overthrown by people living on its western periphery in the vicinity of Xianyang on the Wei River. It is unclear whether the defeat resulted from the internal rebellion of a distant Shang province or by the rebellion of an outside group of people forced by nomadic pressures to settle in or near the Shang state (as is suggested by one 3000-year-old text). Whatever the case, the new dynasty did not create an entirely new civilization; it incorporated the existing network of towns and officials. It was on the foundation of the Shang dynasty that the following Zhou dynasty established China's first empire.

Men make their own history, but they do not make it just as they please; they do not make it under circumstances chosen by themselves, but under circumstances directly encountered, given and transmitted from the past.

K. Marx (1963)

THE ROOTS OF CHINESE CUISINE

Ancient culinary ritual and traditions

Archaeologists often study containers of fired clay, stone, and metal to decipher information about chronology or past technologies; however, the main function of these vessels was the preparation and serving of food and drink. The pottery and bronze vessels of the Shang and Zhou dynasties provide one perspective on ancient Chinese culinary traditions. This archaeological perspective is supplemented vividly by historical texts and inscriptions from these times. For example, *The Three Lis* or the *Three Books of Rites*, solemn texts from the Han period (206 B.C. to A.D. 220) that record ritual and courtly behavior from ancient China, provide detailed descriptions of food production and feasts, including the types and amounts of food and wine served for certain occasions. Oracle bone and bronze vessel inscriptions from the Shang period include written characters that refer to certain foods, rituals, and cooking techniques and whose shapes suggest ancient practices.

It is not surprising that many groups of people are strongly concerned with food. However, according to K. C. Chang, the Chinese are more concerned with food and eating than any other people. He points out that in contemporary China, a familiar greeting is: "Have you eaten?" Chang believes this preoccupation has a long history, as do many Chinese culinary traditions. According to one account, when a duke asked Confucius (551–479 B.C.) about military strategy, the sage replied, "I have indeed heard about matters pertaining to meat stands and meat platters, but I have not learned military matters" (Chang, 1973, p. 496). In ancient China, knowledge and skill in the preparation of food and drink were important personal characteristics. King T'ang, the founder of the Shang dynasty, chose a cook as his prime minister. According to several Zhou texts, a cooking vessel called the *ting* cauldron was the primary symbol of the state. Along with differences in dress and adornment, part of the definition of a "barbarian" or a non-Chinese was a person who did not prepare and consume food in the customary manner. Included in the *Three Books of Rites* is a personnel roster of the king's palace; almost 60% of the 4000 people responsible for the king's private residential quarters were involved with food and wine, with specialists assigned to menu preparation, table service, meat, fish, game, shellfish and turtles, wine, fruits and vegetables, pickling, and salt.

The dualism between *yin* and *yang*, central to much of contemporary Chinese culture, is also present in the categorization of food. A basic dichotomy exists between food and drink. Food is further divided into grain food and "dishes" that are combinations of meat and vegetables. These distinctions, and their associated rules, are integral to the Chinese way of eating today and seem not to have changed much since Zhou times. In the past as well as today, the basic or essential meal consists of grain and water. The basic word *shih*, for food (as opposed to drink), also, in a narrower sense, refers to grain. Meat and vegetable dishes are considered secondary in importance and are to be eaten in moderation.

The historical texts indicate that eating together was a major enjoyment in ancient China. Yet it also was a serious social affair, with strict rules to be observed, including correct table manners and an etiquette regarding the appropriate foods to be served at specific occasions. In Shang and Zhou times, people from the upper ranks ate individually, kneeling on mats. The number of dishes served to an individual was in large part determined by one's rank and age. Utensils and serving platters were placed beside the individual in specific arrangements, certain foods on the right and others on the left. In addition, rules specified the arrangement of certain foods on the serving vessels and how they were presented at the table. Children were trained early to eat with their right hands. In late Zhou times, crunching bones with one's teeth, eating too quickly, slurping down soup, and picking one's teeth were all specified as inappropriate etiquette.

In one contemporary Chinese cookbook, twenty methods for heating food are mentioned. Many of these procedures, including boiling, steaming, and roasting, were also important in Zhou texts. Yet the ancient accounts do not mention stir-frying, which is prevalent today. Nevertheless, in the past as well as the present, it is the preparation before cooking that is essential to Chinese cuisine. The word for cooking in the Zhou texts literally means "to cut and cook." Great significance is placed on the art of mixing flavors and ingredients into distinctive soups and stews before they are heated.

Social class was a major factor in dietary variation. Peasants relied on a basic grain diet, using the platters and vessels associated with such food. According to the textual record, the meat dishes were intended for rituals or upper-class feasts. Meat was usually dried, cooked, or pickled. A few recipes for elaborate dishes of Shang and Zhou times are known; these are for the so-called Eight Delicacies, which were prepared specifically for the elderly. They included the Rich Fry (pickled meat over rice), the Similar Fry (pickled meat over millet), the Bake (baked stuffed pig or ram), the Pounded (pounded meat fillets softened by pickle and vinegar), the Steeped (newly killed beef steeped in wine), the Grill (dried meat seasoned with cinnamon, ginger, and salt), the Soup Balls (fried cakes of meat and rice), and the Liver and Fat (roasted dog liver cooked in fat).

In ancient Chinese cooking, each variety of food and drink was associated with different ceramic and bronze vessels. There were vessels for boiling and simmering and others for steaming. For serving and eating, ladles and chopsticks were used, although hands were employed as often as chopsticks. Special cups for water and wine also were made. In the era of the Shang dynasty, bronze vessels were used only to serve grains and drinks made from grain, but never to serve meat. The most important vessels for meat dishes were made from wood, basketry, and pottery.

Most excavated Zhou period burial assemblages contain ceramic vessels. The great majority of these graves do not include just one or two containers, but a whole range of different vessel forms. Chang has reasoned that most of these individuals were interred with a set of containers for cooking and serving grain, serving meat, and for drinking. Chang's deduction would have been difficult, if not impossible, to derive without the careful juxtaposition of texts with archaeology. Together, these complementary records are serving to uncover the deep traditions of Chinese cuisine.

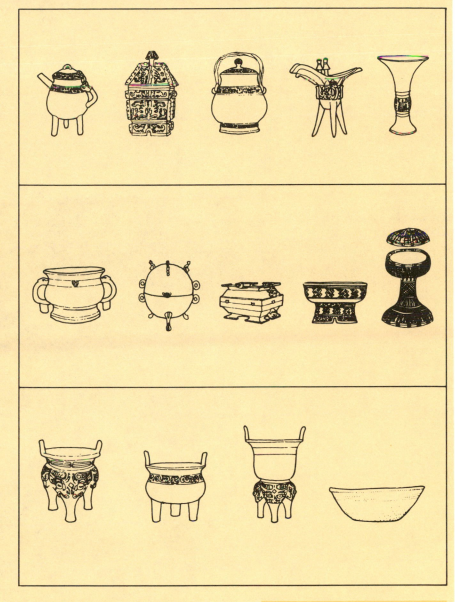

Examples of Shang and Zhou food and drinking vessels: drinking vessels (top), serving vessels (center), cooking vessels (bottom).

Xianyang

Terracotta soldiers and the Qin dynasty

A terracotta soldier guarding the tomb of Shih Huang Ti.

The Zhou dynasty (1122 to third century B.C.) marks the beginning of imperial China and the traditions that persisted for the next 2000 years and into the present. Zhou society was highly stratified at its center, with the king and a royal court at the top. Away from this core, the adjacent areas were divided into partially independent provinces, and administration was enacted by semifeudal lords who had great control over their local domains. Periodic civil wars erupted between these lords and the king.

The Chinese state during the Three Dynasties (including the early Zhou) was built on a hierarchical network of large lineages in which the distance away from the main male line of descent determined relative political status and access to power. Each walled town was inhabited primarily by the members of a particular lineage.

The second half of the Zhou period was characterized by great political change and upheaval, with warring states and shifting capitals. It was also a time

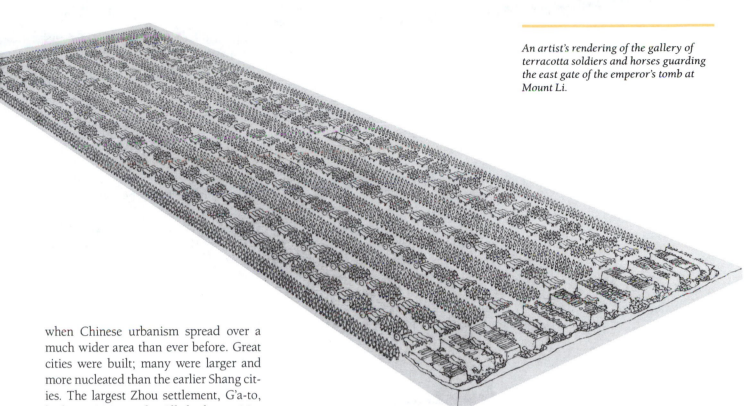

when Chinese urbanism spread over a much wider area than ever before. Great cities were built; many were larger and more nucleated than the earlier Shang cities. The largest Zhou settlement, G'a-to, had 270,000 people. All the large cities were walled. By 600 B.C., iron casting was practiced, and iron agricultural tools were in use. Large irrigation works were constructed, and wet-rice irrigation became increasingly important. Changes in agricultural technology enabled rapid increases in population density. Late Zhou socioeconomic structure placed great emphasis on the taxation of peasants in lieu of labor drafts. Kinship bonds began to diminish, and territorial units and bureaucracies gained in importance. Late Zhou was the time of Confucius, who preached order, deference, and family ties, perhaps in response to rapid social transition and transformation. While large-scale political integration remained relatively weak and fragmentary, a single system of measurement was adopted across most of China. There was increased interregional trade and commercial activity, as well as greater cultural unity.

By the third century B.C., the descendants of the western Zhou kings ruled an increasingly small area outside their original homeland. As the Zhou polity weakened, other states rose in influence. The expansion of the Qin polity and its short-lived dynasty (221 to 207 B.C.) eclipsed the Zhou, along with five other contemporary states.

Shih Huang Ti inherited the throne of the Qin kingdom at age 13 in 246 B.C. During the first twenty-five years of his reign, he frequently engaged in battle, eventually conquering six other major kingdoms. For this reason, six was considered the lucky number of the Qin. Through military prowess, Shih Huang Ti unified China into a single imperial kingdom in 221 B.C. and declared himself China's first emperor. The empire was ruled from the capital city of Xianyang (she-on'yong), to which he forced over 100,000 royal and wealthy families from throughout the empire to move. Shih Huang Ti had luxurious palaces built in Xianyang that were replicas of royal residences in the conquered states. By moving local lords to Xianyang, the feudal aristocracy was forcibly detached from the land and its people, weakening their power. This move also served to centralize the Qin empire by concentrating economic and political power in a single capital.

According to historical records, Shih Huang Ti was an ambitious and ruthless emperor. He built the Great Wall along China's northern periphery by joining walls that had been constructed by earlier feudal states. Although the traditional view is that the wall was to protect the newly formed empire from the nomadic herders of Asia to the north, others have suggested that its principal function was to prevent heavily taxed peasants from escaping taxes and conscription. The 2400-km (1500-mile) wall, built by 700,000 conscripts and wide enough for six horses abreast, remains the longest fortification anywhere. Many men perished while working on the wall, inspiring some to call it "the longest cemetery in the world." Shih Huang Ti also established China's first standing army, a body that may have contained more than a million people.

To weaken regional autonomy, Shih Huang Ti destroyed the feudal structure that had existed for centuries. Because he saw Confucian philosophy as a threat to his authority, all the books of this school were burned, and Confucian scholars who refused to accept his reforms were buried alive.

The centralizing tendencies of Shih Huang Ti included increasing codification of a Chinese legal system and the standardization of Chinese character writing, so that the written language could be understood throughout the empire. Weights and measures, coins, and the gauges of chariot wheels were increasingly regulated and made more homogeneous. Paper was invented during the Qin dynasty. In the grave of one Qin official, more than 1200 bamboo slips were found, bound into a series of books and containing an explicit legal code specifying particular crimes and their punishments. In addition to intensified road building, a canal system was constructed by Shih Huang Ti to enhance communication and transportation. The canal system was one of the greatest inland water communications systems in the ancient world, and several canals are still functioning today.

As soon as Shih Huang Ti became emperor, he began building his tomb. According to history, 700,000 laborers from all parts of the country worked for thirty-six years on the project, a virtual subterranean palace for the emperor to live in for eternity. According to early Chinese historians (the tomb itself has not yet been excavated), the tomb was filled with models of palaces, pavilions, and of-fices. All the country's major waterways were reproduced in quicksilver within the tomb, as were heavenly constellations. His outer coffin was made of molten copper, and fine vessels, precious stones, and other rarities were buried with him.

The emperor's burial tomb, called Mount Li, was at one time 46 m (150 ft) tall. Built in the center of a spirit city, an area enclosed by an inner wall, it contained sacred stone tablets and prayer temples. Beyond this area was an outer city enclosed by a high rectangular stone wall 7 m (23 ft) thick at the base. The total complex covered 200 ha (500 acres). Today most of the walls and temples have been removed.

About 1370 m (4500 ft) east of Mount Li, recent excavations have revealed one of the most astonishing ancient spectacles. Guarding the east side of the emperor's tomb is a brick-floored, 1.2-ha (3-acre) gallery of terracotta soldiers and horses. Collapsed pillars indicate that a roof once covered the underground battlefield. In the royal tombs of the previous Shang dynasty, kings and high-ranking officials were interred with living warriors, women, servants, and horses. This practice, which had ceased for centuries prior to the Qin dynasty, evidently was revived in symbolic fashion by Shih Huang Ti.

Although only part of the gallery has been excavated, it is estimated that between 6000 and 7000 terracotta figures were buried, along with terracotta horses and wooden chariots. The warriors, who carried real weapons—swords, spears, and crossbows—are all slightly larger than life-size, arranged in battle formations, and dressed in uniforms of various rank. Traces of pigment indicate that the uniforms were brightly colored. Of the excavated figures, none look exactly alike; their facial expressions vary, suggesting that they were realistic portraits of each individual in the emperor's honor guard. Even the horses were very finely crafted, appearing alert and tense, as they would be in battle.

The army and horses are supplemented by a rich artifact assemblage, including gold, jade, and bronze objects, linen, silk, bamboo and bone artifacts, pottery utensils, and iron agricultural

tools. Elemental analysis on the swords has revealed that they were made from an alloy of copper, tin, and thirteen other elements.

Shih Huang Ti always lived and worked in guarded secrecy, because several assassination attempts were made on his life. Only a few trusted ministers ever knew where he was. He died on a journey to the eastern provinces, and his death was kept a secret from all except his youngest son. His prime minister and his chief eunuch (castrated male) apparently plotted to keep the death secret for their own ambitious reasons. They wanted the emperor's youngest son to succeed to the throne, instead of an older brother, as Shih Huang Ti had decreed. The councilors reasoned that they could more easily influence and manipulate the younger son. The brother, who had been exiled to the northwestern frontier to help build the Great Wall, was sent a fake order to commit suicide, which he did, paving the way for the younger son to become the new emperor. Nevertheless, Shih Huang Ti's efforts to expand his domain to both the north and the south sapped his treasury, so Qin preeminence was short-lived.

While the Qin dynasty was brief, China's first episode of unification was not. Qin rule was followed by the Han dynasty which lasted for about 400 years (206 B.C. to A.D. 220). The Han unification was in part made possible by technological innovations that were developed in Zhou times: iron tools, wet-rice irrigation, the ox-drawn plow, improved roads, and the crossbow. Under the Han dynasty, China continued as a unified empire, but with greater political stability. The economy was prosperous, and a standardized coinage circulated throughout China.

During the Han dynasty, China became even more densely settled. The world's first census in the years A.D. 1 and 2 lists the population of the empire as 57,700,000, with cities of up to 250,000 people. One late Han city may have contained as many as a half a million people. The decisions made by the Han monarchs were implemented through 1500 administrative provinces, each of which was centered at a walled town. No other political system of its era—not even the Roman empire—was as massive in size or bureaucratic complexity.

GREAT ZIMBABWE

*An important trading center in
southcentral Africa*

The ancient Egyptian state, with its close ties to the Mediterranean world, had few direct contacts with regions far to the south and west. Only the area down to the Nile's first rapids (near the present Aswan Dam) was ruled consistently by the pharaohs, although slaves, ebony, and ivory were brought from further south. Early in the last millennium B.C., following New Kingdom penetrations into Upper Nubia, the Nubian kingdom of Kush (in what is now the Sudan) arose. The Kushites were ethnically and linguistically different from the Egyptians, and they had their own tomb style. Later Egypt came briefly under Kushite control, and the intermingling of these two East African cultures intensified. In the fourth century B.C., following an episode of Egyptian control, a major center on this portion of the southern Nile was established at Meroë. For almost a millennium (until the fourth century A.D.), the Meroitic kingdom maintained trade connections with both the Mediterranean world and the southern Sahara. Yet after its collapse, the fertile grasslands around Meroë became the homeland for more rural lifeways. To the west, state-level societies did not develop on the southern fringes of the Sahara Desert until the first millennium A.D. In southern Africa, relatively egalitarian political formations were even more resilient.

Prior to 3000 B.C., the Sahara received considerably more rainfall than it does today. **Pastoralists**, exploiting wild cereal grasses, were widespread during the fourth millennium B.C.; the camps of these prehistoric hunters and cattle herders have been found along the shores of what were once shallow lakes. Subsequent desiccation led to the southward movement of the Saharan peoples into sub-Saharan Africa. They brought with them their cattle and eventually domesticated local sorghum and millet.

The spread of farming and domesticated animals into southern Africa is thought to have coincided with the appearance of ironworking and the spread of Bantu-speaking peoples. In much of Africa (except Egypt), iron was the first metal to be used. This contrasts with the pattern of metalworking in most of the Old World and suggests that ironworking was introduced from the north. The great efficiency of iron tools may account for the rapid spread of this technology throughout Africa upon its introduction. Prior to the spread of farmers into southern Africa during the Early Iron Age, the area was occupied by hunter-gatherers whose only tools were stone.

Peasant farmers first settled in south-central Africa, in what is now Zimbabwe (zim-bob'way), during the fourth century A.D. Northeast of the Kalahari Desert, Zimbabwe is high plateau country (1200 to 1500 m, 4000 to 5000 ft) bounded by rivers. The gently rolling plains are cool and well-watered, covered with savanna woodlands that are free of the disease-carrying tsetse fly, the scourge of equatorial Africa. Mineral deposits are abundant. Iron ores, widespread throughout much of southern and eastern Africa, are present, as are copper and gold.

The querns and grindstones found in these early farming villages indicate that grain was harvested. Sheep and goats were kept, but hunting continued to pro-

A map of Africa, with places and names mentioned in the text.

vide an important source of meat. People lived in permanent villages, some as large as several hectares, located on open ground, with little apparent concern for defense. Their huts were constructed of a wooden framework covered over with mud. The presence of slag fragments suggests that ironworking was a common skill. Such small iron artifacts as arrowheads, razors, beads, and rings are found in every village. Copper items were rarer; usually no more than a few beads or small strips have been recovered in any one excavation. Handmade ceramics were produced, of which there were several distinct regional variants. Contact with the east coast of Africa is indicated by the presence of glass trade beads and occasional marine shells.

Cattle were introduced into south-central Africa around the ninth or tenth century A.D. Cattle became important both culturally and economically. As in many African societies today, the size of one's cattle herd was probably a sign of status and a basic means of converting grain surpluses into more permanent kinds of wealth. The advent of cattle herding did not eliminate hunting. Grain crops — particularly sorghum, finger millet, cowpeas, and ground beans — also were cultivated. The banana was introduced from Indonesia by trans-Indian traders around the ninth century A.D.

During the later prehistory of Africa (in the last thousand years), complex states emerged in the central and southern regions. One group, the Karanga, was led by powerful chiefs, priests, and traders. They had contacts with societies outside the continent, and at the advent of written history, several of them were still actively involved with foreign merchants.

The most famous and largest site of the Karanga, Great Zimbabwe, is located in the central region of Zimbabwe, on a

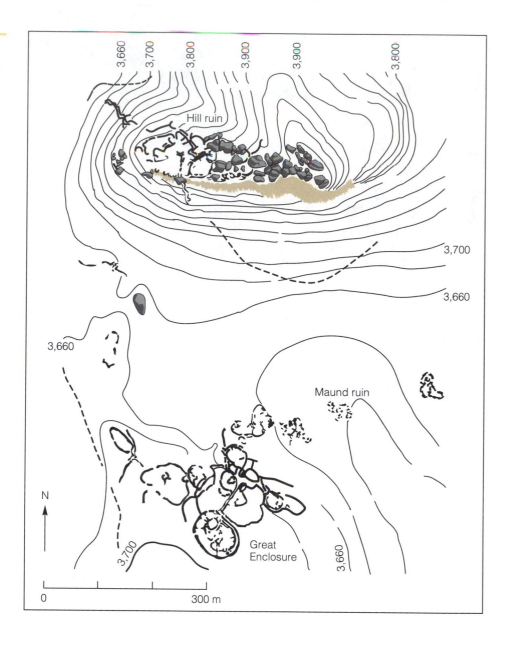

tributary stream that eventually drains into the Indian Ocean. The area is comprised of granite hills, some of which are enormous, bare, rounded domes. Because of their size, these granite features affect rainfall patterns, so that the prevailing southeasterly winds drop more rain here than in neighboring areas. To the north, the site is bounded by a narrow ridge of granite that forms a 91-m (300-ft) cliff, strewn with enormous boulders. Just south of the Great Zimbabwe ruins, the land descends into drier, more open grasslands suitable for cattle. Slabs that break off the granite domes provide abundant building material.

The Karanga began to build stone structures, including field walls, terraces, and stone enclosures, sometime after A.D. 1000. The first stone structures at Great Zimbabwe, built around A.D. 1250, were placed on top of the high cliff, possibly for defense. Simple stone walls enclosed platforms on which sat pole-and-mud houses. The walls do not follow an obvious plan. The only openings are narrow doorways, topped with simple stone lintels. The quality of the walls varies, from uncoursed sections of irregularly shaped rocks to coursed walls of granite blocks that were carefully matched.

The buildings at the site consist of two groups, one on the steep, rocky cliff, and the other on the adjacent valley floor. On the cliff, called the Hill Ruin, well-coursed walls were linked to natural boul-

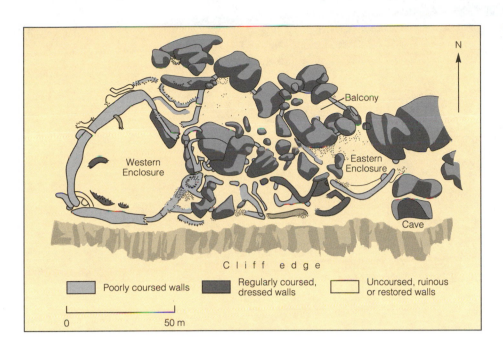

Poorly coursed walls Regularly coursed, dressed walls Uncoursed, ruinous or restored walls

0   50 m

ders, forming a series of easily defended enclosures. The largest and most substantial structure on the hill, called the Western Enclosure, consisted of two curved walls, over 9 m (30 ft) high, circling an area greater than 45 m (150 ft) in diameter. On the other end of the clifftop was a smaller structure, the Eastern Enclosure, bounded by boulders on the north and a stone wall on the south. Inside this structure were groups of circular stone platforms that held many monoliths. The presence of figurines, including seven carved soapstone birds, suggests that this enclosure was the ceremonial center of the site. The carved birds, about 36 cm (14 in.) high, were situated on top of 1-m (3-ft) stone columns. Nothing like these stone carvings have been found elsewhere.

In the valley below, larger, free-standing walled enclosures were built surrounding circular pole-and-mud houses. This pattern is especially clear at the Maund Ruin on the edge of the site, where twenty-nine separate stone walls were built. The walls abut ten circular dwelling huts, forming nine separate courtyards, each entered through doorways in the stone walls. These enclosures form single, functional units. Both in the valley and on the hill, large middens of domestic garbage have accumulated outside most of the enclosures.

One enclosure on the opposite end of the valley from the Hill Ruin, the Great Enclosure, was especially large and complex, with a perimeter wall over 10 m (33 ft) high and 5 m (16 ft) thick. The outer wall was over 240 m (800 ft) long, forming an irregular ellipse with a diameter of 89 m (292 ft). The top of the wall is decorated with a band of two lines in a chevron pattern. There are several entrances into the enclosure on the north and west sides of the wall. Containing more stonework than all the rest of the ruins at Great Zimbabwe combined, this wall is the largest prehistoric structure in sub-Saharan Africa. Several other smaller walled enclosures are situated within this outer wall, containing dwellings that housed the ruler and his family. The most striking construction inside the Great Enclosure is a solid circular stone tower rising 10 m (33 ft) from its base, which is 6 m (20 ft) in diameter. Called the Conical Tower, this structure was surrounded by platforms and large monoliths. The function of these monoliths, also associated with the Hill Ruin, remains somewhat of a mystery. Their distribution was not random; they were placed in areas having a sacred character.

Great Zimbabwe is the most elaborate and largest—40 ha (100 acres)—of the more than 150 similar stone structures constructed across the high granite region

The Great Enclosure and other ruins at Great Zimbabwe.

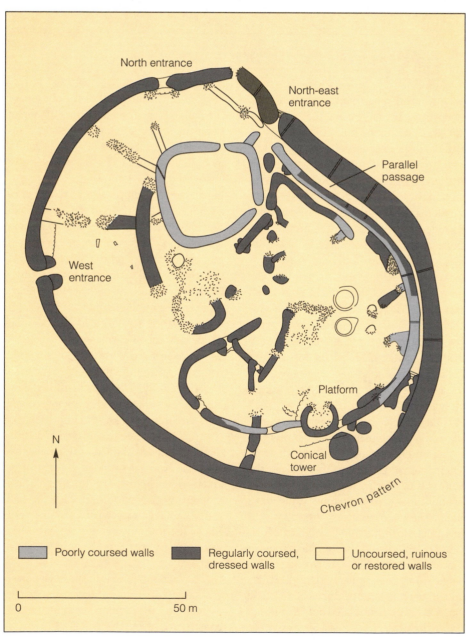

North entrance

North-east entrance

Parallel passage

West entrance

Platform

N

Conical tower

Chevron pattern

Poorly coursed walls

Regularly coursed, dressed walls

Uncoursed, ruinous or restored walls

0   50 m

The Great Enclosure.

of the Zimbabwe plateau. Many of these sites were small, having between one and five small enclosures surrounded by free-standing walls. The pottery at all these sites was relatively similar to that found at Great Zimbabwe.

The architectural florescence at Great Zimbabwe was linked to the development of a powerful and strong political authority. The construction of the extensive stone walls clearly required an organized labor effort. Centralized control of expanded trade links with Indian Ocean polities may have been an important factor, and Great Zimbabwe became an important commercial center, both locally and regionally. Specialized craftspeople made simple forged iron tools, such as hoes, axes, and arrowheads. They alloyed copper with tin and made coiled wire bracelets and pins, needles, and razors, and used imported gold to make bracelets, anklets, and beads. These metals were worked at a small scale in certain enclosures set aside for specific tasks. The presence of large numbers of spindle whorls, made from both potsherds and soapstone, indicate that cotton textiles were woven at Great Zimbabwe.

The prosperity of Great Zimbabwe was based largely on its role in coastal and long-distance trade. Exchange with Africa's east coast, which was visited by Arab and Indian merchants, provided a large number of exotic objects, including Persian and Chinese pottery, Near Eastern glass, and cowrie shells from the beaches of the Indian Ocean. These items were prestige goods and were essential to demonstrate rank. Porcelain, glass, and trinkets were found in one hoard at Great Zimbabwe in association with iron gongs, hoes, and seashells. The latter items are still recognized in the region today as symbols of chiefly authority. The traders at Great Zimbabwe also received products from the surrounding area, through either patronage or tribute. Copper was imported from the northern edge of the plateau in the form of standardized ingots. With the initiation of goldworking, the gold trade on the plateau became important by the late twelfth or early thirteenth century.

Zimbabwe reached its period of greatest influence between A.D. 1350 and 1450. The balance of power then shifted to a more northerly center on the Zambezi River. The increasing importance of copper from the north may have been a factor in redirecting trade. Later, trade and communication routes, focused on the Zambezi, may have bypassed Great Zimbabwe. The Portuguese penetrated the area in the sixteenth century and established a fort on the east coast. Their attempt to control the gold exchange of southcentral Africa further disrupted trade, and the Karanga empire disintegrated by the end of the century. Today Karanga ruins stand tall in the plateau country of Zimbabwe. The word *zimbabwe* means "stone houses" or "venerated houses," and the Karanga used it to identify the houses of chiefs. It is these ruins that now give their name to a contemporary nation.

EPILOG
THEORIES OF STATE DEVELOPMENT

*Changing views on the rise of
complex polities and urban societies*

Decades ago, the late V. Gordon Childe described the essence of what we mean by civilization in a list of ten characteristics (even if he did not succeed in providing a scientifically precise or universally acceptable definition). Charles Redman, of Arizona State University, subsequently organized Childe's indices into a list of primary and secondary characteristics. The primary characteristics are economic, organizational, and demographic in nature and suggest fundamental changes in societal structure. These include: (1) cities — dense, nucleated demographic concentrations; (2) full-time labor specialization; (3) state organization, based on territorial residence rather than kin connections; (4) class stratification — the presence of a privileged ruling stratum; and (5) the concentration of surplus. According to Redman, Childe's secondary characteristics serve to document the existence of the primary criteria. They are: (1) monumental public works; (2) long-distance exchange; (3) writing; (4) arithmetic, geometry, and astronomy; and (5) highly developed, standardized artwork.

Childe's criteria, particularly the secondary ones, are certainly not without problem. For example, the Inca, who established the largest pre-Columbian New World empire, did not have a standardized system of writing. Conversely, many societies that are not consensually recognized as civilizations built monumental edifices, engaged in long-distance exchange, crafted wonderful (and reasonably standardized) artwork, and were very aware of astronomical cycles. Even the primary criteria are subject to discussion, as kinship is known to have played a very strong organizational role in both Native American and early Chinese civilizations. Although it is next to impossible using archaeological data to distinguish full-time craft specialization from part-time specialization, occupational specialization (of an unknown degree of intensity) is often found at archaeologically known sites that are not traditionally conceptualized as civilizations. Nevertheless, Childe's criteria not only provide a valuable starting point for discussion, but the majority of them can be examined archaeologically. To the researcher, they provide a more useful beginning point than, for example, the frequently cited definition of the state as an institution that monopolizes force, a characteristic that cannot be subjected to straightforward archaeological investigation.

Given the difficulties in defining the state and civilization, as well as the evident variety in human societies and sequences of societal change, it is not really surprising that no single, satisfactory explanation has been developed to account for these transformations. In anthropology, current interpretive perspectives can be subdivided into integrative and coercive models. Integrative approaches emphasize coordination and regulation as roles of emergent institutions. The alternative coercive theories stress the role of the developing state in the resolution of intrasocietal conflicts that emerge from disparities in wealth. These alternative frameworks have their philosophical roots at least as early as the fifth century B.C., when the Greek writer Thucydides described the Peloponnesian War and its combatants. Thucydides compared different organizational frameworks, contrasting the democratic and the oligarchic. The former, typified by Athens under the ruler Pericles, was characterized by government through cooperation, with the populace described as benefiting from state policies and services. Sparta, which typified the latter, more coercive governing structure, ruled by the propertied class that controlled decision making in order to maintain their disproportionate wealth.

Most states integrate as well as coerce, although their degree of dependence on different governing strategies certainly can vary. For archaeologists, as well as other social and historical scientists, the decipherment of different organizational strategies is a promising domain for research. Yet in modeling the evolution of early states, researchers should recognize that governmental strategies can undergo change. For example, institutions may initially develop to serve integrative or regulative tasks. Once established, they may become more coercive either in the face of new challenges or to maintain whatever benefits their decision makers may have accrued. Therefore, the functions served by a governing institution may not provide a complete picture of why that institution arose in the first place.

The above line of discussion contrasts the explanatory merits of integrative versus coercive frameworks. A second analytical pathway compares the relative utility of different "prime-movers," key factors that are proposed to account for many, if not all, cases of state development. Robert Carneiro's circumscription theory, discussed in Chapter Seven, uses warfare as a key prime-mover. The late Karl Wittfogel proposed water control (irrigation) as the key variable in the rise of the "hydraulic state." Wittfogel saw water as having unique properties, essential for agriculture in the dry lands where many of the world's early states developed, yet manipulable by people in ways that other environmental resources are not. Nevertheless, although large-scale canal irrigation systems were eventually utilized in the domains of many early states (such as in Mesopotamia), the temporal sequence of state formation and the construction of these grand irrigation networks is not clear. In other areas, like Mexico's Valley of Oaxaca (Chapter Seven), it appears that most pre-Columbian water-control devices could have been managed by a few households at most. Recent ethnographic research also indicates that large-scale irrigation networks do not necessarily require centralized administration.

A third prime-mover, demographic pressure, places the causal primacy for political change on imbalances between a human population and its available food supply. Influenced by the work of agricultural economist Esther Boserup, proponents of this view have turned the work of Thomas Malthus on its head. In the late eighteenth century, Malthus argued that the advent of agriculture led to the production of food surpluses, thereby making human population growth possible and increasing the availability of leisure time. Yet anthropological work, spearheaded by Carneiro, Marshall Sahlins, of the University of Chicago, and Richard Lee, of the University of Toronto, questioned the long-held dogma surrounding surplus and leisure time. As Kent Flannery synthesized:

> The cold ethnographic fact is that the people with the most leisure time are the hunters and gatherers, who also have the lowest productivity; even primitive farmers don't produce a surplus unless they are forced to, and thus the challenge is getting people to work more, or more people to work. With better technology, people simply work less; what produces surplus is the coercive power of real authority, or the demands of elaborate ritual.
>
> (Flannery, 1972, pp. 405–406)

Recently anthropologists have questioned the arguments of Lee and Sahlins concerning leisure time. They note that most hunting-and-gathering populations suffer seasonal or periodic shortages of food or frequently lack certain key resources, like fat or protein. Yet the fact remains that, except when encouraged, few hunting-and-gathering or village people produce a great deal more than their families require.

Primarily concerned with the contemporary Third World (where runaway demographic growth is not unusual), Boserup argues that technological changes and increased productivity also could be spurred by excessive population. Archaeological adherents of Boserup's position view ancient population growth as an independent variable and the principal cause of social and economic transformations. As we saw in many of the site discussions in this chapter and in Chapters Seven and Eight, demographic growth often coincided with episodes of great social change, and in many regions it was an important

The regularities set forth by Steward, and the models constructed by Wittfogel, Carneiro, and others, have guided a great deal of fruitful research leading to knowledge about the material forces important in the rise of complex chiefdoms and states. What constructs, however, will guide us in the future?

H. T. Wright (1986)

variable. Yet correlation does not equal causality. What is not clear in most cases is the nature of the interconnections—whether population growth was the cause or the consequence of political and economic transitions.

In rural, preindustrial contexts where child labor can be economically valuable even at early ages, increases in tribute and the labor demands on households (often associated with political development) can spur cycles of demographic growth, as families opt to have more children. In other words, political and economic strategies can greatly influence demographic change. In many of the cases that we have examined, the nucleation of population around an emerging center also may have been spurred by in-migration, as people were inclined or coerced to settle near an increasingly powerful institution.

Furthermore, population growth does not necessarily imply population pressure, the latter being a notoriously difficult concept to measure. Archaeological and historical findings from many areas indicate that long-term population change is neither regular, uniform, nor ever-increasing, making it theoretically problematic to assume continuous and autonomous growth. Finally, in several cases, archaeological findings have shown that regional populations were markedly below any reasonable estimate of available agrarian production at the time of early state development.

Exchange also has been advanced as a prime-mover, although, like warfare, it is practically a human universal and therefore too broadly defined to account for the development of the state. Thus the occurrence of exchange is not as evolutionarily significant as are the nature and mode of the transactions, whether they are monopolized or controlled and by whom, the volume of the transactions involved, and the kinds of items moved (and their local importance). Until these considerations are empirically considered and refined theoretically, exchange cannot be convincingly employed as a prime-mover in state development.

Today most archaeologists have adopted multivariate approaches, recognizing that the process of state development was probably triggered by a suite of factors (including some of the prime-movers), rather than a single causal stimulus in each instance, and that even the same set of factors may not have been involved in each case. The examples of state formation discussed in these chapters illustrate that factors such as population growth, new technologies, changing exchange and interaction (including warfare) patterns, and shifts in the organization of labor and specialization were often intertwined with episodes of managerial restructuring; and yet we have sorted out neither the specific interlinkages between these factors nor their relative importance in each case. If we concede that the rise of new forms of government are often accompanied by other significant (and interdependent) shifts at both higher and lower scales (e.g., households, boundary relations), then the analytical tasks in front of us seem all the more challenging.

Nevertheless the study of the state has made tremendous progress during the last decades. Recent archaeological surveys, large-scale excavations, the study of ancient households, and ethnohistoric breakthroughs, which have helped us to unravel some of the ideological changes that made new managerial formations possible, have enriched the empirical foundation necessary to examine this key societal transformation. If these contributions continue apace (especially in the face of our dwindling, threatened archaeological record) and a series of crucial definitional and theoretical challenges are met, the opportunity for taking giant steps forward in our understanding lies immediately ahead.

SUGGESTED READINGS

Baines, John, and Jaromír Málek. 1980. *Atlas of ancient Egypt.* New York: Facts on File. A well-illustrated overview of ancient Egyptian civilization.

Chang, K. C. 1986. *The archaeology of ancient China.* New Haven: Yale University Press. A synthesis of the archaeology and early history of ancient China.

Garlake, Peter S. 1973. *Great Zimbabwe*. London: Thames & Hudson. A descriptive discussion of a key site in Africa.

Kenoyer, Jonathan M. 1991. The Indus Valley tradition of Pakistan and western India. *Journal of World Prehistory* 5:331–385. A timely overview by an areal specialist.

Redman, Charles L. 1978. *The rise of civilization: From early farmers to urban society in the ancient Near East*. San Francisco: Freeman. A classic review of the ancient Near East.

Schmandt-Besserat, Denise. 1978. The earliest precursor of writing. *Scientific American* 238(6):50–59. A groundbreaking article on early writing in Southwest Asia.

Wright, Henry T. 1986. The evolution of civilizations. In *American archaeology, past and future*, ed. D. J. Meltzer, D. D. Fowler, and J. A. Sabloff. Washington, DC: Smithsonian Institution Press. A current synthesis of archaeological interpretations.

Yoffee, Norman, and George L. Cowgill, eds. 1988. *The collapse of ancient states and civilizations*. Tucson: University of Arizona Press. A comparative collection of scholarly papers by experts from several disciplines.

10

PREHISTORIC EUROPE

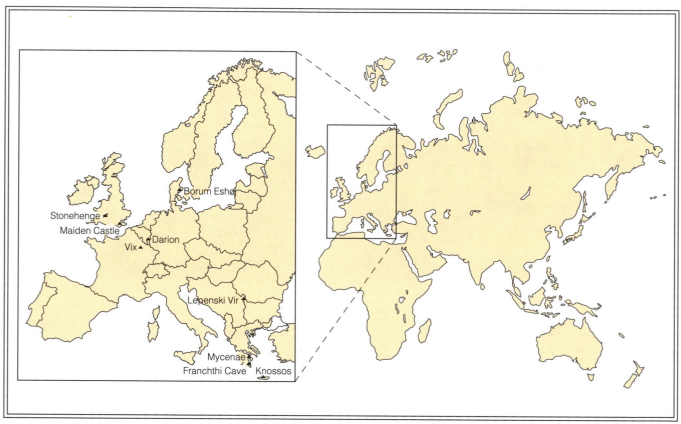

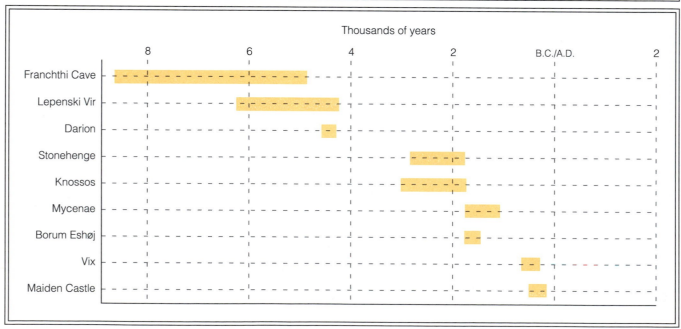

FROM THE FIRST FARMERS TO THE ROMAN EMPIRE

The prehistory of Europe, from the appearance of the first farmers to the historic events of the Roman conquest, is the story of the spread of agriculture, technological innovation, and the development of economically and politically powerful groups. This period extends from roughly 6000 B.C. until shortly after the birth of Christ. It is of interest to us today because many of the basic tenets of western civilization come largely from prehistoric Europe. Languages, customs, traditions, forms of government, and many of our fundamental solutions to the uncertainties of the world emerged in Europe during this time. This period is also of interest because, in the span of about 5000 years, we can trace the development of human societies from small, simple bands of hunter-gatherers to large, complex states with thousands of citizens.

The very earliest evidence for domesticated plants and animals in Europe is found near the end of the seventh millennium B.C. Incipient farming communities appeared in the Aegean area and Greece, with domesticated plants and animals, architecture, and ceramics brought or borrowed from the Near East (Southwest Asia). It is important to remember that, in the prehistory of Europe, most of the major innovations appeared initially in the southeast of the continent and moved gradually to the north and west. These major innovations included domesticated plants and animals, pottery, metallurgy, and writing. The earliest agriculture in southeastern Europe appeared shortly before 6000 B.C., while the earliest agriculture in northwestern Europe did not arrive until around 3000 B.C.

Excavations at the site of Franchthi Cave document the introduction of agriculture to southeastern Europe in the seventh millennium B.C. During the sixth millennium, agriculture and pottery followed two main pathways from Greece and the Aegean into the rest of Europe: by land into the center of the continent and by sea along the north coast of the Mediterranean. The combination of pottery, mud-brick houses, and domestic plants and animals spread quickly to the Balkan Peninsula of southeastern Europe (the present countries of Yugoslavia, Romania, Hungary, and Bulgaria) via the Danube River by 5500 B.C. In the other direction, the caves and rock shelters along the Mediterranean shore contain distinctive pottery and the bones of domesticated sheep after 6000 B.C. The coastal location and irregular distribution of these sites suggests an adoption of agriculture products arriving by sea. The fifth millennium B.C. witnessed the flowering of Neolithic cultures in southeastern Europe, with the appearance of large settlements, elaborate religious systems, copper mining, and extensive trade networks. An archaeological site at Lepenski Vir provides evidence of such societies.

The two-pronged spread of agriculture continued between 5000 and 4000 B.C. The coastal branch moved inland from the Mediterranean shore to Spain, France, and Italy. By 4500 B.C., changes in plants, architecture, and farming practices permitted further expansion of the Balkan branch from Hungary into the valleys of central Europe. The expansion may not always have been a peaceful one. At the early Neolithic site of Darion in northeastern Belgium, there is evidence that the first farmers in this area had to fortify their villages.

CONTENTS

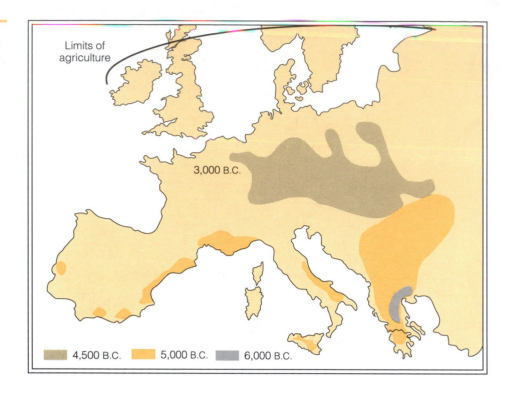

The fourth millennium B.C. witnessed the final adoption of farming by peoples in northwestern Europe: the Netherlands, northern Germany, northern Poland, southern Scandinavia, and Britain. These groups begin to develop local traditions as independent societies. Both warfare and trade are hallmarks of this period in northwestern Europe. Only those northerly areas of Scandinavia above the limits of cultivation did not partici-pate in the transition to agriculture.

The third millennium B.C. witnessed a number of major innovations from the farmers of Europe, including the introduction of bronze, new weapons, the wheel, draft animals and the plow and ox cart, the horse and chariot, and extensive maritime contacts. Secondary animal products, such as milk and wool, became important for food and raw materials. Neolithic farming societies in western Europe erected large, stone tombs and monumental constructions, such as those at Stonehenge.

The second millennium B.C. was important in the Aegean area. First on Crete and later in Greece, Bronze Age lords directed powerful polities. The palaces of Knossos and Mycenae provide evidence of the vitality of these early states. The palace economy involved writing systems, craft specialization, taxation, and extensive trade networks. This commerce attracted goods and materials from most of temperate Europe to the Aegean. The second millennium B.C. is also the time of the Bronze Age north of the Alps. Large polities arose in those areas where raw materials and trade routes coincided. The tombs of elite individuals under large earthen mounds in southern England, Czechoslo-vakia, and southern Scandinavia are evidence of local wealth and high status in these areas. The Danish site of Borum Eshøj provides an example of these tombs and societies.

The first millennium B.C. is known as the Iron Age, because of the introduction of this new metal. The classical civilizations of Greece and Rome arose in the Mediterranean during this time. These literate polities are the subjects of classical archaeology. North of the Alps, prehistory continued somewhat longer. In temperate western Europe, Celtic and Germanic tribes with distinctive traditions and art styles were present during the Iron Age. The fortresses of these warrior societies, known by the Roman name **oppida**, dotted the landscape of western Europe, centers of trade and warfare. The princess burial at Vix in France documents the wealth and interaction of those Celtic elite. The discipline

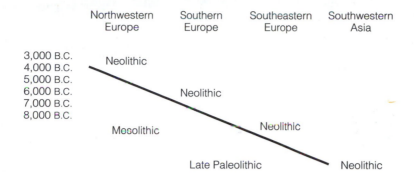

	Northwestern Europe	Southern Europe	Southeastern Europe	Southwestern Asia
3,000 B.C.	Neolithic			
4,000 B.C.				
5,000 B.C.				
6,000 B.C.		Neolithic		
7,000 B.C.				
8,000 B.C.			Neolithic	
	Mesolithic			
		Late Paleolithic		Neolithic

A chronology of the spread of agriculture into Europe. Agriculture arrived in northwestern Europe after 4000 B.C.

of the legions finally overwhelmed the Celts, as Julius Caesar and his successors carried the legacy of Rome to western Europe. The fortress of Maiden Castle in southern England, for example, was razed by the legions around 44 B.C. Only those areas north and east of the Rhine River remained free of Roman rule and continued a tribal way of life for a short while longer. Iron Age sacrifices and executions preserved in bogs from this area provide a startling glimpse of some early Europeans and a fitting conclusion to our journey through prehistoric Europe.

FRANCHTHI CAVE

The Neolithic comes to Europe

Franchthi (fraunk'tee) Cave in southern Greece provides evidence for the introduction of agriculture to the European continent. Today the cave sits at the coast, overlooking the Argolid Gulf. Across the Aegean lie the coast of Turkey and the Near East. In the early Holocene, however, the Aegean Sea was some distance from the cave, and a fairly level plain stood where the waters are now.

Investigations at the cave led by Thomas Jacobsen, of Indiana University, revealed layers of trash and other debris that contained a detailed picture of human residence over the last 20,000 years. The early Mesolithic inhabitants of Franchthi exploited a wide range of terrestrial and marine resources at the end of the Pleistocene. Evidence for the hunting of red deer and other large game animals, the collecting of marine mollusks and land snails, and the use of several wild types of plants, including greens, pistachio nuts, and almonds, and several wild grasses, is found in the cave deposits. The variety and seasonal availability of the foods at the site suggest that the cave was occupied year-round by this time.

Later Mesolithic levels at the site indicate an increasing dependence on marine foods. Bones from large tuna comprise about 50% of all animal remains in some layers at the cave. (Tuna, measuring up to 2.5 m, or 8 ft, in length and weighing up to 200 kg, or 450 lb, lived only in the deeper waters of the Aegean.) In addition, obsidian used for some artifacts at Franchthi came from the island of Melos 150 km (100 mi) away. The bones of tuna and the presence of obsidian document the seafaring abilities of these peoples as long as 10,000 years ago.

The major layers at Franchthi Cave.

Period	Sea Level	Percentage of Wild Animal Bones				Fish	Plants	Years B.P.
Late Mesolithic	−25 m	Deer			Pig	Large and common	Wild barley, vetch, and lentils	ca. 8500
Middle Mesolithic		Deer			Pig	Small and rare	Wild barley, vetch, and lentils	ca. 10,500
Early Mesolithic		Deer	Horse	Goat	Pig	Small and rare	Wild barley, vetch, and lentils	
Hiatus								
Late Paleolithic	−50 m	Deer	Horse	Cattle	Goat	—	Wild barley, vetch, and lentils	ca. 12,500
Upper Paleolithic	−90 m	Deer	Horse			—	—	ca. 22,000

Several lines of evidence point to the increasing use of vegetable foods around 6500 B.C., despite the absence of domesticated crops. Carbonized plant remains become more abundant in the cave deposits at this time. Some stone blades have **sickle polish** along their edges. This thick polish is deposited when blades are used to cut the stems of such plants as grasses and reeds. The presence of sickle polish indicates that the inhabitants of the cave were harvesting plants in substantial quantities. Coriander seeds are also found among the plant remains from this period. Coriander is a plant that grows as a weed in cultivated or disturbed areas; its presence suggests that crops may have been cultivated. Finally, the lentils preserved from this level at Franchthi are large, the size of the later domesticated variety.

By 6000 B.C., domesticated plants and animals were present at Franchthi. Sheep and goats were found in the cave levels from this period, as well as domesticated wheats and barley. Earlier species had by now disappeared, including wild oats. Red deer and tuna were less common among the animal remains. The occupation area increased in size at this time. A terrace in front of the cave was now used for the construction of structures, as a small farming community, with a population of maybe seventy-five people, grew up here. Contacts with other areas increased. New exotic materials, such as marble, are found in the cave deposits from this time.

There are several possible scenarios for the introduction of agriculture from the Near East to Europe. One involves the movement of people bringing domesticates to colonize Greece and the Aegean islands. Another possibility would be the adoption of exotic domesticates and pottery by the indigenous peoples of southeastern Europe. The introduction of domestic plants and animals and pottery does not disrupt other aspects of life; there is some continuity in the previous way of life at the cave. It seems unlikely that the inhabitants changed with the arrival of the Neolithic. Perhaps the domesticated plants and animals were introduced by seafarers from Turkey or the Near East looking for exotic materials to trade or exchange. Whatever the initial mechanism for the introduction, these new materials and ideas initiated a series of changes that would eventually be felt throughout Europe. Within 3000 years of their first record in Greece, farming societies replaced hunter-gatherers across most of the continent. The story of that transition will be discussed in the following pages.

Franchthi Cave, on the coast of the Aegean in southern Greece (left), and a view down the "chimney" of Franchthi cave at the excavations below (right).

LEPENSKI VIR

Early settlers in the Iron Gates of the Danube

Lepenski Vir, located on a low terrace in the gorge of the Iron Gates of the Danube River in Yugoslavia.

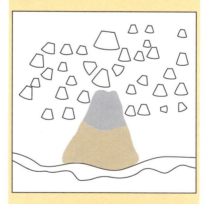

One phase of settlement at Lepenski Vir. The alignment of the structures and their arrangement around one larger house and the central plaza (shaded) suggest both planning and cooperation in the community.

Some 60 km (40 mi) downriver from the city of Beograd, Yugoslavia, the slow waters of the Danube funnel into a much narrower torrent, as they cut through a gorge in the Carpathian Mountains known as the Iron Gates. The combination of the steep-sided mountains and the fast-paced river fosters an extraordinarily rich and diverse environment along the 100-km (60-mi) stretch.

The area is isolated and difficult to enter. High mountain ridges shelter the gorge from the extremes of summer heat and winter chill. The river mists, warm soils, and moderate seasons protect an unusual vegetation and animal life that have changed little since the Pleistocene. Northern species of trees, such as birch and spruce, survive alongside more Mediterranean varieties, such as hackberry

and beech. The forests here were full of game, particularly red deer, and the river was full of fish. Where the waters of the Danube rush into the narrow channel of the gorge, whirlpools stir up the bottom sediments, providing rich nourishment for fish. Danubian carp and catfish are enormous in this area; sturgeon migrating upstream from the Black Sea may reach a weight of 200 kg (450 lb).

In the 1960s, the Yugoslavian and Romanian governments began construction of a hydroelectric plant to tap the enormous power of the river. Archaeologists working ahead of construction searched the shores of the Danube to document the prehistoric sites that would be submerged by the waters rising behind the dam. Lepenski Vir (la-pen′ski-veer′) is the name given to one of the great whirlpools in the middle of this gorge. On the sunny right bank opposite the whirlpool is a broad, arc-shaped shelf of rock that lies between the river and the steep, forested cliffs of the gorge. On this shelf the archaeologists uncovered one of the more remarkable sites in all of Europe—and one about which controversy over its precise age and significance continues.

The excavators identified two major phases in the stratigraphy of 3 m (10 ft) of deposits at the site, each with evidence of substantial house construction and remarkable artifacts. Most of the site belongs to the early Neolithic culture of southeastern Europe, dating to perhaps 5500 B.C. In the lowest level, approximately twenty structures were found in irregular rows on a series of terraces, a total area of some 60 by 30 m (200 by 100 ft). Deer, pig, and abundant fishbones document the diet of the inhabitants. A central plaza lies amid the houses, adjacent to the shoreline. The settlement also had one larger building located near the center of the village. In the upper levels at the site, there are changes in domestic architecture; houses had indoor ovens, perhaps for baking bread. Domestic sheep are present, and there is evidence that obsidian and *Spondylus* shell were imported from the Adriatic or Aegean sea. The basic plan of the community and houses, however, remains the same.

The residential structures range from 5 to 30 sq m (50 to 325 sq ft) in floor area (the equivalent of a modern medium-sized room). The trapezoidal huts often included an elaborate stone-lined hearth and red plastered floors. The plaster floor was surrounded by large post holes, indicating a substantial timber superstructure. The broader sides of the houses faced the river, while the narrower ends often contained an area of stone paving, sometimes with elaborately carved river boulders—Europe's oldest known stone sculptures. These large boulders are carved with curvilinear designs, often with the faces of half-human, half-fish creatures. Skulls and other parts of human heads were recovered in areas between houses, while the remainders of the skeletons were found beneath the house floors. In one case, the body of an old man was laid out in a grave with the head of an

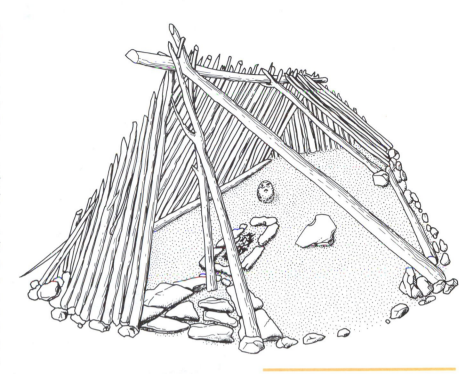

older woman (minus her lower jaw), an aurochs skull at his or her shoulder, and a deer skull near his or her hand.

Lepenski Vir and other sites in the Iron Gates indicate that local hunting-gathering communities gradually shifted to farming, as agriculture spread from Greece into southeastern Europe. The layout of the settlement at Lepenski Vir, its permanent nature, and the houses, burials, sculpture, and other remains suggest that this was a very unusual settlement of some sort, perhaps a center for the larger, more dispersed population of the gorge.

Today the original location of Lepenski Vir lies beneath the waters of the dammed Danube, but the site can still be visited as a national monument of Yugoslavia. In 1969, as the water rose slowly behind the hydroelectric dam, many of the structures and other remains at Lepenski Vir were raised almost 30 m (100 ft) up the side of the gorge to the plateau above. A small museum stands adjacent to the new site, and an elaborate roof protects the reconstructed archaeological remains.

An artist's reconstruction of the super-structure of the trapezoidal houses at Lepenski Vir. Note the hearth and sculpture in the plastered floor of the structure.

One of the stone statues from a house floor at Lepenski Vir.

DARION

Farmers invade central Europe

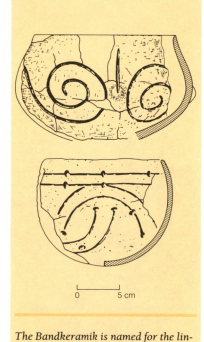

The Bandkeramik is named for the linear bands of decoration found on hemispherical pottery bowls from these sites. The heavy line on the right of each bowl shows the shape of the wall.

Although early farming adaptations moved westward very quickly from the Near East into southeastern Europe and the Mediterranean Basin, the first crops and domesticated animals did not appear in central Europe before 4500 B.C. Practices that had been successful in the southern portion of the continent had to be modified to cope with a cooler, moister climate, pronounced seasons, heavier forest, and different soil conditions. Much of the material culture of these early farmers, in fact, reflects a major adjustment to the climatic and environmental conditions of interior Europe.

Southeastern Europe is much like the Near East. Rainfall is limited, and the climate is generally of the Mediterranean type, with cool winters and hot summers. In central and northern Europe, however, cold winters and heavy rain are more typical. Crops are planted in the spring and harvested in the fall. Early or late killing frosts are a hazard for farmers; varieties of crops with a short growing season are essential. Cultivation practices in central and northern Europe focus on wheat and lentils; barley is rare in the cooler climate and shorter growing season of temperate Europe. The flat-roofed houses that accumulated on the tells of more arid southeastern Europe became longhouses with peaked roofs in central Europe. The larger houses could accommodate interior storage areas and protect the grains, seeds, and silage that had to survive the winter; the peaked roof carried away the rainwater and melting snow. Cattle and pigs, rather than sheep and goats, were the primary domestic animals in central Europe during the Neolithic.

The first Neolithic communities in central Europe are known as **Bandkeramik**. The Bandkeramik had its origin around 4500 B.C. in villages along the middle Danube and its tributaries in eastern Hungary. From this core area, farmers migrated east, north, and west, to the loess-covered valleys of central Europe to Belgium, southern Poland, and the Ukraine. These loess soils of central Europe are among the most fertile on the continent, having been under cultivation since the arrival of the first farmers. The millennia of plowing have virtually destroyed the surface of the early Bandkeramik settlements. Nevertheless, deep pits, ditches, and post holes from the settlements have survived and contain some evidence from this period.

Remarkable is the very rapid expansion of the Bandkeramik. Within a period of a few hundred years around 4500 B.C., small farming villages appear for the first time in an area stretching from Hungary, to Belgium, to southern Poland, and to Ukraine. The uniformity of the architecture, artifacts, burials, and settlement plan characterizing these settlements is impressive. Each site contains a very similar set of houses, cemeteries, pottery, and exotic goods.

Ceramic vessels from this period are distinctively decorated with ribbons of incised, linear bands, hence the name Bandkeramik. This pottery is unpainted, in contrast to some of the spectacular vessels found in southeastern Europe at this time. Vessel shapes are limited to hemispherical bowls, vases, and a few other forms. Bandkeramik communities consist of small groups of longhouses, each one 6 m wide

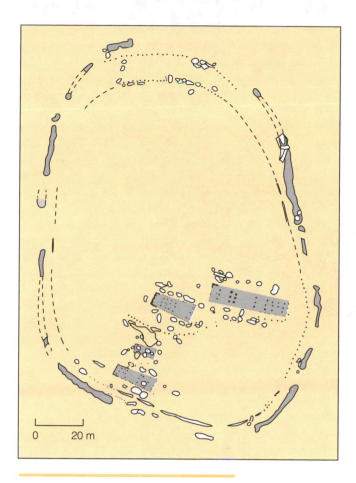

The hamlet of Darion. The heavy dashed line marks the location of the palisade around the settlement. Houses are located in the southern third of the enclosure.

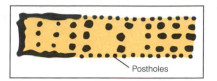

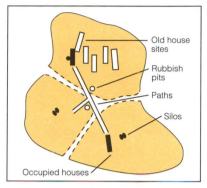

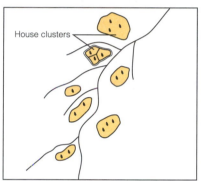

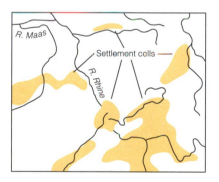

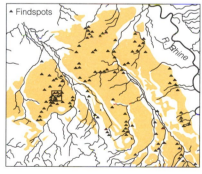

Levels of Bandkeramik settlements, showing the house, the hamlet, the community, and local and regional settlement patterns from top to bottom.

and 8 to 40 m long (20 ft wide and 25 to 130 ft long) (the size of one or two train cars), built with a framework of oak or pine timbers covered with wattle-and-daub walls and a thatched roof. Economy was based on cattle herding and on the hoe cultivation of cereals in narrow strips of land near rivers and streams. Cemeteries associated with the Bandkeramik villages were generally small. The burial populations indicate that men had a longer life expectancy than women. Exotic goods were limited, but *Spondylus* shell from the Mediterranean is found at many sites. Axes of a stone from a single source in Poland or Bulgaria also show up over a very wide area of central Europe.

Much of the Bandkeramik colonization of central Europe was a peaceful process, with the expanding farming population moving into relatively unoccupied

areas of dense forest. However, in some areas there appears to have been conflict between the incoming farmers and the indigenous inhabitants, indicated from recent investigations at the site of Darion. Excavation and analysis by Daniel Cahen, of the Royal Institute of Natural Science of Belgium, documents the layout of this settlement. A fairly typical Bandkeramik hamlet with only a few large houses, Darion is unusual, however, in that a fortified palisade and ditch encircles the houses and some fields, raising significant questions about the peaceful nature of the process of Neolithic colonization. What is also unusual for this area is the compelling evidence for village specialization in production. Characteristic debris from the manufacture of pottery, flint blades, and stone adzes varies greatly between villages, suggesting that these products were

Clusters of Bandkeramik settlements in northeastern Belgium. The location of Darion is marked. Notice the separation of late Mesolithic and early Neolithic Bandkeramik sites in this area.

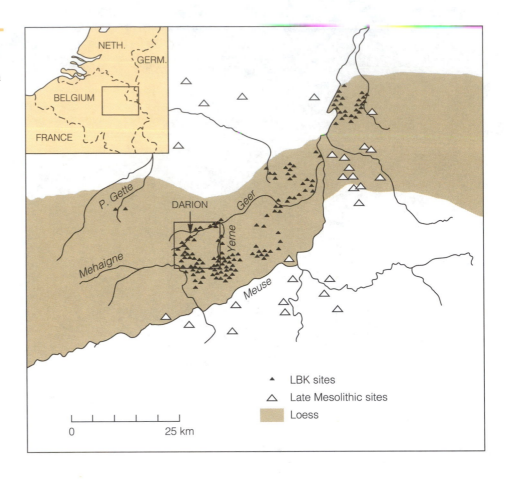

Labor costs for Darion fortifications.

Basic Costs Per Unit

Earth-moving: 1.1 cu m/person-day (8-hr day).
Tree-felling and trimming; one 35 cm diameter tree felled with stone adze = 0.5 person-hours; trimming and sizing 1 post = 0.25 person-hours; thus 11 posts (cut, trimmed, and sized) per person-day.
Hauling and emplacing posts: 1 post per 0.67 person-hours or 12 posts per day

Construction Labor

Ditch, 1600 cu m x 1.1 cu m/person-day: 1450
Palisade
   Post-cutting and trimming: 500 posts at 11 posts/person-day: 45
   Hauling and emplacing: 500 posts at 12 posts/person-day: 42
   Excavation of foundation trench and pot holes, 110 cu m: 100
Miscellaneous carpentry and construction (est.): 30

Total Labor Costs (person-days): 1667

1667 person-days is the equivalent of one person working for almost 5 years, or 10 people working for 5.6 months, or 25 people working for slightly more than 2 months.

being made in different villages and exchanged among the communities.

There is also intriguing evidence that Darion was an outpost on a border between groups of farmers and hunter-gatherers. Darion is located along a small stream in eastern Belgium, with several nearby sites from the same period. Although the landscape and environment are very similar in all directions, there were no Bandkeramik sites north of the line formed by Darion and its neighbors. This situation suggests a frontier or border between two groups in conflict and may well explain the palisade around the settlement at Darion.

Vere Gordon Childe was arguably one of the most prolific and influential archaeologists of the twentieth century, in spite of the fact that he did not obtain a professional position until age 35. Both brilliant and eccentric, he published almost one book a year during the thirty years of his career, many dealing with the prehistory of Europe. His work has been translated into thirteen languages and read by hundreds of thousands of people.

Childe traveled widely and read well in several languages. Profoundly influenced by Marxism, as a social philosopher he utilized the prehistory of Europe as a means for understanding the evolution of society. His contributions to archaeology are enormous, particularly his sweeping view of the past, his ability to cross modern political boundaries and synthesize events and processes that characterized changes in prehistoric society.

Born in 1892 in New South Wales, Australia, Childe studied at the University of Sydney and then sailed to England to attend Oxford University at age 22. Childe completed his undergraduate degree in archaeology in 1917. He returned briefly to Australia at that time, but lost his position as Secretary to the Premier of New South Wales in a change of government. He went back to England in 1921 and, through a series of minor jobs, continued his interests in prehistory. In 1925, he published *The Dawn of European Civilization,* which established his reputation almost overnight. Prehistoric archaeology was still largely an amateur pastime, practiced by the wealthy. In 1927, Childe took the position of Abercromby Professor of Archaeology at the University of Edinburgh. The volumes he published during these early years in Edinburgh rewrote European prehistory and emphasized Childe's diffusionist view that new inventions and ideas had reached Europe from the east — "the irradiation of European barbarism by Oriental civilization" (Childe, 1928, p. 24). His books at that time included *The Aryans: A Study of Indo-European Origins* (1927), *The Most Ancient East: The Oriental Prelude to European Pre-*

history (1928), *The Danube in Prehistory* (1929), and *The Bronze Age* (1930).

Focusing on the prehistory of Scotland in the late 1920s and early 1930s, Childe conducted excavations at the Neolithic site of Skara Brae in the Orkney Islands. He moved to the Institute of Archaeology at the University of London in 1946, where he remained as Director until his retirement. His pace of publication never slackened as he considered the *idea* of prehistory, rather than the details of prehistory itself, presenting a popular prehistory to the public. *Man Makes Himself* (1936), *What Happened in History* (1942) (which sold over 300,000 copies), and *Society and Knowledge* (1956) were some of the more important titles during this period.

Childe retired from the Institute in 1956 and returned to his native Australia for the first time in thirty-five years. After six months in Australia, he jumped 1000 feet to his death at the foot of Govett's Leap in the Blue Mountains. A letter from Childe, opened in 1968, revealed his deep disillusionment with Australian society and a serious concern with aging and loss of memory. Kruschev's revelations about Stalin and the Soviet invasion of Hungary in 1956 may have caused a loss of faith in Marxism as Childe's political philosophy. Friends and colleagues also reported a profound sense of loneliness that Childe carried with him to his death.

V. GORDON CHILDE, 1892–1957

A prolific career, but a lonely life

The most original and useful contributions that I may have made to prehistory are certainly not novel data rescued by brilliant excavation from the soil, or by patient research from dusty museum cases, nor yet well founded chronological schemes nor freshly defined cultures, but rather interpretative concepts and methods of explanation.

V. Gordon Childe, *Retrospect* (1958)

You stood on the sheer rocky edge of silence, where the stark light burned; the dialogue with life was ended, you saw the many-coloured thing swing out below you, far and splendid; and you upon the dizzying ledge let go, went down went down, and died. You saw that temple opening wide, you entered through the shining door where words weren't needed any more.

Jack Lindsay, in Green (1981)

THE MEGALITHS OF WESTERN EUROPE

Trademark tombs of the first farmers

The largest series of aligned menhirs in Europe at Carnac. There are more than 3000 standing stones at the site.

Almost as soon as agriculture reached the Atlantic coast of western Europe, farming societies began to erect large structures made of long stone slabs and boulders. These **megaliths**, as they are called, usually involved a burial area in or on the ground, surrounded by a chamber of large stones laid atop one another without mortar. The entire stone tomb was then buried beneath a mound of earth, creating an artificial cave. Often a covered passage at the edge of the mound provided an entrance for subsequent burials and rituals.

Tens of thousands of these structures are found along the coast of the Atlantic and the North Sea (in Spain, Portugal, France, Belgium, the Netherlands, Ireland, Britain, Germany, Denmark, and Sweden). The megaliths are distributed in a curious, patchy pattern that defies explanation. Different traditions of pottery manufacture and house construction are associated with these monuments; apparently different groups of people built the same kinds of tombs.

The absence of metal objects in these structures makes it clear that they predate the Bronze Age of western Europe. Radiocarbon dates indicate an age of between 4000 and 2000 B.C., during the Neolithic, and most were built early in this period. Varying greatly in size and in the number of stones used for construction, they were all built to withstand the test of time: to last for many generations as monuments. The megaliths fall into three major groups: menhirs, henges, and dolmens.

Menhirs are large, standing stones, erected either singly or collectively in linear arrangements. Standing stones, either intentionally shaped or existing naturally as long narrow blocks that can be set upright in the ground, range in height from less than 1 m to several meters (3 to 12 ft). The largest known menhir comes from the town of Locmariaquer on the peninsula of Brittany in France. No longer standing, this stone has fallen and broken into five huge pieces that lie on the ground. Originally this stone was 23 m (75 ft) long,

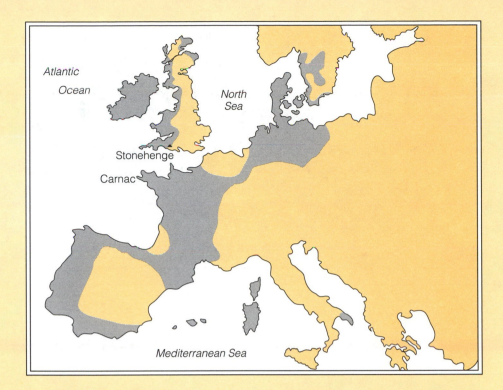

Distribution of megalithic tombs (shaded areas) in western Europe and the location of Stonehenge, England, and Carnac, France.

the height of a six-story building, and weighed at least 350 tons.

Perhaps the most impressive of the stone lines is found at Carnac, also in Brittany, where almost 3000 large stones have been arranged in thirteen parallel lines, stretching almost 6 km (4 mi) across the landscape. The stones are smaller at the eastern end of the arrangement, around 1 m (3 ft) high, and reach up to 4 m (13 ft) at the western end. The purpose of these linear arrangements is unclear, but they may have been intended to measure the cycles of the moon and predict eclipses. What is striking is that a smaller arrangement of wooden poles could easily have been used in place of such massive stone sentinels.

Henge monuments, or circles, are defined by the presence of an enclosure, usually made by a circular ditch and bank system, up to 500 m (1600 ft) in diameter. Not all the henges contain stones; some appear to have held large timber structures. Stone circles, found primarily in the British Isles, are a special form of alignment with a definite astronomical significance. While the best known of these is at

Stonehenge, hundreds of other stone circles dot the landscape of northern England and Scotland.

A **dolmen** is a megalithic tomb or chamber with a roof. Large stones and piles of earth were used to create these chambers. In spite of the enormous amount of labor required to obtain the stones and move them to the site of the tomb, the entire structure was often buried under a mound of earth. Megalithic dolmens range from small, single-chamber stone structures to enormous hills of rock and soil that may hide a number of rooms and crawlways. Passage graves and gallery graves are two types of larger tombs. A **passage grave** is entered via a long, low, narrow passage that opens into a wider room, generally near the center of the structure. A **gallery grave**, or long tomb, lacks an entrance passage, and the burial room or rooms form the entire internal structure.

The earliest examples of megalithic tombs come from Brittany, dating to 4000 B.C., at the time of the transition to agriculture in this area. The first large tombs in Scandinavia were earthen long barrows

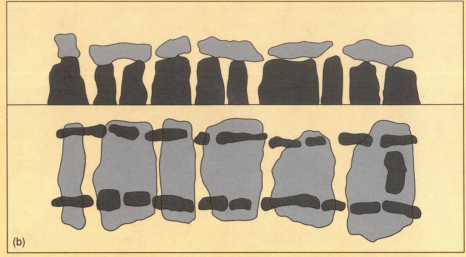

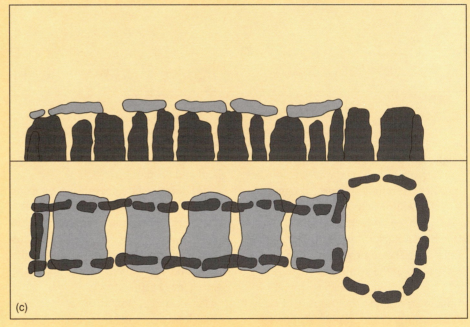

The three major types of megalithic tombs in western Europe: (a) dolmen, (b) gallery grave, (c) and passage grave.

(mounds) with a single log tomb inside, appearing to imitate the plans of Neolithic houses. These earthen structures, intended for the burial of a single individual, were quickly transformed into larger, stone chambers for the collective burial of a number of individuals. The tombs often had a movable stone door that could be opened to permit the interment of new bodies. Remains of the previous occupants were pushed aside to make room. It has been suggested that these tombs were intended for all the members of a related group of farmsteads or hamlets, where the tomb symbolized the collective and co-operative nature of the group.

The tombs served an important purpose for the living, as well. Such "cults of the dead" likely involved both ancestor worship and property rights. Elaborate burial ritual and monument construction reinforced the cult. Ancestor veneration may have supported claims to agricultural fields for local communities of farmers. The construction of a permanent burial monument provided dramatic evidence of one's tenure in place and the inheritance of rights to the land.

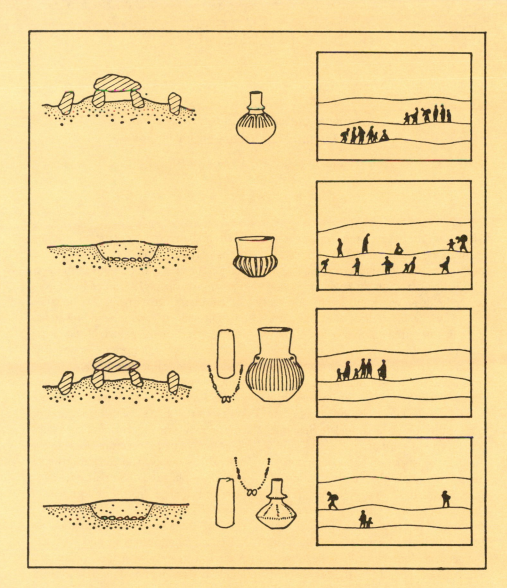

A model of the relationship between population density, grave goods, and type of tomb in Neolithic Denmark. Megalithic tombs occur in areas with higher population clustering; more grave goods occur in areas with fewer people.

Part of the ritual associated with a cult of the dead apparently dictated that burials be placed in large stone tombs after lengthy ceremonies and activities elsewhere. Only the bones of the deceased were placed in the tombs; the flesh had decomposed or had been removed prior to entombment. The tombs do not appear to have been major repositories for wealth or elaborate furnishings for the dead. Grave goods are rare; usually only a few pots, stone tools, and bones are found. There is, however, evidence that pottery vessels with food and drink were regularly placed at the entrance of the tombs as ceremonial offerings for the deceased.

Megalithic structures provide dramatic and enduring evidence of the impact of agriculture on the inhabitants of western Europe. Construction of monumental architecture is one clue to the increasing complexity of societies in this area. Shortly after farming was adopted, a strong trend toward localization appeared. In spite of the evidence of a widespread cult, such as megalithic burials, various regional styles in material culture arose in conjunction with the fortification of settlements and increasing evidence for warfare. This pattern was exacerbated in the succeeding Bronze and Iron Ages.

STONEHENGE

A temple to the sun and "observatory" on England's Salisbury Plain

Construction technique at Stonehenge. Wooden scaffolding was probably used to raise the lintel stone into place.

The most impressive prehistoric monument in the British Isles, and perhaps all of Europe, is at Stonehenge on the plains of Salisbury in southern England. Stonehenge holds an enormous fascination, as much for the mysterious aura that surrounds it as for the impressive feat of construction. Some of the stones have been taken away over the centuries; many have fallen and lie half-buried in the earth. Other stark, brooding, grey stones still stand, arranged in circles and arches that outline this "observatory" of late Neolithic and Bronze Age Britain.

The construction and elaboration of Stonehenge took place over a period of more than 1000 years, from approximately 2750 to 1500 B.C. The earliest monument was first defined by a circular bank and ditch, almost 100 m (330 ft) in diameter, cut into the chalk of the subsoil. The bank on the inside of the circle would have stood almost 2 m high, piled up with material dug from the ditch. A level entrance to the circle was left on the northeast side. Inside this circle and bank were placed the fifty-six Aubrey holes, named after their seventeenth-century discoverer, regularly spaced around the perimeter. These holes were filled shortly after their original excavation, and their purpose is unknown. Cremation burials were placed in a few of the depressions, and also in the bank and ditch areas somewhat later. The Heel Stone was brought to the site at this time and erected outside the circle to the northeast. This irregular boulder stands almost 5 m (16 ft) above ground level and weighs at least 35 tons.

During a second stage of construction, around 2150 B.C., an "avenue" some 500 m (1600 ft) long and 15 m (50 ft) wide, flanked on either side by an earthen ditch and bank, was constructed, running to the northeast from the circle of Stonehenge. The Heel Stone stands in this avenue, approximately 100 m (330 ft) from the circular embankment. Two parallel, crescent-shaped rows of standing stones were erected in the center of the circle, along with several upright stones. The blue-tinted volcanic dolerite came from a source some 250 km (150 mi) distant in the Prescelly Mountains of southern Wales. Certainly part of their journey was by water, but the movement of such large stones was a major accomplishment. The individuals involved in the various construction phases of Stonehenge must have numbered in the hundreds or thousands.

The third stage of construction involved major additions around 2000 B.C. A circle of carefully shaped pillars and lintels of Sarsen sandstone replaced the earlier crescent of blue stones. Huge columns of this sandstone were quarried as far away as 30 km (20 mi) from Stonehenge, shaped into pillars, and dragged to the site. The larger pillars weigh as much as 50 tons and were likely moved on oak rollers. A system of scaffolding was probably used to raise the stones into position.

Inside the circle, five **trilithons** (two upright pillars with a crosspiece on the top) of Sarsen stone were erected in a horseshoe-shaped arrangement. One of these trilithons is distinctly taller than the other four, standing 8 m high. The lintel on this trilithon is 5 m long and over 1 m thick. More standing stones were added near the entrance and inside the periphery of the ditch. Slightly later, a new circle of standing blue stones was placed inside the horseshoe of trilithons. In the final stage of construction, a ring of bluestone pillars

The megalithic monument that is Stonehenge, on the Salisbury Plain in southern England.

An aerial view of Stonehenge.

STONEHENGE   **469**

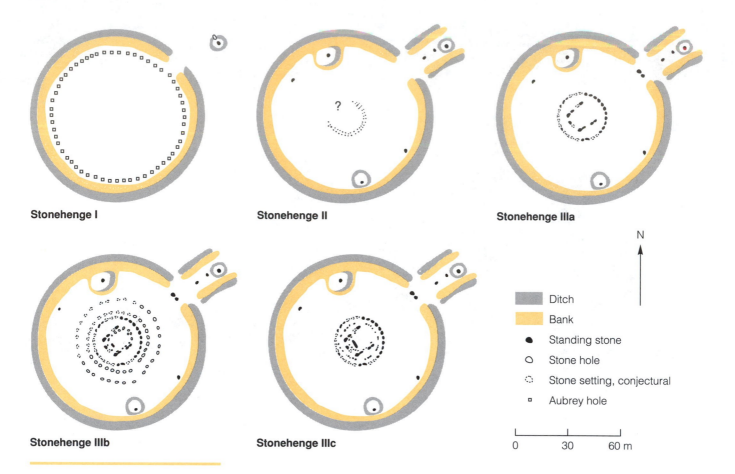

Stonehenge I

Stonehenge II

Stonehenge IIIa

Stonehenge IIIb

Stonehenge IIIc

N

▨	Ditch
▨	Bank
●	Standing stone
○	Stone hole
⬭	Stone setting, conjectural
▫	Aubrey hole

0   30   60 m

The major construction stages at Stonehenge, between 2750 and 1500 B.C.

was raised inside the Sarsen circle, but outside the horseshoe. In addition, two rings of large holes were dug around the outer circle. These may also have held standing stones that are now missing.

Stonehenge functioned in part as an observatory to record the summer solstice. On the 21st or 22nd of June, the sun rises directly over the Heel Stone. Morning sunlight passes across the Heel Stone, through the double standing stones at the entrance, bisects the two horseshoes of standing stones, and reaches the altar stone in the very center of the circle. Today the sun just misses the exact top of the Heel Stone; a result of changes in the Earth's axis since construction. This shift was used in 1905 by the Royal Astronomer Sir Norman Lockyer, to estimate the date of the monument at 1900 B.C., an accurate prediction made many years before other methods of absolute dating were available.

Some have argued that Stonehenge was an astronomical "computer," used to record lunar and stellar alignments. A popular theory is that the circles of stones and holes could have been used to predict lunar eclipses. There is no strong evidence, however, for any alignment other than the summer solstice.

Stonehenge has become a problem for British archaeology in recent years. Although it is a mecca for tourists, just behind the Tower of London in popularity, the wear and tear wrought by visitors has lead to more careful regulation of the monument grounds. Years of post–World War II tourism had dire consequences; inquisitive fingers had worn down the engravings on the stones, and the weight borne by millions of feet had worn the ground down to the chalk bedrock. At the summer solstice in late June, huge festivals celebrated the season and watched present-day Druids celebrate the sunrise. Today most of the monument is not immediately accessible; walkways direct the visitor past the mute sentinels of the past. While such means of protection distance the visitor from the stones, they do serve to help ensure that Stonehenge and its heritage will remain for the future as a monument to and from the ancient Britons.

The wine dark waters of the Aegean Sea bathe the shores of Turkey to the east and Greece to the north and west. The long, mountainous island of Crete marks the southern border of this part of the sea, which is splattered with small rocky and volcanic islands. These islands, the summits of a submerged mountain range, generally have thin, poor soil and a dry climate.

These rugged and barren conditions may actually have been an asset for the early inhabitants. The absence of large areas of fertile farmland meant that crops other than cereals had to be cultivated. Wheat was grown in more sheltered areas with deeper soils, but grapes, olive trees, and sheep flourished on the rocky slopes of these islands. Olives are remarkably nutritious and provide oil that can be burned, worn, used for cooking, or eaten. Grapes are not only a delicious fruit but are also essential for the fermentation of wine. These crops became important export items for economies of these small islands. The inhabitants must have also relied on the sea for fish and other foods; sailing and knowledge of the sea would have been essential.

Seafaring and trade permitted the movement of goods and food between islands and between the islands and the mainland. The obsidian at Franchthi Cave on mainland Greece was brought from the distant Aegean island of Melos at least 10,000 years ago. The strategic location of Crete and the Aegean islands along the main avenues of sea trade allowed the inhabitants to become the middlemen in moving goods between the civilizations of Egypt and the Near East and the inhabitants of Europe.

The demand for wine, olive oil, pottery, textiles, and other goods enhanced the economic well-being of the islands. A pattern also seems to have been established early in the Aegean, in which raw materials were taken to the islands and made into finished products. Some craftspeople used the potter's wheel to make fine ceramic vessels. Other workers carved stone, bone, and ivory seals for economic transactions, produced wooden tools, sculpted figurines and bowls of

THE AEGEAN BRONZE AGE

Heroes of Homer's legends

The locations of important Minoan and Mycenaean sites in the Aegean region. The shaded area in the lower-right corner indicates the zone of major ash fall from the eruption of the volcanic island of Thera.

marble, obsidian, and other colorful stones, or created jewelry and other luxury items. After 3000 B.C., the craftspeople of the Aegean also began to make objects of metal: bronze, silver, and gold. Smiths produced bronze tools and weapons by the thousands for both local use and export. This metal was the signature material of the Bronze Age, and its production was one of the primary reasons for the growth of the economy and political power in the Aegean area.

The discovery and use of metals in the Old World was a relatively slow process. A very few small pieces of copper, in the form of jewelry, appeared in the Near East by 7000 B.C. at early Neolithic sites. This was native copper, simply hammered from its original shape into a new form. The melting and casting of copper began in southeastern Europe and the Near East shortly before 4000 B.C. Copper mines were opened in Yugoslavia, and various copper artifacts, axes, and jewelry found their way throughout much of Europe. Gold objects also began to appear in the fourth millennium B.C.

Bronze was discovered, probably by accident, shortly before 3000 B.C. Bronze is a mixture of copper and tin or arsenic. Copper ores sometimes contain arsenic, one of the alloys of bronze. In all likelihood, early smiths discovered that those ores that included arsenic produced a slightly harder material, easier to cast. Further experimentation must have lead to the discovery of tin as another alloy, and bronze metallurgy was underway. Bronze has several advantages over copper. Bronze can be recycled repeatedly, while copper loses its tensile strength in recasting. Bronze holds an edge much better than copper, and most of the early bronze objects were weapons: swords, daggers, spearheads, and arrowheads.

The advent of metallurgy, first of copper and then of bronze, silver, and gold, greatly increased trade and the movement of goods across the Aegean and the rest of Europe. Copper, tin, and gold from sources in Ireland and England moved across the English Channel, down the Seine and Rhone rivers in France, to the Mediterranean for shipment to the Aegean. Copper ores and ingots from the Carpathian Mountains of Czechoslovakia were brought overland through the Brenner Pass in the Alps to the shores of Greece. Amber from the Baltic and North Sea coasts of Denmark and Poland was also imported to the Aegean. Other commodities, including furs and slaves, may have also traveled to the Aegean in exchange for finished bronze weapons, pottery vessels, bronze, and gold jewelry.

The Aegean Bronze Age dates from approximately 3000 to 1000 B.C., ending with the beginning of the Iron Age and the rise of the classical Greek civilization of Plato and Homer. There were two major centers of development and power in the Aegean, one on Crete and one on mainland Greece.

The civilization that emerged on the island of the Crete was known as the Minoan and reached its peak between 2000 and 1450 B.C. During this period, the Minoans dominated the Aegean through sea power and the control of trade in the eastern Mediterranean. The seats of power on Crete were in the palaces and villas, residences of the local rulers who directed this early state. Defensive fortifications were not needed by the islanders, because they were protected by their ships. Three different writing systems were used on Crete, including an early hieroglyphic system, replaced around 1700 B.C. by a writing system known as Linear A. Another writing system, Linear B, is related to archaic Greek and was developed on mainland Greece and later introduced to Crete by the Mycenaeans.

The Mycenaeans controlled most of the Aegean between 1500 and 1100 B.C. and took over Crete after 1450 B.C. The Mycenaean civilization was dominated by a series of hilltop fortresses, or **citadels**,

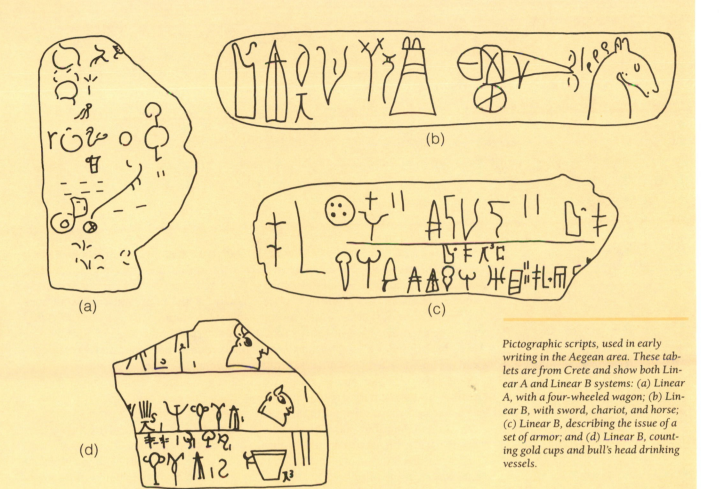

(a)

(b)

(c)

(d)

Pictographic scripts, used in early writing in the Aegean area. These tablets are from Crete and show both Linear A and Linear B systems: (a) Linear A, with a four-wheeled wagon; (b) Linear B, with sword, chariot, and horse; (c) Linear B, describing the issue of a set of armor; and (d) Linear B, counting gold cups and bull's head drinking vessels.

interconnected by roads. These citadels were ruled by powerful warrior kings, whose graves are among the richest ever uncovered in Europe. Episodic alliances among the citadels led to greater political, economic, and military power, and the Mycenaeans became the major force in the Aegean after 1500 B.C. The collapse of Mycenaean power and the abandonment of the heavily fortified citadels after 1100 B.C. is one of the more intriguing mysteries of Aegean archaeology.

The Bronze Age in the Aegean marks a watershed in the prehistory of Europe. In the Mediterranean basin, early civilizations rose in the Aegean, mainland Greece, and later on the Italian Peninsula. These societies were literate, ruled by kings, inhabited large towns, fielded armies and navies, collected taxes, and established laws—all the trappings of state-level polities. These states controlled trade over large areas and extracted a variety of raw materials and other products from the rest of Europe.

North of the Alps, there was much less political integration; societies operated at a tribal or chiefdom level, on a smaller scale. This pattern continued essentially until the Roman conquest of France and much of Britain, shortly before the birth of Christ. The Romans introduced writing systems and true statecraft in northwestern Europe for the first time. Prehistory ends much earlier south of the Alps, where the literate civilizations of Greece, in the first half of the first millennium B.C., and of Rome, in the second half, dominated the Mediterranean basin.

Knossos

The mythical halls of the Minotaur on the island of Crete

Sir Arthur Evans, the keeper of the Asmolean Museum in Oxford, England, traveled to Crete in 1894 and discovered an extensive group of ruins at a place known as Knossos (kuh'nos-sus). The remains covered almost 2.5 ha (6 acres) and were buried under a low mound of soil and collapsed walls. Beginning in 1900, Evans spent the remaining thirty-five years of his life excavating at Knossos. He also restored those areas he had excavated, rebuilding the walls and repainting the plaster in the vivid colors that had been preserved in the ruins. Today the palace that he uncovered is a monument to his labor and his vision of the restoration.

The first Bronze Age palace at Knossos was erected around 3000 B.C. on top of 7 m (22 ft) of Neolithic deposits that had accumulated for several thousand years. A series of palaces was built, one palace on top of the other, each larger and more elaborate, as the settlement and administrative structure grew. Knossos covers almost 25,000 sq m (6 acres, an area the size of large basketball arena), in a complex of buildings and construction that included the palace itself, several surrounding large mansions, and many smaller houses, connected by roads.

The palaces were the centers of the Minoan state. The palace was laid out and built according to a plan, with a large, rectangular central court surrounded by myriad rooms, numerous corridors, a maze of courtyards, grand staircases, private apartments, administrative chambers, enormous storerooms, baths, and a sophisticated plumbing system. The complex of rooms and buildings housed many of the administrative, economic, aesthetic, and religious facets of the government. Many of the important craft workshops were also located in the palace or housed in adjacent buildings. Functional space was carefully designed and separated according to residential, administrative, storage, religious, and manufacturing areas. The palace was a multistory building with extensive basement storerooms. Long narrow chambers in these warehouses held enormous storage jars, or *pithoi* (singular, *pithos*) along the walls for oils, wine, and other liquids, and stone-lined pits in the floor were filled with wheat and other cereals. It is clear from this arrangement that the palace complex controlled the economic activities of the state.

Frescoes and murals decorate the walls of the palace, depicting various aspects of Minoan life. Shrines are scattered throughout the palace as well, documenting the integration of church and state in the early civilizations of the Aegean. Much has been made of the open-bodice costumes of the goddesses and the acrobatic bullfighters who are often depicted. Religious ceremonies appear to have combined several elements including the bull, a sacred axe, snakes, and other elements.

The ruins of the palace of Knossos on Crete (right). The standing walls were reconstructed by Sir Arthur Evans.

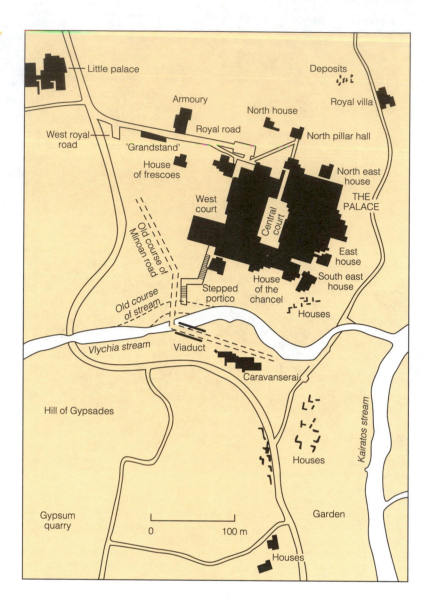

The plan of Knossos around 1900 B.C., which included the palace, a number of adjacent mansions, smaller houses, and other buildings, along with a system of paved roads. The original settlement at this location was a Neolithic village at the juncture of the two streams.

The extensive network of trade that was directed from Knossos and the other Minoan centers is evidenced by the variety of raw materials found in the palace: copper from Cyprus and Turkey; ivory, amethyst, carnelian, and gold from Egypt; lapis lazuli from Afghanistan; amber from Scandinavia. These commodities, and the Cretan ships that carried them, were the foundation of the wealth and power of the Minoan state. The Egyptians feared the "great green sea," yet the sturdy Minoan ships with their deep keels and high prows weathered the storms of the Mediterranean and controlled the sea lanes.

The palace of Knossos was destroyed at least twice in its history. The first destruction, in 1700 B.C., was marked by extensive wall collapse and evidence from a major fire. Many of the other palaces and

villas on Crete show evidence of similar destruction at the same time; it seems clear that a major earthquake must have struck the island. The second level of destruction at Knossos dates to approximately 1450 B.C. and marks the end of the Minoan civilization in the Aegean. The palace was reoccupied following this episode, but now the pottery and other artifacts indicate the presence of Mycenaeans from the mainland in control of the palace. Other palaces on Crete also were destroyed at this time, but not simultaneously, as in 1750 B.C. The reason for this last episode of destruction and the collapse of the Minoans is not as clear, but it may involve both the growing power of the Mycenaeans and a major natural catastrophe, the eruption of the island of Thera.

Thera (thare'a), or Santorini as it is known today, is one of many Aegean islands of volcanic origin, an accumulation of magma, lava, and ash that gradually rose from the sea floor. In 1700 B.C., Thera was a huge volcanic cone, some 20 km (13 mi) in diameter at the base, rising perhaps 1500 m (5000 ft) comparable in size and appearance to Mt. Fujiyama in Japan. The volcano must have been relatively stable at that time, since its lower sides were heavily inhabited. The large town of Akrotiri, stood on its flank at the seaside.

Today most of the former island is gone; the volcanic cone has disappeared, and only small remnants of its coast stand above sea level. These 300-m (1000-ft) cliffs are a layer cake of the ash and lava that accumulated as the volcano grew. Akrotiri is located at the edge of these cliffs, buried beneath the ash.

Thera erupted in 1628 B.C. with enormous energy, spewing rock, cinders, and ash over much of the eastern Mediterranean. This initial eruption must have lasted some days, as the town of Akrotiri was abandoned and the inhabitants fled. Then, perhaps suddenly, when the mountain had spewed out most of its insides, the cone collapsed into the sea with what must have been a huge explosion of hot magma. The mountain blew apart, leaving only the crescent of small islands that mark its former outline.

There are only a few instances on record of the explosion of volcanoes. The explosive self-destruction of Mt. St. Helens in the western United States in the early 1980s was well documented; the force of that explosion leveled large areas in its path. However, only one side of Mt. St. Helens collapsed and blew outward.

Perhaps a better comparison to the eruption of Thera comes from the island of Krakatoa in the South Pacific. Krakatoa, off the coast of Java, was only about one-quarter the size of Thera. When this island volcano blew up in 1883, the results of the explosion were felt at great distances. The thunder of the final explosion was heard in Australia, more than 3000 km (2000 mi) away. Seismic tidal waves, created by the eruption, drowned hundreds of villages along the coast of Java and Sumatra, killing 36,000 people. The blast cracked brick buildings more than 100 km (60 mi) away. Three days after the final explosion of Krakatoa, volcanic ash was still falling on the decks of ships up to 2000 km (1200 mi) away. The volcanic dust blown into the atmosphere was responsible for remarkable sunsets reported in Paris and throughout Europe, as the sun filtered through the fine dust for several years after the eruption.

Thera is only about 100 km (60 mi) from the north shore of Crete, where its massive explosion probably had direct effects on the Minoan inhabitants. The cataclysmic eruption likely had two major impacts. The ash fall of possibly 10 cm or more (3 in.) on the eastern end of Crete may have destroyed crops and fields for several years. The ash fall likely took place in spring, after crops were planted. Large tidal waves, tens of meters high, from the collapse and accompanying earthquakes would have raked the near shore of Crete. If the Minoan fleet, the source of sea trade and power, was on the north side of the Crete, it could have been wiped out in a single blow.

What is confounding, however, is the fact that the evidence for the demise of Minoan civilization—the final abandonment and burning of the palaces and the disappearance of certain pottery styles and other local artifacts in 1450 B.C.—did not take place for almost 200 years after the eruption of Thera. Whether or not the disastrous eruption weakened the economic and political base of Crete sufficiently to lead eventually to its demise is unclear. Nonetheless, the explosion must certainly have been the single most dramatic natural event in the lives of the prehistoric peoples of Crete and the eastern Mediterranean.

THE ERUPTION OF THERA

An island explodes in the eastern Mediterranean in 1628 B.C.

The island of Thera (known today as Santorini) and the location of the excavations at Akrotiri. The crescent shape of the island is a remnant of the volcanic cone that exploded here some 3500 years ago.

MYCENAE

*Fortress of the warrior kings of
Bronze Age Greece*

An aerial photograph of the citadel of Mycenae in Greece. The grave circles are in the foreground.

The Bronze Age in Europe, and its accompanying weaponry, ushered in a period of conflict and warfare in which the skills, attitude, and power of the militant seemed to take precedence over other aspects of society. A new warrior class emerged during this period; weapons and armor are the primary burial goods, and martial and hunting scenes dominate decorative art. This presence is strongly visible in the Bronze Age citadels of southern Greece, the "halls of the heroes." These are the people, so vividly described in *The Illiad* of Homer, who sailed to Troy and eventually sacked the city around 1250 B.C. This is the civilization of Agamemmon and Ulysses. These early Greeks gradually wrested power away from Crete and the Minoans and came to dominate the Aegean between 1600 and 1100 B.C., a time known as the Mycenaean period in prehistoric archaeology.

The early rulers of the citadel of Mycenae (my-seen′ee) were buried in **shaft graves,** pits 6 to 8 m (20 to 25 ft) deep, cut into the soft rock of their hilltop settlement. Groups of shaft graves were enclosed in a circle of standing limestone slabs. Two such grave circles have been excavated at Mycenae, and several tombs were found in each shaft. The walls of the tombs were lined with brick or stone, and the entire structure was covered with a timber roof. At a later date, the shaft was reopened and another tomb added. A total of nineteen individuals were buried in the six shaft graves of grave circle A at Mycenae, two to five people in each shaft. There were nine men, eight women, and two children.

The quantity of gifts and offerings in these graves was remarkable, including precious metals and stone in the form of weapons, vessels, masks, and other objects. Ninety swords were found in the graves of three individuals. Amber from northern Europe, ivory from Africa, silver from Crete, glass from Egypt, and great amounts of gold were entombed along with these early rulers.

Heinrich Schliemann, excavator of the graves, described the opening of one of the shafts in a letter to a friend in 1876:

> There are in all five tombs, in the smallest of which I found yesterday the bones of a man and a woman covered by at least five kilograms of jewels of pure gold, with the most wonderful archaic, impressed ornaments; even the smallest leaf is covered with them. To make only a superficial description of the treasure would require more than a week. Today I emptied the tomb and still gathered more than 6/10 kilogram of beautifully ornamented gold leafs; also many earrings and ornaments representing an alter with two birds. . . .

There were also found two scepters with wonderfully chiselled crystal handles and many large bronze vessels and many gold vessels.

> (Schliemann, in Vermeule, 1972, p. 86)

By 1400 B.C., a new kind of grave, the vaulted, beehive-shaped *tholos* tomb, was constructed for the major rulers. A number of these architectural wonders still stand today. The Treasury of Atreus at Mycenae is the finest example of such a tomb. The roof of the vault stands more than 13 m (40 ft) above the floor, with a diameter of 15 m (50 ft). The dramatic doorway is 5 m (16 ft) high, and the lintel across this door weighs over 100 tons. The structure was buried under a hill of rubble, intended to conceal it. Unfortunately its contents were robbed long ago.

Many major and minor settlements from this time period were scattered across southern Greece. A sophisticated system of graveled roads for chariots and carts, with stone bridges and culverts,

The massive outer walls of the citadel, enclosing one of the shaft grave circles and several of the elite burials at the site.

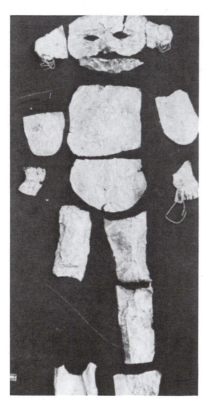

connected these towns. The Mycenaean towns were heavily fortified with monumental stone walls. Major citadels from this period existed in Mycenae, Tiryns, Pylos, and Thebes. At the citadel of Tiryns, the great walls are 15 m (50 ft) thick with internal passages.

At Mycenae, the hilltop was leveled and terraced to hold the walls of the fortress as well as the inhabitants of the palace and town. A long, narrow road, flanked by high stone walls, leads up to the entrance to the citadel, called the Lion Gate because of the enormous stone sculpture of two lions crowning the gate. The massive **Cyclopean** stone walls of Mycenae encircle an area 1100 m (3500 ft) in diameter (the equivalent of two city blocks), enclosing the palace of the king as well as a number of residences and other structures. The Mycenaean palaces combined many of the administrative, military, and manufacturing functions of the kingdom within the residence of the ruler. Workshops for crafts, guardrooms, storerooms, and kitchens were attached to the rear of the palace. There was a small postern gate at the rear of the citadel. Fresh water in time of siege was available from a cistern, found at the bottom of a rock-cut tunnel and staircase deep inside the hill of Mycenae. This reservoir stored water brought from distant hills.

The surrounding villages supplied crops and meat, men and materials to the lord of the citadel. This information comes from the preserved clay tablets with Linear B script. These abstract signs were enscribed on tablets of soft clay. In some fortunate instances, these tablets were burned in fires that swept the citadels, and the fire-hardened clay has been preserved. The inscriptions have been deciphered, and their contents are known. The texts are largely economic, dealing with inventories, shipments, and quotas of items to be paid to the palace in tribute. At the palace of Pylos, where a major horde of tablets was preserved, a list of different occupations in the kingdom is recorded: bakers, bronze smiths, carpenters, heralds, masons, messengers, potters, and shepherds. Many other craft skills are also evidenced in the artifacts and architecture of the citadel: delicate ivory carving, fresco painting, metal inlay, and weapons manufacturing.

The collapse of the Mycenaeans remains a mystery, unrelated to drought or outside conquest, perhaps simply the result of a culmination of centuries of conflict and competition. After 1100 B.C., Athens began to assert its importance in Greece as the center of a new industry of iron making, and the citadels of the Mycenaeans fell into ruin. The beginnings of Iron Age civilization in classical Greece take form until the golden age of Athens, the exploits of Perikles, the thoughts of Socrates and Plato, the inventions of Archimedes, the writings of Homer, and the foundations of much of Western civilization, between 600 and 300 B.C.

HEINRICH SCHLIEMANN, 1822–1890

The man with the golden touch

Heinrich Schliemann.

Heinrich Schliemann, the discover of Troy and the Mycenaean civilization, was born into poverty in Germany. Clever and quick, he eventually became a wealthy international trader in commodities in St. Petersburg, Russia. He must have been quite a remarkable individual, described by others in terms ranging from brilliant to megalomaniacal. Schliemann was fascinated with the story of the Trojan War and learned ancient Greek so he could read Homer in the original language. At age 50, he left his businesses to pursue a vision of the Aegean — specifically, to find the Troy of Priam and Helen. Schliemann believed Homer had described actual events in the past and that Troy was a real citadel, located somewhere on the coast of Turkey. Excavating a mound there known as Hissarlik, Schliemann indeed discovered the ancient walls of Troy and a treasure of precious metals and jewels, including almost 9000 gold rings and a crown with more than 16,000 individual pieces of gold.

After ten years at Troy, Schliemann's interests turned toward Greece and the citadel of Mycenae. Inside the famous Lion Gate at Mycenae are a series of large, stone-lined circles, originally thought to be a meeting place or council area of some kind. Thinking they might be grave monuments, Schliemann began to dig. He eventually uncovered five royal graves in rock-cut shafts beneath the circle. Again he stumbled onto a remarkable treasure of gold and rare stones buried with the former rulers of this citadel. The grave goods from Mycenae are among the most spectacular finds from the Bronze Age: gold and bronze masks and drinking cups, necklaces, earrings, a crystal bowl carved in the shape of a goose, swords and daggers with gold and lapis inlays. In addition, the corpses were apparently covered with hundreds of leaves, flowers, butterflies, and stars cut from thin sheets of gold. Schliemann was also convinced that he had found the gold death mask and body of Agamemnon, murdered by his wife's lover when he returned from the conquest of Troy. That individual was not Agamemnon, but these remains document the wealth of Mycenae and its rulers.

The Bronze Age North of the Alps

Feeding growing populations

One of the more pronounced trends in the European Neolithic was regionalization, the development of distinctly local traditions. This pattern contrasted with the initial farming cultures, which were widespread and similar. Settlements of the first cultivators in western Europe were generally in the open and unprotected; pottery styles were similar across very large areas; trade in exotic materials was on a small scale. Very quickly, however, the growth of population and the emergence of permanent field systems resulted in conflict and competition between groups. By 2000 B.C., the continent was occupied by well-entrenched farming populations making stone tools and pottery, cultivating, trading, and fighting.

Settlements from the later Neolithic were often located in defensive positions and heavily fortified. Pottery styles became more limited in their distribution. At the same time, trade and exchange expanded in scope. A variety of materials and finished goods moved long distances across parts of Europe. The processes of obtaining raw materials for items, manufacturing trade items, and moving the finished materials became important parts of Neolithic economic systems. Flint, for example, was mined in Denmark, Belgium, and England and ground into fine polished axes for trade.

Metals appeared later in the northern part of Europe than in the Aegean area. Copper first appeared north of the Alps around 3000 B.C., coming primarily from the southeast. Bronze objects began to appear in graves and cemeteries of farming settlements in this area after 2000 B.C. By this time, Bronze Age cultures in the eastern Mediterranean had developed into major political entities through a process of alliance, sea power, and the control of trade.

Much of the rest of Europe was involved in the movement of materials and goods into the economic magnet of the eastern Mediterranean. Gold, copper, and tin from Ireland and the British Isles moved across southern England and the English Channel, down the Seine and Rhone rivers in France to the Mediterranean, and by ship to the east. Copper and tin from the Carpathian Mountains in Czechoslovakia traveled overland, across the Alps at the Brenner Pass, and into the Adriatic Sea to move by ship to Crete, Greece, and the Near East. Amber, aromatic resins, and furs moved from southern Scandinavia toward Czechoslovakia and eventually into the Aegean.

A number of new objects and ideas were introduced along these corridors of trade. The third millennium B.C. in northern and western Europe witnessed a number of major innovations, including bronze and gold, the plow, the ox as a draft animal, the horse, the wheel, the ox cart, the chariot, and new weapons. Secondary animal products, such as milk and wool, became more important and fostered new industries. Greater dependence on stock raising is seen in the archaeological rec-

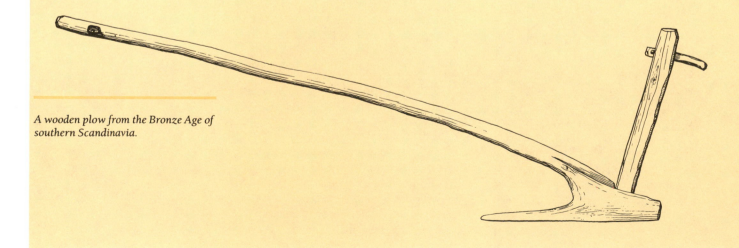

A wooden plow from the Bronze Age of southern Scandinavia.

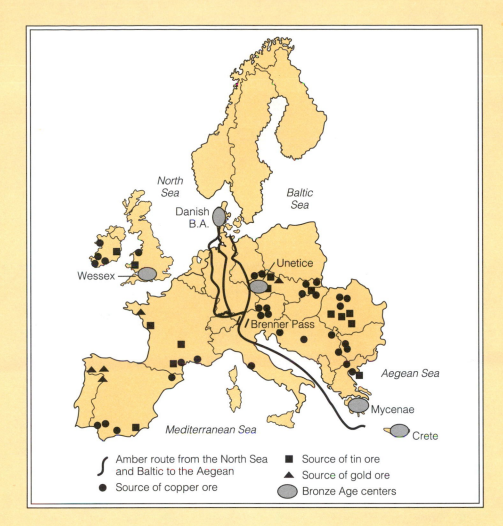

The major sources for gold, copper, tin, and amber in Europe and some of the trade routes to the Mediterranean. Three of the major centers of the Bronze Age north of the Alps were in southern England, Denmark, and western Czechoslovakia.

Map labels:
North Sea
Baltic Sea
Danish B.A.
Unetice
Wessex
Brenner Pass
Aegean Sea
Mycenae
Crete
Mediterranean Sea

Legend:
Amber route from the North Sea and Baltic to the Aegean
● Source of copper ore
■ Source of tin ore
▲ Source of gold ore
⬭ Bronze Age centers

ord, and a pattern of **transhumance** characterized many communities during the Bronze Age north of the Alps.

Wealthy and powerful nonegalitarian societies arose at the heads of these important trade routes in the early Bronze Age after 2000 B.C. The Wessex culture in England elaborated the construction of Stonehenge and raised hundreds of burial mounds across the Salisbury Plain. The Unetice culture in Czechoslovakia, known from a number of "princely" burials, dominated central Europe. The Bronze Age in Denmark and southern Sweden was spectacular in terms of the amount of fine metal objects that are buried in many funerary mounds and caches.

Most of what is known about the Bronze Age comes from large burial mounds (barrows) or in caches of metal objects hidden in the ground; very few actual houses or settlements have been discovered or excavated. Such information provides a limited but spectacular view of only a small, wealthy segment of Bronze Age society.

BORUM ESHØJ

A Bronze Age barrow in Denmark

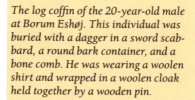

The log coffin of the 20-year-old male at Borum Eshøj. This individual was buried with a dagger in a sword scabbard, a round bark container, and a bone comb. He was wearing a woolen shirt and wrapped in a woolen cloak held together by a wooden pin.

Two Bronze Age barrows (burial mounds) along the coast of Denmark.

Bronze Age barrows dot the landscape of southern Scandinavia. These high, circular mounds were often dramatically placed on the horizon to emphasize the importance of the buried individuals. In a few instances, barrows have preserved their contents to the present, providing a glimpse of the elite of Bronze Age society in northwestern Europe. Dressed in their finest clothing, wearing jewelry, and equipped with weapons, the deceased individuals were placed in a coffin near the center of the mound. Made from a huge log of oak, split in half and hollowed out inside, the coffin was covered under a cairn or pile of stones and buried under a mound of cut sods and soil. The mosslike coverings of these tombs sometimes sealed the contents from the air, and the log coffins quickly filled with groundwater. These conditions have preserved both the coffins and the contents in remarkable fashion.

Borum Eshøj (bore′um-es-hoy) was one of the largest Bronze Age barrows in Denmark, located a little north of the present city of Aarhus. The original mound was almost 9 m (30 ft) high (equivalent to a three-story building) and 40 m (130 ft) in diameter. The barrow was first opened in 1875 by the landowner who was removing the rich soil of the

mound for his fields. Three oak coffins were eventually removed from the mound, containing an elderly man, a younger man, and a woman. The central log coffin in the mound was 3 m (10 ft) long and contained the body of a 50-to-60-year-old man, lying on a cowhide. The man wore a wool cap over a head of hair once blond, now stained black by tannic acid. His chin, also stained dark, was clean-shaven, and his teeth were in good condition. He was dressed in a wool skirt with a rope belt. The body of the younger man, age 20, was buried in a wool shirt held together by a leather belt and a wooden button. This person was buried with a bronze dagger placed in a wooden scabbard for a sword, a bone comb, a round bark container, and a wooden pin to fasten his cloak.

The burial of the elderly woman was extremely well preserved. The woman was between 50 and 60 years old and 1.57 m (5′2″) tall. The first item found when the coffin was opened was a cowhide with the hairs still intact. Beneath the hide was a woolen rug on top of the body of the woman. She was buried wearing a skirt and tunic of brown wool, a tasselled belt, and a hairnet of wool thread with her long hair still inside. A comb made of horn was found next to her hair. Various bronze ob-

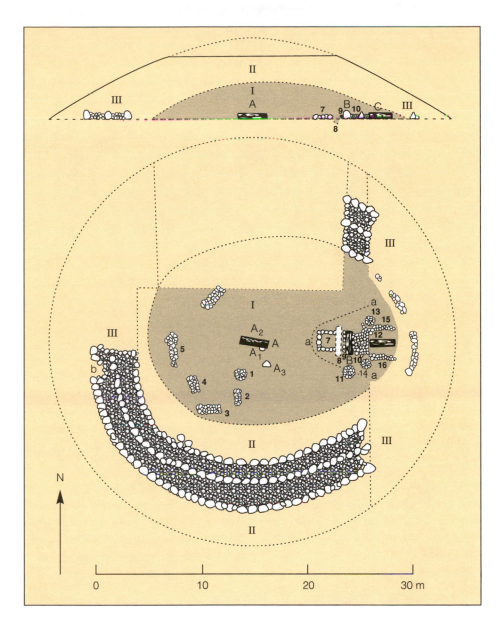

jects were also in the coffin, including a pin, a dagger with a horn handle, a belt disk, and rings for the fingers, arms, and neck.

Bronze Age barrows were built for the wealthier members of society and erected near where the living had died. The distribution of thousands of such barrows in Denmark provides some information on the use of the landscape and the organization of society in the early Bronze Age. The larger numbers of barrows are located in areas of more productive farmland in Denmark, evidence of the important relationship between the control of agricultural resources and wealth.

The amount of metal in these burials provides some indication of the wealth of the deceased individuals, as well. The metal is either bronze or gold. Gold was more valuable; only 1 g (0.04 oz) of gold is found for every 1000 g (2.2 lb) of bronze. There are pronounced differences between the sexes and between individuals. Male graves are more common than female ones, and they contain more wealth. Some individuals were buried with lots of bronze and gold and some without any, suggesting that social differentiation was pronounced in this area. All the bronze and gold in southern Scandinavia was imported, because this was an area lacking in most metal ores. An elite segment of the population probably had control over most of the resources as well as the trade.

A woolen woman's tunic and belted skirt from one of the log coffins.

VIX

*A princess burial from
the late Hallstatt Iron Age*

*A bronze head from a La Tène crema-
tion grave near Koblenz, Germany;
4.6 cm high.*

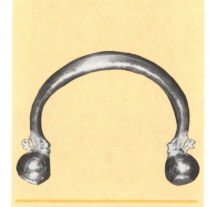

*The imported gold collar found with
the princess burial at Vix.*

Iron making was discovered in Turkey shortly before 2000 B.C. The technology was likely well guarded for some time, for military advantage. Iron has a melting temperature of over 3000°C, and sophisticated furnaces and smelting techniques are needed to reduce iron ores. The new metal was used initially for stronger, more durable weapons and later for more practical tools and equipment. Iron came to Europe around the beginning of the first millennium B.C., slightly earlier in the eastern Mediterranean, slightly later in the northwestern part of the continent.

The Iron Age in western Europe, the time of the Celtic tribes, is divided into two major phases: Hallstatt and La Tène. Hallstatt, the earlier portion of the Iron Age, lasted from approximately 1000 to 500 B.C., centered in Austria and southern Germany and Czechoslovakia. Salt and iron mines in these regions during the early Iron Age led to economic boom times. The La Tène period followed Hallstatt. The major concentrations of sites from this period are found in eastern France and Switzerland. This Celtic Iron Age came to an end in most of western Europe shortly before the birth of Christ with the Roman conquest of France (Gaul) by Caesar in 43 B.C. Most of England was conquered by Claudius slightly later. Remnants of the Celtic traditions remained in Ireland for centuries, however, untouched by the Roman empire. Germanic tribes in central and northern Europe also remained in the Iron Age at the fringe of the Roman Empire for many centuries.

Both Hallstatt and La Tène are defined primarily by types of pottery and styles of artistic decoration. In general, there is a Celtic art style found throughout western Europe at this time. Designs from the La Tène period are flamboyant and hypnotic. Complex patterns of concentric circles, spirals, and meanders, and a variety of birds and animal figures, decorate metal and ceramic objects. Disembodied heads with almond-shaped eyes and fierce moustaches; long, fanciful horses' heads; willowy statues of women—all characterize the tradition. Weapons, tools, jewelry, and everyday equipment are ornamented with this distinctive art.

This art style, along with certain religious practices and beliefs, was shared by a number of large societies in western Europe. These groups were headed by strong leaders and organized along specific lines. In some areas, there were elected magistrates. Julius Caesar, who encountered these groups in battle and in negotiations, wrote about their social structure, describing three major divisions below the king: an aristocratic class of warriors and priests, the common people, and slaves.

The tombs of the elite of Celtic society are among the best-known finds from this period. The grave at Vix (vee) was excavated in 1953 by René Joffroy at the foot of an Iron Age hill fort known as Mont Lassois in northern France. A princess was buried here beneath an earthen mound along the headwaters of the Seine around 500 B.C. A large square chamber had been dug into the earth and lined with wooden planks; the tomb was filled and covered with a mound. The body of a 35-year-old woman was placed on the bed of a ceremonial cart or hearse in the center of the grave. The wheels of the cart were removed and stacked against the sides of the tomb. Her body was covered with a leather blanket, and a bronze-headed staff was placed across her body. Buried with a heavy gold diadem or collar, probably made in Spain, she was wearing Baltic amber beads, locally made bronze brooches, and other pins and jewelry.

In the tomb was a wealth of exotic funerary offerings. A huge bronze **krater** (a vessel for mixing and storing wine), more than 1.5 m (5 ft) high, 208 kg (450 lb) in weight, with a volume of some 280 gal, was set in one corner of the grave. Crafted in a Greek bronze workshop, probably in southern Italy, the krater was designed to be dismantled for transport, and the assembly instructions were in Greek. The design around its rim depicts Greek warriors and horse-drawn chariots. A number of bronze, silver, and gold bowls were placed alongside the krater, including a bronze Etruscan flagon from Italy and two painted pottery cups from Attic Greece.

The sources for the various materials found in the princess grave at Vix point to the extensive trade of materials that was taking place in Europe at this time. The Rhone is the largest river in Europe that connects with the Mediterranean. The river provides a major corridor from the south into temperate Europe. The modern city of Marseille, at the mouth of the Rhone in southern France, was originally a Greek colony called Massilia, founded in 600 B.C. Wine from the Aegean was imported to Massilia for shipment into western Europe. Various goods and materials from the continent were exported through this colony to the eastern Mediterranean. The quantity of materials flowing through this port must have been remarkable. Fragments of a garment of Chinese silk, found in a Hallstatt tomb in Germany, are one example of the extent of trade at this time.

The princess grave at Vix lies below the Iron Age oppida at Mont Lassois, one of the major political and commercial centers of late Hallstatt Europe. Mont Lassois dominates the Upper Seine valley at the point where the river becomes navigable, with the Rhone River and its tributaries nearby to the east. Thus Mont Lassois is at a strategic point in the main route of commerce between the western Mediterranean and the Atlantic coast of western

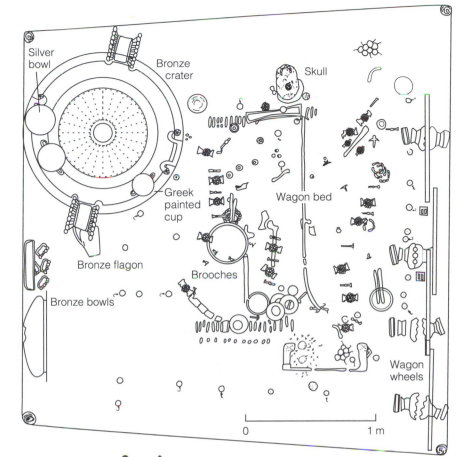

The ground plan of the princess burial from Vix. The wagon bed in the center was used as a burial platform, and the wheels of the wagon were placed along the wall to the right. An enormous bronze vessel was placed in the upper-left corner of the tomb, along with a number of other vessels.

The bronze krater (vessel) from the tomb at Vix, 1.5 m high and more than 200 kg.

France, and the English Channel and the British Isles. Iron ores, along with the wood for charcoal to reduce the ores, are also readily available in this area. The richness of the gifts in the tomb of the princess at Vix, some 500 km (300 mi) north of Marseille, suggests that the Greeks were giving gifts to the elite of Celtic society in order to obtain favorable trading status and secure commerce.

MAIDEN CASTLE

The end of the Celtic Iron Age

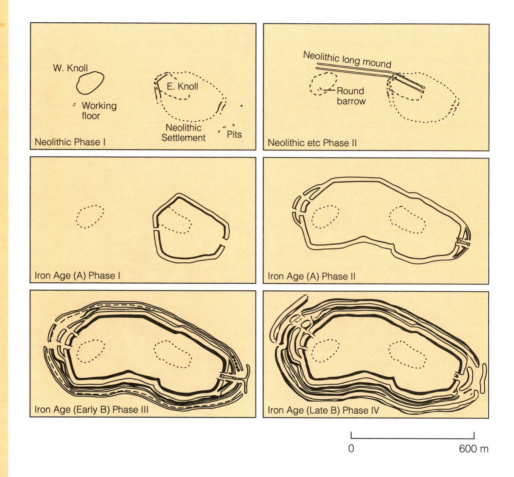

Wheeler's interpretation of the construction phases at Maiden Castle, from the Neolithic through the Iron Age.

The largest settlements from the Iron Age in Europe are defended hilltops, found throughout southern Germany, France, and Britain. The Romans frequently remarked on the strength of the Gaelic walls that surrounded these hilltops. Greek and Roman writers reported on the ferocity of the Celtic defenders, describing the bold *gaesatae*, spearmen who went naked into battle. Roman statues commemorated the valor of the Celts as fair-haired warriors with drooping moustaches. In a famous sculpture, a defeated Celt puts himself to the sword rather than surrender to the Romans. That the Romans should so admire the character of their boisterous and aggressive enemy is itself a remarkable statement about the Celts.

Hundreds of Iron Age hill forts are found in Britain and Ireland, in sizes ranging from less than an acre to many hectares. These hill forts served as both population centers and retreats during the Iron Age, distinguished by the fortifications that surround them with one or more walls. Maiden Castle is one of the

largest hill forts in Britain, in its final form enclosing an area of almost 18 ha (45 acres). Maiden Castle sits atop a high, saddleback hill in the Downs of Dorset, near the south coast of England. Sir Mortimer Wheeler began excavations there from 1934 to 1937. After his college studies, Wheeler served as a young officer in World War I, the commander of a battery in the Royal Artillery. Returning at the end of the war to head the archaeology section of the National Museum of Wales, in 1925 he became Director of the London Museum. His excavations at Maiden Castle were intended both to reveal the past history of the site and to train new students in archaeology. Wheeler was one of the major figures in British archaeology, highly respected both for the quality of his work and his concern with the education of archaeologists.

Wheeler's forte was the **stratigraphic section**, the excavation of trenches and squares across manmade features to reveal the sequence and methods of construction. It is this vertical wall, or profile of excavated trenches and squares, that provides the information essential to understanding the past history of a site. Recording these sections in photographs and drawings provides a permanent record of the stratigraphy of events for the archaeologist to interpret. Wheeler's precise excavations and recording have revealed much about the prehistory of Maiden Castle, from the Neolithic to the Roman conquest of Britain.

The hilltop was first used around 3000 B.C. as a Neolithic camp; an enormous barrow was erected here during the same period, overlooking the adjacent valley. The Neolithic long barrow ran for over 450 m (1500 ft) across the hilltop, marked by two parallel ditches, each 5 m (16 ft) wide, 15 m (50 ft) apart. Bronze Age remains are absent from the hilltop. By 350 B.C. in the Iron Age, fortifications begin to appear around a growing market center on the hilltop.

The first fort at Maiden Castle was univallate (having one wall) and enclosed some 6 ha (15 acres). Dense evidence of

Maiden Castle, Dorset, England, showing the fortifications of multiple walls and ditches.

A Roman catapult arrowhead lodged in the back of one of the defenders of Maiden Castle.

occupation is present; perhaps as many as 2000 to 4000 people lived there. The large hill forts like Maiden Castle appear to have had administrative, religious, economic, and residential functions in a proto-urban context, an early form of the walled town. There are several distinct areas inside Maiden Castle. An Iron Age shrine or temple was uncovered on the most prominent part of the hilltop. This structure was later replaced by a Roman temple, documenting the continuity of religious significance and focus at the hillforts. Residential structures dot the hilltop. Large pits were dug into the chalk, as deep as 3 m (10 ft), for storage, water reservoirs, and other purposes. Excavations also revealed the parallel ruts of wagon wheels crossing the defended interior; the standard wheel-to-wheel distance in the later Iron Age was 1.46 m (4.79 ft).

By 50 B.C., shortly before the first Roman invasion of Britain, the fortifications were enormously expanded, and the enclosed area inside the hill fort tripled in size. The final set of fortifications consisted of an enormous set of three concentric banks and two ditches enclosing almost 18 ha (45 acres). A fourth bank was added at the south end for additional protection. The term **multivallate** describes large hill forts with complex defenses of multiple ditches and ramparts. Some of the walls at Maiden Castle stand as high as 20 m (65 ft) today. These walls had a 4-m-high foundation of stone, on which stood a massive wooden palisade. A narrow, serpentine, and dangerous path guards the entrance at the eastern end of the hilltop. At the entrance were wooden gates, 4 m (13 ft) wide. Some 22,000 sling stones were found in caches near the walls of Maiden Castle, documenting one of the important defensive weapons in use.

In spite of its massive defenses and preparations against attack, Maiden Castle fell to Roman legions and their siege artillery in A.D. 43. Wheeler's depiction of the final hours of the defenders of Maiden Castle is a masterpiece of archaeological interpretation and prose:

> It was now easy to reconstruct the succession of events. Before the close fighting began, the regiment of catapults or *ballistae*, which habitually accompanied a legion on campaign, put down a barrage across the gateway, causing casualities at the outset. Following the barrage, the Roman infantry advanced up the slope, cutting its way from rampart to rampart, tower to tower. In the innermost bay of the entrance, a number of huts had been recently built; these were now set alight, and under the rising clouds of smoke the gates were stormed. But resistance had been obstinate and the attack was pushed home with every savagery. The scene became that of a massacre in which the wounded were not spared. Finally, the gates were demolished and the stone walls which flank them reduced to the lowly and ruinous condition in which we found them, nineteen centuries later.
>
> (Wheeler, 1943, p. 47)

A Roman catapult arrowhead, found in the back of the skeleton of one of the defenders of Maiden Castle, poignantly marks the end of the Celtic Iron Age in western Europe and its replacement by Rome.

THE BOG PEOPLE

Iron Age cadavers from the peat — "creatures from the black lagoons"

Grauballe Man, found in a Danish bog in 1952. His throat had been cut, and he was placed naked in the waters of the Grauballe bog around 20 B.C.

Archaeologists rarely find flesh on the bones of the past. Much of what we know about our ancestors and their lifeways comes from the detective work of piecing together information from fragments of pots and tools, bones and buried skeletons — the broken, discarded, and buried remains of what life once created. Unusual situations, especially in the case of preserved human bodies from the past, immediately capture our attention. These discoveries emphasize the fragile nature of our human condition and generate much interest in the past.

Among the most remarkable series of preserved bodies from long ago are the "bog people" from northern Europe. Several hundred individuals have been found in the peat bogs of northern Germany and southern Scandinavia, dating to the centuries around the birth of Christ. These bogs have marvelous preservative powers. The accumulation of peat and organic detritus filling the swamps and mires contains tannic acid from the needles of coniferous trees. Also used for tanning hides, tannic acid is essentially responsible for the preservation and color of the skin of the bog bodies. Because the bogs are waterlogged, they create an environment in which bacteria cannot break down soft tissues.

The bog bodies are normally not the result of accidental drowning or disappearance. They are a curious consequence of the beliefs and practices of early Iron Age society. These people viewed the bogs as sacred places where sacrifices were to be made to the gods. Long braids of human hair were cut off and thrown in to the bogs in one gesture of offering. Weapons and jewelry of bronze, iron, and gold were also placed in the mire to appease the gods. Sacrificial individuals were also intentionally executed and placed in the bogs. Some of the bodies found in the bogs were victims of violent death. Lindlow Man, found in England in 1984, was bludgeoned with an axe, strangled, and finally his throat was cut.

One of the best-known examples is the Tollund Man, exhumed from the bogs of Denmark by P. V. Glob of the Danish National Museum. Tollund Man was placed in the murky waters of a peat bog in central Denmark almost 2000 years ago. As Glob describes, the body was very well preserved, even his eyelashes and whiskers were readily visible. Tollund Man died by strangulation; a thin leather garrotte was found still tight around his neck. He was naked except for a small leather cap and a belt around his waist. Tollund Man was well groomed when he died, and his hands were soft and uncalloused, unaccustomed to hard labor. His last meal was a gruel of many different kinds of seeds and grains. He died in spring, and his execution is thought to be related to the rites and rituals of Iron Age society that required sacrifice and offerings for the resurrection of the year and the bounty of the Earth. In fact, he may have been a priest charged as the ceremonial caretaker for a goddess of spring.

In the peat cut, nearly seven feet down, lay a human figure in a crouched position, still half buried. A foot and a shoulder protruded, perfectly preserved but dark brown in color like the surrounding peat, which had dyed the skin. Carefully we removed more peat, and a bowed head came into view. As dusk fell, we saw in the fading light a man take shape before us. He was curled up, with legs drawn under him and arms bent, resting on his side as if asleep. His eyes were peacefully shut . . . his brows were furrowed and his mouth showed a slightly irritated quirk, as if he were not overpleased by this unexpected disturbance of his rest.

P. V. Glob, *The Bog People* (1970)

EPILOG
LESSONS FROM PREHISTORIC EUROPE

The growth of European civilization

The story of European prehistory from the advent of agriculture to the beginning of written history is one of spectacular growth and change. As we have seen, the introduction of agriculture resulted in major changes in European society and economy over the six millennia before Christ. The initial spread of farming was slow, over a period of roughly 3000 years, as the new plant and animal species were adjusted to the more temperate climatic conditions of the European mainland. The first farming communities in Europe are known from Greece and date to around 6000 B.C. By 3000 B.C., farming reached its climatic limits in southern Scandinavia and Britain and penetrated to the coasts of western Europe. By that time, virtually all the cultivable areas of Europe were inhabited by farming populations, and hunter-gatherers survived only in the more northerly and marginal areas.

The third and second millenium B.C. in Europe witnessed increased trade, and more powerful societies in the eastern Mediterranean influenced the entire continent. Early states in Mesopotamia, the Nile Valley, and the Aegean were voracious consumers

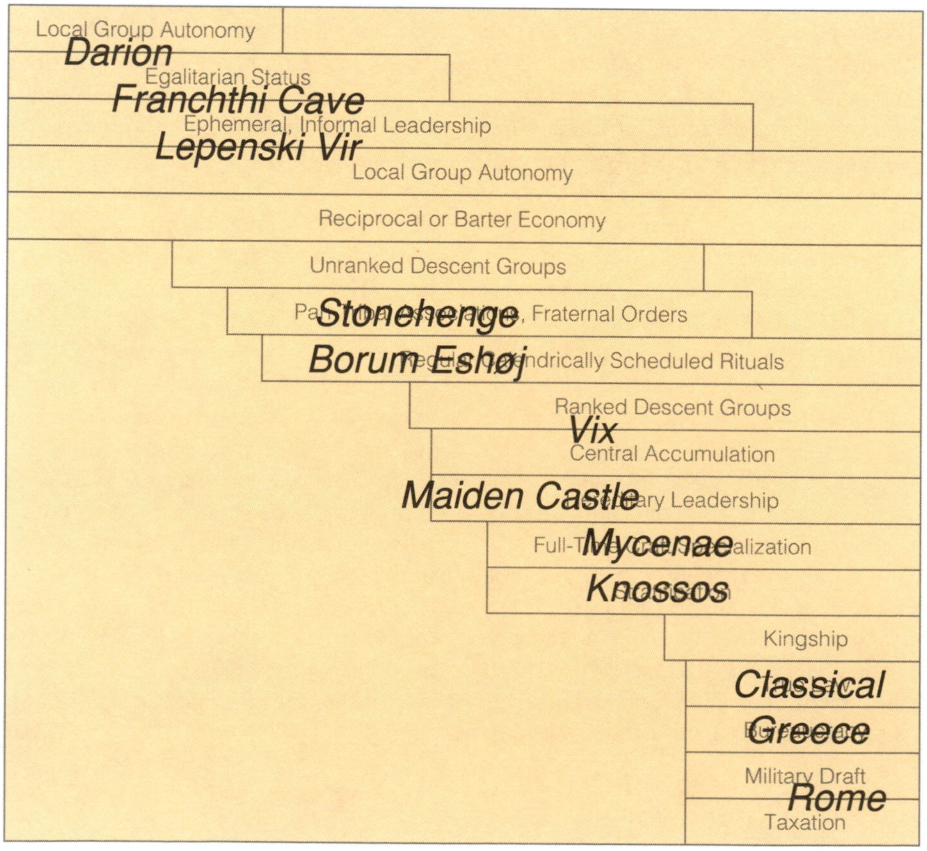

The evolution of European society.

Local Group Autonomy
Darion
Egalitarian Status
Franchthi Cave
Ephemeral, Informal Leadership
Lepenski Vir
Local Group Autonomy
Reciprocal or Barter Economy
Unranked Descent Groups
Pan-Tribal Sodalities, Fraternal Orders
Stonehenge
Calendrically Scheduled Rituals
Borum Eshøj
Ranked Descent Groups
Vix
Central Accumulation
Maiden Castle
Hereditary Leadership
Full-Time Craft Specialization
Mycenae
Knossos
Kingship
Classical
Greece
Military Draft
Rome
Taxation

of rare and exotic materials, including such metals as bronze and gold, amber and other rare stones, furs and pelts, and other items from temperate Europe. The third millennium also witnessed a number of major changes in technology and transportation, including the manufacture of bronze weapons and jewelry, the widespread adoption of the plow and the wheel, and the use of draft animals, such as the ox and the horse. Secondary animal products, such as milk and wool, became important items in the economy. Weapons and militaristic motifs dominate the symbols of status and prestige in European society during this period, as local warfare and conflict contrasted strongly with the long-distance patterns of trade and cooperation.

The introduction of iron after 1000 B.C. brought new tools and weapons everywhere. Mines for iron ore in the Alps mean that the sources for raw materials were closer to the Mediterranean, as Greece and then Italy saw the rise of very powerful city-states and empires in the centuries before Christ. North of the Alps, Europe was home to the more diffuse political groups of the Celts and the Germanic "tribes," until the Roman conquest and the spread of Christianity initiated the beginnings of the historic periods of the Dark Ages, the Rennaissance, and eventually the Industrial Era.

SUGGESTED READINGS

Chadwick, John. 1976. *The Mycenaean world.* Cambridge: Cambridge University Press. A classic treatise on the Mycenaeans, with particular emphasis on the written language.

Chippendale, Christopher. 1983. *Stonehenge complete.* Ithaca, NY: Cornell University Press. A well-illustrated compendium on the evolution of Stonehenge and our understanding of it.

Coles, John M., and Anthony F. Harding. 1979. *The Bronze Age in Europe.* London: Methuen. Details of the Bronze Age civilizations of Europe, with an emphasis on areas north of the Alps.

Powell, T. G. E. 1980. *The Celts.* London: Thames & Hudson. An updated classic on the Celtic peoples of Europe and their art.

Whittle, Alastair. 1985. *Neolithic Europe: A survey.* Cambridge: Cambridge University Press. A synthesis of the evidence on the Neolithic of Europe.

IN CONCLUSION

There is no present or future—only the past, happening over and over again—now.

Eugene O'Neill,
A Moon for the Misbegotten

Perhaps the best way to conclude this book is to ask the question, What have we learned? We know that archaeology includes stunning museum pieces, travel, and exotic places. Archaeology is puzzles, mysteries, and detective work. Archaeology is a number of intriguing methods for getting answers about the past, and a stimulating career in which any number of interests can be accommodated by the variety of times, places, and ways in which people lived in the past. Archaeology is digging holes and recovering architecture and artifacts. Archaeology is good, dirty fun.

But there are larger lessons from the past. The Spanish-American philosopher Santyana wrote that those who cannot remember the past are condemned to repeat it. Certainly there are lessons about the long span of our prehistory on Earth and about the evolution of our species and our behavior. In terms of the vastness of geological or archaeological time, our own role as humans on the planet is miniscule indeed. Yet the impact of our species is immeasurable. Although relative newcomers to Earth's history, we have an obligation and a responsibility toward all that is around us. Humans have tremendous destructive power as well as creative abilities. Through looting, careless development, and the wanton destruction of archaeological resources, we even have the potential to eliminate our abilities to reconstruct and understand the human past.

Society has so much to learn from its ancestors—their successes and failures—and contemporary archaeology is developing the tools and techniques to examine this ancient record carefully and with the degree of objectivity that science requires.

A corollary to the immensity of prehistoric time is the tempo of change. The rate of change in our societies and in ourselves is ever-increasing. Numbers and diversity of species increased almost geometrically through the Earth's history. If we consider the passage of time as a straight line, the major milestones in the evolution of life occur more and more frequently as we approach the present. The complexity and rate of change in our own human prehistory are clearly accelerating. We took our first steps some 4 to 5 million years ago, made our first tools 2 to 3 million years ago, first buried our dead perhaps 100,000 years ago, painted on the walls of caves some 25,000 years ago, domesticated plants and animals 10,000 years ago, built cities and began to write on clay about 5000 years ago, and began to harness fossil fuels and machinery less than 500 years ago.

The pace of life, science, and living has become so rapid that today almost everything around us changes in the short period between birth and death. It becomes more and more difficult to understand or cope with changes in the society that fostered us. We must deal with what philosopher and visionary Alvin Toffler has called future shock:

> By now the accelerative thrust triggered by man has become the key to the entire evolutionary process on our planet. The rate and direction of the evolution of other species, their very survival, depends on decisions made by man. Yet there is nothing inherent in the evolutionary process to guarantee man's own survival.
>
> Throughout the past, as successive stages of social evolution unfolded, man's awareness followed rather than preceded the event. Today unconscious adaptation is no longer

adequate. Faced with the power to alter the gene, to create new species, to populate the planets, or depopulate the earth, man must now assume conscious control of evolution itself. Avoiding future shock as he rides the waves of change, he must master evolution, shaping tomorrow to human need. Instead of rising in revolt against it, he must, from this historic moment on, anticipate and design the future.

(Toffler, 1970, p. 438)

Perhaps the final lesson of archaeology is a lingering sense of hope and future. Our strongest feelings from what we as archaeologists have learned remain a basic optimism for our species. In every way we are artifacts, manufactured over a very long period of time, created by the experiences of our ancestors. We have been on the planet for several million years. In that time, we have evolved from a chimpanzee-like ape to the person on the moon. We have expanded geographically and survived under a wide range of conditions. There is an unusual quality about the human species, the enormous potential in the human intellect, with its remarkable inventiveness for coping with change. Large brains and creativity managed to get us through a very long and difficult journey in the past. For that very reason, the future should be just as exciting.

APPENDIX

COMMON MEASUREMENT CONVERSIONS AND EQUIVALENTS

LENGTH or HEIGHT

1 centimeter = 0.394 inches
1 inch = 2.54 centimeters
1 meter = 3.281 feet
1 foot = 0.305 meters
1 meter = 1.0936 yards
1 yard = 0.9144 meters
1 kilometer = 0.6214 miles
1 mile = 1.6094 kilometers

APPROXIMATE EQUIVALENTS	Feet	Meters
Average Person	5.5	1.7
Height of Basketball Basket	10	3.0
High-Diving Platform	32.8	10
Bowling Alley	60	18
Ten-Story Building	100	30
Arc de Triomphe	164	50
High Ski Jump	196.8	60
Football Field	300	91
Washington Monument	555	169
Golf Course	20,000	6098

AREA

1 square centimeter = 0.155 square inch
1 square inch = 6.452 square centimeters
1 square meter = 10.764 square feet
1 square foot = 0.0929 square meters
1 square meter = 1.196 square yards
1 square yard = 0.8361 square meters
1 square kilometer = 0.386 square mile
1 square mile = 2.59 square kilometers
1 hectare = 10,000 square meters
1 hectare = 2.47 acres
1 acre = 0.405 hectare

APPROXIMATE EQUIVALENTS	Length	Width	Square Feet	Square Meters	Acres	Hectares
Average Bedroom	12 ft	10 ft	120	11	.0027	0.0011
Soccer Goal Post	24 ft	8 ft	192	18	.0045	0.0018
Doubles Tennis Court	36 ft	78 ft	2808	261	.0645	0.0261
Basketball Court	84 ft	45.75 ft	3843	357	.0882	0.0357
Average House Lot	80 ft	80 ft	6400	595	.1469	0.0595
Baseball Infield	90 ft	90 ft	8100	753	.1859	0.0753
Olympic Pool	50 m	21 m	11,298	1050	.2594	0.1050
Football Field	300 ft	60 ft	18,000	1673	.4132	0.1673
Hockey Rink	200 ft	100 ft	20,000	1859	.4591	0.1859
Soccer Field	100 m	80 m	86,080	8000	1.9760	0.8000
Union Square, New York City			430,400	40,000	9.8800	4.0000
City Block	700 ft	700 ft	490,000	45,539	11.2481	4.5539

	Miles	Miles	Square Miles	Acres	Hectares
Churchill Downs (Horse Race Track)	1.25	oval	0.018522	11.849	4.797
Indianapolis Race Track	2.5	oval	0.4112	263.057	106.501
Central Park, New York City	2.5	0.5	1.25	799.663	323.750
Manhattan Island	12.5	2.5	22	14,074.060	5698.000

VOLUME

1 cubic centimeter = 0.061 cubic inches
1 cubic inch = 16.39 cubic centimeters
1 cubic meter = 35.314 cubic feet
1 cubic foot = 0.0283 cubic meter
1 cubic meter = 1.308 cubic yards

APPROXIMATE EQUIVALENTS	Cubic Meters
Refrigerator	2
Home Bathroom	10
UPS Delivery Truck	25
School Bus	50
Large Room	100
Medium-Size House	1000
Small Church	10,000
Modern Oil Tanker	100,000

DENSITY

25 People/square kilometer	0.2 Person/Soccer field	65 People/square mile
500 People/square kilometer	4 People/Soccer field	1300 People/square mile
5000 People/square kilometer	40 People/Soccer field	13,000 People/square mile

GLOSSARY

Abri (French) A rock overhang or shelter in which the depth of the shelter is less than twice the width of the opening. A cave has a depth more than twice the width of its opening.

Absolute dating A method of assigning archaeological dates in calendar years, so that an age in actual number of years is known or can be estimated.

Accelerator mass spectrometer (Ams) A scientific instrument for measuring the mass of accelerated atomic particles by separating and counting individual carbon atoms; used to measure the ratio of ^{14}C to ^{12}C atoms in very small samples (less than 0.01 g) to determine radiocarbon age.

Acheulean A major archaeological culture of the Lower Paleolithic, named after the site of St. Acheul in France. A hallmark of the Acheulean is the handaxe.

Achieved status Social status and prestige attributed to an individual according to achievements or skills rather than inherited social position. *See also* Ascribed status.

Acropolis (Greek) A raised complex of palaces and courtyards, especially in Mesoamerica and Greece.

Adena A burial mound complex that developed in the Ohio River Valley toward the end of the last millennium B.C.

Adobe A mud mixture used to make sun-dried bricks for buildings in arid areas.

Adze A heavy, chisel-like tool.

Alloying A technique of combining or mixing two or more metals to make an entirely new metal; for example, mixing copper and tin creates bronze.

Annealing The process of heating and gradually cooling metal (or other materials) to reduce brittleness and enhance toughness.

Anthropomorphic Having human form or attributes.

Alpaca A domesticated South American herbivore with long, soft wool.

Altiplano (Spanish) The high-altitude plain between the eastern and western ridges of the Andes in Peru.

Anasazi One of three major cultural traditions of the American Southwest during late prehistoric times. The Anasazi were centered in the northern Southwest, on the high plateau of the Four Corners region.

Archaeoastronomy The study of ancient alignments and other aspects of the archaeological record and their relationship to ancient astronomical knowledge and events. Archaeoastronomical investigation refers to research conducted by archaeoastronomers.

Archaeology The study of the human past, combining the themes of time and change.

Archaeozoology The study of animal remains from archaeological sites.

Archaic The term used for the early Holocene in the New World, from approximately 6000 B.C. until 1500 to 1000 B.C.

Articulated A term describing the relationship of bones in the skeleton. Articulated bones are found in their original position, indicating that the body or part thereof was buried intact.

Artifact Any object or item created or modified by human action.

Ascribed status Social status and prestige attributed to an individual at birth, regardless of ability or accomplishments. *See also* Achieved status.

Assemblage The set of artifacts and other remains found on an archaeological site or within a specific level of a site.

Association The relationship between items in an archaeological site. Items in association are found close together and/or in the same layer or deposit. Often used for dating purposes, as items found in association are assumed to be of the same age.

Atlantean column A carved human figure serving as a decorative or supporting column, such as at the Mesoamerican site of Tula.

Atlatl A spearthrower, or wooden shaft, used to propel a spear or dart; first appeared in the Upper Paleolithic, also used in the precontact New World.

Australopithecine The generic term for the various species of the genus *Australopithecus*, including *afarensis, africanus, robustus,* and *boisei.*

Bajo (Spanish) A broad, flat, clay-lined depression in the Maya lowlands that fills with water during the rainy season.

Ball court An I-shaped or oval prehispanic structure, found throughout Mesoamerica and the southwestern United States, that was the site of ritual ballgames.

Bandkeramik An archaeological culture of the early Neolithic of central Europe. The term refers to the style of pottery from this culture: linear bands of incised designs on hemispherical bowls.

Bas-relief Sculptural relief, in which the figures project slightly from the background.

Bifacial A term describing flaked stone tools in which both faces or sides are retouched to make a thinner tool. *See also* Unifacial.

Bipedalism The human method of locomotion, walking on two legs. One of the first human characteristics to distinguish the early hominids, as opposed to quadrupedal, walking on four legs.

Bitumen A black or brown tarlike, waterproof substance, often used for painting or making a container water-tight, or as an adhesive.

Blade A special kind of flake with two parallel sides and a length at least twice the width of the piece. The regular manufacture of blades characterized the Upper Paleolithic, with an efficient way of producing mass quantities of cutting edge.

Boustropedon An ancient method of writing, in which the lines run alternatively from right to left on one line and from left to right on the next line.

Bow-drill A device for perforating beads or other small objects, in which a bow is used to rotate the shaft of the bit.

Breccia The accumulated materials from cave deposits that harden into a conglomerate rock, including sediments, rocks, and the bones of animals.

Brow ridge That part of the skull above the eye orbits. This ridge of bone was particularly pronounced in the early hominids, when cranial capacity was less and the forehead absent or sloping. Brow ridges are largely absent in *Homo sapiens sapiens.*

Bulla (plural **bullae**) (Latin) A hollow clay sphere or envelope that was used to enclose clay tokens in ancient Mesopotamia.

Burin A stone tool with right-angle edges used for planing and engraving.

Cacao A bean of the cacao tree, which is native to Mesoamerica; used to make chocolate. Cacao beans also were used as money by the Aztec.

Cache A collection of artifacts, often buried or associated with constructed features, that has been deliberately stored for future use.

Calibrated dates Dates resulting from the process of calibration, the correction of radiocarbon years to calendar years, by means of a curve or formula derived from the comparison of radiocarbon dates and tree rings from the bristlecone pine. Calibration extends approximately 6000 years into the past. (The radiocarbon dates in this book are not calibrated.)

Camelid A ruminant mammal—such as camel, llama, and extinct related forms—having long legs and two toes.

Cannibalism The practice of eating human flesh.

Carnelian A red or reddish variety of chalcedony (a translucent variety of quartz) that is used in jewelry.

Cayman A tropical American alligator.

Cenote The Maya term for a sinkhole, a natural well in the Yucatán that provides water for drinking and bathing.

Cenozoic The most recent geological era of the last 65 million years, sometimes called the age of the mammals.

Chac mool A life-size stone figure in a reclining position, with flexed legs and head raised and turned to one side. They served as altars and often were placed in temple doorways to receive offerings.

Charnel house A house in which the bodies of the dead are placed.

Chert A dull-colored, sub-tranluscent rock resembling flint that was often used for making flaked stone tools.

Chicha A South American beer made from maize.

Chichimec A term loosely applied to the peoples who lived beyond the northern limits of Mesoamerica; nomadic people, considered to be uncivilized barbarians.

Chinampa (Spanish) An agricultural field created by swamp drainage or land fill operations along the edges of lakes. This intensive form of agriculture was especially prevalent in the Basin of Mexico; but also was employed elsewhere in the Central Highlands of Mexico.

Circumscription The process or act of being enclosed by either environmental boundaries, such as mountains, oceans, and rivers, or social boundaries, such as neighboring groups of people.

Citadel A hilltop fortress. Citadels are the characteristic settlement of the ruling elite of Mycenaean civilization, between 1700 and 1100 B.C.

Cleaver A companion tool of the handaxe during the Acheulean period. Cleavers have a broad leading edge, while handaxes come to a point.

Clactonian A term used for assemblages from the Lower Paleolithic, lacking handaxes and characterized by large flakes with heavy retouch and notches.

Clovis An archaeological culture during the Paleoindian period in North America, defined by a distinctive type of fluted point; named for the original find spot near Clovis, New Mexico.

Codex (plural **codices**) (Latin) A handpainted book on bark paper or animal skins that was folded like a screen. In Mesoamerica, codices, which record historical, religious, and tribute information, were made both before and after the Spanish conquest.

Comal (Spanish) A flat, ceramic griddle used for cooking tortillas.

Conquistador (Spanish) A conqueror; referring to the Spanish explorers who conquered Mexico in the early 1500s and also ventured into the southern United States.

Coprolite Fossilized human feces.

Corbell A type of construction technique for building false arches, in use in Greece and Mesoamerica prior to the introduction of the true Roman arch with a keystone. Corbelling involves offset layers of stones that eventually close the ceiling of a room or building. The interior looks something like the underside of a stone staircase.

Cord-marking [Cord-impressed] A decorative technique in Jomon Japan and elsewhere, in which cord or string is wrapped around a paddle and pressed against an unfired clay vessel, leaving the twisted mark of the cord.

Core A term used in lithic studies to describe the stone from which other pieces or flakes are removed. Core tools are shaped by the removal of flakes.

Cultigen A cultivated plant.

Cultivation The human manipulation or fostering of a plant species (often wild) to enhance or ensure production, involving such techniques as clearing fields, preparing soil, weeding, protecting plants from animals, and providing water to produce a crop.

Cultural resource management The survey and/or excavation of archaeological and historical remains threatened by construction and development. Also called CRM or rescue archaeology.

Culture A uniquely human means of non-biological adaptation; a repertoire of learned behaviors for coping with the physical and social environment.

Cuneiform A writing system of ancient Mesopotamia involving a series of wedge-shaped marks to convey a message or text.

Cutmark A trace left on bone by a stone or metal tool used in butchering a carcass; one of the primary forms of evidence for meat eating by early hominids.

Cyclopean From Cyclops, the mythical giant, referring to the huge stone walls of Mycenaean tombs and fortresses.

Danzantes (Spanish) Dancers; life-size carvings of captives or prisoners of war depicted in bas-relief on stone slabs at San José Mogote and Monte Albán, Oaxaca.

Débitage (French) A term referring to all the pieces of shatter and flakes produced and not used when stone tools are made. Also called lithic waste or waste material.

Dendrochronology The study of the annual growth rings of trees as a dating technique to build chronologies.

Descent group All the individuals related to one another through a previous common ancestor; a lineage or clan. In some instances, this common ancestor may be a mythical being in the distant past.

Dolmen A generic term for a megalithic tomb or chamber with a roof. *See also* Gallery grave; Passage grave.

Domestication The taming of wild plants and animals by humans. Plants are farmed and become dependent on humans for propagation; animals are herded and their feeding often becomes dependent on their human caretakers.

Dryopithecine The generic term for the Miocene fossil ancestor of both the living apes and modern humans, found in Africa, Asia, and Europe.

E group An arrangement of buildings designed to mark the position of the rising sun during important solar events, such as equinoxes and solstices in Mesoamerica.

Edge hypothesis A revised version of the population pressure hypothesis about the origins of agriculture, suggesting that the need for more food was initially felt at the margins of the natural habitat of the ancestors of domesticated plants and animals. Sites like Ali Kosh, with early dates for agriculture and located in a marginal area, support this theory.

Effigy A representation or image of a person or animal.

Egalitarian A term that refers to societies lacking clearly defined status differences between individuals, except for those due to sex, age, or skill.

El Niño (Spanish) A warm water countercurrent that periodically appears off the Peruvian coast, usually soon after Christmas, and alters the normal patterns of water temperature, flow, and salinity. These changes diminish the availability of nutrients to marine life, causing large schools of fish and flocks of sea birds to either migrate or die.

Endocast A copy or cast of the inside of a skull, reflecting the general shape and arrangement of the brain and its various parts.

Epigraphy The study of inscriptions.

Epiphysis (plural **epiphyses**) The end of a long bone in humans and other mammals, which hardens and attaches to the shaft of the bone with age.

Epoch A subdivision of geological time, millions of years long, representing units of eras.

Equinox A time when the sun crosses the plane of the equator, making night and day the same length all over Earth, occurring about March 21 and September 22.

Era A major division of geological time, tens or hundreds of millions of years long, usually distinguished by significant changes in the plant and animal kingdoms. Also used to denote later archaeological periods, such as the prehistoric era.

Estrus The cycle of female sexual receptivity in many species of animals. The female is sexually receptive only a few days a month or year, rather than continually. Estrus is absent in the human female.

Ethnocentrism Evaluating other groups or societies by standards that are relevant to the observer's culture.

Ethnography The study of contemporary cultures through first-hand observation.

Ethnohistory The study of ancient (often non-Western) cultures using evidence from documentary sources and oral traditions, and often supplemented with archaeological data. Traditionally, ethnohistorians have been concerned with the early history of the New World, the time of contact, and later settlement and colonization by Europeans.

Evolution The process of change over time due to shifting conditions of the physical and cultural environment, involving mechanisms of mutation and natural selection. Human biology and culture evolved during the Pliocene, Pleistocene, and Holocene.

Facade The face, or front, of a building.

Flake A type of stone artifact produced by removing a piece from a core through chipping. Flakes are made into a variety of different kinds of tools or used for their sharp edges (without further retouch).

Flint A fine-grained, crystalline stone that fractures in a regular pattern, producing sharp-edged flakes; highly prized and extensively used for making flaked stone tools.

Flintknapping The process of making chipped stone artifacts; the striking of stone with a hard or soft hammer.

Floodwater farming A method of farming that recovers floodwater and diverts it to selected fields to supplement the water supply.

Flotation A technique for the recovery of plant remains from archaeological sites. Sediments or pit contents are poured into water or heavy liquid; the lighter, carbonized plant remains float to the top for recovery, while the heavier sediments and other materials fall to the bottom.

Fluted point The characteristic artifact of the Paleoindian period in North America. Several varieties of fluted points were used for hunting large game. The flute refers to a large channel flake removed from both sides of the base of the point to facilitate hafting.

Folsom An archaeological culture during the Paleoindian period in North America, defined by a distinctive type of fluted point and found primarily in the Great Plains.

Fossil The mineralized bone of an extinct animal. Most bones associated with humans in the Pliocene, Pleistocene, and Holocene are too young to have been mineralized, but the term *fossil skull* or *fossil bone* is often used generically in these cases as well.

Frieze A decorative band or feature, commonly ornamented with sculpture, usually near the top of a wall.

Galena A common, heavy mineral that is the principal ore of lead.

Gallery grave A megalithic tomb lacking an entrance passage; the burial room or rooms form the entire internal structure; found in Neolithic western Europe. *See also* Dolmen; Passage grave.

Glacial A cold episode of the Pleistocene, in contrast to a warmer interglacial period. Also referred to as an ice age. The classic European sequence of the Günz, Mindel, Riss, and Würm glacials has recently been revised, with the recognition of a large number of cold/warm oscillations in the Pleistocene. *See also* Interglacial.

Glyph (Greek) A carving; a drawn symbol in a writing system. A glyph may stand for a syllable, a sound, an idea, a word, or a combination of these.

Glume The tough seed cover of many cereal kernels. In the process of the domestication of wheat, the tough glume becomes more brittle, making winnowing easier.

Gorget A circular ornament, flat or convex on one side and concave on the other; usually worn over the chest.

Grave goods The items that are placed in graves to accompany the deceased.

Guano Bird excrement.

Half-life A measure of the rate of decay in radioactive materials; essentially, half the radioactive material will disappear within the period of one half-life.

Hammerstone A stone used to knock flakes from nodules and cores; part of the tool kit of a flintknapper.

Handaxe The characteristic artifact of the Lower Paleolithic: a large, teardrop-shaped stone tool bifacially flaked to a point at one end and a broader base at the other, for general-purpose use that continued into the Middle Paleolithic.

Hard hammer technique A percussion technique for making stone tools, by striking one stone, or core, with another stone, or hammer. *See also* Soft hammer technique.

Hematite A common heavy mineral that is the principal ore of iron.

Hemp A tall annual plant whose tough fibers are used to make coarse fabrics and ropes.

Henge A monument defined by the presence of an enclosure, usually made by a circular ditch and bank system, up to 500 m in diameter. Henges were erected during the Neolithic and early Bronze Age in western Europe.

Hierarchical A term referring to societies that have a graded order of ranks, statuses, or decision makers.

Hieroglyph Originally, the pictographic script of ancient Egypt; any depictive, art-related system of writing, such as that of Mesoamerica. Also refers to an individual symbol.

Hohokam One of three major cultural traditions of the American Southwest during late prehistoric times. The Hohokam were centered in the deserts of southern Arizona.

Holocene The most recent geological epoch, which began 10,000 years ago with the close of the Pleistocene and continues today. Some describe this epoch only as a warmer episode between glacial periods.

Also called Recent, Postglacial, and Present Interglacial.

Hominid The term used to describe only the human members of the primates, both fossil and modern forms.

Hominoidea The taxonomic term used to describe the human and ape members of the primates, both fossil and modern forms.

Hopewell Interaction Sphere A complex trade network involving goods and information that connected distinct local populations in the midwestern United States from approximately 200 B.C. to 400 A.D.

Huaca An Andean term for pyramid.

Hunter-gatherer A hunter of large wild animals and gatherer of wild plants, seafood, and small animals, as opposed to farmers and food producers. Hunting-gathering characterized the human subsistence pattern prior to the domestication of plants and animals and the spread of agriculture. Also called food collectors, foragers.

Hyoid bone A delicate bone in the neck that anchors the tongue muscles in the throat.

Iconography The study of artisitic representations or icons that usually have religious or ceremonial significance.

Ideograph A written symbol that represents an abstract idea rather than the sound of a word or the pictorial symbol of an object (pictograph).

In situ (Latin) A term describing archaeological remains found in the same location where they were abandoned or dropped. *In situ* finds have presumably not been later moved by human or natural forces. Also called primary position. *See also* Secondary position.

Incensario (Spanish) An incense burner made of pottery and sometimes stone, used in Mesoamerican religious and political ceremonies.

Inflorescence The flowering part of a plant.

Interglacial A warm period of the Pleistocene, in contrast to a colder period called a glacial.

Isotope One of several different atomic states of an element; for example, carbon occurs as ^{12}C, ^{13}C, and ^{14}C, also known as carbon-14 or radiocarbon.

Isotopic technique A technique for absolute dating that relies on known rates of decay in radioactive isotopes, especially carbon, potassium, and uranium.

Jasper A high-quality flint, often highly colored, often used as a raw material for the manufacture of stone tools, beads, and other ornaments.

Jet A compact, black coal that can be highly polished; used to make beads, jewelry, etc.

Jomon The archaeological culture of late Pleistocene and early Holocene Japan. Primarily associated with groups of hunter-gatherers, but recent evidence suggests that these groups were practicing some rice cultivation.

Kiln A furnace or oven for baking or drying objects, especially for firing pottery.

Kiva A semisubterranean ceremonial room found at sites throughout the American Southwest.

Krater A large metal vessel for mixing and storing wine, traded over a large part of Europe during the Iron Age.

Lactational amenorrhea The suppression of ovulation and menstruation during breast feeding.

Laguna (Spanish) Lagoon; a manmade depression in Mesoamerica that may have begun as a borrow pit for the construction of an earthen mound. They were often lined with waterproof bentonite blocks and may have been used for ritual bathing.

Lapis lazuli A semiprecious stone of deep blue color, used and traded widely in antiquity in the form of beads, pendants, and inlay.

Levallois A technique for manufacturing large, thin flakes or points from a carefully prepared core, first used during the Lower Paleolithic and remaining common during the Middle Paleolithic. The method wasted flint and was generally not used in areas of scarce raw materials.

Lintel A horizontal beam of wood or stone that supports the wall above a doorway or window.

Lithic Pertaining to stone, or rock. Paleolithic means old stone; Neolithic means new stone; microlithic means small stone; megalithic means giant stone.

Living floor The actual surface of occupation at a prehistoric site, sometimes preserved under unusual conditions of deposition.

Llama A woolly South American ruminant camelid, used as a beast of burden.

Locomotion A method of movement, such as bipedalism.

Loess Wind-blown silt deposited in deep layers in certain parts of the northern hemisphere.

Lomas (Spanish) Vegetation that is supported by fog in otherwise arid environments.

Long Count The Classic Maya system of dating that records the total number of days elapsed from an initial date in the distant past (3114 B.C.). The system is based on multiples of 20, beginning with the *kin* (1 day), *uinal* (20 kins or 20 days), *tun* (18 uinals or 360 days), *katun* (20 tuns or 7200 days), and *baktun* (20 katuns or 144,000 days).

Longhouse A wooden structure that is considerably longer than it is wide; served as a communal dwelling, especially among Native North Americans in the Northeast and on the Northwest Coast.

Lost wax casting A technique for casting metal in which a sand or clay casing is formed around a wax sculpture. Molten metal is poured into the casing, melting the wax. The cooling metal takes on the shape of the "lost" wax sculpture preserved on the casing.

Maguey Any of several species of cactus, an important source of fiber and needles, which were used to make rope and clothing in Mesoamerica. The heart of the plant can be roasted and the sap used to make mescal and tequila.

Mano The hand-held part of a stone-milling assembly for grinding maize or other foods.

Manuport A natural stone carried into an archaeological site and used without significant modification as a seat, anvil, pillow, and the like; recognized as exotic to the specific location where found.

Marketing An exchange system that frequently involves currencies and generally extends beyond close kinsmen and a small group of trading partners. Market participants try to minimize their costs and maximize their returns to make a profit.

Megalith (Greek) A large stone monument.

Menhir A large, standing stone, erected either singly or collectively in a linear arrangement.

Mesoamerica The region consisting of central and southern Mexico, Guatemala, Belize, El Salvador, and the western parts of Honduras and Nicaragua that was the focus of complex, hierarchical states at the time of Spanish contact. The people of this area shared a basic set of cultural conventions. Also called Middle America.

Mesolithic The period of time of hunter-gatherers in Europe, North Africa, and parts of Asia between the end of the Pleistocene and the introduction of farming; the Middle Stone Age.

Mesquite A tree or shrub of the southwestern United States and Mexico whose beanlike pods are rich in sugar.

Metallurgy The art of separating metals from their ores.

Metate The stone basin, often trough-shaped, or lower part of a stone-milling assembly for grinding maize or other foods.

Microband A small family group of hunter-gatherers.

Midden An accumulated pile of refuse near a dwelling or in other areas of a site.

Milankovitch forcing A term describing the phenomenon considered to be the prime reason for glacial fluctuations and climatic change. Changing factors are the distance between the Earth and the sun and the tilt of the Earth's axis, which play major roles in the amount of sunlight reaching the Earth, atmospheric temperature, and the expansion and retreat of continental glaciation. The cyclical nature of variation in these factors was recognized by a Yugoslav mathematician named Milutin Milankovitch.

Millennium (plural **millennia**) A period of 1000 years. The millennia before Christ run in reverse; the first millennium goes from 0 to 1000 B.C., the second from 1000 to 2000 B.C., and so on.

Mississippian The collective name applied to the societies that inhabited portions of the eastern United States from approximately A.D. 700 to 1600. Mississippian peoples practiced an agricultural way of life, constructed earthen platform mounds, and shared certain basic cultural conventions.

Mit'a system A means of tribute in prehispanic Andean South America that involved the use of conscripted laborers to complete discrete organizational tasks.

Mitochondrial DNA Genetic material in the mitochondria of human cells that mutates at a relatively constant rate. Because mitochondrial DNA is inherited only from the mother, it provides an unaltered link to past generations. The number of mutations separating two individuals should be a function of how far back in time they share a common maternal ancestor.

Mitmaq A system of colonization used by the Inca to minimize provincial rebellion by moving people around to break up dissident groups.

Mogollon One of three major cultural traditions of the American Southwest during late prehistoric times. The Mogollon were centered in the mountainous areas of southeastern Arizona and southwestern New Mexico.

Moiety A division of society into two distinct social categories or groups, often on the basis of kinship or descent.

Montaña (Spanish) The word for mountain, specifically refers to the wet, tropical slopes of the Amazonian Andes.

Mousterian A term describing the stone tool assemblages of the Neanderthals during the Middle Paleolithic. Named after the type site of Le Moustier in France. *See also* Acheulean.

Multidisciplinary Referring to a project or study that incorporates scientists from a number of disciplines into the research team, including archaeozoologists, geoarchaeologists, paleoethnobotanists, palynologists, physical anthropologists, and the like. Classic examples of such projects include the Koobi Fora project, the investigations of Star Carr, and the Braidwood project on early agriculture in the natural habitat of the Near East.

Multivallate A term describing complex defenses of multiple ditches and ramparts at large Iron Age hill forts.

Mural art One of the two major categories of Paleolithic art, along with portable art. Mural art consists of painting, engraving, and sculpting on the walls of the caves, shelters, and cliffs of southwestern Europe; one of the hallmarks of the Upper Paleolithic.

Natural habitat hypothesis A theory about the origins of agriculture associated with Robert Braidwood, suggesting that the earliest domesticates appeared in the area their wild ancestors inhabited.

Necropolis (Greek) Cemetery.

Neolithic New Stone Age; describes early farmers with domesticated plants and animals, ground stone tools, permanent villages, and often pottery.

Net-sinkers A small weight attached to fishing nets.

Nome A geographical province incorporated within the ancient Egyptian state.

Oasis hypothesis A theory about the origins of agriculture associated with V. Gordon Childe and others, suggesting that domestication began as a symbiotic relationship between humans, plants, and animals at oases during the desiccation of the Near East at the end of the Pleistocene.

Obsidian Translucent, grey to black or green, glasslike rock from molten sand; produces extremely sharp edges when fractured and was highly valued for making stone tools.

Oldowan A term used to describe the earliest kinds of stone tools from the end of the Pliocene and the early Pleistocene, discovered at Olduvai Gorge. Oldowan assemblages contain various types of unifacial and bifacial pebble tools and flakes.

Olmec The Aztec name for the late prehispanic inhabitants of the Gulf Coast region of Mexico. This term has been extended by archaeologists to describe the sites, monuments, and art found in the same region during the Formative period. Aspects of this art style and related motifs have a wider distribution across Mesoamerica during the Early and Middle Formative periods (1150 to 700 B.C.). This broader distribution is called the Olmec Horizon.

Oppida (Latin) Massive fortifications in western Europe, often on hilltops or bluffs built for defensive purposes during the Iron Age; described in some detail and often conquered by the Romans.

Optical emission spectroscopy A technique used in the analysis of the elemental composition of artifacts. Material is heated to a high temperature, causing its electrons to release light of a particular wavelength, depending on what elements are present. Because of different characteristic wavelengths for different elements, it is possible to determine what elements are present in the tested material.

Oracle bone An animal bone with cracks (due to heating) or other markings, used to foretell the future.

Osteodontokeratic A controversial term used by Raymond Dart to describe the kinds of materials in their natural state that may have been used as tools by early hominids, such as bone, tooth, and horn.

Paleoanthropology The branch of anthropology that combines archaeology and physical anthropology to study the biological and behavioral remains of the early hominids.

Paleoethnobotany The study of plant remains from archaeological sites.

Paleoindian The period of large game hunters in North America at the end of the Pleistocene. Remains are characterized by the presence of fluted points and frequently the bones of extinct animals.

Palisade A fence of posts or stakes erected around a settlement for defensive purposes.

Palynology The study of pollen for the reconstruction of past climate and environment; also called pollen analysis.

Papyrus An ancient type of paper made from the papyrus plant, used by the ancient Egyptians for writing.

Passage grave A megalithic tomb entered via a long, low, narrow passage that opens into a wider room, generally near the center of the structure. *See also* Dolmen; Gallery grave.

Pastoralism The shepherding of animals as a subsistence strategy. Generally associated with a mobile lifeway.

Patrilocal A residence pattern in which married couples live with or near the husband's family.

Pectoral An ornament worn across the chest, especially for defensive purposes.

Percussion flaking The technique for producing stone artifacts through striking or knapping crystalline stone with a hard or soft hammer, as opposed to pressure flaking.

Petroglyph A drawing that has been carved into rock.

Petty state A small, socially stratified political unit prevalent in Mesoamerica at the time of the Spanish conquest. Similar political formations have been found in other regions as well.

Phonetic Pertaining to the sounds of speech.

Photomicrograph A photograph of a microscopic object, taken through a microscope.

Pictograph A written or painted symbol that more or less portrays the represented object. *See also* Ideograph.

Pithos (plural *pithoi*) A large clay storage jar.

Pithouse A prehistoric semisubterranean dwelling in which the lower parts of the walls are the earthen sides of a shallow pit. The top part of the walls often consisted of a framework of poles intertwined with small twigs, covered with mud.

Pleistocene The geological epoch from 2 m.y.a. to 10,000 B.P., characterized by oscillations in climate between warm and cold, the expansion of continental ice sheets, significant changes in sea level, and much of the evolution of the human species.

Pliocene The geological epoch from 6 to 2 m.y.a., which witnessed the appearance of the first hominids.

Plio/Pleistocene A combination term used to describe the time between the appearance of the earliest hominids during the Pliocene and the beginning of Pleistocene.

Pochteca A privileged, hereditary class of long-distance Aztec traders.

Pollen diagram A graph showing the percentages of different species of pollen in a stratigraphic sequence; summarizes both the species and the proportions of the various groups of plants found in each sample.

Polychrome Multicolored; describing pottery that has been decorated with three or more colors.

Population pressure hypothesis A theory about the origins of agriculture espoused by Lewis Binford in terms of an equilibrium between people and food, a balance that could be upset either by a decline in available food or an increase in the number of people; because climatic and environmental changes appeared to be minimal in the Near East, population increase upset the balance, forcing people to turn to agriculture as a way to produce more food.

Portable art One of the two major categories of Paleolithic art, along with mural art. Portable art includes all decorated materials that can be moved or carried; found throughout Europe and much of the Old World.

Postglacial The most recent geological epoch, which began 10,000 years ago with the close of the Pleistocene and continues today. Some describe this epoch only as a warmer episode between glacial periods. Also called Holocene, Present Interglacial, and Recent.

Post mold The circular remains, often just a dark stain in the soil, of a wooden post that formed part of the frame of prehistoric structures. Also called a post hole.

Potlatch A large feast among Northwest Coast Indians that included the display and dispersal of accumulated wealth to the assembled guests.

Potsherd A fragment of a clay vessel.

Prehistory In general, the human past; specifically, the time before the appearance of written records.

Provenience The established position of an artifact. In the context of a specific site, the horizontal and vertical locations of an object in relation to an established coordinate system. When the position of a specific object is known to archaeologists, it is considered well-provenienced.

Primate The order of animals that includes lemurs, tarsiers, monkeys, apes, and humans, characterized by grasping hands, flexible limbs, and a highly developed sense of vision.

Pueblo A stone-masonry complex of adjoining rooms found in the American Southwest.

Puna (Spanish) High grassland plateaus in the Peruvian Andes.

Quern A stone grinding surface for preparing grains and other plant foods and for grinding other materials.

Quetzal A bird native to the humid mountain forests of Mesoamerica, prized for its brilliant feathers.

Quipu The Inca term for a numerical device consisting of a horizontal string from which a series of smaller cords hung. The Inca used the *quipu* to record numbers by tying knots at various intervals along the strings.

Rachis The stem that holds seeds to the stalk in wheat and other plants; changes from brittle to tough when wheat is domesticated.

Radiocarbon dating An absolute dating technique based on the principle of decay of the radioactive isotope of carbon, carbon-14. Also called carbon dating.

Radiopotassium dating An absolute dating technique based on the principle of decay of the radioactive isotope of potassium, ^{40}K. Can be used for materials ranging in age from 500,000 years ago to the age of the oldest rocks in the universe. Also called potassium-argon dating.

Recent The most recent geological epoch, which began 10,000 years ago with the close of the Pleistocene and continues today. Some describe this epoch only as a warmer episode between glacial periods. Also called Holocene, Postglacial, and Present Interglacial.

Reciprocity The exchange of goods between known participants, involving simple barter and face-to-face exchanges.

Red ochre An iron mineral that occurs in nature, used by prehistoric peoples in powdered form as a pigment for tanning animal skins; often found in burials from the late Paleolithic and Mesolithic.

Redistribution The accumulation and dispersal of goods through a centralized agency, individual, or institution.

Reducing atmosphere The oxygen-deficient atmosphere that is achieved in kilns for baking pottery or smelting ores.

Reduction technique In archaeology, a manufacturing process involving the removal of materials from a core that becomes the finished product; includes techniques like flintknapping or wood carving; as opposed to additive technique. Also called subtractive technique.

Refitting A technique for putting back together the scattered pieces of stone, pottery, or bone at an archaeological site to study patterns of manufacturing and disposal.

Relative dating A technique used to *estimate* the antiquity of archaeological materials, generally based on association with materials of known age or simply to say that one item is younger or older than another. *See also* Absolute dating.

Repoussé The process of forming a raised design on a thin sheet of metal by placing it over a mold and hammering it in place.

Retouch The shaping or sharpening of lithic artifacts through percussion or pressure flaking; a technique of flint-knapping.

Rhizome An edible, rootlike subterranean plant stem.

Sacbe The Maya term for a raised causeway constructed of stone blocks and paved with gravel and plaster.

Sarcophagus A stone coffin, usually decorated with sculpture or inscriptions.

Scapulimancy The ancient practice of seeking knowledge by reading cracks on bones. Symbols were written on an animal's scapula (shoulder blade); the bone was heated until a series of cracks formed, then diviners interpreted the pattern of cracking to foretell the future.

Scheduling The process of arranging the extraction of resources based on their availability and the demands of competing subsistence activities.

Seasonality A term that refers to the changing availability of resources according to the different seasons of the year.

Secondary position A term describing archaeological remains that have been moved by natural or human activity from their original location of deposition, as opposed to *in situ*, or primary position. *See also In situ.*

Sedentism The transition from a mobile way of life to living in more permanent contexts, such as villages.

Setaria A wild grass with edible seeds.

Sexual division of labor The cooperative relationship between the sexes in hunter-gatherer groups.

Shaduf An Egyptian bucket-and-lever lifting device that allows water to be raised a few feet from a well or ditch into fields and gardens.

Shaft grave A vertical tunnel cut into rock in which the tombs of Mycenaean elite were placed.

Shaman An anthropological term for a spiritualist, curer, or seer.

Shell midden A mound of shells accumulated from human collection, consumption, and disposal. Shell middens are the dumps of shells from oysters, clams, mussels or other species that are found along coasts and rivers, usually dating to the Holocene.

Shicra The Inca word for meshed bags containing rocks, used as fill in the reconstruction of ancient Andean structures.

Sickle A tool for cutting the stalks of cereals, especially wheat. Prehistoric sickles were usually stone blades set in a wood or antler handle.

Sickle polish A clear polish that forms along the edges of flakes and blades used as sickles to cut reeds, grass, wheat, and other long-stemmed plants.

Slash and burn A type of farming in which the ground is cleared by cutting and burning the vegetation on the spot. The burned vegetation serves as a natural fertilizer. The field is farmed until yields decrease; then it is allowed to lie fallow. Also called swidden farming.

Slate A fine-grained rock, with a dull, dark bluish-gray color, that tends to split along parallel cleavage planes, often producing thin plates or sheets.

Social hypothesis A theory about the origins of agriculture suggesting that domestication was the solution to a social problem, allowing certain individuals to accumulate food surplus and to transform those foods into more valued items, such as rare stones, metals, or alliances.

Sodality An organizational unit of human society that cross-cuts generational relationships. Generally organized by age and sex for special purpose groups, such as a dance society or fraternity. *See also* Descent group.

Soft hammer technique A flintknapping technique that involves the use of a hammer of bone, antler, or wood, rather than stone. *See also* Hard hammer technique.

Solifluction A phenomenon in which freezing and thawing of the ground results in slippage of the surface.

Solstice The time of year when the sun is at its greatest distance from the equator, occurring about June 21 and December 22.

Sondage (French) A test excavation or test pit made at an archaeological site to determine the content and/or distribution of prehistoric materials.

Southern Cult A network of interaction, exchange, and shared information present over much of the southeastern (and parts of the midwestern) United States from around A.D. 1200 until the early 1500s. Also called Southeastern Ceremonial Complex.

Spindle whorl A cam or balance wheel on a shaft or spindle for spinning yarn or thread from wool, cotton, or other material; usually made of clay.

Split inheritance An Andean practice by which the successor to the throne inher-

ited only the office of the dead ruler, while his junior kinsmen received the lands, palace, and personal wealth of the dead ruler.

State A form of government with an internally specialized and hierarchically organized decision-making apparatus. States generally have three or more administrative levels. Societies that have state institutions are referred to as state societies or state-level societies.

Status differentiation Inequality in human society in which certain individuals or groups have access to more resources, power, and roles than others. Differentiation occurs through ranking of descent groups or the creation of classes of people. *See also* Egalitarian.

Steatite Soapstone, a variety of talc with a soapy or greasy feel, often used to make containers or carved ornaments.

Stela (plural **stelae**) (Latin) An erect stone monument that is often carved.

Stone boiling The process of heating stones in a fire and then adding them to containers to boil water or cook other foods.

Stratigraphic section The excavation of trenches and squares across manmade features to expose a cross section of the deposits and reveal the sequence and methods of construction.

Stucco A type of plaster, often made of lime, used for decoration.

Talud-tablero (Spanish) An architectural style characteristic of Teotihuacan during the Classic period, in which recessed rectangular panels (the *tablero*) are separated by sloping aprons (the *talud*).

Tampu A roadside lodging and storage place situated along the Inca road system, roughly one day's walk apart.

Tell A mound composed of mud-bricks and refuse, accumulated as a result of human activity. The mound of Jericho built up at a rate of roughly 26 cm per 100 years, almost a foot a century.

Temper A nonplastic material (such as sand, shell, or fiber) that is added to clay to improve its workability and to reduce breakage during drying and firing.

Temporal marker A morphological type, such as a design motif on pottery or a particular type of stone tool, that has been shown to have a discrete and definable temporal range.

Teosinte (Aztec *Teocentli*) A tall annual grass, native to Mexico and Central America, that is the closest relative of maize.

Terracotta A hard, brownish-orange earthenware of fine quality that is often used for architectural decorations, figurines, etc.

Tholos tomb A large, behive-shaped tomb, constructed using the corbel arch technique, dating to the Mycenaean civilization of Greece.

Tlachtli The Aztec word for their ritual ballgame.

Totem pole A pole or post that has been carved and painted with totems or figures, such as animals, that serve as the emblems of clans or families. Native Americans of the Pacific Northwest often erected these poles in front of their houses.

Transhumance A pattern of seasonal movement usually associated with pastoralists who take their herds to mountains in the summer and valleys in winter; more generally, a regular pattern of seasonal movement by human groups.

Trilithon A massive stone lintel occurring in prehistoric structures, such as Stonehenge and the *tholos* tombs in Greece.

Tuber A fleshy, usually oblong or rounded outgrowth (such as the potato) of a subterranean stem or root of a plant.

Tuff A deposit of volcanic ash that can be used for a variety of purposes. Some tuff deposits harden and become a type of soft rock.

Tumpline A strap that is passed over the forehead or the chest to facilitate the transportation of a heavy load carried on the back.

Tzompantli Aztec term for skull rack. The Aztec often placed the skulls of sacrificial victims on a wooden pole or frame; in some cases, large blocks of stone were sculpted to look like skull racks.

Unifacial A term describing flaked stone tools in which only one face or side is retouched to make a sharp edge. *See also* Bifacial.

Village A permanent, sedentary community of less than 1000 people. Although villages existed in the later Paleolithic and Mesolithic, they were more common during and after the Neolithic.

Wadi (Arabic) A dry streambed.

Waranqa A subdivision of the Inca empire that was used for administrative purposes, consisting of 1000 taxpayers.

Wattle and daub A building technique that uses a framework of poles, interspersed with smaller poles and twigs. The wooden frame is then plastered with mud or a mud mixture.

Were-jaguar A representation of a deity that is half jaguar and half human. The were-jaguar was a common symbol in Preclassic Mesoamerica.

Wet-site excavation The technique of excavating waterlogged sites by pumping water through garden hoses to spray the dirt away and expose archaeological features and artifacts.

Wheel-thrown pottery Pottery that is made using the potter's wheel.

Woodhenge A circular feature demarcated by large upright timbers, probably used by prehistoric groups as astronomical observatories.

Ziggurat A large pyramid in Mesopotamia consisting of many stepped levels.

Zoomorphic Having animal form or attributes.

REFERENCES

Aaris-Sørensen, K., and E. Brinch Petersen. 1986. The Prejlerup aurochs — an archaeozoological discovery from Boreal, Denmark. *Striae* 24:111–117.

Adams, D. 1980. *The hitchhiker's guide to the galaxy.* New York: Harmony.

Adams, R. E. W., W. E. Brown, and T. P. Culbert. 1981. Radar mapping, archeology and ancient Maya land use. *Science* 213:1457–1463.

Adams, R. Mc. 1981. *Heartland of cities.* Chicago: University of Chicago Press.

Aikens, C. M., and T. Higuchi. 1982. *The prehistory of Japan.* New York: Academic Press.

Aikens, R. J. C. 1956. *Stonehenge.* Baltimore: Pelican.

Aitken, M. J. 1985. *Thermoluminescence dating.* New York: Academic Press.

Akazawa, T. 1980. Fishing adaptation of prehistoric hunter-gatherers at the Nittano site, Japan. *Journal of Archaeological Science* 7:325–344.

Allchin, B., and R. Allchin. 1982. *The rise of civilization in India and Pakistan.* Cambridge: Cambridge University Press.

Ames, K. M. 1981. The evolution of social ranking on the Northwest Coast of North America. *American Antiquity* 46:789–805.

Ammerman, A. J., and L. L. Cavalli-Sforza. 1984. *The Neolithic transition and the genetics of populations in Europe.* Princeton: Princeton University Press.

Anawalt, P. R. 1982. Understanding Aztec human sacrifice. *Archaeology* 35(3): 38–45.

Anderson, A. 1987. Recent developments in Japanese prehistory: A review. *American Antiquity* 61:270–281.

Arens, W. 1979. *The man-eating myth: Anthropology and anthropophagy.* New York: Oxford University Press.

Audouze, F. 1987. The Paris basin in Magdalenian times. In *The Pleistocene Old World: Regional perspectives,* ed. O. Soffer. New York: Plenum Press.

Aveni, A. F. 1986. The Nazca lines: Patterns in the desert. *Archaeology* 39(4): 32–39.

Banning, E. B., and B. F. Byrd. 1987. Houses and changing residential units: Domestic architecture at PPNB 'Ain Ghazal, Jordan. *Proceedings of the Prehistoric Society* 53:8–65.

Bar Yosef, O. 1986. The walls of Jericho: An alternative explanation. *Current Anthropology* 27:157–162.

Bar-Yosef, O. and A. Belfer Cohen. 1992. Foraging to farming in the Mediterranean Levant. In *Transitions to agriculture in prehistory,* ed. A. B. Gebauer and T. D. Price. Madison, WI: Prehistory Press.

Barber, R. L. N. 1988. *The cyclades in the Bronze Age.* Iowa City: University of Iowa Press.

Bareis, C. J., and J. W. Porter, eds. 1984. *American Bottom archaeology.* Urbana: University of Illinois Press.

Barker, G. 1985. *Prehistoric farming in Europe.* Cambridge: Cambridge University Press.

Bayard, D. 1971. *Non Nok Tha: The 1968 excavation procedure, stratigraphy, and a summary of evidence.* University of Otago: Studies in Prehistoric Anthropology, Vol. 4. Dunedin, NZ.

Bayard, D. 1980. East Asia in the Bronze Age. In *The Cambridge encyclopedia of archaeology,* ed. A. Sherratt. New York: Crown.

Beadle, G. 1980. The ancestry of corn. *Scientific American* 242:112–119.

Becker, M. J. 1979. Priests, peasants, and ceremonial centers: The intellectual history of a model. In *Maya archaeology and ethnohistory,* ed. N. Hammond and G. R. Willey. Austin: University of Texas Press.

Bellwood, P. 1978. *Man's conquest of the Pacific.* Oxford: Oxford University Press.

Bellwood, P. 1990. Foraging towards farming: A decisive transition or a millennial blur? *Review of Archaeology* 11:14–24.

Bender, B. 1978. Gatherer-hunter to farmer: A social perspective. *World Archaeology* 10:204–222.

Bennett, W. C. 1934. Excavations at Tiahuanaco. *Anthropological Papers of the American Museum of Natural History* 34(3):359–494.

Bennett, W. C. 1947. The archaeology of the central Andes. In *Handbook of South American Indians: Vol. 2, The Andean civilizations,* ed. J. Steward. Washington, DC: Smithsonian Institution, Bureau of American Ethnology, Bulletin 143.

Benson, E. P., ed. 1968. *Dumbarton Oaks conference on the Olmec.* Washington, DC: Dumbarton Oaks.

Benson, E. P., ed. 1971. *Dumbarton Oaks conference on Chavín.* Washington, DC: Dumbarton Oaks.

Benson, E. P., ed. 1981. *The Olmec and their neighbors: Essays in memory of Matthew W. Stirling.* Washington, DC: Dumbarton Oaks.

Berger, R., R. Chohfi, A. V. Zegarra, W. Yepez, and O. F. Carrasco. 1988. Radiocarbon dating Machu Picchu, Peru. *Antiquity* 62:707–710.

Bernal, I. 1965. Archaeological synthesis of Oaxaca. In *Handbook of Middle American Indians, Vol. 3: Archaeology of southern Mesoamerica,* ed. G. R. Willey. Austin: University of Texas Press.

Bernal, I. 1980. *A history of Mexican archaeology: The vanished civilizations of Middle America.* London: Thames & Hudson.

Bicchieri, M. G. 1972. *Hunters and gatherers today.* New York: Holt, Rinehart & Winston.

Bickerton, D. 1991. *Language and species.* Chicago: University of Chicago Press.

Binford, L. R. 1983. *In pursuit of the past.* New York: Thames & Hudson.

Binford, L. R., and S. R. Binford. 1966. A preliminary analysis of functional variability in the Mousterian of Levallois facies. In *Recent studies in paleoanthropology,* eds. J. D. Clark and F. C. Howell. *American Anthropologist,* special issue 68 (2,2):238–295.

Binford, L. R. 1984. *In pursuit of the past: Decoding the archaeological record.* New York: Thames & Hudson.

Binford, L. R., and C. K. Ho. 1985. Taphonomy at a distance: Zhoukoudien, the cave home of Beijing man. *Current Anthropology* 26:413–442.

Bingham, H. 1915. The story of Machu Pichhu: The Peruvian expeditions of the National Geographic Society and Yale University. *National Geographic* 27(2):172–216.

Bingham, H. 1948. *Lost city of the Incas.* New York: Duell, Sloan & Pearce.

Black, D. 1931. On an adolescent skull of *Sinanthropus pekinensis* in comparison with an adult skull of the same species and with other hominid skulls, recent and fossil. *Palaeontologica Sinica,* Series D, Vol. 7, Fasicule 2.

Blanton, R. E. 1978. *Monte Albán: Settlement patterns at the ancient Zapotec capital.* New York: Academic Press.

Blanton, R. E. 1983. The ecological perspective in highland Mesoamerican archaeology. In *Archaeological hammers and theories,* eds. J. A. Moore and A. S. Keene. New York: Academic Press.

Blumenschine, R. J. 1987. Characteristics of the early hominid scavenging niche. *Current Anthropology* 28:383–407.

Bogucki, P. 1988. *Forest farmers and stockherders.* Cambridge: Cambridge University Press.

Bordaz, J. 1971. *Tools of the Old and New Stone Age.* New York: American Museum of Natural History.

Bordes, F. 1968. *The Old Stone Age.* New York: McGraw-Hill.

Bordes, F. 1972. *A tale of two caves.* New York: Harper & Row.

Bordes, F., and D. de Sonneville-Bordes. 1970. The significance of variability in Paleolithic assemblages. *World Archaeology* 2:61–73.

Boserup, E. 1965. *The conditions of agricultural growth: The economics of agrarian change under population pressure.* Chicago: Aldine.

Bowen, D. Q. 1978. *Quaternary geology.* Oxford: Pergamon Press.

Bowen, D. Q. 1978. *Quaternary geology.* Oxford: Pergamon Press.

Braidwood, R. J. 1960. The agricultural revolution. *Scientific American* 203(3):130–148.

Braudel, F. 1970. History and the social sciences: The long term. *Social Science Information* 9:145–174.

Browman, D. L. 1981. New light on Andean Tiwanaku. *American Scientist* 69(4):408–419.

Brunhouse, R. L. 1973. *In search of the Maya.* New York: Ballantine Books.

Bryan, A. L. 1978. *Early man in America from a circum-Pacific perspective.* Edmonton: Archaeological Researches International.

Bryan, A. L. 1986. *New evidence for the Pleistocene peopling of the Americas.* Orono, ME: Center for the study of Early Man.

Burger, R. L. 1984. *The prehistoric occupation of Chavín de Huantar, Peru.* Berkeley: University of California Press.

Burger, R. L. 1985. Concluding remarks: Early Peruvian civilization and its relation to the Chavín horizon. In *Early ceremonial architecture in the Andes,* ed. C. B. Donnan. Washington, DC: Dumbarton Oaks.

Burl, A. 1976. *Stone circles of the British Isles.* New Haven: Yale University Press.

Butzer, K. W. 1980. Civilizations: Organisms or systems? *American Scientist* 68:148–160.

Butzer, K. 1982. *Archaeology as human ecology.* Cambridge: Cambridge University Press.

Calnek, E. E. 1976. The internal structure of Tenochtitlan. In *The Valley of Mexico: Studies in pre-Hispanic ecology and society,* ed. E. R. Wolf. Albuquerque: University of New Mexico Press.

Campbell, B. G. 1982. *Humankind emerging,* 3rd ed. Boston: Little, Brown.

Cann, R. L., M. Stoneking, and A. C. Wilson. 1987. Mitochondrial DNA and human evolution. *Nature* 325:31–36.

Carneiro, R. L. 1970. A theory of the origin of the state. *Science* 169:733–738.

Caso, A., and I. Bernal. 1965. Ceramics of Oaxaca. In *Handbook of Middle American Indians, Vol. 3: Archaeology of southern Mesoamerica,* ed. G. R. Willey. Austin: University of Texas Press.

Chakrabarti, D. 1980. Early agriculture and the development of towns in India. In *The Cambridge encyclopedia of archaeology,* ed. A. Sherratt. New York: Crown.

Chang, K. C. 1973. Food and food vessels in ancient China. *Transactions of the New York Academy of Sciences* 35(6):495–520.

Chang, K. C. 1977. Chinese archaeology since 1949. *Journal of Asian Studies* 36(4):623–646.

Chang, K. C. 1977a. The continuing quest for China's origins, I: Early farmers in China. *Antiquity* 30(2):116–123.

Chang, K. C. 1977b. The continuing quest for China's origins, II: The Shang civilization. *Antiquity* 30(3):187–193.

Chang, K. C. 1981. In search of China's beginnings: New light on an old civilization. *American Scientist* 69:148–160.

Chang, K. C. 1989. Ancient China and its anthropological significance. In *Archaeological thought in America,* ed. C. C. Lamberg-Karlovsky. Cambridge: Cambridge University Press.

Chesterton, G. K. 1933. *All I survey: A book of essays.* London: Methuen.

Childe, V. G. 1950. The urban revolution. *The Town Planning Review* 21:3–17.

Childe, V. G. 1956. *A short introduction to archaeology: Man and society.* London: F. Muller.

Childe, V. G. 1958. Retrospect. *Antiquity* 32:69–74.

Cieza de León, P. 1959. *The Incas,* trans. H. de Onis, ed. V. von Hagen. Norman: University of Oklahoma Press.

Clark, G. A., and J. M. Lindley. 1989. The case for continuity: Observations on the biocultural transition in Europe and western Asia. In *The human revolution: Behavioural and biological perspectives on the origins of modern humans,* eds. P. A. Mellars and C. B. Stringer. Edinburgh: Edinburgh University Press.

Clark, J. D. 1970a. *Kalambo Falls.* Cambridge: Cambridge University Press.

Clark, J. D. 1970b. *The prehistory of Africa.* London: Thames & Hudson.

Clark, J. D., and S. A. Brandt, eds. 1984. *From hunters to farmers.* Berkeley: University of California Press.

Clark, J. D., and J. W. K. Harris. 1985. Fire and its roles in early hominid lifeways. *African Archaeological Review* 3:3–28.

Clark, J. E. 1986. From mountains to molehills: A critical review of Teotihuacan's obsidian industry. In *Research in Economic Anthropology, Supplement 2,* ed. B. L. Isaac. Greenwich, CT: JAI Press.

Clark, J. G. D. 1954. *Excavations at Star Carr.* Cambridge: Cambridge University Press.

Clark, J. G. D. 1972. *Star Carr: A Case Study in Bioarchaeology.* Reading, MA: Addison-Wesley.

Coe, M. D. 1977. *Mexico,* 2nd ed. New York: Praeger.

Coe, M. D. 1984. *The Maya,* 3rd ed. London: Thames & Hudson.

Coe, M. D., and R. A. Diehl. 1980. *In the land of the Olmec: The archaeology of San Lorenzo Tenochtitlan.* Austin: University of Texas Press.

Coe, M., D. Snow, and E. Benson. 1986. *Atlas of ancient America.* New York: Facts on File.

Coe, W. R. 1965. Tikal: Ten years of study of a Maya ruin in the lowlands of Guatemala. *Expedition* 8:5–56.

Coe, W. R. 1967. *Tikal: A handbook of the ancient Maya ruins.* Philadelphia: University Museum.

Coe, W. R., and W. A. Haviland. 1982. Introduction to the archaeology of Tikal, Guatemala. *University Museum Monograph 46.* Philadelphia: University of Pennsylvania.

Coggins, C. 1979. A new order and the role of the calendar: Some characteristics of the Middle Classic period at Tikal. In *Maya archaeology and ethnohistory,* ed. N. Hammond. Austin: University of Texas Press.

Cohen, M. N. 1977. Population pressure and the origins of agriculture: An archaeological example from the coast of Peru. In *The origins of agriculture*, ed. C. Reed. The Hague: Mouton.

Cole, S. 1975. *Leakey's luck: The life of Louis Seymour Bazett Leakey, 1903–1972*. New York: Harcourt Brace Jovanovich.

Coles, J. M. 1982. The Bronze Age in northwestern Europe. *Advances in World Archaeology* 1:265–321.

Coles, J. M., and E. S. Higgs. 1969. *The archaeology of early man*. London: Faber & Faber.

Conkey, M. W. 1980. The identification of prehistoric hunter-gatherer aggregation sites: The case of Altamira. *Current Anthropology* 21:609–630.

Conkey, M. W. 1981. A century of Paleolithic cave art. *Archaeology* 34:20–28.

Conrad, G. W. 1981. Cultural materialism, split inheritance, and the expansion of ancient Peruvian empires. *American Antiquity* 46:3–26.

Coope, G. R. 1975. Climatic fluctuations in northwest Europe since the Last Interglacial, indicated by fossil assemblages of Coleoptera. In *Ice Ages: Ancient and modern*, ed. A. E. Wright and F. Moseley. Liverpool: Seel House Press.

Cordell, L. S. 1979. Prehistory: Eastern Anasazi. In *Handbook of North American Indians, Vol. 9: Southwest*, ed. A. Ortiz. Washington, DC: Smithsonian Institution Press.

Costantini, L. 1984. The beginning of agriculture in the Kachi Plain: The evidence of Mehrgarh. In *South Asian archaeology 1981*, ed. B. Allchin. New York: Cambridge University Press.

Cowan, C. W., and P. J. Watson. 1992. *Origins of agriculture in world perspective*. Washington, D.C.: Smithsonian Institution Press.

Cowgill, G. L. 1975. Population pressure as a non-explanation. In *Population studies in archaeology and biological anthropology*, ed. A. C. Swedlund. *American Antiquity, Memoir* 30:127–131.

Crawford, G. W., and H. Takamiya. 1990. The origins and implications of late prehistoric plant husbandry in northern Japan. *Antiquity* 64:889–911.

Crook, J. H. 1972. Sexual selection, dimorphism, and social organization in the primates. In *Sexual selection and the descent of man, 1871–1971*, ed. B. Campbell. Chicago: Aldine.

Culbert, T. P. 1988. Political history and the Maya glyphs. *Antiquity* 62(234): 135–152.

Culbert, T. P., and D. S. Rice, eds. 1990. *Precolumbian population history in the Maya lowlands*. Albuquerque: University of New Mexico Press.

Dahlin, B. H. 1984. The colossus in Guatemala: The Preclassic Maya city of El Mirador. *Archaeology* 37(5):18–25.

Dales, G. F. 1986. Some fresh approaches to old problems in Harappan archaeology. In *Studies in the archaeology of India and Pakistan*, ed. J. Jacobson. New Delhi: Oxford and IBH Publishing.

D'Altroy, T. N., and T. K. Earle. 1985. Staple finance, wealth finance, and storage in the Inka political economy. *Current Anthropology* 26(2):187–206.

Dart, R. 1925. *Australopithecus africanus:* The man-ape of South Africa. *Nature* 115:195–199.

Dart, R. 1953. The predatory transition from ape to man. *International Anthropological Linguistics Review* 1:201–218.

Dart, R. 1956. Cultural status of the South African man-apes. *Smithsonian Report* 4240:325–26.

Darwin, C. 1981. *The descent of man, and selection in relation to sex*. With an introduction by John Bonner and Robert M. May. Princeton, NJ: Princeton University Press.

Day, M. 1977. *Guide to fossil man*. London: Cassell.

Deacon, H. 1989. Late Pleistocene paleoecology and archaeology in the southern Cape, South Africa. In *The human revolution*, eds. P. A. Mellars and C. B. Stringer, pp. 547–564. Princeton: Princeton University Press.

Dearborn, D. S. P., and K. J. Schreiber. 1986. Here comes the sun: The Cuzco-Machu Picchu connection. *Archaeoastronomy* 9(1–4):15–37.

Dearborn, D. S. P., K. Schreiber, and R. E. White. 1987. Intimachay: A December solstice observatory at Machu Picchu, Peru. *American Antiquity* 52(2): 346–352.

de Borhegyi, S. F. 1980. The pre-Columbian ballgames: A pan-Mesoamerican tradition. *Contributions in Anthropology and History: 1.* Milwaukee: Milwaukee Public Museum.

de Lumley, H. 1969. A Paleolithic camp at Nice. *Scientific American* 220(5):42–50.

De Mortillet, G. 1872. Classification des ages de la pierre. *Comptes rendues congress International d'Anthropologie et d'Archéologie prehistorique, VI session*, pp. 432–444. Brussels.

Dennell, R. C. 1983. *European economic prehistory: A new approach*. London: Academic Press.

Dennell, R. C. 1983. *European economic prehistory: A new approach*. New York: Academic Press.

Deuel, L. 1977. *Memoirs of Heinrich Schliemann*. New York: Harper & Row.

Díaz del Castillo, B. 1956. *The discovery and conquest of Mexico*. New York: Farrar, Straus & Giroux.

Diehl, R. A. 1976. Pre-Hispanic relationships between the Basin of Mexico and north and west Mexico. In *The Valley of Mexico*, ed. E. R. Wolf. Albuquerque: University of New Mexico Press.

Diehl, R. A. 1981. Tula. In *Supplement to the handbook of Middle American Indians*, ed. J. A. Sabloff. Austin: University of Texas Press.

Diehl, R. A. 1983. *Tula: The Toltec capital of ancient Mexico*. London: Thames & Hudson.

Diehl, R. A., and R. A. Benfer. 1975. Tollan: The Toltec capital. *Archaeology* 28(2):112–124.

Diehl, R. A., and J. C. Berlo, ed. 1989. *Mesoamerica after the decline of Teotihuacan, A.D. 700–900*. Washington, DC: Dumbarton Oaks.

Dillehay, T. 1984. A late Ice-Age settlement in southern Chile. *Scientific American* 254(4):100–109.

Dillehay, T. 1987. By the banks of the Chinchihuapi. *Natural History* 4:8–12.

Dillehay, T. 1989. *Monte Verde, a late Pleistocene settlement in Chile*. Washington: Smithsonian Institution Press.

Dixon, J. E., J. R. Cann, and C. Renfrew. 1968. Obsidian and the origins of trade. *Scientific American* 211(3):44–53.

Donnan, C. B. 1976. *Moche art and iconography*. Los Angeles: UCLA Latin American Center Publications.

Donnan, C. B., ed. 1985. *Early ceremonial architecture in the Andes*. Washington, DC: Dumbarton Oaks.

Drennan, R. D., P. T. Fitzgibbons, and H. Dehn. 1987. The Tehuacán Valley and the Teotihuacan obsidian industry. Paper presented at the annual meeting of the Society for American Archaeology.

Drucker, P. 1955. *Indians of the Northwest Coast*. New York: McGraw-Hill.

Drucker, P., R. Heizer, and R. Squier. 1959. Excavations at La Venta, Tabasco. *Bureau of American Ethnology, Bulletin 170*. Washington, DC: Smithsonian Institution.

Dubois, E. 1894. *Pithecanthropus erectus, eine Menschenahnliche Ubergangsform aus Java*. Cologne: Batavia.

Duby, G. 1974. *The early growth of the European economy: Warriors and peasants* from the seventh to the twelfth century. Ithaca, NY: Cornell University Press.

Dye, D. 1989. Death march of Hernando de Soto. *Archaeology* 42(3):27–31.

Elvin, M. 1973. *The pattern of the Chinese past.* Stanford, CA: Stanford University Press.

Engel, F. A. 1976. *An ancient world preserved.* New York: Crown.

Fagan, B. M. 1989. *People of the earth: An introduction to world prehistory,* 6th ed. Glenview, IL: Scott, Foresman.

Fairservis, W. A. 1983. The script of the Indus Valley civilization. *Scientific American* 248(3):58–66.

Fairservis, W. A. 1986. A review of the archaeological evidence in connection with the identity of the language of the Harappan script. In *Studies in the archaeology of India and Pakistan,* ed. J. Jacobson. New Delhi: Oxford and IBH Publishing.

Falk, D. 1984. The petrified brain. *Natural History* 93(9):36–39.

Farnsworth, P., J. E. Brady, M. J. deNiro, and R. S. MacNeish. 1985. A re-evaluation of the isotopic and archaeological reconstructions of diet in the Tehuacán Valley. *American Antiquity* 50:102–116.

Feder, K. L., and M. A. Park. 1989. *Human antiquity.* Mountain View, CA: Mayfield.

Fedigan, L. M. 1986. The changing role of women in models of human evolution. *Annual Review of Anthropology* 15:25–66.

Feinman, G. M., S. A. Kowalewski, L. Finsten, R. E. Blanton, and L. Nicholas. 1985. Long-term demographic change: A perspective from the Valley of Oaxaca. *Journal of Field Archaeology* 12:333–362.

Feldman, R. A. 1983. From maritime chiefdom to agricultural state in formative coastal Peru. In *Civilization in the ancient Americas: Essays in honor of Gordon R. Willey,* eds. R. M. Leventhal and A. L. Kolata. Albuquerque: University of New Mexico Press.

Finlayson, W. D. 1985. The 1975 and 1978 rescue excavations at the Draper site: Introduction and settlement patterns. *National Museum of Man Mercury Series,* Paper #130. Ottawa: Archaeological Survey of Canada.

Finney, F. A., and J. B. Stoltman. 1991. The Fred Edwards site: A case of Stirling phase culture contact in southwestern Wisconsin. In *New Perspectives on Cahokia,* ed. J. B. Stoltman. Madison, WI: Prehistory Press.

Fish, S. K., and S. A. Kowalewski, eds. 1990. *The archaeology of regions: A case for full-coverage survey.* Washington, DC: Smithsonian Institution Press.

Fitting, J. E. 1978. Regional cultural development, 300 B.C. to A.D. 1000. In *Handbook of North American Indians, Vol. 15: Northeast,* ed. W. C. Sturtevant and B. G. Trigger. Washington, DC: Smithsonian Institution Press.

Flannery, K. V. 1968. Archaeological systems theory and early Mesoamerica. In *Anthropological archeology in the Americas,* ed. B. J. Meggers. Washington, DC: Anthropological Society of Washington.

Flannery, K. V. 1968. The Olmec and the Valley of Oaxaca: A model for interregional interaction in formative times. In *Dumbarton Oaks conference on the Olmec,* ed. E. Benson. Washington, DC: Dumbarton Oaks.

Flannery, K. V. 1972. The cultural evolution of civilizations. *Annual Review of Ecology and Systematics* 3:399–426.

Flannery, K. V. 1972. The origins of the village as a settlement type in Mesoamerica and the Near East: A comparative study. In *Man, settlement, and urbanism,* ed. P. J. Ucko, R. Tringham, and G. W. Dimbleby. London: Duckworth.

Flannery, K. V. 1973. The origins of agriculture. *Annual Review of Anthropology* 2:271–310.

Flannery, K. V., ed. 1986. *Guilá Naquitz: Archaic foraging and early agriculture in Oaxaca, Mexico.* New York: Academic Press.

Flannery, K. V., and J. Marcus. 1976. Evolution of the public building in Formative Oaxaca. In *Cultural change and continuity: Essays in honor of James Bennett Griffin,* ed. C. Cleland. New York: Academic Press.

Flannery, K. V., and J. Marcus. 1983. The growth of site hierarchies in the Valley of Oaxaca: Part 1. In *The cloud people: Divergent evolution of the Zapotec and Mixtec civilizations,* eds. K. V. Flannery and J. Marcus. New York: Academic Press.

Flinders Petrie, W. M. 1904. *Methods and aims of archaeology.* London: Macmillan.

Foley, R. 1987. Hominid species and stone-tool assemblages: How are they related? *Antiquity* 61:380–392.

Ford, J. A., and C. H. Webb. 1956. Poverty Point: A Late Archaic site in Louisiana. *Anthropological Papers,* vol. 46, part 1. New York: American Museum of Natural History.

Ford, R. I., ed. 1984. *The origins of plant husbandry in North America.* Ann Arbor: University of Michigan Museum of Anthropology.

Foster, M. S., and P. C. Weigand, eds. 1985. *The archaeology of west and northwest Mesoamerica.* Boulder, CO: Westview Press.

Fowler, M. L. 1975. A pre-Columbian urban center on the Mississippi. *Scientific American* 232:92–101.

Fowler, M. L. 1991. Mound 72 and Early Mississippian at Cahokia. In *New perspectives on Cahokia,* ed. J. B. Stoltman. Madison, WI: Prehistory Press.

Fowler, M. L., and R. L. Hall. 1978. Late prehistory of the Illinois area. In *Handbook of North American Indians, Vol. 15: Northeast,* ed. W. C. Sturtevant and B. G. Trigger. Washington, DC: Smithsonian Institution Press.

Frankfurt, H. 1956. *The birth of civilization in the Near East.* Garden City, NY: Doubleday.

Funk, R. E. 1978. Post-Pleistocene adaptations. In *Handbook of North American Indians, Vol. 15: Northeast,* ed. W. C. Sturtevant and B. G. Trigger. Washington, DC: Smithsonian Institution Press.

Gábori, M. 1976. *Les civilisations du Paléolithique moyen entre les Alpes et l'Oural.* Budapest: Akadémiai Kaidó.

Galinat, W. C. 1971. The origin of maize. *Annual Review of Genetics* 5:447–478.

Gamble, C. 1986. *The Paleolithic settlement of Europe.* Cambridge: Cambridge University Press.

Gargett, R. H. 1989. Grave shortcomings: The evidence for Neanderthal burial. *Current Anthropology* 30:157–190.

Garlake, P. S. 1980. Early states in Africa. In *The Cambridge encyclopedia of archaeology,* ed. A. Sherratt. New York: Crown.

Garrod, D. A. E., and D. M. A. Bate. 1937. *The stone age of Mount Carmel.* Oxford: Clarendon Press.

Geddes, D. 1985. Mesolithic domesticated sheep in west Mediterranean Europe. *Journal of Archaeological Science* 12:25–48.

Geertz, C. 1963. The transition to humanity. *Anthropological Series* 3:1–9. Washington, DC: Voice of America, United States Information Service.

Gibson, J. L. 1974. Poverty Point: The first North American chiefdom. *Archaeology* 27:97–105.

Gibson, J. L. 1987. The Poverty Point earthworks reconsidered. *Mississippi Archaeology* 22:15–31.

Gimbutas, M. 1977. Varna, a sensationally rich cemetery of the Karanova culture about 4500 B.C. *Expedition* 19:39–47.

Gingerich, P. D. 1985. Nonlinear molecular clocks and ape-human divergence times. In *Hominid evolution: Past, present, and future*, ed. P. V. Tobias. New York: A. R. Liss.

Gleeson, P., and G. Grosso. 1976. Ozette site. In *The excavation of water-saturated archaeological sites (wet sites) on the Northwest Coast of North America*, ed. D. R. Croes. Ottawa: Archaeological Survey of Canada.

Gleeson, P., and M. Fisken. 1977. *Ozette archaeological project, interim final report, phase X*. Pullman: Washington Archaeological Research Center, Washington State University.

Glob, P. V. 1970a. *The bog people*. Ithaca, NY: Cornell University Press.

Glob, P. V. 1970b. *The mound people*. Ithaca, NY: Cornell University Press.

Glover, I. C. 1977. The Hoabinhian: Hunter-gatherers or early agriculturalists in Southeast Asia? In *Hunters, gatherers, and first farmers beyond Europe*, ed. J. V. S. Megaw. Leicester: Leicester University Press.

Glover, I. C. 1980. Agricultural origins in East Asia. In *The Cambridge encyclopedia of archaeology*, ed. A. Sherratt. New York: Crown.

Goodall, J. 1986. *The chimpanzees of Gombe Reserve*. Cambridge: Harvard University Press.

Gorman, C. H. 1970. Excavations at Spirit Cave, North Thailand: Some interim interpretations. *Asian Perspectives* 13:79–107.

Gorman, C. H. 1971. The Hoabinhian and after: Subsistence patterns in Southeast Asia during the Late Pleistocene and Early Recent periods. *World Archaeology* 2(3):300–320.

Gorman, C. H. 1977. A priori models and Thai prehistory: A reconsideration of the beginnings of agriculture in southeastern Asia. In *The origins of agriculture*, ed. C. A. Reed. The Hague: Mouton.

Goudie, A. 1983. *Environmental change*. Oxford: Clarendon Press.

Gowlett, J. A. J. 1984. *Ascent to civilization: The archaeology of early man*. New York: Knopf.

Gowlett, J. A. J. 1984. Mental abilities of early man. In *Community ecology and human adaptation in the pleistocene*, ed. R. A. Foley. London: Academic Press.

Gowlett, J. A. J. 1987. The archaeology of accelerator radiocarbon dating. *Journal of World Prehistory* 1:127–170.

Graham, I. 1967. *Archaeological explorations in El Petén, Guatemala*. Middle American

Research Institute, Publication 33. New Orleans: Tulane University.

Graham, I. 1976. John Eric Sidney Thompson, 1898–1975. *American Anthropologist* 78(2):317–320.

Grayson, D. K. 1987. Death by natural causes. *Natural History* 5:8–12.

Green, M. W. 1981. The construction and implementation of the cuneiform writing system. *Visible Language* 15(4): 345–372.

Green, S. 1981. *Prehistorian: A biography of V. Gordon Childe*. Bradford-on-Avon: Moonraker Press.

Griffin, J. B. 1967. Eastern North American archaeology: A summary. *Science* 156:175–190.

Griffin, J. B. 1980. Agricultural groups in North America. In *The Cambridge encyclopedia of archaeology*, ed. A. Sherratt. New York: Crown.

Griffin, J. B. 1983. The Midlands. In *Ancient North Americans*, ed. J. Jennings. San Francisco: Freeman.

Grove, D. C. 1981. The formative period and the evolution of complex culture. In *Supplement to the handbook of Middle American Indians, Vol. 1*, ed. J. A. Sabloff. Austin: University of Texas Press.

Grove, D. C. 1984. *Chalcatzingo: Excavations on the Olmec frontier*. London: Thames & Hudson.

Gumerman, G. J., ed. 1991. *Exploring the Hohokam: Prehistoric desert peoples of the American Southwest*. Dragoon, AZ: Amerind Foundation. (and Albuquerque: University of New Mexico Press.)

Gumerman, G. J., and E. W. Haury. 1979. Prehistory: Hohokam. In *Handbook of North American Indians, Vol. 9: Southwest*, ed. A. Ortiz. Washington, DC: Smithsonian Institution Press.

Haas, J. S. 1982. *The evolution of the prehistoric state*. New York: Columbia University Press.

Haas, J., S. Pozorski, and T. Pozorski, eds. 1987. *The origins and development of the Andean state*. Cambridge: Cambridge University Press.

Haddingham, E. 1979. *Secrets of the Ice Age*. London: Walker & Co.

Hall, R. L. 1977. An anthropocentric perspective for eastern United States prehistory. *American Antiquity* 42(4):499–518.

Halloway, R. L. 1983. Cerebral brain endocast pattern of *Australopithecus afarensis*. *Nature* 303:420–422.

Hammond, N. 1977. Sir Eric Thompson, 1898–1975: A biographical sketch and bibliography. In *Social process in Maya*

prehistory: Studies in honour of Sir Eric Thompson, ed. N. Hammond. London: Academic Press.

Hammond, N. 1982. *Ancient Maya civilization*. New Brunswick, NJ: Rutgers University Press.

Hammond, N. 1987. The discovery of Tikal. *Archaeology* 40(3):30–37.

Hantman, J. L. 1990. Between Powhatan and Quirank: Reconstructing Monacan culture and history in the context of Jamestown. *American Anthropologist* 92:676–690.

Harlan, J. R. 1967. A wild wheat harvest in Turkey. *Archaeology* 20(3):197–201.

Harlan, J. R., J. M. J. de Wet, and A. B. L. Stemler, eds. 1976. *Origins of african plant domestication*. The Hague: Mouton.

Harlan, J. R., and D. Zohary. 1966. Distribution of wild wheats and barley. *Science* 153:1074–1080.

Harner, M. 1977. The enigma of Aztec sacrifice. *Natural History* 86:47–52.

Harrison, R. J. 1980. *The Beaker Folk*. London: Thames & Hudson.

Hastings, C. M., and M. E. Moseley. 1975. The adobes of Huaca del Sol and Huaca de la Luna. *American Antiquity* 40: 196–203.

Hastorf, C. A. and V. S. Popper. 1989. *Current paleoethnobotany*. Chicago: University of Chicago Press.

Haury, E. W. 1976. *The Hohokam: Desert farmers and craftsmen*. Tucson: University of Arizona Press.

Haury, E. W. 1986. HH-39: Recollections of a dramatic moment in southwestern archaeology. In *Emil W. Haury's prehistory of the American Southwest*, eds. J. J. Reid and D. E. Doyel. Tucson: University of Arizona Press.

Hayden, B. 1990. Nimrods, piscators, pluckers and planters: The emergence of food production. *Journal of Anthropological Archaeology* 9:31–69.

Hedges, R. E. M. 1981. Radiocarbon dating with an accelerator. *Archaeometry* 23:3–18.

Helbaek, H. 1960. The paleoethnobotany of the Near East and Europe. In *Prehistoric investigations in Iraqi Kurdistan*, eds. R. J. Braidwood and B. Howe. Chicago: University of Chicago Press.

Henry, D. 1989. *From foraging to agriculture: The Levant at the end of the Ice Age*. Philadelphia: University of Pennsylvania Press.

Hesse, B. 1982. Slaughter patterns and domestication: The beginnings of pastoralism in western Iran. *Man* 17:403–417.

Higham, C. F. W. 1977. Economic change in prehistoric Thailand. In *The origins of ag-*

riculture, ed. C. A. Reed. The Hague: Mouton.

Higham, C. F. W. 1984. Prehistoric rice cultivation in Southeast Asia. *Scientific American* 250(4):138–146.

Higham, C. F. W. and A. Kijngam. 1982. Prehistoric man and his environment: Evidence from the Ban Chiang faunal remains. *Expedition* 24(4):17–24.

Hill, B., and R. Hill. 1974. *Indian petroglyphs of the Pacific Northwest.* Saanichton, Can: Hancock House.

Hill, J. N. 1970. *Broken K Pueblo: Prehistoric social organization in the American Southwest.* Tucson: University of Arizona Press.

Hillman, G. C., and M. S. Davies. 1990. Measured domestication rates in wild wheats and barley under primitive cultivation, and their archaeological implications. *Journal of World Prehistory* 4:157–222.

Hoffman, M. A. 1976. The city of the hawk. *Expedition* 18:32–41.

Hoffman, M. A. 1983. Where nations began. *Science 83* October:42–51.

Hole, F., K. V. Flannery, and J. A. Neely. 1969. *Prehistory and human ecology of the Deh Luran Plain.* Ann Arbor: University of Michigan Press.

Hood, S. 1973. *The Minoans.* London: Thames & Hudson.

Howell, F. C. 1966. Observations on the earlier phases of the European Lower Paleolithic. *American Anthropologist* 68(2,2):88–201.

Hsu, C. 1965. *Ancient China in transition.* Stanford, CA: Stanford University Press.

Ikawa-Smith, F. 1980. Current issues in Japanese archaeology. *American Scientist* 68:134–145.

Iltis, H. H. 1983. From teosinte to maize: The catastrophic sexual transmutation. *Science* 222:886–894.

Isaac, G. 1977. *Olorgesailie: Archaeological studies of a Middle Pleistocene lake basin in Kenya.* Chicago: University of Chicago Press.

Isaac, G., and R. Leakey. 1979. *Human ancestors. Readings from Scientific American.* San Francisco: Freeman.

Isaac, G. 1984. The archaeology of human origins: Studies of the lower Pleistocene in East Africa, 1971–1981. *Advances in World Archaeology* 3:1–87.

Isbell, W. H. 1978. The prehistoric ground drawings of Peru. *Scientific American* 238:140–153.

Jacobsen, T. 1976. Seventeen thousand years of Greek prehistory. *Scientific American* 234(6):76–87.

Jacobson, J. 1979. Recent developments in South Asian prehistory and protohistory. *Annual Review of Anthropology* 8:467–502.

Jacobson, J. 1986. The Harappan civilization: An early state. In *Studies in the archaeology of India and Pakistan,* ed. J. Jacobson. New Delhi: Oxford and IBH Publishing.

Jarrige, J.-F., and R. H. Meadow. 1980. The antecedents of civilization in the Indus Valley. *Scientific American* 243(2): 122–133.

Jawad, A. J. 1974. The Eridu material and its implications. *Sumer* 30:11–46.

Jefferson, T. 1797. *Notes of the state of Virginia.* London: J. Stockdale.

Jeffries, R. W., and M. Lynch. 1985. Dimensions of Middle Archaic cultural adaptation at the Black Earth site, Saline County, Illinois. In *Archaic hunters and gatherers in the American Midwest,* eds. J. L. Phillips and J. A. Brown. New York: Academic Press.

Jelinek, A. J. 1982a. The Tabun Cave and Paleolithic man in the Levant. *Science* 216:1369–1375.

Jelinek, A. J. 1982b. Obituary for François Bordes. *American Antiquity* 47:785–792.

Jelinek, A. J. 1988. Technology, typology, and culture in the Middle Paleolithic. In *Upper Pleistocene prehistory,* ed. H. Dibble and A. Montet-White. Philadelphia: University of Pennsylvania Press.

Jiménez Moreno, W. 1941. Tula y los Toltecas según las fuentes históricas. *Revista Mexicana de Estudios Antropológicos* 5:79–83.

Joffroy, R. 1962. *Le Trésor de Vix. Historie et porteé d'une grande decouverte.* Paris: Fayard.

Johanson, D. 1976. Ethiopia yields first 'family' of early man. *National Geographic* 150(6):790–811.

Johanson, D. C., and M. A. Eddy. 1981. *Lucy: The beginnings of humankind.* New York: Simon and Schuster.

Jolly, C. 1970. The seed eaters: A new model of hominid differentiation based on a baboon analogy. *Man* 5:5–26.

Jones, C. 1977. Inauguration dates of three Late Classic rulers of Tikal, Guatemala. *American Antiquity* 42:28–60.

Jones, C., and L. Satterthwaite. 1982. *The monuments and inscriptions of Tikal: The carved monuments. Tikal Report 33A. University Museum Monograph 44.* Philadelphia: University of Pennsylvania.

Jurmain, R., H. Nelson, and W. A. Turnbaugh. 1987. *Understanding physical anthropology and archaeology.* Third

Edition. St. Paul, MN: West Publishing Co.

Jurmain, R., H. Nelson, and W. A. Turnbaugh. 1987. *Understanding physical anthropology and archaeology.* Fourth Edition. St. Paul, MN: West Publishing Co.

Keeley, L. H. 1981. *Experimental determination of stone tool uses: A microwear analysis.* Chicago: University of Chicago Press.

Keeley, L. H., and D. Cahen. 1989. Early Neolithic forts and villages in northeastern Belgium: a preliminary report. *Journal of Field Archaeology* 16:157–176.

Keeley, L. H., and N. Toth. 1981. Microwear polishes on early stone tools from Koobi Fora, Kenya. *Nature* 293(8):464–465.

Keightley, D. N., ed. 1983. *The origins of Chinese civilization.* Berkeley: University of California Press.

Kenoyer, J. M. 1984. Shell working industries of the Indus civilization: A summary. *Paleorient* 10(1):49–63.

Kenoyer, J. M. 1985. Shell working at Moenjo-daro, Pakistan. In *South Asian archaeology 1983,* eds. J. Schotsmans and M. Taddei. Naples: Instituto Universitario Orientale.

Kenoyer, J. M. 1988. Recent developments in the study of the Indus civilization. *Eastern Anthropologist* 41(1):65–76.

Kenyon, K. 1954. Ancient Jericho. *Scientific American* 190(4):76–82.

Kenyon, K. 1960. *Excavations at Jericho. I.* Jerusalem: British School of Archaeology.

Kirchhoff, P. 1952. Mesoamerica: Its geographic limits, ethnic composition, and cultural characteristics. In *Heritage of conquest,* ed. S. Tax. New York: The Free Press.

Kirk, R., and R. D. Daugherty. 1978. *Exploring Washington archaeology.* Seattle: University of Washington Press.

Klein, R. G. 1989. *The human career.* Chicago: University of Chicago Press.

Klein, R. G., and K. Cruz-Uribe. 1984. *The analysis of animal bones from archaeological sites.* Chicago: University of Chicago Press.

Klein, R. G., and K. Cruz-Uribe. 1987. Large mammal and tortoise bones from Eland's Bay Cave Province, South Africa. In *Papers in the prehistory of the Western Cape, South Africa,* ed. J. Parkington and M. Hall. British Archaeological Reports, Series 332.

Klima, B. 1962. The first ground plan of an Upper Paleolithic loess settlement in middle Europe and its meaning. In *Courses toward urban life,* eds. R. J. Braidwood and G. R. Willey. Chicago: Aldine.

Klima, B. 1963. *Dolní Vestonice.* Prague: Nakladatelstvi Ceskoslovenske Akademie Ved.

Knight, V. J. Jr. 1990. Social organization and the evolution of hierarchy in southeastern chiefdoms. *Journal of Anthropological Research* 46:1–23.

Kolata, A. L. 1983. The South Andes. In *Ancient South Americans,* ed. J. D. Jennings. San Francisco: Freeman.

Kolata, A. L. 1986. The agricultural foundations of the Tiwanaku state. *American Antiquity* 51(4):748–762.

Kolata, A. L. 1987. Tiwanaku and its hinterland. *Archaeology* 40(1):36–41.

Kramer, S. N. 1988. The temple in Sumerian literature. In *Temple in society,* ed. M. V. Fox. Winona Lake, IN: Eisenbrauns.

Kurtén, B. 1968. *Pleistocene mammals of Europe.* Chicago: Aldine.

Kurtén, B. 1968. *Pleistocene mammals of Europe.* London: Weidenfeld & Nicholson.

Kurtén, B., and E. Anderson. 1980. *Pleistocene mammals of North America.* New York: Columbia University Press.

Laitman, J. T. 1984. The anatomy of human speech. *Natural History* 93(9):20–27.

Lamberg-Karlovsky, C. C., and J. A. Sabloff. 1979. *Ancient civilizations: The Near East and Mesoamerica.* Prospect Heights, IL: Waveland Press.

Lanning, E. P. 1967. *Peru before the Incas.* Englewood Cliffs, NJ: Prentice-Hall.

Larsson, L. 1988. *The Skateholm Project. I. Man and environment.* Lund, Sweden: Almqvist & Wiksell International.

Leakey, M. D. 1971. *Olduvai Gorge.* Cambridge: Cambridge University Press.

Leakey, M. D. 1978. Pliocene footprints at Laetoli, Tanzania. *Antiquity* 52:133.

Leakey, M. D., and R. E. Leakey, eds. 1978. *Koobi Fora research project.* Oxford: Clarendon Press.

Leakey, R., and R. Lewin. 1977. *Origins.* New York: Dutton.

Leakey, R. 1981. *The Making of Mankind.*

Lechevallier, M., and G. Quivron. 1985. Results of the recent excavations at the Neolithic site of Mehrgarh, Pakistan. In *South Asian archaeology 1983,* ed. J. Schotmans and M. Taddei. Naples: Instituto Universitario Orientale.

Lee, R. B. and I. DeVore. 1968. *Man the hunter.* Chicago, Aldine.

Legge, A. J., and P. A. Rowley-Conwy. 1988. *Star Carr revisited.* London: University of London.

LeGros Clark, W. E., and B. G. Campbell. 1978. *The fossil evidence for human evolution.* Chicago: University of Chicago Press.

Lekson, S. H., T. C. Windes, J. R. Stein, and W. J. Judge. 1988. The Chaco Canyon community. *Scientific American* 259(1):72–81.

León-Portilla, M. 1987. Ethnohistorical record for the Huey Teocalli. In *The Aztec Templo Mayor,* ed. E. H. Boone. Washington, DC: Dumbarton Oaks.

Leroi-Gourhan, A. 1957. *Prehistoric man.* New York: Philosophical Library.

Leroi-Gourhan, A. 1968. The archaeology of Lascaux Cave. *Scientific American* 219(4):104–111.

Leroi-Gourhan, A., and M. Brezillon. 1972. Fouilles de Pincevent: Essai d'analyse ethnographique d'un habitat Magdalenien (sec. 36). VII supplément a *Gallia Prehistoria.* Paris: Editions du Centre National de la Recherche Scientifique.

Leroi-Gourhan, A. 1984. *The dawn of European art: An introduction to Paleolithic cave paintings.* Cambridge: Cambridge University Press.

Lewin, R. 1984. *Human evolution: An illustrated introduction.* San Francisco: Freeman.

Lewin, R. 1988. *In the age of mankind.* Washington, DC: Smithsonian Institution Press.

Lindsay, J. 1981. Foreward. In *Prehistorian: A Biography of V. Gordon Childe,* by S. Green, p. ix-xvii. Bradford-on-Avon: Moonraker Press.

Lipe, W. 1983. The Southwest. In *Ancient North Americans,* ed. J. Jennings. San Francisco: Freeman.

Lister, R. H., and F. C. Lister. 1981. *Chaco Canyon, archaeology and archaeologists.* Albuquerque: University of New Mexico Press.

Long, A., B. F. Benz, D. J. Donahue, A. J. T. Jull, and L. J. Toolin. 1989. First direct AMS dates on early maize from Tehuacán, Mexico. *Radiocarbon* 31(3):1035–1040.

Lovejoy, C. O. 1981. The origin of man. *Science* 211:341–350.

Lumbreras, L. 1974. *The peoples and cultures of ancient Peru,* trans. B. J. Meggers. Washington, DC: Smithsonian Institution Press.

Lynch, T. F. 1980. *Guitarrero Cave: Early man in the Andes.* London: Academic Press.

Lynch, T. F., R. Gillespie, J. A. J. Gowlett, and R. E. M. Hedges. 1985. Chronology of Guitarrero Cave, Peru. *Science* 229:864–867.

MacNeish, R. S. 1974. Reflections on my search of the beginnings of agriculture in Mexico. In *Archaeological researches in*

retrospect, ed. G. R. Willey. Cambridge: Winthrop.

MacNeish, R. S. 1978. *The science of archaeology?* North Scituate, MA: Duxbury Press.

MacNeish, R. S. 1981. Tehuacán's accomplishments. In *Supplement to the handbook of Middle American Indians, Vol. 1,* ed. J. A. Sabloff. Austin: University of Texas Press.

MacNeish, R. S., F. A. Peterson, and K. V. Flannery. 1970. *Prehistory of the Tehuacán Valley, vol. 3: Ceramics,* ed. R. S. MacNeish. Austin: University of Texas Press.

Mallowan, M. E. L. 1967. The development of cities, from Al-'Ubaid to the end of Uruk 5. *The Cambridge ancient history, Vol. 1.* Cambridge: Cambridge University Press.

Mallowan, M. E. L. 1977. *Mallowan's memoirs.* London: Collins.

Maloney, B. K., C. F. W. Higham, and R. Bannanurag. 1989. Early rice cultivation in Southeast Asia: Archaeological and palynological evidence from the Bang Pakong Valley, Thailand. *Antiquity* 63:363–370.

Marcus, J. 1976a. *Emblem and state in the Classic Maya lowlands: An epigraphic approach to territorial organization.* Washington, DC: Dumbarton Oaks.

Marcus, J. 1976b. The origins of Mesoamerican writing. *Annual Review of Anthropology* 5:35–67.

Marcus, J. 1980. Zapotec writing. *Scientific American* 242(2):50–64.

Marcus, J. 1983a. The conquest slabs of Building J, Monte Albán. In *The cloud people: Divergent evolution of the Mixtec and Zapotec civilizations,* ed. K. V. Flannery and J. Marcus. New York: Academic Press.

Marcus, J. 1983b. Lowland Maya archaeology at the crossroads. *American Antiquity* 48:454–488.

Marcus, J. 1987. Prehistoric fishermen in the kingdom of Huarco. *American Scientist* 75(4):393–401.

Marcus, J., ed. 1990. *Debating Oaxaca archaeology.* Ann Arbor: University of Michigan, Museum of Anthropology, *Anthropological Papers, No. 84.*

Marshack, A. 1972a. *The roots of civilization.* New York: McGraw-Hill.

Marshack, A. 1972b. Upper Paleolithic symbol and notation. *Science* 178: 817–828.

Martin, P. S., and F. Plog. 1973. *The archaeology of Arizona: A study of the Southwest region.* New York: Natural History Press.

Martin, P. W., and H. E. Wright, Jr. 1967. *Pleistocene extinctions: The search for a cause.* New Haven: Yale University Press.

Marx, K. 1963. *The eighteenth Brumaire of Louis Bonaparte.* New York: International Publishers.

Masuda, S., I. Shimada, and C. Morris. 1985. *Andean ecology and civilization: An interdisciplinary perspective on Andean ecological complementarity.* Tokyo: University of Tokyo Press.

Matheny, R. T., ed. 1980. El Mirador, Petén, Guatemala: An interim report. *New World Archaeological Foundation, Papers* 45.

Matheny, R. T. 1986. Investigations at El Mirador, Petén, Guatemala. *National Geographic Research* 2(3):332–353.

Mathien, F. J., and R. H. McGuire, eds. 1986. *Ripples in the Chichimec Sea: New considerations of Southwestern-Mesoamerican interactions.* Carbondale: Southern Illinois University Press.

Matos Moctezuma, E. 1984. The great temple of Tenochtitlan. *Scientific American* 251(2):80–89.

Mayr, E. 1970. *Population, species, and evolution.* Cambridge, MA: Harvard University Press.

McHenry, H. M. 1982. The pattern of human evolution: Studies on bipedalism, mastication, and encephalization. *Annual Review of Anthropology* 11:151–173.

Mead, J. I., and D. J. Meltzer. 1985. *Environments and extinctions: Man in late glacial North America.* Orono, ME: Center for the Study of Early Man.

Meadow, R. H. 1984. Animal domestication in the Middle East: A view from the eastern margin. In *Animals and archaeology* 3, ed. J. Clutton-Brock and C. Grigson. Oxford: British Archaeological Reports S202.

Meggers, B. J., and C. Evans. 1957. *Archaeological investigations at the mouth of the Amazon.* Washington, DC: Smithsonian Institution, Bureau of American Ethnology, Bulletin 167.

Mellars, P., and C. Stringer. 1989. *The human revolution: Behavioural and biological perspectives on the origins of modern humans.* Edinburgh: Edinburgh University Press.

Mendelssohn, K. 1974. *The riddle of the pyramids.* New York: Praeger.

Milisauskas, S. 1978. *European prehistory.* New York: Academic Press.

Millon, R. 1967. Teotihuacan. *Scientific American* 216:38–48.

Millon, R. 1973. *Urbanization at Teotihuacan, Mexico, Vol. 1: The Teotihuacan map.* Austin: University of Texas Press.

Millon, R. 1976. Social relations in ancient Teotihuacan. In *The Valley of Mexico*, ed. E. R. Wolf. Albuquerque: University of New Mexico Press.

Millon, R. 1981. Teotihuacan: City, state, and civilization. In *Supplement to the handbook of Middle American Indians, Vol. 1: Archaeology,* ed. J. A. Sabloff. Austin: University of Texas Press.

Montague, A. 1964. *The concept of race.* New York: Free Press.

Montellano, B. R. O. 1978. Aztec cannibalism: An ecological necessity? *Science* 200:611–617.

Moore, A. M. T. 1979. A pre-Neolithic farming village on the Euphrates. *Scientific American* 241:62–70.

Moore, A. M. T. 1985. The development of Neolithic societies in the Near East. *Advances in World Archaeology* 4:1–70.

Moore, C. B. 1905. Certain aboriginal remains of the Black Warrior River. *Journal of the Academy of Natural Sciences of Philadelphia* 13:125–244.

Moorehead, W. K. 1922. *The Hopewell mound group of Ohio.* Chicago: Field Museum of Natural History, Publication 211, Anthropological Series 6(5); reprinted in 1968.

Morley, S. G., and G. W. Brainerd. 1956. *The ancient Maya,* 3rd ed. Stanford: Stanford University Press.

Moseley, M. E. 1975a. Chan Chan: Andean alternative of the preindustrial city? *Science* 187:219–225.

Moseley, M. E. 1975b. *The maritime foundations of Andean civilization.* Menlo Park, CA: Benjamin/Cummings.

Moseley, M. E. 1975c. Prehistoric principles of labor organization in the Moche Valley, Peru. *American Antiquity* 40:191–196.

Moseley, M. E. 1983. Central Andean civilization. In *Ancient South Americans,* ed. J. D. Jennings. San Francisco: Freeman.

Moseley, M. E., and K. C. Day, eds. 1982. *Chan Chan: Andean desert city.* Albuquerque: University of New Mexico Press.

Muller, J. 1983. The Southeast. In *Ancient North Americans,* ed. J. Jennings. San Francisco: Freeman.

Mulvaney, D. J. 1975. *The prehistory of Australia.* 2nd ed. Baltimore: Pelican.

Murra, J. V. 1962. Cloth and its function in the Inca state. *American Anthropologist* 64:710–728.

Murra, J. V. 1972. El "control vertical" de un máximo de pisos ecológicos en la economia de las sociedades andinas. In *Visita de la provincia de Leon de Huanuco (1562), Vol. 2,* ed. J. V. Murra. Huanuco, Peru: Universidad Nacional Hermilio Valdizan.

Neitzel, J. 1989. The Chacoan regional system: Interpreting the evidence for social complexity. In *The sociopolitical structure of prehistoric southwestern societies,* eds. S. Upham, K. G. Lightfoot, and R. A. Jewett. Boulder, CO: Westview Press.

Nicholas, L. M., and G. M. Feinman. 1989. A regional perspective on Hohokam irrigation in the lower Salt River Valley, Arizona. In *The sociopolitical structure of prehistoric southwestern societies,* eds. S. Upham, K. G. Lightfoot, and R. A. Jewett. Boulder, CO: Westview Press.

Nissen, H. J. 1986. The archaic texts from Uruk. *World Archaeology* 17(3):317–334.

Nissen, H. J. 1988. *The early history of the ancient Near East, 9000–2000 B.C.* Chicago: University of Chicago Press.

Oakley, K. P. 1955. Fire as a Paleolithic tool and weapon. *Proceedings of the Prehistoric Society* 21:36–48.

Oates, J. 1980. The emergence of cities in the Near East. In *The Cambridge encyclopedia of archaeology,* ed. A. Sherratt. New York: Crown.

O'Connor, D. 1980. Egypt and the Levant in the Bronze Age. In *The Cambridge encyclopedia of archaeology,* ed. A. Sherratt. New York: Crown.

O'Shea, J. 1980. Mesoamerica: From village to empire. In *The Cambridge encyclopedia of archaeology,* ed. A. Sherratt. New York: Crown.

Otto, M. P. 1979. Hopewell antecedents in the Adena heartland. In *Hopewell archaeology: The Chillicothe conference,* eds. D. S. Brose and N. Greber. Kent, OH: Kent State University Press.

Parkington, J. E. 1972. Seasonal mobility in the Late Stone Age. *African Studies* 31:223–43.

Parkington, J. E. 1981. Stone tools and resources: A case study from South Africa. *World Archaeology* 13:16–30.

Parkington, J. E. 1984. Changing views of the Later Stone Age of South Africa. *Advances in World Archaeology* 3:89–142.

Parpola, A. 1986. The Indus script: A challenging puzzle. *World Archaeology* 17(3):399–419.

Parsons, J. R. 1972. Archaeological settlement patterns. *Annual Review of Anthropology* 1:127–150.

Paul, A., and S. A. Turpin. 1986. The ecstatic shaman theme of Paracas textiles. *Archaeology* 39(5):20–27.

Pearsall, D. 1989. *Paleoethnobotany*. Orlando, FL: Academic Press.

Pearsall, D. 1992. The origins of plant cultivation in South America. In *Origins of agriculture in world perspective,* eds. C. W. Cowan and P. J. Watson. Washington, DC: Smithsonian Institution Press.

Pearson, R., and A. Underhill. 1987. The Chinese Neolithic: Recent trends in research. *American Anthropologist* 89(4):807–822.

Peebles, C. S., and C. A. Black. 1987. Moundville from 1000–1500 A.D. as seen from 1840 to 1985 A.D. In *Chiefdoms in the Americas,* eds. R. D. Drennan and C. A. Uribe. Lanham, MD: University Press of America.

Peebles, C. S., and S. Kus. 1977. Some archaeological correlates of ranked society. *American Antiquity* 42:421–448.

Perony, D. 1930. Le Moustier. *Revue Anthropologique* 14.

Perrot, J. 1966. Le Gisement Natoufien de Mallaha (Eynan), Israel. *L'Anthropologie* 47:437–484.

Peterson, I. 1988. Tokens of plenty. *Science News* 134:408–410.

Pfeiffer, J. E. 1977. *The emergence of society*. New York: McGraw-Hill.

Pfeiffer, J. E. 1985. *The emergence of humankind*. New York: Harper & Row.

Phillipson, D. 1977. *The later prehistory of eastern and southern Africa*. London: Heinemann.

Phillipson, D. 1980. Iron Age Africa and the expansion of the Bantu. In *The Cambridge encyclopedia of archaeology,* ed. A. Sherratt. New York: Crown.

Phillipson, D. 1985. *African archaeology*. Cambridge: Cambridge University Press.

Pilbeam, D. 1985. Distinguished lecture: Hominoid evolution and hominoid origins. *American Anthropologist* 88:295–312.

Possehl, G. L. 1990. Revolution in the urban revolution: The emergence of Indus urbanization. *Annual Review of Anthropology* 19:261–282.

Price, T. D. 1987. The Mesolithic of western Europe. *Journal of World Prehistory* 1:225–305.

Price, T. D., ed. 1989. *The chemistry of prehistoric bone*. Cambridge: Cambridge University Press.

Price, T. D., and Brinch Petersen, E. 1987. A Mesolithic community in Denmark. *Scientific American* 255(3):111–121.

Prufer, O. 1964. The Hopewell cult. *Scientific American* 211(6):90–102.

Puleston, D. E. 1973. Ancient Maya settlement patterns and environment at Tikal, Guatemala: Implications for subsistence models. Ph.D. dissertation, University of Pennsylvania, Philadelphia.

Puleston, D. E. 1977. The art and technology of hydraulic agriculture in the Maya lowlands. In *Social processes and Maya prehistory,* ed. N. Hammond. New York: Academic Press.

Puleston, D. E. 1978. Terracing, raised fields, and tree cropping in the Maya lowlands: A new perspective on the geography of power. In *Prehispanic Maya agriculture,* ed. P. D. Harrison and B. L. Turner II. Albuquerque: University of New Mexico Press.

Quilter, J. 1985. Architecture and chronology at El Paraíso, Peru. *Journal of Field Archaeology* 12:279–297.

Quilter, J., B. Ojeda, D. M. Pearsall, D. H. Sandweiss, J. G. Jones, and E. S. Wing. 1991. Subsistence economy of El Paraíso, an early Peruvian site. *Science* 251:277–283.

Quilter, J., and T. Stocker. 1983. Subsistence economies and the origins of agriculture. *American Anthropologist* 85(3):545–562.

Rambo, A. T. 1991. The study of cultural evolution. In *Profiles in cultural evolution: Papers from a conference in honor of Elman R. Service,* eds. A. T. Rambo and K. Gillogly. Ann Arbor, MI: Anthropological Papers, Museum of Anthropology, University of Michigan, No. 85.

Randsborg, K. 1975. Social dimensions of early Neolithic Denmark. *Proceedings of the Prehistoric Society* 41:105–118.

Raymond, J. S. 1981. The maritime foundations of Andean civilization: A reconsideration of the evidence. *American Antiquity* 46(4):806–821.

Redman, C. 1978. *The rise of civilization: From early farmers to urban society in the ancient Near East*. San Francisco: Freeman.

Redmond, E. M. 1983. *A fuego y sangre: Early Zapotec imperialism in the Cuicatlán Cañada, Oaxaca*. Ann Arbor: University of Michigan, Museum of Anthropology, Memoirs 16.

Reed, C. A., ed. 1977. *The origins of agriculture*. The Hague: Mouton.

Reid, J. J. 1986. Emil W. Haury: The archaeologist as humanist and scientist. In *Emil W. Haury's prehistory of the American Southwest,* eds. J. J. Reid and D. E. Doyel. Tucson: University of Arizona Press.

Renfrew, C. 1974. *Before civilization*. New York: Knopf.

Renfrew, J. 1973. *Palaeoethnobotany*. New York: Columbia University Press.

Rice, G. 1987. La Ciudad: A perspective on Hohokam community systems. In *The Hohokam village: Site structure and organization,* ed. D. E. Doyel. Glenwood Springs, CO: Southwestern and Rocky Mountain Division of the American Association for the Advancement of Science.

Rindos, D. 1984. *The origins of agriculture: An evolutionary perspective*. New York: Academic Press.

Robson, J. R. K., R. I. Ford, K. V. Flannery, and J. E. Konlande. 1976. The nutritional significance of maize and teosinte. *Ecology of Food and Nutrition* 4:243–249.

Roe, D. 1981. *The Lower and Middle Paleolithic periods in Britain*. London: Routledge & Kegan Paul.

Rolland, N., and H. L. Dibble. 1990. A new synthesis of Middle Paleolithic variability. *American Antiquity* 55:480–499.

Rollefson, G. O. 1985. The 1983 season at the Early Neolithic site of 'Ain Ghazal. *National Geographic Research* Winter: 44–62.

Ronen, A., ed. 1982. *The transition from Lower to Middle Paleolithic and the origin of modern man*. Oxford: British Archaeological Reports.

Roosevelt, A. C., R. A. Housley, M. Imazio da Silveira, S. Maranca, and R. Johnson. 1991. Eighth millennium pottery from a prehistoric shell midden in the Brazilian Amazon. *Science* 254:1621–1624.

Rosman, A., and P. G. Rubel. 1971. *Feasting with mine enemy: Rank and exchange among Northwest Coast societies*. New York: Columbia University Press.

Rowe, J. H. 1947. Inca culture at the time of Spanish conquest. In *Handbook of South American Indians: Vol. 2, The Andean civilizations,* ed. J. H. Steward. Washington, DC: Smithsonian Institution, Bureau of American Ethnology, Bulletin 143.

Rowe, J. H. 1967. What kind of settlement was Inca Cuzco? *Nawpa Pacha* 5:59–76.

Rowe, J. H. 1987. Machu Pijchu: A la luz de los documentos del siglo XVI. *Kuntur* 4:12–20.

Ruddiman, W. F., and J. E. Kutzbach. 1991. Plateau uplift and climatic change. *Scientific American* 264(3):66–75.

Ruz Lhuillier, A. 1973. *El Tempo de las Inscripciones: Palenque*. Mexico, D.F.: Instituto Nacional de Antropología e Historia.

Sabloff, J. A. 1990. *The new archaeology and the ancient Maya*. New York: Freeman.

Sahagún, F. B. 1950–1982. *Florentine codex: General history of the things of New Spain*, trans. A. J. O. Anderson and C. E. Dibble (11 vols.). Santa Fe, NM: School of American Research, and Provo: University of Utah.

Sahlins, M. D. 1968. Notes on the original affluent society. In *Man the hunter*, eds. R. B. Lee and I. DeVore, pp. 85–89. Chicago: Aldine.

Sahlins, M. D. 1972. *Stone Age economics*. Chicago: Aldine.

Sanders, W. T., and B. Price. 1968. *Mesoamerica: The evolution of a civilization*. New York: Random House.

Sanders, W. T., J. R. Parsons, and R. S. Santley. 1979. *The Basin of Mexico: Ecological processes in the evolution of a civilization*. New York: Academic Press.

Sarich, V. 1983. Retrospective on hominid macromolecular systematics. In *New interpretations of ape and human ancestry*, eds. R. L. Ciochon and R. S. Corrucini. New York: Plenum Press.

Sauer, C. O. 1952. *Agricultural origins and dispersals*. New York: The American Geographical Society.

Scarborough, V. L., and D. R. Wilcox, eds. 1991. *The Mesoamerican ballgame*. Tucson: University of Arizona Press.

Schele, L., and M. E. Miller. 1986. *The blood of kings: Dynasty and ritual in Maya art*. Fort Worth, TX: Kimball Art Museum.

Schmandt-Besserat, D. 1980. The envelopes that bear the first writing. *Technology and Culture* 21(3):357–385.

Schmandt-Besserat, D. 1990. Accounting in the prehistoric Middle East. *Archeomaterials* 4(1):15–23.

Service, E. R. 1975. *Origins of the state and civilization: The process of cultural evolution*. New York: Norton.

Sharer, R. J., and D. C. Grove, eds. 1989. *Regional perspectives on the Olmec*. Cambridge: Cambridge University Press.

Sherratt, A., ed. 1980. *The Cambridge encyclopedia of archaeology*. New York: Crown.

Shutler, R., Jr. 1983. *Early man in the New World*. Beverly Hills: Sage Publications.

Siemens, A. H., and D. E. Puleston. 1972. Ridged fields and associated features in southern Campeche: New perspectives on the lowland Maya. *American Antiquity* 37:228–239.

Simons, E. 1972. *Primate evolution*. New York: Macmillan.

Simpson, G. G. 1967. *The meaning of evolution*. New Haven: Yale University Press. Revised edition.

Singer, R., and J. Wymer. 1982. *The Middle Stone Age at Klasies River Mouth in South Africa*. Chicago: University of Chicago Press.

Skelton, R. R., H. M. McHenry, and G. M. Drawhorn, 1986. Phylogenetic analysis of early hominids. *Current Anthropology* 27:21–43.

Smith, B. D. 1986. The archaeology of the southeastern United States: From Dalton to de Soto, 10,500–500 B.P. *Advances in World Archaeology* 5:1–92.

Smith, B. D. 1989. Origins of agriculture in eastern North America. *Science* 246:1566–1571.

Smith, C. E. 1980. Plant remains from Guitarrero Cave. In *Guitarrero Cave*, ed. T. F. Lynch. New York: Academic Press.

Smith, F. H., and F. Spencer, eds. 1984. *The origins of modern humans*. New York: A. R. Liss.

Soffer, O. 1985. *The Upper Paleolithic of the central Russian plains*. New York: Academic Press.

Solecki, R. 1971. *Shanidar: The first flower people*. New York: Knopf.

Solheim, W. G., II. 1972a. An earlier agricultural revolution. *Scientific American* 226:34–41.

Solheim, W. G., II. 1972b. Early man in Southeast Asia. *Expedition* 14(3):25–31.

Spence, M. W. 1974. Residential practices and the distribution of skeletal traits in Teotihuacan, Mexico. *Man* 9:262–273.

Spence, M. W. 1981. Obsidian production and the state in Teotihuacan. *American Antiquity* 46(4):769–787.

Spencer, C. S. 1982. *The Cuicatlán Cañada and Monte Albán: A study of primary state formation*. New York: Academic Press.

Spooner, B., ed. 1972. *Population growth: Anthropological implications*. Cambridge, MA: MIT Press.

Srejevic, D. 1972. *Europe's first monumental sculpture: New discoveries at Lepenski Vir*. New York: Stein & Day.

Srejevic, D., and Ljubinka Babovic. 1983. *Umetnost Lepenskog Vira*. Beograd: Srpska Akademija Nauka.

Stephens, J. L. 1841. *Incidents of travel in Central America, Chiapas, and Yucatán*, 2 vols. New York: Harper & Row. (Reprinted by Dover, 1962.)

Stephens, J. L. 1843. *Incidents of travel in Yucatán*, 2 vols. New York: Harper & Row. (Reprinted by Dover, 1963.)

Steponaitis, V. 1983. *Ceramics, chronology, and community patterns: An archaeological study at Moundville*. New York: Academic Press.

Steponaitis, V. 1986. Prehistoric archaeology in the southeastern United States, 1970–1985. *Annual Review of Anthropology* 15:363–304.

Steponaitis, V. 1991. Contrasting patterns of Mississippian development. In *Chiefdoms: Power, economy, and ideology*, ed. T. Earle. Cambridge: Cambridge University Press.

Stirling, M. W. 1943. Stone monuments of southern Mexico. Washington, DC: Smithsonian Institution, *Bureau of American Ethnology, Bulletin* 138.

Streuver, S., ed. 1971. *Prehistoric agriculture*. New York: Natural History Press.

Stringer, C. B. 1985. Middle Pleistocene hominid variability and the origin of Late Pleistocene humans. In *Ancestors: the hard evidence*, ed. E. Delson. New York: A. R. Liss.

Stringer, C. B. 1988. *The Neanderthals*. London: Thames & Hudson.

Stringer, C. B. 1990. The emergence of modern humans. *Scientific American* 259(12):98–103.

Sudgen, D. E., and B. S. John. 1976. *Glaciers and landscape*. London: E. Arnold.

Susman, R. L. and J. T. Stern. 1982. Functional morphology of *Homo habilis*. *Science* 217:931–934.

Swaminathan, M. S. 1984. Rice. *Scientific American* 250(1):80–93.

Tanner, N. 1981. *On becoming human*. London: Cambridge University Press.

Tattersal, I., C. Delson, and J. V. Couvering, eds. 1988. *Encyclopedia of human evolution and prehistory*. New York: Garland.

Tauber, H. 1981. ^{13}C evidence for dietary habits of prehistoric man in Denmark. *Nature* 292:332–333.

Taylor, R. E. 1988. *Radiocarbon Dating*. New York: Academic Press.

Taylour, W. 1989. *The Mycenaeans*. London: Thames & Hudson.

Te-k'un, C. 1959. *Archaeology in China, Vol. I: Prehistoric China*. Cambridge: W. Heffer & Sons.

Te-k'un, C. 1960. *Archaeology in China, Vol. 2: Shang burials*. Cambridge: W. Heffer & Sons.

Te-k'un, C. 1966. *Archaeology in China: New light on prehistoric China*. Cambridge: W. Heffer & Sons.

Tello, J. C. 1943. Discovery of the Chavín culture in Peru. *American Antiquity* 9:135–160.

Thomas, D. H. 1978. *Archaeology*. Holt, Rinehart & Winston.

Thomas, D. H. 1983. *The archaeology of Monitor Valley 2: Gatecliff Shelter*. New York: American Museum of Natural History.

Thomas, D. H. 1989. *Archaeology*. New York: Holt, Rinehart & Winston.

Thompson, D. E., and J. V. Murra. 1966. The Inca bridges in the Huánuco region. *American Antiquity* 31:632–639.

Thompson, J. E. S. 1963. *Maya archaeologist*. Norman: University of Oklahoma Press.

Tobias, P. 1971. *The brain in hominid evolution*. New York: Columbia University Press.

Toffler, A. 1970. *Future shock*. London: Pan Books.

Topic, T. L. 1982. The Early Intermediate period and its legacy. In *Chan Chan*, eds. M. E. Moseley and K. C. Day. Albuquerque: University of New Mexico Press.

Topping, A. 1978. The first emperor's army, China's incredible find. *National Geographic* 153(4):440–459.

Toth, N. 1987. The first technology. *Scientific American* 256(2):112–121.

Trigger, B. G. 1980. *Gordon Childe: Revolutions in archaeology*. New York: Columbia University Press.

Trigger, B. G. 1978. Early Iroquoian contacts with Europeans. In *Handbook of North American Indians, Vol. 15: Northeast*, eds. W. C. Sturtevant and B. G. Trigger. Washington, DC: Smithsonian Institution Press.

Trigger, B. G. 1980. Archaeology and the image of the American Indian. *American Antiquity* 45:662–675.

Trigger, B. G., B. J. Kemp, D. O. O'Connor, and A. B. Lloyd. 1983. *Ancient Egypt: A social history*. Cambridge: Cambridge University Press.

Tringham, R. 1971. *Hunters, fishers, and farmers of Eastern Europe 6000–3000 B.C.* London: Hutchinson University Library.

Trinkhaus, E., ed. 1990. *The emergence of modern humans*. Cambridge: Cambridge University Press.

Trinkhaus, E., and W. W. Howells. 1979. The Neanderthals. *Scientific American* 241:94–105.

Tuck, J. A. 1978a. Northern Iroquoian prehistory. In *Handbook of North American Indians, Vol. 15: Northeast*, eds. W. C. Sturtevant and B. G. Trigger. Washington, DC: Smithsonian Institution Press.

Tuck, J. A. 1978b. Regional cultural development, 3000 to 300 B.C. In *Handbook of North American Indians, Vol. 15: Northeast*, eds. W. C. Sturtevant and B. G. Trigger. Washington, DC: Smithsonian Institution Press.

Turner, B. L. II, and P. D. Harrison, eds. 1983. *Pulltrouser Swamp: Ancient Maya habitat, agriculture, and settlement in northern Belize*. Austin: University of Texas Press.

Tylor, E. B. 1960. *Anthropology*. Ann Arbor, MI: University of Michigan Press (originally published in 1881).

Ubelaker, D. H. 1978. *Human skeletal remains*. Washington, DC: Taraxacum Press.

Ucko, P. J., and A. Rosenfeld. 1967. *Paleolithic cave art*. London: Weidenfeld & Nicholson.

U.S. Congress, Office of Technology Assessment. 1986. *Technologies for prehistoric and historic preservation*. OTA-E-319. Washington, DC: U.S. Government Printing Office.

Vaillant, G. C. 1966. *Aztecs of Mexico*. Harmondsworth: Pelican.

Vermeule, E. 1972. *Greece in the Bronze Age*. Chicago: University of Chicago Press.

Villa, P. 1982. Conjoinable pieces and site formation processes. *American Antiquity* 47:276–290.

Wainwright, G. 1989. *The henge monuments*. London: Thames & Hudson.

Walker, A. 1981. Diet and teeth: Dietary hypotheses and human evolution. *Philosophical Transactions of the Royal Society of London* B292:57–64.

Wallace, A. R. 1869. *Malay archipelago*. New York: Harper and Brothers.

Warren, P. 1975. *The Aegean civilizations*. Oxford: Elsevier Phaidon.

Warrick, G. A. 1983. Reconstructing Iroquoian village organization. *National Museum of Man Mercury Series*, Paper #124. Ottawa: Archaeological Survey of Canada.

Warrick, G. A. 1988. Estimating Ontario Iroquoian village duration. *Man in the Northeast* 36:21–60.

Watson, W. 1960. *Archaeology in China*. London: Max Parrish.

Weaver, M. P. 1981. *The Aztecs, Maya, and their predecessors: Archaeology of Mesoamerica*. New York: Academic Press.

Wenke, R. J. 1984. *Patterns in prehistory*. Oxford: Oxford University Press.

Wheeler, R. E. M. 1943. *Maiden Castle, Dorset*. London: Society of Antiquaries 12.

Wheeler, R. E. M. 1968. *The Indus civilization*. Cambridge: Cambridge University Press.

Wheeler, T. S., and R. Maddin. 1976. The techniques of the early Thai metalsmith. *Expedition* 18(4):38–47.

White, J. C. 1982. *Discovery of a lost Bronze Age: Ban chiang*. Philadelphia: University of Pennsylvania Press.

White, L. A. 1959. *The evolution of culture*. New York: McGraw-Hill.

Wilcox, D. R., T. R. McGuire, and C. Sternberg. 1981. *Snaketown revisited*. Arizona State Museum Archaeological Series 155. Tucson: University of Arizona.

Willey, G. R. 1953. *Prehistoric settlement in the Virú Valley, Peru*. Washington, DC: Smithsonian Institution Press.

Willey, G. R. 1966. *An introduction to American archaeology*, vol. 1: North and Middle America. Englewood Cliffs, NJ: Prentice-Hall.

Willey, G. R. 1971. *An introduction to American archaeology*, vol. 2: *South America*. Englewood Cliffs, NJ: Prentice-Hall.

Willey, G. R. 1974. The Classic Maya hiatus: A rehearsal for the collapse? In *Mesoamerican archaeology: New approaches*, ed. N. Hammond. London: Duckworth.

Wills, W. H. 1988. Early agriculture and sedentism in the American Southwest: Evidence and interpretations. *Journal of World Prehistory* 2(4):445–488.

Wilmsen, E. N. 1974. *Lindenmeier: A Pleistocene hunting society*. New York: Harper & Row.

Wilmsen, E. N. 1978. *Lindenmeier, 1934–74*. Washington, DC: Smithsonian Institution Press.

Wilson, D. J. 1981. Of maize and men: A critique of the maritime hypothesis of state origins on the coast of Peru. *American Anthropologist* 83(1):93–120.

Wing, E. S. 1980. Faunal remains. In *Guitarrero Cave: Early man in the Andes*, ed. T. S. Lynch. New York: Academic Press.

Wittfogel, K. 1957. *Oriental despotism*. New Haven: Yale University Press.

Wood, J. W., D. Lai, P. L. Johnson, K. L. Campbell, and I. M. Masler. 1985. Lactation and birth spacing in highland New Guinea. *Journal of Biosocial Science, Supplement* 9:159–173.

Woodman, P. C. 1981. A Mesolithic camp in Ireland. *Scientific American* 245(2):120–132.

Woolley, C. L. 1954. *Excavations at Ur*. London: Benn.

Wright, G. A. 1969. *Obsidian analyses and prehistoric Near Eastern trade: 7500–3500 B.C.* Ann Arbor: University of Michigan Museum of Anthropology.

Wright, H. E. 1971. Late Quaternary vegetational history of North America. In *The Late Cenozoic ice ages*, ed. K. K. Turekian. New Haven: Yale University Press.

Wright, H. T., and G. A. Johnson. 1975. Population, exchange and early state formation in southwestern Iran. *American Anthropologist* 77:267–289.

Wymer, J. 1968. *Lower Paleolithic archaeology in Britain*. London: John Baker.

Yen, D. E. 1977. Hoabinhian horticulture: The evidence and the questions from northwest Thailand. In *Sunda and Sahul: Prehistoric studies in Southeast Asia, Mela-nesia, and Australia,* eds. J. Allen, J. Golson, and R. Jones. London: Academic Press.

Yen, D. E. 1982. Ban Chiang pottery and rice. *Expedition* 24(4):51–64.

Yerkes, R. W. 1988. The Woodland and Mississippian traditions in the prehistory of midwestern North America. *Journal of World Prehistory* 2(3)307–358.

INDEX

CREDITS
(continued from copyright page)

T (top), M (middle), B (bottom), L (left), R (right).

Introduction p. 2, negative no. 108781 Courtesy Department of Library Services, American Museum of Natural History. **Chapter 1** p. 11T, photo by Bob Campbell; pp. 11B, 13, John Reader/ Science Photo Library; p. 16L, redrawn from original drawings by Bobbie Brown in *Lucy: The Beginnings of Humankind* by Donald C. Johanson and Maitland Edey, 1981, Simon and Schuster; p. 16R, © Institute of Human Origins, photo by Dr. Donald Johanson; p. 17L, R, John Reader/Science Photo Library; p. 18, *Mosaic*, Volume 10, no. 2, March/April 1979; p. 20, Al Nomura/Institute of Human Origins; p. 22, Courtesy Transvaal Museum, South Africa; p. 23L, John Reader/Science Photo Library; p. 23R, Illustration from *Human Evolution* 2/ed. by Joseph Birdsell. Copyright © 1975, 1981 by Harper & Row, Publishers, Inc. Reprinted by permission of HarperCollins Publishers; p. 24, Bernard Price Institute for Palaeontological Research, University of the Witwatersrand, Republic of South Africa; p. 25, from C. K. Brain. 1981. *Who Were the Hunters or the Hunted?* Chicago: The University of Chicago Press. Reprinted with permission of the publisher; p. 26, Baron Hugo van Lawick © 1963 National Geographic Society; p. 29T, *Olduvai Gorge, Volume 3* by Mary Leakey, 1971, Cambridge University Press. Reprinted with permission of the publisher; p. 30, John Reader/Science Photo Library; p. 31, Robert F. Sisson © 1961 National Geographic Society; p. 33, John Reader/Science Photo Library; p. 34L, R, photos by Pat Shipman and Richard Potts; p. 36, From "The First Technology" by Nicholas Toth. Copyright © 1987 by Scientific American, Inc. All rights reserved; p. 39, Warren Garst/Tom Stack and Associates. **Chapter 2** p. 44B, National Museums of Kenya; p. 45B, McKern and McKern, *Living Prehistory*. Copyright © 1974, Benjamin/Cummings Publishing Company; p. 46, © T. Douglas Price; p. 47B, from A. Leroi-Gourhan. 1957. *Prehistoric Man*. New York: Philosophical Library. Reprinted with permission of the author; p. 49, John Reader/Science Photo Library; p. 50B, negative no. 298897. Courtesy Department Library Services, American Museum of Natural History; p. 52, courtesy Professor Huang Weiwen, Institute of Vertebrate Paleontology and Paleoanthropology, Bejing; p. 53, negative no. 335794. Courtesy Department of Library Services, American Museum of Natural History; p. 58, courtesy Henry de Lumley, Musée National d'Histoire Naturelle, Paris; p. 60T, © T. Douglas Price; p. 61, from "A Paleolithic Camp in Nice" by Henry de Lumley. Copyright © 1969 by Scientific American, Inc. All rights reserved; p. 62, Reproduced with permission of the Trustees of the British Museum; p. 63, from F. Bordes. 1968. *The Old Stone Age*. New York: McGraw-Hill, Inc. Reprinted with permission of the publisher; p. 64, 65T, 65B, courtesy F. Clark Howell; p. 66T, courtesy Leslie G. Freeman; p. 67, source material courtesy Richard Klein; p. 68, After Aaris-Sørensen and Brinch Petersen, STRIAE, 24:111–117, 1986, photo: Geert Brovad; p. 70, 71T, courtesy J. Desmond Clark; p. 71B, from J. D. Clark. 1970. *The Prehistory of Africa*. London: Thames and Hudson. Reprinted with permission of the author; p. 72T, 72B, 73L © Laurence Bartram; p. 73R, photo by Karen B. Strier; p. 76B, John Reader/Science Photo Library. **Chapter 3** p. 80T, Staatliches Museum für Naturkunde Stuttgart; p. 80B,

Laboratoire de Préhistoire du Musée de l'Homme, Paris, courtesy Henry de Lumley; p. 84, negative no. 124667. Courtesy Department of Library Services, American Museum of Natural History; pp. 86–87, Peabody Museum of Natural History, Yale University. Painted by Rudolph F. Zallinger; p. 88, courtesy Hilary Deacon; p. 89B, © T. Douglas Price; p. 91, source material courtesy Richard Klein; p. 93, courtesy Musée de l'Homme, Paris; p. 95T, from *Shanidar: The First Flower People* by Ralph S. Solecki. Copyright © 1971 by Ralph S. Solecki. Reprinted by permission of Alfred A. Knopf, Inc.; p. 95B, Reprinted by permission from page 439 of *Understanding Physical Anthropology and Archaeology*, Third Edition by Robert Jurmain, Harry Nelson, and William Turnbaugh, copyright © 1987 by West Publishing Company. All rights reserved; p. 96, from F. Bordes. 1968. *The Old Stone Age*. New York: McGraw-Hill, Inc.; p. 99B, Reconstruction of *Homo Sapiens Neanderthalensis* by Jay H. Matternes © copyright 1981; pp. 101, 103T, courtesy Ralph Solecki; p. 103B, redrawn from Clark Spencer Larsen and Robert M. Matter, *Human Origins: The Fossil Record*, p. 175, copyright © 1985 by Waveland Press, Inc., Prospect Heights, Illinois. Second Edition published 1991. Used by permission from the publisher; p. 105B, Courtesy Institute of Archaeology, University College, London; pp. 106, 107L, 107B, © T. Douglas Price; p. 107R, courtesy Arthur Jelinek; p. 109, courtesy Anne Birgette Gebauer; p. 111, © Thomas Hoepker/Magnum Photos; p. 113, courtesy Peter Vang Petersen, National Museum, Copenhagen; p. 114, courtesy Peter Vemming Hansen; p. 115, G. LaPlace. 1974. *La Typologie Analytique et Structurale*. Paris: Editions du Centre National de la Recherche Scientifique; p. 116, Courtesy of Archeologicky Ústav, Brno, Czechslovakia; p. 117T, 118T, 118M, 119B, B. Klima. 1963. *Dolni Vestonice*. Prague: Czechslovakian Academy of Science; p. 117B, Collection of the Institute für Ur- und Frühgeschichte, University Tübingen, Germany; p. 118B, H. Müller-Karpe. 1966. *Handbuch vor Vorgeschichte*. Munich: C. H. Beck; p. 119T, negative no. 69368fr.15. Courtesy Department of Library Services, American Museum of Natural History; p. 120, © Bruno Barbey/Magnum Photos; p. 122R, E. Hadingham. 1979. *Secrets of the Ice Age*. After C. Barrière 1975, figure 17. New York: Walker and Co.; p. 122L, Illustration by Zdenek Burian. Reprinted with permission of Eva Hochmanová-Burianová; pp. 123, 124, Photo Jean Vertut, Issy-les-Moulineaux, France; p. 125T, from A. Leroi-Gourhan. 1982. *The Dawn of European Art: An Introduction to Paleolithic Cave Painting*. New York: Cambridge University Press. Reprinted with permission of the publisher; p. 125B, E. Haddingham. 1979. *Secrets of the Ice Age*. New York: Walker and Co.; p. 126, negative no. 39686, photo: Kirschner. Courtesy Department Library Services, American Museum of Natural History; p. 127T, A. Leroi-Gourhan. 1982. *The Dawn of European Art: An Introduction to Paleolithic Cave Painting*. New York: Cambridge University Press; p. 127B, Drawing of Gravettian Venus by Ann Hatfield from the book *Plato Prehistorian* by Mary Settegast, published by The Rotenberg Press, 1986; p. 128, courtesy George Weidenfeld & Nicholson Limited, Publishers. Photo by Henri Leroi-Gourhan; p. 129T, B, reprinted with permission of the publisher, Editions du Centre National de la Recherche Scientifique; p. 130, 131B, courtesy Alexander Marshack; p. 131T, negative no. 2A17536. Courtesy Department of Library Services, American Museum of Natural History; p. 134, from "Elephant Hunting in North America" by C. Vance Haynes, Jr. Copyright © 1966 by Scientific American. All rights reserved; p. 135, courtesy George Frison; p. 136, 139B, © Tom Dillehay; p. 140T, photo by Vance T. Holliday; p. 140B, D. H. Thomas. 1978. *Archaeology*. NY:

courtesy Ruth Kirk; p. 287B, courtesy Allan May. **Chapter** 7 pp. 296, 309T, 310, 316B, from K. V. Flannery and J. Marcus, eds. *The Cloud People: Divergent Evolution of the Zapotec and Mixtec Civilizations.* New York: Academic Press. Courtesy Joyce Marcus; pp. 297, 299T, 299B, 304, 312, from K. V. Flannery and J. Marcus, eds. *The Cloud People: Divergent Evolution of the Zapotec and Mixtec Civilizations.* New York: Academic Press. Courtesy Kent V. Flannery and Joyce Marcus; p. 298, courtesy Linda Nicholas; p. 301, Richard H. Stewart © National Geographic Society; p. 305, reprinted from *In the Land of the Olmec: The Archaeology of San Lorenzo Tenochtitlan, Volume I,* by Michael Coe and Richard Diehl, copyright © 1980. By permission of the author and the University of Texas Press; pp. 307B, 308, Project El Mirador, photo provided courtesy of Dr. Ray Matheny; p. 309B, reproduced, with permission, from the Annual Review of Anthropology, Volume 5, © 1976 by Annual Reviews, Inc.; p. 311, courtesy Linda Nicholas; p. 317M, from E. Redmond. 1983. "*A Fuego y Sangre:* Early Zapotec Imperialism in the Cuicatlán Cañada, Oaxaca." *University of Michigan, Museum of Anthropology, Memoirs.* 16. Reprinted with permission; p. 317B, from C. Spencer. 1982. *The Cuicatlán Cañada and Monte Albán.* Reprinted with permission of the author, photo provided by the author; p. 321B, courtesy Linda Nicholas; p. 323T, courtesy Jennifer Blitz; p. 323B, stone relief panel from the ballcourt at El Tajin, figure 23 from *The Sculpture of El Tajin, Veracruz, Mexico* by Michael Kampen, 1972, University of Florida Press; p. 325, The University Museum, University of Pennsylvania, Tikal Project, negative no. 65-4-125; p. 327T, The University Museum, University of Pennsylvania, Tikal Project, negative no. 65-4-1094; p. 327B, The University Museum, University of Pennsylvania, Tikal Project, negative no. 67-4-80; p. 329, from *Science,* "Prehistoric Raised-Field Agriculture in the Maya Lowlands," by B. L. Turner; Volume 213; pages 399–405; July 1981. Copyright 1981 by the AAAS; p. 330, 331, reprinted from John S. Henderson, *The World of the Ancient Maya.* Copyright © 1981 by Cornell University Press. Used by permission of the publisher, Cornell University Press; p. 332, Andromeda Oxford Ltd.; p. 333T, S. G. Morley, G. W. Brainerd, revised by R. J. Sharer. 1983 *The Ancient Maya,* 4th ed. Stanford: Stanford University Press. Owned by Simon Greco; p. 333B, Drawing courtesy Merle Greene Robertson; p. 334, Courtesy of the Pre-Columbian Art Research Institute, photo by Irmgard Groth; p. 336, 337T, Andromeda Oxford Ltd.; p. 337B, from *Everyday Life of the Aztecs* by Warwick Bray, 1986. Reproduced by permission of the publishers, B. T. Batsford Ltd., London; p. 339T, courtesy Linda Nicholas; p. 340, courtesy Susan Kepecs; p. 341, Bates Littlehales © 1961 National Geographic Society; p. 342B, courtesy Linda Nicholas; p. 343T, reprinted from *The Ancient Maya,* Fourth Edition, by Sylvanus Griswold Morley and George W. Brainerd; revised by Robert J. Sharer with the permission of the publishers, Stanford University Press. © 1946, 1947, 1956, and 1983, by the Board of Trustees of the Leland Stanford Junior University; p. 343B, courtesy Susan Kepecs; pp. 345, 347 from *Everyday Life of the Aztecs* by Warwick Bray, 1986. Reproduced by permission of the publishers, B. T. Batsford Ltd., London; p. 348, photograph by David Hiser with overlay by Ned M. Seidler © National Geographic; p. 349, *Codex Florentino: Illustrations for Sahagun's Historia General de las Cosas de Nueva España* edited by Francisco del Paso y Troncoso, Vol. 5, Madrid, 1905; p. 350, F. Beardan. 1982. *The Aztecs of Central Mexico: An Imperial Society.* New York: Holt, Rinehart, Winston. **Chapter 8** p. 358, M. E. Moseley. 1975. *The Maritime Foundations of Andean Civilization.* Menlo Park: Benjamin-Cummings. Reprinted with permission of the author; p.

359, reproduced from *Journal of Field Archaeology* with permission of the Trustees of Boston University; p. 360T, courtesy Jeffrey Quilter, Ripon College; p. 360B, M. E. Moseley. 1975. *The Maritime Foundations of Andean Civilization.* Menlo Park: Benjamin-Cummings. Reprinted with permission of the author; p. 362, R. A. Feldman, Ph.D. dissertation, Harvard University; p. 363T, 364, from G. R. Willey. 1971. *Introduction to American Archaeology: South America.* Englewood Cliffs, NJ: Prentice-Hall. Reprinted with permission of the author; p. 363B, from *Ancient South Americans,* by Jesse D. Jennings. Copyright © by W. H. Freeman and Company. Reprinted by permission; p. 365, Dumbarton Oaks Research Library and Collections, Washington, D.C.; p. 367T, Courtesy Theresa Lange Topic, Trent University; p. 367B, negative no. 334913. Courtesy Department of Library Services, American Museum of Natural History; p. 368, negative no. 122461. Photo by E. L. Bailey. Courtesy Department of Library Services, American Museum of Natural History; p. 369B, reproduced by permission of the Society for American Archaeology from *American Antiquity* 40, 1975; p. 370, reproduced, with permission, from Christopher B. Donnan, *Moche Art and Iconography* (Los Angeles: UCLA Latin American Center Publications, 1976), Figure 104a; p. 371, Bates Littlehales © 1964 National Geographic Society; p. 373B, Andromeda Oxford Ltd.; p. 374, Peabody Museum, Harvard University, photograph by E. C. Pickering. Courtesy President and Fellows of Harvard College. All Rights Reserved; p. 375T, Peabody Museum, Harvard University. Courtesy President and Fellows of Harvard College; p. 375B, Bennett, W. 1947. *Handbook of South American Indians,* Volume 2. J. Stewart, ed. Page 126. Washington, D.C.: Government Printing Office; p. 377R, Andromeda Oxford Ltd.; p. 378, negative no. 334878. Courtesy Department of Library Services, American Museum of Natural History; p. 379, courtesy Alan L. Kolata; p. 382, from *Ancient South Americans,* by Jesse D. Jennings. Copyright © 1983 by W. H. Freeman and Company. Reprinted by permission; p. 383T, B, courtesy Jennifer Blitz; p. 385, John Hyslop, American Museum of Natural History; p. 386, from C. Morris and D. Thompson. 1985. *Huánaco Pampa: An Inca City and its Hinterland.* London: Thames and Hudson. Reprinted with permission of the authors; p. 387, from R. W. Keatinge, ed. 1988. *Peruvian Prehistory.* New York: Cambridge University Press. Reprinted with permission of the publisher and the owner of the material, Craig Morris; p. 388, courtesy Donald E. Thompson; p. 389T, B, from C. Morris and D. Thompson. 1985. *Huánaco Pampa: An Inca City and its Hinterland.* London: Thames and Hudson. Reproduced with permission of the authors; p. 391, negative no. 330282. Courtesy Department of Library Services, American Museum of Natural History; p. 392T, B, courtesy Jennifer Blitz; p. 393, courtesy Leopold Pospisil, Yale University, Peabody Museum of Natural History, and the National Geographic Society. **Chapter 9** p. 399, reproduced, with permission, from the Annual Review of Ecology and Systematics, Volume 3, © 1972 by Annual Reviews, Inc.; p. 402, from *Art of the Ancient Near East* by Seaton Lloyd, copyright © 1961 Thames and Hudson, page 259, Praeger Publishers, an imprint of Greenwood Publishing Group, Inc., Westport, CT. Reprinted with permission; p. 403, © State Antiquities and Heritage Organization, Baghdad; p. 404, Nöldecke, A. 1936. *Uruk Vorbericht* 7, Figure 5; p. 405, Nöldecke, A, A. von Haller, H. Lenzen, and E. Heinrich. 1937. *Abhandlungen der Preussischen Akademie der Wissenschaften.* Figure 1. Berlin: Verlag der Akademie der Wissenschaften; p. 406, courtesy Gregory Johnson, Hunter College of the City University of New York; pp. 407, 409, courtesy Denise Schmandt-Besserat. With permission of Deutsches

Archäologisches Institut, Abteilung Baghdad; p. 410, courtesy Département des Antiquités Orientales, Musée du Louvre, Paris. Photograph courtesy Denise Schmandt-Besserat; p. 414, from *Civilizations Anciennes du Pakistan*. 1989. Bruxelles: Musées Royaux d'Art et d' Histoire; p. 415T, from M. Wheeler. 1968. *The Indus Civilization*. New York: Cambridge University Press. Reprinted with permission of the publisher; pp. 415B, 416, Courtesy George Dales and the Harappa Project, University of California at Berkeley; p. 420, Ashmolean Museum, Oxford; p. 421, Giraudon/Art Resource, N.Y.; p. 422, K. Mendelssohn. 1974. *The Riddle of the Pyramids*. New York: Praeger Publishers. Copyright © Thames and Hudson 1974. Reprinted with permission of Henry Holt and Company; p. 423, from Michael A. Hoffman, "Where Nations Began." *Science 83*. October, 1983, pp. 42–51. Copyright 1982 by the AAAS; p. 424, Giza pyramids plateau from the air, photo courtesy Museum of Fine Arts, Boston; p. 425, Lovell Johns/ Andromeda Oxford Ltd.; p. 426, acc. no. 11.1738, pair statue of Mycerinus and His Queen, from Giza, dynasty IV, 2599–1571 B.C., slate schist, H (complete statue): 54-1/2 in. Harvard-MFA Expedition. Courtesy, Museum of Fine Arts, Boston; pp. 428, 429, K. Mendelssohn. 1974. *The Riddle of the Pyramids*. New York: Praeger Publishers. Copyright © Thames and Hudson 1974. Reprinted with permission of Henry Holt and Company; p. 432T, from K. C. Chang. 1986. *Studies of Shang Archaeology*. New Haven: Yale University Press; p. 432B, from *Wen-wu*, 1984, no. 4, p. 7; p. 433T, B, courtesy of the Institute of History and Philology, Academia Sinica, Taiwan; p. 437, from K. C. Chang, "Food and Vessels in Ancient China," *Transactions of the New York Academy of Sciences* 35 (6) 1973. Reprinted with permission of the annals of the New York Academy of Sciences; pp. 438, 441, courtesy Audrey Topping; p. 439, Yang Hsien-Min © 1978 National Geographic Society; pp. 444, 445, 446B, P. Garlake. 1973. *Great Zimbabwe*. London: Thames and Hudson; p. 446T, © Robert Holmes 1989; p. 447, Walter Meayers Edwards © 1992 National Geographic Society. **Chapter 10** pp. 457TL, TR, Courtesy Thomas Jacobsen, Indiana University; pp. 458T, 459T, 459B, courtesy Dragoslav Srejovic; p. 460, from S. Milisauskas. 1978. *European Prehistory*. Reprinted with permission of the publisher and the author; p. 462, reprinted from *Journal of Field Archaeology* with permission of the Trustees of Boston University; p. 463, Royal Commission on Ancient Monuments, Scotland; p. 464, from *Ancient Europe from the Beginnings of Agriculture to Classical Antiquity* by Stuart Piggott. Reprinted with permission of Edinburgh University Press; p. 467, reproduced with the permission of the Prehistoric Society; pp. 468, 470, C. Chippendale. 1983. *Stonehenge Complete*. London: Routledge; p. 469T, negative no. 269817. Photo by G. H. Sterwood. Courtesy Department of Library Services, American Museum of Natural History; p. 469B, Cambridge University Collection, © British Crown copyright 1991/MOD reproduced with the permission of the Controller of Her Britannic Majesty's Stationery Office; p. 475, photo: John Bennet; p. 473, from E. Vermeule. 1972. *Greece in the Bronze Age*. Chicago: The University of Chicago Press. Reprinted with permission of the publishers; p. 478, Royal Hellenic Air Force and M. Paraskevaïdes; pp. 479, 480T, courtesy of Jack Davis; p. 480B, photo by J. McCredie. Courtesy National Museum, Athens; p. 481, The Bettmann Archive; p. 482, from J. Jensen. 1979. *Bronzealderen*, Volume 1. Copenhagen: Sesam. Reprinted with permission of the publisher; p. 484T, published by permission of the Danish National Museum; p. 484B, four bronze age barrows along the coast of Denmark. From *Danish Prehistoric Monuments* by P. B. Glob, 1971, page 27, figure 4. Reprinted with permission of Glydendal, Copenhagen; p. 485T, from P. B. Glob. 1970. *The Mound People*. Ithaca, NY: Cornell University Press. Originally published by Glydendal, Copehagen; p. 486T, from T. G. E. Powell. 1983. *The Celts*. Plate 29. London: Thames and Hudson. Reprinted with permission of the publisher; pp. 486B, 487B, Cliché Musée Archéologique de Châtillon sur Seine; p. 487T, from T. Champion, C. Gamble, S. Shennan, and A. Whittle. 1984. *Prehistoric Europe*. London: Academic Press. Reprinted with permission of the publisher; p. 488, 490, Society of Antiquaries of London; p. 489, Ashmolean Museum, Oxford; p. 491, Forhistorisk Museum, Denmark. **Color insert** Plates 1, 2, 3, John Reader/ Science Photo Library; Plate 4, Jean Vertut, Issy-les-Molineaux, France; Plate 5, National Museum of Denmark; Plate 6, photo by Peter Dorrell and Stuart Laidlaw, courtesy University of London, Institute of Archaeology. Photo provided courtesy of Gary Rollefson, San Diego State University; Plate 7, courtesy Bruce F. Benz, Universidad de Guadalajara; Plate 8, courtesy Dr. Thomas F. Lynch; Plates 9, 10, 11, 12, courtesy Linda M. Nicholas; Plate 13, © Kenneth Garrett 1982. All rights reserved; Plate 14, reproduced by courtesy of the Trustees of the British Museum; Plate 15, Bodleian Library, Oxford University; Plate 16, Dumbarton Oaks, Pre-Columbian Studies, Washington, D.C.; Plate 17, courtesy Jennifer Blitz; Plate 18, © Robert Frerck/Woodfin Camp and Associates. All rights reserved; Plate 19, reproduced by courtesy of the Trustees of the British Museum; Plate 20, © Dilip Mehta/ Woodfin Camp and Associates. All rights reserved; Plate 21, PHOTRI, Inc.; Plate 22, © Robert Holmes 1989; Plate 23, D. Cahen and L. Keeley; Plate 24, Hellenic Republic, National Archaeological Museum, Athens; Plate 25, reproduced by courtesy of the Trustees of the British Museum; Plate 26, Silkeborg Museum, Denmark.